HANDBOOK OF BIBLICAL HEBREW

HANDBOOK
of
BIBLICAL HEBREW

An Inductive Approach Based on the Hebrew Text of Esther

by

WILLIAM SANFORD LaSOR

WILLIAM B. EERDMANS PUBLISHING COMPANY
Grand Rapids, Michigan

First published 1979 in three volumes by Wm. B. Eerdmans Publishing Co.
This one-volume paperback edition published 1988 by
Wm. B. Eerdmans Publishing Co., 255 Jefferson Ave. SE, Grand Rapids, MI 49503

Printed in the United States of America

ISBN 0-8028-0444-6

Reprinted, January 1989

TO
MY STUDENTS
AND ESPECIALLY TO
THOSE WHO SERVED AS
MY TEACHING ASSISTANTS
WHO HAVE TAUGHT ME MORE THAN I TAUGHT THEM
THIS WORK IS
GRATEFULLY AND LOVINGLY
DEDICATED

Acknowledgements

Fig. 3 is reproduced from M. Burrows, ed., *The Dead Sea Scrolls of St. Mark's Monastery*, Vol. I (New Haven: American Schools of Oriental Research, 1961).

Fig. 6 is reproduced from †R. Kittel *et al.*, eds., *Biblia Hebraica* (3d ed., Stuttgart: Privilegierte Württembergische Bibelanstalt, 1937).

Fig. 7 is reproduced from *Biblical Archaeology Review*, Sept.-Oct., 1978.

Fig. 8 is reproduced from K. Elliger and W. Rudolph, eds., *Biblia Hebraica Stuttgartensia* (Stuttgart: Deutsche Bibelstiftung, 1977).

This work was set in Times Roman and LaSor Hebrew 11 point on 13 and 10 point on 12, on the Photon Pacesetter. Layout design and typography by the author.

TABLE OF CONTENTS

Table of Contents

ILLUSTRATIONS IN PARTS 2 AND 3

PUBLISHER'S NOTE

The *Handbook of Biblical Hebrew* was originally published in three volumes. Volume One contained Part 1, the lessons themselves. Volume Two contained Part 2, the grammar; Part 3, the tables and paradigms; and Part 4, the basic vocabulary. The third volume was a twenty-page booklet containing the Hebrew text of the Book of Esther. This arrangement made it very convenient for students to carry out the author's intention that they have open before them both the lesson itself and the supporting material related to the lesson.

The economics of modern publishing, regrettably, have made such an arrangement an impractical luxury. In order to keep the *Handbook* in print at a price students can afford, we have had to combine all three volumes into a single binding. The convenience of having two volumes open at once must give way to the relative inconvenience of paging back and forth from the first half of the volume to the second.

Readers should be aware that, although we have retained the author's original references to Volumes One and Two in his explanation of how to use the *Handbook,* those designations now refer to the first and second halves of the single volume. The pagination begins again at "1" for Parts Two and Three; Part Four, as before, is paginated as "*1", "*2", and so on. The Book of Esther is paginated as it would be read in Hebrew: the first page is at the back of the volume, moving forward to p. 18.

Although we regret having had to sacrifice the greater convenience of the multi-volume format, we are pleased to be able to keep this useful *Handbook* available for a new generation of students.

THE PUBLISHER

PREFACE

This *Handbook* is designed to be a complete tool for the student who wishes to learn Biblical Hebrew. It combines lessons, grammar, basic vocabulary, and learning methodology. The student who follows the method faithfully will not only learn the elements of Hebrew, but in addition, and more important, he or she will learn *how to observe and how to learn by observation.* In addition, the *Handbook* is keyed to the classical 28th edition of the Kautzsch-Cowley *Gesenius' Hebrew Grammar* for fuller study of many points. It has been set up in 80 lessons, each lesson on two facing pages so as to be completely visible at a glance, planned for a course of 90 class-hours. Thus it can be covered in a 3-hour course in 30 weeks (whether semesters or quarters) or (as I have done many times) in a 15-hour course in six weeks.

The *method* is largely *inductive,* i.e. working from the text to the grammar. The learned William Rainey Harper did much to develop this method of language study, and for decades his work on Hebrew has been well recognized, going through many editions. However, this method has fallen somewhat into disrepute. In my opinion, this was due more to improper use of the inductive method than to the method itself. See my article, "The Inductive Method of Teaching Hebrew — Its Advantages and Its Pitfalls," *Hebrew Abstracts,* 15 (1974) 108-119, for fuller discussion. I have tried to remedy this defect in using the inductive method by requiring *more synthesis* of what is learned inductively.

The inductive method has advantages and disadvantages. First of all, *it holds student interest,* because the student is at once into reading the language. The learning of paradigms, rules of grammar and syntax, vocabulary, and other features of conventional language study for a year (more or less) before ever reading connected text can kill the interest of all but the most persistent student. Moreover, much that is taught is *useless.* Who has not learned pluperfect or other forms he has not seen in years of reading? Who has not learned to write, "My aunt's male elephant loves my uncle's female elephant," only to find that he never has had the chance to use that literary gem? The inductive method is free from these faults. The student learns only what he or she encounters.

On the other hand, many students *observe without integrating their observations.* After a year of inductive study they cannot tell what they have seen. (This, contrary to the false idea among many language teachers, does not necessarily mean ignorance of the language. Many persons can read, speak, and even write a language well, who have no grammatical integration of the language.) As a result, teachers and students conclude that the inductive method does not work. I strongly disagree, and I have the experience and evidence to back up my opinion.

This work started out as "Notes on Biblical Hebrew" in 1950, and developed into *Hebrew Handbook,* which went through two or three revisions. It has been used to teach more than 2,000 students at Fuller Theological Seminary, and an unknown number at other institutions. I used the same method to develop my *Handbook of New Testament Greek,* which went through several revisions (1963-1969) and was brought out by Eerdmans in 1973. I have used the same method, with various amounts of helps available to the students, to teach Old Babylonian, Biblical Aramaic, New Testament Syriac, several other Aramaic dialects, Ugaritic, Phoenician, Ethiopic, Old South Arabic, and, most recently, Sumerian. I may have omitted one or two others. Without hesitation I state categorically, *the system works.* I make no claim that this is the *best* method; I simply say that, *if it is used properly, it produces excellent results.*

Perhaps the greatest obstacle to the inductive method is *what it demands* of both teacher and student. The teacher must be ready to *face* (not necessarily to *answer*; he or she can say frankly, "I don't know; I'll try to work it out and give you the answer tomorrow") *any question at any time.* Preparing tomorrow's lesson is easily done when the lesson is on the *Pe Guttural* verb. But when the teacher is faced with students who will ask anything from the utterly stupid to the most discerning question, the teacher must know the language and the *Handbook* thoroughly. At the same time, the student must think for him/herself. He/she must learn to observe and to question. The student is faced with a vast amount of heterogeneous material *from the very start.*

This is an advantage, however. When learning a language by the conventional method, the student finds the work increasingly more difficult as he/she learns more material. He/she tends to forget what he/she learned a few weeks ago. But when learning by the inductive method he/she will never find it more difficult than it is between the tenth and twentieth lessons. From that point on, learning is almost entirely by repetition of things already observed, and there is little chance to forget, for the student is constantly using what has already been seen.

The learning of a language involves at least three things – more, if you plan to speak and write in that language. First is the *meaning of words,* those units of thought that compose the message being expressed. Some teachers seem to think that all a student needs for this is a dictionary of word-for-word equivalents – but this obviously is extremely limited. To read with understanding, the student needs to know how the meaning of a word is affected by its context.

Next, for an inflected language the student needs to be able to identify correctly the *changes in form* that indicate the relationship of a word to its context. The student can achieve a degree of success by memorizing paradigms, or he or she can learn the same thing by encountering the word in many contexts. We all learned our mother-tongue by this inductive method, therefore it is *not* necessary to learn paradigms. Learning paradigms is faster – but is it better in the long run? Teachers will argue this point at length without convincing one another. I would simply point out that in any case it is still necessary to learn to read in context.

Third, and most important, the student needs to understand the meaning that is conveyed by the *putting together of these inflected words into a meaningful group,* or what the Greeks called "syntax." According to the "classical" method of teaching a language, syntax always comes last (if at all), and since it is of little meaning to the student without contexts, it is rarely mastered. Again, it is only when the student begins to read connected passages that syntax begins to make sense.

I have been asked many times, "Why did you use Esther?" For one thing, it is a story, with literary character, a plot, denouement, etc. This makes it interesting. Masculine and feminine forms, as well as singular and plural, are used throughout the work. (Much of the narrative material in the rest of the Hebrew Bible is seriously lacking in feminine forms.) Esther presents little difficulty in theological or textual matters. When we begin with the first chapter of Genesis, we immediately encounter all sorts of discussions concerning theology, historicity, cosmology, etc., when we ought to be learning the elements of Hebrew. Esther is long enough to present most of what the first-year student needs to know, with enough repetition to impress certain points on the student's mind. Some might object that Esther is late Hebrew, but the difference between Esther and, let us say, Genesis is not all that great. The vocabulary of Esther is excellent, containing about 500 words, most of which are of high frequency and relatively few of low frequency. That is to say, the student is constantly encountering words that will be needed wherever he or she turns in the Hebrew Bible. And, since I have included readings from other portions of the Bible, including several chapters from Genesis, the student will have opportunity to read Hebrew other than that of Esther.

I have a deep debt of gratitude that should be expressed. First and foremost I am indebted to my mentor at Dropsie University, Dr. Cyrus Gordon, for introducing me to the reduction of observations to simple rules. Some of the "Rules" herein are in the form in which he gave them to us; others have been reworked by me or by one of my assistants, particularly by my now-colleague, Dr Frederick Wm. Bush; still others have been formulated from my own observations. Most of these I have not learned from Grammars, and some are not to be found in any Grammar; they are proof that an observant student can learn many things *directly from the text.*

Starting in 1950, I applied the principle that "the best way to learn a subject well is to teach it," by giving my best students the responsibility of teaching sections of Hebrew. These *Teaching Assistants* or *Teaching Fellows* were continually feeding back to me the reactions to the method, pointing out places where clarification was needed, helping to make the length of lessons more reasonable, and in many other ways helping make this *Handbook* what it is today. To review their names is to give a veritable Who's Who, for quite a number of them have gone on to be teachers and administrators of excellence that would make any teacher proud. Some of them got their first experience in teaching in this manner. At least two of them have gone on to their eternal reward. My former assistants are: David Allan Hubbard (my first, and now the president of our Seminary), †Robert H. Emery, †Robert B. Laurin, Robert P. Dugan Jr, Marvin Webster, Haskell I. Stone, Gerald Swaim, Frederick W. Bush, Roy Hayden, Dwight Paine, John D. Koeker, Kurt G. Jung, Duncan W. McIntosh, Richard J. Saley, George VanAlstine, J. William Whedbee, Willard A. Parker, D. Dale Gerard, Ronald F. K. Ching, Timothy P. Owen, Glenda Fisk, Roger Fung, William Jeffrey Sweeney, W. Allan Gravely, Thomas F. Johnson, Michael F. Kopesec, David Lee Foxgrover, Kent A. Meads, Walter C. Wright Jr, Stephen J. Kobernik, Howard J. Loewen, Gary A. Tuttle, Gerald Sheppard, Edward E. Breeden, Robin A. Moore, Timothy E. Udd, Gerald H. Wilson, Richard C. Meyer, David M. Watson, B. Michael Blaine, Kenneth Brewster, Karen L. Hammeras, John H. Hull, Garth Moller, John C. Puckett, Mark A. Sereduck, Eugene Carpenter, Robert S. Goffigon, and Dawn Waring. If I have lost any names from this list, it is entirely unintentional and regrettable, but trying to reconstruct the details of three decades is a difficult task.

To some of these associates I have a particular indebtedness. Gary Tuttle, Gerald Wilson, and David Watson worked long and hard over numerous details in the revision. David Watson checked over the Basic Vocabulary, adding numbers and word-counts wherever they were lacking. Thomas McAlpine struggled, as I have done, to try to put the Synoptic Paradigms into some form that would be both useful and pleasing to the eye. Dawn Waring and Leon Mashchak opaqued the negatives from which the page-plates were made. Michael Blaine carried countless pages and galleys back and forth between the Seminary and Church Press. All of the recent teaching assistants have worked with and taught from these pages and have furnished me with numerous corrections that need to be made. And again, if I have forgotten anyone, I truly am sorry. Hearty thanks to each one who helped.

Finally, I want to thank Allan Farson of Church Press, Glendale, for creative ideas and much time and patience in making possible the typography in this *Handbook.* He designed the photographic disk used on the Photon by which the type was photographically set. Working with me, he created the beautifully clear Hebrew font, which he has graciously named "LaSor Hebrew." He patiently taught me how to set the type (by typewriter and punched tape), and he helped me work out countless mistakes. That many others remain I have no doubt. If anyone thinks he or she is infallible, try setting type for a book like this! I must add, also, my warm appreciation to William B. Eerdmans Jr for his willingness to venture the publication of my Handbooks.

To God be the greater glory!

William Sanford LaSor

Altadena, California
19 April 1978

PREFACE TO VOLUME TWO

Because of the nature of this *Handbook* I feel that it is in order to preface the second volume with a few words of explanation and caution. In the classical method of teaching Hebrew (or any language), a study of grammar comes first, hence teachers and students may turn to this volume first. In the method which I have used, and on which this *Handbook* is developed, the student should work from the lessons in Volume One to the referenced portions of Volume Two. He or she should only attempt to learn *what is actually being encountered* in the reading. Browsing in the second volume is not discouraged, but to make each encounter *meaningful* – and only by such encounters is learning achieved – the grammar should be learned through the reading of Hebrew passages.

Be sure you understand the *numbering system*, especially the logic of it, when you use this volume. Read §06.ff until it makes sense and then look at the Table of Contents, and notice the grammatically logical arrangement of the material. Since we are learning in context, and not by subjects, the participle – to take just one example – is not covered in any one place. Rather, the description and use of the participle are scattered among the various portions of phonology, morphology, and syntax, and the syntax of the participle is divided according to the various heads of syntax. I do not suggest that this is the best way to treat the participle. If you want to study the participle all at one time, I recommend that you turn to *Gesenius' Hebrew Grammar*. I might add one further word. If the numbering at times seems to have interruptions, it is because I have tried to design a system that will fit all my projected handbooks, including Aramaic, Syriac, and Old Babylonian – and, hopefully, others that my former students may add to the series.

I would reiterate what I said in the first volume concerning my use of *transliteration*. My goal is to see the student recognize דִּבֵּר as *dabbēr*, and *dabbēr* as דִּבֵּר, so that he/she has an immediate sound-and-sight identification of the Hebrew word. It can be done, and I have seen it work. It cannot be done, however, without the whole-hearted participation of both teacher and student in the process. Remember, students who are just learning Hebrew cannot recognize Hebrew orthography with the facility that seasoned Hebraists have acquired. But do not stop with transliteration. Keep at it until you can read and pronounce Hebrew with facility. At a number of points I have dared to challenge long-accepted views. This is not due to any desire on my part to be original, for I am by nature very conservative. Rather, it comes from wide reading of texts in many Semitic languages. When I have set forth a differing position, I have done so on the basis of dozens – perhaps scores – of supporting data. But, since my method is to encourage the student to learn by observation and to challenge the accepted position by what he/she encounters in his/her reading, I make no plea for acceptance of my novel ideas. Test them. If the reading of much Hebrew supports them, good. If not, that's even better. To prove an idea wrong is the first step toward finding the right solution to a problem.

The *paradigms*, like much of the rest of this *Handbook*, are unlike those we find in other Hebrew grammars. The reason: I have attempted to set down synoptic paradigms, i.e. comparable forms that will help the student to see what is *similar* and what is *different* about them. It is less important, in my opinion, to know the entire paradigm of the "strong" verb than it is to know precisely wherein the various "weak" verbs differ from it. Therefore I have arranged, let's say, the D-imperfect in such a way that the comparison of the CCC, CGC, NGC, C'C, and other types of verbal roots can be seen at a glance. If you want the customary paradigms, there are plenty of First-Year Hebrew books that have them.

The *Basic Vocabulary* is given in two different forms. In Volume One it is arranged by basic vocabulary groups, to be learned with the lessons in the course of study. In this volume the Basic Vocabulary is printed in alphabetical order, with complete references to the Brown-Driver-Briggs *Lexicon.* In the word groups, the words are given in both Hebrew orthography and transliteration. In the alphabetical list, only Hebrew orthography is used. There's a reason: when learning the word, the student should know how to pronounce it; but when looking up a word he/she must be able to find it in its Hebrew form.

In order to get this work finished (I have been working on the actual production of this edition for just short of four years), I have omitted an index. I regret this, and have tried to compensate for it to some degree by giving a rather thorough Table of Contents. Almost any subject can be found there, and cross-references in the relevant sections will lead to other sections where there is further comment on the matter. Besides, the beginning student, following the method I have set forth, really does not need a detailed index. Only the advanced student needs it. I hope to have an index in the next printing of this work, should there be one.

That there are many errors, when there are so many figures and references, I am certain. I shall welcome your calling them to my attention, and try to correct them in any future printing.

Now, please turn to Volume One and begin with Lesson 1. And may God bless you as you seek to learn more about Him through His word, the Hebrew Bible!

William Sanford LaSor

Labor Day 1978

abs. absolute
acc. accented, accusative
adj. adjective, adjectival
adv. adverb, adverbial
Akk. Akkadian
Arab. Arabic
Aram. Aramaic
art. article
attrib. attributive
BDB Brown-Driver-Briggs *Lexicon*
Bib. Biblical
c conversive, see p.59
c. construct
c common (m. and f.)
C consonant, see §29.02
cent. century
cf. compare
cl. clause, closed
cohort. cohortative
coll. collective
comp. complementary
cond. condition(al)
conj. conjunction, conjunctive
cons. consonant(al)
conv. conversive, converted
cstr. construct
CT Consonantal Text
d. dual
D *Piʿel*, cf. §28.12
dat. dative
d.d.o. definite direct object
d.o. distant open
def. definite
demon. demonstrative
denom. denominal
dir. direct
disc. discourse
du. dual
e.g. for example
energ. energic
Eng. English
esp. especially
Est. Esther
ET English translations
Eth. Ethiopic (Geʿez)
EV English Version(s)
f., ff. following
f. feminine
fda, fdc, fds fem. dual abs., cstr., suf.
fem. feminine
fig. figure
fpa, fpc, fps fem. plur. abs., cstr., suf.
fsa, fsc, fss fem. sing. abs., cstr., suf.
ft. foot, feet
fut. future
G *Qal*, cf. §28.12
GCC cf. §29.02
gen. genitive
Gen. Genesis
Ger. German
Ges. Gesenius Hebrew Grammar
Gk. Greek
GNB Good News Bible
GNP gender, number, person
GNS gender, number, state
Gp *Qal* passive, cf. p.59
gram. grammar/-atical
H *Hiphʿil*, cf. §28.12
Heb. Hebrew
Hp *Hophʿal*, cf. §28.12
HtD *Hithpaʿel*, cf. §28.12
i.e. that is
imperf. imperfect
impers. impersonal
impf. imperfect
impv. imperative
ind. indirect
indef. indefinite
indir. indirect
inf. infinitive
interrog. interrogative
intr. intransitive
intrans. intransitive
IPA International Phonetic Association
juss. jussive
kg. kilogram(s)
KJV King James' Version
Kt *kᵉṯîḇ*, written
L *Poʿel*, cf. §28.121
Lat. Latin
lb., lbs. pound(s)
lit. literally
loc. local, locative
LXX Septuagint

Abbreviations

m. masculine m. meter(s)
mda, mdc, mds masc. du. abs., cstr., suf.
mid. middle
mpa, mpc, mps masc. pl. abs., cstr., suf.
msa, msc, mss masc. sg. abs., cstr., suf.
MT Masoretic Text
N *Niph'al*, cf. §28.12
n. neuter, note
neg. negative
neut. neuter
n.o. near open
nom. nominative
num. number, numeral
obj. object, objective
OPers Old Persian
OSE Old South Arabic
p passive, plural
pace with due respect to
part. particle
pass. passive
perf. perfect
Pers. Persian
PGN person, gender, number
Phoen. Phoenician
phr. phrase
pl. plural
plur. plural
pred. predicate
preform. preformative
prep. preposition
pr.n. proper noun
pres. present
pron. pronoun
PS Proto-Semitic
ptcp. participle, participial
Q q^{e}*rî*, read
R *Pilpel*, cf. §28.121
Ṙ. Rule (number)
rad. radical
rel. relative
RSV Revised Standard Version
s suffixed, suffixial, cf. p.59
s singular
Sem. Semitic
sg. singular
sing. singular
st. abs. absolute state
st.cstr. construct state
suf. suffix, suffixial
Swed. Swedish
syll. syllable(s)
t infixed *t*, cf.§28.12
T. Table (number)
tr. transitive
trans. transitive
u.c. unaccented closed
Uger. Ugaritic
un.cl. unaccented closed
v vowel, cf. §16.3
vb. verb
VDC Verb Diagnosis Chart
voc. vocative
WCC *Pe Waw*, cf. §29.02
x times
YCC *Pe Yod*, cf. §29.02
2, 3, etc. see p.59
* hypothetical form
+ is eqaivalent to
< develops from
> develops into, becomes
/ or
+ is equivalent to
+ ? is equivalent to what?

ADDITIONS AND CORRECTIONS

To Part 1

p.6, ¶ 6, l.1 read §11.15
p.10, ¶ 3, l.1 read לְ|מָלְ|כוֹ
p.16, ¶ 5, l.3 read m.p.c.
p.16, ¶ 7, l.1 read m.p.c.
p.19, ¶ 4, l.3 read *wā-îš*
p.21, ¶ 9, l.4 read לַמֶּלֶךְ
p.21, 4 ll. f.b. read תּוֹכַחַת
p.24, ¶ 4, l.4 read suf.
p.29, 1 line f.b. read שֶׁבֶת
p.34, ¶ 2, l.5 read Root is *ʿśy*
p.39, ¶ 5, l.4 read עָשָׂה
p.41, 5 ll. f.b. readיְכַבֵּב
p.41, 4ll. f.b. read תְּכַבֵּב
p.51, ¶ 4, l.7 read *yišlōaḥ*
p.54, ¶ 1, l.6 read *ʾmn*
p.60 ¶ 6, l.1 read –תַ
p.63 1 line f.b. read כָּמוֹהָ
p.66 ¶ 5, l.1 read (a) 2:10²
p.70 ¶ 5, l.2 read 'And
p.75 ¶ 6, l.1 read *yešnô*
p.83 2 lines f.b. read הַגּוֹרָל
p.109 4 lines f.b. read אֵלַי
p.113 add Learn the words in BVG 1-11, 34-45.
p.113 delete repetion f. b. of p.112.
p.135 ¶ 5, l.1 read *šṓmaʿ*
p.156 last ¶ read *ʿal*
p.158 ¶ 5, l.1 read וְאָבִיו
p.166 ¶ 5, l.3 read *Ges.* §101*l*

To Part 2

§11.122 l.6, *omit*) *after* 213
§11.17 l.4, *read* MSS
§11.411 l.2, *read* מֹשֶׁה
p.19 *add* §11.413 The *Biblia Hebraica Stuttgartensia* does not follow these rules for the pointing of שׁ.
§11.441 l.1, *read* dāḡēš
§11.442 l.2, *likewise*
§11.443 l.1, *read* MSS; l.3, *read dāḡēš*
§11.7 ll.3,5, *read BH³*; *add BHS* has added a much larger quantity of marginal *mᵉsôrôṯ*.
§12.5 l.12, *read* [i̱]
§13.62 l.2, *add space after ḥāwāʰ*
§14.3 l.3, *add* (*before* ptcp.)
§15.131 l.1, *read* segolate
§15.231 l.2, *omit* (*before* §17.12
§15.721 l.3, *read* בַּיִת
§17.311 l.3, *read Qumrân*
§21. l.2, *read* indicate
§22.13 l.2, *read* §§27.117
§23.121 l.4, *read* with sg. with pl.
§23.123 l.2, *read* + קְטָלָה > קְטַלְתָּהּ
§23.221 ll.5, *read *nagb*
§24.5 l.2, *read* N-14
§24.6 l.3, *read* N-15
§26.232 l.3, *read ʾālep̄*
§27.212 l.2, *read* הֵבַנְתִּי
§27.22 l.2, *read* CaCaCa
§27.42 l.5, *read* prothetic

§27.422 l.4, *read* CCuCû

§27.721 l.2, *read* *C*^{e}*CāCaṯkā*

§27.722 l.2, *read* *C*^{e}*CaCtínî*

§28.211 l.1, *read* D10

§28.3 l.8, *read* lie';

§28.51 l.10, *add* HtD65 (same as HtD60)

§28.52 l.8, *add* An analysis of these forms in BDB suggests that some of them are probably tG rather than (H)tD, cf. §28.54.

§29.02 l.25, *read* נ in 1st

§29.211 l.3, *read* תְּאֻכַּל

§29.311 l.7, *read* יוֹצִיח

§29.321 l.3, *read* G20

§29.412 l.2, *add* Cf. §27.6511.

§29.631 l.17, *read* קָם §29.6318

§29.6313 l.3, *add* Cf. also §15.64.

§29.6326 l.2, *add* (before Pôlēl)

§29.633 l.3, *delete* n *to read* from

§29.641 l.2, *read* Examples

§29.71 l.14, *delete* 3

§30.1231 l.1, *insert* § *before* 30.113

§30.21 l.3, *read* "*his*

§30.311 l.10, *read* §35.5

§30.3222 l.1, *read* §30.3222

§30.3393 l.3, *read* *stands*

§31.11 l.1, *add* [ ] *to read* [was]

§31.122 l.1, *add* [ ] *to read* [is]

§31.125 l.1, *add* [ ] *to read* [is]

§31.27 l.2, *read* *my covenant*

§31.31 l.2, *read* אֱלֹהַּ

§31.33 p.146, *delete repetition of this section*

§31.5 l.1, *read* can be determined only by

§32.372 l.2, *for* *ʾôhēḇ* *read* *ʾôyēḇ*

§32.421 l.2, *delete* a *before* 'and

§32.5113 ll.1-4, *delete* the passage quoted *and substitute* Exod. 10:3, עַד־מָתַי מֵאַנְתָּ לֵעָנוֹת 'How many times do you refuse to humble yourself ...?'

§32.5142 l.5, *add* Cf. §38.644.

§32.5218 l.4, *add* Cf. §32.82.

§32.5311 l.5, *add* Cf. §38.552.

§33.1111 l.4, *read* *raḡlîm*

§33.1114 l.4, *for* soul *read* voice

§33.124 *at end insert* §§33.125, .126 from p.173

§33.125 *belongs on* p.172

§33.126 *belongs on* p. 172

§34.13 l.3, *for* §38.31 *read* §38.81

§35.422 l.3, *read* *while*

§36.112 l.2, *read* *hahôl*^{e}*ḵîm baḥōšeḵ*

§36.152 l.2, *read* *b*^{e}*ḵol-yôm*

Part 1
LESSONS

TO THE TEACHER

You may pick up a copy of this *Handbook*, look at the Table of Contents, examine the detailed presentation of Phonology, the unusual Synoptic Paradigms, and the quantity of Hebrew to be read (about 15 chapters), and be tempted to put it aside with the comment, "It won't work!" Or you may have had some experience with "the inductive method," and found that, while it is certainly a more enjoyable method of learning, nothing is really learned. At the end of the course the student still does not know the language. Well, before you make a decision, please let me have this chance of explaining what this method entails and how it is expected to work.

The method used in this *Handbook*, simply described, is *to begin with the context.* Orthography, phonology, morphology, syntax, and vocabulary are all learned by encountering the various elements in a connected passage. This method, of course, plunges the student into everything all at once. It is like teaching a person to swim by throwing him or her into a deep lake. Obviously, some planned approach is necessary. In this *Handbook* certain features indicate the approach I use.

Transliteration is used, along with Hebrew orthography. You and I, after years of experience, can look at a Hebrew word and pronounce it almost as easily as we can pronounce a word in Roman characters – but the student has not yet reached that stage. Some years ago, my friend Dr. G. Douglas Young attempted to reduce all Hebrew to transliteration for his grammar. His argument was basically sound: the student could read, recall, and reproduce transliteration much more readily than he could do the same with Hebrew characters. The basic flaw in that system is obvious: only Dr. Young's work was transliterated. To read the Bible, the student must read Hebrew orthography. I have attempted to use both, sometimes Hebrew without transliteration, sometimes only transliteration, and often both side by side. The goals are to learn the approximate and recognizable sound of a word from the start, and to learn to read Hebrew as soon as possible. Teachers who look upon Hebrew orthography as an esoteric mystery will resent transliteration. I consider my task to teach, rather than to impress my students with a self-awarded Master of Mysteries.

Learning is through *repetition*, rather than through attempted mastery at the first encounter. At this point, I would caution the teacher *not* to expect mastery of each new item as it is introduced. Repetition is built into the system. Not every encounter is meaningful, and nothing is learned through meaningless encouters. I have attempted to build in many meaningful encounters of the more significant elements of the language. Please don't ignore them. Remember that some students learn more slowly than others.

The *more frequent elements* of the language receive *more emphasis*. For example, about 10% of the vocabulary makes up about 90% of the text on any given page. Therefore, the student who knows 850 high-frequency words will read much better than one who knows 850 words drawn at random. I stress frequency vocabulary. The same fact is true, *mutatis mutandis*, of other elements of the language. Why spend as much time on the Hithpalpel as on the Qal imperfect? Why not emphasize the things that the student will see most often? In Volume 2 of this *Handbook*, I have attempted to include everything significant, so the student has access to it. In addition, I have given copious references to *Gesenius' Hebrew Grammar* (ed. E. Kautzsch, trans. A. E. Cowley, 2d ed. 1910). But in the lessons, I have concentrated on the more common phenomena. The *Handbook* is designed to be used by working from the lessons to the grammar, not the reverse.

Each lesson has a primary purpose, but this is not the total purpose of that lesson. The teacher should use the lesson to make encounters with the indicated subject as meaningful as possible. Do not attempt, however, to use that as an occasion to present material other than that which is in the lesson.

Along about Lesson 12, the student begins to be overwhelmed by the amount of material being presented. For the next fifteen or twenty lessons, he or she will need a great deal of understanding and encouragement. Those of us who have been through the system several times know that this takes place, and that it always comes out satisfactorily – but students do not know that, and some drop the course at this point. What is happening is simply this: the quantities of new material must be assimilated at the student's own pace. Nothing is gained by *reducing* the pace; it is *repetition* that counts. But the student needs your help to assure him or her that a learning plateau has been reached, and that there will be a period of no apparent progress until assimilation at that level is nearly complete. Then once again there will be noticeable progress.

All learning is *in context*. The context, however, is not artificial, composed perchance by one who does not use the language naturally, but rather it is the actual language of those who used it as their mother-tongue. For this reason, I refuse to ask the students to compose sentences in Hebrew. To do so is to impress errors on the student's mind. And, frankly, most of us who teach Biblical Hebrew do not have sufficient fluency in the language to speak or write in it. I differentiate here between Biblical and Modern Hebrew.

Most of all, I attempt to make the learning process *enjoyable*. Not *easy*, but *enjoyable*. The student should have a constant feeling that he or she is learning a very useful tool, that there is a sound reason for learning elements of phonology (no pun intended!) as well as morphology and syntax, and that the teacher's role is to teach, to help to learn, and to encourage, not to test, to criticize, and to ridicule. The worst epitaph I can imagine is one that would read, "He loved to teach, but he taught his students to hate the subject."

I have used proverbs, pithy sayings, and scriptural portions as space-fillers. Some of these may profitably be used to illustrate points in the lessons; others may be memorized. But, above all, teach *what is in the lesson.*

Encourage the student to keep some systematic record of his or her observations. The major weakness of the inductive method is the lack of a synthesizing process. I have endeavored to compensate for this by synthetic illustrations, but the student should carry this out by entering observed phenomena systematically in a notebook, both in Hebrew characters and in transliteration. Teach the student to observe, and he or she will be learning the rest of his or her life.

The ear to hear and the eye to see, The Lord made both of them.	אֹזֶן שֹׁמַעַת וְעַיִן רֹאָה יהוה עָשָׂה גַם־שְׁנֵיהֶם׃

Proverbs 20:12

1

Purpose: To get acquainted with the *Handbook* and the method.
Materials: Handbook, Parts 1, 2, 3, and 4

Since this course is designed for *inductive* study, let's get acquainted with the *Handbook* inductively. Note that it is divided into four parts. For your convenience, Part 1 has been bound separately. Parts 2, 3, and 4 have been bound as Volume 2. You will normally work with Vol. 1 open to the lesson you are studying (as you are doing right now), and you will be referring continually to Vol. 2 for information that is designed to help you learn certain points in the lesson. *Note the order:* Always work from the lesson to the grammar, not the reverse.

Now turn to Vol. 2. The front portion (Part 2) is the *Grammar.* It is divided into three divisions: Phonology, Morphology, and Syntax. Note that these 3 divisions are subdivided into many sections (indicated by the sign § 'section,' followed by numbers). Look at §10: it defines Phonology. Don't bother to learn it now, since this is simply a familiarization run on the *Handbook.* Now look at §20, where Morphology is defined. Next look at §30. What is defined there? Turn now to §06ff and read about the numbering system. Look over the examples at the bottom of that page. What have you learned?

Turn to Part 3, Tables and Paradigms. Leaf through it and get an idea of what is contained there. Note that the Paradigms are "synoptic." If you don't know the meaning of "paradigm" and "synoptic," where would you look? Do it. In most grammars, paradigms give all significant examples of a particular type of a verb or a noun. In this *Handbook,* we get a synoptic view of a certain feature of several different types, e.g. the "G-stem" of "regular" and "irregular" verbs. You are *not* expected to memorize entire paradigms; rather, you are expected to *observe* (and, of course, learn) the significant characteristics of forms so you can recognize them quickly and accurately.

Now look at Part 4, Basic Vocabulary. In this *Handbook,* we stress the learning of a *basic* vocabulary (i.e. the words that occur most frequently in a language). About 10% of the words occur about 90% of the time. Of the more than 8,600 words in the OT vocabulary, only about 1,100 (about 12.5%) occur 25 times or more. Obviously, these are the words to learn first. The basic vocabulary is arranged alphabetically, and each word is numbered (following the numbering of *Strong's Concordance*). In addition a letter-and-number symbol indicates the word's frequency. All words that occur 15x or more (except proper names) are listed. Beginning with Lesson 4, you will be learning groups of words. These groups, fitted to the lessons, will be found in the back of Vol. 1.

Now, how do we go about studying? We go through each *Lesson,* point by point. We look up the references to the Grammar and the Tables and Paradigms. We observe, record observations, compare our records, learn a few points, and move on. Concentrate on a *few* points in each lesson. *Do not try to learn everything* in a lesson, but work to the limit of your own ability. Repetition has been built into the *Handbook*, so if you do not learn a point in one lesson, you will have many more opportunities to learn it.

Learning is *repetition*. We have deliberately–even mechanically–built repetition into the *Handbook*. Not only are there periodic reviews, but each point that is introduced will be repeated in subsequent lessons, then ignored for several lessons, and then reintroduced for relearning. If it takes 5 meaningful encounters to learn a point, we have built in 10 or even 15 encounters that are designed to be meaningful. If you get bored by such repetition, remember that another student needs that extra encounter to learn the matter. If after several lessons, you find that you no longer need to look up §13.111, skip it. If you can look at a Hebrew word and tell at a glance its form, its root, and other details that are significant for the understanding of that word in its context, pass on to the next. Just remember, some learn more slowly, some more rapidly. You should work at your own pace.

We shall make use of *synthetic* materials (grammars, lexicons, commentaries, etc.), in order to draw upon knowledge already gained—for no one in his right mind would seek to cover the entire field of human knowledge inductively. At the same time, we must not let the conclusions arrived at by other students blunt our own observations of the data.

Keep a *notebook*, and record carefully your observations. Periodically review and rearrange them, until you have a small grammar of your own. Inductive learning breaks down if the student fails to synthesize what he observes inductively.

Plan to spend *two hours* on each lesson. Make the time count. Don't spin your wheels, but keep learning new points. Jot down points that are not clear. Learn to ask questions of the text, and soon it will be answering you. If you are weak in English grammar, spend time on §30ff. The first 25-30 lessons will be the hardest, especially from about Lesson 12 on. The reason: you are continually encountering new items, far more rapidly than you can assimilate them. From about Lesson 30 on, you will encounter few *new* items, but you will be constantly reviewing what you have previously seen (and probably not learned, or not fully understood). *Stay with it!* There is no *easy* way to learn a language. The inductive method can be *more enjoyable* and, properly used, can be more *effective*.

Read over §§01.-05, §§10., 10.1, 10.2, 10.3, 10.4.

2

Purpose: To start learning the alphabet and the pointing
Materials: Esther 1:1

וַיְהִ֗י בִּימֵ֣י אֲחַשְׁוֵר֑וֹשׁ ה֣וּא אֲחַשְׁוֵר֗וֹשׁ הַמֹּלֵךְ֙ מֵהֹ֣דּוּ וְעַד־ א
כּ֔וּשׁ שֶׁ֛בַע וְעֶשְׂרִ֥ים וּמֵאָ֖ה מְדִינָֽה׃

וַיְהִי[1]—Hebrew is read *from right to left* (←), see §11., §11.1. Consonants: ו *wāw*, י *yôḏ*, ה *hê*, י *yôḏ*. Compare (cf.) ו and י. See TABLE B. Vowels: ַ *pattāḥ*, ְ *š^{e}wâ*, ִ *ḥîrîq*. For vowels see TABLE C. Accent under ה, *ṭip̄ḥâ*, §11.53. Read §§11.5-.521. Final *yôḏ* is a vowel lengthener, §11.2. Transliteration, *wa-y^{e}-hî^{y}*. 'And it was.'

בִּימֵי[2]—ב *bêṯ*, מ *mêm*; you should recognize *yôḏ* (1:1[1]). Vowels: *ḥîrîq*, ֵ *ṣērê*. Note בּ with *dāḡēš*, §§11.44, .441. Accent, *mûnāḥ*, §11.54. י without vowel is a vowel letter, §11.21. *bî^{y}-mê^{y}* 'in the days of.'

אֲחַשְׁוֵרוֹשׁ[3]—א *'ālep̄* (§12.51, §12.35), ח *ḥêṯ* (§§12.331, .341), שׁ *šîn* (pronounce *sheen;* §11.41). ו *wāw*, ר *rêš*, וֹ *ḥôlām-wāw* (§11.3231). ֲ *ḥăṭap̄-pattāḥ* (§11.32); you have had the others. ֑ is *'aṯnāḥ* (§11.533, §11.55). וֵ: *wāw* with vowel must be consonantal. וֹ could be *wō* or *ô^{w}*—but note the ר. Since it has no vowel written under it, וֹ must be its vowel. ֲ is a short vowel (§14.2); וֹ is a long vowel (§14.1). *'ă-ḥaš-wē-rô^{w}š* 'Ahasuerus.'

הוּא[4]—*hê*, spirant, §12.42. §11.54. No vowel under ה, but וּ *šûrûq* follows, §11.324. א is quiescent, §13.55. *hû'* 'he, that.'

אֲחַשְׁוֵרוֹשׁ[5]—See 1:1[3]. Note *r^{e}ḇî^{a}'* over ר, §11.534. א is a stop, §12.411. ח, שׁ, consonantal ו, and ר are spirants, §12.421. ו *w*, originally a bilabial, §12.31. ר *r* probably uvular, §12.341, originally alveolar flap, §12.321. שׁ *š*, sibilant, §12.322.

הַמֹּלֵךְ[6]—ל *lāmed*, §11.15. ךְ *kap̄ sôp̄îṯ* 'final kaph,' §11.131; if it has no vowel, it is always written with shewa. מּ, with strong dagesh, §11.431, read §11.43. Note ֹ *ḥôlām*, §11.323. Read §§12.-12.22, and start using §12.5. Accent is postpositive, §11.571. *ham-mô-lēḵ* 'the (one) ruling.'

מֵהֹדּוּ[7]—First letter? vowel? §12.5. §11.32. Second letter? vowel? accent? §11.54. ד *dāleṯ* with *dāḡēš*: read §11.44. Dagesh both doubles and hardens, §11.43, §11.442. וּ *šûrûq*. *mē-hōd-dû* 'from India.'

וְעַד־כּוּשׁ[8]—ע *'áyin* (not Y!), strong glottal stop, §12.351. ־ *maqqēp̄*, §11.45. כּ *kap̄* with dagesh, cf. 1:1[6], §11.131, and read §11.44 carefully. This is the light dagesh, §11.441. Note וְ and וּ—which is consonant, which is vowel letter? (1:1[4]). Note that ד and שׁ at word-end have no vowels. Accent, *zāqēp̄-qāṭôn*, §11.535. *w^{e}-aḏ—kû^{w}š* 'and unto Cush.'

שֶׁבַע[9]—ב is *rāp̄ê*, read §11.44, §11.443. ע is pronounced how? Squeeze your glottis! Accent conjunctive; read §11.57. *šé-ḇa‘* 'seven.'

וְעֶשְׂרִים[10]—שׂ *śîn,* §11.41. Note שׁ and שׂ. ם *mêm sôp̄ît,* §11.131. ◌ֶ *s*ᵉ*ḡôl,* §11.32. ◌ִי *ḥîrîq-yôḏ,* §14.13, §11.322. First *š*ᵉ*wâ* is vocalic, second is silent (read §15.251). *w*ᵉ*-‘es-rî*ʸ*m* 'and 20.'

וּמֵאָה[11]—◌ָ *qāmāṣ gāḏôl,* §11.321. וּ *šûrûq* is the only vowel that stands at beginning of word, §16.3f. Review §11.21, §11.53. *û-mē-'ā*ʰ 'and 100.'

מְדִינָה׃[12]—נ *nûn.* ׃◌ֽ *sillûq* and *sôp̄ pāsûq,* read §11.531, §11.46. *m*ᵉ*-ḏî*ʸ*-nā*ʰ 'province(s).'

The following consonants have appeared: א ב ב ד ד ה ו ח י כ ך ל מ ם נ ע ר שׂ שׁ. Be sure you know them, names, transliteration, pronunciation, and how to write them (TABLE D).

The following vowels have appeared: ◌ְ ◌ָ ◌ֶ ◌ֵ ◌ַ ◌ִ ◌ָה ◌ֵי ◌ִי וֹ וּ. Know their names and values (TABLE C).

Note carefully: ב כ ר ד י ו נ ו ח ה ד ך שׁ שׂ.

Read over §§01.—04. Read over §§10.—10.442.

Learn the terms: consonant, vowel, diphthong, transliteration, quiescent, vowel lengthener, conjunctive, disjunctive (accent); dagesh, begadkepat, athnaḥ, sillûq, sôph pasûq.

Learn to write Hebrew clearly and accurately. *Write* the letters; don't *draw* them. Omit serifs and shading, just as you do when writing English.

with serifs and shading: A B C D E F G H I J
with serifs, no shading: A B C D E F G H I J
no serifs, no shading: A B C D E F G H I J

ABCDE ABCDE ABCDE
אבגדה אבגדה אבגדה
שמע ישראל שמע ישראל שמע ישראל

אבגדהוזחטיכךלמםנןסעפףצץקרשת

3

Purpose: To learn the orthography
Materials: Esther 1:2

2 בְּיָמִים הָהֵם כְּשֶׁבֶת ׀
הַמֶּלֶךְ אֲחַשְׁוֵרוֹשׁ עַל כִּסֵּא מַלְכוּתוֹ אֲשֶׁר בְּשׁוּשַׁן הַבִּירָה׃

בְּיָמִים[1]—בּ, read carefully §11.441, §12.4, .41. What vowel follows? §11.32. Read carefully §11.431. Compare מּ and ם and read §11.13f. Read §11.2. *bay-yā-mîʸm* 'in the days.'

הָהֵם[2]—For *qāmāṣ gāḏôl* read §11.32, Table C. For *ṣērê* §11.32, and for *'aṯnāḥ* §11.533. Read §11.5. *hā-hēm* 'the those' 'in those days.'

כְּשֶׁבֶת ׀[3]—For כּ §11.441. For ְ §15.25, .2521. שֶׁ §11.41, §11.54, §17.11. Read §17. ב read §12.422, §11.443. ת is also spirantized, §12.422. For | §11.72. Note that it cannot be a major pause here. *kᵉ-šé-ḇeṯ* 'when the sitting of.'

הַמֶּלֶךְ[4]—Cf. 1:1[6]. מּ §11.431, §13.31. Read §11.43 and §13.3. For ֶ read §11.54, §11.57. Read also §17.11, and start to notice where stress-accent is placed. For ךְ §11.1311; note where the shewa is placed. Read §16.363. What is an *allophone*? §10.23. Read §11.44. *ham-mé-leḵ* 'the king.' With the preceding word the phrase means 'when the king [was] sitting.'

אֲחַשְׁוֵרוֹשׁ[5]—Material will be omitted as we progress. This word occurred twice in 1:1[3 5]. If you have any problems, review the notes in Lesson 2.

עַל[6]—Learn to pronounce ע as an emphatic glottal stop. Accent is conjunctive §11.521, 11.54. *'al* 'upon.'

כִּסֵּא[7]—Note כּ and סּ: which dagesh is a hardener and which is a doubler? Review §11.431, §11.441. Make it a point to learn this *now*. א is quiescent §15.54. Is accent conjunctive or disjunctive? §11.521. *kis-sē'* '[the] throne of.'

מַלְכוּתוֹ[8]—Note וּ §11.324, §11.3231. Both כ and ת are spirantized, §11.44. Accent is *zāqēp̄ qāṭôn*, like a shewa on top of the letter §11.535. *mal-ḵûʷ-ṯôʷ*, his kingship/royalty.'

אֲשֶׁר[9]—Note *ḥaṭap̄ pattāḥ* ֲ. Read carefully §11.325, §15.253, §15.42. Learn which sounds (letters) are *gutturals*. Is שׁ *šîn* or *śîn*? §11.41. Accent conj. or disj.? §11.521. *'ă-šer* 'which.'

בְּשׁוּשַׁן[10]—New letter ן *nûn sôp̄îṯ* §11.131. Is dagesh in בּ strong or light? §11.43ff. Is shewa vocal or silent? §16.35. Is וּ a vowel (*ûʷ*) or a geminate consonant (*ww*)? How can you tell? §11.433. Note: if וּ is a geminate consonant, *it must have a vowel with it*–is there one? In an accented syllable, *qāmāṣ* must be *ā*, §15.11, cf. §11.321. What kind of accent? *b^e-šû^w-šan* 'in Susa.'

הַבִּירָה׃''—After vowel, dagesh in בּ must be strong (doubling) §16.3612, therefore syllable must be *closed* §16.11, and the vowel a *normal short* vowel §14.232. Start to master Table E. For ִי cf. §§11.2, .21, .211. ָ is *ā*, §15.11, cf. §14.2. ָה is a vowel, §11.21. Note ֽ – silluq, §11.531 it looks like metheg (§11.58), but where is silluq found?. Soph pasuq ׃, §11.46. *hab-bî^y-rā^h*, 'the palace/citadel.'

New consonants: ת ס ן.

Note carefully the differences: ד ר ל ת ח ה ם ס ן ו י.

Long vowels thus far: ָה, ֵי, וֹ, וּ/. Read §14., §14.1, §14.13.

Short vowels thus far: ַ ָ ֶ ֵ ֹ ֻ ָ. Read §14.2, §14.232.

Know the meanings: closed syllable, open syllable, geminate consonant; begadkepat, athnaḥ, silluq, soph pasûq; light dagesh, strong dagesh; stop, spirant, spirantization. Put them in your notebook.

Transliterate from Heb. characters to Roman Zephaniah 3:8, using the system of transliteration found in Tables B and C. You will have difficulty with the shewa and the dagesh, but these will be cleared away in the next few lessons. Concentrate on getting a useful phonetic equivalent for the Heb. orthography.

לָכֵן 8
חַכּוּ־לִי נְאֻם־יְהוָה לְיוֹם קוּמִי לְעַד כִּי מִשְׁפָּטִי לֶאֱסֹף
גּוֹיִם לְקָבְצִי מַמְלָכוֹת לִשְׁפֹּךְ עֲלֵיהֶם זַעְמִי כֹּל חֲרוֹן אַפִּי
כִּי בְּאֵשׁ קִנְאָתִי תֵּאָכֵל כָּל־הָאָרֶץ׃

RULES

1a. A *dagesh* in a *begadkepat* at the beginning of a word or following a shewa is a light dagesh, indicating stopped pronunciation (§11.44). A dagesh in any other letter, or in a begadkepat in any other position, is a strong dagesh, indicating a geminate (doubled) consonant (§11.43). A strong dagesh in a begadkepat both doubles and hardens it (§11.442).

1b. Consonants with shewa, except begadkepat and ט, frequently lose the strong dagesh (§13.41). This particularly applies to י.

4

Purpose: To study syllabification and vowel quantity
Materials: Esther 1:3

בִּשְׁנַת שָׁלוֹשׁ לְמָלְכוֹ עָשָׂה מִשְׁתֶּה לְכָל־שָׂרָיו וַעֲבָדָיו 3
חֵיל ׀ פָּרַס וּמָדַי הַפַּרְתְּמִים וְשָׂרֵי הַמְּדִינוֹת לְפָנָיו׃

1:3 בִּשְׁנַת [1]—Always start from the *end* of a word to syllabify. Every syllable must begin with a consonant (read §16.3). Read §16. בִּשְׁ|נַת, 2 syllables, both closed, §§16.11, .32.33. The word is *in construct,* hence has no primary stress-accent (Rule 3), §25.4, .42. Both syllables are *unaccented closed,* §16.33. The word is composed of the prep. *b*^{e}- + *š*^{e}*nat̲,* hence a zero shewa, §15.2522, §16.3624. The *ḥîrîq* ִ develops from 2 shewas, §15.651. Read §15.243. *biš-nat̲* 'in the year of.'

שָׁלוֹשׁ [2]—שָׁ|לוֹשׁ, primary accent on ultima, §16.1. Pure long vowel, §14.1, .11, written full (§11.322, .3231. The *penult* (§16.1) is open, §16.32; since it is immediately before the stress-accent, it is *near-open,* §16.321, .3211. Be sure you know this thoroughly. A short vowel normally lengthens in a near-open syllable, hence *šā-lô*^{w}*š* 'three.'

לְמָלְכוֹ [3]—לְ|מָלְ|כוֹ, 3 syllables, read §16.2. Ultima open, accented, pure-long vowel; penult closed, unaccented; antepenult open, hence distant-open, §16.3212. Look at the short vowels: in the penult מָלְ, therefore ָ must be *qāmāṣ-ḥăṭûp̄,* short *o,* §11.321. Shewa in distant open (d.o.) is a reduced vowel, §15.252. כ is spirantized after silent shewa, §15.2522. *l*^{e}*-mol-k̲ô*^{w} 'to (= of) his ruling.'

עָשָׂה [4]—עָ|שָׂה, ultima accented (open), penult near-open, hence lengthened, ה is a vowel-letter, §11.2. *'ā-śā*^{h} 'he made.'

מִשְׁתֶּה [5]—Note dagesh in תּ: since this is a begadkepat, the dagesh could be light or strong, §11.43ff. But since it follows shewa, it must be light, Rule la. Study §16.3622. Review §11.441. The shewa must be a syllable divider, §15.251, and שׁ must close a syllable. For ֶ in accented syllable, read §15.732, .7322. Review §11.535. *miš-tê*^{h} 'a banquet.'

לְכָל־שָׂרָיו [6]—Syllabify, working from end. What does maqqeph (§11.45) tell you about accent on לְכָל? §17.121. Then what is ָ? §11.321, §14.23, .231. Is the shewa silent or vocal? §15.25, .252. Whis syllable is near-open (n.o.)? §15.12. The combination רָיו is pronounced [raw] or [rav], read §13.52, .525. *l*^{e}*-k̲ol-śā-rā*^{y}*w* 'for all his princes.'

וַעֲבָדָיו [7]—Syllabify, identify each syllable (acc., n.o., d.o., cl). There are 2 d.o. syll., neither with simple shewa. Read §15.253, then §15.653 (Rule 21). Review §11.58f, §15.23, §15.12, §14.31, and 1:3[6]. What does ֲ tell you? §11.533. *wa-'ă-b̲ā-d̲ā*^{y}*w* 'and his servants.'

|חֵיל[8]—One syll., §16.2, a monophthong §15.7, in cstr., hence no primary accent (Rule 3), cf. §15.7324. Review §11.54, §11.72. *ḥêʸl* 'the might of.'

פָּרַ֫ס[9]—Syllabify, identify each syll. Note pattaḥ in acc. cl. The mark * above ר is a Masoretic note (§11.7), telling us that *qāmāṣ* is found in some texts. Which would you expect? Rule 13. *pā-ras,* 'Persia.'

וּמָדַ֗י[10]—Syllabify, identify syllables. How many vowels and diphthongs? Therefore, how many syllables? Learn §16.2 *now.* Read §16.31, review §15.12, §14.33, §15.72. Loan-words often do not follow the rules. *ûʷ-mā-ḏay* 'and Media.'

הַפַּרְתְּמִים[11]—Syllabify. There are 2 begadkepats with dagesh: read §§11.441, .442 carefully, and identify the strong dagesh (Rule 1a). Read §15.2511 carefully. You should have cvc-cvc-cv-cvc. For n.o. with shewa, possibly §15.241, but this is a loan word. Review §14.13. *hap-par-tᵉ-mîm* 'the nobles.'

וְשָׂרֵ֫י[12]—Without further instruction, *you are expected to syllabify every word in the next several lessons,* until you can do it easily and accurately. Review §17.12. Word in cstr., hence שָׂ may be compensation vowel §15.14. Note §15.73. *wᵉ-śā-rêʸ* 'and [the] princes of.'

הַמְּדִינ֖וֹת[13]—Identify the long vowels. §11.322, §11.3231, §14.1. Which dagesh? §16.3612. Does §16.3622 apply? *ham-mᵉ-ḏîʸ-nôʷṯ* 'the provinces.'

לְפָנָֽיו׃[14]—How many vowels? How many syllables? Is the shewa a syllable? §16.21. Does the begadkepat that follows have dagesh?. Cf. 1:2[13]. *lᵉ-pā-nāʸw* '[were] before him.'

New consonants: כ פּ פ ת; new vowel: ָ (*o*); diphthongs: ָו ֵי ָיו.

Know the meanings of: closed, open, accented, unaccented, near-open, distant-open, lengthened, reduced, pure-long vowel, lengthened short vowel, zero shewa.

Learn Rules 1a, 3, 13.

Syllabify Est. 1:1.

Memorize the words in Vocabulary Group 1.

3. Words joined by maqqeph and words in construct have only one major accent (§17.12).

יִרְאַת יְהוָה רֵאשִׁית דָּעַת
The fear of the Lord is the beginning of wisdom.
(Prov. 1:7)

Purpose: To introduce morphology
Materials: Esther 1:4

4 בְּהַרְאֹתוֹ אֶת־עֹשֶׁר כְּבוֹד מַלְכוּתוֹ וְאֶת־יְקָר תִּפְאֶרֶת
גְּדוּלָּתוֹ יָמִים רַבִּים שְׁמוֹנִים וּמְאַת יוֹם׃

Read carefully §§20.-20.31.

בְּהַרְאֹתוֹ [1]—Syllabify all words. בְּ|הַרְ|אֹ|תוֹ. Be sure you understand why it is divided in this manner. Read §§20.1,.12, 20.2,.212. -בּ is a preposition (§30.35). וֹ- is a pronominal suffix, §23.121, §30.312. The balance is a verb, to be discussed in later lessons. א is defective, §11.324f, תוֹ is *plene* $\hat{o}^{w}$, §11.322. Read §11.3241. Review §11.534, §17. 'In his causing to see' = 'when he showed.'

אֶת־עֹשֶׁר [2]—For עשׁ see §11.411. Note maqqeph, §11.45. We have here the beginning of a chain of constructs (§36.31f). Read §17.12f carefully. Accent on ר is postpositive (§11.571), and since the stress-accent (secondary) is on the penult, the accent is repeated over עֹ. Review §11.52f, §11.45. אֶת is the sign of the definite direct object (d.d.o.), §34.113. 'The wealth of.'

כְּבוֹד [3]—Cstr., hence כְּ is d.o. §17.121. בוֹד is unacc. cl., hence long $\hat{o}^{w}$, §15.22. 'The glory of.'

מַלְכוּתוֹ [4]—וֹ- is pron. suf., 1:4[1], §23.21. \וּת\ indicates an abstract idea, '-ship, -ness,' §24.56. The root is מלך *m-l-k*, §20.3. *It will be easier to learn a basic vocabulary if you learn to group words from the same root.* A pron. suf. makes a word definite, §30.3222, §36.523. If the last word in cstr. is definite, all words in the chain are def., §36.31-.312. 'His kingship' = 'the wealth of the glory of his kingship.'

וְאֶת־יְקָר [5]—w^{e} is d.o., *'et* unacc.cl., y^{e} is d.o. in cstr. §17.121. The word $y^{e}q\hat{a}r$ has the same form in abs. and cstr., hence $\hat{a}$ must be long (Rule 2a). 'And the costliness of.'

תִּפְאֶרֶת [6]—תִּפְ|אֶ|רֶת with accent on penult, a segolate (§17.11). ֶ-ֶת is a fem. morpheme, §25.131; for development, see §15.61. Originally the word was something like **tip'artu.* 'The beauty/adornment of.'

גְּדוּלָּתוֹ [7]—וֹ is what morpheme? §23.121. ָת- is an original fem. sg morpheme, preserved in cstr. and suf. forms (as well as fem. of segolates), §25.13. Is the word definite? What does this do to the chain of cstrs.? §36.3131. Review §11.53. 'His greatness.' [Note that the word 'greatness' is fem. (abstract), but the pron. suf. is masc.]

יָמִים רַבִּים [8]—We shall begin to study words in phrases. Note the ending ִים– and read §25.12. This is a masc. pl. absolute (m.p.a.) morpheme. Note position of adjective: in Heb. it regularly follows the noun it modifies, §30.32, §36.12, and is in concord (i.e. it agrees in gender, number, and state), §36.11.

שְׁמוֹנִים [9]—ִים– is what morpheme? §25.12. Syllabify and identify each syllable. The pl. of '8' is '80'–don't ask why! §26.26.

וּמְאַת יוֹם׃ [10]—*û*^{w}*-m*^{e}*-aṯ*, §16.3. ַת– is what morpheme? §25.13. *yô*^{w}*m* < **yawm*, §15.72ff. Review §11.531. 'Eighty and one hundred of day' = '180 days.'

This is just an *introduction* to morphology. We must study it from now on, until every morpheme is quickly apparent. If you have not yet started a notebook, do so now. Record your observations until you no longer need to do so (which should be for at least the next 40 lessons!)

New consonants: גּ ק. Review others. Note differences: כ נ ג.

Note these words: הַמֶּלֶךְ 1:1[6], הַמֶּלֶךְ 1:2[4], לְמָלְכוֹ 1:3[3], and מַלְכוּתוֹ 1:4[4]; what do you see? Read §20.2. What is the common *root* of these words? What does it mean? *Don't look it up until you have tried to figure it out!* Learn to use your power of reasoning.

Now go back over Lessons 2–4 and analyze –ל and –ו similarly. See if you can figure out the morphemes ִים– and וֹת–. Look for other morphemes. You may see some that are not there, but at least you're looking.

Learn Rules 2, 4, and 5. Learn the basic vocabulary in Group 2.

13a. Short vowels normally *lengthen* in accented or near-open syllables, and *reduce* in distant-open syllables (§15.11, §15.12, §15.23)

13b. Compensatory vowels do not reduce (§15.233).

13c. The original vowel of a segolate does not reduce in sg. cstr. (§15.232). It does, however, reduce in pl. abs. forms.

13d. In many forms, *ṣērê* does not reduce (§15.223).

פּוֹרֵעַ מוּסָר מוֹאֵס נַפְשׁוֹ.

He who ignores instruction despises himself.

(Prov. 15:32)

6

Purpose: To study the behavior of short-vowels
Materials: Esther 1:5

ה וּבִמְלוֹאת ׀ הַיָּמִים
הָאֵלֶּה עָשָׂה הַמֶּלֶךְ לְכָל־הָעָם הַנִּמְצְאִים בְּשׁוּשַׁן הַבִּירָה
לְמִגָּדוֹל וְעַד־קָטָן מִשְׁתֶּה שִׁבְעַת יָמִים בַּחֲצַר גִּנַּת בִּיתַן
הַמֶּלֶךְ׃

1:5 וּבִמְלוֹאת [1]—Masoretic note (§11.61) calls attention to unusual form. Correct form is given in the *qᵉrê* in bottom margin (§16.31). Form here is built by analogy. -ו is conjunction, §30.36. -ב is prep., §30.35. §20.2, §20.211, §22.41. Balance is a verb, in cstr., hence no major accent (Rule 3). Now note the vowels: וֹ is pure-long (Rule 2a). *wᵉḇᵉmᵉ-* developed to *ûʷ-ḇim-* under Rule 8 (§16.31) and Rule 19 (§15.651). §11.5, .521, .54. 'and in the filling of.'

הַיָּמִים הָאֵלֶּה — ־ִים §25.231. ·הַ is def. art. §22.2. So is הָ. Start to master Table G. For אֵלֶּה note accent; *'ēl-* is acc. cl., hence vowel is lengthened (R. 13). *-lêʰ* is a monophthong §15.7, §15.73; this word is an exception to §15.7322. In a similar way work out the vowels in *hay-yā-mîʸm*. For the demonstrative pronoun, see §30.3123, and for concord §§36.11, .12. Review §11.534. 'the days the these.' With the previous word, read 'when these days were filled.'

עָשָׂה הַמֶּלֶךְ [3]—Cf. 1:3[4], 1:2[4]. Read §30.33, §30.31. In future lessons we shall omit words which you are supposed to know without explanation, but be sure you can explain them. הַמֶּלֶךְ is a segolate, §24.21. Such words do not lengthen ֶ under accent, §15.232. Read §15.35, §17.11. Is שׂ *šîn* or *śîn*? Explain the vowels in עָשָׂה. 'He made, the king' = 'the king made.'

לְכָל־הָעָם [4]—Identify the def. art., note vowel, see Table G. 1:5[2]. -לְ is a prep., §20.2. For כָּל see 1:3[6]. Which *qāmāṣ*? What kind of syllable? For עָם, §15.133. 'for all the people.'

הַנִּמְצְאִים [5]—See §15.2511, and then syllabify. ·הַ 1:5[2], §22.2. ־ִים is what morpheme? §25.231. נ is a stem-indicator (to be discussed when we get to verbs) often passive, and the word is a participle (ptcp.), §30.382, a verbal adjective, hence in concord with הָעָם. As in Eng., 'people' can be sg. or pl.; here pl., 'the [ones who are] being found.' The form should be **nimṣā'îm,* cf. §15.241f.

בְּשׁוּשַׁן הַבִּירָה [6]—(a) 1:2[10]. This word is always vocalized with *pattāḥ*. For בּ §22.4. (b) 1:2[11]. §22.2 ־ָה is fem. sg. absolute morpheme, §25.13, .131.

לְמִגָּדוֹל וְעַד־קָטָן [7]—(a) *l*^{e}- 1:5[4]. *migg-* for *ming-*, read §13.1, .111, Rule 11. §22.42. *gāḏôl* is an adj. used substantivally, §30.31, §24.4, .41. Explain each vowel. (b) *w*^{e} is a conjunction, §30.36, §22.1. *ʿaḏ* is a prep., §30.35f. *qāṭān* is adj. used substantivally (§30.31). Explain the quantity of each vowel (§15). *l*^{e}*min* . . . *w*^{e}*ʿaḏ* is an idiom, 'from . . . to;' 'from great to small' is a merism, meaning 'everybody.'

מִשְׁתֶּה [8]—Cf. 1:3[5]. There is no indefinite article in Heb. For *-tê*^{h} §15.7322 and Table F.

שִׁבְעַת יָמִים [9]—(a) ־ַת *-aṯ* is what morpheme? §25.13, .131. Does this tell us how to relate the two words? R.3. 1:1[9]. (b) *-î*^{y}*m* is what morpheme? 1:2[1], 1:4[8]. Note 1:4[10] '100 of day'; here '7 of days.' With numbers 2-9 use pl. nouns, from 10 up, use sg. Don't ask why!

בַּחֲצַר גִּנַּת בִּיתַן הַמֶּלֶךְ׃ [10]—Note the vowels: all short vowels are reduced except in closed syllables or in the last word. This is your clue to a chain of constructs, §36.31. (a) Read §15.653. *ba-* is what morpheme? 1:5[1]. (b) What morpheme is *-aṯ*? §25.13, .131, 1:5[9]. (c) Long vowels do not reduce, §15.22. (d) 1:2[4]. 'in the court of the garden of the house of the king.'

New consonants: צ ט. Note differences: א ע צ מ ט.

Study the accents in this verse and note how they break up the sentence into phrases and clauses. Read over §§11.5–11.59.

Learn Rules 2a, 10b, 11, 19.

Learn the basic words in Group 3.

Analyze the following words: יוֹם 1:4[11], בַּיָּמִים 1:2[1], הַיָּמִים 1:5[2], בִּימֵי 1:1[2]. Make notes in your notebook. Do the same with וּמֵאָה 1:1[11] and וּמְאַת 1:[10], and with שֶׁבַע 1:1[9] and שִׁבְעַת 1:5[9]. How many observations can you list? How many morphemes have you identified?

11. Nun נ assimilates to a following consonant when no vowel separates (§13.111).

19. When two successive simple (vocal) shewas would occur, the first becomes *ḥîrîq* and the second becomes zero-shewa (§15.651).

לֵךְ־אֶל־נְמָלָה עָצֵל רְאֵה דְרָכֶיהָ וַחֲכָם׃
Go to the ant, O sluggard; consider her ways, and be wise.
(Prov. 6:6)

Purpose: To introduce the segolates
Materials: Esther 1:6

6 חוּר ׀ כַּרְפַּס וּתְכֵלֶת אָחוּז בְּחַבְלֵי־בוּץ וְאַרְגָּמָן
עַל־גְּלִילֵי כֶסֶף וְעַמּוּדֵי שֵׁשׁ מִטּוֹת ׀ זָהָב וָכֶסֶף עַל רִצְפַת
בַּהַט־וָשֵׁשׁ וְדַר וְסֹחָרֶת׃

1:6 חוּר ׀[1]——Masoretic note calls attention to the large *ḥêṯ*. The reason for the large letter is no longer known. וּ is a long vowel, §14.1. For *pāsêq,* 1:1[3]. Closed syllable, §16.33. 'white cotton/linen.'

כַּרְפַּס[2]—Review R.1 (why?). Two closed syllables; we would expect *qāmāṣ* in the ultima. Why? §16.3. 'fine linen.'

וּתְכֵלֶת[3]—Syllabify *û^{w}-ṯ^{e}-ḵē-leṯ*. Read and apply §16.31, §16.3212, §17.1, §17.11, §16.33. Now study carefully §15.61. Be sure you understand anaptyxis, §15.61, .611 and doubly-closed syllable, §16.34. Rules 4, 5, 6b. The word originally was probably **tukiltu* or *tikiltu. 'and violet/blue.'

אָחוּז[4]—Syllabify, read §16.3211, §16.33. Identify the long vowel. This is a passive participle (pass. ptcp.),§30.382. 'seized/held.'

בְּחַבְלֵי־בוּץ[5]—Maqqeph, §11.45. R. 3. §17.121. (a) *b^{e}-ḥaḇ-lê^{y}*. Identify each syllable and each vowel. Read §14.3, §15.7, §15.72ff, .73ff, §16.33, §15.23. Cf. 1:5[1, 10]. ֵי is masc. pl. cstr. (m.p.c.) morpheme. Take it away, and you have *ḥabl*–a doubly-closed syllable. Rule 6b would suggest a development to *ḥéḇel,* a segolate, §16.3432. (b) What kind of vowel? 'With bands/cords of *βυσσος* (fine linen).'

וְאַרְגָּמָן[6]—וְ|אַרְ|גָּ|מָן, identify each syllable (acc. cl., n.o., d.o., u.c.), and explain each vowel, whether it is lengthened (§15.1) or reduced (§15.2). Start to work on the Short-Vowel Chart (SVC), Table E. Read §16.3622, §16.361. 'and purple.'

עַל־גְּלִילֵי כֶסֶף[7]—Note m.p.c. morpheme (ֵי) and maqqeph, recall R. 3. What is true of all syllables except the next-to-last? (a) Prep., §30.35, u.c. §16.33. (b) Which dagesh? §11.44f. Both *yôḏ*s are vowel letters, §11.21. Which is a long vowel (§14.13) and which is a monophthong (§15.73)? §11.322. What is the m.p.c. morpheme? §25.421. Cf. 1:6[5]. (c) כ is spirantized because the word is closely joined to the preceding which ends in a vowel-sound. Originally **kaspu* (cf. Akk. *kaspum*), the word has become a segolate, §15.611. Study carefully §15.61. 'on rings of silver.'

וְעַמּוּדֵי שֵׁשׁ[8]—(a) ֵי tells us what? 1:6[7]. §25.421. What does this tell us about the stress-accent? §17.121. Which dagesh in מּ? R.1. What does this do to preceding syllable? §16.3611. What kind of vowel is וּ ? §14.13. Since it is a d.o. syll., וּ

cannot be a short vowel, §15.23. (b) What accent is under שׁ֖? §11.53. What does this tell us? §11.533. Syllabify. 'and pillars of marble.'

מִטּוֹת[9] | זָהָב וָכֶסֶף—(a) Two syllables–why? §16.361, .3613. Neither can reduce–why? §15.243, §15.22. Hence the *form* does not tell us whether the word is in cstr., but the *context* does. Note *pāsêq*, 1:2[3]. (b) Syllabify *zā-hā<u>b</u>*, §16.3211, .33. R. 13. (c) וָ, note vowel, §16.3211. כֶּסֶף, note where the accent is–a fairly reliable clue to a segolate, §15.611. Here we find one ruling noun (§36.311) with two governed nouns (§36.312). Read §36.313. We therefore probably should read 'beds of gold-and-silver' rather than 'beds of gold and (other beds) of silver.'

עַל רִצְפַת[10]—(a) Prep. in cstr. followed by noun. (b) Note vowels: both short, §15.243. Which dagesh in פּ? Master Rule 1a *now*. Identify the morpheme ַת. 'upon a pavement of.'

בַּהַט־וָשֵׁשׁ[11]—(a) Note vowels and accent, §15.61. The guttural accounts for the *a*-vowels, §15.43. This type of noun is often classified as a segolate, §15.611; more accurately, it develops by anaptyxis, §15.61. (b) 1:6[8]. Note vowel under ו. Perhaps 'porphyry and marble.'

וְדַר וְסֹחָרֶת[12]—(a) The vowels suggest a cstr., but the following ו makes this impossible. *dar* is doubly-closed, cf. Arab. *durru,* hence §15.112, R.6a. The conj. *wa* does not always lengthen in n.o. (b) Note silluq and soph pasuq, §11.531. The word is *in pause,* hence the original *a*-vowel has lengthened (§15.131), possibly **suḥartu* > *sōḥéret*, pausal *sōḥā́ret*. Here four nouns are governed by one ruling noun (*regens*), hence we are to understand that the floor was composed of (inlays? of) porphyry and marble, and mother-of-pearl and tortoise-shell (?), possibly a mosaic. The meanings of the words are uncertain.

New letters: ז ף ץ. All letters have now appeared. Compare: ק ף ע ץ ו ז.

Go back over Lessons 2–6 and list all the segolates you can recognize. This type of noun is very common, so you should learn to recognize it as soon as possible.

Learn Rules 6a, 10d, 14, 16.

Learn the basic vocabularly in Group 4.

14. Short *a* does not lengthen in *erstwhile doubly-closed syllables* except in pause (§15.111, cf. §15.132).

16. In *near-open* syllables, *i-* or *u*-class short vowels *reduce* to shewa when preceded by a long *syllable* or by no syllable at all (§15.241).

8

Purpose: To Learn the Short-Vowel Chart
Materials: Esther 1:7-8

7 וְהַשְׁקוֹת בִּכְלֵי זָהָב וְכֵלִים
8 מִכֵּלִים שׁוֹנִים וְיֵין מַלְכוּת רָב כְּיַד הַמֶּלֶךְ׃ וְהַשְּׁתִיָּה
כַדָּת אֵין אֹנֵס כִּי־כֵן ׀ יִסַּד הַמֶּלֶךְ עַל כָּל־רַב בֵּיתוֹ
לַעֲשׂוֹת כִּרְצוֹן אִישׁ־וָאִישׁ׃

1:7 וְהַשְׁקוֹת[1]—Read §§ 14., 14.1, 14.2, .21, .22, .23, 15., 15.1. וְ|הַשְׁ|קוֹת *w*^{e}*-haš-qô*^{w}*t̠*. Always syllabify from the *end* of the word. Ultima is acc. cl., pure-long vowel. Penult is unaccented closed (u.c.), short-vowel is normal, §14.232. Antepenult is distant-open (d.o.), short-vowel reduces, §15.2, §15.23, R.13. Turn to Table E, and be sure you can find the syllable and the vowels. 'and drinking/causing to drink.'

בִּכְלֵי זָהָב[2]—בִּ|כְ|לֵי זָ|הָב. Note ־ֵי: what morpheme? §25.433. Cstr. (§25., §36.31, .325). Only one major accent. *hāb̠* is acc. cl., §15.11. *zā* is n.o., §15.12. Cf. 1:6[9]. *lê*^{y} is monophthongized, hence short-vowel rules do not apply (but diphthong rules do!). *bik̠* develops from (<) *b*^{e}*k̠*^{e}, §15.53, §15.651. 'in/with vessels of gold.'

וְכֵלִים מִכֵּלִים שׁוֹנִים[3]—There is no sign of a cstr. chain, so we treat each word separately. (a) *w*^{e}*-k̠ē-lî*^{y}*m* d.o. §15.23, §16.3212, n.o. §15.12, §16.3211, acc. §15.11. 'and vessels.' (b) *mik-kē-lî*^{y}*m,* u.c. §14.232, n.o. §15.12, *mikk* < *min* + *k,* §13.111, R.11. Figure out the meaning. (c) *šô*^{w}*-nî*^{y}*m,* penult has pure-long vowel (§15.21), read §15.22. Ultima has pure-long vowel. 'differing.'

וְיֵין מַלְכוּת רָב[4]—The monophthong ־ֵי tells us that this is cstr. (Table F), hence *w*^{e}*-yê*^{y}*n mal-k̠ût̠,* d.o. §16.3212, Monophthong §15.7, .71, .73, .7324. u.c. §14.232, acc. cl. §15.11. Be sure you understand how to find these syllables and vowels on Table E-*û*^{w}*t̠* is fem. §24.56. *rāb̠* is masc., hence it cannot modify *malk̠ût̠*; it must therefore modify *yê*^{y}*n*, §36.11. 'much wine of royalty' = 'much royal wine.'

כְּיַד הַמֶּלֶךְ׃[5]—Vowels in *k*^{e}*-yad̠* are unaccented or reduced, suggesting cstr. Find them on Table E. (a) ־כְּ is a prep., יָד 'hand,' = 'according to the generosity of.' (b) 1:2[6]. Note accent, note segols, rev. §15.611, §15.61.

1:8 וְהַשְּׁתִיָּה כַדָּת [1]—*w*^{e}*-haš-š*^{e}*-t̠î*^{y}*-yā*^{h}. Identify each syllable, d.o., u.c., long, acc., and explain each vowel. Table E, §14.232, §15.11, §§15.2, .21, .22. Note form of def. art. (Table G). ־ָה is fem., §25.13. 'and the drinking.' (b) *kad-dāt̠*. Identify syllables, explain vowels. *kadd-* < *k*^{e} + def. art., §13.521. '[was] according to the decree.'

אֵין אֹנֵס [2]—(a) Accent (§11.54), monophthong (§14.32), Table F, = cstr. 'nonexistence of' = 'there is/was not.' (b) *'ōnēs,* defective writing, §11.3241. This is a participle (ptcp.), §24.23, §27.611, .6111. *ô* < *â,* §14.11, §15.31, 'compelling';

the king's decree concerning the drinking was 'there is no compelling.'

כִּֽי־כֵ֖ן | יִסַּ֣ד הַמֶּ֑לֶךְ [3]—(a) *kî^y* conj. (§30.362), pure-long vowel, §15.22. 'for, because.' (b) *k̲ēn,* adv. (§30.34), acc.cl., spirantized כ because closely joined to previous word which ends in a vowel. 'thus.' (c) Verb, see §15.113. Rule 15. 'he ordained, commanded.' (d) Segolate, CvCC, §24.21, §15.61, .611.

עַ֥ל כָּל־רַ֣ב בֵּית֔וֹ [4]—(a) Prep., §14.232, §30.35f. (b) This is in a chain of cstrs., hence u.c., hence *qāmāṣ-ḥăṭûp̄* (§11.321). 'every.' (c) u.c., §14.232. 'great (one).' (d) **bayt* (CaYC) > *báyiṯ,* §24.212, §15.72. However, the added suffix *-ô* causes an accent shift with resulting change of the diphthong: **baytô* > *bê^yṯô^w,* §15.73, .7324. 'his house.'

לַעֲשׂ֖וֹת [5]—*la-'ă-śô^wṯ* < **l^e-'^e-śô^wṯ;* read §15.4, .42, R. 10b, and §15.653, R. 21. The form is an infinitive construct (inf. cstr.), §27.65. 'to do.'

כִּרְצ֥וֹן אִֽישׁ־וָאִֽישׁ׃ [6]—*k^e-r^e-ṣô^wn* > *kir-ṣô^wn,* §15.651. 'according to the will/pleasure of.' (b) *'î^yš* contains a long vowel; the metheg is used with a long vowel in a closed syllable before maqqeph (*Ges.* §16*f*). 'a man.' (c) *wā-'î^yš,* vowel of conj. ו often lengthens (but not always) in near-open. אִֽישׁ־וָאִֽישׁ is distributive, 'each individual man.'

Your primary task in this lesson is *to master the Short-Vowel Chart* (Table E). *Do it.* Many of the problems of recognizing verb and noun forms will not be understood until you understand the rules governing vocalic alteration. Look over the major points in §15 (i.e., the sections with one and two decimals, §15.1, §15.11, etc.).

Learn the words in Vocabulary Group 5.

The Short-Vowel Chart

	a-type vowel	*i*-type vowel	*u*-type vowel
Unaccented closed	◌ַ	◌ֶ/◌ִ	◌ָ/◌ֻ
Accented or Near-open	◌ָ	◌ֵ	◌ֹ
Distant-open	◌ְ	◌ְ	◌ְ
" with gutturals	◌ֲ/◌ֱ	◌ֱ/◌ֲ	◌ֳ

9

Purpose: To study the definite article
Materials: Esther 1:9-10

9 גַּם וַשְׁתִּי הַמַּלְכָּה עָשְׂתָה
י מִשְׁתֵּה נָשִׁים בֵּית הַמַּלְכוּת אֲשֶׁר לַמֶּלֶךְ אֲחַשְׁוֵרוֹשׁ׃ בַּיּוֹם
הַשְּׁבִיעִי כְּטוֹב לֵב־הַמֶּלֶךְ בַּיָּיִן אָמַר לִמְהוּמָן בִּזְּתָא
חַרְבוֹנָא בִּגְתָא וַאֲבַגְתָא זֵתַר וְכַרְכַּס שִׁבְעַת הַסָּרִיסִים
הַמְשָׁרְתִים אֶת־פְּנֵי הַמֶּלֶךְ אֲחַשְׁוֵרוֹשׁ׃

1:9 גַּם וַשְׁתִּי הַמַּלְכָּה [1]—(a) Conj., v.1571, BDB 168 gives root as *gmm*. §30.36f. (b) Pr. n. 'Vashti,' not bound by the *w* > *y* shift, §12.66. (c) *ham-mal-kā*^{h}, v. (vocab., see Part 4) 4436. Def. art. is –ּהַ, §22.2, .231. Start to study Table G. ָה– is fem. sg. abs. (fsa) morpheme, §25.1, .13. If מֶלֶךְ is 'king,' what is מַלְכָּה?

עָשְׂתָה [2]—*ʿā-ś*^{e}*-ṯā*^{h}, a verb, study Rules 15 and 17 and §11.581. 'she made.'

מִשְׁתֵּה נָשִׁים [3]—Note ֵה–, §15.7323, Table F, cstr., 1:3[5], voc. 4961. (b) ים– is mpa morpheme, but the word means 'women.' The morphological gender does not always indicate the sex gender, §15.1. Gen. of reference, §36.3212. Voc. 802.

בֵּית הַמַּלְכוּת [4]—(a) *bê*^{y}*ṯ* for *b*^{e}*ḇê*^{y}*ṯ* 'in the house of,' cf. BDB 108, 1a. (b) *ham-mal-ḵûṯ*, 1:2[8], note def. art., §22.2. If the last word in a cstr. relation is definite, the preceding word is definite, §36.3122. 'In the house of the royalty' = 'in the royal house.'

אֲשֶׁר לַמֶּלֶךְ [5]—(a) Relative pronoun (rel. pron.), 1:2[9], note syllables and vowel quantities. §30.3128, §38.42. *ʾăšer* modifies 'the royal house,' §30.2, which is its antecedent, §30.313. (b) *lammélek̲* < *l*^{e} + *hammélek̲*, §22.24, learn §13.521 now. *ʾăšer l*^{e}- 'which [was] to ...' = 'which belonged to ...'; an adj. clause, §30.323.

1:10 בַּיּוֹם הַשְּׁבִיעִי [1]—(a) *bayy-* suggests what? §13.521, §22.24. **yawm* > *yô*^{w}*m*, §24.212. 'in the day.' (b) Do you see a def. art.? We had שֶׁבַע in 1:1[9]; the form with *î-î* is an ordinal numeral, §24.55; for numeral adj., §30.32; voc. 7637. Note that def. art. is repeated on an adj. in concord, §36.11.

כְּטוֹב לֵב־הַמֶּלֶךְ—(a) *k*^{e}- 1:2[3], 'as, when.' *ṭô*^{w}*ḇ* adj. 'good' voc. 2896, CvC §24.12. This word is used as a predicate adjective, §30.321. (b) *lēḇ* 'heart,' voc. 3820, < *libb-*, §13.42. Note maqqeph, §11.45. The *ṣêrê* does not reduce in this word, §15.223. Since המלך is def., this word is also def., 'the heart of the king.' With pred. adj., translate 'when the heart of the king (was) good.'

בַּיָּיִן [3]—*bayy-* suggests what? §22.24. *yáyin* 'wine' (3196) is CaYC, §24.212, but here in pause, §11.53311.55. 'with (the) wine.'

אָמַ֫ר [4]—Verb, 'he said' (559), R. 15.

לִמְהוּמָן ... וְכַרְכַּס [5]—l^e- introduces indirect object, §30.22, §35.1. Use the 7 names to review alphabet, vowels, and short-vowel rules.

שִׁבְעַת הַסָּרִיסִים [6]—(a) 1:5[9]. (b) Def. art.? *sârîs* 'eunuch, official' (v.5631). Metheg is often replaced by other weak accents, *Ges.* §16*f.* Cf. 1:5[9]: does this mean '7 of the eunuchs' or 'the 7 eunuchs'? §36.325.

הַֽמְשָׁרְתִ֔ים [7]—Article? *m^ešārēṯ* 'ministering' (v.8334) is D participle (ptcp.), §24.33f. Review §13.38, §15.15f, §15.233, Rule 13b. Note *mûnāḥ* for *méṯeḡ*, cf. 1:10[6].

אֶת־פְּנֵי [8]—(a) Prep. 'with, close by' (v.854, BDB 816, II 2). (b) *pānî^ym* (pl.) 'face,' in cstr. often = 'before,' §36.42.

Review the def. art. in previous notes: 1:2[1, 2], 1:5[2], 1:8[2]? These were selected because they illustrate different points. What do you see? How many other def. arts. can you find in 1:2, 1:5, 1:8?

Study Table G carefully. You should now recognize: –·הַ, –·בַּ, –·בַ, –הָ.

Learn the words in vocabulary group 6.

---

hammōlēḵ	הַמֹּלֵךְ	*hāhēm*	הָהֵם
bayyāmîm	בַּיָּמִים	*hā'ēllê^h*	הָאֵלֶּה
kaddâṯ	כַּדָּת	*hā'ām*	הָעָם
lammélek	לַמֶּלֶךְ	*beḥāṣēr*	בֶּחָצֵר

21. When *simple (vocal) shewa* would occur before *compound shewa,* the simple shewa is changed to the normal short vowel of the same vowel-class as the compound shewa (§15.653).

22. When *compound shewa* would occur before simple (vocal) shewa, the compound shewa develops to its corresponding normal short vowel, and the simple shewa becomes zero shewa (§15.2532).

אֹהֵב מוּסָר אֹהֵב דָּעַת וְשׂוֹנֵא תוֹכַחַת בָּעַר׃
Whoever loves discipline loves knowledge,
but he who hates reproof is stupid.
Proverbs 12:1

10

Purpose: To Introduce Noun Morphology
Materials: Esther 1:11

לְהָבִיא אֶת־ 11
וַשְׁתִּי הַמַּלְכָּה לִפְנֵי הַמֶּלֶךְ בְּכֶתֶר מַלְכוּת לְהַרְאוֹת הָעַמִּים
וְהַשָּׂרִים אֶת־יָפְיָהּ כִּי־טוֹבַת מַרְאֶה הִיא׃

Read §20.–20.5 before working on the text.

1:11 לְהָבִיא אֶת־וַשְׁתִּי הַמַּלְכָּה [1]—(a) l^e + inf. cstr. 'to cause to enter, to bring,' in indirect discourse, §38.82. (b) 1:4[2]. 1:9[1]. 'Vashti' is definite (pr. n.) and dir. obj. of verb, §34.1, .113. (c) 1:9[1]. Basic pattern of this type of noun is CaCC (an *a*-vowel after the first consonant, no vowel between 2d and 3d consonants). In msa and msc, anaptyxis occurs, §24.21.

לִפְנֵי הַמֶּלֶךְ [2]—(a) l^e- + $p^e n\hat{e}^y$ 'to the face of' > *prep.* 'before.' Cf. 1:3[14]. It is followed by its object, §30.351. (b) Basic pattern is CaCC *malk*, but this develops to *mélek̲* (Rule 6b), §24.21. This is a *segolate* (Lesson 7).

בְּכֶתֶר מַלְכוּת [3]—(a) You should recognize b^e- -בְּ. *kéṯer* 'crown' (v.3804 3x in OT, 3x in Est. [3/3]) is CvCC. It could be *katr* or *kitr*—possibly the latter (Arab. has both *katr* and *kitr,* Aram. has *kitrâ*). It is a segolate, §24.21. (b) 1:2[8]. Basic pattern is CaCC + ût, §24.56.

לְהַרְאוֹת הָעַמִּים וְהַשָּׂרִים [4]—(a) -לְ + inf. cstr., 'to cause to see, to show.' (b) Note form of def. art. *'ammî* has mpa *-îm* ־ִים morpheme, §25.231. Basic form of the noun *'amm* is CvC², with geminate 2d rad., §24.214. §13.42 applies (Rule 6a): *'amm* > *'am,* then Rule 14 applies, §15.111, עַם, pausal or with def. art. *'ām* עָם, 1:5[4]. This is the first object of the verb (§34.3). (c) Note conj. and def. art., note mpa morpheme. What remains is שַׂר. The basic form is **śarr* (cf. Σαρρα), CaC², §24.214, but ר resists gemination (§13.38) and there is compensation (§15.14). The first obj. of the verb is compound (§34.115).

אֶת־יָפְיָהּ [5] —(a) §34.113. The verb takes two objects, §§34.3, .35, *whom* he caused to see and *what* he caused them to see. (b) Basic form CuCY *yopy,* §24.213, but §15.67 (R.9) applies > $y^e p\hat{\imath}$ יְפִי (§15.241, R. 16) 'beauty' (v.3808, 19/1). ־ָהּ *-āh* is 3fs suffix 'her'; note *mappîq* (§11.42). 'to cause *the peoples and the princes* to see *her beauty.*'

כִּי־טוֹבַת מַרְאֶה הִיא׃ [6]—(a) *kî* conj. 'because,' introduces causal clause, §30.3623. (b) *ṭôḇaṯ* ends with fsc morpheme *-aṯ* ־ַת, 1:10[2]. Pattern is CvCat, §24.121. (c) *mar'ê*[h] 'appearance, sight' (4758); pattern maCCaY *mar'ay,* §24.33. Nouns can be formed with preformative *mêm.* (d) Pers. pron. 3fs 'she' §21.1. The copula is omitted, and a verbless clause results, §31., the subj. is הִיא §31.121, and the pred. is a pred. adj. phrase, §31.23. 'for she [was] good of appearance.'

Read carefully: §25.11, §25.231, §25.41, §§25.421, .424, §§25.4211, .4212.

Know these morphemes: *-îm* ־ִים, *ê^{y}* ־ֵי, *-ê^{h}* ־ֶה, *-ē^{h}* ־ֵה.

Learn the words in Group 7.

Study the following noun types and their morphology. Enter them in your notebook, and add others as you see them. *Begin* (do not attempt to master at this time) the study of noun formation and gender-number-state (GNS) morphology.

CaC	yad	*yaḏ*	יַד	1:7	m.s.c.
CaCat	šanat	*š^{e}naṯ*	שְׁנַת	1:2	f.s.c.
CiCat	mi'at	*mē'ā^{h}*	מֵאָה	1:1	f.s.a.
		m^{e}'aṯ	מְאַת	1:4	f.s.c.
CaC^{2}	'amm	*'ām*	עָם	1:3	m.s.a. + הָ
		'ammîm	עַמִּים	1:11	m.p.a.
CaC^{2}at	gannat	*ginnaṯ*	גִּנַּת	1:5	f.s.c.
CiC^{2}	libb	*lēḇ*	לֵב	1:10	m.s.c.
CaCC	malk	*méleḵ*	מֶלֶךְ	1:2	m.s.a.
	kasp	*késep̄*	כֶּסֶף	1:6	m.s.a.
CaCCat	malkat	*malkā^{h}*	מַלְכָּה	1:11	f.s.a.
CaWC	yawm	*yôm*	יוֹם	1:10	m.s.a.
CaYC	yayn	*yā́yin*	יָיִן	1:10	m.s.a. (paus.)
		yên	יֵין	1:7	m.s.c.
CiCG	šib'	*šéḇa'*	שֶׁבַע	1:1	f.s.a. (num.)
CiCGat	šib'at	*šiḇ'aṯ*	שִׁבְעַת	1:5	m.s.c. (num.)
CiCC	kitr	*kéṯer*	כֶּתֶר	1:11	m.s.c.
CuCC	'uθr	*'ṓšer*	עֹשֶׁר	1:4	m.s.c.
CaCaC	ðahab	*zāhāḇ*	זָהָב	1:6	m.s.a.
	dabar	*d^{e}ḇar*	דְּבַר	1:12	m.s.c.
CaCiG	ḥaṣir	*ḥăṣar*	חֲצַר	1:5	f.s.c. (!)
CâCiC	mâlik	*môlēḵ*	מֹלֵךְ	1:1	m.s.a.
	'ânis	*'ônēs*	אֹנֵס	1:8	m.s.a.
CaCâC	gadâl	*gāḏôl*	גָּדוֹל	1:5	m.s.a.
	kabâd	*k^{e}ḇôḏ*	כְּבוֹד	1:4	m.s.c.
CaCîCat	madînat	*m^{e}ḏînā^{h}*	מְדִינָה	1:1	f.s.a.
miCCaY	mištay	*mištê^{h}*	מִשְׁתֶּה	1:3	m.s.a.
CaCCût	malkût	*malḵûṯ*	מַלְכוּת	1:11	f.s.a.

4. Original short vowels in final open syllables have generally vanished (§§15.51, .52).

11

Purpose: To study feminine noun morphology
Materials: Esther 1:12

וַתְּמָאֵן הַמַּלְכָּה 12
וַשְׁתִּי לָבוֹא בִּדְבַר הַמֶּלֶךְ אֲשֶׁר בְּיַד הַסָּרִיסִים וַיִּקְצֹף
הַמֶּלֶךְ מְאֹד וַחֲמָתוֹ בָּעֲרָה בוֹ׃

1:12 וַתְּמָאֵן הַמַּלְכָּה [1]—(a) Verb, 'and she refused,' subject follows, §30.111. (b) 1:11[1], fsa morpheme -*ā*^{h} ־ָה. Read §25.12 carefully. §33.1. וַשְׁתִּי is in apposition, §30.251.

לָבוֹא [2]—Inf. cstr., 'to enter'; complementary inf. after 'refused,' §34.82.

בִּדְבַר הַמֶּלֶךְ [3]—(a) *d*^{e}*ḇar* has reduced or normal short vowels, hence no major accent. Why? R.13a. Normal pattern CaCaC *dāḇār,* §24.22; 'word, affair' (v.1697). 'And the queen, Vashti, refused to enter into (participate in?) the king's matter' or 'to enter at the king's command.'

אֲשֶׁר בְּיַד הַסָּרִיסִים [4]—(a) 1:2[9], §21.3. (b) *yaḏ* (is it cstr.?), pattern CvC §24.12, lengthens under accent to *yāḏ* יָד. 'by the hand of' = 'by.' (c) 1:10[6]. Probably a loan-word, pattern either CvC^{2}vC or Cv̂Cv̂C; in either case there is no possible reduction of vowels in cstr., suff., or pl. forms.

וַיִּקְצֹף הַמֶּלֶךְ מְאֹד [5]—(a) Verb 'and he was angry,' subj. follows. (b) What kind of noun formation? §24.21. §33.1f. (c) Adv. 'exceedingly' (v.3966); §35.2, §30.34. Possibly developed from a noun, **mi'âd.*

וַחֲמָתוֹ [6]—Conj., §30.36f. Suf. (s0) *–ô* §36.52. The rest is *ḥămāṯ,* with fsc *-at* morpheme §25.12. The abs. would be **ḥāmā*^{h} or *ḥēmā*^{h}, since the guttural would obscure the reduced vowel. We find it as *hēmā*^{h} (v.2534), according to BDB 404, from *y*^{e}*ḥēmā*^{h} with apheresis §13.51. For our purposes, we can analyze the word that we have, not the hypothetical form. It is fem. of CvCat type §24.122. Note what happens when adding the suffix: accent shifts, n.o. lengthens, d.o. reduces, influence of guttural (§15.42, R. 10b). Be sure you understand this; it is almost impossible to locate the lexicon form if you cannot reconstruct it from the textual form.

בָּעֲרָה בוֹ׃ [7]—(a) Verb, 'she/it burned,' subj. precedes, 'his wrath burned.' For concord, §33.11. Note influence of guttural on penult. (b) Prep. + s0 וֹ– 'in him.' The prep. phrase is adverbial, §30.341, §30.354, §30.412. It tells *where* his anger burned.

Read carefully: §§25.12, .131, .232, .422, .425, .52, .54.

Go back over 1:1-11 and look for fem. nouns. Note the following:
מֵאָה 1:1[11], מְאַת 1:4[10], מְדִינָה 1:1[12], הַמְּדִינוֹת 1:3[13], תִּפְאֶרֶת 1:4[6]; גְּדוּלָּתוֹ 1:4[7]; תְּכֵלֶת
1:6[3]; מִטּוֹת 1:6[9]; בִּשְׁנַת 1:3[2]. Why have I selected these words? Can you identify every one? Make notes of your observations.

Learn the words in Group 8.

Study the following noun types and their morphology. Enter them in your notebook, and add others as you see them.

m.s.a.	m.s.c.	m.p.a.	m.p.c.
dāḇār 1:21 דָּבָר	*d^e^ḇar* 1:12 דְּבַר	*d^e^ḇārîm* 2:1 דְּבָרִים	*diḇrê^y^* 2:23 דִּבְרֵי
yāḏ 2:21 יָד	*yaḏ* 1:7 יַד	*yāḏîm* יָדִים	*y^e^ḏê^y^* 3:9 יְדֵי
yôm 1:4 יוֹם	*yôm* 9:18 יוֹם	*yāmîm* 1:4 יָמִים	*y^e^mê^y^* 2:12 יְמֵי
ʿam 1:22 עַם	*ʿam* 3:6 עַם	*ʿammîm* 1:11 עַמִּים	*ʿammê^y^* עַמֵּי
raḇ רַב	*raḇ* 1:8 רַב	*rabbîm* 1:4 רַבִּים	*rabbê^y^* רַבֵּי
		kēlîm 1:7 כֵּלִים	*k^e^lê^y^* 1:7 כְּלֵי
		śārîm 1:11 שָׂרִים	*śārê^y^* 1:3 שָׂרֵי

f.s.a.	f.s.c.	f.p.a.	f.p.c.
*ṭôḇā^h^* 1:19 טוֹבָה	*ṭôḇaṯ* 1:11 טוֹבַת	*ṭôḇôṯ* טוֹבוֹת	*ṭôḇôṯ* 2:2 טוֹבוֹת
*mēʾā^h^* 1:1 מֵאָה	*m^e^ʾaṯ* 1:4 מְאַת	*mēʾôṯ* 9:6 מֵאוֹת	
*šānā^h^* 9:21 שָׁנָה	*š^e^naṯ* 1:3 שְׁנַת		
*rabbā^h^* 1:20 רַבָּה		*rabbôṯ* 2:8 רַבּוֹת	
*m^e^ḏînā^h^* 1:1 מְדִינָה		*m^e^ḏînôṯ* 1:3 מְדִינוֹת	*m^e^ḏînôṯ* 1:16 מְדִינוֹת

	Masculine		Feminine			
sg.abs.	–	–	*–ā^h^*	or *–t*	ָה	ֶ ֶת
sg.cstr	—	–	*—aṯ*	or *—t*	ַת	ֶ ֶת
pl.abs.	*–îm*	ִים	*—ôṯ*		וֹת–	
pl.cstr.	*—ê*	ֵי	*—ôṯ*		וֹת–	

Purpose: To review your progress to this point
Materials: Esther 1:1-12, Tables, Rules

At this time there is value in reading (rather rapidly) the entire Phonology part of the *Handbook,* §§10.–17.41. Some of the §§ that meant little when you first encountered them, will now be meaningful. Skip over the others. Mark for further study any that need it.

Be sure you know the meanings of all terms used so far, both Eng. and Heb. terminology. When starting any new field of study, one of your great problems is "vocabulary control," which means the vocabulary of that particular field. Our present field is language, specifically Hebrew.

Be sure you know the alphabet. Go over Zephaniah 3:8, which contains all letters of the alphabet, all vowel signs except ֳ, all final letters, and all of the important accents (except *'ôlê wᵉyôrēḏ*). If you can do it completely, you know the orthography.

Study Tables B and C. Students who fail to get the details of orthography at this stage do a lot of wheel-spinning through most of the rest of the course.

Study Tables E and F. Be sure you know Rule 13.

Be able to identify pure-long vowels written full; start to work on distinguishing pure-long written defectively from lengthened short, and lengthened short written with false *plene* from pure-long. This will take many more meaningful encounters.

Be able to recognize the mpa and mpc morphemes, and also the fsa, fsc, and fpa morphemes.

Be able to recognize all bound prepositions (–בְּ, –כְּ, –לְ, –מִ) and the conjunction (–וְ).

Be able to spot possible construct forms from reduction of vowels.

Know the meanings of the words in Basic Vocabulary Groups 1-8.

Pronounce the following Hebrew characters:

ע	[y] as in *yet*	[ts] as in *hats*	[ʔ] as in *unh-unh*
שׁ	[ʃ] as in *shish*	[s] as in *sis*	[ts] as in *hats*
ף	[p] as in *pep*	[f] as in *fife*	[q] as in *kook*
ט	[m] as in *mom*	[t] as in *taught*	[ts] as in *hats*
ם	[m] as in *mom*	[s] as in *sis*	[k] as in *kick*
פּ	[p] as in *pep*	[f] as in *fife*	[b] as in *bob*
ס	[m] as in *mom*	[s] as in *sis*	[k] as in *kick*
ח	[h] as in *hah*	[x] as in *ach!*	[t] as in *tat*
א	[ks] as in *kicks*	[ʔ] as in *naïve*	[w] as in *wow*
ג	[g] as in *gig*	[z] as in *zoo*	[n] as in *none*

Transliterate from Roman to Hebrew characters:

'ēṯ	*qēṣ*	*bêʸṯ*
'ēṯ	*'ēṣ*	*'aḏ*
'ēṭ	*gan*	*yaḏ*
kāp̄	*dôr*	*sārîs*
qôp̄	*ṣûm*	*śārîm*

Transliterate from Hebrew to Roman characters:

קֶצֶף	יִכְתֹּב	הַזֶּה
עָמַר	יִכָּתֵב	הַכְּתָב
וַתִּשָּׂא	יְכַתֵּב	גִּנְזֵי
וַתְּצַוֵּהוּ	פַּתְשֶׁגֶן	יֻצַּע
הֶחֱרַשְׁתִּי	טַבַּעְתּוֹ	הָאֲחַשְׁדַּרְפְּנִים

Check the words that *have* the definite article:

הַיּוֹם	לַעֲשׂוֹת	הָעָם
בַּיַּיִן	הֶגְלָה	בָּעֶרֶב
לַמֶּלֶךְ	בֶּחָצֵר	הָמָן
לְהָבִיא	וְהַנַּעֲרָה	לְבַדּוֹ
כָּרֵת	מִתְהַלֵּךְ	בַּחֹדֶשׁ

5. A doubly-closed syllable never occurs within a word and rarely occurs at word-end (§16.34).

6. When a doubly-closed syllable would result from the loss of a short vowel (Rule 4), one of the following occurs:
   a. If a geminate consonant would result, it loses gemination (§13.42);
   b. If a consonantal cluster would result, an anaptyctic vowel is inserted (§15.61);
   c. In a few cases, the doubly-closed syllable remains (§16.3423).

13

Purpose: To examine the student's progress
Materials: Esther 1:1-12, student's notebook

The first hour examination will be given at this point. It will be thorough but (we hope!) not unfair.

1. You will be asked to transliterate from Hebrew to Roman characters, and from Roman to Hebrew, both consonants and vowels. This is to test your knowledge of the orthography and your ability to read Hebrew text. You may get Zeph. 3:8.

2. You will be tested on your knowledge of the Short-Vowel Chart and short-vowel rules, by being given forms to point. You will also be tested on pure-long vowels and diphthongs.

3. You will be asked to identify the definite article, with or without prepositions, in the normal form and in the forms before gutturals. You may be given words to point to show that you know these details.

4. You will be asked to identify morphemes, both bound- and free-form, both prefixed and suffixed.

5. You will be questioned about the significance of the most important conjunctive and disjunctive accents.

6. You will be asked to translate simple clauses either from Est. 1:1-12 or closely similar clauses. This is to test your ability to put together the words in context and get meaning therefrom.

7. You will be tested on the basic vocabulary to date.

Do your own best–that is all that is expected of you.

2a. *Pure-long vowels* do not reduce except in originally-closed syllables (§15.22), where they become the corresponding short vowel, subject to the short-vowel rules (§15.222)

2b. Long *â* became long *ô* in the Canaanite dialects (§14.11).

8. The conjunction —וְ, when it occurs before labials (בּ, מ, פּ, called *bumep̄*), or before consonants with shewa, develops to vocalic וּ *û*; before yod with shewa, however, long *î* is formed (§15.652).

Given	Point	Given	Point
דָּבָר	דבר הַמֶּלֶךְ	מַיִם	המים
כֹּל	כלָּם	אִמּוֹ	אם
נַפְשִׁי	נפש	עוֹלָם	העולם
קוֹל	קל יְהוָה	כֹּל	כל־יום
ʿammî	עמי	*báyiṯ*	בית
lᵉ + *ʿăḇōḏ*	לעבד	*kᵉ* + *kᵉṯōḇ*	ככתב

Be able to recognize all bound prepositions (–בּ, –כּ, –ל, –מֵ) and the conjunction (–ו).

Identify the following morphemes:

—ֵי	כְּ—	—ֶֶת
הַ·—	—וֹ	הָ—
וְ—	—ַת	לְ—
—ָה	—ָיו	בְּ—
—ִים	—וֹת	—ָהּ

What is the *significance* of each of the following?

silluq	revia‘	metheg
maqqeph	zaqeph-qaṭon	athnaḥ

Translate the following:

דְּבַר הַמֶּלֶךְ	בִּשְׁנַת שֶׁבַע	מִכָּל־עֲבָדָיו
עַמִּים רַבִּים	שָׂרִים טוֹבִים	לַמַּלְכָּה הַטּוֹבָה

Behold, how good and how pleasant
for brothers to dwell in unity!
(Psa. 133:1)

הִנֵּה מַה טּוֹב וּמַה נָּעִים
שֶׁבֶת אַחִים גַּם יָחַד.

14

Purpose: To introduce the Hebrew verb
Materials: Esther 1:1–12

We now begin to study the Hebrew verbal system. Read §27., §27.1, and §27.11. Read §§30.33, .332. If you are weak in Eng. grammar, read §§30.–30.339.

אָמַר, 1:10[4], means 'he said.' It is third person, masculine singular, perfect, of the simple stem (G or Qal). All of these data are indicated by the vowel pattern and the presence or absence of preformatives. In this *Handbook* we call such a form 'G10'–which is much easier to write. G = G-stem, 1- = perfect, -0 = 3 masc. sing. The full system is given in §27.151, but we shall not attempt to learn it just yet. The G10 pattern is CaCaC > *CāCaC*. Note operation of Rule 15.

עָשָׂה, 1:5[3], 'he made,' is also G10. Rule 15 is not operative, since the ultima is open, *CāCā^h*. The perfect is *not a tense,* but rather it indicates *completed action.* The tense of the action must be determined from the context, §27.1111. The perfect is most frequently translated by an Eng. past tense.

בָּעֲרָה, 1:12[7], is 3 fem. sg. (G11). The subject is fem., hence the verb form is fem. The 3fs perf. (11) is indicated by the morpheme -*ā^h* ָה. See §27.221, but don't try to learn it now.

עָשְׂתָה, 1:9[2], is also G11. In verbs that have -*ā^h* ָה for G10 (called CCY or *Lamed Hê* verbs), the G11 morpheme is -*tā^h* ָתה. All other verbs have the regular G11 ending, so you must learn the regular ending first, then the CCY ending. CCY verbs are very common.

צִוָּה, 1:8[3], 'he commanded,' is also perf. 3ms, but it is built on the D stem (*Pi'el*), hence is D10. Read §28 carefully, and look over §28.1–but don't try to learn it yet.

הַנִּמְצְאִים, 1:1[5], is a ptcp. built on the N stem (*Niph'al*). The N stem often has a passive meaning. Here the word means 'the being-found ones' or 'those that (were) found.' The ptcp. has no tense; you must get the tense from context.

לְהָבִיא, 1:11[1], and לְהַרְאוֹת, 1:11[4], are infinitives construct (inf. cstr.), built on the H stem (*Hiph'il*). The H stem usually has a causative meaning, 'to cause to enter' (= 'to bring in') and 'to cause to see' (= 'to show').

So far we have seen the G, D, H, and N stems. There is also the HtD (*Hithpa'el*) as well as some less-common stems. The *root* of the word gives us the basic meaning; the *stem* gives some special significance. Now read §§27.115–.1153.

The names of the stems give us a clue to their morphology. The G (ground) stem, or Qal (קַל 'light') is the basic form and generally has the basic root-meaning.

The D (doubled) stem doubles the middle radical. *yissad̲* from the root *ysd,* shows this gemination. Hebrew grammarians used the verb פָּעַל for their basic paradigm, and unfortunately it cannot show the doubling in *pi'ēl* because of the guttural. The D stem often gives an idea of repetition, intensity, or the like. יִסַּד 'he commanded,' and וַתְּמָאֵן, 1:12[1], 'and she refused' both convey some intensity or repetition.

The H stem is basically formed by the addition of a preformative ה–, hence הִפְעִיל *hip̄'îl.* Besides indicating causation, this stem can turn an intransitive verb into a transitive (§§30.3391f).

The N stem is basically formed by the addition of a preformative נ–, hence נִפְעַל or *nip̄'al.* Besides indicating the passive voice (§30.334, .3342), it sometimes indicates a reflexive sense (§30.3343).

Most of the finite (§30.3321) verbs that we have seen so far are perfs. (10s or 11s), but we have also seen two impfs., וַיְהִי 1:1[1], and וַתְּמָאֵן 1:12[1]. The *imperfect* (§27.3) indicates *incomplete action/state.* We indicate it by 2- in the tens place, hence G20 would be G imperf. 3ms, and G21 G imperf. 3fs. In Bib. Heb., however, it is possible to *convert* the impf. to have the force of a perf. by adding –ַּו to the verb. Both of these verbs are thus converted, and we indicate this fact by adding 'c' before the indicator: Gc20, Dc21.

We have also seen several infs. cstr. (G65, H65), and a number of ptcps. (G50, N55, and Gp50, 'p' after the stem symbol indicates 'passive').

It is therefore obvious that we have a bit of a job ahead of us to learn how to distinguish the elements that are indicated by verb morphology. There are certain vowel patterns, and there are person–gender–number (PGN) morphemes (preformative and sufformative), and there are also stem indicators. How do we go about learning to recognize these morphemes? When a Hebrew heard *watt^{e}mā'ēn lāb̲ô'* how did he immediately recognize the tense, voice, mood, person, and number of the verb, plus the fact that it was followed by a complementary infinitive? This will be our task for the next 12 or more lessons.

Read §27.15. Know precisely what is required when parsing a verb. Start to become familiar with Paradigm V-1.

Learn the basic words in Group 9.

תֵּן לְחָכָם וְיֶחְכַּם עוֹד

Give instruction to a wise man and he will be still wiser.

(Prov. 9:9)

15

Purpose: To study the G stem of the verb
Materials: Esther 1:13-14

13 וַיֹּאמֶר הַמֶּלֶךְ
לַחֲכָמִים יֹדְעֵי הָעִתִּים כִּי־כֵן דְּבַר הַמֶּלֶךְ לִפְנֵי כָּל־יֹדְעֵי
14 דָּת וָדִין׃ וְהַקָּרֹב אֵלָיו כַּרְשְׁנָא שֵׁתָר אַדְמָתָא תַרְשִׁישׁ
מֶרֶס מַרְסְנָא מְמוּכָן שִׁבְעַת שָׂרֵי ׀ פָּרַס וּמָדַי רֹאֵי פְּנֵי
הַמֶּלֶךְ הַיֹּשְׁבִים רִאשֹׁנָה בַּמַּלְכוּת׃

1:13 וַיֹּאמֶר הַמֶּלֶךְ לַחֲכָמִים[1]— (a) Start to learn the process of "stripping" a verb form. Here we see וַ-יֹ-אמֶר. -וַיְ is the conj., but with pattaḥ and the strong dagesh, it is a "conversive" or "converting" waw. Read §32.53. In this form (with dagesh) it occurs only on the imperfect. Read §32.52. The impf. is formed by adding preformatives to the root, and for some PGNs, a sufformative. Read §20.212, §20.3. The preformative here is -י *y*–, §§27.3, .31, .311. v.559, 'and he said.' (b) This is the defined subj. of the verb, §§33., 33.1. (c) Note -לַ, prep. and def.art., Table G. Note -ִים. חָכָם v.2450, 'wise (man).'

יֹדְעֵי הָעִתִּים [2]—(a) G ptcp. mpc (G57) of יָדַע, v.3045. Read §27.61. The vowel pattern of G50 is CâCiCu > *CôCēC yôḏē*^{a}ʿ. The clue to look for is long *ô* (often written defectively) after the first radical. Read §§27.6111, .6112. Read §30.382. 'knowers of.' (b) Note -הָ and see Table G. Note -ִים, §25.231. עֵת v.6256 'time,' obj. of the ptcp. The clause, 'knowers of the times,' modifies 'wise men,' §36.7.

כִּי־כֵן דְּבַר הַמֶּלֶךְ [3]—(a-b) Cf. 1:8[3]. (c-d) Cf. 1:12[3].

לִפְנֵי כָּל־יֹדְעֵי| דָּת וָדִין׃ [4]—(a) 1:11[2]. (b-c) 1:13[2], review notes on ptcp. (d) 1:8[1]. (e) v.1779 'law.' 'For thus [was] the word of the king before all who know custom and law.'

1:14 וְהַקָּרֹב—(a) Identify the bound-form morphemes. קָרֹב v.7138, here written defectively, 'near,' used substantivally, §30.31.

אֵלָיו[2]—Prep. אֶל v.413, always in the form אֵלַי* with suff. -ָיו, Table H. 'unto him.'

כַּרְשְׁנָא ... מְמוּכָן[3]—7 pr.n., use them to review consonants, vowels, and accents. Be sure you can read proper nouns! You cannot recognize them if you can't read them. They are not included in the basic vocabulary.

שִׁבְעַת שָׂרֵי ׀ פָּרַס וּמָדַי[4]—(a) 1:5[9]. What morpheme is -ַת? §25.422. (b) 1:3[6]. -ֵי is what morpheme? §25.424. (c-d) 1:3[9,10]. Since a pr.n. is definite (§30.3144), the cstr. chain is def. Is this 'seven of' or 'the seven'?

רֹאֵי פְּנֵי הַמֶּלֶךְ [1]—(a) *rô'ê*^{y}: note clues, long *ô* after 1st rad. = G ptcp., ־ֵי mpc, hence G57, v.7200. 'The ones seeing' = 'those who saw.' Read §38.43. (b) פָּנִים (pl.) 'face,' v.6440. In this form (mpc), this word is often used as a prep., but not here. 'the face of the king,' §36.322.

הַיֹּשְׁבִים [6]—Strip the form הַ—ִים, identify the morphemes. The remainder is יֹשֵׁב < יָשַׁב, v.3427, cf. 1:2[3]. What clue do you see after 1st rad.? Does transliteration *yôšēḇ* help you?. §27.6111, 'the ones sitting/dwelling.'

הָרִאשֹׁנָה בַּמַּלְכוּת׃ [7]—(a) *rî'šônā*^{h}, quiescent א, §13.523, *-ôn* §24.431, adv. *-ā*^{h} (identified as fem. in BDB 912), 'foremost.' (b) Note —ַּבַּ: what morpheme is hidden? §13.521. Cf. 1:2[8], v.4438.

Analyze the following forms: הַמֶּלֶךְ 1:1[6], שׁוֹנִים 1:7[3], אֹנֵס 1:8[2].

Analyze the following: וַיִּקְצֹף 1:12[5], cf. 1:13[1].

Start to memorize the G10 and G20 morphemes, §§27.21, .31. Learn them as *recognition elements:* ככב י 'he will ...,' ככב 'he did ...,' etc.

Learn the basic words in Group 10.

CaCaC	> *CāCaC*	*qāṭal*	קָטַל
CaCiC	> *CāCēC*	*kāḇēḏ*	כָּבֵד
CaCuC	> *CāCōC*	*qāṭōn*	קָטֹן
yaCCuC	> *yiCCōC*	*yiqṭōl*	יִקְטֹל
yiCCaC	> *yiCCaC*	*yiḵbaḏ*	יִכְבַּד
yaCCiC	> *yiCCēC*	*yittēn*	יִתֵּן

עַל שְׁלשָׁה דְבָרִים הָעוֹלָם קַיָּם:
עַל הָאֱמֶת, עַל הַדִּין , וְעַל הַשָּׁלוֹם.
On three things the world is established:
on truth, on justice, and on peace.
(פרקי אבות א)

16

Purpose: To learn more of the G stem
Materials: Esther 1:15-16

טו כְּדָת מַה־לַּעֲשׂוֹת
בַּמַּלְכָּה וַשְׁתִּי עַל ׀ אֲשֶׁר לֹא־עָשְׂתָה אֶת־מַאֲמַר הַמֶּלֶךְ
16 אֲחַשְׁוֵרוֹשׁ בְּיַד הַסָּרִיסִים׃ וַיֹּאמֶר מוּמְכָן לִפְנֵי הַמֶּלֶךְ
וְהַשָּׂרִים לֹא עַל־הַמֶּלֶךְ לְבַדּוֹ עָוְתָה וַשְׁתִּי הַמַּלְכָּה כִּי
עַל־כָּל־הַשָּׂרִים וְעַל־כָּל־הָעַמִּים אֲשֶׁר בְּכָל־מְדִינוֹת
הַמֶּלֶךְ אֲחַשְׁוֵרוֹשׁ׃

1:15 כְּדָת[1]—Cf. 1:8[1]—what difference do you see between the form here and in 1:8?

מַה־לַּעֲשׂוֹת[2]-(a) Interrog. pron., §21.42f. (b) לַ–עֲשׂ–וֹת. Note dagesh, §13.3, §13.36. Only two radicals are seen, ע–שׂ, hence one is missing, but is it the 1st, 2d, or 3d? Clue: ל—וֹת is almost certainly an inf. cstr. (G65) of a verb with 3d rad. weak (CCY). Read §29., §29.7. Note §29.71, to which you will return often. Read §32.38. Root is *'ss*, v.6213. 'What to do?' = 'what shall we do?' At this point, review עָשָׂה 1:3[4], which is G10, and עָשְׂתָה, 1:9[2], which is G11. Look at §29.71 again, and locate the CCY endings.

בַּמַּלְכָּה[3]—Cf. 1:12[1].'With the queen.'

עַל ׀ אֲשֶׁר [4]—(a) v.5921. (b) v.834. Together, they form an idiom, 'because that,' cf. BDB 758 IIIa.

לֹא־עָשְׂתָה [5]—(a) Neg. part., v.3939, §35.221. (b) Can you work it out without going back to 1:9[2]? Learn *now* that ־תָה– with 2 rads. is G/D/H/N/HtD 11 morpheme of CCY verbs. 'She did not do.'

אֶת־מַאֲמַר ... בְּיַד הַסָּרִיסִים׃ [6]—(a) Sign of d.d.o., §34.113. Why is the word that follows definite? §30.3144. (b) *ma'ămar* msc of מַאֲמָר (3982 3/3) 'commandment,' a noun built on the pattern maCCaC, §24.33. (e-f) 1:12[4]. 'Because she did not do the commandment of king A. (delivered) by the eunuchs.'

1:16 וַיֹּאמֶר מוּמְכָן לִפְנֵי הַמֶּלֶךְ וְהַשָּׂרִים [1]—(a) Review 1:13[1]. This is an 'CC verb, §29.21, note especially §29.212. Conv. waw has caused accent shift, §17.341. **ya'mir* > **yâ'mēr* > *yô'mēr*, with conv. waw *wayyṓ'mer*. This word is so very common, that you should learn וַיֹּאמֶר 'and he said.' (b) Masoretic note calls attention to misspelling מומכן for מְמוּכָן*. (e) 1:11[4].

לֹא עַל־הַמֶּלֶךְ לְבַדּוֹ[2]—(a) 1:15[5]. (b) *'al* prep. 'against,' v.5921, BDB 757 II 7d. (c) *l^e-badd- -ô*, analyze the elements. בַּד v.905, 'alone': 'not against the king alone.'

עָוְתָה[3]—Cf. 1:15[5]. Here the verb is ʿ-*w-y* עָוָה (v.5753) 'to do wrong, be perverse. The form is G11 of CCY, as the ending ־תָה tells us. Because of the very high frequency of CCY verbs, start to master them *today*: 'she has done wrong.'

כִּי עַל־כָּל־הַשָּׂרִים [4]—(a) After a neg. 'but,' v.3588, BDB 474 3e. (b) 1:16[2]. You should be able to work this out.

וְעַל־כָּל־הָעַמִּים[5]—(a) Note that the prep. is repeated. This is more common, but we sometimes find one prep. governing two objects. Cf. 1:16[2]. (c) 1:5[4], v.5971.

אֲשֶׁר בְּכָל־מְדִינוֹת [6]—(a) Relative clause, §38.4, modifying 'all the princes' and 'all the peoples.' (b) *kol* before pl. = 'all': 'in all the provinces of the king.'

Analyze the following forms:

כְּשֶׁבֶת *k^{e}šeḇeṯ* G65 of *yšb* with *k^e*-, §§29.3, .322:

לְמָלְכוֹ *l^{e}molḵô*, 1:3[3], G65 of *mlk* with *l^e*-, §§27.65f.

וּבִמְלוֹאת *ûḇimlô^{w}ʾṯ*, §1:5[1], G65 (irreg.) of *mlʾ*, read §29.22, §29.2213.

לָבוֹא *lāḇôʾ*, 1:12[2], G65 (irreg.) of *bwʾ*, §29.54, §29.6, §29.631.

Learn the basic vocabulary in Group 11.

Study the following verb developments:

CCC	מלך	**yamluk*	>	*yimlōḵ*	יִמְלֹךְ
CCC	כבד	**yikbad*	>	*yiḵbaḏ*	יִכְבַּד
ʾCC	אלף	**tiʾlap*	>	*teʾlap̄*	תֶּאֱלַף
ʾCC	אמץ	**yiʾmaṣ*	>	*yeʾĕmaṣ*	יֶאֱמַץ
ʾCC	אסר	**yaʾsur*	>	*yeʾsōr*	יֶאְסֹר
				or *yeʾĕsōr*	יֶאֱסֹר
GCC	חפך	**yahpuk*	>	*yahăp̄ōḵ*	יַחֲפֹךְ
GCC	חמס	**yaḥmus*	>	*yaḥmōs*	יַחְמֹס
GCC	חלם	**yaḥlum*	>	*yaḥălōm*	יַחֲלֹם
GCC	חנן	**yiḥnan*	>	*yeḥĕnan*	יֶחֱנַן
GCC	עבד	**yaʿbud*	>	*yaʿăḇōḏ*	יַעֲבֹד
GCC	ערב	**yiʿrab*	>	*yeʿĕraḇ*	יֶעֱרַב
NCC	נדר	**yandur*	>	*yiddōr*	יִדֹּר
NCC	נגש	**yingaš*	>	*yiggaš*	יִגַּשׁ
NCC	נתן	**yintin*	>	*yittēn*	יִתֵּן
WCC	יעף	**yiyʿap*	>	*yî^{y}ʿap̄*	יִיעַף
WCC	ילד	**taylid*	>	*têlēḏ*	תֵּלֵד
YCC	ישר	**yiyšar*	>	*yî^{y}šar*	יִישַׁר

Purpose: To introduce derived stems of verb forms
Materials: Esther 1:17-18

17 כִּי־יֵצֵא דְבַר־הַמַּלְכָּה עַל־כָּל־הַנָּשִׁים
לְהַבְזוֹת בַּעְלֵיהֶן בְּעֵינֵיהֶן בְּאָמְרָם הַמֶּלֶךְ אֲחַשְׁוֵרוֹשׁ אָמַר
לְהָבִיא אֶת־וַשְׁתִּי הַמַּלְכָּה לְפָנָיו וְלֹא־בָאָה׃ וְהַיּוֹם הַזֶּה 18
תֹּאמַרְנָה ׀ שָׂרוֹת פָּרַס־וּמָדַי אֲשֶׁר שָׁמְעוּ אֶת־דְּבַר הַמַּלְכָּה
לְכֹל שָׂרֵי הַמֶּלֶךְ וּכְדַי בִּזָּיוֹן וָקָצֶף׃

1:17 כִּי־יֵצֵא[1]—(a) Conj., v.3588, 'for, because,' introduces causal clause, §30.3623. (b) *yêṣē' < *yayṣi'u,* yaCCiC or *yaqtil* impf. of *yṣ',* v.3318, 'to go out.' The verb is YCC < *WCC. Read §29.3, §29.321. Now read §27.33. Since most grammars fail to distinguish the *yaqtil*-type of impf., this formation is often misunderstood. The impf. here is not converted, hence may be translated as a future, §32.522, 'it shall go out.'

עַל־כָּל־הַנָּשִׁים[2]—(a) The preps. אֶל and עַל often interchange, particularly in the later books; but cf. BDB 757. Here it seems to mean 'unto.' (c) 1:9[3]. The morpheme ◌ִים *-îm* is mpa, but this word means 'women' (listed under אִשָּׁה in BDB 61). The word is fem., and takes fem. adjs..

לְהַבְזוֹת בַּעְלֵיהֶן בְּעֵינֵיהֶן[3]—(a) *l^{e}-haḇz-ôṯ,* לְ—וֹת could be 65 (inf. cstr.) of CCY, §29.71. That leaves הבז of which only 2 can be radicals (in CCY the 3d rad is weak), hence ה must be a stem indicator of H stem, §28.3, cf. §32.82. בָּזָה 'to despise,' v.959, cf. 1:18[7] below, H 'to cause to despise.' (b) *ba'ăl-ê^{y}-hen,* from בַּעַל 'lord, master, husband,' v.1167. ◌ֵי tells us that it is mps (§25.5) and the הֶן– is 3fp (s6), 'their husbands.' Note that in Heb. the pron. suf. is in concord with its antecedent; in French it is in concord with the word it modifies, *son mari* 'her husband,' *sa femme* 'his wife.' (c) *b^{e}-'ên-ê^{y}-hen,* from עַיִן 'eye,' v.5989, mps6 (masc. pl. with 3fp suffix.), 'their (f) eyes,' 'to make their husbands despicable in their eyes.'

בְּאָמְרָם[4]—*b^{e}-'omr-ām,* prep., G65, s5. For *'omr < *'umur,* cf. §27.65, §27.652. Study this carefully. 'In their saying' = 'when they say,' §35.421. What follows is direct discourse, §38.31.

אָמַר[5]—Rule 15. No preformative or sufformative = G stem, and vowel pattern CaCaC indicates G10, 'he said'; subj. precedes. What follows is indirect discourse, §38.82.

לְהָבִיא אֶת־וַשְׁתִּי ... לְפָנָיו[6]—(a) *l^{e}- hāḇî'* gives 3 clues: the prep. –לְ, which often signals an inf. cstr., the –הָ, which may signal an H stem, and the –ִי, which often indicates an H stem. There are other possibilities, but we should start with the most likely. Since there is no indication of loss of first radical and no indication of loss of 3d rad. (points that you will learn by analyzing many verbs), we may assume that it comes from *bw'* בּוֹא 'to enter,' v.935. Cf. 1:11[1]. H65 of בּוֹא. (b) v.853, ddo., §34.113. (e) 1:3[14].

וְלֹא־בָ֫אָה׃[7]—(a) Conj. and neg. part. (b) ־ָה could be one of several morphemes: replacement for weak 3d rad. (CCY, G10), fsa of noun, or 11 of verb. Note accent, which indicates that it is not a noun or a G10. It is G11 (perf. 3fs) of בּוֹא, Cv̂C, see §29.6, §§29.63f. In verbs of this category (Cv̂C), G11 is accented in the penult, and G51 on the ultima. 'and she did not come.'

1:18 וְהַיּוֹם הַזֶּה [1]—(a) 1:4[10]. (b) זֶה demon. pron. 'this,' v.2088, §21.2, cf. 1:2[12]. Note position of pron. and concord (agrees in gender, number, definiteness).

תֹּאמַ֫רְנָה[2]—נָה—ת are afformatives that indicate 3fp (26) or 2fp (28) of impf., §27.31. The balance is אמַר, which has no indication of D, H, N, or HtD stem, hence must be G. Context requires G26 of אמר 'they (f) will say,' referring to the women, 1:17[2].

שָׂרוֹת[3]—If שָׂרִים is 'princes,' what is this? What morpheme is וֹת–? §25.232. Since the vowels cannot reduce (ָ is a compensation vowel), there is nothing but the accent ֣ to indicate cstr., 'the princesses of Persia and Media.'

אֲשֶׁר שָֽׁמְעוּ [4]—(a) Introduces rel. cl., §38.4. (b) Note וּ— and no preformative. This can be 15, 16 (§27.21) or 37 (§27.422), and only the vowel under the 1st rad. tells the difference. Here is it ָ, hence it must be G15/16, and context requires the 3fp or G16. שָׁמַע 'he heard,' v.8085. In context, this must be translated as future perfect, 'and all the princesses who shall have heard ... shall say.'

לְכֹל שָׂרֵי הַמֶּלֶךְ[5]—Indirect object after verb of saying, §35.11. You should be able to work it out. What the ladies will say is left unsaid—any married man will know!

וּכְדַי[6]—For *û*, Rule 8. *kᵉ*-, 'like, as.' The expression is cryptic, and many explanations have been given, possibly 'according to the abundance of' (BDB, reading וּכְדֵי). For דַּי 'enough,' see v.1767.

בִּזָּיוֹן וָקָצֶף׃ [7]—(a) *bizzay* + *ôn*, 'contempt' (963 1/1), cf. 1:17[3](a). (b) *qéṣep̄*, pausal *qā́ṣep̄*, 'wrath,' v.7110, cf. 1:12[5](a). 'and (there will be) like plenty of contempt and wrath.'

Start to work in earnest on Paradigm V-1.

Analyze the following verbs:
בָּעֲרָה, *bāʿărāʰ*, 1:12[7], ה— with ָ under 1st rad., G11 of *bʿr*, §27.21.
עָשְׂתָה, 1:9[2], תָה— with ָ under 1st rad. = ? §29.7131.
עָוְתָה, 1:16[3].

Learn the vocabulary in Group 12.

18

Purpose: To continue study of the Hebrew verb
Materials: Esther 1:19-20

אִם־עַל־הַמֶּלֶךְ טוֹב 19
יֵצֵא דְבַר־מַלְכוּת מִלְּפָנָיו וְיִכָּתֵב בְּדָתֵי פָרַס־וּמָדַי וְלֹא
יַעֲבוֹר אֲשֶׁר לֹא־תָבוֹא וַשְׁתִּי לִפְנֵי הַמֶּלֶךְ אֲחַשְׁוֵרוֹשׁ
וּמַלְכוּתָהּ יִתֵּן הַמֶּלֶךְ לִרְעוּתָהּ הַטּוֹבָה מִמֶּנָּה׃ וְנִשְׁמַע כ
פִּתְגָם הַמֶּלֶךְ אֲשֶׁר־יַעֲשֶׂה בְּכָל־מַלְכוּתוֹ כִּי רַבָּה הִיא
וְכָל־הַנָּשִׁים יִתְּנוּ יְקָר לְבַעְלֵיהֶן לְמִגָּדוֹל וְעַד־קָטָן׃

1:19 אִם־עַל־הַמֶּלֶךְ טוֹב [1]—(a) Conj., 'if,' v.518; introduces a condition §38.6. (d) 1:11[6]. This is a common cliché to a superior. The clause is verbless (§31), 'if (it is) good.'

יֵצֵא דְבַר־מַלְכוּת [2]—(a) 1:17[1]. There it is impf. (G20), but here context suggests jussive (G40, §30.3355); there is no formal difference in this word. 'let there go forth.' (b-c) Cf. 1:7[4]; here 'a royal word.'

מִלְּפָנָיו [3]—*min* + *l*^{e}- + *p*^{e}*nê* + s0, lit. 'from (reference) to face of him' = 'from before him,' an idiom found 73x in OT (BDB 817 II 5).

וְיִכָּתֵב [4]—*w*^{e}*yikkāṯēḇ* < **w*^{e}*yinkāṯēḇ,* possibly < **w*^{e}*y*^{e}*hinkāṯēḇ,* read §28.4 on N stem. Clues to the N perf.: preformative n —נ, with *i* < *a* under the preformative. Clues to the N imperf., strong dagesh in 1st rad. and vowel pattern yiC^{2}āCēC. What clues do you see here?. This could be N20 (—·יִ) or N40 (juss.); context suggests juss., 'and let it be written.' The *wāw* cannot be conversive, for on impf. it would be –·וַ, and it cannot stand on juss. כתב 'to write,' v.3789.

בְּדָתֵי פָרַס־וּמָדַי [5]—(a) Note ־ֵי. You should know the word (1:8[1]). (b-c) You should know this expression (1:3[9 10]).

וְלֹא יַעֲבוֹר [6]—(a) You should know (v.3939). (b) Written with a false plene (§11.3241), it may confuse you. —י indicates a 3ms impf. (20) form, §27.21. Vowel pattern yaCCuC, §27.32, usually > *yiCCōC yiqtōl* (Rule 18), but with GCC verbs (§29.lf.), Rule 10c applies > *yaGăCōC. Study this carefully.* עבר 'to cross over, pass away,' v.5674. 'and it shall not pass away.'

אֲשֶׁר לֹא־תָבוֹא [7]—(a) Introduces indir. disc. BDB 833.8, or possibly final clause (§30.3624). (b) —תָ: morpheme is either impf. 3fs (21) or 2ms (22), §27.31. There is no indication that this is CCY (21/22 of CCY ends in -ê^h). It could be CC^2 or CvC, but the final א rules out the former, so we try בוא, v.935, 'to enter.' Subj. follows, 'Vashti,' hence verb is G21, and clause is translated 'Vashti shall not enter.' The form could be G41 (juss.), 'Let Vashti not enter,' but לא is usually used with indicative and אל with juss. (you haven't learned this yet), hence this is indic.—לא + indic. is a strong prohibition.

וּמַלְכוּתָהּ יִתֵּן [8]—(a) ־ָהּ *-āh* (with mappiq, §11.42) is 3fs suffix (s1), hence 'her royalty.' (b) *yittēn* < **yintēn* (R.11), yaCCiC, §27.334. Preformative —י must be 20, and *i*-vowel under preformative is a fairly sure sign of G20. Strong dagesh (R.1a) suggests that a consonant has been assimilated. It could be an N stem, but the vowel-pattern does not confirm this. It could be D10 of **ytn*, or G20 of *ntn*. In a case like this, we try both for fit. G20 of נתן 'to give,' v.5414, fits context. It could be G40 (juss.). Object precedes, subj. follows: 'her kingdom let the king give.'

לִרְעוּתָהּ [9]—*l^{e}-r^{e}'ût-āh*, with R.19. רְעוּת (7466 6/1) 'friend, neighbor.'

הַטּוֹבָה מִמֶּנָּה׃ [10]—(a) Def. art. used like rel. pron. What does *-ā^{h}* suggest? Cf. טוֹב, 1:10[2]. It is in concord with 1:19[10], §36.1f. (b) Possibly < *min* + *min* + *hā^{h}*, with reduplication of the prep. (v.4480), 'from her.' This is מִן of comparison, §38.71. 'The good from her' = 'who is better than she.'

1:20 וְנִשְׁמַע פִּתְגָם הַמֶּלֶךְ [1]—(a) *w^{e}-nišma'*: *ni— —a—* = niCCaC. The preformative can be impf. 1cp (29) or N perf 3ms (N10); context favors the latter. See §28.42. שמע 'to hear' (v.8085), N10 'it shall be heard.' The subj. is more closely defined by the next word. (b) *pitgām* (Pers. *patigâma*) 'edict' (6599 2/1), in cstr. with following word.

אֲשֶׁר־יַעֲשֶׂה [2]—(a) Rel.pron., modifying *pitgām*. (b) ־ֶה—יַ. We see only 2 rads. and the form ends in ־ֶה, hence it must be 20 of CCY. The vowel pattern could be H20 of CCY or G/H20 of GCY, §29.11. Since this verb has a guttural in 1st rad., our first try will be G20 of עָשָׂה, 'he shall make.'

כִּי רַבָּה הִיא [3]—(a) Causal, 'for,' §38.53 (b) masc. *rab*, fem. *rabbā^{h}*, hence CvC^{2} type noun/adj. (v.7227). Here it is pred. adj., §30.321, §31.23. (c) Independent pron. 3ms, §21.1 (v.1931b), 'she, it (f).' Subj. of the verbless clause, §31.12. A copula is not used in Heb. but must be added in translation: 'for it (is) great.'

וְכָל־הַנָּשִׁים יִתְּנוּ יְקָר לְבַעְלֵיהֶן [4]—(a-b) 1:9[3], 1:17[2]. (c) וּ—יִ must be impf. 3mp (25), §27.31. Strong dagesh in 1st rad. suggests assimilated *nûn* < **yint^{e}nû*, G25 of נתן, cf. 1:19[9]. Subj. precedes and is fem.; possibly the *-îm* ending attracted a masc. form of the verb. Context suggests that juss. (G45) is possible, 'let all the women give.' (d) 1:4[5]. (e) 1:17[3]. לְמִגָּדוֹל וְעַד־קָטָן׃ [5]—Cf. 1:5[7].

Analyze the following verbs:

יִסַּד *yissad*, 1:8[3]. Careful! There are some YCC verbs, and the –יְ can be the 1st rad. Can this be a D10 form?

וַתְּמָאֵן, 1:12[1]. –וַ tells us what? —תְּ tells us (1) form is 21/22 and (2) it is D (shewa under preformative, vowel pattern), §28.21.

לְהַרְאוֹת, 1:11[4]: וֹת—לְ suggests 65 of CCY, §29.71, but that leaves הרא. The ה must therefore be stem indicator, hence H65 of *r'y* רָאָה.

Learn the vocabulary in Group 13.

19

Purpose: To continue analysis of the Hebrew verb
Materials: Esther 1:21-22

21 וַיִּיטַב
הַדָּבָר בְּעֵינֵי הַמֶּלֶךְ וְהַשָּׂרִים וַיַּעַשׂ הַמֶּלֶךְ כִּדְבַר מְמוּכָן׃
22 וַיִּשְׁלַח סְפָרִים אֶל־כָּל־מְדִינוֹת הַמֶּלֶךְ אֶל־מְדִינָה וּמְדִינָה
כִּכְתָבָהּ וְאֶל־עַם וָעָם כִּלְשׁוֹנוֹ לִהְיוֹת כָּל־אִישׁ שֹׂרֵר
בְּבֵיתוֹ וּמְדַבֵּר כִּלְשׁוֹן עַמּוֹ׃

1:21 וַיִּיטַב הַדָּבָר [1]—(a) *way - yî[y]ṭaḇ: yi—a–* is yiCCaC type of YCC verb. Read §29.3 carefully. Look at יֵצֵא, 1:17[1], and compare with יִיטַב. Read §29.33 and then read carefully §29.331. In this *Handbook* we distinguish WCC from true YCC. WCC verbs often lose 1st rad. י in G impf., and YCC verbs usually keep 1st rad י in the same forms. יטב (v.3190) 'to be good'; subj. follows. (b) 'The word, thing' (v.1697). What does *wāw* conv. do to tense of verb?

בְּעֵינֵי הַמֶּלֶךְ וְהַשָּׂרִים [2]—(a)1:17[3], CaYC-type noun, §24.212. In cstr. with *two* nouns, contrary to normal grammar, *Ges.* §128*a*.

וַיַּעַשׂ [3]—Note carefully *way - yáʻaś,* note accent. This is *apocopated;* read §13.533 and Rules 5,6. Read §17.341. Apocopation is a common feature of CCY verbs with wāw conv. and impf. Decide now to learn this. 'and he did.' *yiGCay* > *yaGăCê[h]* יַעֲשֶׂה + *way* > *wayyáʻaś* וַיַּעַשׂ

כִּדְבַר מְמוּכָן׃[4]—(a) Note vowels, *kiḏbar* < *k[e]ḏ[e]ḇar*, R.19. –כְּ prep., 'according to.' It is necessary to study the wide range of meanings the preps. have. (b) Note spelling and cf. 1:16[1] and Masoretic note there.

1:22 וַיִּשְׁלַח סְפָרִים [1]—(a) –וַ tells us what?. *yi--a-* suggests yiCCaC, here yiCCaG, a CCG-type verb, §29.13. שלח v.7971, 'to send.' What form here? §27.31. How should you translate it? (b) *s[e]pārîm* is pl. of *sēper,* v.5612, 'document,' a CiCC-type noun. Why is אֵת omitted? §34.113.

אֶל־כָּל־מְדִינוֹת הַמֶּלֶךְ [2]—How does the accent here and that of the following word help us? (a) אֶל v.413, 'unto.' Which is correct? 'The king sent documents unto all the cities,' or '... unto every city,' or 'and he sent documents to all the cities of the king.'

אֶל־מְדִינָה וּמְדִינָה כִּכְתָבָהּ [3]—(a-c) Cf. 1:8[6]; this is distributive, = 'to each province.' (d) *k[e]- k[e]ṯāḇ -āh* , prep. + כְּתָב v.3792 'writing,' cf. 1:19[4]. 'according to its writing.'

וְאֶל־עַם וָעָם כִּלְשֹׁנוֹ[4]—(a-c) Distributive. (b,c) Note vowels: עָם is pausal form. Translate. (d) *k^e-l^ešôn-ô.* לָשׁוֹן v.3956, 'tongue,' CvCv̂C-type noun. Why is it *kilšônô* but *kik̲t̲^eb̲āh?* Why are the suffixes different? What are their antecedents?

לִהְיוֹת כָּל־אִישׁ[5]—(a) *l^e- h^eyôt̲:* ל—וֹת could be an inf. cstr. (65) of a CCY, §29.71. Work from there; what consonants remain? What would the root be? Is היה the right answer? Does it make sense in context (v.1961)? (b-c) כֹּל before sing. means 'every.' This phrase is subj. of the inf., 'every man to be....'

שֹׂרֵר בְּבֵיתוֹ[6]—(a) *-ô-ē-* CôCēC is G50 pattern, §27.611. שׂרר is prob. a denominal verb from שַׂר. meaning 'to be prince, ruler' (8323 5/1). ר was heard as geminate by LXX translators (*Σαρρα* = שָׂרָה). An *r* can be prolonged when it is trilled, but not when it is guttural (contrast Span. and Ital. *r* with Ger. and Fr.). Tiberian Heb. (i.e. Masoretic) was guttural, cf. Matt. 26:73.

וּמְדַבֵּר[7]—*û- m^ed̲abbēr: m^eCaC²iC* is the pattern of D50, §28.21. Your clues are: (1) shewa under preformative, (2) *-a-i-* vowel pattern, and (3) dagesh in middle radical—*in this order!* דִּבֵּר 'he spoke,' v.1696; 'and speaking.'

כִּלְשׁוֹן עַמּוֹ׃[8]—(a) 1:22[4]. (b) 1:16[5]. Does the dagesh in עַמּוֹ explain why the sing. is עַם? Rules 6a and 14. 'and speaking according to the tongue of his [not his wife's] people.'

Be sure you have recorded in your notebook all the verb forms that we have encountered. Now it is time to categorize them and to work seriously on methodical verb analysis. You will make very slow progress if you do not master the verbal system outline at this point!

In the following forms, כ stands for any strong consonant. Can you recognize the forms?

ככַב	יִכְכֹּכ	תִּכְכַּכ	יִכְכְּכוּ
כּוֹכֵב	יִכֵּכ	יַעֲסֹם	יִכְּכוּ
כָּכָה	יִכְכֶּה	מְכַכְּכִים	יִסָּסֵם
תְּסַכֵּכ	לִכְכוֹת	לְהָכִיכ	לְהַכְּכוֹת

Learn the words in Group 14.

---

20. In originally closed accented syllables, in certain forms original short *i* becomes short *a* (§15.33).

20

Purpose: To learn to use the Verb Diagnosis Chart
Materials: Verb Diagnosis Chart, student's notebook

Note: Some students and instructors find the VDC of little value. In my experience, it has been very useful, and a few former students report that they still use it for difficult forms. I have no zeal for the VDC, but I am certain that there is no substitute for developing a *methodical approach* to verb analysis. The following steps, with or without the VDC, are of primary importance.

Preliminary steps

1. Remove all prepositions and suffixes. If there is a prep., form must be a verbal noun. If there is a suf., vowel pattern may have to be restored, using SVC.

2. Identify all preformatives and sufformatives. *You cannot parse a verb form if you do not know these morphemes.* If there is a preformative –י, –ת, –א, or –נ, the form is impf. (20) or juss. (40). If there is a sufformative but no preformative, the form is perf. (10) or impv. (32).

3. Identify any stem-indicator (strong dagesh, stem preformative or the effect of one). Stem preformatives are –ה, –נ, –הִת, and –הִנ, or resultant forms with PGN preformatives added to stem preformatives (e.g. –יִת, –אֶת, etc.), assimilation of *nûn,* ellision (syncopation) of –הָ–, and other phonetic alterations.

4. What remains is the *root* or one or two radicals of the root. Step 2 has given us PGN and possibly other data, such as stem, aspect (tense), voice, and mood, and Step 3 has given us the stem if the form is a derived stem. But the parsing of a verb is not complete until the root is given, for it is impossible to know the meaning of the word without knowing its root (unless, of course, you grow up with the language).

5. Are there apparent causes for irregularity? Is there a guttural, a *rêš*, signs of a hollow verb (*CûC, CîC*), signs of first radical weak (*WCC, YCC*) or third radical weak (*CCY*), a dagesh indicating an assimilated *nûn* or a compensation vowel giving the same clue? Carefully check each step.

Parsing procedure

6. Easiest to recognize are HtD and D forms of the "strong" verb (CCC, plus GCC and CCG and some forms of CC^2 and NCC). See Table 1 of VDC.

a. Is there a preformative –הִת, –תִת, –אֶת, –נִת, of –מִת? The form is HtD, §28.5. Is there any sign of metathesis and/or assimilation, §28.53? The middle radical should be doubled (that's the D in HtD), but if it is a guttural or *rêš* or if it has a shewa, doubling may be absent.

b. Is there a strong dagesh in the second radical? If everything else seems to be in order, the form is either D or Dp (Pi'el or Pu'al), §28.2. However, be sure you have the second *radical* and not just the second consonant in the word. The N perf. of NCC or CC² verbs, the N32 of strong verbs, certain forms of CC² verbs, etc., may have a dagesh in the second consonant. It is for this reason that you *must* be able to identify the preformatives (steps 2 and 3).

c. Is there a shewa under the preformative? This is often a better indicator of the D than the gemination of the middle radical, see §§28.21, .22. However, beware of pronominal suffixes which may pull the accent to the end of the word, leaving a shewa under the first radical. You may mistake the radical for a sufformative, particularly if it is י, ת, א, נ, or מ.

d. Is there there the correct vowel pattern? Short *a* after the first radical is HtD or D active, *u* (usually *o*, ָ, *qāmāṣ ḥāṭûp̄*) after the 1st rad. is Dp (HtDp is very rare, §28.52).

7. Is the *first radical* doubled? See Table 2 of VDC. This is a fairly sure sign of the N stem, §28.4.

a. The N perf. and ptcp. will have preformative stem indicator, hence no doubling of 1st rad.

b. When the *nûn* is assimilated, doubling the 1st rad., the vowel pattern confirms the clue: —*i*—*ā*—*ē*—, —ִ—ָ—ֵ—.

c. Be sure three radicals are present; NCC and CC² forms may have the first apparent radical doubled (see Table 7 of VDC).

d. In GCC verbs, gemination is impossible, but compensatory lengthening may give the clue; check the vowel pattern.

8. Is there a *silent shewa* under the 1st radical? In other words, does the preformative and the first radical form a closed syllable? See Table 3 of VDC. The form may be G20/40, H or Hp, N10/60; look for further clues.

a. Start with H or Hp. H/Hp10/60 will have the preformative -ה. The other H forms will have *pattāḥ* under the preformative, and Hp forms will have *qāmāṣ-ḥāṭûp̄*.

b. The N forms will have preformative *nûn*. Study the vowel pattern. niCCaC is N10, niCCāC is N50, niCCôC is N60.

c. G20/40 forms will have *i* under the preformative. GCC verbs, of course, do not fall into this category (see Table 4 of VDC).

continued on next page

9. Is there *both* a preformative *and* a vowel under the first radical? Make further analysis.

a. If there is a shewa under the preformative, it is probably a D; see step 6c above or Table 1 of VDC.

b. If the first radical is a guttural, the form may be N or G. Check the vowel pattern (step 7b, Table 2 VDC) for N.

c. If 7a and 7b are negative and there is a guttural in 1st rad., the form is G impf. or juss.

d. If the form is *not* GCC, have you overlooked a pron. suf. that has shifted accent?

10. Are there three radical consonants, no sufformative, all consonants separated by vowels? The form can only be G, D/Dp of CGC or CC², or you have not identified a pre-/suf-formative.

a. If the form is CGC, it could be D or Dp perf. Check the vowel pattern. The D has an *i*-vowel under the first radical; the Dp10 has a *u*-vowel.

b. The G10 has an *a*-vowel under the 1st rad.

c. The G50 has a long *ô* after the 1st rad. It is possible to confuse this with a Pô'ēl (§28.6), but such forms are comparatively rare.

d. The Gp50 has long *û* after 2d rad., and the G60 has long *ô* after 2d rad.

e. The G12/13/14/19 of CCY have long *î* after 2d rad.—don't let this mislead you to identify the form as H. See Table 3 VDC and step 8a above.

f. Is there a shewa under the first radical? The form may be G17/18, G32/65. Look for further clues.

g. Is there an *i* vowel under 1st rad.? The form may be D10 of CGC or G33/37. Look for further clues.

11. If *only two radicals* are present, see Tables 6-10 of Verb Diagnosis Chart and follow these steps.

12. Does the form end in ־ָה, ־ֶה, ־וֹת, or a pron. suf.? It can only be CCY (see Table 6 VDC).

a. Read carefully §§29.7-.723.

b. Take all of the form up to and including the 2d rad. and apply the steps above (or Tables 1-5 VDC).

13. Is the *first radical* doubled? Careful! Do not confuse this with step 7, which is

for *three* radicals; this is only for forms with *two* radicals. The form can be NCC, CC², or N stem of CvC. See Table 7 VDC.

a. If first vowel is *u* (ֻ), form is Hp of NCC, §29.43.

b. If first vowel is *o* (ָ), form is Hp60 of CC², with "Aramaic" doubling, §29.5115.

c. If first vowel is *a* (ַ), form is H (but not Hp) of NCC, §29.4.

d. If first vowel is *i* (ִ), note the second vowel, use Table 7 VDC.

14. Is the *second radical* doubled? Remember, we are dealing here *only* with forms that have only *two* radicals showing. The form is either CC² or D of CCY. See Table 8 VDC.

a. For CC², read through §§29.5ff.

b. For CCY, review §§29.7ff.

c. Beware of נָתַתִּי, the only verb that assimilates its *third radical nûn*, §29.44.

15. Is there a preformative? There are a number of possibilities. Study Table 9 VDC carefully. It will take some time to master this category.

a. If there is *ô* (וֹ or ֹ) in preformative, it is H or N of WCC, §29.32.

b. If there is *ê* (ֵ for יֵ) in preformative, it is WCC (§29.321) or possibly YCC (*Ges.* §70*c*, Rem. 1).

c. If there is *û* (וּ) in preformative, it is Hp of WCC, CvC, or CC².

d. In other cases, follow Table 9 of VDC carefully. Note that G and H forms are often remarkably similar.

16. Are there *just two radicals* with no preformative? See Table 10 VDC.

a. If the consonants are separated by ִי, form is CîC, §29.64.

b. If the consonants are separated by וֹ, form is CûC, §29.63ff.

c. In other cases, use Table 10 VDC

17. Is *only one radical* present? Form is NCY or G65 of נתן. See Table 11 VDC.

a. If the separating vowel is *a* (ַ), form is H.

b. If the separating vowel is *i* (ִ), form is G20 or H10.

c. If the vowel is *ē* (ֵ), form is G40.

d. If the vowel is *u* (ֻ), form is Hp10.

Using the verbs in your notebook, start analyzing them by using these steps.

Learn the words in Vocabulary Group 15.

Verb Diagnosis Chart

If *three* radicals are present, use Tables 1-5.

1 Middle radical doubled; ± *hiṯ*- stem-indicator

cac^{2}ēc	*dabbēr*	דִּבֵּר	D32[3]	CCC
cac^{2}ôc	*yassôr*	יַסֹּר	D60	
cic^{2}ac	*limmaḏ*	לִמַּד	D10	
	yissaḇ	יִסַּב		T.7
cic^{2}ác-	*biššáltā*	בִּשַּׁלְתָּ	D12	CCC
cic^{2}ēc	*ʿiwwēr*	עִוֵּר	D10	
cic^{2}ᵉcv	*kibbᵉḏû*	כִּבְּדוּ	D15	
	tissᵉḇû	תִּסְּבוּ		T.7
cuc^{2}ac	*puqqaḏ*	פֻּקַּד	Dp10	
	huggaš	הֻגַּשׁ		T.7
cuc^{2}ôc	*quṭṭôl*	קֻטּוֹל	Dp60	CCC
***y*ᵉcac^{2}ac**	*yᵉḡallaḥ*	יְגַלַּח	D20	CCG
***y*ᵉcac^{2}ēc**	*yᵉḏabbēr*	יְדַבֵּר	D20	CCC
	nᵉbaššēl	נְבַשֵּׁל	D29	
	mᵉḏabbēr	מְדַבֵּר	D50	
ʾăcac^{2}ēc	*ʾăḵappēr*	אֲכַפֵּר	D24	
***y*ᵉcac^{2}ᵉc-**	*tᵉḏabbᵉrûn*	תְּדַבְּרוּן	D27	
	mᵉḇaššᵉlîm	מְבַשְּׁלִים	D55	
***y*ᵉcic^{2}ēc-**	*yᵉsibbēnî*	יְסִבֵּנִי		T.8
***y*ᵉcuc^{2}ac**	*yᵉḇuqqaš*	יְבֻקַּשׁ	Dp20	CCC
	tᵉḇuššal	תְּבֻשַּׁל	Dp21[7]	
mᵉcuc^{2}āc	*mᵉp̄uzzār*	מְפֻזָּר	Dp50	
mᵉcuc^{2}ᵉc-	*mᵉlummᵉḏêʸ*	מְלֻמְּדֵי	Dp57	

***h*itcac^{2}ac**	*hiṯʾannap̄*	הִתְאַנַּף	HtD10	CCC
	tiṯhaddar	תִּתְהַדַּר	HtD42	
	yiṯgabbār	יִתְגַּבָּר	HtD20	CCG
	yiṯhallᵉḵû	יִתְהַלְּכוּ	HtD25	
***h*iṯcac^{2}ēc**	*ʾeṯhallēḵ*	אֶתְהַלֵּךְ	HtD24	
	hiṯhallēḵ	הִתְהַלֵּךְ	HtD32[3]	
	hiṯḥannēn	הִתְחַנֵּן	HtD10[3]	GCC
	miṯhallēḵ	מִתְהַלֵּךְ	HtD50	
***h*ictac^{2}ēc**	*mistattēr*	מִסְתַּתֵּר	HtD50	R.12
	hištabbēᵃḥ	הִשְׁתַּבֵּחַ	HtD65	R.12
	niṣṭaddēq	נִצְטַדֵּק	HtD29	R.12
hotcac^{2}ac	*huṭṭammāʾāʰ*	הֻטַּמְּאָה	HtDp11	R.12
***h*itc^{2}ac^{2}ēc**	*middabbēr*	מִדַּבֵּר	HtD50	R.12
	ʾeddammêʰ	אֶדַּמֶּה	HtD24	CCY

2 First radical doubled; with preformative or stem-indicator

***y*ic^{2}ācac**	*yiwwadaʿ*	יִוָּדַע	N20	CCG
	hiššāmaʿ	הִשָּׁמַע	N32[2]	CCG
***y*ic^{2}ācac-**	*tiqqāṭálnā*	תִּקָּטַלְןָ	N26[8]	CCC
***y*ic^{2}ācēc**	*yikkāṯēḇ*	יִכָּתֵב	N20	CCC
	tillāḥēm	תִּלָּחֵם	N21[7]	
	hiqqāḇēṣ	הִקָּבֵץ	N32[2]	
hic^{2}ācôc	*hinnāṯôn*	הִנָּתוֹן	N60	
***y*ic^{2}ācᵉcv**	*yillāḥămû*	יִלָּחֲמוּ	N25	CGC
hic^{2}îc	*higgîḏ*	הִגִּיד		T.7
tic^{2}ōccā	*tissōḇnā*	תִּסֹּבְנָה		T.7
***y*ic^{2}ᵉcv**	*yippᵉlû*	יִפְּלוּ		T.7
	yiggᵉlû	יִגְּלוּ		T.6
huc^{2}ac	*huggaḏ*	הֻגַּד		T.7

[1] 32 = 60
[2] 32 = 65
[3] 32 = 60 = 65
[4] 10 = 32 = 60 = 65
[5] 60 = 65
[6] 15 = 16
[7] 21 = 22
[8] 26 = 28
[9] 40 = c20
[10] 20 = 40
[11] 10 = 50
[12] CWC = CYC
y-/h- = any preformative

If *less than three* radicals are present, use Tables 6-11

3 1st and 2d radicals *not* separated by vowel

yaccac	*yaṣmaḥ*	יַצְמַח	H40[9]	CCG
yaccēc	*yalbēš*	יַלְבֵּשׁ	H21[7]	CCC
nā	*taqṭēlnā*	תַּקְטֵלְנָה	H26[8]	
yaccîc	*talbîš*	תַּלְבִּישׁ	H21[7]	
’eccac	*’elbaš*	אֶלְבַּשׁ	G24	
’eccōc	*’eḏrōš*	אֶדְרֹשׁ	G24	
yiccac	*yiškaḇ*	יִשְׁכַּב	G20*a*	CCC
yiccāc	*yimṣā’*	יִמְצָא	G20*u*	CC’
yiccōc	*yisgōr*	יִסְגֹּר	G20*u*	CCC
yicc^{e}c-	*yišr^{e}ṣû*	יִשְׁרְצוּ	G25	
yō’cac	*yō’mar*	יֹאמַר	G20	’CC
yuccac	*yušlaḵ*	יֻשְׁלַךְ	Hp20	CCC
haccēc	*haḇdēl*	הַבְדֵּל	H32[3]	
haccîc	*halbîš*	הַלְבִּישׁ	H65	
-v̂	*haḇdîlû*	הַבְדִּילוּ	H37	
heccác-	*heḵlámnû*	הֶכְלַמְנוּ	H19	
hiccác-	*hilbáštā*	הִלְבַּשְׁתָּ	H12	
hiccēc	*himṣē’ṯ*	הִמְצֵאת	H13	CC’
hiccîc	*hiḏrîḵ*	הִדְרִיךְ	H10	CCC
hoccac	*hohpaḵ*	הָהְפַּךְ	Hp10	
hoccēc	*hoḥtēl*	הָחְתֵּל	Hp60	
huccac	*huškaḇ*	הֻשְׁכַּב	Hp10	
hucc^{e}c-	*hušl^{e}kû*	הֻשְׁלְכוּ	Hp15	
maccîc	*maḏrîḵ*	מַדְרִיךְ	H50	
moccac	*mošlaḥ*	מָשְׁלָח	Hp50	
muccāc	*mušlāḵ*	מֻשְׁלָךְ	Hp50	
neccac	*nehpaḵ*	נֶהְפַּךְ	N10	GCC
niccac	*niḵbaḏ*	נִכְבַּד	G29	CCC
	nišmar	נִשְׁמַר	N10	
niccāc	*nistār*	נִסְתָּר	N10 paus.	
	nip̄rāṣ	נִפְרָץ	N50	
	nimṣā’	נִמְצָא	G29/N10	
niccac-	*nišmartem*	נִשְׁמַרְתֶּם	N17	
niccēc-	*niqrḗ’ṯî*	נִקְרֵאתִי	N14	CC’
nicc^{e}c-	*nip̄q^{e}ḥû*	נִפְקְחוּ	N15	CCC
niccōc	*niḵtōḇ*	נִכְתֹּב	G29	CCC
niccôc	*nilḥôm*	נִלְחֹם	N60	

6 Only 2 radicals: Note ending; Up to and including 2d rad., Tables 1-5

	—$\bar{a}^{h}$	־ָה	10	CCY
Up to and	—e^{h}	־ֶה	20/50	CCY
including	—$\bar{e}^{h}$	־ֵה	32	CCY
2d radical,	—*îṯ*	־ִית	12	CCY
in Tables	—$\bar{o}^{h}$	־ֹה	60	CCY
1 to 5.	—*ôṯ*	־וֹת	65	CCY
Read	—*ûy*	־וּי	p50	CCY
§§29.7ff.	—*tā*	־ְתָה	11	CCY

4 1st and 2d radicals separated and *with* preformative or stem-indicator

cacăcēc	*haḥărēš*	הַחֲרֵשׁ	H32[3]	GCC
cacăcîc	*haḥăṭî’*	הַחֲטִיא	H60	GCC
	yaḥălîp̄	יַחֲלִיף	H20	GCC
	maḥărîš	מַחֲרִישׁ	H50	GCC
cacăcōc	*ya‘ăḇōr*	יַעֲבֹר	G20*u*	GCC
cacac^{e}cv	*yahar^{e}ḡû*	יַהַרְגוּ	G25	GCC
cecĕcac	*ye’ĕhaḇ*	יֶאֱהַב	G20*a*	GCC
	neḥĕlāṣ	נֶחֱלָץ	N10	GCC
cecĕcîc	*he‘ĕmîḏ*	הֶעֱמִיד	H10	GCC
cecĕcōc	*’eḥĕḇōš*	אֶחֱבֹשׁ	G24*u*	GCC
cecec^{e}cv	*teḥeṭ^{e}’û*	תֶּחֶטְאוּ	G27	GCC
cēcācēc	*yē’āḵēl*	יֵאָכֵל	N20	’CC
c^{e}cacēc	*y^{e}ḇahēl*	יְבַהֵל	D20[10]	CGC
c^{e}cācēc	*t^{e}mā’ēn*	תְּמָאֵן	D21[7]	CGC
	m^{e}ḇārēḵ	מְבָרֵךְ	D50	CGC
c^{e}cācaccv	*t^{e}hārā́ḡnā*	תְּהָרַגְנָה	G26	GCC

5 All radicals separated; *no* preformative or stem-indicator

cácac	*dá‘aṯ*	דַּעַת		T.10
cācac	*’āmar*	אָמַר	G10*a*	CCC
	nāsaḇ	נָסַב		T.9
cācáccv	*’āḇáḏtî*	אָבַדְתִּי	G14	CCC
cācāc	*qārā’*	קָרָא	G10	CC’
	‘āśā^{h}	עָשָׂה		T.6
	nāsāḇ	נָסָב		T.9
cācēc	*kāḇēḏ*	כָּבֵד	G10*i*[11]	CCC
	bārēḵ	בָּרֵךְ	D32[3]	CGC
cācîcv	*‘āśîṯā*	עָשִׂיתָ		T.6
cācōc	*qāṭōn*	קָטֹן	G10*u*[11]	CCC
cācôc	*nāṯôn*	נָתוֹן	G60	CCC
cācûc	*’āḥûz*	אָחוּז	Gp50	CCC
cécec	*šéḇeṯ*	שֶׁבֶת		T.10
cēcac	*bēraḵ*	בֵּרַךְ	G10	CGC
cic^{e}cv	*šim^{e}‘û*	שִׁמְעוּ	G37	CCC
coc^{e}cv	*mol^{e}ḵô*	מָלְכוֹ	G65s0	CCC
cōcac	*bōraḵ*	בֹּרַךְ	Dp10	CGC
côcac	*sôḇaḇ*	סוֹבַב	Lp10	CC[2]
côcēc	*môlēḵ*	מֹלֵךְ	G50	CCC
	sôḇēḇ	סוֹבֵב	L10	CC[2]
c^{e}cac	*š^{e}ma‘*	שְׁמַע	G32*a*	CCG
c^{e}caccv	*q^{e}ṭaltem*	קְטַלְתֶּם	G17	CCC
	ḥăzáqnā^{h}	חֲזַקְנָה	G38	GCC
c^{e}cōc	*š^{e}lō^{a}ḥ*	שְׁלֹחַ	G65[2]	CCG

If *less than three* radicals are present, use Tables 6-11

7 Only 2 radicals, 1st radical doubled

yac^{2}ēc	*yassēḇ*	יַסֵּב	H20	CC^2
	tappēl	תַּפֵּל	H40	NCC
yac^{2}îc	*yassîṯ*	יַסִּית	H20	CWC
	taggîḏ	תַּגִּיד	H22[7]	NCC
yic^{2}ac	*yimmal*	יִמַּל	G20[10]	CC^2
	yiggal	יִגַּל	N40	CC^2
	yissag	יִסַּג	N20	CWC
	tigga'	תִּגַּע	G21[7]	NCC
	nittan	נִתַּן	N10	NCC
	yiqqaḥ	יִקַּח	G20	לקח
yic^{2}ác^{2}û	*yiqqállû*	יִקַּלּוּ	N25	CC^2
yic^{2}āc	*tiśśā'*	תִּשָּׂא	G21[7]	NC'
	tiggāl	תִּגָּל	N40	T.6,2
yic^{2}ācû	*yiqqāwû*	יִקָּווּ	N15	T.6,2
yic^{2}ōc	*yimmōl*	יִמֹּל	N20	CWC
	yiddōḏ	יִדֹּד	G20	NC^2
	nissōḇ	נִסֹּב	N29	CC^2
'ec^{2}ōc	*'eddōm*	אֶדֹּם	G24	CC^2
yuc^{2}ac	*yuṣṣa'*	יֻצַּע	Hp20	YṢC
hac^{2}ac	*hannaḥ*	הַנַּח	H32	CWC
hac^{2}ēc	*haṣṣēl*	הַצֵּל	N32	NCC
hac^{2}ôc	*hakkôṯ*	הַכּוֹת	N65	NCY
hic^{2}ēc	*hissēḇ*	הִסֵּב	N60[5]	CC^2
hic^{2}îc	*higgîḏ*	הִגִּיד	H10	NCC
	hinnî^{a}ḥ	הִנִּיחַ	H10	CWC
huc^{2}ôc	*himmôl*	הִמּוֹל	N60	CWC
.	*hiqqôm*	הִקּוֹם	N60	CC^2
hic^{2}ocv	*himmṓlû*	הִמּוֹלוּ	N37	CWC
hic^{2}û	*hiṣṣû*	הִצּוּ	H15	NCY
hoc^{2}ac^{2}v	*hoššammā^h*	הָשַּׁמָּה	Hp60	CC^2
huc^{2}actv	*huggáštî*	הֻגַּשְׁתִּי	N14	NCC
mac^{2}écet	*maggéḏeṯ*	מַגֶּדֶת	H51	NCC
mac^{2}îc	*maggî^{a}'*	מַגִּיעַ	H50	NCC
nic^{2}ac	*nittan*	נִתַּן	N10	NCC
	nissaḇ	נִסַּב	N29	CC^2
nic^{2}actv	*niggáštā*	נִגַּשְׁתָּ	N12	NCC
nic^{2}ōc	*nissōḇ*	נִסֹּב	G29	CC^2
	nimmōl	נִמּוֹל	N10	CWC
nic^{2}ōcîm	*nimmōlîm*	נִמֹּלִים	N55	CWC
nic^{2}ôc	*nimmôl*	נִמֹּל	N10	CWC

[1]32=60
[2]32=65
[3]32=60=65
[4]10=32=60=65
[5]60=65
[6]15=16
[7]21=22
[8]26=28
[9]40=c20
[10]20=40
[11]10=50
[12]CWC = CYC
y-/h- = any preformative

8 Only 2 radicals, 2d radical doubled

cac^{2}v	*ḥáttā^h*	חַתָּה	G11	CC^2
	qállû	קַלּוּ	G15	CC^2
	máttā	מַתָּ	G12	CWC
	máttî	מַתִּי	G14	CWC
cac^{2}v-	*sabbū́nî*	סַבֻּנִי	G15s4	CC^2
	sabbṓṯî	סַבּוֹתִי	G14	CC^2
	ḥannōṯ	חַנּוֹת	G65	CC^2
cāc^{2}v	*rā́bbā^h*	רָבָּה	G11	CC^2
	dā́mmû	דָּמּוּ	G15	CC^2
cic^{2}v	*tillû*	תִּלּוּ	D15	CCY
cōc^{2}v	*sṓbbî*	סֹבִּי	G33	CC^2
	ḥṓttû	חֹתּוּ	G37	CC^2
yācéc^{2}v	*yāhḗllû*	יָהֵלּוּ	H15	CC^2
yācóc^{2}v	*tāmṓddû*	תָּמֹדּוּ	G27	CC^2
	nāḇṓzzû	נָבֹזּוּ	G49	CC^2
yēcóc^{2}v	*yērṓmmû*	יֵרֹמּוּ	N15	CC^2
y^{e}cac^{2}v	*y^{e}ḇallû*	יְבַלּוּ	D25	CCY
y^{e}cic^{2}ê-	*y^{e}sibbḗnî*	יְסִבֵּנִי	H25s4	CC^2
	t^{e}ḥillé^{y}nā^h	תְּחִלֶּינָה	H26	CC^2
y^{e}cuc^{2}v	*t^{e}hummēm*	תְּהֻמֵּם	G22s5	CC^2
	l^{e}hummām	לְהֻמָּם	G65s5	CC^2
	t^{e}subbé^{y}nā^h	תְּסֻבֶּינָה	G26[8]	CC
hacic^{2}ôt-	*haḥillṓṯā*	הַחִלּוֹתָ	H12	CC^2
hēcác^{2}v	*hēsábbû*	הֵסַבּוּ	H15	CC^2
hēcéc^{2}v	*hēḥḗllû*	הֵחֵלּוּ	H15	CC^2
hēcóc^{2}v	*hērṓmmû*	הֵרֹמּוּ	N37	CC^2
nacác^{2}v	*nāsábbû*	נָסַבּוּ	N15	CC^2
	nātáttā	נָתַתָּ	G12	NCC
nācéc^{2}v	*nāsḗbbā^h*	נָסֵבָּה	N11	CC^2
nācóc^{2}v	*nāqṓṭṭû*	נָקֹטּוּ	N15	CWC
	nābṓzzā^h	נָבֹזָּה	G49	CC^2

11 only *one* radical, with preformative or stem-indicator

cac	*haḵ*	הַךְ	H32	NCY
	taṭ	תַּט	H40	NCY
	yaḵ	וַיַּךְ	Hc20	NCY
cac^{2}v	*hakkû*	הַכּוּ	H37	NCY
	yaššê^h	יַשֶּׁה	H20	NCY
	makkîm	מַכִּים	H55	NCY
cāc	*'āṭ*	אָט	G24	NCY
cēc	*yēṭ*	יֵט	G40[9]	NCY
	tēṭ	וַתֵּט	Gc21	NCY
cic^{2}v	*yiṭṭû*	וַיִּטּוּ	Gc25	NCY
cuc^{2}v	*tukkû*	תֻּכּוּ	Hp27	NCY
	hukkā^h	הֻכָּה	Hp10	NCY
	mukkā^h	מֻכָּה	Hp51	NCY

Verb Diagnosis Chart

If *three* radicals are present, use Tables 1-5

9 — 2 radicals separated by vowel, *with* preformative or stem-indicator

yā**cac**	*nāsaḇ*	נָסַב	N10	CC[2]
	yāšaḇ	יָשַׁב		T.5
yā**cēc**	*yāqēl*	יָקֵל	H20	CC[2]
	yāqēm	יָקֵם	H40	CWC
	yāḡēl	יָגֵל	G40	CYC
yā**cîc**	*'āqîm*	אָקִים	H20	CWC[12]
	yāḡîl	יָגִיל	G20	CYC
yā**cōc**	*yāsōḇ*	יָסֹב	G20	CC[2]
	yāmōṯ	יָמֹת	G40	CWC
yā**côc**	*tāḇô'*	תָּבוֹא	G21[7]	CWC
yā**cûc**	*'āṣûm*	אָצוּם	G24	CWC
	yāḏû^{a}ʿ	יָדוּעַ		T.5
yá**cac**	*-yáʿan*	וַיַּעַן		T.6,4
cécec	*léḏeṯ*	לֶדֶת	G65	WCC
yê**cac**	*yêḏaʿ*	יֵדַע	G20	WCC
yế**cec**	*yếšeḇ*	יֵשֶׁב	G20	WCC
yê**cēc**	*yêṭēḇ*	יֵיטֵב	H40	YCC
	yêṣē'	יֵצֵא	G20	WCC
yê**cîc**	*têṭîḇ*	תֵּיטִיב	H21[7]	YCC
yí**cec**	*yíḡel*	יִגֶל	G40	CCY
yî́**cec**	*yî́qeṣ*	וַיִּיקֶץ	Hc20	YCC
yî**cac**	*yîṭaḇ*	יִיטַב	G20	YCC
yô**cēc**	*tôsēp̄*	תּוֹסֵף	H40	WCC
	yôšēḇ	יוֹשֵׁב	G50	YCC
yô**cîc**	*yôšîḇ*	יוֹשִׁיב	H20	WCC
yû**cac**	*yûsaḇ*	יוּסַב	Hp20	CC[2]
	yûšaḇ	יוּשַׁב	Hp20	WCC
	yûqam	יוּקַם	Hp20	CWC

*y^{e}***cac**	*y^{e}ṣaw*	יְצַו	D40	CCY
*yiṯ***cac**	*yiṯgal*	יִתְגַּל		T.6,1
mē**c**ē**c**	*mēsēḇ*	מֵסֵב	H50	CC[2]
mē**c**î**c**	*mēqîm*	מֵיקִים	H50	CWC[12]
mê**c**î**c**	*mêṭîḇ*	מֵיטִיב	H50	YCC
mû**c**ā**c**	*mûšāḇ*	מוּשָׁב	Hp50	WCC
nā**cac**	*nāsaḇ*	נָסַב	N10	CC[2]
	nāṯan	נָתַן		T.5
nā**c**ā**c**	*nāsāḇ*	נָסָב	N50	CC[2]
nā**c**ē**c**	*nāsēḇ*	נָסֵב	N10	CC[2]
nā**c**ô**c**	*nāqôm*	נָקוֹם	N10[11]	CWC[12]
	nāṯôn	נָתוֹן		T.5
nô**c**ā**c**	*nôšāḇ*	נוֹשָׁב	H20[10]	WCC
	nôḏaʿ	נוֹדַע	N10[11]	WCC
nô**c**î**c**	*nôšîḇ*	נוֹשִׁיב	H20	WCC
hā**c**ē**c**	*hāšēḇ*	הָשֵׁב	H32[1]	CWC
	hāsēḇ	הָסֵב	H32[3]	CC[2]
hā**c**î**c**	*hāḇî'*	הָבִיא	H65	CWC
hē**cac**	*hēsaḇ*	הֵסַב	H10	CC[2]
hē**c**ē**c**	*hēḥēl*	הֵחֵל	H10	CC[2]
hecĕcv	*heḥĕlî*	הֶחֱלִי	H11	CCY
hē**c**î**c**	*hēḇî'*	הֵבִיא	H10	CWC
hê**c**î**c**	*hêṭîḇ*	הֵיטִיב	H60[4]	YCC
hô**c**î**c**	*hôḏî^{a}ʿ*	הוֹדִיעַ	H65[4]	WCC
	hôšîḇ	הוֹשִׁיב	H10	WCC
hû**cac**	*hûḥal*	הוּחַל	Hp10	CC[2]
	hûšaḇ	הוּשַׁב	Hp10[4]	WCC
	hûqam	הוּקַם	Hp10[4]	CWC

10 — 2 radicals, *no* preformative

cac	*tam*	תַּם	G10	CC[2]
	gaš	גַּשׁ	G32	NCC
	daʿ	דַּע	G32	WCC
	gal	גַּל	D32	CCY
	qaḥ	קַח	G32	לקח
cacc-	*gašnā^{h}*	גַּשְׁנָה	G38	NCC
	tammû	תַּמּוּ		T.8
cá**c**ac	*daʿaṯ*	דַּעַת	G65	WCC
cā**c**	*qām*	קָם	G10	CWC
	bān	בָּן	G10	CYC
câ**c**	*qâm*	קָם	G50	CWC
	qâmê^{y}	קָמֵי	G57	CWC
	bân	בָּן	G50	CYC
cē**c**	*mēṯ*	מֵת	G10[11]	CWC
	šēḇ	שֵׁב	G32	WCC
	tēṯ	תֵּת	G65	נתן

	lēḵ	לֵךְ	G32	הלך
	tēn	תֵּן	G32	נתן
cē**c**v	*mḗṯā^{h}*	מֵתָה	G11	CWC
cē**cc**	*ṣē'ṯ*	צֵאת	G65	WC'
cé**c**et	*šéḇeṯ*	שֶׁבֶת	G65	WCC
	géšeṯ	גֶּשֶׁת	G65	NCC
cî**c**	*bîn*	בִּין	G65[2]	CYC
	śîm	שִׂים	Gp50	CYC
cō**c**	*šōḵ*	שֹׁךְ	G32[2]	CC[2]
cô**c**	*bôn*	בֹּן	G60	CYC
	qôm	קוֹם	G60	CWC
cû**c**	*qûm*	קוּם	G32[2]	CWC
	qûm	קוּם	Gp50	CWC
c^{e}**c**v	*g^{e}šî*	גְּשִׁי	G33	NCC
	š^{e}ḇû	שְׁבוּ	G37	WCC
	l^{e}ḵû	לְכוּ	G37	הלך
*y*v**cc**^{e}	*wayyašq^{e}*	וַיַּשְׁקְ	Hc20	CCY
	wattēḇk^{e}	וַתֵּבְךְּ	Gc20	§29.721
	wayyišb^{e}	וַיִּשְׁבְּ	Gc20	"

21

Purpose: To study the D stem
Materials: Esther 2:1-3a

ב **Cap. II.** ב

אַחַר הַדְּבָרִים הָאֵלֶּה כְּשֹׁךְ חֲמַת הַמֶּלֶךְ אֲחַשְׁוֵרוֹשׁ זָכַר א
אֶת־וַשְׁתִּי וְאֵת אֲשֶׁר־עָשָׂתָה וְאֵת אֲשֶׁר־נִגְזַר עָלֶיהָ׃
וַיֹּאמְרוּ נַעֲרֵי־הַמֶּלֶךְ מְשָׁרְתָיו יְבַקְשׁוּ לַמֶּלֶךְ נְעָרוֹת בְּתוּלוֹת 2
טוֹבוֹת מַרְאֶה׃ וְיַפְקֵד הַמֶּלֶךְ פְּקִידִים בְּכָל־מְדִינוֹת 3
מַלְכוּתוֹ

2:1 אַחַר הַדְּבָרִים הָאֵלֶּה[1]—(a) Prep. 'after' (v.310), *'*aḥḥar* with implied doubling, §15.1411. (b) –הַ· §22.2. ־ִים §25.231. (c) 1:5[2], §21.2. Cf. §36.11. This is a prep. phrase used adverbially.

כְּשֹׁךְ חֲמַת[2]—(b) In the Letteris text, this is pointed as though from *śkk*, but BDB 1013 lists it under *škk* 'to be assuaged' (7918 5/2). k^e + *šōḵ*, cōc, Table 10 VDC, CC[2] G65. On CC[2], §29.51. k^e- + inf. cstr., 'when, while.' (b) 1:12[6], note vowels and ־ַת; what do they tell us?. §25.13. You know the next words. 'When the anger of the king decreased.'

זָכַר אֶת־וַשְׁתִּי[3]—(a) Three consonants, no pre- or sufformative, căcac in Table 5 VDC. The vowel pattern indicates G10 of CCC, §27.221, from *zkr* 'to remember' (v.2142). The subj. is in the verb form, §§32., .1, .113, mentioned in previous clause. (b) Why אֶת? Is Vashti definite? Why?

וְאֵת אֲשֶׁר־עָשָׂתָה[4]—(a) Note pointing. This indicates a second dir. obj. in a compound obj., §34.115. (b-c) Noun cl. used as obj., §34.12, §21.3. 'He remembered *what she had done.*' (c) תָה— indicates 11 of CCY, §29.7131. The pausal form is found here with *zāqēp̄-qāṭôn*, §17.2231.

וְאֵת אֲשֶׁר־נִגְזַר עָלֶיהָ׃[5]—(a) 3d obj. of compound object, §34.115. (b-d) Noun cl., obj. of verb, §34.12. (c) *ni*— is G29 or N10, §27.31, §28.42. *gzr* 'to cut, divide, decide' (1504 13/1). (d) עַל always takes the form עלי when adding a suf. Cf. 1:14[2]

2:2 וַיֹּאמְרוּ נַעֲרֵי[1](a) *way-* tells us what? §22.13, §27.117. י—וּ tells us what? §27.31. *yô'm^{e}rû* < **ya'mirû* ya'CiC, §29.2, §29.212. Cf. 1:13[1]. Subj. follows. (b) ־ֵי = ? §25.424. נַעַר (v.5288) here 'servants.' CaGC type noun, §24.21, .211.

מְשָׁרְתָיו[2]—Cf. 1:10[7]. ־ָיו = ? §23.121. ——מְ = ? §28.21, Table 1 VDC. m^e–ā—, note §15.141. Don't expect to find a dagesh in every D form.

יְבַקְשׁוּ לַמֶּלֶךְ[3]—(a) וּ—יְ, this could be 25 or 45 (jussive, §27.5f.); context tells. Note shewa under preform.: a strong clue of D. §28.21. ק usually omits dagesh when with reduced vowel (shewa); you must learn the vowel patterns, here

y^e-a-^{e}-û. D25/45 of *bqš*, D 'to seek' (v.1245). (b) l^e-, §36.4121. 'Let them seek for (on behalf of) the king.'

נְעָרוֹת בְּתוּלוֹת[4]—(a) *naʿărāʰ* (v.5291), f. of נַעַר, §24.211, note the pl., §24.215. (b) Adj. in concord, note GNS (gender, number, state), §36.11. *b^e^tûlāʰ* 'unmarried woman, virgin' (v.1330). Noun type, §24.241. Attrib. adj., §36.1. Note position of adj. 'virgin maidens.'

טוֹבוֹת מַרְאֶה׃[5]—(a-b) 1:11[6]; what difference do you see? ־ַת = ? ־וֹת = ? §25.14, §25.232. (b) מַ—ה tells two things: -*êʰ* is 20/50 of CCY, §29.71, Table 6 VDC; *ma*- is H ptcp., §28.31. Hence form is H50 of *r'y* ראה. However, it is usually taken as a noun, here in apposition with *n^eʿărôṯ*, §36.6.

2:3 וְיַפְקֵד הַמֶּלֶךְ פְּקִידִים[1]—(a) וְ, is this *wāw* conv.? §22.1, .13. –ַ suggests H20/40,-n§28.31, .313. The vowel pattern -*a*--*ē*- could be Hc20 (conv. impf.) or H40 (juss.). Which is it? *pqd* H 'to appoint' (v.6485). (c) CvCv̂C-type noun, §24.24, cf. §15.21. *p^eqîḏ* 'officer, one appointed' (6496 13/1). Why is there no את?. 'and let the king appoint appointees.'

בכל־מדינות מלכותו[2]—(a) 'all' or 'every' ?. (b) 1:1[12]. (c) 1:3[4].

Go over the D stem (§28.22ff) and spot the identifying morphemes.

CiC²ēC	*qiṭṭēl*	קִטֵּל
CēGēC	*bē'ēr*	בֵּאֵר
m^eCaC²ēC	*m^eqaṭṭēl*	מְקַטֵּל
m^eCāGēC	*m^ešārēṯ*	מְשָׁרֵת

Start to familiarize yourself with Paradigm V-4.
Go back over previous lessons and look for D-stem forms. Analyze them.

Learn the basic vocabulary in Group 16.

---

9. At word-end, original *-cw > -*cû* and *-cy > -*cî* (§15.67).

10a. *Gutturals* reject dagesh (§11.432); before א, ע, and ר there is compensatory lengthening (§15.141).
 b. Gutturals do not take simple vocal shewa (§15.42).
 c. Gutturals often vocalize a silent shewa (§15.421).
 d. Gutturals prefer *a*-class vowels, especially before them (§15.43).
 e. At word-end, ע, ח, or הּ (*heʰ with mappiq*) attract pattaḥ furtive after *i*- or *u*-class vowels (§15.4321).
 f. *i* > *e* (*ḥîrîq* > *s^egôl*) before nonfinal gutturals (§15.434).
 g. Initial א prefers *i*-class vowels when near the accent (§15.433).
 h. א at word-end and frequently at syllable-end is quiescent (§15.54).

22

Purpose: To study the G stem
Materials: Esther 2:3b-4

וְיִקְבְּצוּ אֶת־כָּל־נַעֲרָה־בְתוּלָה טוֹבַת מַרְאֶה אֶל־
שׁוּשַׁן הַבִּירָה אֶל־בֵּית הַנָּשִׁים אֶל־יַד הֵגֶא סְרִיס הַמֶּלֶךְ
שֹׁמֵר הַנָּשִׁים וְנָתוֹן תַּמְרוּקֵיהֶן׃ וְהַנַּעֲרָה אֲשֶׁר תִּיטַב 4
בְּעֵינֵי הַמֶּלֶךְ תִּמְלֹךְ תַּחַת וַשְׁתִּי וַיִּיטַב הַדָּבָר בְּעֵינֵי
הַמֶּלֶךְ וַיַּעַשׂ כֵּן׃

2:3b וְיִקְבְּצוּ [3]—*way-*, §22.13, tells us what aspect (tense)?. §32.5, .52. Will it be translated past or future? §32.53. *yi——û* is what PGN (person, gender, number)? §27.31. Will you translate it 'they,' 'we, or 'you'? *yiCC^eCû,* Table 3 VDC, no vowel between 1st and 2d radicals, *i*-vowel under preformative, G25/45, §32.35. *qbṣ* 'gather, collect' (v.6908). 'Let them gather.'

אֶת־כָּל־נַעֲרָה־בְתוּלָה [4]—(a) This tells us what?. כֹּל is used to determine a noun, *Ges.* §117*c.* (c-d) What is the difference between this and 2:2[4]?

טוֹבַת מַרְאֶה [5]—(a-b) 1:11[6].

אֶל־ שׁוּשַׁן הַבִּירָה [6]—1:2[10.11].

אֶל־בֵּית הַנָּשִׁים [7]—(b) 1:8[4]. Table F. (c) 1:17[1].

אֶל־יַד הֵגֶא סְרִיס [8]—(b) 1:7[5] (c) Pr.n. Hegai. (d) Note that ָ has reduced, cf. 1:10[6]. Note how the directions get increasingly precise.

שֹׁמֵר הַנָּשִׁים[9]—(a) For שׁ, §11.411. Vowel pattern –ֹ–ֵ– strongly suggests G50, §27.61, cf. §27.6, .6111. *šmr* 'to watch, keep, protect' (v.8104). Read §27.6112. This is cstr., G52.

וְנָתוֹן תַּמְרוּקֵיהֶן׃ [10]—(a) *nāṯôn, -ā-ô-* is vowel pattern of G60, §27.64. Read §§30.381, .3812, §32.39f; 'to give.' (b) *tamrûq* is taCCûC, §24.36, *mrq* 'to scour, polish,' *tamrûq* 'detergent' (8562 4/3). For הֶן–, §23.121. The heavy ending takes the accent.

2:4 וְהַנַּעֲרָה[1]—(a) Compare the forms in 2:2[4] and 2:3[4]. Identify them.

אֲשֶׁר תִּיטַב בְּעֵינֵי [2]—(a) Rel. cl. (b) *t*—— can be 3fs or 2ms impf (20/40). The pattern *ti-a-* is G20/40 of yiCCaC type, Table 3 VDC. *tiYCaC* is YCC. If you can't work it out, see 1:21[1]. (c) 1:21[2]

תִּמְלֹךְ[3]— —ת is 21/22 or 41/42. *ti--ō-* is G of yaCCuC type, §27.321. The vowel following the 2d rad. is called the *thematic* (or *theme*) vowel, §27.231. At this point you should begin to get familiar with "Barth's Law," §27.331f. What does the root מלך mean? 1:1[6], 1:3[3]. Is the form 3fs or 2ms? How can you tell?

תַּ֫חַת וַשְׁתִּי[4]—(a) Denominal prep. 'under,' v.8478, here 'in the place of, as the successor to.'

וַיִּיטַב הַדָּבָר בְּעֵינֵי[5]—(a) Work it out. Then cf. 1:21[1]. (a-d) 1:21[12].

וַיַּ֫עַשׂ כֵּן׃[6]—(a) Note –ַּ. *yá'aś*: *yá–*, only 2 radicals. The accent is like CvCC nouns (*ná'ar*), hence no true vowel separates the consonants, hence it is not the 2d rad. that is lost. There is no lengthening of preformative vowel, hence it is unlikely that the 1st rad. is lost. That suggests CCY, §29.7), and we should think at once of the possibility of apocopation, §29.72. Review 1:21[3] carefully. (b) 1:8[3].

This is a good place to try to nail down the G stem, particularly the G impf.

yaCCuC	*yiqṭōl*	יִקְטֹל
yiCCaC	*yik̲bad̲*	יִכְבַּד
yaCCiC	*yittēn*	יִתֵּן
yaGCuC	*yaḥălōm*	יַחֲלֹם
yaCCuG	*yišlaḥ*	יִשְׁלַח
	yišlôᵃḥ	יִשְׁלֹחַ
yaYCi'	*yêṣē'*	יֵצֵא
yiYCaC	*yîʸṭab̲*	יִיטַב

Go back over previous lessons and analyze the G-stem verbs you have encountered. Make plenty of notes in your notebook. You will always have trouble until you conquer the G stem of the verb.

Learn the basic vocabulary in Group 17.

---

23. The connecting vowel of a pronominal suffix, if any, takes the accent (§17.32). If a shewa precedes the suffix, it is zero shewa and the ךָ of the suffix is spirantized.

24. In verbal forms, thematic *a* in G-perf. generally yields thematic *u* in G-impf., andnthematic *i* or *u* in G-perf. yields thematic *a* in G-impf. (§27.331).

25. In G-impf., the vowel of the preformative is determined usually by the thematic vowel, as follows: thematic *a* preformative *i*, thematic *i* or *u* preformative *a* (§27.332).

23

Purpose: To study the H stem
Materials: Esther 2:5-6

אִישׁ יְהוּדִי הָיָה בְּשׁוּשַׁן הַבִּירָה ה
וּשְׁמוֹ מָרְדֳּכַי בֶּן יָאִיר בֶּן־שִׁמְעִי בֶּן־קִישׁ אִישׁ יְמִינִי׃ אֲשֶׁר 6
הָגְלָה מִירוּשָׁלַיִם עִם־הַגֹּלָה אֲשֶׁר הָגְלְתָה עִם יְכָנְיָה
מֶלֶךְ־יְהוּדָה אֲשֶׁר הֶגְלָה נְבוּכַדְנֶאצַּר מֶלֶךְ בָּבֶל׃

2:5 אִישׁ יְהוּדִי הָיָה [1]—(a) 1:8[6]. Indef., 'a man,' §30.3223. (b) ־ִי— is a gentilic (a people of a place), §22.55. *y^{e}hûḏ* 'Judah, Judea,' hence, 'Jew.' The word in in apposition with (a). (c) *–ā–ā^h* tells us two things: *-ā^h* ־ָה– is 10 of CCY, §29.71. and the vowel after the 1st rad. tells us that it is G. *hy^h* 'to be' (v.1961).

בְּשׁוּשַׁן הַבִּירָה [2]—1:2[10,11].

וּשְׁמוֹ מָרְדֳּכַי [3]—(a) *û,* §16.31. *š^{e}m* + *ô,* from *šēm,* §15.121, R. 16, 'name' (v.8034). (b) Pr.n. 'Mordecai,' מָרְ is unaccented closed, Table E.

בֶּן יָאִיר בֶּן־שִׁמְעִי בֶּן־קִישׁ [4]—A genealogy, not necessarily complete. Jair may have been his father, and Shimei and Kish more remote ancestors. Note בֵּן but בֶּן in cstr.

אִישׁ יְמִינִי׃ [5]—(a) Cstr.–why not reduced vowel? (b) For *ben-y^{e}mînî,* Benjamite.

2:6 אשר הגלה[1]—(a) Rel. cl., modifying 2:5[1]. (b) *ho--ā^h:* note *-ā^h*, Table 6 of VDC, §29.71. Note *hoḡ-* (un. cl, therefore *qāmāṣ ḥăṭûp̄*, sign of Hp[ass.], §28.32. *gl^y* גלה (v.1540), here 'to go into exile'; Hp 'was caused to go ..., was taken exile.'

מִירוּשָׁלַיִם [2]—*mî-* from *min* + *y^e*-. *y^{e}rûšāláyim,* pr. n.— can you figure it out? This is a prep. phrase used adverbially ('he was taken *from where?*').

עִם־הַגֹּלָה [3]—(a) עִם prep. 'with' (v.5973); do not confuse it with עַם. (b) *hag* + *gôlā^h:* CôCê^h is masc., CôCā^h fem., G51 of *gl^y,* 2:6[1]. The fem. is often an abstract noun, here 'the exile' (v.1473). Another prep. phr. used adverbially.

הָגְלְתָה [4]—Note ־ָתה, sign of 11 of CCY, §29.71. Learn the CCY indicators now. Note –הָג: if ־ָ is *o* and not *ā,* this is Hp, §28.32. Now cf. 2:6 . Why is this form fem.? The subj. is אֲשֶׁר, but its antecedent is הַגֹּלָה.

עִם יְכָנְיָה מֶלֶךְ־יְהוּדָה [5]—(a) 2:6[3]. (b) Pr.n., *y^{e}ḵonyā^h*–can you figure it out? (d) *y^{e}hûḏā^h* syncopated later > *yûḏā^h;* can you figure it out?

הֶגְלָה[6]—ה-ָ is what of CCY? §29.71. -הִ (or -הֶ) is sign of H (act.), §28.31. Now compare *heglāʰ* הֶגְלָה with *hoglāʰ* הָגְלָה. The subj. follows.

נְבוּכַדְנֶאצַּר מֶלֶךְ בָּבֶל׃ [7]—(a) *nᵉbûkadneṣṣar*–can you figure it out? (c) *bābel* from Akk. *bab ilim* 'gate of god' = Babylon.

This is a good time to work on the H stem. Get familiar with Paradigm V-5.

Study these forms:

hiCCîca	*hiqṭîl*	הִקְטִיל
yᵉhaCCîCu	*yaqṭîl*	יַקְטִיל
yᵉhaCCîC	*yaqṭēl*	יַקְטֵל
mᵉhaCCîC	*maqṭēl*	מַקְטֵל
hiCCaY (?)	*heglāʰ*	הֶגְלָה
huCCaC	*hoqṭal*	הָקְטַל

Analyze the following:

הֶגְלָה	2:6[6]	וַיַּמְלִיכֶהָ	2:17[6]
הָגְלָה	2:6[1]	וּבְהַגִּיעַ	2:12[1]
הִגִּידָה	2:10[1]	בְּהַרְאֹתוֹ	1:4[1]
הָגְלְתָה	2:6[4]	לְהָבִיא	1:11[1]
תַּגִּיד	2:10[4]	בְּהִשָּׁמַע	2:8[2]
וַיַּפְקֵד	2:3[1]	לְהַרְאוֹת	1:11[4]
וַיַּגֵּד	2:22[2]	וְהַשְׁקוֹת	1:7[1]
וַיָּשֶׂם	2:17[5]	לְהָיוֹת	1:22[1]
וַיַּעַשׂ	2:18[1]	לְהַבְזוֹת	1:17[3]

Memorize the basic vocabulary in Group 18.

---

17. In finite verbal forms *without sufformatives*, the accent is on the *ultima* (§17.21). In such forms *with sufformatives*, the following rules prevail:
a. If the *ultima* is *closed*, the accent is on the ultima, and the form follows the short-vowel chart (§17.221).
b. If the *ultima* is *open* and the *penult* is *long*, the accent is on the *penult*, and the form follows the short-vowel chart (§17.222).
c. If the *ultima* is open and the *penult* is *short*, in *nonpausal* forms the accent is on the *ultima*, the vowel of the *penult* reduces to shewa, and the vowel of the antepenult has its pausal form (lengthened) and is marked by metheg (§17.223).
d. Under the same conditions (17c) but in *pausal form*, the accent is on the *penult*, and the form follows the short-vowel chart (§17.2231).

18. Short *a* frequently attenuates to short *i* in unaccented closed syllables (§15.32).

Purpose: To study the N stem
Materials: Esther 2:7-8

7 וַיְהִי אֹמֵן
אֶת־הֲדַסָּה הִיא אֶסְתֵּר בַּת־דֹּדוֹ כִּי אֵין לָהּ אָב וָאֵם
וְהַנַּעֲרָה יְפַת־תֹּאַר וְטוֹבַת מַרְאֶה וּבְמוֹת אָבִיהָ וְאִמָּהּ
8 לְקָחָהּ מָרְדֳּכַי לוֹ לְבַת׃ וַיְהִי בְּהִשָּׁמַע דְּבַר־הַמֶּלֶךְ וְדָתוֹ
וּבְהִקָּבֵץ נְעָרוֹת רַבּוֹת אֶל־שׁוּשַׁן הַבִּירָה אֶל־יַד הֵגָי
וַתִּלָּקַח אֶסְתֵּר אֶל־בֵּית הַמֶּלֶךְ אֶל־יַד הֵגַי שֹׁמֵר הַנָּשִׁים׃

2:7 וַיְהִי אֹמֵן אֶת־הֲדַסָּה [1]—(a) 1:1[1]. This form is somewhat difficult to analyze, and since it is very common, you would do better to memorize it *now*. Gc20 of היה. Analysis: *yôḏ* with shewa drops dagesh (R.1b), hence this is way- (conv. *wāw*). CCY apocopates in conv. impf. (c20) and juss. (40), *way* + *yihyêʰ* > **wayyihy*, §29.72. *-cy* > *-cî*, **wayyihî* (R.9); application of R.16 > **wayyᵉhîʸ*, and application of R.1b > *wayᵉhîʸ*. (b) Vowel pattern *-ô-ē-*, G50, §27.6122, of *ʾamn* 'to be firm, support, rear, foster' (v.539). G10 + G50 denotes continuous or habitual action in past time (§32.511), 'he was (had been) supporting.' (c-d) Pr.n. 'Hadassah.'

הִיא אֶסְתֵּר [2]—(1:20[3], §21.1f.). Verbless cl., 'she/that (was) Esther.' (b) Pr.n.

בַּת־דֹּדוֹ [3]—(a) **bin* 'son' + *-t* > **bint* (cf. Arab. *bint*) 'daughter' > **bitt* > **bit* > *baṯ* (v.1323). Explain each step. (b) *dôḏ* 'uncle' (v.1730). Whose uncle? What was Esther's relationship to Mordecai?

כִּי אֵין לָהּ אָב וָאֵם [4]—(a) Causal (v.3588), §38.53. (b) 1:8[2]. *ʾên lᵉ-* = 'he/she does/did not have.' (c) Prep. + s1, §23.121. (d) *ʾāḇ* 'father' (v.1); CvC-type noun, §24.12. (e) *ʾēm* 'mother' (v.517); CiC²-type noun, §24.214.

וְהַנַּעֲרָה יְפַת־תֹּאַר [5]—(a) 2:2[4]. (b) Cf. 1:11[5]; here יָפֶה adj. 'fair, beautiful' (v.3303), fem. יָפָה, f. cstr. יְפַת. (c) *tṓʾar* 'outline, form' (v.8389); CuCC-type noun. Note postpositive accent, repeated on stressed syllable, §11.571.

וְטוֹבַת מַרְאֶה [6]—Cf. 1:11[6]. Verbless cl., §31. Compound pred., §30.123. 'The maiden (was) (1) beautiful of form and (2) good of appearance' (= 'shapely and comely').

וּבְמוֹת אָבִיהָ וְאִמָּהּ [7]—(a) *û* + *bᵉ-* + *môṯ*. Table 10 VDC shows that G65 of CûC would be מוּת; the form here therefore must be a noun < *mā́weṯ* 'death' (v.4194). 'And on the death of' followed by two governed nouns. (b) 2:7[4](d); note that אָב adds ִי when adding suf., *ʾāḇî-*, §23.121. (c) 2:7[4](e); אֵם with suf. restores gemination: *ʾimm-*. Why *ʾāḇî-hā* but *ʾimm-āh*? §23.121.

לְקָחָהּ מָרְדֳּכַי לוֹ לְבַת׃ [8]—(a) *Watch out!* הָ- is s1, §23.122, not sufformative. The accent shift has altered the vowel quantities, §27.72. G10 *lāqáḥ* + *āh* > *lᵉqāḥāh*. *lqḥ* 'to take' (v.3947). (b) 2:5[3]. Subj. of preceding verb, 'Mordecai took.' (c) Indir. obj. (like dat. of reference) 'for himself.' (d) 'for a daughter' 2:7[3].

2:8 וַיְהִי [1]—Note the *rᵉbîaʿ*. Cf. 1:1[1]. 'And it was,' και εγενετο.

בְּהִשָּׁמַע דְּבַר־הַמֶּלֶךְ וְדָתוֹ [2]—(a) *û* + *ḇᵉ* + *hiššāmaʿ*. 1st rad. geminate, Table 2 VDC; it must be N stem. **hin-* is found only in N32/65, and *bᵉ-* is found only on 65, hence N65. The vowel pattern hiC²āCēC is affected by guttural > hiC²āCaG. 'In the being heard of' = 'when was heard.' *šmʿ* 1:18[4]. (b-c) 1st obj. of N65. (d) 2d obj. (compound) of N65. Note that the obj. of the inf. cstr. becomes the subj. in Eng. trans.: 'in the being heard of the word' = 'when the word was heard.'

וּבְהִקָּבֵץ נְעָרוֹת רַבּוֹת [3]—(a) *û* + *ḇᵉ* + *hiqqāḇēṣ*, see notes on 2:8[2](a). Can you see a similarity? Here hiC²āCēC. qbṣ, 2:3[3]. (c) 1:20[3]. Why is form different here? On translation, see previous note.

אֶל־שׁוּשַׁן הַבִּירָה אֶל־יַד הֵגָי [4]—(a-c) 1:2[10 11]. (d-f) 2:3[8]. Note different spellings, הֵגֶא, הֵגַי, and pausal הֵגָי.

וַתִּלָּקַח אֶסְתֵּר אֶל־בֵּית הַמֶּלֶךְ [5]—(a) *wat* + *tillāqaḥ* tiC²āCaG, cf. 2:8[2]. —וַ tells us what? Doubled 1st rad. tells us what? (Table 2 VDC). Preformative tells us what? —ת is 21/22, and the subj. that follows tells us that it is 21, hence N21 of *lqḥ* (2:7[8]). (b) 2:7[2]. (c-e) Cf. 2:3[7]. Translate the clause.

אֶל־יַד הֵגַי שֹׁמֵר הַנָּשִׁים׃ [6]—(a-c) 2:3[8] and 2:8[4]; note spelling. (d-e) 2:3[9].

Analyze the following forms: הַנִּמְצְאִים 1:5[5]. וַיִּכָּתֵב 1:19[4]. נִשְׁמַע 1:20[1]. נִגְזַר 2:1[5].

niCCaC	*niqṭal*	נִקְטַל
yᵉhanCaCiCu		
> yiC²āCēC	*yiqqāṭēl*	יִקָּטֵל
naCCaCu	*niqṭāl*	נִקְטָל
hanCaCiCu	*hiqqāṭēl*	הִקָּטֵל

Read §28.4. Work on the peculiarities of the N stem.

Learn the words in Basic Vocabulary Group 19.

7. Syllables do not begin with consonantal clusters, except in forms of the word for 'two' (§16.35).

25

Purpose: To review for the examination
Materials: Esther 2:9-10

9 וַתִּיטַב הַנַּעֲרָה בְעֵינָיו וַתִּשָּׂא חֶסֶד לְפָנָיו וַיְבַהֵל אֶת־
תַּמְרוּקֶיהָ וְאֶת־מָנוֹתֶהָ לָתֵת לָהּ וְאֵת שֶׁבַע הַנְּעָרוֹת
הָרְאֻיוֹת לָתֶת־לָהּ מִבֵּית הַמֶּלֶךְ וַיְשַׁנֶּהָ וְאֶת־נַעֲרוֹתֶיהָ
י לְטוֹב בֵּית הַנָּשִׁים׃ לֹא־הִגִּידָה אֶסְתֵּר אֶת־עַמָּהּ וְאֶת־
מוֹלַדְתָּהּ כִּי מָרְדֳּכַי צִוָּה עָלֶיהָ אֲשֶׁר לֹא־תַגִּיד׃

2:9 וַתִּיטַב הַנַּעֲרָה בְּעֵינָיו[1]—(a) See 1: 21[1]: what is the difference? Work out the parsing (§27.15). Then cf. 2:4[2]. (b) How is this related to the verb? §32.113. Cf. 2:4[5]. (c) What is the difference betwen בְּעֵינָיו here and בְּעֵינֵי in 1:21[2]?

וַתִּשָּׂא חֶסֶד לְפָנָיו[2]—(a) Note the dageshes, R. 1a. *wat-* tells what? (§22.13). Then *tiśśā'* must be what aspect (tense)? Therefore only 2 radicals are present, for the second *t* must be a preformative. If you do not understand the logic here, you need much more study of the points covered. תּ must be geminate, *tt*. Conv. *wāw* of this form only stands before impf., therefore *t*— indicates 21/22 form. First *radical* (שׂ) is doubled; Table 7 VDC indicates that yiC^2aC is G20 of NCC. Verb is therefore *nś'* 'to lift up, carry' (v.5375). (b) *ḥéseḏ* is a very rich word (v.2618), but here it simply means 'favor'; idiom 'to take up favor, to be liked.' (c) 1:17[6]

וַיְבַהֵל[3]—Cf. R.1b. *way(y)-* tells us what? §22.13. Preformative with shewa tells us what? §28.21. Vowel pattern *y^e-a-ē-* tells us what? §28.21. Why no dagesh in 2d rad.? R.10a. Look at Table 4 VDC. Identify as Dc20 of CGC. Why no compensatory lengthening? §15.1411. בלה D 'to hasten' (v.926).

אֶת־תַּמְרוּקֶיהָ וְאֶת־מָנוֹתֶיהָ [4]—(a-b) 2:3[10]. What suffix here? §23.121. (d) *mānā^h* 'part, portion' (4490 13/3). Note fps *-ôṯê* –וֹתֶי– §25.54.

לָתֵת לָהּ[5]—(a) לָ|תֵת prep. + G65 of נתן. This is difficult, so it is best to memorize לָתֵת 'to give.' **n^{e}ṯin* (G65) > **tin* + *t* (§13.513) > **tint* > **titt* (R.11) > **tiṯ* (R.6a) > *tēṯ* (R.13a). For shift of accent, §17.35. (b) Pron. + s1, indir. obj.

וְאֵת שֶׁבַע הַנְּעָרוֹת[6]—(a) 2d compound obj. after וַיְבַהֵל, 'to hasten (1) her detergents and her portions, and (2) the seven maidens....' (b) Cf. 1:10[6]. Here the noun is f. so the num. adj. has the "masc." form, §26.23.

הָרְאֻיוֹת לָתֶת־לָהּ[7]—(a) *hā* + *r^e'ûyy* + *ôṯ*. *rā'ûy* is Gp50 of CCY, §27.63, §29.71. The pl. may double the *yôḏ* (also *r^e'ûyôṯ*, BDB 906). The pass. of 'to see' is 'to be seen, to seem, to appear'; here 'seemly,' modifying נְעָרוֹת. (b-c) 2:9[5].

וַיְשַׁנֶּהָ וְאֶת־נַעֲרוֹתֶיהָ [8]—(a) Can this be conv. *wāw*? R.1b. *yᵉšannê* + *hā*, §23.122. Preformative with shewa, 2d rad. doubled, it must be D20/40. The 3d rad. lost, it must be CCY. If you don't know why, go back over your notes on verbs in your notebook. Dc20s1 of *šny* G 'to double,' D 'to remove' (v.8138). (b) 2d compound obj.: 'he removed (l) her and (2) her maidens. Note form of suffix; on verb it is accusative, on noun genitive.

לְטוֹב בֵּית הַנָּשִׁים׃ [9]—(a) 'to the good of' = 'to the best (part) of.' On superlative, §36.3262.

2:10 לֹא־הִגִּידָה אֶסְתֵּר [1]—(a) Neg. adv., negating either a following word or a clause. (b) *higgîḏāʰ*: *-āʰ* could be an 11 ending of CCY, §29.71. hiC– could be H perf., §28.31. For hic²îc, Table 7 VDC, which identifies form as H10 of NCC. The ָה then must be 3fs (11), and correct parse is H11 of *ngd* H 'to declare, tell, proclaim' (v.5046). (c) Subj. of verb.

אֶת־עַמָּהּ וְאֶת־מוֹלַדְתָּהּ [2]—Note the compound obj. (a-b) and (c-d). (b) *ʿamm* + s1, 'her people.' (d) *môladt* + s1; *môladt* > *môlēḏeṯ* < **mawladt*, WCC. The form can be parsed as H51 of *yld*, but it is listed as a noun 'kindred' (v.4137) from **wld* > *yld* 'to bear, give birth'

כִּי מָרְדֳּכַי צִוָּה עָלֶיהָ [3]—(a) Causal, 1:17[1]. (b) 2:5[3]. (c) Note וָּ: the ָ tells us that ו is *wāw* with strong dagesh, hence *ṣiwwāʰ*, cf. §11.433. Then *-āʰ* cannot be an 11 morpheme, hence it must be 10 of CCY, Table 6 VDC, §29.71. cic²āʰ must be D10 of CCY (note that ָה is for *all* 10 morphemes in CCY, G10, D10, H10, N10). *ṣwy* צוה 'to give charge/command' (v.6680). (d) The verb does not take direct object of the person: 'Mordecai gave charge to her.'

אֲשֶׁר לֹא־תַגִּיד׃ [4]—(a) Introduces indirect discourse. (b) לֹא + impf. is a strong prohibition. (c) *taggîḏ*, cf. 2:10[1]. Here *pattāḥ* under preformative may be a sign of H20/40. —ת is 21/22/41/42. tac²îc, Table 7 VDC, must be H21/22; tac²ēc would be H41/42, cf. *yap̄qēḏ*, 2:3[1]. 'that she should not declare.'

In view of the upcoming exam, you should use this occasion to review verbs. If you are weak in any particular area(s), now is the time to work specifically. Can you identify the following?

כָּבַב	יִכְכֹּב	תִּכְכַּב	תִּכְכַּבְנָה
יַעֲכֹב	יֹאכֵב	כֹּכֵב	כְּכֹב
לְכַבֵּב	מַכְכִּיב	נִכְכַּב	נִכְכָּב
לְכַכּוֹת	בְּכָכְכֶם	כָּכַבְתָּ	כְּכַבְתֶּם
וַיֵּכֶב	וַיִּיכַב	כָּכוֹב	

Learn the basic words in Group 20.

26

Purpose: To review the student's progress to this point
Materials: Esther 1:1–2:10

The second hour examination should be given at this point, and it should deal mainly with the verb. Elements of phonology that are significant for verb morphology, noun morphemes that are used on participles, and similar material, will be included.

Read: §§30.12ff, 30.33–.3394, 30.38–.382.
Read: §§32., .11, .12, .31, .35, .38, .4, .5, .51, .52.
Read *carefully* §32.53.

Now, let's get the morphology in hand.
Read: §§27., .11, .1111, .1112, .1121, .1131, .1134.
Read §§27.114, .211; *memorize* §27.21 and §27.31.
Read: §§27.115, .1153, §§28., 28.1, and work carefully on Paradigm V-1.

Read: §§28.2, .21; §§28.3, .31; §§28.4, .42, .421
Read: §§29., .01, .02.

This review should be fairly meaningful to you, since you have encountered the forms and meanings in the last 12 lessons. You will have to review many more times to gain an ability to handle the verb with facility. There is no substitute for careful analysis and observation. You should havenseparate pages for various types of verbs, and you should have all verbs recorded and arranged to show **similarities and differences. You should also be studying the synoptic paradigms in the *Handbook*.**

You should be able to answer questions like the following:

1. Identify the following preformatives and sufformatives: —י, —א, וּ—, וּ—י, הָ—, הָ— (only 2 other consonants present), —תְּ, תֶּם—, תָּה— (only 2 other consonants present), נָה—תְּ, תָּ—.

2. Know the operation of Rules 1a, 1b, 2a, 9, 10a-f, 11, 13b, 15, 18, 20.

3. Know the meanings of technical terms used in connection with the study of the Heb. verb.

4. Know the thematic vowels and their general significance in the perf. (CaCaC, CaCiC, CaCuC), and in the imperf. (yaCCuC, yiCCaC, yaCCiC).

5. Parse the following, using the indicators (§27.151, reprinted below).

נִקְדַּשׁ   הִבְדִּיל   דִּבֵּר   אָכַל
תִּגָּנֹב   הִמְשַׁלְנוּ   צִוָּה   אָכַלְתָּ
גָּלְתָה   תְּקַבֵּץ   יִצְדַּק   יִרְגַּז
תֵּצֵא   תִּתֵּן   יַעֲבֹר   תִּיטַב
מְבַקְשׁוֹת   מְדַבְּרִים   אָחוּז   מַשְׁלִימִים
שָׁמוּעַ   גֹּלֶה   סַפֵּר   הָשְׁלַךְ

Know all the basic vocabulary in Groups 1-20.

TABLE OF INDICATORS

Stem	Conjugation	PGN	Perf.	Impf.	Impv.	Juss./ Cohort.	Ptcp.	Inf.	Pron. Suf.	PGN
G	qtl	3 ms	10	20	--	40	50 m.s.a.	60 inf.abs.	s0	3 ms
Gp	qtl pass.	3 fs	11	21	--	41	51 f.s.a.		s1	3 fs
N	nqtl	2 ms	12	22	32	42	52 m.s.c.		s2	2 ms
D	qttl	2 fs	13	23	33	43	53 f.s.c.		s3	2 fs
Dp	qttl pass.	1 cs	14	24		44			s4	1 cs
HtD	htqttl									
HtDp	" pass.	3 mp	15	25	--	45	55 m.p.a.	65 inf.cstr.	s5	3 mp
H	hqtl	3 fp	16	26	--	46	56 f.p.a.		s6	3 fp
Hp	hqtl pass.	2 mp	17	27	37	47	57 m.p.c.		s7	2 mp
HtŠ		2 fp	18	28	38	48	58 f.p.c.		s8	2 fp
		1 cp	19	29	--	49			s9	1 cp

c *after stem indicator and before the number,* indicates *wāw* conversive; *wāw* conj. not indicated.
s *after the number* plus suffix indicator indicates pron. suf.
e.g. וַיִּתְּנָהּ is identified as Gc20s1 of נתן, which is much simpler than writing 'third masculine singular, imperfect, of נתן, with 3 fem. sing. suf. and *wāw* conversive.'

Those who wait on YHWH shall renew strength,
they shall ascend on wings like the eagles,
they shall run and not grow weary,
they shall walk and not grow faint.

וְקֹוֵי יהוה יַחֲלִיפוּ כֹחַ
יַעֲלוּ אֵבֶר כַּנְּשָׁרִים
יָרוּצוּ וְלֹא יִיגָעוּ
יֵלְכוּ וְלֹא יִיעָפוּ׃

(Isaiah 40:31)

27

Purpose: To study the numerals
Materials: Esther 2:11-13

11 וּבְכָל־
יוֹם וָיוֹם מָרְדֳּכַי מִתְהַלֵּךְ לִפְנֵי חֲצַר בֵּית־הַנָּשִׁים לָדַעַת
12 אֶת־שְׁלוֹם אֶסְתֵּר וּמַה־יֵּעָשֶׂה בָּהּ׃ וּבְהַגִּיעַ תֹּר נַעֲרָה
וְנַעֲרָה לָבוֹא ׀ אֶל־הַמֶּלֶךְ אֲחַשְׁוֵרוֹשׁ מִקֵּץ הֱיוֹת לָהּ כְּדָת
הַנָּשִׁים שְׁנֵים עָשָׂר חֹדֶשׁ כִּי כֵּן יִמְלְאוּ יְמֵי מְרוּקֵיהֶן שִׁשָּׁה
חֳדָשִׁים בְּשֶׁמֶן הַמֹּר וְשִׁשָּׁה חֳדָשִׁים בַּבְּשָׂמִים וּבְתַמְרוּקֵי
13 הַנָּשִׁים׃ וּבָזֶה הַנַּעֲרָה בָּאָה אֶל־הַמֶּלֶךְ אֵת כָּל־אֲשֶׁר
תֹּאמַר יִנָּתֵן לָהּ לָבוֹא עִמָּהּ מִבֵּית הַנָּשִׁים עַד־בֵּית הַמֶּלֶךְ׃

2:11 וּבְכָל־יוֹם וָיוֹם[1]—(a-c) This is distributive, 'each day.' 1:8[6], 1:22[34]. Note the vowel: וָיוֹם. It does not always lengthen in near-open with the conj.

מָרְדֳּכַי מִתְהַלֵּךְ[2]—(a) 2:5[3]. (b) *mithallēk*, note מת- and -ל-, Table 1 VDC. For HtD, read §§28.5, .51, .511. Preformative מ- is often the sign of a ptcp. (not G). הלך 'to walk' (v.1980), in HtD 'to walk back and forth.'

לִפְנֵי חֲצַר בֵּית־הַנָּשִׁים [3]—(a) 1:11[2]. (b) Note vowels; what should the quality tell us? 1:5[10]. (c-d) You should know this.

לָדַעַת אֶת־שְׁלוֹם אֶסְתֵּר [4]—(a) l^e + *dá'at*. Cf. 1:2[3]. תַ- could be "ballast," §13.513. If so, there are only 2 rads., cf. Table 10 VDC. The form is WCC or YCC with apheresis, §13.511, and anaptyxis, §15.61. Your clues are the prep. l^e- and the *-t*, §29.322. ידע 'to know' (v. 3045). With -ל the inf. cstr. often expresses purpose, §38.54. (c) *šālôm* 'peace, welfare' (v. 7965). What does the reduced vowel tell us? §25.42f. (b-d) Noun clause, obj. of inf. cstr.. 'in order to know Esther's welfare.'

וּמַה־יֵּעָשֶׂה בָּהּ׃[5]—(a) Indef. pron., §21.5, 'whatever' (v. 4100), subj. of following verb. (b) יֵעָשֶׂה *yēʿāśê^h*, note dagesh, §13.36. הֶ- could be 20 of CCY, §29.71. Learn this *now*. Guttural in 1st rad. resists gemination, with compensatory lengthening (R.10a), hence vowels indicate N stem, §28.42; Table 4 VDC also identifies as N20 of GCC. (a-c) Noun cl., 2d compound obj. of *dá'at* 'to know ... whatever would be done with her.' Note that in Heb., since the subjunctive has disappeared, you must get the mood from the context (§27.1132).

2:12 וּבְהַגִּיעַ תֹּר נַעֲרָה וְנַעֲרָה[1]—(a) *û* + b^e + *haggî^{a}'*. הַ- could be H stem indicator; if so, only 2 rads. are present, 1st geminate, suggesting NCC, §28.31. A prep. occurs on a verb form only in the inf. cstr., hence H65. Table 7 VDC. Read §15.4321. נגע H 'to arrive, reach' (v.5060). (b) *tôr* 'turn' (8447 4/2). (c-d) Distributive, §31.112, 33.125. 'In the reaching of the turn of maiden and maiden' = 'when each girl's turn arrives.'

לָבוֹא ׀[2]—(a) 1:12[2].

מִקֵּץ הֱיוֹת לָהּ[3]—(a) *min* + *qēṣ* 'end' (v.7093), cstr., note *ṣêrê*, §15.223. (b) וֹ– could be fpa/c or 65 of CCY, Table 6 VDC. *hĕyôṯ* is G65 of *hy^h* היה 'to be.' 'From the end of being to her ... 12 months' = 'at the end of her 12-month period.'

כְּדָת הַנָּשִׁים שְׁנֵים עָשָׂר חֹדֶשׁ [4]—(a) 1:8[1]; *dâṯ* should not reduce in cstr. (R. 2a), cf. 9:13[4]. (b-c) Numeral, §26.2, '12,' composed of (b) *šnêm*, the form of '2' used in '12'; note the initial cluster, §16.351, (v.8147); and *ʿāśār* the form of '10' used in the teens (v.6235b). Read §26.25. (d) *ḥōḏeš* 'month' (v.2320); CuCC-type noun, §24.21. Note that the sg. form is used with numbers from 10 up (1:1[12]), §36.14.

כִּי כֵּן יִמְלְאוּ [5]—(a-b) 1:8[3]. (c) וּ— יִ— = ? —ְ = ? מלא, cf. 1:5[1] (v.4390). 'For thus they fulfilled'; subj. follows.

יְמֵי מְרוּקֵיהֶן [6]—(a)1:1[2], §24.212; pl. of *yôm* is irregular, as if from **y^{e}wāmîm* > *yāmîm* (v.3117). (b) Cf. 2:3[10], note difference; *mārûq* 'scouring, rubbing' (4795 1/1).

שִׁשָּׁה חֳדָשִׁים בְּשֶׁמֶן הַמֹּר [7]—(a) *šiššā^h* '6' (v.8337), §26.234. The 'fem.' form with *-ā^h* is used with masc. noun, §36.141. (b) 2:12[4](d), *ḥōḏeš*, pl. *ḥŏḏāšîm*, Paradigm N-3. R. 10b. (c) *b^e*- + *šémen* 'oil (vegetable)' (v. 8081), cstr., but segolates do not reduce in cstr., §15.232. (d) *ham* + *mōr* 'myrrh' (4753 12/1), Akk. *murru*, Gk. *μύῤῥα*.

וְשִׁשָּׁה חֳדָשִׁים בַּבְּשָׂמִים וּבְתַמְרוּקֵי הַנָּשִׁים׃ [8]—(a,b) 2:17[7]. (c) *b^e*- + *hab* + *b^{e}śāmîm*, pl. of בֹּשֶׂם 'balsam' (v. 1314). (d) 2:3[10].

:13 וּבָזֶה הַנַּעֲרָה בָּאָה[1]—(a) *û* + *bā* + *zê^h*, §21.2. 'and in this (manner).' (c) Note carefully: *bā́ā^h* is G11, and *bāʾā́^{h}* is G51, cf. 1:17[7]. Learn this *now*. 'The maiden (is) entering.'

אֵת כָּל־אֲשֶׁר תֹּאמַר[2]—(a) The grammar is distorted, for the noun cl. which begins as object becomes the subject of the main verb, possibly by attraction to the nearer verb: '*all* that she shall say *shall be given*.' (d) *tôʾmar* < **taʾmir*, ya'CiC (R. 10d). —ת = ? Parse it.

יִנָּתֵן לָהּ [3]—(a) Note accent, §17.35. Normalize it *yinnāṯēn*, 1st rad. doubled, sign of N stem, Table 2 VDC. N20 of *ntn*, 2:3[10].

לָבוֹא עִמָּהּ [4]—(a) 1:12[2]. (b) *ʿimm-*, 2:6[3].

מִבֵּית הַנָּשִׁים עַד־בֵּית הַמֶּלֶךְ׃ [5]—(b) Note dagesh in בּ. What does this suggest? R. 11. (c) Cf. 1:5[7].

Learn the basic words in Group 21.

28

Purpose: To study the participle
Materials: Esther 2:14-15

14 בָּעֶרֶב ׀ הִיא בָאָה וּבַבֹּקֶר הִיא שָׁבָה אֶל־בֵּית הַנָּשִׁים
שֵׁנִי אֶל־יַד שַׁעַשְׁגַז סְרִיס הַמֶּלֶךְ שֹׁמֵר הַפִּילַגְשִׁים לֹא־
תָבוֹא עוֹד אֶל־הַמֶּלֶךְ כִּי אִם־חָפֵץ בָּהּ הַמֶּלֶךְ וְנִקְרְאָה
טו בְשֵׁם׃ וּבְהַגִּיעַ תֹּר־אֶסְתֵּר בַּת־אֲבִיחַיִל ׀ דֹּד מָרְדֳּכַי אֲשֶׁר
לָקַח־לוֹ לְבַת לָבוֹא אֶל־הַמֶּלֶךְ לֹא בִקְשָׁה דָּבָר כִּי אִם
אֶת־אֲשֶׁר יֹאמַר הֵגַי סְרִיס־הַמֶּלֶךְ שֹׁמֵר הַנָּשִׁים וַתְּהִי
אֶסְתֵּר נֹשֵׂאת חֵן בְּעֵינֵי כָּל־רֹאֶיהָ׃

2:14 בָּעֶרֶב ׀ הִיא בָּאָה [1]—(a) For b^e- + *hā* + *'éreḇ* 'evening' (v.6153), with syncopation §13.521, and compensatory lengthening §15.14. For | §11.72. Anaptyxis, §15.6. Noun is GvCC type, §24.211. (b) Pers. pron., §21.1 (c) 1:13[1]; is this G51 or G11? בּוֹא, v.935. ה ָ cannot be a radical, for הִיא is fem., hence there are only 2 rads. The root cannot be CCY, for then we would have תָה– in 11 or ה ֶ– in 51. There is no way it can be 1st rad. weak in this form. Therefore it must be Cv̂C. Be sure you can follow the logical steps in indentifying such a form.

וּבַבֹּקֶר הִיא שָׁבָה [2]—(a) Identify the morphemes. Is there a def. art.? The accent is prepositive, §11.571. *bṓqer* 'morning' (v. 1242), is CuCC-type noun, §24.21. (c) *šûḇ* 'to return' (v.7725), Cv̂C verb: G51 and G11 are distinguished by accent, §29.6318. 'In the evening she is entering and in the morning she is returning.'

אֶל־בֵּית הַנָּשִׁים שֵׁנִי [3]—(a-c) You can now do this without help. (d) *šēnî* 'second' (v.8145), an ordinal numeral, §26.32. We would expect a def. art., since בֵּית is def. because of the noun it governs. 'To the second harem.'

אֶל־יַד שַׁעַשְׁגַז סְרִיס הַמֶּלֶךְ [4]—(a-c) Cf. 2:8[6]; note the differences and explain them. (c) Pr. n. 'Shashgaz.' (d-e) You can do.

שֹׁמֵר הַפִּילַגְשִׁים [5]—(a-b) Cf. 2:8[6]. *šômēr*, pattern *-ô-ē-* is G50, §24.24, §27.611. (b) *pîlégeš* 'concubine' (v.6370), a 4-consonant form, §03.12, §24.28, which has developed similar to a segolate < **pîlagš*, note the pl. When the girl entered the king's house she was בְּתוּלָה; when she returned she was פִּילֶגֶשׁ. She left the (first) house of the women; she returned to the second. She was first under Hegai; later she was under Shaashgaz. With exquisite reserve the story is fully told—yet devoid of sensual details.

לֹא־תָבוֹא עוֹד [6]—(a) 1:17[7]. (b) *tāḇô'*, —ת can be 21/22 or 41/42. Table 9 VDC suggests G20 of CWC, but context requires 21. (c) *'ôḏ* 'again' (v.5750), modifying the verb, §35.2. 'She shall not enter again.'

כִּי אִם־חָפֵץ בָּהּ הַמֶּלֶךְ[7]—(a-b) After a neg. *kî 'im* usually means 'except' (v.3588). (b) *ḥāpēṣ,* pattern is G10/50 of CaCiC, a stative verb. Read §27.23f, and note well §27.232. חפץ 'to delight, take pleasure' (v.2654), followed by prep. –בְּ, see (d). (e) Subject. 'Except the king was delighted with her.'

וְנִקְרְאָה בְשֵׁם׃[8]—(a) נ—ָה, *n—āʰ,* with 3 rads. between, therefore most likely N stem perf. 3ms, or N11 of *qr'* 'to call' (v. 7121). *wᵉ-* could be simple or conversive, §27.117. If we read, 'unless the king was delighted with her and she was called by name,' it is simple *wāw.* The Masoretic note calls attention to ָ, but no good reason is given. (b) 2:5[3]. Note application of R.16 in *šᵉmô,* 2:5[3]. *bᵉ-* 'with, in,' here is better translated 'by.'

2:15 וּבְהַגִּיעַ תֹּר־אֶסְתֵּר בַּת־אֲבִיחַיִל דֹּד מָרְדֳּכַי[1]—(a) 2:12[1]; go over the analysis again. (b-c) Cf. 2:12[1]. Now it's Esther's turn. (d-e) Name formula, like Swed. *Svensdotter.* (f-g) Cf. 2:7[3].

אֲשֶׁר לָקַח־לוֹ לְבַת[2]—(a-c) Cf. 2:7[8]. (b) *lā́qaḥ;* CāCaC is G10 pattern; accent has shifted because of proximity of next accent, §17.35. (a) is obj. of verb, 'whom he took to him for a daughter.'

לָבוֹא אֶל־הַמֶּלֶךְ[3]—Cf. 2:12[2].

לֹא בִקְשָׁה דָּבָר[4]—(b) *biqᵉšāʰ.* We see 4 consonants; *bᵉ-* could be prep., but only on 65 and the pattern is wrong. *-āʰ* could be 11 sufformative. The *i*-vowel with 1st rad. suggests D stem, but there is no gemination of 2d rad. Is there a reason? R.1b. *biqqᵉšāʰ* is D11 of *bqš,* 'he sought' (v.1245), cf. 2:2[3]. 'She did not seek a thing.'

כִּי אִם אֶת־אֲשֶׁר יֹאמַר[5]—(a-b) 2:14[7](a-b). (c-d) Noun clause, obj. of verb which is understood from previous clause. (e) *yômar* < **ya'mir,* 'CC. Cf. 2:13[2](d). What is the difference between the two forms? For the following words, cf. 2:8[6] or 2:3[8].

וַתְּהִי אֶסְתֵּר נֹשֵׂאת חֵן[6]—(a) Cf. וַיְהִי in 1:1[1]; what is וַתְּהִי? Cf. Rule 1b. (c) G51 of CC' verb. Normally CôCēCt > CôCéCeṯ, but the א quiesces > CôCē't *nôśē'ṯ.* For *nś',* 2:9[2]. (d) *ḥēn* 'favor, grace, acceptance' (v.2580).

בְּעֵינֵי כָּל־רֹאֶיהָ׃[7]—(a) 1:21[2]. (c) *rô'ēʸ* + *hā. CôCēʰ* is G50 pattern of CCY. Learn it *now.* ֶיהָ is masc. pl. of the noun, and 3fs suf. of the pronoun, 'the (ones) seeing her.' A ptcp., particularly when definite, often serves as a relative clause, 'in the eyes of all *who saw her.*'

Learn the words in Group 22.

Love your neighbor as yourself. וְאָהַבְתָּ לְרֵעֲךָ כָּמוֹךָ.

Lev. 19:18

29

Purpose: To study the *wāw*-conversive
Materials: Esther 2:16-18

16 וַתִּלָּקַח אֶסְתֵּר אֶל־
הַמֶּלֶךְ אֲחַשְׁוֵרוֹשׁ אֶל־בֵּית מַלְכוּתוֹ בַּחֹדֶשׁ הָעֲשִׂירִי הוּא־
17 חֹדֶשׁ טֵבֵת בִּשְׁנַת־שֶׁבַע לְמַלְכוּתוֹ׃ וַיֶּאֱהַב הַמֶּלֶךְ אֶת־
אֶסְתֵּר מִכָּל־הַנָּשִׁים וַתִּשָּׂא־חֵן וָחֶסֶד לְפָנָיו מִכָּל־הַבְּתוּלֹת
18 וַיָּשֶׂם כֶּתֶר־מַלְכוּת בְּרֹאשָׁהּ וַיַּמְלִיכֶהָ תַּחַת וַשְׁתִּי׃ וַיַּעַשׂ
הַמֶּלֶךְ מִשְׁתֶּה גָדוֹל לְכָל־שָׂרָיו וַעֲבָדָיו אֵת מִשְׁתֵּה
אֶסְתֵּר וַהֲנָחָה לַמְּדִינוֹת עָשָׂה וַיִּתֵּן מַשְׂאֵת כְּיַד הַמֶּלֶךְ׃

2:16 וַתִּלָּקַח אֶסְתֵּר [1]—(a) Work out the analysis and then look at 2:8[5]. Note the use of *wāw* to invert the tense significance. Read §27.117f. When parsing a form with conversive *wāw,* you identify the *form* (here impf.) and not the meaning (here past time). Use a 'c' before the symbol: Nc21. You should be able to do the rest to the next note.

בַּחֹדֶשׁ הָעֲשִׂירִי [2]—(a) Is there a def. art.? R.10a. §15.1411. 2:12[7]. (b) *hā* + *'ăśîrî:* the pattern *—î–î* suggests an ordinal number, §26.32. עשר gives us the idea of 'ten,' hence ordinal '10th' (v.6224). Note concord, §36.11. Note word order, §26.87. 'In the month the tenth' = 'in the 10th month.'

הוּא־חֹדֶשׁ טֵבֵת [3]—(a) Demon. pron., §21.2. Noun clause, 'that (is) the month Tebet,' §31.122. (b) Cstr., but a segolate, §15.232. (c) Pr.n. 'Tebet,' 10th month counting from Nisan (Mar.), hence about January. Since the pr. n. is definite, the noun in cstr. is def., §36.3121.

בִּשְׁנַת־שֶׁבַע לְמַלְכוּתוֹ׃ [4]—(a) b^e + $š^e na\underline{t}$, R.19. $šānā^h$ 'year' (v.8141). Note carefully §26.871. (b) 1:1[9]. 'In the year of 7' = ? (c) If Ahasuerus = Xerxes I, this would be 479 BC, but scholars are divided on this identification.

2:17 וַיֶּאֱהַב [1]—Note *wāw* and strong dagesh, §22.13. This can only be on the impf., and always converts the meaning of impf. to that of the corresponding perf. —י 3ms, vowel pattern is yiCCaC of 'CC. אהב 'to love' (v. 157). This verb is often pointed אָהֵב, which is stative vocalization, and G20 form agrees with this (cf. Barth's law, §27.331). The theory is good, but formal statives (i.e. having the form of a stative) often, as here, take direct objects.

מִכָּל־הַנָּשִׁים [2]—מִן of comparison, cf. 1:7[3], 1:19[11]. 'More than all the women.'

וַתִּשָּׂא־חֵן וָחֶסֶד [3]—(a) 2:9[2]. What kind of *wāw*? §27.117. (b) 2:15[6](d). (c) 2:9[2].

מִכָּל־הַבְּתוּלֹת [4]—(a) מִן of comparison, 2:17[2]. (b) 2:3[4](d). What difference(s) do you see in the two forms?

וַיָּשֶׂם כֶּתֶר־מַלְכוּת בְּרֹאשָׁהּ [5]—(a) Note *wāw*. Note shift of accent, Rule 27. The impf. without conv. *wāw* would be *yāśîm* יָשִׂים, CîC verb. G20 and H20 fall together in this type verb, §§29.6, .64, .6413. Note especially §29.641. שִׂים 'to place' (v. 7760). (b-c) 1:11[3]. (d) בְּ|רֹאשׁ|ָ־הּ, *rôʾš* 'head' (v. 7218). 'And he put the royal crown on her head.'

וַיַּמְלִיכֶהָ תַּחַת וַשְׁתִּי׃ [6]—(a) Note *wāw*. Preformative with *a* (—ַי) tells us what? Long *î* after 2d rad. (–י—) is a clue to what? Table 3, VDC. Note the connecting vowel; cf. Table H. The root *mlk* gives the idea of reigning, being king; what would the H stem mean? (b-c) 2:4[4].

2:18 וַיַּעַשׂ [1]— Work it out. Note accent: what does it suggest? When you get stuck, try 1:21[3].

מִשְׁתֶּה גָדוֹל [2]—(a) 1:3[5]. (b) 1:5[7]. Does the adj. agree in GNS? Then how is it used? §36.11. For the next phrase, 1:3[67].

אֵת מִשְׁתֵּה אֶסְתֵּר [4]—(a) Why is אֵת used here and not before 2:18[2]? (b-c) Note ־ֵה and see Table F. Cf. 1:9[3].

וַהֲנָחָה לַמְּדִינוֹת עָשָׂה [5]—(a) *hănāḥāʰ* 'holiday' (2010 1/1), root *nwḥ* 'to rest,' an H-formation noun, §24.31, obj. of verb (c)—note word order. (c) ־ָה: G51 of Cv̂C or G10 of CCY? The form could be either (but not G11 of Cv̂C because of accent), so unless you recognize the word you may have to look up both עוּשׂ and עָשָׂה, and fit the proper word with the context. Note that the *wāw* conv. *cannot* be used unless the verb stands *first* in the clause.

וַיִּתֵּן מַשְׂאֵת כְּיַד הַמֶּלֶךְ׃ [6]—(a) Can יִתֵּן be D10 of *ytn*? §27.117. What else could cause gemination of ? Table 7 VDC. Cf. 1:19[9]—is there a difference? (b) *maśʾēṯ* (v.4864), from *nśʾ*, usually means an 'uprising' or something taken by force or authority, but here (and Gen. 43:34; Jer. 40:5) it must mean something like 'gift.' (c-d) 1:7[5].

Learn the basic words in Group 23.

Analyze the following:

		וַיִּתֵּן	2:18[1]
וַיֹּאמֶר	1:13[1]	וַתִּשָּׂא	2:9[2]
וַיֹּאמְרוּ	2:2[1]	וַיִּשְׁלַח	1:22[1]
וַיִּיטַב	1:21[1]	וַיִּקְצֹף	1:12[5]
וַתִּיטַב	2:9[1]	וַיֶּאֱהַב	2:17[1]
וַיְהִי	1:1[1]	וַיַּעַשׂ	1:21[3]
וַתְּהִי	2:15[6]	וַיָּשֶׂם	2:17[5]
וַיְבַהֵל	2:9[3]	וַיְשַׁנֶּהָ	2:9[8]
וַתְּמָאֵן	1:12[1]	וַיַּמְלִיכֶהָ	2:17[6]

30

Purpose: To translate infinitives and participles
Materials: Esther 2:19-21

וּבְהִקָּבֵץ בְּתוּלוֹת שֵׁנִית וּמָרְדֳּכַי יֹשֵׁב בְּשַֽׁעַר־הַמֶּֽלֶךְ׃ 19
אֵין אֶסְתֵּר מַגֶּדֶת מֽוֹלַדְתָּהּ וְאֶת־עַמָּהּ כַּאֲשֶׁר צִוָּה עָלֶיהָ כ
מָרְדֳּכָי וְאֶת־מַאֲמַר מָרְדֳּכַי אֶסְתֵּר עֹשָׂה כַּאֲשֶׁר הָיְתָה
בְאָמְנָה אִתּֽוֹ׃ בַּיָּמִים הָהֵם וּמָרְדֳּכַי יוֹשֵׁב בְּשַֽׁעַר־ 21
הַמֶּלֶךְ קָצַף בִּגְתָן וָתֶרֶשׁ שְׁנֵֽי־סָרִיסֵי הַמֶּלֶךְ מִשֹּׁמְרֵי הַסַּף
וַיְבַקְשׁוּ לִשְׁלֹחַ יָד בַּמֶּלֶךְ אֲחַשְׁוֵרֹֽשׁ׃

2:19 וּבְהִקָּבֵץ בְּתוּלוֹת שֵׁנִית [1]— *û* + *b*[e] + *hiqqāḇēṣ*: Note that –ה is not H-stem. 1st rad. doubled, clue to N (VDC 2). –הִנ is N32/65; prep. –ב tells us it is 65, temporal, §35.421. (b) 2:2[4]. (c) 2:14[3]. The fem. form (note ת–) is used as an adverb, 'a second time.' There is no reason why this word should present a problem (see older commentaries). Under the polygamous system in vogue, the king must have ordered a collection of virgins several times during his reign. A study of the commentaries at this point, as at many others, should convince any serious student (1) that he should learn to handle the text himself, and not depend on others, and (2) that he should let the text speak for itself.

וּמָרְדֳּכַי יֹשֵׁב בְּשַֽׁעַר־הַמֶּֽלֶךְ׃[2]— – – ֵ ֹ וּ– tells us what? §27.61f., 1:2[3];1:14[6]. (c) *šáʿar* 'gate' (v.8179). Does short vowel reduce in cstr.? Why not? §15.232. RSV: 'When the virgins were gathered together the second time, Mordecai was sitting at the king's gate.' *b*[e]- + inf. cstr. 'in the being gathered to' = 'when (were) gathered.' RSV does not give right impression, however. A new phase of the story is being introduced, and what Mordecai was doing is an incidental part of it.

2:20 אֵין אֶסְתֵּר [1]–(a) 1:8[2]. אַיִן usually is the neg. part. used with ptcps. 'nonexistence of, is not' (v.369). (b) Note accent; we would join this with next word. Compare this construction with 2:10, *lôʾ* + H11.

מַגֶּדֶת[2]—Fem. of G ptcp. (G51) is often formed by adding *-t* ת–, hence *maggîd* + *t* > **maggidt* (R. 2a) > *maggéḏeṯ* (R. 6b). –מַ (with *pattāḥ*) is a strong clue for H50, §27.61, §28.31. If we remove ת—מ, what are the 3 rads.? (VDC 8). נגד 2:10[1]. 'Esther (was) not making known, telling'—i.e. she had not done so, and still was not doing so.

מֽוֹלַדְתָּהּ וְאֶת־עַמָּהּ [3]—(a) a:10[2]. We would expect אֵת before it, cf. 2:10[2]. (c) 2:10[2].

כַּאֲשֶׁר צִוָּה עָלֶיהָ מָרְדֳּכָי [4]—(a) 'according as.' (b) Parse first, then 2:10[3]. Does this verb take a dir. obj.? (d) Note position of subj., cf. 2:10[3]. The student with ethical sensitivity need not be offended by this statement. Unless asked, Esther would not be required to offer the information. Furthermore, in parts of Iran, even to the present, the custom of maintaining a pretense (*kitmân* or *taqiyya*) is practised for the sake of peace. Oftentimes, both parties are fully aware of the true situation, yet they observe the custom. From Ahasuerus' reaction to Esther's "revelation" in Chap. 7, we may suspect that this ancient custom was even then being observed.

וְאֶת־מַאֲמַר [5]—(a) Obj. well before the verb. (b) §24.33, 1:15[6].

עֹשָׂה [6]—Note *ô* after 1st rad., §24.23f, §27.61. 1:5[3]. Ptcp. expresses continued activity: 'the word of Mordecai she was observing.'

כַּאֲשֶׁר הָיְתָה [7]—(a) 2:20[4]. (b) תָה–, §29.71. Form here is used like our perf.: 'as she had been (doing).'

בְאָמְנָה אִתּוֹ׃ [8]—(a) Note carefully! Is it *b̲[e]'ām[e]nā[h]* or *b̲[e]'omnā[h]*? How can you tell? §11.584. Cf. 1:1[3], 1:17[1]. 2:7[1]. אָמְנָה is fem. of G65, 'bringing up, tutelage' (545 1/1) However, it is possible that ־ָה is s1, for ־ָהּ > ־ָה in some instances, cf. *Ges.* §91*e*. (b) *'ēt̲, 'ittô* is to be distinguished from *'ēt̲, 'ôt̲ô* (cf. v.853 and v.854).

2:21 בַּיָּמִים הָהֵם [1]— This can be used of a reference to the past, or to the future. In the latter usage it is often an eschatological formula.

וּמָרְדֳּכַי יֹשֵׁב בְּשַׁעַר־הַמֶּלֶךְ [2]—(b) Written full, ־ֹו־ should give you no trouble. Cf. 2:19[2]. The ptcp. can be used for repeated as well as continuous activity: 'M. sat there every day.'

קָצַף בִּגְתָן וָתֶרֶשׁ [3]—(a) – ־ַ ־ָ should be easy to recognize, §27.22. Cf. 1:12[5]. Verb in 3ms with compound subj. is permitted when verb precedes, §33.121. (b,c) Pr. nouns, 'Bigthan, Teresh.' Note vocalization of –וָ before accent.

שְׁנֵי־סָרִיסֵי הַמֶּלֶךְ [4]— With the help of 1:10[6], 1:5[9], and 2:14[4], you should be able to do this.

מִשֹּׁמְרֵי הַסַּף [5]— (a) Cf. 2:3[9]. What is the ending here? (b) *sap̄* (R.14) 'threshold, doorway' (v.5592).

וַיְבַקְשׁוּ לִשְׁלֹחַ יָד [6]— (a) 2:15[4]. (b) 1:22[1] *š[e]lō[a]ḥ yād̲ b[e]*- is an idiom, 'to lay a hand on, stretch out a hand against, do harm to.' Finish the verse.

Learn the words in Group 24.

מַה שֶּׁשָּׂנוּא עָלֶיךָ אַל תַּעֲשֶׂה לַחֲבֵרְךָ.

What is hateful to you, don't do to your neighbor.'

(Hillel)

31

Purpose: To study the Imperfect
Materials: Esther 2:22-23

22 וַיִּוָּדַע הַדָּבָר
לְמָרְדֳּכַי וַיַּגֵּד לְאֶסְתֵּר הַמַּלְכָּה וַתֹּאמֶר אֶסְתֵּר לַמֶּלֶךְ
בְּשֵׁם מָרְדֳּכָי׃ וַיְבֻקַּשׁ הַדָּבָר וַיִּמָּצֵא וַיִּתָּלוּ שְׁנֵיהֶם עַל־ 23
עֵץ וַיִּכָּתֵב בְּסֵפֶר דִּבְרֵי הַיָּמִים לִפְנֵי הַמֶּלֶךְ׃

2:22 וַיִּוָּדַע הַדָּבָר [1]—(a) Note וּ: since it has a vowel ָ, it cannot be *šûrûq*, but must be *wāw* and strong dagesh, hence *wayyiwwāḏa'*. Do you see 3 radicals? What about the first? Does the pattern resemble yaC²āCēC? Why *pattāḥ* under ד? Does CCG have anything to do with it? §29.13. You should know ידע; make it passive. (b) Subj. of verb, 'the matter was known to M.'

וַיַּגֵּד לְאֶסְתֵּר [2]—(a) Do you see 3 radicals? י must be a preformative–why? §22.13. With *a*-vowel, –ַיּ suggests what stem? §28.31. Is the dagesh in גּ light or strong? R.1a. Why is it here? (R.11). H20 יַגִּיד, H40 עֶגֶד, R.2a. VDC–7. (b) Indir. obj. 'And he told (it) to Esther.'

וַתֹּאמֶר [3]—1:13[1]. 2:2[1]; can you work it out?

בְּשֵׁם [4]—Cstr., but ֵ is not reduced, cf. 2:5[3]. Esther gave Mordecai credit when reporting the plot.

2:23 וַיְבֻקַּשׁ [1]—Note pattern: –ַ–ֻ–ְיְ; shewa under preformative, probably D; *u*-vowel under 1st rad., passive; entire pattern, positive D-pass. VDC–1. Dpc20. בקשׁ, 2:15[4], 2:2[3]. 'And it was sought.'

וַיִּמָּצֵא [2]—Pattern –ֵ–ָּ–ִיִ should be enough for you to parse it quickly. VDC–2. 1:5[5]. 'And it was found.'

וַיִּתָּלוּ שְׁנֵיהֶם עַל־עֵץ [3]—(a) Note וּ-–ָּ–ִיִ, and cf. 2:23[2]. This *could* be Nc25 of a CCY—do you think it is? §29.7, .713. תלה (v.8518) 'to hang.' (b) *šnêhem*, s5 on the word for '2.' 'The two of them were hanged.' (d) *'ēṣ* 'tree' (v.6086). Historical monuments indicate that death by impaling on a stake was commonly used. תלה may have this meaning.

וַיִּכָּתֵב [4]—Note –ֵ–ָּ–ִיִ: what does it tell you? 2:23[23]. Cf. 1:19[4].

בְּסֵפֶר דִּבְרֵי הַיָּמִים לִפְנֵי הַמֶּלֶךְ׃ [5]—(a-c) The journal or day-book of royal records; cf. the title of 1-2 Chronicles, 2 Kgs. 14:28, etc. (d) 'Before,' or possibly 'in the presence of,' so that A. saw it written.

This is a good place to go over your notebook and synthesize your observations of imperf. forms, particularly the N imperfs. that you have seen.

Read through §§20.–20.5.
Read the following:

§§21., .1, .2, .3, .4, .5
§§22., .1, .2, .3, .4, .41
§§23., .1, .121, .122

Review the following:

§§24., .1, .2, .3, .4, .5, .6
§§25., .1, .2, .3, .4, .5
§§30.311, .312

Go over the following:

§§24.21, .215, .22, .221, .23, .24, .25, .26, .27, .28
§§24.3, .31, .33, .4, .5

Learn the words in Group 25.

Analyze the following verbs (using VDC if it helps you):

יַעֲבוֹר	וַיְבַהֵל	וַיִּמָּצֵא	יֹאמַר	תָּבוֹא
יַעֲשֶׂה	וַיְבַקְשׁוּ	וַיִּוָּדַע	תֹּאמַר	תָּבֹא
וַיֶּאֱהַב	וַיְבַקֵּשׁ	וַתִּלָּקַח	תֹּאמַרְנָה	
וַיִּשְׁלַח	וַתְּמָאֵן	וַיִּתָּלוּ	וַיֹּאמֶר	וַיָּשֶׂם
וַיִּיטַב	וַיְשַׁנֶּהָ	יִנָּתֵן	וַיֹּאמְרוּ	וַיַּעַשׂ
וַיִּקְצֹף	וַתְּהִי	תַּגִּיד	וַתֹּאמֶר	תַּגִּיד
יִמָּלְאוּ	וַיְהִי	וַיִּכָּתֵב		

Suggested genealogy of Mordecai and Esther

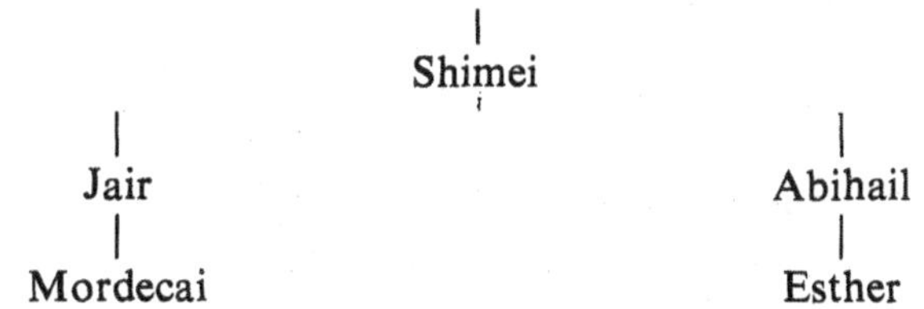

שְׁמַע עֵצָה וְקַבֵּל מוּסָר
לְמַעַן תֶּחְכַּם בְּאַחֲרִיתֶךָ׃
Listen to advice and accept instruction,
that you may gain wisdom for the future.
Proverbs 19:20

32

Purpose: To introduce the HtŠ-stem
Materials: Esther 3:1-3

ג CAP. III. ג

אַחַר ׀ הַדְּבָרִים הָאֵלֶּה גִּדַּל הַמֶּלֶךְ אֲחַשְׁוֵרוֹשׁ אֶת־הָמָן א
בֶּן־הַמְּדָתָא הָאֲגָגִי וַיְנַשְּׂאֵהוּ וַיָּשֶׂם אֶת־כִּסְאוֹ מֵעַל כָּל־
הַשָּׂרִים אֲשֶׁר אִתּוֹ׃ וְכָל־עַבְדֵי הַמֶּלֶךְ אֲשֶׁר־בְּשַׁעַר הַמֶּלֶךְ 2
כֹּרְעִים וּמִשְׁתַּחֲוִים לְהָמָן כִּי־כֵן צִוָּה־לוֹ הַמֶּלֶךְ וּמָרְדֳּכַי
לֹא יִכְרַע וְלֹא יִשְׁתַּחֲוֶה׃ וַיֹּאמְרוּ עַבְדֵי הַמֶּלֶךְ אֲשֶׁר־ 3
בְּשַׁעַר הַמֶּלֶךְ לְמָרְדֳּכָי מַדּוּעַ אַתָּה עוֹבֵר אֵת מִצְוַת
הַמֶּלֶךְ׃

3:1 אַחַר ׀ הַדְּבָרִים הָאֵלֶּה [1]—Cf. 2:1. (a) R.10a. (b-c) R.1a. R.13.

גִּדַּל [2]—(a) Note CiC²aC – ֵ ַ: it can only be what? Table 1 VDC, §28.21. Note that there are *two* vocalizations of this stem. גדל 'to be large, great;' D 'to make large, magnify' (v.1431). Note that the D stem often has a causative force like the H stem.

אֶת־הָמָן בֶּן־הַמְּדָתָא הָאֲגָגִי [3]—(a) Dir. obj. of verb. (b) Pr.n. 'Haman.' (c-d) Patronymic (name of father), 'son of Hammedatha.' (e) Gentilic (name of *gens* or race), note —*î* ִי—, §24.55, 'the Agagite.' This may suggest that the arch-villain was descended from Agag.

וַיְנַשְּׂאֵהוּ [4]—Note suf. ֵהוּ, see Table H. Note pattern – ַ – ְ: this should tell you the form. Note (1) shewa under preformative, (2) dagesh in middle radical, (3) *a*-vowel under 1st rad., §28.21. 'And he lifted him up.'

וַיָּשֶׂם אֶת־כִּסְאוֹ [5]—(a) Try to work it out. Then look at VDC Table 9. Then see 2:17[5]. (c) 12[7]. What suffix here? 'Ane he [the king] placed his [Haman's] chair/throne.'

מֵעַל כָּל־הַשָּׂרִים אֲשֶׁר אִתּוֹ׃ [6]—(a) *min* + *ʿal* 'from over' = 'higher than.' (b) *kol* with pl. = ? Note extended width of ל: certain letters (א ה ל ם ת, and in MSS also ד ר כ) are expanded to fill out the line. In printed texts these are used at line-end, but in MSS even within the line. (e) 2:20[8]. Translate.

3:2 וְכָל־עַבְדֵי הַמֶּלֶךְ [1]—(b) Cf. 1:3[7].

אֲשֶׁר־בְּשַׁעַר הַמֶּלֶךְ [2]—Cf. 2:19[2]. This is a relative clause, defining the servants (answers *which servants?*).

כֹּרְעִים [3]—Note pattern ֹ ְ ִים; the long *ô* after the 1st rad. should help you, §27.611. כרע 'to bow down' (v.3766). The ptcp. often indicates continuing activity, 'were bowing down.'

וּמִשְׁתַּחֲוִים לְהָמָן [4]—(a) Note this form carefully! *mištaḥăwîm* < **mit̠šaḥăwîm*; this is generally listed under **שחה** as HtD, but actually it is HtŠ (Hishtaph'el) of **חוה** *ḥwy*, §28.13. **חוה** HtŠ 'to bow down, worship' (v.7817). (b) Indir. obj.

כִּי־כֵן צִוָּה־לוֹ הַמֶּלֶךְ [5]—(a-b) 1:8[3]. (c) 2:10[3]. Note the prep. used here.

לֹא יִכְרַע [6]—(a) Note neg. adv., generally used with finite verbs in perf. and impf. §35.221. (b) Note –ַ–ְ–ִי: your clues are (1) *i* under preformative, (2) no vowel between 1st and 2d rad. VDC Table 3. yiCCaC or *yiqtal* type impf., §27.333. For *kr*ʿ cf. 3:2[3].

וְלֹא יִשְׁתַּחֲוֶה׃ [7]–(b) ה‍ֶ— could be 20 of CCY, in which case ו and ח are the other two rads. This leaves *yištă–* as preformative, metathesized from **yit̠šă-*. Cf. 3:2[4]. Note the difference between the ptcp. ('the servants *were bowing down*') and the impf. ('but M. *would not bow down*').

3:3 וַיֹּאמְרוּ [1]—2:2[1]. For rest of clause, 2:2[1 2].

מַדּוּעַ אַתָּה עוֹבֵר [2]—(a) Interrog. adv. 'why?' (v.4069), prob. from *mah yādûa*ʿ 'what (is) known?'—but learn it as a word. (b) Independent pers. pron. 2ms (p2), §21.1 (c) Pattern tells us what? **עבר** has many meanings, here 'transgressing, disobeying' (v.5674).

אֵת מִצְוַת [3]–(a) What does this tell us? (b) *m-* (–מ) formation noun (§24.33) from **צוה**, *miṣwāh* 'commandment' (v.4687). Usually in pl. when used of God's commandments. What does ‍ַת tell us? Note expanded ת, cf. 3:1[6].

Learn the words in basic vocabulary Group 26.

Note the following uses of the participle:
הוּא אֲחַשְׁוֵרוֹשׁ הַמֹּלֵךְ מֵהֹדּוּ ... 'that (was the) Ahasuerus *who was ruling* from India ...' (1:1)
הָעָם הַנִּמְצְאִים בְּשׁוּשַׁן 'the people *who were found* in Susa' (1:5)
לַחֲכָמִים יֹדְעֵי הָעִתִּים 'to wise men *who know* the times' (1:13)
רֹאֵי פְּנֵי הַמֶּלֶךְ '*who see* the king's face' (1:14)
הַיֹּשְׁבִים רִאשֹׁנָה בַּמַּלְכוּת '*who sit* first in the kingdom' (1:14)
מְשָׁרְתָיו '*who serve* him' (2:2)
Note that in every case the ptcp. is defined (definite).

Take my instruction	קְחוּ־מוּסָרִי
instead of silver,	וְאַל־כָּסֶף
And knowledge	וְדַעַת
rather than choice gold.	מֵחָרוּץ נִבְחָר׃

Proverbs 8:10

33

Purpose: To study "weak" verbs
Materials: Esther 3:4-6

וַיְהִי בְּאָמְרָם אֵלָיו יוֹם וָיוֹם וְלֹא שָׁמַע אֲלֵיהֶם 4
וַיַּגִּידוּ לְהָמָן לִרְאוֹת הֲיַעַמְדוּ דִּבְרֵי מָרְדֳּכַי כִּי־הִגִּיד לָהֶם
אֲשֶׁר־הוּא יְהוּדִי׃ וַיַּרְא הָמָן כִּי־אֵין מָרְדֳּכַי כֹּרֵעַ 5
וּמִשְׁתַּחֲוֶה לוֹ וַיִּמָּלֵא הָמָן חֵמָה׃ וַיִּבֶז בְּעֵינָיו לִשְׁלֹחַ יָד 6
בְּמָרְדֳּכַי לְבַדּוֹ כִּי־הִגִּידוּ לוֹ אֶת־עַם מָרְדֳּכָי וַיְבַקֵּשׁ הָמָן
לְהַשְׁמִיד אֶת־כָּל־הַיְּהוּדִים אֲשֶׁר בְּכָל־מַלְכוּת אֲחַשְׁוֵרוֹשׁ
עַם מָרְדֳּכָי׃

3:4 וַיְהִי בְּאָמְרָם אֵלָיו יוֹם וָיוֹם [1]—(a) Cf. 1:1[1]. היה is GCY, doubly weak (the medial *y* is strong). Treat it as GCC §29.11 and CCY §29.7–or better yet, learn the most common forms for immediate recognition. (b) 1:17[4]. 'CC, cf. §29.21. The Masoretic note reads *k^e'omrām*. (d-e) Idiom, 'day by day.'

וְלֹא שָׁמַע אֲלֵיהֶם [2]—(b) *šāmar*: what does the pattern tell us? – ַ ָ. CCG §29.13. Cf. 1:18[4]. (c) אֶל + s5, cf. 1:14[2]. 'And so it was, when they spoke to him daily and he did not listen to them.'

וַיַּגִּידוּ לְהָמָן [3]—(a) Conj. -ו here is better translated 'that.' Look at *wayyaggēḏ*, 2:22[2]. In that case, the syllable was originally closed and R.2a applies. Here the ending *-û* prevented a closed syllable, so the rule does not apply. ו– – –י tells us what §27.31. – י ÷ יַ tells us what? (1) ַ under preformative, (2) dagesh in first visible rad. (could it be §13.111?), (3) long *î* before final rad. §28.31. Look at §29.42. 2:10[1]. (b) Indir. obj. 'And they told (it) to Haman.'

לִרְאוֹת [4]—*l^e* + *r^e'ôṯ*: וֹת– can be 65 of CCY, §29.71. Does this fit here? Complete the parsing. 1:14[5]. Doubly weak, C'C = CGC, §29.12, and CCY, §29.7 *l^e*- + 65 indicates purpose, 'in order to see.'

הֲיַעַמְדוּ דִּבְרֵי מָרְדֳּכַי [5]—(a) -הֲ is interrog. part., go over §22.3. The verb is GCC; note that secondary opening develops to a full vowel, study §15.2532, §15.321, §15.421, R.10c. In *yaqtul* and *yaqtil* impfs., you may be fooled by the *pattāḥ* under the preformative. עמד 'to stand' (v.5975). Direct question is used for indirect: 'to see, "would the affairs of M. stand?" ' = 'to see whether ... would stand.'

כִּי־הִגִּיד לָהֶם [6]—(a) Causal, 'for, because.' (b) –הִ–ִי– looks like H10, but what is dagesh doing in גּ? Table 7 VDC. You should now know the meaning of this verb. v.5046. (c) Indir. obj., 'for he had declared to them.'

אֲשֶׁר־הוּא יְהוּדִי׃ [7]—(a) Here conj., 'that,' introduces indirect discourse, §38.82. (b-c) Noun cl., 'he (was) a Jew,' §§31.11, .21. (c) 2:5[1].

3:5 וַיַּרְא הָמָן [1]—(a) *way-yar'*, with apocopation < *yir'ê^h*, §29.72, §13.533. *Ges.* §75*q* says *pattāḥ* under *yôḏ* is due to influence of ר, but possibly it is an application of R.20. CC' verbs, see §29.22. (b) Subj. of verb. 'And Haman saw.'

כִּי־אֵין מָרְדֳּכַי כֹּרֵעַ [2]—(a) Conj. 'that,' introducing indir. disc. after a verb of *seeing*, or a noun cl. as obj. of 'he saw.' (b) Note the neg. part. used before ptcps. 2:20[1]. (d) R.10c. The rest of the cl. you have had in a similar form, 3:2[3 4].

וַיִּמָּלֵא הָמָן חֵמָה׃ [3]—(a) – – ִיִּ: (1) dagesh in 1st rad., (2) vowel pattern. VDC Table 2. מלא 1:5[1] (b) Subj. (c) Acc. of material after verb of *filling*.

3:6 וַיִּבֶז בְּעֵינָיו [1]—(a) Note anaptyxis, *wayyíḇez*. This suggests what? §29.72. < *yiḇzê^h* יִבְזֶה, CCY, cf. 1:17[3]. (b) ָיו is s0 added to du. or pl., Table H. Cf. 1:17[3], 1:21[2]. 'And it was contemptible in his eyes.'

לִשְׁלֹחַ יָד בְּמָרְדֳּכַי לְבַדּוֹ [2]—(a-b) 2:21[7]. (d) 1:16[2]. 'To lay his hand on M. alone.'

כִּי־הִגִּידוּ לוֹ אֶת־עַם מָרְדֳּכָי [3]—(a) 'For.' (b) Cf. 3:4[6], 3:4[3]. Now figure this form out. Subj. is indefinite. (c) Indir. obj. (d-f) Dir. obj., cf. 2:10[2]; here cstr. 'For they had made known to him M.'s people.'

וַיְבַקֵּשׁ הָמָן —(a) – ֵ ַּ ְיְ: (1) shewa under preform., (2) dagesh in mid. rad., (3) vowel pattern = what? §28.21. (b) Subj. of verb.

לְהַשְׁמִיד אֶת־כָּל־הַיְּהוּדִים [5]—(a) *l^e* + *hašmîḏ*. *ha – –î–* suggests what? VDC Table 3. Learn to observe such "little" differences. Complementary inf. after 'he sought.' (b-d) Dir. obj. of inf. cstr., 'to destroy all the Jews.' (d) Pl., cf. 3:4[7], 2:5[1]

אֲשֶׁר בְּכָל־מַלְכוּת [6]—(a) Rel. pron. introduces rel. cl. modifying היהודים. (b) Before *malkûṯ* what does *kol* mean? (c) Cstr. before next word. You should be able to do the rest.

Learn the words in Group 27.

---

12. In HtD forms, when the first radical is a dental or a sibilant, metathesis, assimilation, or both occur (§13.112, §13.61)

דֶּרֶךְ אֱוִיל יָשָׁר בְּעֵינָיו וְשֹׁמֵעַ לְעֵצָה חָכָם׃

The way of a fool is right in his own eyes,
but a wise man listens to advice.
Proverbs 12:15

7 בַּחֹדֶשׁ הָרִאשׁוֹן הוּא־חֹדֶשׁ נִיסָן בִּשְׁנַת
שְׁתֵּים עֶשְׂרֵה לַמֶּלֶךְ אֲחַשְׁוֵרוֹשׁ הִפִּיל פּוּר הוּא הַגּוֹרָל
לִפְנֵי הָמָן מִיּוֹם ׀ לְיוֹם וּמֵחֹדֶשׁ לְחֹדֶשׁ שְׁנֵים־עָשָׂר הוּא־
8 חֹדֶשׁ אֲדָר׃ וַיֹּאמֶר הָמָן לַמֶּלֶךְ אֲחַשְׁוֵרוֹשׁ יֶשְׁנוֹ
עַם־אֶחָד מְפֻזָּר וּמְפֹרָד בֵּין הָעַמִּים בְּכֹל מְדִינוֹת מַלְכוּתֶךָ
וְדָתֵיהֶם שֹׁנוֹת מִכָּל־עָם וְאֶת־דָּתֵי הַמֶּלֶךְ אֵינָם עֹשִׂים
וְלַמֶּלֶךְ אֵין שֹׁוֶה לְהַנִּיחָם׃

3:7 בַּחֹדֶשׁ הָרִאשׁוֹן הוּא־חֹדֶשׁ נִיסָן [1]—(a) 2:12[4] (b) 1:14[7], 'first' (v.7223). The adj. follows the noun it modifies and is in concord (agreement in gender, number, and definiteness). (c) Demon. pron., used as rel. pron. (§21.2), 'that (is).' (e) Nisan, the first month (late March or April), cf. 2:16[3].

בִּשְׁנַת שְׁתֵּים עֶשְׂרֵה [2]—(a) 2:16[4]. (b-c) In 2:12[4] masc. *šnêm ʿāśār,* here fem. *štêm ʿeśrē^h,* §26.25. Note, there are no *ordinals* above 10, cf. §26.872. The numerals are generally adjs. in use, but are basically substantives, cf. §26.2. (b) Cf. 2:14[4](b). (c) Cf. 2:12[4](c). This would be 474 B.C., but see 2:16[4].

הִפִּיל פּוּר הוּא הַגּוֹרָל [3]—(a) *hippîl: hi-–î–* = ? §29.4. Cf. *higgîḏ,* 3:4[6]. נפל 'to fall' (v.5307), H 'to cast, throw down.' (b) *pûr* (loanword) 'lot, chance' (6332 8/8). (c-d) Appositional cl., §36.6, a noun cl., 'that (is) the lot,' explaining the meaning of *pûr.* (d) *gôrāl* 'lot' (v.1486).

לִפְנֵי הָמָן [4]—The defined subj. of *hippîl* is Ahasuerus, but what the significance of casting a lot before Haman is, we are not told. In the light of 3:13 we may assume that it anticipates the story by telling the means of selecting the day of the genocide.

מִיּוֹם ׀ לְיוֹם וּמֵחֹדֶשׁ לְחֹדֶשׁ שְׁנֵים־עָשָׂר [5]—(a-b) Note form of מִן. Probably the lot was cast to select the specific day. We need not assume that it was cast every day for a year. (c-d) Note form of מִן. We would expect מִחֹדֶשׁ, similar to מִחוּץ (R.10a). Again we may assume that the lot was cast to select the month. (e) Cf. 2:12[4]. It is possible that a word or phrase has been dropped out, for this is not smooth.

הוּא־חֹדֶשׁ אֲדָר׃ [6]—(a) Cf. 3:7[1]. Adar was the 12th and, (except for years with intercalary Second Adar [Ve'adar]), the last month.*

---

*According to one system of calendration, the New Year began with Tishrî, the 7th month (as it does today in the Jewish calendar). But whether the year began with Nisan or Tishrî, the numbering of the months was constant; Nisan is always the 1st month, and Adar the 12th.

3:8 וַיֹּאמֶר [1]—You should have no trouble with this clause.

יֶשְׁנוֹ ׳ עַם־אֶחָד [2]—(a) *yēš* יֵשׁ 'existence of' (v.3426), may serve as a verb. It takes pron.sufs., here s0. 'Existence of it' = 'it exists, there is.' (c) Num. *'eḥad* 'one' (v.259), cf. §26.211, §26.81. 'One people,' more than simply 'a people,' as the following words show.

מְפֻזָּר וּמְפֹרָד בֵּין הָעַמִּים [3]—(a) *m*^{e}*puzzār:* (1) *mêm* with shewa, (2) *u*-vowel under 1st rad., (3) doubled 2d rad. = ? Table 1 VDC. פזר 'to scatter abroad' (6340, 10/1). (b) *m*^{e}*pōrād*: (1) *mêm* with shewa, (2) *u*-vowel under 1st rad. with compensatory lengthening, (3) mid. rad. rejects dagesh, = ?. Table 4 VDC. פרד N 'to be divided' (v.6504). (c) Pre. *bên* 'between' (v.996), governing the following word. We would say, 'among the peoples.'

בְּכֹל מְדִינוֹת מַלְכוּתֶךָ [4]—(a) *kōl* before pl. is translated how? (b) f.p.c., §25.422. (c) s2 with connecting vowel preserved by pausal accent, Table H.

וְדָתֵיהֶם שֹׁנוֹת מִכָּל־עָם [5]—(a) *dāṯ* is fem., but pl. is *dāṯîm*, and suffixial form is *dāṯê-*, here fps5. 1:8[1]. (b) *šôn-ôṯ*, f.p.a.; long vowel in *šôn-* suggests G50, cf. *šônîm* in 1:7[3]. 'And their laws (are) differing from [those of] all [other] people.'

וְאֶת־דָּתֵי הַמֶּלֶךְ אֵינָם עֹשִׂים [6]—(a-c) Obj. of עשים. (b) f.p.c., cf. 3:8[5]. (c) Cf. *yešnô*, 3:8[2]. *'ên* + s5 'nonexistence of them' 'they are not.' (d) *'ôśî*, cf. *šônîm*, 1:7[3]. On the use of אין + ptcp., cf. *Ges.* §152*l,m*. The idea seems to be, 'they habitually do not keep the king's laws.'

וְלַמֶּלֶךְ אֵין שֹׁוֶה לְהַנִּיחָם׃ [7]—(a) Like dat. of reference, 'as for the king.' (b) אין negates the ptcp. (c) שֹׁוֶה: note *ḥôlām* on *šîn*, not over *wāw*, which has *s*^{e}*gôl*. *šôwê*^{h}: ־ֶה could be 50 of CCY–are there other clues? שָׁוָה 'he resembled' (v.7737), but here 'it is not like (him), it is not fitting.' (d) *l*^{e} + *hannîḥ* + *ām: hannî*^{a}*ḥ* is H65 of *nû*^{a}*ḥ*, with Aramaic doubling, §29.5115. Study this carefully. נוח 'to rest' (v.5117), H65s5 'to give them rest.'

Read over §30.251, §§30.32–30.324, §§36.–36.14.

Learn the basic words in Group 28.

---

26. When adding a consonantal sufformative (i.e. one which begins with a consonant) to a CC^2 verb which ends in a geminated consonant, the consonantal cluster which would occur is avoided by the insertion of a long vowel before the sufformative, namely וֹ (*ô*) in the perf. and ־ֵי (*ê*^{y}) in the impf. (§15.64).

Purpose: To study the numerals
Materials: Esther 3:9-12a

9 אִם־עַל־הַמֶּלֶךְ טוֹב יִכָּתֵב
לְאַבְּדָם וַעֲשֶׂרֶת אֲלָפִים כִּכַּר־כֶּסֶף אֶשְׁקוֹל עַל־יְדֵי עֹשֵׂי
10 הַמְּלָאכָה לְהָבִיא אֶל־גִּנְזֵי הַמֶּלֶךְ׃ וַיָּסַר הַמֶּלֶךְ אֶת־טַבַּעְתּוֹ
מֵעַל יָדוֹ וַיִּתְּנָהּ לְהָמָן בֶּן־הַמְּדָתָא הָאֲגָגִי צֹרֵר הַיְּהוּדִים׃
11 וַיֹּאמֶר הַמֶּלֶךְ לְהָמָן הַכֶּסֶף נָתוּן לָךְ וְהָעָם לַעֲשׂוֹת בּוֹ
12 כַּטּוֹב בְּעֵינֶיךָ׃ וַיִּקָּרְאוּ סֹפְרֵי הַמֶּלֶךְ בַּחֹדֶשׁ הָרִאשׁוֹן
בִּשְׁלוֹשָׁה עָשָׂר יוֹם בּוֹ

3:9 אִם־עַל־הַמֶּלֶךְ טוֹב[1]—This should give you no difficulty. 1:19[1].

יִכָּתֵב לְאַבְּדָם[2]—*yikkāṯēḇ:* ־ ִ ּ ָ ֵ י, note dagesh and vowel pattern. VDC–2. (b) *l^e'abb^{e}ḏām*: ־ָם is s5 (Table H); ־לְ suggests what? Note dagesh in בּ: is it strong or light? R.16. CaC^{2}ēC (VDC Table 1) is what? CaC^{2}ōC is what? Which is it here? אבד D 'to kill' (v.6).

וַעֲשֶׂרֶת אֲלָפִים כִּכַּר־כֶּסֶף[3]—(a) Num., §26.24 (v.6235). (b) Num. אלף 'thousand' (v.504), in form a segolate, plur. after '10,' lit. 'ten of thousands.' (c) *kikkar* 'talent' (v.3603), sing. after a number above 10 (read §26.9), cstr. with following word. A talent was about 30 kg. (66 lbs.). (d) 1:6[9].

אֶשְׁקוֹל עַל־יְדֵי עֹשֵׂי הַמְּלָאכָה[4]—(a) Written fully (read §11.3241), but it is not a true long vowel. ־ ־ ־ ֶא is what? §27.321. שקל 'to weigh (out)' (v.8254). (c) *y^{e}ḏê^y*: ־ֵי is what? יָד 'hand' (v.3027). (d) Written defectively for ־ֹ־ֵי, only 2 rads., but *ô* after the first suggests G50. Ending is what? (e) *m^{e}lā'ḵā^h* 'work, business' (v.4399). 'I shall weigh into the hands of the doers of the work.'

לְהָבִיא אֶל־גִּנְזֵי הַמֶּלֶךְ׃[5]—(a) Cf 1:11[1]. (c) *g^{e}nāzîm* (only pl.) 'chests, treasury' (1595, 3/2). Note form here and explain.

3:10 וַיָּסַר הַמֶּלֶךְ אֶת־טַבַּעְתּוֹ[1]—(a) Note accent shift: *way* + *yāsēr* > **wayyāser* VDC–9), but there is influence of ר on last vowel. סור 'to turn aside,' H 'to remove' (v.5493). (b) Subj. (c-d) Obj. *ṭabba'ṯ* + *ô* could develop from *ṭabbá'aṯ* or from *ṭabb^e'ā^h*; v.2885 gives the former, 'signet-ring, seal.'

מֵעַל יָדוֹ[2]—(a) *min* + *'al*. If we read carefully, we shall note that Heb. is often more precise in its use of preps. than Eng. A. did not take the signet *from* his hand, but *from upon* his hand. (b) You should be able to analyze this word and translate it.

וַיִּתְּנָהּ[3]—*way* + *yitt^{e}n* + *āh* (note *mappîq*). Explain each morpheme. Parse the word and translate. The indirect obj. follows.

צֹרֵר הַיְּהוּדִים׃[4]—(a) —ֵ–ו– (written defectively, §11.324), tells us what? צרר 'to be hostile to, harass' (v.6887c). On the analogy of עשי המלאכה we conclude that this is G52 (m.s.c.) and that (b) is in gen., rather than G50 with dir. obj. 'The harasser of the Jews.'

3:11 וַיֹּאמֶר הַמֶּלֶךְ לְהָמָן[1]—You should be able to analyze and translate this clause.

הַכֶּסֶף נָתוּן לָךְ[2]—(a) Def. because previously mentioned, 'the silver,' 1:6[9]. (b) –ָ–ו–ַ is what pattern? §27.13, VDC Table 5. (c) Indir. obj. Note the pausal form (Table H). 'The silver is given to you.'

וְהָעָם לַעֲשׂוֹת בּוֹ כַּטּוֹב בְּעֵינֶיךָ׃[3]—(a) Second of compound subj., §30.113. Note the pausal form with the def. art. and read §15.133. (b) ל––וֹת suggests what? §35.423. (c) s0 agrees with its antecedent, 'the people ... it'; we might say 'them.' (d-e) Cf. 1:21[1]·2. Can you figure this out? *kaṭṭôḇ* with def. art., 'according to the good' = 'according to what is good.'

3:12a וַיִּקָּרְאוּ סֹפְרֵי הַמֶּלֶךְ בַּחֹדֶשׁ הָרִאשׁוֹן[1]— (a) 2:14[8]; parse. (b) *sôpēr* 'scribe' (G50 of ספר, v.5608). (d) 2:12[4]. (e) 3:7[1].

בִּשְׁלוֹשָׁה עָשָׂר יוֹם בּוֹ[2]— (a-b) Cf. 2:12[4], 1:3[1], §26.25. (d) What is the antecedent of the pronoun?

Learn the words in Group 29.

Analyze the following:

2:2[4]	שְׁנֵי־סָרִיסֵי הַמֶּלֶךְ
2:19[3]	שֵׁנִית
2:14[3]	בֵּית הַנָּשִׁים שֵׁנִי
2:12[4]	שְׁנֵים עָשָׂר חֹדֶשׁ
1:3[1]	בִּשְׁנַת שָׁלוֹשׁ
2:12[7]	שִׁשָּׁה חֳדָשִׁים
1:6[9]	שִׁבְעַת יָמִים
1:10[6]	שִׁבְעַת הַסָּרִיסִים
2:16[4]	בִּשְׁנַת שֶׁבַע
2:9[6]	שֶׁבַע הַנְּעָרוֹת
1:10[1]	בַּיּוֹם הַשְּׁבִיעִי
1:1[9.12]	שֶׁבַע וְעֶשְׂרִים וּמֵאָה מְדִינָה
1:4[9.10]	שְׁמוֹנִים וּמְאַת יוֹם
2:16[2]	בַּחֹדֶשׁ הָעֲשִׂירִי

הֲלֹא־חָכְמָה תִקְרָא וּתְבוּנָה תִּתֵּן קוֹלָהּ׃

Does not wisdom call, does not understanding raise her voice?

Proverbs 8:1

Purpose: To review some of the things we have learned
Materials: Esther 3:12b-13

וַיִּכָּתֵב כְּכָל־אֲשֶׁר־צִוָּה הָמָן אֶל
אֲחַשְׁדַּרְפְּנֵי־הַמֶּלֶךְ וְאֶל־הַפַּחוֹת אֲשֶׁר ׀ עַל־מְדִינָה וּמְדִינָה
וְאֶל־שָׂרֵי עַם וָעָם מְדִינָה וּמְדִינָה כִּכְתָבָהּ וְעַם וָעָם
כִּלְשׁוֹנוֹ בְּשֵׁם הַמֶּלֶךְ אֲחַשְׁוֵרֹשׁ נִכְתָּב וְנֶחְתָּם בְּטַבַּעַת
13 הַמֶּלֶךְ׃ וְנִשְׁלוֹחַ סְפָרִים בְּיַד הָרָצִים אֶל־כָּל־מְדִינוֹת
הַמֶּלֶךְ לְהַשְׁמִיד לַהֲרֹג וּלְאַבֵּד אֶת־כָּל־הַיְּהוּדִים מִנַּעַר
וְעַד־זָקֵן טַף וְנָשִׁים בְּיוֹם אֶחָד בִּשְׁלוֹשָׁה עָשָׂר לְחֹדֶשׁ
שְׁנֵים־עָשָׂר הוּא־חֹדֶשׁ אֲדָר וּשְׁלָלָם לָבוֹז׃

3:12 וַיִּכָּתֵב כְּכָל־אֲשֶׁר־צִוָּה הָמָן [4]-(a) Est. 1:19[4]. The subj. is indefinite. (b) *kᵉ*- 'according to.' (d) –וּ– is it *šûrûq* or *wāw* with strong dagesh? 2:10[3]. (e) Subj. of verb. Translate.

אֶל אֲחַשְׁדַּרְפְּנֵי־הַמֶּלֶךְ [5]—(b) From Gk. σατράπης, OPers *ḫšaθrapāvan* 'ruler, satrap' (323 4/3).

וְאֶל־הַפַּחוֹת [6]—(b) *peḥāʰ* (v.6346), prob. < **peḥḥāʰ*, pl. **paḥḥôṯ*. Review guttural rules, §15.4ff.

וְאֶל־שָׂרֵי עַם וָעָם [7]—(a-b) You should be able to do this. What morpheme is ֵי-? (c-d) 1:22[4]. Note the use of cstr. before two closely-joined governed nouns.

מְדִינָה וּמְדִינָה כִּכְתָבָהּ וְעַם וָעָם ׀ כִּלְשׁוֹנוֹ [8]—Review notes in 1:22.

בְּשֵׁם הַמֶּלֶךְ אֲחַשְׁוֵרֹשׁ נִכְתָּב [9]—(a) 2:5[3], 2:22[4]. Note that ֵ does not reduce in cstr., but it does in suffixial *šᵉmô*. (d) Masoretic note calls attention to *qāmāṣ* (pausal, §15.134) with *zāqēp̄ qāṭôn;* N10, not N50, 'it was written.'

וְנֶחְתָּם בְּטַבַּעַת הַמֶּלֶךְ׃ [10]—(a) Note influence of guttural, niccāc > negcāc. Note vowels and see VDC Table 3. חתם 'to seal' (v.2856). Is it N10 or N50? (b) 3:10[1].

3:13 וְנִשְׁלוֹחַ סְפָרִים בְּיַד הָרָצִים [1]—(a) niccôc VDC Table 3, §28.42. שׁלח 1:22[1], 2:22[7]. (b) 1:22[1]. (c) *bᵉyaḏ,* idiom = 'by.' (d) רוץ (v.7323) 'to run'; §§29.631, .6318. This form is used as a noun, 'runners, courriers.' 'And documents to be sent....'

אֶל־כָּל־מְדִינוֹת הַמֶּלֶךְ [2]—See 1:22[2].

לְהַשְׁמִיד לַהֲרֹג וּלְאַבֵּד [3]—(a) –הַ–ִי–, note the vowel with ה. Explain the following: –הִ, –הַ. Now note vowel after 2d rad: if ִ, what is it? if ִי, what? VDC T.3. §28.31. *šmd* H 'to annihilate, exterminate' (v.8045). (b) Note ––ֲ, cf. §27.65f. *hrg* 'to kill, slay' (v.2026). (c) Cf. 3:9². – ּ –ְ –לְ, §28.21. Use this opportunity to compare the inf. cstr. forms.

אֶת־כָּל־הַיְּהוּדִים [4]—Dir. obj. of the 3 preceding infs.

מִנַּעַר וְעַד־זָקֵן טַף וְנָשִׁים [5]—(a) *na'ar* 'youth' (v.5288). What morpheme is prefixed? §22., §22.42. (b) 1:5⁷. (c) *zāqēn* 'old person' (v.2205), §24.22. (d) *ṭap̄* (coll.) 'little children' (v.2945). (e) 1:9³. What morpheme is ־ִים? What gender is this word? §25.1.

בְּיוֹם אֶחָד [6]—Is this the same as יוֹם רִאשׁוֹן? Is אֶחָד cardinal or ordinal? §§26.2, .3. Do you translate it 'in one day' or 'on the first day'?

בִּשְׁלוֹשָׁה עָשָׂר לְחֹדֶשׁ שְׁנֵים־עָשָׂר [7]—(a-b) Cf. 3:12³. (c-e) Cf. 3:7⁵. Which month is this?

הוּא־חֹדֶשׁ אֲדָר [8]—See 3:7⁶.

וּשְׁלָלָם לָבוֹז׃ [9]—(a) *šᵉlālām* could be G10s5 of *šālal* or the noun *šālāl* with s5; context prefers the noun. *šālāl* 'booty, spoil' (v.7998). (b) cōc is G65 of CC²; cûc is G65 of CWC (VDC T.10). *bzz* 'to plunder, spoil' (v.962).

Study the following:

G10 cācac, + suf. > cᵉcācām, *qᵉṭālām*
G65 cucuc > cᵉcāc, + suf. > coccām, *qoṭlām, 'omrām*
CāCāC-type noun + suf. > cᵉcācām, *dᵉb̲ārām*

Memorize the words in vocabulary Group 30.

Note the following uses of the perfect:
עָשָׂה הַמֶּלֶךְ ... מִשְׁתֶּה 'the king *made* a banquet' (1:5)
כִּי־כֵן יִסַּד הַמֶּלֶךְ ... לַעֲשׂוֹת 'for thus the king *decreed* to do' (1:8)
גַּם וַשְׁתִּי ... עָשְׂתָה מִשְׁתֵּה נָשִׁים 'Vashti also *made* a women's banquet' (1:9)
לֹא־עָשְׂתָה אֶת־מַאֲמַר הַמֶּלֶךְ 'She *did not do* the king's command' (1:15)
וְלֹא־בָאָה 'and she *did not come*' (1:17)
אֲשֶׁר שָׁמְעוּ אֶת־דְּבַר הַמַּלְכָּה 'who *heard* the king's word' (1:18)
Note the consistent translation in *past* tense. Read §32.51.

He who heeds instruction
is on the path to life,
but he who rejects reproof
goes astray.

אֹרַח לְחַיִּים
שׁוֹמֵר מוּסָר
וְעֹזֵב תּוֹכַחַת
מַתְעֶה׃

Proverbs 10:17

Purpose: To review some of the things we have seen
Materials: Esther 3:14-15

14 פַּתְשֶׁגֶן הַכְּתָב
לְהִנָּתֵן דָּת בְּכָל־מְדִינָה וּמְדִינָה גָּלוּי לְכָל־הָעַמִּים לִהְיוֹת
15 עֲתִדִים לַיּוֹם הַזֶּה׃ הָרָצִים יָצְאוּ דְחוּפִים בִּדְבַר הַמֶּלֶךְ
וְהַדָּת נִתְּנָה בְּשׁוּשַׁן הַבִּירָה וְהַמֶּלֶךְ וְהָמָן יָשְׁבוּ לִשְׁתּוֹת
וְהָעִיר שׁוּשָׁן נָבוֹכָה׃

3:14 פַּתְשֶׁגֶן הַכְּתָב [1]—(a) *paṯšeḡen* 'copy' (6572 3ε). (b) k^e*ṯāḇ* 'writing' (v.3792, 9x in Est.). Explain the vowels in each word.

לְהִנָּתֵן דָּת [2]—(a) Note accent and read §17.35. Normal form *hinnāṯēn*, clues: *hin-*, dagesh in 1st rad. (VDC T.2). Does –לְ tell you whether it is 32 or 65?. (b) You should know this. This sounds like documentary form, 'a copy of the writing to be given (as) law.' The following words you should know–but be sure to go over them!

גָּלוּי לְכָל־הָעַמִּים [3]—(a) For *–ûy* וּי– see §29.71. גלה, cf. 2:6[1], here means 'revealed, laid bare.' (b-c) Why pl.? How would you translate it?.

לִהְיוֹת עֲתִדִים לַיּוֹם הַזֶּה׃ [4]—(a) 1:22[5]. (b) *'āṯîḏ* 'prepared, ready' (6264 6/2). The pattern CāCîC is an 'Aram.-type' pass. ptcp., see §24.2441. (c-d) Cf. 1:18[1]. What is different here?

3:15 הָרָצִים יָצְאוּ [1]—(a) 3:13[1]. Note form of def. art. and review Table G. (b) *y---û*. Careful! Is *y–* a preformative (§20.212) or a radical? Look at the vowels, ָ-ְ-וּ is the pattern of what form? §27.221. Learn this *now*.

דְחוּפִים בִּדְבַר [2]—(a) CāCûC is what pattern? (VDC T.5) §27.63. *dḥp* 'to hasten' (1765 4/3). Why plural? What does it modify? (b) Note prep. b^e-, denoting agency or means. Explain vowels. Note accent ֥.

וְהַדָּת נִתְּנָה [3]—(a) You know this word. (b) Be careful! $CiC^{2e}Cā^h$ could be D11 of *ntn*. But suppose the –תְּ– is the result of assimilation, and –נִ is a stem indicator–what would it be? §28.42. D10 is *nittēn*, N10 is *nittan*, but in the 11 forms, the vowel of the penult reduces and the forms lose distinction. Which makes sense in context? For the next words, cf. 1:2[10,11].

יָשְׁבוּ לִשְׁתּוֹת [4]—(a) Cf. 1:15[1] יָצְאוּ. Note vowels here. Can you figure out the form? *yšb* 'to sit, dwell,' 1:2[3]. (b) וֹת–ְ– should now "ring a bell." שׁתה (cf. 1:8[1]) 'to drink' (v.8354).

וְהָעִ֫יר שׁוֹשַׁ֫ן נָבֽוֹכָה׃ [5]—(a) Cf. v.5892, fem. gender. (b) In apposition with the preceding word (§30.251). (c) *nāḇôḵāʰ* or perhaps *nâḇôḵāʰ*, VDC–9. בּוּךְ 'to perplex, confound' (943 3/1). Accent on N11 should be *nā-ḇṓ-ḵāʰ*, and N51 should be *nᵉ-ḇô-ḵā́ʰ*. Accents here are perplexing.

Study the following carefully:

G25 CCY yiCCû: *yiglû* יִגְלוּ, *yiṣʼû* יִצְאוּ.
G25 NCC yiC²ᵉCû: *yittᵉnû* יִתְּנוּ, *yiṣṣᵉʼû* יִצְּעוּ
G25 YCC yîCᵉCû: *yîʸṭᵉḇû* יִיטְבוּ, **yîʸṣᵉʼû* יִיצְאוּ
G25 WCC yēCᵉCû: *yêṣᵉʼû* יֵצְאוּ
G25 CWC yāCûCû: *yāqûmû* יָקוּמוּ, **yāṣúʼû* יָצוּאוּ.

Take some of the verbs we have had, and make similar comparative studies. Get so you know what to look for as identifying clues.

Learn the basic vocabularly in Group 31.

Read the following sections *carefully*:

§§27.–27.1112
§§27.114–27.1141
§§27.115, .1153
§§27.2, .21, .221, .232, .233
§§27.3, .31, .321, .333, .334

Read the following:

§28.1
§28.2, .21
§§28.3, .31
§§28.4, .42
§§28.5, .51
§§29., 29.02
§§32.51, .52, .53, .54
§§32.8, .81, .82, .83, .84

לֹא־יַחְפֹּץ כְּסִיל בִּתְבוּנָה כִּי אִם־בְּהִתְגַּלּוֹת לִבּוֹ׃
A fool takes no pleasure in understanding, but only in expressing his opinion.
Proverbs 18:2

38

Purpose: To review what we have been studying
Materials: Esther 4:1-3

CAP. IV. ד

ד

א וּמָרְדֳּכַי יָדַע אֶת־כָּל־אֲשֶׁר נַעֲשָׂה וַיִּקְרַע מָרְדֳּכַי אֶת־
בְּגָדָיו וַיִּלְבַּשׁ שַׂק וָאֵפֶר וַיֵּצֵא בְּתוֹךְ הָעִיר וַיִּזְעַק זְעָקָה
2 גְדוֹלָה וּמָרָה׃ וַיָּבוֹא עַד לִפְנֵי שַׁעַר־הַמֶּלֶךְ כִּי אֵין לָבוֹא
3 אֶל־שַׁעַר הַמֶּלֶךְ בִּלְבוּשׁ שָׂק׃ וּבְכָל־מְדִינָה וּמְדִינָה מְקוֹם
אֲשֶׁר דְּבַר־הַמֶּלֶךְ וְדָתוֹ מַגִּיעַ אֵבֶל גָּדוֹל לַיְּהוּדִים וְצוֹם
וּבְכִי וּמִסְפֵּד שַׂק וָאֵפֶר יֻצַּע לָרַבִּים׃

4:1 וּמָרְדֳּכַי יָדַע אֶת־כָּל־אֲשֶׁר נַעֲשָׂה [1]—(b) Remember that –י can be a radical! Note the pattern, ַ־ָ־ֳ. (f) Examine each of the following suggestions, both for morphology and for context: G29 of CCY, N10 of CCY, G11 of NCC, D11 of CGC. Review Rule 10c,d, §28.42, §29.121, §29.42, §29.71. (c-f) Rel. cl., obj. of *yāḏaʿ*. (d-e) Subj. of *naʿăśā*^{h}, 'all that was (had been) done.'

וַיִּקְרַע מָרְדֳּכַי אֶת־בְּגָדָיו [2]—(a) Is *yiqraʿ* yiqtal or yaqtul?. Don't confuse *qrʿ* קרע with *qrʾ* קרא or with *krʿ* כרע. *qrʿ* 'to tear' (v.7167). (b) *béḡeḏ* 'garment' (v.899); what suffix? on sing. or plur.? (Table H). §24.215.

וַיִּלְבַּשׁ שַׂק וָאֵפֶר[3]—(a) לבשׁ 'to put on (clothing), clothe (self)' (v.3847). (b) *śaq* 'sackcloth' (v.8242). (c) *ʾēper* (coll.) 'ashes' (v.665).

וַיֵּצֵא בְּתוֹךְ הָעִיר [4]—(a) Review 1:17[1]. Is this form yiqtal, yaqtul, or yaqtil? (b) *b*^{e}- + *tāweḵ*, cstr. *tôḵ* (Table F), 'midst' (v.8432). (c) 3:15[5].

וַיִּזְעַק זְעָקָה גְדוֹלָה וּמָרָה׃ [5]—(a) *zʿq* 'to cry, cry out' (v.2199). (b) *z*^{e}*ʿāqā*^{h} 'cry' (v.2201). Cognate accusative (§30.22) (the verb is intrans.), 'to cry a cry.' (c) Adj., modifying (b), 1:5[7]. (d) Adj., also modifying (b), §30.21. *mar(r)*, f. *mārā*^{h} 'bitter' (v.4751). Cf. Exod. 15:23; Ruth 1:20.

4:2 וַיָּבוֹא עַד לִפְנֵי שַׁעַר־הַמֶּלֶךְ [1]—(a) Cf. 1:19[7]. What is the difference? (b-c) 1:1[3], 1:19[3]; contrast *millipānā*^{y}*w* '(from) before him' and *ʿaḏ lipnê*^{y} 'until before' = 'as far as in front of.' (d) 2:19[2].

כִּי אֵין לָבוֹא [2]—(a) Causal. (b) אֵין + inf. cstr. 'there is not to enter' = 'one does not enter.' Cf. Ewald, *Syntax*, §321c.

בִּלְבוּשׁ שָׂק׃ [3]—(a) *b*^{e}- + *l*^{e}*ḇûš* 'clothing' (v.3830). Is the word in cstr.? (b) 4:1[3].

4:3 מְקוֹם אֲשֶׁר דְּבַר־הַמֶּלֶךְ וְדָתוֹ מַגִּיעַ [1]— (a) *māqôm* 'place' (v.4725), *m*– formation noun, §24.33, from קוּם, cstr. before rel. pron. (b) Here, 'where.' In earlier Heb.,

מְקוֹם would not be needed, cf. 2 Sam. 7:7, *bᵉkōl ʼăšer-hiṯhallákṯî* 'in every place I walked.' (f) מַגִּיעַ, cf. הִגִּיעַ in 2:12[1]. Preformative *m–* suggests what form? '(Any) place where the word of the king and his decree (were) reaching.'

אֵבֶל גָּדוֹל לַיְּהוּדִים [2]—(a) *ʼḗḇel* 'mourning' (v.60). (b) How is this word related to the clause? (a-c) Noun clause. 'Great mourning (was) to the Jews.' Translate smoothly.

וְצוֹם וּבְכִי וּמִסְפֵּד [3]—(a) *ṣôm* 'fasting' (v.6685). (b) *bᵉḵî* 'weeping' (v.1065). (c) *mispēḏ* 'wailing' (v.4553). How do these words fit the preceding clause?

יֻצַּע לָרַבִּים׃ [4]—If you have forgotten the words preceding the verb, cf. 4:1[3]. (a) *yuṣṣaʻ*, note the *u*-vowel. CuC²aC is Dp10, hence this could be Dp10 of *yṣʻ*. yuC²aC could also be Hp20 of *nṣʻ*. Read carefully §29.34, and see §29.3411. *yṣʻ* 'to lay, spread' (3331 4/1). 'Sackcloth and ashes were (lit. was) spread for the multitude.'

Learn the words in Group 32.

Note the following *passive participles*:
אָחוּז בְּחַבְלֵי־בוּץ '*held* with linen cords' (1:6)
הַכֶּסֶף נָתוּן לָךְ 'the money *is given* to you' (3:11)
גָּלוּי לְכָל־הָעַמִּים '*revealed* to all the peoples' (3:14)
דְּחוּפִים בִּדְבַר הַמֶּלֶךְ '*hastened* by the king's word' (3:15)
עַם־אֶחָד מְפֻזָּר וּמְפֹרָד בֵּין הָעַמִּים 'a certain people *scattered* and *dispersed* among the peoples' (3:8)
Read §32.3712.

Note the following uses of the *jussive*:
וּמַלְכוּתָהּ יִתֵּן הַמֶּלֶךְ לִרְעוּתָהּ 'and *let* the king *give* her royalty to her fellow woman' (1:19)
יְבַקְשׁוּ לַמֶּלֶךְ נְעָרוֹת '*let* them *seek* maidens for the king' (2:2)
וְיַפְקֵד הַמֶּלֶךְ פְּקִידִים 'and *let* the king *appoint* appointees' (2:3)
Note how the juss. is translated. Read §32.35f.

בַּחֵיק יוּטַל אֶת־הַגּוֹרָל וּמֵיְהוָה כָּל־מִשְׁפָּטוֹ׃
The lot is cast in the lap, but from YHWH is His every judgment.
Proverbs 16:33

39

Purpose: To review some things we have seen
Materials: Esther 4:4-6

4 וַתָּבוֹאינָה נַעֲרוֹת
אֶסְתֵּר וְסָרִיסֶיהָ וַיַּגִּידוּ לָהּ וַתִּתְחַלְחַל הַמַּלְכָּה מְאֹד
וַתִּשְׁלַח בְּגָדִים לְהַלְבִּישׁ אֶת־מָרְדֳּכַי וּלְהָסִיר שַׂקּוֹ מֵעָלָיו
5 וְלֹא קִבֵּל׃ וַתִּקְרָא אֶסְתֵּר לַהֲתָךְ מִסָּרִיסֵי הַמֶּלֶךְ אֲשֶׁר
הֶעֱמִיד לְפָנֶיהָ וַתְּצַוֵּהוּ עַל־מָרְדֳּכָי לָדַעַת מַה־זֶּה וְעַל־
6 מַה־זֶּה׃ וַיֵּצֵא הֲתָךְ אֶל־מָרְדֳּכָי אֶל־רְחוֹב הָעִיר אֲשֶׁר
לִפְנֵי שַׁעַר־הַמֶּלֶךְ׃

4:4 וַתָּבוֹאינָה נַעֲרוֹת אֶסְתֵּר וְסָרִיסֶיהָ[1]—(a) Masoretic note points out the excessive *yôḏ*; *q*^{e}*rê wattāḇōnā*^{h}. נָה—ת = ? §27.31. Cf. 1:18[2]. Subj. of verb is compound, §30.113. The nearer subj. is fem., hence the verb form. (b-d) In Bib. Heb. it is impossible to say, 'the maids and eunuchs of Esther.' Regularly the construction would be 'the maids of E. and her eunuchs.' (d) ֶ‑יהָ is sl on pl., cf. Table H.

וַיַּגִּידוּ לָהּ[2]—(a) Here the verb is 3mp. Cf. 3:4[3]. (b) What suffix? Table H.

וַתִּתְחַלְחַל הַמַּלְכָּה מְאֹד[3]—(a) *wat-tiṯhalḥal* is HtRc21, with reduplication of 1st and 2d rads., usually called Hithpalpēl and treated as HtD, §28.5f. This stem is found mainly with CC^2 and CWC verbs, and often has the idea of turning or twisting. *ḥûl* 'to turn, twist, writhe' (v.2342). (c) *m*^{e}*'ôḏ* 'exceedingly' (v.3966).

וַתִּשְׁלַח בְּגָדִים[4]—(a) Cf. 1:22[1]; what is different about this form? Parse; translate. (b) Cf. 4:1[2], בְּגָדָיו. What is the difference?

לְהַלְבִּישׁ אֶת־מָרְדֳּכַי[5]—(a) Cf. 4:1[3]. *ha—î–* tells us what?. If G means 'to put on clothing,' what does H mean? (b-c) *lbš* is intransitive in G, trans. in H, §28.3.

וּלְהָסִיר שַׂקּוֹ מֵעָלָיו[6]—(a) Cf. 3:10[1]. *l*^{e}*ha-î–*, VDC T.9. If G means 'to turn aside' (intrans.), what might H mean?. (b) Note strong dagesh. Does this explain vowel in שַׂק? (c) Note compound prep., *mē'al–* 'from upon.'

וְלֹא קִבֵּל׃[7]–(a) Neg. part., the form usually used with finite verbs in perf./impf. (b) *qibbēl*, cic^{2}ēc: do you recognize it? Note vowel under 1st rad., VDC–1. קבל 'to receive' (6901 13/3).

4:5 וַתִּקְרָא אֶסְתֵּר לַהֲתָךְ[1]—(a) We have had the verb קרא, 3:12[1]. Can you parse it? R.15, §29.22. (b) Subj. (c) Indir. obj.

מִסָּרִיסֵי הַמֶּלֶךְ אֲשֶׁר הֶעֱמִיד לְפָנֶיהָ[2]—(a) מִן partitive, 'from among, one of.' (d) *he'ĕmîḏ*, note vowels, R.10f, §29.11, R.10c. hiCCîC > *hiqṭîl*, but with GCC >

heʿĕmîḏ. Learn this *now*. **עמד** 'to stand' (v.5975), in H 'whom he stood (stationed) before her.'

וַתְּצַוֵּהוּ עַל־מָרְדֳּכָי [3]—(a) Note ו and וּ–which is vowel and which is consonant?. ־ֵהוּ is s0 acc. suf. on impf. (Table H). –**תְּצַו** suggests what stem? What are the clues? Parse. 'And she commanded him concerning M.'

לָדַעַת מַה־זֶּה וְעַל־מַה־זֶּה׃ [4]–(a) 2:11[4], §29.32. (b-c) Note strong dagesh after מַה, *maʰ-zzêʰ*, 'what (is) this?' (d-f) *ʿal-maʰ* 'on account of what?' = 'why?' 'And why (is) this?'

4:6 וַיֵּצֵא הֲתָךְ אֶל־מָרְדֳּכָי [1]—(a) 1:17[1]. Note the difference and explain it. (b) 4:5[1].

אֶל־רְחוֹב הָעִיר [2]— (b) *rᵉḥôḇ* 'broad place, plaza, street' (v.7339). (c) 3:15[5].

אֲשֶׁר לִפְנֵי שַׁעַר־הַמֶּלֶךְ׃ [3]— You should be able to do this without help.

Study Rules 24, 25.

Learn the words in Group 33.

Note the following ways of expressing the interrogative:
מִי בֶּחָצֵר '*Who* (is) in the court?'
מַה־נַּעֲשָׂה '*What* was done?'
לְמִי יַחְפֹּץ הלמך לַעֲשׂוֹת יְקָר '*To whom* would the king delight to do honor?'
הֲיַעַמְדוּ דִּבְרֵי מרדכי 'Would Mordecai's words stand up?' (הֲ)
מַדּוּעַ אַתָּה עוֹבֵר אֵת מִצְוַת המלך '*Why* are you transgressing the king's command?'
אֵיכָכָה אוּכַל '*How* shall I be able ...?'

Note carefully every interrogative clause that you encounter. Learning comes only from meaningful encounters.

הַאֲמִינוּ בַּיהוָה אֱלֹהֵיכֶם וְתֵאָמֵנוּ הַאֲמִינוּ בִנְבִיאָיו וְהַצְלִיחוּ׃
Believe in the LORD your God, and you will be established;
believe his prophets, and you will succeed.
2 Chronicles 20:20

Purpose: To examine the student's progress
Materials: Esther 2:11–3:15

The Mid-Year (Mid-Course) Examination is to be given at this point. It should be a thorough review of just about everything. At this point the student has encountered almost everything that he will see in narrative Hebrew. The exam should point out what he *needs to learn.* In the coming lessons, there will be constant review, and if the student is aware of *what to study*, he will make much better progress.

Since the verb is the biggest obstacle to most students, this will be stressed.

Note the following uses of the *imperfect*:
כִּי־יֵצֵא דְבַר־הַמַּלְכָּה 'for the queen's word *shall go forth*' (1:17)
תֹּאמַרְנָה שָׂרוֹת פָּרַס־וּמָדַי 'The princesses of Persia and Media *shall say*' (1:18)
וְלֹא יַעֲבוֹר 'and it *shall not pass away*' (1:19)
לֹא־תָבוֹא וַשְׁתִּי לִפְנֵי הַמֶּלֶךְ 'Vashti *shall not come in* before the king' (1:19)
אֲשֶׁר יַעֲשֶׂה בְּכָל־מַלְכוּתוֹ 'which he *shall cause to be done* in all his kingdom' (1:20)
Note that the impf. is consistently translated in the *future* tense. Read §32.52f.

Note the following uses of the *converted imperfect*:
וַיִּיטַב הַדָּבָר ... וַיַּעַשׂ הַמֶּלֶךְ ... וַיִּשְׁלַח סְפָרִים ... 'and the matter *was good* ... and the king *did* ... and *he sent* documents ...' (1:21-22)
Note that the conv. impf. is consistently translated in *past* tense. Read §32.533.

Go over the following verbs.

שָׁמַע	3:4[2]	וַיֹּאמֶר	3:8[1]	וַיַּרְא	3:5[1]
יֵצְאוּ	35[1]	וַיֹּאמְרוּ	3:3[1]	וַיִּבֶז	3:6[1]
יֵשְׁבוּ	3:15[4]	וַיִּתְּנָהּ	3:10[3]	וַיְהִי	3:4[1]
יִכְרַע	3:2[3]	הֲיַעַמְדוּ	3:4[5]	עוֹבֵר	3:3[2]
אֶשְׁקוֹל	3:9[4]	וַיָּשֶׂם	3:1[5]	נָתוּן	3:11[2]
כֹּרֵעַ	3:5[2]	וַיָּסַר	3:10[1]	לִשְׁלוֹחַ	3:6[2]
כֹּרְעִים	3:2[3]	לִרְאוֹת	3:4[4]	לַהֲרֹג	3:13[3]
גִּדַּל	3:1[2]	וַיְבַקֵּשׁ	3:6[4]	מְפֻזָּר	3:8[3]
בִּקְשָׁה	2:15[4]	וַיְבַקְשׁוּ	2:21[6]	מְפֹרָד	3:8[3]
צִוָּה	3:2[5]	וַיְבֻקַּשׁ	2:23[1]	לְאַבֵּד	3:13[3]
				לְאַבְּדָם	3:9[2]
הִגִּיד	3:4[6]	וַיָּשֶׂם	3:1[5]	לְהַשְׁמִיד	3:6[5]
הִגִּידוּ	3:6[3]	וַיָּסַר	3:10[1]	לְהָבִיא	3:9[5]
הִפִּיל	3:7[3]	וַיַּגִּידוּ	3:4[3]	מַגֶּדֶת	2:20[2]
וַיַּגֵּד	2:22[3]	וַיַּמְלִיכֶהָ	2:17[6]	וּבְהַגִּיעַ	2:12[1]

וְנָתַתֶּם	3:12[10]	יִכָּתֵב	3:9[2]	לְהַנִּיחָם	3:8[7]
נִכְתָּב	3:12[9]	יֵעָשֶׂה	2:11[5]	לְהִנָּתֶן –	3:14[2]
נִתְּנָה	3:15[3]	יִנָּתֶן –	2:13[3]	וּבְהִקָּבֵץ	2:19[1]
וְנִקְרְאָה	2:14[8]	וַתִּלָּקַח	2:16[1]	וְנִשְׁלוֹחַ	3:13[1]
וַיִּקָּרְאוּ	3:12[1]	וַיִּוָּדַע	2:22[1]	נְבוֹכָה	3:15[5]
וַיִּתָּלוּ	2:23[3]	וַיִּמָּצֵא	2:23[2]	וַיִּמָּלֵא	3:5[3]

מִתְהַלֵּךְ	2:11[2]	וַתִּתְחַלְחַל	4:4[3]	מִשְׁתַּחֲוֶה	3:5[2]

צֹרֵר	3:10[4]	נָתוּן	3:11[2]	בָּאָה	2:13[1]
עוֹבֵר	3:3[1]	גָּלוּי	3:14[3]	שָׁבָה	2:14[2]
שֹׁוֶה	3:8[7]	נֹשֵׂאת	2:15[6]	עָשָׂה	2:20[6]
עֹשִׂים	3:8[6]	רֹאֶיהָ	2:16[1]	עֹשֵׂי	3:9[4]
שֹׁנוֹת	3:8[5]	דְּחוּפִים	3:15[2]	רָצִים	3:13[1]

לִשְׁלֹחַ	3:6[2]	בְּאָמְרָם	3:4[1]	לְהַשְׁמִיד	3:6[5]
לִשְׁתּוֹת	3:15[4]	לְאַבְּדָם	3:9[2]	לְהָבִיא	3:9[5]
הֱיוֹת	2:12[3]	וּלְאַבֵּד	3:13[3]	וּבְהַגִּיעַ	2:12[1]
לִהְיוֹת	3:14[4]	וּבְהִקָּבֵץ	2:19[1]	לְהִנָּתֵן	3:14[2]
לָדַעַת	2:11[4]	בְּאָמְנָה	2:20[3]	לַהֲרֹג	3:13[3]
לִרְאוֹת	3:4[4]	לְהַנִּיחָם	3:8[7]	לַעֲשׂוֹת	3:11[3]

Know all the words in basic vocabulary groups 1–33.

עֹבֵד אַדְמָתוֹ יִשְׂבַּע־לָחֶם וּמְרַדֵּף רֵיקִים חֲסַר־לֵב׃

He who tills his land will have plenty of bread,
but he who follows worthless pursuits has no sense.

Proverbs 12:11

41

Purpose: To review the Infinitive Construct
Materials: Esther 4:7-10

וַיַּגֶּד־לוֹ מָרְדֳּכַי אֵת כָּל־אֲשֶׁר קָרָהוּ 7
וְאֵת ׀ פָּרָשַׁת הַכֶּסֶף אֲשֶׁר אָמַר הָמָן לִשְׁקוֹל עַל־גִּנְזֵי
הַמֶּלֶךְ בַּיְּהוּדִיִּים לְאַבְּדָם׃ וְאֶת־פַּתְשֶׁגֶן כְּתָב־הַדָּת אֲשֶׁר־ 8
נִתַּן בְּשׁוּשָׁן לְהַשְׁמִידָם נָתַן לוֹ לְהַרְאוֹת אֶת־אֶסְתֵּר וּלְהַגִּיד
לָהּ וּלְצַוּוֹת עָלֶיהָ לָבוֹא אֶל־הַמֶּלֶךְ לְהִתְחַנֶּן־לוֹ וּלְבַקֵּשׁ
מִלְּפָנָיו עַל־עַמָּהּ׃ וַיָּבוֹא הֲתָךְ וַיַּגֵּד לְאֶסְתֵּר אֵת דִּבְרֵי 9
מָרְדֳּכָי׃ וַתֹּאמֶר אֶסְתֵּר לַהֲתָךְ וַתְּצַוֵּהוּ אֶל־מָרְדֳּכָי׃

4:7 וַיַּגֶּד־לוֹ [1]—Note *maqqēp̄,* normal form וַיַּגֵּד. Cf. וַיַּגִּידוּ 4:4[2]. R.2a. §15.22. The conv. impf. is *not* built on the impf., but on an originally-closed form like the juss. Subj. follows.

אֵת כָּל־אֲשֶׁר קָרָהוּ [2]—(a-d) Obj. (= ind. disc.) of 4:7[1], the first of a compound obj. (d) *qārāhû* G10s0 of קרה 'he met, it befell' (v.7136); do not confuse it with קרא (they sound alike). 'All that befell him, happened to him.' Note that the ה in this form is not the radical, but the suffix. §15.432. §29.713.

וְאֵת ׀ פָּרָשַׁת הַכֶּסֶף [3]—(a-c) Second of compound obj. Note *pāsêq.* (b) *pārāšat* is obviously in cstr., hence the *qāmāṣ*s must be either long vowels or compensation vowels. *pārāšā*^{h} 'total, sum, declared amount' (6575 2/2).

אֲשֶׁר אָמַר הָמָן [4]—Rel. cl. defining הכסף. (c) Subj. of (b).

לִשְׁקוֹל [5]—Note ל–, R.19. False plene, §11.322). *šuqul* cucuc = G65 (§27.65). 'He said to weigh,' = 'he said that he would weigh,' indirect discourse. For the following words, 3:9[5].

בַּיְּהוּדִיִּים לְאַבְּדָם׃ [6]—(a) ב– of price, *Ges.* §119*p*, 'to pay for.' The Kt (§11.61) is the basic form of the pl. of a gentilic, y^{e}*hûḏî* + *îm*; the Qr is the developed form, y^{e}*hûḏî*^{y}*m*; note the violation of R.1b. (b) Cf. 3:13[3]. The form here has what suf.? R.16.

4:8 וְאֶת־פַּתְשֶׁגֶן [1]—3:14[1].

אֲשֶׁר־ נִתַּן בְּשׁוּשָׁן לְהַשְׁמִידָם [2]—(a) What kind of clause?. (b) $CiC^{2}aC$ would be D10–but is it? What would N10 of NCC look like? G29 of NCC? N29 of CC^{2}? (c) ב–, place where, 'in.' (d) 3:6[5]. What is ָם–? ל– + 65 indicates purpose.

נָתַן לוֹ [4]—(a) Who is the subj.? (b) ל– before substantive, indirect object.

לְהַרְאוֹת אֶת־אֶסְתֵּר [5]—(a) l^{e} + 65, purpose. להַ|רא|ות, If *-ôṯ* tells us that the form is 65 of CCY (§29.71), why can't ה be a radical? 1:11[4]. Note that there is no syncopation (§13.5221). (b-c) The H-stem of transitive verbs takes two objects, one of which (the nearer) may take **אֶת**. 'To show (it) to Esther,' = 'to cause E. to see (it).'

וּלְהַגִּיד לָהּ[6]—(a) *l*[e] + *haggîḏ* < **hangîḏ* (r.11), VDC–7. (b) Ind. obj.

וּלְצַוּוֹת עָלֶיהָ לָבוֹא[7]—(a) Note carefully! **ו** can be *û* or *ww*; here it is followed by a vowel **וֹ**, so it must be a consonant, *l*[e]*ṣawwôṯ,* cf. 3:2[5]. (b) **צוה** does not take a dir. obj., but requires a prep., 2:20[4]. (c) Ind. disc.

4:8 לְהִתְחַנֶּן־לוֹ[1]—(a) *l*[e] + *hiṯḥannen,* with *nāsôḡ 'āḥôr* (§17.35), obviously HtD, and after –ל obviously 65. **חנן** 'to be gracious,' HtD 'to beseech, make supplication to, seek mercy' (v.2603). (b) Is this 'from him,' 'on his behalf,' or 'to him'?

וּלְבַקֵּשׁ מִלְּפָנָיו עַל־עַמָּהּ׃[9]—(a) CaC^{2}ēC could be what forms? VDC–2. Can you tell which it is here? 2:2[3]. (b) *min* + *l*[e] + *p*[e]*nê* + s0. BDB 816-819. (c) *'al* 'on account of' (5921), see BDB 752-759. (d) CaC^2 + s1.

4:9 You should be able to do 4: 9 without help.

4:10 וַתֹּאמֶר[1]—Note the incomplete way **אמר** is often used. When we use the Eng. verb *to say,* we expect something to follow, even if only *it.* Here it is better to translate the verb 'and she told' (even though that should be וַתַּגֵּד). **התך** is pr.n., 4:5[1].

וַתְּצַוֵּהוּ[2]—(a) For *-ēhû* Table H. For **צוה** 4:8[7], 3:2[5]. For —ת, §27.31. Who gave the command? To whom was it given? Note that while **צוה** requires a prep. before a noun-object, it can take a pron. suf. for object. 'And E. said (= told it) to H., and she commanded him (to go tell it) to M.'

Use this lesson to review the inf. cstr., its morphology and its syntax. You have not had *everything* about the inf.cstr. at this point, but you have had *most* of the common uses.

Learn the words in Group 34.

Note the following uses of the infinitive construct:
וַיִּבֶז בְּעֵינָיו לִשְׁלֹחַ יָד בְּמָרְדֳּכַי לְבַדּוֹ – *What* was contemptible?
וְלַמֶּלֶךְ אֵין שֹׁוֶה לְהַנִּיחָם – *What* is not suitable or fitting? To whom?

מַשְׂכִּיל עַל־דָּבָר יִמְצָא־טוֹב
וּבוֹטֵחַ בַּיהוה אַשְׁרָיו׃

He who gives heed to the word will prosper, and happy is he who trusts in YHWH.

Proverbs 16:20

Purpose: To review verb stems
Materials: Esther 4:11-13

11 כָּל־
עַבְדֵי הַמֶּלֶךְ וְעַם מְדִינוֹת הַמֶּלֶךְ יֽוֹדְעִים אֲשֶׁר כָּל־אִישׁ
וְאִשָּׁה אֲשֶׁר־יָבוֹא אֶל־הַמֶּלֶךְ אֶל־הֶחָצֵר הַפְּנִימִית אֲשֶׁר
לֹֽא־יִקָּרֵא אַחַת דָּתוֹ לְהָמִית לְבַד מֵאֲשֶׁר יֽוֹשִׁיט־לוֹ הַמֶּלֶךְ
אֶת־שַׁרְבִיט הַזָּהָב וְחָיָה וַאֲנִי לֹא נִקְרֵאתִי לָבוֹא אֶל־
12 הַמֶּלֶךְ זֶה שְׁלוֹשִׁים יֽוֹם׃ וַיַּגִּידוּ לְמָרְדֳּכָי אֵת דִּבְרֵי אֶסְתֵּר׃
13 וַיֹּאמֶר מָרְדֳּכַי לְהָשִׁיב אֶל־אֶסְתֵּר אַל־תְּדַמִּי בְנַפְשֵׁךְ
לְהִמָּלֵט בֵּית־הַמֶּלֶךְ מִכָּל־הַיְּהוּדִים׃

4:11 כָּל־עַבְדֵי הַמֶּלֶךְ וְעַם מְדִינוֹת הַמֶּלֶךְ יֽוֹדְעִים[1]—Note this long clause. (a) כל is in cstr. with modifiers (1) עבדי המ׳ and (2) עם מדינות המ׳. (b) *'ab̲d̲ê^y* mpc of *'éb̲ed̲*, 1:3[7], §24.241. (d-f) Chain of cstrs., last word is def., therefore all are def., 'the people of the provinces of the king.' (g) *yôḏ^e'îm: -ô--* is what pattern? Pl. because it agrees with (b-c) and (d-f). §27.6.

אֲשֶׁר כָּל־אִישׁ וְאִשָּׁה [2]—(a) Pron. introduces ind. disc., 'knows *that* ....' (b) Modifies (c) and (d), (c-d) serving as a single expression, 'every (any) man and (or) woman.' (c) *'îš* 'man' (v.376), root **'š* (CvC), 1:8[6]. (d) *'iššā^h* 'woman' (v.802), root **'nθ* (Arab. *'unθay, θ > š* §12.65, *nš > šš* §13.111). The cstr. *'éšet̲* 'wife of' probably is fem of *'îš > 'išt* (R.2a).

אֲשֶׁר־יָבוֹא [3]—(a) Introduces rel. cl. (b) *yāCôC,* CvC verb (§29.63). With yaCCuC or yaCCiC impf. of this type of verb, the *a* of the preformative remains (the syllable is not closed, hence R.18 does not apply). Don't confuse it with the clue to the H-stem.

אֶל־הֶחָצֵר הַפְּנִימִית [4]—(b) The gender of the noun must be determined by the adj. חצר appears to be masc., but the ת– on (c) proves that it is fem. 1:5[10], 2:11[3]. Table G. (c) *p^{e}nîmî* 'inner' (v.6442), CvCîCî pattern, often used for ordinals, §26.3. Note concord (§36.11).

אֲשֶׁר לֹֽא־יִקָּרֵא [5]—(a) How is this particle used here? (c) Dagesh in 1st rad., vowel pattern, VDC–3. If this is not a *yqtl* perf. (cf. Akk. *iprus*), it has to be taken as = fut. perf., 'who shall enter, who shall not have been called.'

אַחַת דָּתוֹ לְהָמִית[6]—(a) §31., 'one (is) his law.' §26.21, §13.1, §13.113, §15.1411, §16.3431. (c) *hā–î–* looks like H-stem of a verb with 2 rads., prob. CvC. Does it fit? מות (v.4191) 'to die,' H 'to put to death.'

לְבַד מֵאֲשֶׁר יוֹשִׁיט־לוֹ [7]—(a) *lbd* 1:16[2], BDB 94. followed by מִן 'in separation from, apart from, besides,' *Ges.* §119*c*. (b) Analyze it. (c) יָשַׁט 'he held out, stretched forth' (3447 3/3); WCC, hence in H *yaw* > *yô*, §29.311.

אֶת־שַׁרְבִיט הַזָּהָב וְחָיָה [8]—(b) Without def. art. *šarbîṭ* would appear to be a pr. n., but see 5:2[5]; 'scepter' (8275 4/4). There is no explanation of spirantized *ḇ* after dagesh; possibly it is a loan-word with original [v]. Scepters were often named. (c) 1:7[2]; in concord, therefore *šarḇîṭ* must be def. (see also אֵת). (d) *ḥāyāʰ* 'to live' (v.2421). Do not confuse חיה with היה. Gc10, 'and he shall live,' §32.54.

וַאֲנִי לֹא נִקְרֵאתִי לָבוֹא [9]—(a) Note *rᵉbîᵃʿ* 'and as for me' (§21.1). (c) *ni-–-tî*: נ-– could be 29, but what about תי-? If it is 14, then what is *ni*-? Could it be a stem morpheme? Note נ-–-תי, cf. נִקְטַלְתִּי, and compare the vowels under 2d rad. The CC' root leaves the syllable open. N14, 'I have not been called.' §29.22. (d) Purpose, or possibly ind. disc.

זֶה שְׁלוֹשִׁים יוֹם׃ [10]—(a) Demon. pron., §21.2, in sing. to agree with *yôm*. (b) The pl. of '3' is '30' (v.7970), §26.26. With numbers above 10, the noun is sing., §26.84, hence 'these 30 days.'

4:12 You should be able to do 4:12. If you need help on the verb, cf. 4:4[2].

4:13 לְהָשִׁיב [1]—(a) Cf. 3:9[5], 1:11[1]. This has to be H65 of CvC—explain why. שׁוּב 'to return, turn; (H) to return, bring back' (v.7725). 2:14[2].

אַל־תְּדַמִּי בְנַפְשֵׁךְ [2]—(a) *'al* negates juss., a milder form of command. §35.222. (b) Look at this form carefully. Afformatives ת--י, §27.31. Look at the clues: shewa, dagesh, *a*-vowel—what stem? What rad. is missing? What type of verb? דמה 'to be like; (D) to imagine' (v.1819). D43. (c) ב|נפש|ך, *nép̄eš* 'soul, self, life' (v.5315), with s3; 'with/in your soul.'

לְהִמָּלֵט בֵּית־הַמֶּלֶךְ [3]—(a) hiC²āCēC should now be familiar (VDC–2). מלט N 'to escape' (v.4422). (c) = בבית, 1:9[4]. 'Don't imagine in your soul to escape' = '. . . that you will escape,' inf. of ind. disc.

מִכָּל־הַיְּהוּדִים׃ [4]—(a) *min* of comparison, 'more than (other) Jews' = 'Don't think that you will be safer.'

Be sure you know the principal characterstics of verb-stem morphology. Students struggle with the Heb. verb for years, just because they fail to learn *what to look for* in each form. The basic patterns are your best friends in this problem.

Memorize the words in Group 35.

43

Purpose: To review verb "tenses"
Materials: Esther 4:14-16

כִּי אִם־הַחֲרֵשׁ 14
תַּחֲרִישִׁי֮ בָּעֵת הַזֹּאת֒ רֶוַח וְהַצָּלָה יַעֲמוֹד לַיְּהוּדִים֙ מִמָּקוֹם
אַחֵר וְאַתְּ וּבֵית־אָבִיךְ תֹּאבֵדוּ וּמִי יוֹדֵעַ אִם־לְעֵת כָּזֹאת
הִגַּעַתְּ לַמַּלְכוּת׃ וַתֹּאמֶר אֶסְתֵּר לְהָשִׁיב אֶל־מָרְדֳּכָי׃ טו
לֵךְ֩ כְּנ֨וֹס אֶת־כָּל־הַיְּהוּדִים הַנִּמְצְאִים בְּשׁוּשָׁן וְצוּמוּ עָ֠לַי 16
וְאַל־תֹּאכְלוּ וְאַל־תִּשְׁתּוּ שְׁלֹשֶׁת יָמִים֙ לַיְלָה וָיוֹם גַּם־אֲנִי
וְנַעֲרֹתַי אָצוּם כֵּן וּבְכֵן אָבוֹא אֶל־הַמֶּ֙לֶךְ֙ אֲשֶׁר לֹא־כַדָּת
וְכַאֲשֶׁר אָבַדְתִּי אָבָדְתִּי׃ 17

4:14 כִּי אִם־הַחֲרֵשׁ תַּחֲרִישִׁי֮ [1]—(a-b) *kî 'im* often means 'except,' especially after a neg. Here, however, the words are not joined; they mean 'for if.' אִם 'if,' etc. (v.518), BDB 49f. (c) *haḥărēš* < **haḥrēš* (R.10c) haCCēC, VDC–3, inf. abs. (H60, §28.31). חרשׁ 'to be silent, dumb' (v.2790). (d) *taḥărîšî* ־ִי—תּ = 23, ־ִי־ִ־תַּ = H23. For the use of H60 + H23 see §35.6. 'Surely if you keep silent.'

בָּעֵת הַזֹּאת֒ [2]—(a) b^e + *hā*, §13.521, + *'ēṯ* 'time' (v.6256). (b) Demon. pron (§21.2), note concord, including def. art. 'In this time.'

רֶוַח וְהַצָּלָה יַעֲמוֹד לַיְּהוּדִים֙ מִמָּקוֹם אַחֵר [3]—(a) *réwaḥ* 'deliverance, relief' (7305 2/1), cf. §24.21. (b) *haṣṣālā^h* 'deliverance' (2020 1/1), root *nṣl*, cf. §24.31. (c) *yaqtul* of GCC yaGăCōC, with false plēnē (§11.3241). For *'md*, 3:4[5]. (e) *min* + *māqôm* 'place' (v.4725), §24.33, from קום. (f) *'aḥēr* 'other, another' (v.312).

וְאַתְּ וּבֵית־אָבִיךְ תֹּאבֵדוּ [4]—(a) §21.1, < **'anti*, note strong dagesh, *'att^e*, §16.341, §16.363. (c) *'āḇ* always has *yôḏ* when adding suffix. 2:7[4,7]. *Ges.* p.282. (d) Note athnaḥ. Read §29.212, §15.631. ־וּ—תּ is 27, §27.31. R.17 only applies in non-pausal forms. For אבד, 3:13[3].

וּמִי יוֹדֵעַ אִם־לְעֵת כָּזֹאת הִגַּעַתְּ לַמַּלְכוּת׃ [5]—(a) Interrog. pron, §21.4, R.10e. מִי 'who?' (v.4310). (c) 'If, whether.' (d) 4:14[2]. (e) 4:14[2]. Is there a def.art.? §22.41. (f) *higgá'aṯ* < **hinga't*, R.11, R.10c, exception to R.5. ת——ה must be H13, NCC, §27.21, §28.31. נגע 2:12[2]. Read §32.5122.

4:15 You should be able to do this verse. Cf. 4:13. For להשׁיב, cf. 4:13[1].

4:16 לֵךְ֩ כְּנוֹס [1]—(a) *lēḵ* < **h^{e}lēḵ*, §13.512, §27.4. הלך 2:11[2].(b) *k^{e}nōs*, G32 < *CiCuC*, §24.22. כנס 'to gather, assemble' (3664 11/1). Note asyndeton, §30.364. Dir. obj. follows.

הַנִּמְצְאִים בְּשׁוּשָׁן [2]—See 1:5[5].

וְצוּמוּ עָלַי [3]—(a) —*û* could be 15/16/37, §27.41. The *û* between the two radicals tells us it is 37, see VDC–10. צום 'to fast' (v.6684). (b) עַל always has *yôd* with suffix, *'alay* + *î* > *'alay*, §15.72. 'On my behalf, for me.'

וְאַל־תֹּאכְלוּ וְאַל־תִּשְׁתּוּ [4]—(a) 4:13[2]. (b) ת—ו is 27/47 (§27.31). Review §29.212. For אַל and juss., §32.353. 'Don't eat.' (d) Note morphemes. Two rads., 1st syll. closed (G or H), and ִ tells us it is G. §29.713. שתה 3:15[4]. Note change of subj. from sing. (you, Mordecai) to plur. (you, all Jews).

שְׁלֹשֶׁת יָמִים לַיְלָה וָיוֹם [5]—(a) Num., §26.23; cstr., §36.14. (b) *yôm*, pl. *yāmîm*, §24.212. Note pl. after nums. 3-9. (c) *láy-lā^h* 'night' (v.3915), cf. §§23.2, .23. (BDB 538 rejects this explanation, but fails to account for [1] penultimate accent and [2] the frequent use of this word adverbially.)

גַּם־אֲנִי וְנַעֲרֹתַי אָצוּם כֵּן [6]—(a) 'Also' (v.1571). (b-c) Note order. (c) Form is fps4, written defectively. (d) —א is 24, cf. 4:16[3]. The pattern could be Gp50, so beware! (e) 'Thus' (v.3651).

וּבְכֵן אָבוֹא אֶל־הַמֶּלֶךְ [7]—(a) ו|ב|כן 'and in this manner. (b) This verb is irregular; we would expect *'āCûC* like *'āṣûm*, §29.63f.

אֲשֶׁר לֹא־כַדָּת [8]—(b-c) Rel. cl., verbless, 'which (is) not according to law.'

וְכַאֲשֶׁר אָבַדְתִּי אָבָדְתִּי׃ [9]—(a) When,' §36.41. (b) תִּי- - - - is 14, vowel pattern is G. (c) Note pausal form, cf. R.15. This could be fut.perf., 'and when I have perished, I have perished' (§32.5133), or contrary-to-fact condition, 'and if I perish I perish' (§32.5141).

Learn the words in Group 36.

Note the following pronominal suffixes:

b^enô *his* son
bānā^yw *his* sons
b^enî *my* son
bānê^yḵā *your* sons
binḵā *your* son
b^enôṯā^yw *his* daughters

הַחֵקֶר אֱלוֹהַּ תִּמְצָא
אִם עַד־תַּכְלִית שַׁדַּי תִּמְצָא׃
Can you find out the deep things of God?
Can you find out the limit of the Almighty?
Job 11:7

Purpose: To work on the verb
Materials: Esther 4:17–5:2

וַיַּעֲבֹר מָרְדֳּכָי וַיַּעַשׂ כְּכֹל אֲשֶׁר־
צִוְּתָה עָלָיו אֶסְתֵּר׃

CAP. V. ה

ה
א וַיְהִי ׀ בַּיּוֹם הַשְּׁלִישִׁי וַתִּלְבַּשׁ אֶסְתֵּר מַלְכוּת וַתַּעֲמֹד בַּחֲצַר
בֵּית־הַמֶּלֶךְ הַפְּנִימִית נֹכַח בֵּית הַמֶּלֶךְ וְהַמֶּלֶךְ יוֹשֵׁב עַל־
2 כִּסֵּא מַלְכוּתוֹ בְּבֵית הַמַּלְכוּת נֹכַח פֶּתַח הַבָּיִת׃ וַיְהִי
כִרְאוֹת הַמֶּלֶךְ אֶת־אֶסְתֵּר הַמַּלְכָּה עֹמֶדֶת בֶּחָצֵר נָשְׂאָה
חֵן בְּעֵינָיו וַיּוֹשֶׁט הַמֶּלֶךְ לְאֶסְתֵּר אֶת־שַׁרְבִיט הַזָּהָב אֲשֶׁר
3 בְּיָדוֹ וַתִּקְרַב אֶסְתֵּר וַתִּגַּע בְּרֹאשׁ הַשַּׁרְבִיט׃

4:17 וַיַּעֲבֹר מָרְדֳּכָי [1]—(a) Young's Concordance lists 73 different ways עבר is translated in KJV. This word needs careful study. Here it could mean: 'M. *transgressed* (the king's command)'; '*crossed over* (the street)'; '*proceeded with* (E.'s command),' etc. *Meanings are derived from contexts, not from lexicons.* Good lexicons supply references to the contexts for our study.

וַיַּעַשׂ כְּכֹל [2]—(a) You should know this form. §29.72. §32.53. (b) k^e + *k̲ōl*; ־כְּ 'according to.'

אֲשֶׁר־צִוְּתָה עָלָיו אֶסְתֵּר׃ [3]—(a) Rel. pron., used how? (b) ־תָה־ is what morpheme? §29.7131. Is ־וְ־ vocalic or consonantal *wāw*?

5:1 וַיְהִי ׀ בַּיּוֹם הַשְּׁלִישִׁי [1]—(a) You should know this word thoroughly. If you don't, learn it *now.* 3:4[1]. (b-c) Note use of ordinal as adj., §36.14. For morphology, §26.32.

וַתִּלְבַּשׁ אֶסְתֵּר מַלְכוּת [2]—(a) *yiqtal* type Gc20 of לבש (v.3847). §32.533. (b) How related to verb? How do you know?. (c) 1:2[8]. How does 'royalty, queenship' fit here? In Eng. we would use either an adv. or a prep., but learn to observe how it is done in Heb.

וַתַּעֲמֹד בַּחֲצַר בֵּית־הַמֶּלֶךְ הַפְּנִימִית [3]—(a) 4:14[3]. Parse form, translate. (b) 4:11[4]. Explain the different pointing. (c-d) 'Palace.' (e) Does this modify בית or חצר? How do you know? Cf. 4:11[4].

נֹכַח [4]—(a) Noun used as prep, see BDB 647, 'in front of' (v.5227). CuCG-type noun, §24.211. This word in in cstr. with and governing the following word, which is also in cstr.

וְהַמֶּ֫לֶךְ יוֹשֵׁב עַל־כִּסֵּא מַלְכוּתוֹ בְּבֵית הַמַּלְכוּת [5]—(b-e) Cf. 1:2[3,6,7,8]. (f-g) Is this 'in the royal house,' 'in the house of royalty,' or 'in the house of the kingship' ? Note בבית, not בית, and cf. 1:9[4], 4:13[3].

נֹכַח פֶּתַח הַבָּיִת׃ [6]—(a) 5:1[4]. (b) 'Door, doorway' (v.6607), CvCG-type noun; cf. *pattāḥ*, name of the open vowel /a/.

5:2 וַיְהִי כִרְאוֹת [1]—(a) 5:1[1]. ?אם לא עכשו, אימתי (b) Cf. 3:4[4], 3:4[1], 2:20[8]. The 65 + -כְּ
often means 'when,' but more strictly 'as, while'; the 65 + -בְּ means 'when.'
You should be able to work out the rest of the clause.

עֹמֶ֫דֶת בֶּחָצֵר [2]—(a) The fem. of CôCēC is usually CôCeCt when a ptcp. (G51), which > CôCéCet, *'ômédet*. (b) Is there a def. art. on this word?. Table G.

נָשְׂאָה חֵן בְּעֵינָיו [3]—(a) ־ָ־ָ־ָה is what form? (b) 2:15[2]. (c) Do you know the full significance of ־ָיו ?

וַיּוֹשֶׁט הַמֶּ֫לֶךְ לְאֶסְתֵּר אֶת־שַׁרְבִיט הַזָּהָב [4]—(a) Note *wayyôšeṭ* (R.27), cf. *yôšîṭ* in 4:11[7]. Long *ô* in such forms suggests H of WCC, §29.321. Note sub., indir. obj., dir. obj., of verb. Be sure you can identify each and tell how you know. Cf. 4:11[8].

וַתִּקְרַב אֶסְתֵּר [5]—(a) ---ת can be what morpheme? §27.31. --ַ-ִת is what type of impf.? §27.333. קרב 'to draw near' (7126), cf. קָרוֹב 1:14[1]. (b) How is this word related to verb? §33.1.

וַתִּגַּע בְּרֹאשׁ הַשַּׁרְבִיט׃ [6]—(a) Cf. 2:12[1]. G 'to touch,' parse, translate. (b) 2:17[5]. Note use of prep. after נגע. (c) 4:11[8].

Learn the words in Group 37.

Study the following forms:

וַתָּשֶׂם
וַתּוֹסֶף
וַתְּדַבֵּר
וַתִּפֹּל
וַתֵּבְךְּ
וַתִּתְחַנֶּן
וַתָּקָם
וַתַּעֲמֹד
וַתֹּאמֶר

Study the following forms:

לְהַקְהִיל
לְהַשְׁמִיד
לַהֲרֹג
לִהְיוֹת
לְהִנָּקֵם
לְהִנָּתֵן
לְהָשִׁיב
לְהַעֲבִיר

שְׁמַע יִשְׂרָאֵל יְהוָה אֱלֹהֵינוּ יְהוָה | אֶחָד׃
Hear, O Israel, the Lord our God, the Lord is one.
Deuteronomy 6:4

45

Purpose., To introduce exegesis
Materials: Genesis 1:1-5, BDB lexicon

For the exegesis lessons we recommend that you work from your own Hebrew Bible, to get used to it. Masoretic accents will have to be supplied from your Bible.

Exegesis is the art and skill of *bringing out* (ἐξ + ἄγω) the meaning of a passage, specifically the meaning which the author intended to convey. It is both an art and a skill—an art that requires ability to perceive subtle shades of expression, structure, balance, contrast, etc., and a skill that needs to be learned, practiced, and developed. It cannot be learned by simply reading commentaries, any more than swimming or cooking can be learned by simply reading books or watching someone else. We can learn much from observation, but to succeed, we must get in and do it personally.

The first step in *grammatico-historical exegesis* is with the text itself, the words in their context, both as to form and syntax.

Gen. 1:1 בְּרֵאשִׁית בָּרָא אֱלֹהִים[1]—(a) *rē'šîṯ*- 'beginning' (v.7225). No def. art., hence it could be cstr. (with a finite verb—distinctly a possibility in Sem. languages). BDB 912. (b) 'He created' (v.1254), always of divine activity, but not exclusively *ex nihilo* (out of nothing), BDB 135. (c) 'God,' pl. form of אֱלֹהַּ (v.430, 433), BDB 43f., used of rulers, angels, gods (with pl. adjs. and vb. forms) and of God (with sg. adjs. and vb. forms). The pl. is explained as (1) a vestige of polytheism, (2) royal pl., (3) community of persons, either (a) God and his court, or (β) in the godhead. Use of sg. concord seems to rule out (1) and (3a).

אֵת הַשָּׁמַיִם וְאֵת הָאָרֶץ׃[2]—(a,c) Sign of def. dir. obj., §34.113, hence compound obj., §34.115. (b) 'Heavens' (v.8064), BDB 1029. (d) 'Earth' (v.776), BDB 75f.(b + d) Possibly a merism for 'everything, the universe, the earth beneath and the sky overhead.'

1:2 וְהָאָרֶץ הָיְתָה תֹהוּ וָבֹהוּ[1]—(a) The center of interest is earth, not the heavens. All that follows is phenomenologically (but not necessarily physically) geocentric, i.e. as it appears to us on earth.(b) G11 in concord with (a). היה is not a mere copula (§31.3), but rather emphasizes the former state, '*was*,' in the beginning of creation.(c) V.8414, BDB 1062. (d) BDB 96. Note accents. Note form of –ו before ב when near-open, not conforming to R.8.

וְחֹשֶׁךְ עַל־פְּנֵי תְהוֹם[2]—(a) 'Darkness' (v.2822). The cl. is verbless, §31. (d) 'Abyss' (v.8415), possibly cognate with Akk. *Ti'âmat*, the underground waters, cf. BDB 1062f. But the place of Ti'âmat in the Bab. creation story is far different from that of *tᵉhôm.*

וְרוּחַ אֱלֹהִים מְרַחֶפֶת עַל־פְּנֵי הַמָּיִם׃[3]— (a) 'Wind, breath, spirit' (v.7307), BDB 924ff, esp. 925.9, 926.9e.(a-b) Cstr. could be 'the wind from God,' 'the breath which is God's,' 'the divine Spirit,' etc.(c) D51 of רחף 'to hover' (2x, BDB 934). Force of ptcp., '(was) hovering.'

1:3 וַיֹּאמֶר אֱלֹהִים יְהִי אוֹר[1]—(a-b) Note concord in meaning but not in morphology—regular when *'ĕlôhîm* means '(the true) God.' If 1:1[1] is taken as cstr., hence dependent cl., this is the first main cl., 'then God said.'(c) G40 of היה, §27.511, §29.72, §32.35., 'let there be.' In Lat., this is translated *fiat*, hence the term "fiat creation."(d) 'Light' (v.216), not necessarily the light of the sun, moon, and stars, BDB 21.(c-d) Direct discourse or quotation, §38.81. Be sure you understand the jussive. It is significant in Gen. 1.

וַיְהִי־אוֹר׃[2]—(a) Cf. Est. 1:1[1]. Here, however, it is the converse of the היתה of Gen. 1:2 and its darkness, hence, 'Light came into being.'

1:4 וַיַּרְא אֱלֹהִים אֶת־הָאוֹר כִּי־טוֹב[1]—(a) Is this from ירא (v.3372, BDB 431) or from ראה (v.7200, BDB 906ff)? (c-d) What is the relation of this word-group to (a-b)? §34.113. (e) Introduces a noun-clause (§31.13) after verbs of *seeing, hearing, saying,* etc. (v.3588), BDB 471.1a, *Ges.* §157*b*. (f) Pred. adj., §31.23. Supply 'it was' (§31.71).

וַיַּבְדֵּל אֱלֹהִים בֵּין הָאוֹר וּבֵין הַחֹשֶׁךְ׃[2]— (a) ברל 'to be divided, separate' (v.914), but what stem? §28.31. BDB 95. (b) How is this related to (a)? (c,e) Note that בֵּין is repeated, BDB 107.1a,d.

1:5 וַיִּקְרָא אֱלֹהִים | לָאוֹר יוֹם[1]—(a) Parse the verb. (b) Relate to the verb (subj., obj., ind. obj.?). The *pâsēq* | has no significance here (cf. J. Kennedy, *The Note-line in the Hebrew Scriptures* [1903]). (c) Note use of ל– after קרא meaning 'to name,' BDB 896.6e. 'God cried/called "day" to the light.'

וְלַחֹשֶׁךְ קָרָא לָיְלָה[2]—(a) Gen. 1:2[2], 1:5[1](c). (b) In 3d pers. the subj. of verb must be defined unless it is clear from context. §30.3363, §33.212. Identify the subj. (c) Est. 4:16[5], here pausal.

וַיְהִי־עֶרֶב וַיְהִי־בֹקֶר יוֹם אֶחָד׃[3]—(a) Here, more like 'and/so there was.'(b) Est. 2:14[1]. (d) Est. 2:14[2]. (e-f) Cf. Est. 3:8, 13. Either 'one day' or possibly 'day one.' 'The first day' would be הַיּוֹם הָרִאשׁוֹן or יוֹם רִאשׁוֹן.

This exercise loses its point if you fail to study the words in their contexts, their meanings, the syntax, etc. Do *not* start exegesis with a commentary. Commentaries are thought-stoppers. Get all *you* can from the text, start your own thinking, and *then* turn to the commentaries.

Learn the words in Group 38.

46

Purpose: To review afformatives
Materials: Esther 5:3-6

וַיֹּאמֶר לָהּ
הַמֶּלֶךְ מַה־לָּךְ אֶסְתֵּר הַמַּלְכָּה וּמַה־בַּקָּשָׁתֵךְ עַד־חֲצִי
4 הַמַּלְכוּת וְיִנָּתֵן לָךְ׃ וַתֹּאמֶר אֶסְתֵּר אִם־עַל־הַמֶּלֶךְ טוֹב
יָבוֹא הַמֶּלֶךְ וְהָמָן הַיּוֹם אֶל־הַמִּשְׁתֶּה אֲשֶׁר־עָשִׂיתִי לוֹ׃
ה וַיֹּאמֶר הַמֶּלֶךְ מַהֲרוּ אֶת־הָמָן לַעֲשׂוֹת אֶת־דְּבַר אֶסְתֵּר
וַיָּבֹא הַמֶּלֶךְ וְהָמָן אֶל־הַמִּשְׁתֶּה אֲשֶׁר־עָשְׂתָה אֶסְתֵּר׃
6 וַיֹּאמֶר הַמֶּלֶךְ לְאֶסְתֵּר בְּמִשְׁתֵּה הַיַּיִן מַה־שְּׁאֵלָתֵךְ וְיִנָּתֵן
לָךְ וּמַה־בַּקָּשָׁתֵךְ עַד־חֲצִי הַמַּלְכוּת וְתֵעָשׂ׃

5:3 מַה־לָּךְ אֶסְתֵּר הַמַּלְכָּה [1]—(a) *mā*^{h} can be interrog. or indef. (§30.13, §21.5); here interrog. Note dagesh in ל, §13.36. (a-b) Idiom, 'What ails you?' 'What's with you?.' etc. (d) Def. art. used as vocative (§36.66).

וּמַה־בַּקָּשָׁתֵךְ עַד־חֲצִי הַמַּלְכוּת [2]—(a) Here מַה is indef., not interrog., according to Masoretic accents, for the entire clause is joined. (b) *baqqāšā*^{h} 'request, a seeking' (1246 8/7). Note preservation of fem. ת– before suf.; ךְ is s3 (§23.1). Cf. 2:2[3], 2:23[1], 2:15[4], 3:6[4]. (c) *'aḏ* 'until, unto, up to' (v.5704, BDB 723ff). (d) *ḥăṣî* 'half, middle' (v.2677). (e) Cf. 5:1[5]. 'And whatever (is) your request up to half of the kingdom.'

וְיִנָּתֶן לָךְ׃ [3]—(a) *w*^{e} + *yinnāṯēn*, but note effect of next accent (*nāsôg 'āḥôr*, §17.35). Pattern yiC²āCēC, VDC–2. Learn to identify this pattern *now.* Is *wāw* conversive? (§32.53) (b) §23.121.

5:4 אִם־עַל־הַמֶּלֶךְ טוֹב [1]—Cf. 1:19[1].

יָבוֹא הַמֶּלֶךְ וְהָמָן הַיּוֹם [2]—(a) *yāḇô'*: Cf. note on *'āḇô'*, 4:16[7]. This could be G20 or G40, probably the latter: 'Let the king and H. come.' Note verb in sg. with compound subj., §33.12f. (d) *hayyôm* 'today'; Eng. *today* < *the day*).

אֶל־הַמִּשְׁתֶּה אֲשֶׁר־עָשִׂיתִי לוֹ׃ [3]—(b) 1:5[8], maCCaY-type (§24.33, R.18). (d) In CCY verbs, 3d rad. *yôḏ* is preserved in certain forms (§29.712)., learn this *now.* It can't be H (no –ה). It can't be D or N (why not?). 1:5[3], 1:9[2]. (e) Note לָהֶם–E. wouldn't make a משתה for Haman, at least she would not say that to the king, hence this must be address in 3d pers. to the king, following יבוא.

5:5 מַהֲרוּ אֶת־הָמָן [1]—(a) *mahărû* < **mahhărû* (R.10a). ־ֻ ־ָ ־ַ would be G37; ־ֻ ־ֲ ־ַ would be D37. Learn to note such details. מהר D 'to hasten' (v.4116); cf. the name of Isaiah's son (Isa. 8:3). 3cp indef., probably to servants, 'Hurry up Haman.'

לַעֲשׂוֹת אֶת־דְּבַר אֶסְתֵּר[2]—(a) Why not cstr. here? §38.54. (b) Why is את used? Is the phrase def.? Why?

וַיָּבֹא הַמֶּלֶךְ וְהָמָן אֶל־הַמִּשְׁתֶּה[3]—(a) Cf. 5:4[2], here written defectively. Note again the use of sg. verb with compound subj., §33.12.

אֲשֶׁר־עָשְׂתָה אֶסְתֵּר׃[4]—(b) Cf. 1:9[2]. Note word order.

5:6 בְּמִשְׁתֵּה הַיַּיִן[1]—(a) 1:9[3]. Although משתה is generally translated 'feast,' the root שתה means 'to drink,' and the feast is described as משתה היין. For ־ֵה, Table F.

מַה־שְּׁאֵלָתֵךְ וְיִנָּתֵן לָךְ[2]—(a) See notes on 5:3[1]. (b) *šᵉʾēlāʰ* (7596 14/6) 'request, petition,' root שאל (7592). Review §13.36. (c) Cf. 5:3[3].

וּמַה־בַּקָּשָׁתֵךְ עַד־חֲצִי הַמַּלְכוּת[3]—See 5:3[2].

וְתֵעָשׂ׃[4]—*wᵉṯēʿāś* (in pause): —ת can be 21/22/41/42. The subj. is שאלתך, hence vb. is 21/41. Why? תֵּעָשֶׂה < **tiʿʿāśêʰ*, GCY with compensatory lengthening, §15.141, R.10a. But form here is apocopated (§13.533), which is found only in conv. impf. and juss., hence form must be N41, 'let it be done.'

Learn the words in Basic Vocabulary Group 39.

Study the following pronominal suffixes:

בַּעֲלֵיהֶן	שְׁנֵיהֶם	עִמָּהּ	עִמּוֹ	מַלְכוּתֶךָ	עָלַי
בְּעֵינֵיהֶן	לָהֶם	לָהּ	לוֹ	לָךְ	לִי
תַּמְרֻקֵיהֶן	דָּתֵיהֶם	תַּמְרוּקֶיהָ	מַלְכוּתוֹ	בְּעֵינֶיךָ	מוֹלַדְתִּי
	בְּאָמְרָם	יָפְיָהּ	לְמַלְכּוֹ	אָבִיךָ	נְעֻרַתִי
	אוֹתָם	מִמֶּנָּה	מִמֶּנּוּ		מִמֶּנִּי
	עֲלֵיהֶם	מְנוֹתֶיהָ	גְּדוּלָּתוֹ	בַּקָּשָׁתֵךְ	בַּקָּשָׁתִי
	אֵינָם	מוֹלַדְתָּהּ	חֲמָתוֹ	שְׁאֵלָתֵךְ	שְׁאֵלָתִי

הֲיִגְאֶה־גֹּמֶא בְּלֹא בִצָּא
יִשְׂגֶּה־אָחוּ בְלִי־מָיִם׃

Can papyrus grow where there is no marsh?
Can reeds flourish where there is no water?

Job 8:11

47

Purpose: To review morphemes
Materials: Esther 5:7-10

וַתַּ֫עַן *
8 אֶסְתֵּר וַתֹּאמַר שְׁאֵלָתִי וּבַקָּשָׁתִי׃ אִם־מָצָאתִי חֵן בְּעֵינֵי
הַמֶּלֶךְ וְאִם־עַל־הַמֶּלֶךְ טוֹב לָתֵת אֶת־שְׁאֵלָתִי וְלַעֲשׂוֹת
אֶת־בַּקָּשָׁתִי יָבוֹא הַמֶּלֶךְ וְהָמָן אֶל־הַמִּשְׁתֶּה אֲשֶׁר אֶעֱשֶׂה
9 לָהֶם וּמָחָר אֶעֱשֶׂה כִּדְבַר הַמֶּלֶךְ׃ וַיֵּצֵא הָמָן בַּיּוֹם הַהוּא
שָׂמֵחַ וְטוֹב לֵב וְכִרְאוֹת הָמָן אֶת־מָרְדֳּכַי בְּשַׁעַר הַמֶּלֶךְ
וְלֹא־קָם וְלֹא־זָע מִמֶּנּוּ וַיִּמָּלֵא הָמָן עַל־מָרְדֳּכַי חֵמָה׃
10 וַיִּתְאַפַּק הָמָן וַיָּבוֹא אֶל־בֵּיתוֹ וַיִּשְׁלַח וַיָּבֵא אֶת־אֹהֲבָיו
וְאֶת־זֶרֶשׁ אִשְׁתּוֹ׃

5:7 וַתַּ֫עַן אֶסְתֵּר וַתֹּאמַר *[1]—Masoretic * before verse notes that this is the middle verse in Esther. The same fact is noted in the final Masorah at end of Esther. Cf. Fig. 5. (a) *wat* + *táʿan* < *taʿănê*[h], ענה 'to answer' (v.6030). (c) Pausal form; cf. first word in 5:4.

שְׁאֵלָתִי וּבַקָּשָׁתִי׃[2]—(a) Cf. 5:5[2]; what suf. here? (b) Cf. 5:3[2]; what suf. here?. For smooth translation, sc. 'is this.'

5:8 אִם־מָצָאתִי חֵן [1]—(a) 4:14[1]. (b) ־תִי--- is what morpheme? §27.21. ־תִי---ָ is what stem pattern? §27.22. For מצא 1:5[5], 2:23[2], v.4672. (c) 2:15[5]. You should be able to do the next two clauses.

לָתֵת אֶת־שְׁאֵלָתִי וְלַעֲשׂוֹת אֶת־בַּקָּשָׁתִי [2]—(a) Cf. 2:9[5] and note difference in accents. We should note (but not construct a theory on it) that נתן is used with שאלה and עשה with בקשה. Masoretic pointing would seem to make it impossible to take the inf. cls. as subj. of noun cl., with טוב as pred.—but how else to translate it?

יָבוֹא הַמֶּלֶךְ[3]—Cf. 5:5[3].

אֶעֱשֶׂה לָהֶם[4]—(a) ---א is what morpheme? §27.31. ֶה in CCY verb is what morpheme? §29.71. R.10g. (b) Here, להם, cf. 4:4[3] and notes. It is customary to speak to the king in the 3d pers.

וּמָחָר אֶעֱשֶׂה כִּדְבַר הַמֶּלֶךְ׃[5]—(a) *māḥār* 'tomorrow' (v.4279). §24.22. (b) 5:8[4]. (c) *k*[e]- 'according to,' BDB 453ff.

5:9 וַיֵּצֵא הָמָן בַּיּוֹם הַהוּא [1]—(a) Cf. 1:17[1]. What is the difference here? (c-d) Cf. 1:18[1]. 1:2[1] How would you translate the phrase? §30.32.

שָׂמֵחַ וְטוֹב לֵב[2]—(a) *śāmēᵃḥ* is G50 of stative vb., §27.612; note *pattāḥ g*[e]*nûḇā*[h] (§15.4321). Many stative verbs are used in a way that makes it impossible to distinguish between G10 and G50. (bc) 'Good of heart' = 'happy.' *lēḇ* < *libb-*, §24.224.

וְכִרְאוֹת הָמָן אֶת־מָרְדֳּכַי [3]—(a) ־ו here must be translated 'but.'־כ 'when, as.' All of a sudden, Haman's joy is turned to anger.

וְלֹא־קָם וְלֹא־זָע מִמֶּנּוּ [4]—(a) *qām* could be G50 or G10; after **לא** it is more likely perf., §35.221. 'He didn't get up.' (d) *zāʻ* G50 or G10 of **זוע** 'move, tremble' (2111 3/1). (c) **מִן** 'because of' (cf. our idiom 'I was shaking *from* fright'). For *min* + *min* + suf., cf. 1:19[11], §23.1231.

וַיִּמָּלֵא הָמָן עַל־מָרְדֳּכַי חֵמָה׃ [5]—(a) 3:5[3]. (c) 'Against, on account of.' (e) 3:5[3].

5:10 וַיִּתְאַפַּק הָמָן וַיָּבוֹא אֶל־בֵּיתוֹ [1]—(a) *way* + *yiṯʼappēq*: this can only be one form (VDC–1). **אפק** 'restrain self' (662 7/1). (c) Note form here and see 5:5[3]. Be sure you don't get hung up on one to the exclusion of the other!

וַיִּשְׁלַח וַיָּבֵא [2]—(a) Cf. 1:22[1], 4:4[4]. (b) Cf. 5:10[1]. What is the difference between *wayyāḇôʼ* and *wayyāḇēʼ*? between *yaqtul* and *yaqtēl*? §27.321, §28.31, cf. 1:17[6].

אֶת־אֹהֲבָיו [3]—(b) *ʼôhēḇ* would be what form? §24.233. *ʼôhăḇêʸ*? So what is this? Table H. **אהב** 'to love' (v.157), but this form is often a noun, 'friend.'

וְאֶת־זֶרֶשׁ אִשְׁתּוֹ׃ [4]—(b) Pr. n. 'Zeresh.' (c) *ʼišt* is probably fem. of *ʼîš*, §15.222, cf. 4:11[2].

Learn the words in Group 40.

Study the following uses of the negative particles:

lôʼ hēḇîʼāʰ (5:12[1])
lôʼ qibbēl (4:4[7])
lôʼ niqrēʼṯî (4:11[9])
lôʼ qām (5:9[4])
ʼăšer lôʼ yiqqārēʼ (4:11[5])
ʼăšer lôʼ ḵaddāṯ (4:16[8])
ʼêʸn lāḇôʼ (4:2[2])
ʼêʸnénnû šôwêʰ lî (5:13[1])
ʼal tᵉḏammî ḇᵉnap̄šēḵ (4:13[2])
ʼal tōʼḵᵉlû (4:16[4])
ʼal tištû (4:16[4])
ʼal tappēl dāḇār (6:10[5])

Happy is the man who finds wisdom, and the man who gets understanding.

אַשְׁרֵי אָדָם מָצָא חָכְמָה
וְאָדָם יָפִיק תְּבוּנָה׃

Proverbs 3:13

Purpose: To review morphemes
Materials: Esther 5:11-13

וַיְסַפֵּר לָהֶם הָמָן אֶת־כְּבוֹד עָשְׁרוֹ
וְרֹב בָּנָיו וְאֵת כָּל־אֲשֶׁר גִּדְּלוֹ הַמֶּלֶךְ וְאֵת אֲשֶׁר נִשְּׂאוֹ
עַל־הַשָּׂרִים וְעַבְדֵי הַמֶּלֶךְ׃ וַיֹּאמֶר הָמָן אַף לֹא־הֵבִיאָה 12
אֶסְתֵּר הַמַּלְכָּה עִם־הַמֶּלֶךְ אֶל־הַמִּשְׁתֶּה אֲשֶׁר־עָשָׂתָה
13 כִּי אִם־אוֹתִי וְגַם־לְמָחָר אֲנִי קָרוּא־לָהּ עִם־הַמֶּלֶךְ׃ וְכָל־
זֶה אֵינֶנּוּ שֹׁוֶה לִי בְּכָל־עֵת אֲשֶׁר אֲנִי רֹאֶה אֶת־מָרְדֳּכַי
הַיְּהוּדִי יוֹשֵׁב בְּשַׁעַר הַמֶּלֶךְ׃

5:11 וַיְסַפֵּר לָהֶם הָמָן[1]—(a) V.5608, D 'to recount, tell.' Note the pattern – ∸ –ַיְ. You should be able to parse it. Cf. 3:12[1]. (b) Table H. Note word order. Where is the subj. of the verb?

אֶת־כְּבוֹד עָשְׁרוֹ וְרֹב בָּנָיו[2]—(b) 1:4[3]. (c) *'ošrô*; 1:4[2], CuCC > *CŏCeC*,§24.21. (d) *rōb̲* < **rubb*, 'multitude' (v.7230). (e) Note: sg. *bēn* (CiC), pl. *bānîm* (CaC); likewise the fem., sg. *bat̲* < *bint*, §15.33, **(cf. Arab. *bint*), pl. *bānôt̲*.**

וְאֵת כָּל־אֲשֶׁר גִּדְּלוֹ הַמֶּלֶךְ[3]—Note use of n. cl. for dir. obj., §33.6. (d) Cf. 3:1[2], here + s0 (3ms suf.), Table H. 'And all (with) which the king had magnified him.'

וְאֵת אֲשֶׁר נִשְּׂאוֹ[4]—(c) *niśś[e]'ô*: – ∸ –ִ is a strong clue that form is D perf. נִשְּׂאוֹ would be D15, but what is נִשְּׂאוֹ? Table H. For root, 2:9[2], 3:1[4]. 'And how (אשר) he had lifted him up.' You should be able to finish the verse.

5:12 אַף לֹא־הֵבִיאָה אֶסְתֵּר הַמַּלְכָּה עִם־הַמֶּלֶךְ[1]—(a) *'ap̄* 'also' (v.637). (b) Note the neg. part., §35.221. (c) הֵ–ִי–ָה, note clues. הֵ– H perf.; –ָה perf. 3fs (11); 2 radicals, 3d not weak (note –ִי–), and no sign of weak 1st rad. (but it could be YCC defectively written) – so we try ב–א. Does it fit? (d) How is this related to the verb? *'im* 'with' (accompaniment, v.5973). You should be able to do the rest of the cl.

אֲשֶׁר־עָשָׂתָה[2]—(b) Cf. 1:9[2]. Form here is pausal, with a disjunctive accent that is usually relatively weak.

כִּי אִם־אוֹתִי[3]—(a-b) After a neg., *ki 'im* often means 'but, except.' (c) Note *'ēt̲, 'ôt̲-*, sign of def. dir. obj., §23.1233.

וְגַם־לְמָחָר אֲנִי קָרוּא־לָהּ עִם־הַמֶּלֶךְ׃[4]—(a) 1:9[1]. (b) 5:8[5]. Here, something like, 'on (the) morrow.' (c) §21.1. (d) –וּ– –ָ is what pattern? §27.63. (f-g) 5:12[1]. 'And also on the morrow *I* (have been) called by her with the king.'

5:13 וְכָל־זֶה אֵינֶנּוּ שֹׁוֶה לִי[1] — (a-b) 'Yet all this' (RSV). (c) אין + suf., Table H, with *nûn* energ. (§23.1221): 'it is not' (§31.331). (d) Note שׁ, ו, *šôwêʰ* written defectively. שָׁוָה (v.7737), 3:8[7], 'fitting, satisfactory.' §§36.3, .31. (e) Dat. of advantage, 'for me.' Table H.

בְּכָל־עֵת אֲשֶׁר אֲנִי רֹאֶה[2] — (a)'In every (any) time.' §36.15f. (b) *'ēṯ* 'time' (v.6256), 1:13[2], 4:14[2]; < *ʿint. (c) *'ăšer*, here, almost 'when'. §38.51. (d-e) Like a pres. tense, 'I see.' (e) Learn to recognize long vowels written defectively; *rô'êʸ* and *rô'ēʰ* are cstr., but is this? The rest is a ptcp. cl. modifying both the noun *mordᵉḵay* and the verb *rô'êʰ*. §38.43.

Learn the words in Group 41.

Study the following noun modifiers:
בַּחֹדֶשׁ הָעֲשִׂירִי 'in the tenth month'
בִּשְׁנַת שֶׁבַע 'in the seventh year'
כֶּתֶר־מַלְכוּת 'a royal crown'
יֵין מַלְכוּת רָב 'much royal wine'
כִּסֵּא מַלְכוּתוֹ 'his royal throne'
בֵּית הַמַּלְכוּת 'the royal house'
שִׁשָּׁה חֳדָשִׁים 'six months'
וְאֵת שֶׁבַע הַנְּעָרוֹת הָרְאֻיוֹת 'and the seven seemly maids'
נְעָרוֹת בְּתוּלוֹת טוֹבוֹת מַרְאֶה 'good-looking virgin maids'
עֵינֵי מֶלֶךְ 'the king's eyes'
בֵּיתוֹ 'his house'
הַיּוֹם הַזֶּה 'this day'
הַיָּמִים הָאֵלֶּה 'these days'

If YHWH does not build a house, in vain the builders labor on it; if YHWH does not guard a city, in vain the watchman stays awake.	אִם־יהוה לֹא־יִבְנֶה בַיִת שָׁוְא עָמְלוּ בוֹנָיו בּוֹ אִם־יהוה לֹא־יִשְׁמָר־עִיר שָׁוְא שָׁקַד שׁוֹמֵר׃

Psalm 127:1

49

Purpose: To review morphemes
Materials: Esther 5:14–6:2

14 וַתֹּאמֶר לוֹ זֶרֶשׁ אִשְׁתּוֹ וְכָל־
אֹהֲבָיו יַעֲשׂוּ־עֵץ גָּבֹהַּ חֲמִשִּׁים אַמָּה וּבַבֹּקֶר ׀ אֱמֹר לַמֶּלֶךְ
וְיִתְלוּ אֶת־מָרְדֳּכַי עָלָיו וּבֹא עִם־הַמֶּלֶךְ אֶל־הַמִּשְׁתֶּה שָׂמֵחַ
וַיִּיטַב הַדָּבָר לִפְנֵי הָמָן וַיַּעַשׂ הָעֵץ׃

ו CAP. VI. ו

א בַּלַּיְלָה הַהוּא נָדְדָה שְׁנַת הַמֶּלֶךְ וַיֹּאמֶר לְהָבִיא אֶת־
סֵפֶר הַזִּכְרֹנוֹת דִּבְרֵי הַיָּמִים וַיִּהְיוּ נִקְרָאִים לִפְנֵי הַמֶּלֶךְ׃
2 וַיִּמָּצֵא כָתוּב אֲשֶׁר הִגִּיד מָרְדֳּכַי עַל־בִּגְתָנָא וָתֶרֶשׁ שְׁנֵי
סָרִיסֵי הַמֶּלֶךְ מִשֹּׁמְרֵי הַסַּף אֲשֶׁר בִּקְשׁוּ לִשְׁלֹחַ יָד בַּמֶּלֶךְ
אֲחַשְׁוֵרוֹשׁ׃

5:14 וַתֹּאמֶר לוֹ זֶרֶשׁ אִשְׁתּוֹ וְכָל־אֹהֲבָיו [1]— Cf. 5:10[3.4]. Again, note *ḥôlām* in d.o. in אֹהֲבָיו: it must be a long *ô*. Note R.16. (a) Verb; (b) indir. obj., §35.11; (c) subj., §33.1; (d) appositive, §36.6; (e-f) second of compound subj, §33.12. The verb agrees with the nearer subj., §33.111.

יַעֲשׂוּ־עֵץ גָּבֹהַּ חֲמִשִּׁים אַמָּה [2]— (a) In sing. we can distinguish G20 from G40 (cf. §§32.34, .35) of this verb (יַעֲשֶׂה, יַעַשׂ), but in pl. the forms fall together. Here, probably G45, 'Let them make.' Indef. 3mp often = passive, 'Let a tree be made.' (b) *'ēṣ* 'tree' (v.6086), often translated 'gallows,' because of the following clause. Primitive noun (CiC); there is no reason to suppose a root *עצה as BDB 781. (c) *gāḇô*^{a}*h* 'high' (v.1364); note *mappîq* = consonantal *hê*. Note accents: not 'a high tree,' but 'a tree, a high one.' (d) '50' (v.2572), §26.2, §24.261. (e) *'ammā*^{h} 'cubit' (approx. 1.5 ft. or 0.46 m.) (v.520). 'High, 50 cubits.' Note sing. noun, §36.142.

וּבַבֹּקֶר ׀ אֱמֹר לַמֶּלֶךְ [3]— (a) 2:14[2]. CuCC > *CốCēC*, §24.21. For adv. use of prep. phrase, §35.3. (b) Note vowels! – – ָ < CuCuC (R.13a, 16, 10b), the pattern of G32/65. Here, GCC. G32 fits context, 'Say to the king.'

וְיִתְלוּ אֶת־מָרְדֳּכַי עָלָיו [4]— (a) *w*^{e}*yit̲*^{e}*lû*: don't let *yit̲* fool you! You need 3 rads. *yi—û* could be CCY; there is no sign of loss of 1st rad., no sign of medial *wāw* or *yôḏ*. תלה 'to hang' (v.8518). Probably G45, 'Let them hang,' or (indef. 3pl.) = pass., 'Let M. be hanged on it.' Note the form of indirect discourse. (d) Table H. In ancient Persian art, the use of sharpened stakes and impaling is attested. But whether by hanging or by impaling, a 75-ft. (23-m.) tree is hardly necessary. Perhaps it was to be set up on a high place to be seen by all.

וּבֹא עִם־הַמֶּלֶךְ אֶל־הַמִּשְׁתֶּה שָׂמֵחַ [5]— (a) *bô'* can be G32/65 of בוא (it's irregular, remember). In context, impv. is preferred: ‘Say ... and go....’ (f) 5:9[2], §27.612. The ptcp. modifies the verb: *how* he was to go, §35.61. I hope you’re not missing the delightful way this story is being developed!

וַיִּיטַב הַדָּבָר לִפְנֵי הָמָן וַיַּעַשׂ הָעֵץ׃ [6]— (a) Cf. 1:21[1]. Note differences in the following expressions. (c-d) Prep. phr. used adverbially, §35.31. (e) 1:21[3]. (f) 5:14[2], there indef., no special tree; here, def., the tree previously mentioned. §32.221.

6:1 בַּלַּיְלָה הַהוּא נָדְדָה שְׁנַת הַמֶּלֶךְ [1]— (a) 4:16[5]. (a-b) Cf. 5:9[1], §35.31. (c) הָ--- = perf. 3fs (11). The נ– can’t be N-stem, for a word cannot begin with 1st and 2d rads. the same. נדד ‘to flee’ (v.5074). (d) This looks like 3:7[2] (1:3[1]). *šānā[h]* ‘year’ and *šēnā[h]* ‘sleep’ (v.8142) take the same form in cstr. (d-e) Construct phrase (noun phrase) used as subj. (§33.13).

וַיֹּאמֶר לְהָבִיא אֶת־סֵפֶר הַזִּכְרֹנוֹת דִּבְרֵי הַיָּמִים [2]— (b) You should know this. 1:11[1]. §38.82 (d-g) This is probably a title. (e) *hazziḵrônôṯ*, sg. *zikkārôn* ‘remembrance’ (v.2146). Joüon (§18*d,g*) calls the dagesh “spontaneous doubling,” i.e. due neither to extrinsic cause (e.g. assimilation) nor to intrinsic (e.g. denoting intensity). Syntax and accents call for cstr. here, ‘The book of the memorials of the affairs of the days,’ but there is a def. art. on *ziḵrônôṯ*. In advanced Heb. grammar, the student will learn that there are exceptions to rules. The use of the def. art. with a cstr. is not unknown either to Heb. or to Arab. (cf. Wright, *Arabic Grammar*, II, 222A). The book was the king’s chronicles.

וַיִּהְיוּ נִקְרָאִים [3]— (a-b) Note conv. impf. + ptcp.: ‘they were being read.’ (b) With *niqrā’îm*, cf. *nimṣ[e]’îm* 1:1[5].

6:2 וַיִּמָּצֵא כָתוּב [1]— (a) *yimmāṣē’* – do you recognize the pattern? 2:23[2]. (b) *–ā–û–* : do you recognize the pattern? §24.244. ‘And it was found written.’

אֲשֶׁר הִגִּיד מָרְדֳּכַי [2]— (a) ‘Where’ or ‘that.’ (b) 3:4[6] The account concerns (על) Bigthan and Teresh, cf. 2:21[3,4,5]. The Masoretic mark calls attention to a *pattāḥ* in pause (with *’aṯnāḥ*).

אֲשֶׁר בִּקְשׁוּ לִשְׁלֹחַ יָד [3]— Cf. 2:21[6,7]. With בִּקְשׁוּ, cf. בִּקְשָׁה, 2:15[4].

Learn the words in Group 42.

Study the following expressions:

d[e]ḇar hammélek w[e]dāṯô (4:3[1]) ‘the king’s word and law’
na‘ărôṯ ’estēr w[e]sârîsê[y]hā (4:4[1]) ‘Esther’s maids and eunuchs’

50

Purpose: To continue study of exegesis
Materials: Amos 7:10-15; Bible dictionary, atlas

The second element in grammatico-historical exegesis is the understanding of all historical, geographical, and similar elements in a passage. The Bible is unique among religious scriptures in the place it gives to historical and geographical details. The God of the Bible reveals himself in word and action in space and time, hence these details have significance. Some exegetes stress the necessity of identifying the life situation (*Sitz im Leben*) in order to understand the message. This is particularly true in the Prophets.

Amos וַיִּשְׁלַח אֲמַצְיָה כֹּהֵן בֵּית־אֵל[1]— (a) Parse, translate. Cf. Est. 1:22[1]. (b) Amaziah the
7:10 priest, not the king. Cf. *NBD* 29 or any good Bible dictionary. (c) *kôhēn* (> Cohen) 'priest' (v.3548). Is it 'a priest' or 'the priest'? Is it cstr.? §27.6112. (d-e) Bethel ('house of El'), *NBD* 143, *IDB* 1: 191ff. Look at a good Bible Atlas (Grollenberg, *Atlas of the Bible, The Westminster Historical Atlas,* or *The Macmillan Bible Atlas*). Bethel in the south and Dan in the north were cult centers established by Jeroboam ben Nebat, first king of the Northern Kingdom (cf. 1 Kgs. 12:26-30).

אֶל־יָרָבְעָם מֶלֶךְ־יִשְׂרָאֵל לֵאמֹר[2]— (b) y^e*rob̲ʿām* (note *qāmāṣ-ḥăṭûp̄*) 'Jeroboam' – but was it Jeroboam I or II? *NBD* 613f. Note dates of each. (c-d) In apposition (§30.251) with (b). 'Israel' can mean (1) Jacob, (2) the entire people Israel, (3) the entire nation (Judah and Israel, the 12 tribes), or (4) the Northern Kingdom. Which is meant here?. (e) Note form. This may be translated 'quote.'

קָשַׁר עָלֶיךָ עָמוֹס בְּקֶרֶב בֵּית יִשְׂרָאֵל[3]— (a) V.7130, BDB 905, 'to conspire.' (b) Indir. obj. (§35.31). (c) *ʿāmôs* Amos, from Tekoa (Am. 1:1), cf. *IDB*). Was he the father of Isaiah (see Isa. 1:1)? Where was Tekoa? Was Amos a northerner? (d) V.7130, BDB 899.1f. b^e*qéreb̲* often = b^e-. (e-f) BDB 110.5dδ. What does "house of Israel" mean in this context?

לֹא־תוּכַל הָאָרֶץ לְהָכִין אֶת־כָּל־דְּבָרָיו׃[4]— (a-b) Cf. Est. 6:13. Is it 21 (3fs) or 22 (2ms)? (c) How is this word related to (a-b)? What does *hāʾăreṣ* refer to here? the earth? the land under foot? the nation? (b) BDB 466. Here something like 'to sustain, endure, bear.' GNB reads, 'His speeches will destroy the country' – is this a literal translation? (e-f-g) How is this related to (d)? What is the relationship of (d-g) to (a-c)?

7:11 כִּי־כֹה אָמַר עָמוֹס[1]— (a) BDB 471-475. Is this 'that' after a verb of *saying* (ὅτι recitative) or 'because' (ὅτι causal)? (b) V.3541. The formula *kō*^{h} *ʾāmar* ... is often found in the Prophets, frequently with יהוה as subj.

בַּחֶרֶב יָמוּת יָרָבְעָם[2]— (a) *ḥéreb̲* 'sword' (v.2719), בְּ– of instrument 'with,' BDB 89.III.2. Is it 'with a sword' or 'with the sword'? See Table G. (b) VDC–9; מוּת 'to die' (v.4191). (c) How is this related to (b)? Is it 'he caused J. to die with a sword'?

וְיִשְׂרָאֵל גָּלֹה יִגְלֶה מֵעַל אַדְמָתוֹ׃[3]— (a) How used here? Cf. 7:10[2] above. (b) VDC–6, §29.71, Est. 2:6[1]. (c) Parse. (b+c) §35.6. (a-c) Word order for emphasis. (d) *min* + *'al*. (e) *'ăḏāmāʰ* 'ground, land' (v.127); cstr. *'aḏmaṯ* (< *'ăḏᵉmaṯ*, cf. R.19, R.10d).

Amos
7:12 וַיֹּאמֶר אֲמַצְיָה אֶל־עָמוֹס[1]— (b) Cf. 7:10 above. Who said to whom? Make the Heb. give you the translation. Where was Amos – near Jeroboam or near Amaziah?

חֹזֶה לֵךְ בְּרַח־לְךָ אֶל־אֶרֶץ יְהוּדָה[2]— (a) 'Seer' (v.2374), used of prophets, here in derision. (b) G32 of הלך. (c) ברח 'to flee' (v.1272), VDC–5. For asyndeton, §30.364. (d) Impv. is often followed by *lᵉḵā*, "ethical" dative, BDB 515.5.i(b). (g) *yᵉhûḏāʰ* 'Judah.' See art. in *NBD* or *IDB*; find Judah on a map of Israel and Judah in a Bible atlas. Locate Tekoa.

וֶאֱכָל־שָׁם לֶחֶם וְשָׁם תִּנָּבֵא׃[3]— (a) *wᵉ'ĕḵol* (*qāmāṣ-ḥăṭûp̄*), VDC–5; parse, translate. Est. 4:16[4]. (c) *léḥem* 'bread, food' (v.3899), perhaps sarcastically suggesting that Amos expected to earn his living by his prophetic activity. (e) *tinnāḇē'*, VDC–2. נבא N 'to prophesy' (v.5012). (b,d) Repetition of *šām* adds pointed emphasis: *there* eat bread and *there* prophesy.' Is (e) impv.?

7:13 וּבֵית־אֵל לֹא־תוֹסִיף עוֹד לְהִנָּבֵא[1]— (a) For *ûḇᵉbêʸṯ-'ēl*, 'but in Bethel.' Cf. 7:10[1]. (b) *lô'* with impf., §32.5215. (c) *tôsîp̄* < **tawsîp*, VDC–9. יסף 'to add' (v.3254), followed by inf., 'to do again, more,' BDB 728f. After יסף (e) would appear to be pleonastic – but it often occurs. (f) *lᵉhinnāḇē'*, VDC–2, §28.42.

כִּי מִקְדַּשׁ־מֶלֶךְ הוּא[2]— (a) Cf. 7:11[1]. How is *kî* used here? (b) *miqdāš* 'sanctuary' (v.4720), note vowels: abs. or cstr.? §24.33. (d) §21.2. This is a verbless clause, §31. 'For *that* is the king's sanctuary.'

וּבֵית מַמְלָכָה הוּא׃[3]— (b) 'Kingdom' (v.4467); *bêṯ mamlāḵā* is 'palace' or 'capital.' This also is a verbless clause.

7:14 וַיַּעַן עָמוֹס וַיֹּאמֶר אֶל־אֲמַצְיָה[1]— (a) Cf. Est. 5:7[1]. ענה 'to answer' (v.6030). What is the subj.? (c-e) Cf. Am. 7:12[1].

לֹא נָבִיא אָנֹכִי וְלֹא בֶן־נָבִיא אָנֹכִי[2]— (a) *lô'* may be used to negate a noun in a predicate, BDB 519.1b. (b) *nāḇî'* 'prophet' (v.5030). (a-c) Verbless clause. (c) §21.1, v.595. 'I (am) not a prophet.' (e-f) *ben-nāḇî'* 'son of a prophet,' probably meaning a member of a prophetic guild or school.

כִּי־בוֹקֵר אָנֹכִי וּבוֹלֵס שִׁקְמִים׃[3]— (a) After a neg., 'but,' BDB 474.3e. (b) Don't confuse with *bṓqer* (v.1242); *bôqḗr* is denominal (§24.51), from *bāqār* 'cattle, herd' (v.1241), meaning 'herdsman' (951 1/0). (a-c) Verbless cl., 'I (am/was) a herdsman.' (d) G52 (from an unused verb, בלס) 'pincher.' The sycamore fig needs to be bruised to make it edible. (e) *šiqmāʰ*, pl. *šiqmîm* 'sycamore fig' (8256 6/0). (d-e) Verbless cl., subj. omitted (§30.141), supply 'I.'

Note: This lesson is continued on page 109.

51

Purpose: To study direct and indirect discourse
Materials: Esther 6:3-6

וַיֹּאמֶר הַמֶּלֶךְ מַה־נַּעֲשָׂה יְקָר וּגְדוּלָּה 3
לְמָרְדֳּכַי עַל־זֶה וַיֹּאמְרוּ נַעֲרֵי הַמֶּלֶךְ מְשָׁרְתָיו לֹא־נַעֲשָׂה
עִמּוֹ דָּבָר׃ וַיֹּאמֶר הַמֶּלֶךְ מִי בֶחָצֵר וְהָמָן בָּא לַחֲצַר 4
בֵּית־הַמֶּלֶךְ הַחִיצוֹנָה לֵאמֹר לַמֶּלֶךְ לִתְלוֹת אֶת־מָרְדֳּכַי
עַל־הָעֵץ אֲשֶׁר־הֵכִין לוֹ׃ וַיֹּאמְרוּ נַעֲרֵי הַמֶּלֶךְ אֵלָיו הִנֵּה ה
הָמָן עֹמֵד בֶּחָצֵר וַיֹּאמֶר הַמֶּלֶךְ יָבוֹא׃ וַיָּבוֹא הָמָן וַיֹּאמֶר 6
לוֹ הַמֶּלֶךְ מַה־לַּעֲשׂוֹת בָּאִישׁ אֲשֶׁר הַמֶּלֶךְ חָפֵץ בִּיקָרוֹ
וַיֹּאמֶר הָמָן בְּלִבּוֹ לְמִי יַחְפֹּץ הַמֶּלֶךְ לַעֲשׂוֹת יְקָר יוֹתֵר
מִמֶּנִּי׃

6:3 מַה־נַּעֲשָׂה יְקָר וּגְדוּלָּה[1]— (a) Interrogative, §33.23. (b) ־ָה could be 10 of CCY; if so, what is –נ ? Try N10 of עשה in context. Why is there a dagesh in נּ ? §13.36. (c) 1:4[5], 'value, price, honor' (v.3366). (d) $g^e\underline{d}\hat{u}l\bar{a}^h$ 'greatness' (1420 12/3), 1:4[7]. 'What honor was done and greatness to/for M. on account of this?'

וַיֹּאמְרוּ נַעֲרֵי הַמֶּלֶךְ מְשָׁרְתָיו[2]— (b-c) 2:2[1]. (d) 1:10[7].

לֹא־נַעֲשָׂה עִמּוֹ דָּבָר׃[3]— (b) 6:3[1]. (c) *ʿim* 'with' < *ʿimm*; the suf. preserves the gemination. R.5, R.6a. (d) 'a thing.' דבר ... לא 'not a thing, nothing.'

6:4 מִי בֶחָצֵר[1]— (a) Interrog., מִי personal, מָה impers., §21.4. (b) 4:11[4]. Verbless cl., 'Who (is) in the court?' §33.23.

וְהָמָן בָּא לַחֲצַר בֵּית־הַמֶּלֶךְ הַחִיצוֹנָה[2]— (b) *bā'* could be G10 or G50, 'had entered, was entering.' (e) *ḥîṣôn, -ā*[h] 'outer(most)' (v.2435). ־וֹן *-ôn* often adds the superlative idea to a noun or adj., §24.431. What word does it modify? Cf. 4:11[4].

לֵאמֹר לַמֶּלֶךְ[3]— (a) Inf. of purpose, §38.54. l^e + *'ĕmōr* (cf. 5:14[3]) > *lē'mōr*, §15.54.

לִתְלוֹת אֶת־מָרְדֳּכַי עַל־הָעֵץ[4]—(a) Inf. cstr. in indir. disc., §38.82. Direct discourse would be, "... to say, 'Hang Haman' "; indir. disc., "... to say to hang Haman." (e) Why definite? Note following clause.

אֲשֶׁר־הֵכִין לוֹ׃[5]— (b) *hēḵîn*; study the forms in §29.632. כון H 'to set up, erect' (v.3559). (c) Dat. of advantage, 'for him.'

6:5 וַיֹּאמְרוּ נַעֲרֵי הַמֶּלֶךְ אֵלָיו[1]— You should be able to do this. Cf. 6:3[2]. (d) אֶל, like עַל, always brings back an original ־י when adding a suffix, cf. Table H.

הִנֵּה הָמָן עֹמֵד בֶּחָצֵר [2]— (a) *hinnê*^{h} 'behold!' (v.2009). (c) – ֵ –; would you recognize it if it were – ֵ–וֹ–? After הנה we often find the ptcp.

וַיֹּאמֶר הַמֶּלֶךְ יָבוֹא׃ [3]— (c) G20 or G40, here the latter: 'Let him enter.'

6:6 מַה־לַּעֲשׂוֹת בָּאִישׁ [1]— You should be able to do the first 2 clauses. (a-b) 1:15[2]. Why *pattāḥ* under ל ? (c) 'with the man.'

אֲשֶׁר הַמֶּלֶךְ חָפֵץ בִּיקָרוֹ [2]— A rel. cl. defining האיש. (c) *ḥāpēṣ* 'to delight, take pleasure in' (v.2654), note vowels and see §§27.23, .232. It could be G10 or G50 (§27.612). 2:14[7]. (d) 1:4[5], plus what morphemes? b^e + y^e > $bî^y$, §15.652.

בְּלִבּוֹ [3]— Cf. 5:9[2]. Explain form here. אמר בלבו is an idiom meaning 'to think.'

לְמִי יַחְפֹּץ הַמֶּלֶךְ לַעֲשׂוֹת יְקָר [4]— (a) *mî* cannot be inflected (as can, e.g., the Greek pron.), hence *l*^{e}*mî* for 'to whom.' (b) *ḥāpēṣ*, impf. *yaḥpōṣ*. We generally find yiCCaC as impf. of stative verbs (R.24, §27.331). 6:6[2]. 'To whom shall (would) the king delight to do honor?'

יוֹתֵר מִמֶּנִּי׃ [5]— (a) Formally G50 of יתר 'to remain, be left over' (v.3498), but it has become a noun in late Bib. Heb. 'more' (3148 8/1, 7x in Eccl.). (b) Cf. מִמֶּנָּה, ממנו 1:19[4], 5:9[4]. מִן of comparison (§38.74); translate 'more than me.'

Learn the words in Basic Group 44.

The following is the conclusion of Lesson 50, continued from page 107.

Amos

7:15 וַיִּקָּחֵנִי יְהוָה מֵאַחֲרֵי הַצֹּאן [1]—(a) *way|yiq|qā|ḥē|nî*: analyze it. It must be conv. impf.; 1st rad. geminate (VDC–2), hence it could be from *nqḥ*, but don't forget *lqḥ* (§29.45). -*ḗnî* is s4 with connecting vowel, §23.122, §23.1231, R.23. What is left is **yilqaḥ* > *yiqqaḥ*, and the form is Gc20s4 of לקח, cf. Est. 2:7[8]. (b) The sacred name (tetragrammaton) YHWH, read *'ădōnāy* '(my) lord' (§11.63), originally pronounced something like [i̯a-hə-u̯ɛ]. (c) *'aḥărê*^{y}, cf. Est. 2:1[1], + *min*, 'from after, from behind,' BDB 30.4a. (d) *ṣô'n* 'small cattle, flock, sheep and goats.'

וַיֹּאמֶר אֵלַי יְהוָה לֵךְ הִנָּבֵא אֶל־עַמִּי יִשְׂרָאֵל׃ [2]— (a) Who said? (b) *'ēl* + s4, indir. obj. (d) Am. 7:12[2]. (e) Cf. Am. 7:12[3], 7:13[1]; what is the form here? (g) Est. 1:5[4], here + s4. (h) Am. 7:10[2], here in apposition with *'ammî*.

Learn the basic words in Group 43.

52

Purpose: To study the use of prepositions
Materials: Esther 6:7-10

וַיֹּאמֶר הָמָן אֶל־הַמֶּלֶךְ אִישׁ אֲשֶׁר הַמֶּלֶךְ חָפֵץ 7
בִּיקָרוֹ׃ יָבִיאוּ לְבוּשׁ מַלְכוּת אֲשֶׁר לָבַשׁ־בּוֹ הַמֶּלֶךְ 8
וְסוּס אֲשֶׁר רָכַב עָלָיו הַמֶּלֶךְ וַאֲשֶׁר נִתַּן כֶּתֶר מַלְכוּת
בְּרֹאשׁוֹ׃ וְנָתוֹן הַלְּבוּשׁ וְהַסּוּס עַל־יַד־אִישׁ מִשָּׂרֵי הַמֶּלֶךְ 9
הַפַּרְתְּמִים וְהִלְבִּשׁוּ אֶת־הָאִישׁ אֲשֶׁר הַמֶּלֶךְ חָפֵץ בִּיקָרוֹ
וְהִרְכִּיבֻהוּ עַל־הַסּוּס בִּרְחוֹב הָעִיר וְקָרְאוּ לְפָנָיו כָּכָה
יֵעָשֶׂה לָאִישׁ אֲשֶׁר הַמֶּלֶךְ חָפֵץ בִּיקָרוֹ׃ וַיֹּאמֶר הַמֶּלֶךְ י
לְהָמָן מַהֵר קַח אֶת־הַלְּבוּשׁ וְאֶת־הַסּוּס כַּאֲשֶׁר דִּבַּרְתָּ
וַעֲשֵׂה־כֵן לְמָרְדֳּכַי הַיְּהוּדִי הַיּוֹשֵׁב בְּשַׁעַר הַמֶּלֶךְ אַל־
תַּפֵּל דָּבָר מִכֹּל אֲשֶׁר דִּבַּרְתָּ׃

6:7 You should be able to do this entire verse. Cf. 6:6[2].

6:8 יָבִיאוּ לְבוּשׁ מַלְכוּת[1]—(a) *yāḇî'û*: long *î* tells us what? VDC–9. G20/40, here probably juss., 'Let them bring.' (b) *l*[e]*ḇûš* 'clothing,' 4:2[3]. (b-c) How would you translate this idiom? Cf. 1:7[4].

אֲשֶׁר לָבַשׁ־בּוֹ הַמֶּלֶךְ[2]—(a) *'ăšer* cannot be inflected, hence a resumptive prep. phr. is needed (c): *'ăšer* … *bô* = 'in which' (§36.43). (b) *lāḇaš* – do you have any trouble parsing this form? Cf. 4:1[3]. Since the impf. is *yilbaš*, we would expect perf. *lāḇēš* or *lāḇōš* (R.24, §27.331), and the form *lāḇēš* does occur.

וְסוּס אֲשֶׁר רָכַב עָלָיו הַמֶּלֶךְ[3]—(a) *sûs* 'horse' (v.5483). (b) *'ăšer* … *'āla*[y]*w*, cf. note on 6:8[2](a) and §36.43. Translate 'on which.' (c) *rāḵaḇ* 'he mounted and rode' (v.7392); we would say simply, 'on which the king rode.'

וַאֲשֶׁר נִתַּן כֶּתֶר מַלְכוּת בְּרֹאשׁוֹ׃[4]—(a,e) Again, translate 'on whose head,' §36.43. (b) 4:8[2]. (c-d) 2:17[5].

6:9 וְנָתוֹן הַלְּבוּשׁ וְהַסּוּס[1]—(a) –ֹו–ָ is G60 (§27.64); 'and to give' = 'let them give.' (b) 6:8[1]. (c) 6:8[3].

עַל־יַד־אִישׁ מִשָּׂרֵי הַמֶּלֶךְ הַפַּרְתְּמִים[2]—(a-b) 'upon the hand of' = 'by.' RSV 'And let the robes and the horse be handed over to one of the king's most noble princes.' (d) מִן partitive, 'from the princes.' (f) 1:3[11]. The word is in apposition with שרי המלך, to define the princes more closely.

וְהִלְבִּשׁוּ אֶת־הָאִישׁ[3]—(a) ה–ִ–י–ּו must be H15 – do you know why? H of לבש means 'to clothe someone.' This is Hc15, continuing a juss., hence to be translated, 'and let them (the princes) clothe the man ....' (§32.544). You should be able to do the rest of the cl. 6:6[1,2].

וְהִרְכִּיבֻהוּ עַל־הַסּוּס בִּרְחוֹב הָעִיר[4]—(a) Take it apart: וְ|הִרְכִּיבֻ|הוּ. *hirkîḇû* is obviously H15, with final vowel written defectively. Ancient scribes seem to have avoided plēnē writing of one vowel if two were in the form. הוּ– is s0 (Table H). –וְ is conv., hence Hc15s0, continuing a juss., 'and let them mount him on the horse.' (d) *r^{e}ḥôḇ* 4:6[2]. (e) 3:15[5].

וְקָרְאוּ לְפָנָיו[5]—(a) Gc15, see previous notes. A conv. perf. may be used to continue the tense and mood of a previous verb, §§32.542-.546.

כָּכָה יֵעָשֶׂה[6]—(a) *kāḵā^{h}* 'thus' (v.3602), adds a bit of emphasis. (b) This cannot be juss. for it is not apocopated (§29.72). 2:11[5]. You can finish the verse.

6:10 מַהֵר קַח אֶת־הַלְּבוּשׁ[1]—(a) Cf. 5:5[1]. *māhēr* < **mahhēr*, D32, 'Hurry!' (b) *qaḥ* < *l^{e}qaḥ* (§29.45). Cf. 2:7[8]. Form here is G32. **l^{e}qaḥ* could also be G65, but the inf. cstr. adds ballast-*t* after apheresis > *qáḥaṯ*, not found in Est. You should be able to complete the clause.

כַּאֲשֶׁר דִּבַּרְתָּ[2]—(a) 2:20[4]. (b) תָּ--- is what? (§27.21). תָּ-ַ-ִ is what stem? (§28.21). Note *i* > *a* (§15.33). For דבר, 1:22[7]. 'According as you have spoken.'

וַעֲשֵׂה־כֵן לְמָרְדֳּכַי[3]—(a) Be careful! וַ|עֲשֵׂה: *GăCē^{h}* < C^{e}CaC GCY, pattern is impv. (§27.423). The –וַ is *not* conversive! (Conv. *wāw* is only found on impf. and perf.) 'And do thus.' Complete the clause.

הַיּוֹשֵׁב בְּשַׁעַר הַמֶּלֶךְ[4]—(a) Ptcp. with def. art. often used as a relative clause (§38.421), 'who (was) sitting.' Complete the clause.

אַל־תַּפֵּל דָּבָר מִכֹּל אֲשֶׁר דִּבַּרְתָּ׃[5]—(a) אל is the neg. used with juss. (§35.222). (b) *tappēl* < **tanpēl*, vowels are our clues: H42 (§28.31). There is no neg. of impv.; to give a negative command in Heb., the following are used: לא + impv. (very strong), or אל + juss. (less strong). For נפל, 3:7[3]. (c) 'Thing.' 'Don't let a thing fall from all you have spoken.' (f) 6:10[2].

Learn the meanings of the words in Group 45.

Study the following uses of the participle:

hammélek̠ yôšēḇ ʿal kissēʾ malk̠ûṯô (5:1[5]) 'the king was sitting on his throne'
ʾestēr hammalkā^{h} ʿômédeṯ (5:2[2]) 'Queen Esther was standing'
wayyêṣēʾ hāmā ... śāmē^{a}ḥ (5:9[2]) 'and Haman went out rejoicing'
b^{e}k̠ol-ʿēṯ ʾăšer ʾănî rôʾē^{h} ʾeṯ-mord^{e}k̠ay yôšēḇ b^{e}šáʿar hammélek̠ (5:13[2]) 'every time I see M. sitting in the king's gate'
hayy^{e}hûḏîm hannimṣ^{e}ʾîm b^{e}šûšān (4:16[2]) 'the Jews who are found in Susa'
hayy^{e}hûḏî hayyôšēḇ b^{e}šáʿar hammélek̠ (6:10[4]) 'the Jew who sits in the king's gate'
naʿărê hammélek̠ m^{e}šār^{e}ṯā^{y}w (6:3[2]) 'the king's servants who minister to him'

53

Purpose: To review the student's progress
Materials: Esther 4:1–6:10

In the following groups of words, a Rule is illustrated by one of the words. Identify the word that illustrates the Rule.

Rule 2a וְיִּפְקֵד, (b) יִכְתֹּב, (c) יַֽעֲבוֹר, (d) קֹדֶשׁ, (e) עַם
Rule 8. (a) וְכָתוּב, (b) וּתְדַבֵּר, (c) אָצוּם, (d) כְּטוֹב, (e) וּמָרְדֳּכַי
Rule 10c. (a) יֶֽאֱהַב, (b) יֹאמַר, (c) יַֽעֲבֹר, (d) נַֽעֲרָה, (e) עַיִן
Rule 11. (a) מִדְבָּר, (b) וַיִּשָּׂא, (c) מֵאָה, (d) מִכָּל־, (e) בְּהִקָּבֵץ
Rule 14. (a) טַף, (b) הַמֶּלֶךְ, (c) כְּיַד, (d) אֵם, (e) עֵת, (f) חֹק
Rule 16. (a) יוֹדְעֵי, (b) שְׁמוֹ, (c) וַיִּשְׁלַח, (d) הַיּוֹשְׁבִים, (e) יְקַטְּלוּ
Rule 19. (a) בִּשְׁנַת, (b) יִקְטְלוּ, (c) כִּכְתָבָהּ, (d) מִדְבָּר, (e) יִקְטֹל
Rule 21. (a) אֲחַשְׁוֵרוֹשׁ, (b) חֳדָשִׁים, (c) יַֽעֲבֹר, (d) לַֽעֲשׂוֹת, (e) וַֽחֲמֹרוֹ

You will be given a sight passage, similar to the one printed below, and asked a number of questions about it. These questions are such as you should ask yourself when working on a new passage. Observe them carefully.

וַיָּ֫מָת כִּדְבַר־יְהוָ֫ה | אֲשֶׁר־דִּבֶּר אֵלִיָּ֫הוּ וַיִּמְלֹךְ יְהוֹרָם תַּחְתָּיו בִּשְׁנַת שְׁתַּיִם לִיהוֹרָם בֶּן־יְהוֹשָׁפָט מֶלֶךְ יְהוּדָ֑ה כִּי לֹא־הָיָה לוֹ בֵּן׃ וְיֶתֶר דִּבְרֵי אֲחַזְיָהוּ אֲשֶׁר עָשָׂ֑ה הֲלוֹא־הֵמָּה כְתוּבִים עַל־סֵפֶר דִּבְרֵי הַיָּמִים לְמַלְכֵי יִשְׂרָאֵל׃

Parse these verbal forms: וַיָּמָת (1); דִּבֶּר (1); וַיִּמְלֹךְ (1); כְּתוּבִים (4).

Parse these nonverbal forms: כִּדְבַר (1); בִּשְׁנַת (2); דִּבְרֵי (3); הֲלוֹא (4).

Explain the use of these prepositions: כִּדְבַר (1); בִּשְׁנַת (2); תַּחְתָּיו (2), לִיהוֹרָם (2); לוֹ (3); עַל (4); לְמַלְכֵי (4).

Describe or explain the dageshes in: וַיָּמָת (1); כִּדְבַר (1); דִּבֶּר (1); שְׁתַּיִם (2); בֵּן (3); הֵמָּה (4); הַיָּמִים (4).

What is the difference between: יְהוֹרָם (2) and יְהוּדָה (3)? between לֹא (3) and לוֹא (4)?

Which words have a pronominal suffix: אֵלִיָּהוּ (1); תַּחְתָּיו (2); לִיהוֹרָם (2); יְהוּדָה (3); לוֹ (3); דִּבְרֵי (3)?

What is meant by the terms: "perpetual Q^{e}re" – יְהוָה (1); "full (plene) writing" – הֲלוֹא (4); "patronymic" – בֶּן־יְהוֹשָׁפָט (2).

Work out the following proper nouns by transliteration and normalization: אֵלִיָּהוּ (1); יְהוֹשָׁפָט (2); אֲחַזְיָהוּ (3); יִשְׂרָאֵל (5).

What kind of clause is introduced by: אֲשֶׁר (1); כִּי (3); הֲלוֹא (4)?

Parse these verbal forms: וַיָּמָת (1); דִּבֶּר (1); וַיִּמְלֹךְ (1); כְּתוּבִים (4).

Parse these nonverbal forms: כִּדְבַר (1); בִּשְׁנַת (2); דִּבְרֵי (3); הֲלוֹא (4).

Explain the use of these prepositions: כִּדְבַר (1); בִּשְׁנַת (2); תַּחְתָּיו (2), לִיהוֹרָם (2); לוֹ (3); עַל (4); לְמַלְכֵי (4).

Describe or explain the dageshes in: וַיָּמָת (1); כִּדְבַר (1); דִּבֶּר (1); שְׁתַּיִם (2); בֵּן (3); הֵמָּה (4); הַיָּמִים (4).

What is the difference between: יְהוֹרָם (2) and יְהוּדָה (3)? between לֹא (3) and לוֹא (4)?

Which words have a pronominal suffix: אֵלִיָּהוּ (1); תַּחְתָּיו (2); לִיהוֹרָם (2); יְהוּדָה (3); לוֹ (3); דִּבְרֵי (3)?

What is meant by the terms: "perpetual Qᵉre" – יְהוָה (1); "full (plene) writing" – aWlḥ (4); "patronymic" – בֶּן־יְהוֹשָׁפָט (2).

Work out the following proper nouns by transliteration and normalization: אֵלִיָּהוּ (1); יְהוֹשָׁפָט (2); אֲחַזְיָהוּ (3); יִשְׂרָאֵל (5).

What kind of clause is introduced by: אֲשֶׁר (1); כִּי (3); הֲלוֹא (4)?

Which are the more nearly correct translations:
בִּשְׁנַת שְׁתַּיִם (2) 'in the second year' or 'in two years'?
אֲשֶׁר דִּבֶּר אֵלִיָּהוּ (1) 'who spoke unto him,' 'which Elijah spoke' or 'which was the word of Eliyahu'?
וַיִּמְלֹךְ יְהוֹרָם תַּחְתָּיו (1-2) 'and he reigned over Judah in his place,' 'and Jehoram succeeded him as king' or 'and he placed their law under him'?
כִּי לֹא הָיָה לוֹ בֵּן (3) 'when his son was not with him,' 'for he was not with us' or 'since he had no son'?
סֵפֶר דִּבְרֵי הַיָּמִים לְמַלְכֵי יִשְׂרָאֵל (4-5) 'he told those words to the kings of Israel, 'the book of the chronicles of the kings of Israel' or 'to guard those words for the kings of Israel' ?
Who died? (a) Jehoram, (b) Jehoshaphat, (c) Ahaziah, (d) Elijah.
Who had no son? (a) Jehoram, (b) Jehoshaphat, (c) Ahaziah, (d) Judah.
Who reigned in the place of him who died? (a) Jehoram, (b) Jehoshaphat, (c) Ahaziah, (d) Israel.

שִׁפְטוּ־דַל וְיָתוֹם עָנִי וָרָשׁ הַצְדִּיקוּ׃
Give justice to the weak and the fatherless:
Maintain the right of the afflicted and the destitute.
Psalm 82:3

54

Purpose: To note types of clauses
Materials: Esther 6:11-14

וַיִּקַּח הָמָן אֶת־הַלְּבוּשׁ
וְאֶת־הַסּוּס וַיַּלְבֵּשׁ אֶת־מָרְדֳּכָי וַיַּרְכִּיבֵהוּ בִּרְחוֹב הָעִיר
וַיִּקְרָא לְפָנָיו כָּכָה יֵעָשֶׂה לָאִישׁ אֲשֶׁר הַמֶּלֶךְ חָפֵץ בִּיקָרוֹ׃
12 וַיָּשָׁב מָרְדֳּכַי אֶל־שַׁעַר הַמֶּלֶךְ וְהָמָן נִדְחַף אֶל־בֵּיתוֹ אָבֵל
13 וַחֲפוּי רֹאשׁ׃ וַיְסַפֵּר הָמָן לְזֶרֶשׁ אִשְׁתּוֹ וּלְכָל־אֹהֲבָיו
אֵת כָּל־אֲשֶׁר קָרָהוּ וַיֹּאמְרוּ לוֹ חֲכָמָיו וְזֶרֶשׁ אִשְׁתּוֹ אִם
מִזֶּרַע הַיְּהוּדִים מָרְדֳּכַי אֲשֶׁר הַחִלּוֹתָ לִנְפֹּל לְפָנָיו לֹא־
14 תוּכַל לוֹ כִּי־נָפוֹל תִּפּוֹל לְפָנָיו׃ עוֹדָם מְדַבְּרִים עִמּוֹ
וְסָרִיסֵי הַמֶּלֶךְ הִגִּיעוּ וַיַּבְהִלוּ לְהָבִיא אֶת־הָמָן אֶל־הַמִּשְׁתֶּה
אֲשֶׁר־עָשְׂתָה אֶסְתֵּר׃

6:11 וַיִּקַּח הָמָן[1]—(a) *yiqqaḥ* < +*yilqaḥ*, cf. 6:10[1]. לקח behaves as an NCC verb (§29.45). Complete the clause, 6:8[1,3], 6:10[1].

וַיַּלְבֵּשׁ אֶת־מָרְדֳּכַי[2]— (a) Compare יִלְבַּשׁ 4:1[3] and יַלְבִּשׁ. What is the difference? Vowel under preformative tells us what? Vowel after 2d rad. tells us what? Form here is Hc20 – translate it.

וַיַּרְכִּיבֵהוּ בִּרְחוֹב הָעִיר[3]— (a) Analyze it. Cf. 6:9[4]. Note difference in connecting vowels. –ִי–ֵ– tells us what? For the rest of clause, 6:9[4].

וַיִּקְרָא לְפָנָיו[4]— (a) Cf. 6:9[5]. Explain the difference here. You should be able to do the rest of the verse with the help of 6:9[6].

6:12 וַיָּשָׁב מָרְדֳּכַי[1]—(a) *wayyā́šoḇ* (*qāmāṣ ḥăṭûp̄*!) < *yāšûḇ*. Impf. *yāšûḇ* < **yašûbu*, but Gc20 or G40 > *yāšōḇ* (R.2a). With conv. *wāw* accent shifts, *way* + *yāšōḇ* > *wayyā́šoḇ* (R.27). Be sure to note the differences between CWC and WCC/YCC. §32.5311.

וְהָמָן נִדְחָף[2]—(a) Note position of subj. (b) *niḏḥap̄*: the 3 rads. must be ד ח פ, since ף cannot be a sufformative or suffix. נ must therefore be either 29- or N-indicator. Which fits context? For *dḥp*, 3:15[2]. For use of N, §32.83.

אָבֵל וַחֲפוּי רֹאשׁ׃[3]—(a) *'āḇēl* 'mourning' (v.56). (b) *ḥăp̄ûy*: note vowels (cstr., reduced from ָ–*û*–); what must it be? Note 3d rad. *yôḏ*. cf. §29.7. חפה 'to cover' (2645 12/2). Gp50 of CCY –ָ–וּי, of CCW –ָ–וּו (rare). §32.3712. (c) 2:17[5].

6:13 וַיְסַפֵּר הָמָן לְזֶרֶשׁ אִשְׁתּוֹ[1]–(a) 5:11[1]. For balance cf. 5:10[3,4].

אֵת כָּל־אֲשֶׁר קָרָהוּ[2]—(a-c) Obj. of the following verb, §34.1.33. (d) This could be G15 of קָרָה, but no such verb is listed. ־ָהוּ could be s0 (Table H); if so, verb must be CCY. 4:7[2]. §32.5114.

וַיֹּאמְרוּ לוֹ חֲכָמָיו[3]—(a) Review §29.212. Form is yaqtil. (b) Masoretic note calls attention to dagesh, without explanation. It would appear that the words were read as one, *wayyō̆'mᵉrûllô*. §35.111. (c) 1:13[1]; explain form and vocalization. §33.13.

אִם מִזֶּרַע הַיְּהוּדִים מָרְדֳּכַי[4]—(a) Introduces conditional cl., §38.6111; read §38.6. (b) *zéraʿ* 'seed' (v.2233), review §24.211. מִן of origin. (d) Subj. of verbless cl., §31.11, §31.62.

אֲשֶׁר הַחִלּוֹתָ לִנְפֹּל לְפָנָיו[5]—(a-d) Rel. cl., §38.42. 'who . . . before him' = 'before whom.' (b) *haḥillôṯā*: (1) -ה could be stem indicator, §28.3. (2) תָ- must be PGN morpheme (§27.21). (3) -וֹ- after ל with dagesh could be epenthetic (R.26). This leaves a root חלל H 'to begin' (v.2490). This verb generally requires a complement. (c) Note נ, violating R.11, *linpōl*. §§29.412, .42, §27.6511. 3:7[3]. §34.8.

לֹא־תוּכַל לוֹ[6]—This is the main cl. (apodosis) of the condition, §38.612. (b) *tûḵal* is generally identified as Hp22 of יכל (*Ges.* §53*u*, 69*r*), but it is impf. < **tiwkal*, and has no causative significance. יכל 'to be able, prevail' (v.3201). *lô'* + impf. need not be prohibitive; it may be a simple statement, 'you will not prevail over (ל) him.' §32.5211.

כִּי־נָפוֹל תִּפּוֹל לְפָנָיו׃[7]—(a) Adversative, introducing a second apodosis. (b) Pattern tells us what? §27.64. For the use of inf. abs. to strengthen a finite verb, see §35.6. It is difficult to translate, here perhaps 'surely.' (c) VDC–7. Cf. 6:10[5]. Is the form yiqtal or yaqtul?.

6:14 עוֹדָם מְדַבְּרִים עִמּוֹ[1]—(a) עוֹד 'yet, still' (v.5750), can take a pron. suf. and serve in a verbless clause, translated by a form of the verb *to be* (cf. אין, יש). Here + s5, they (were) still speaking.' (b) מְ-ִ-ים there are enough clues for you to parse the form. 6:10[2], 1:22[7]. (c) 6:3[3].

וְסָרִיסֵי הַמֶּלֶךְ הִגִּיעוּ [2]—(a) *wᵉ*- is best translated 'when' in this context. If you have forgotten this word, cf. 1:10[6], 6:2[2]. (c) Cf. 4:14[5], 4:3[1]. וּ- is what morpheme? Is it any different than הִ-ִי-וּ? Be sure you recognize the basic morphemes, regardless of where they occur.

וַיַּבְהִלוּ לְהָבִיא אֶת־הָמָן[3]-(a) Note the clues: וַיְ-ַ-ִ-וּ. (1) *way*- tells us what? §32.53. (2) ַ under preformative, ִ after 2d rad. (written fully or defectively?) tell us what? VDC–3. (3) י---וּ tells us what? §27.31. For בהל 2:9[3]. (b) §34.8. You should recognize the form. 3:9[5].

אֶל־הַמִּשְׁתֶּה [4]—This clause should be fairly easy. Cf. 5:12[1,2].

Learn the words in BVG–46.

55

Purpose: To introduce exegesis of poetry
Materials: Micah 6:6-8

This lesson serves not only to study a great prophetic passage, but also to introduce Hebrew poetry. Fundamental to Heb. poetry is *parallelism,* generally found in a *distich* composed of two *stichs* (*stichoi*), or a *tristich* composed of three stichs. The parallelism may be expressed by stichs that are synonymous, or antithetical, or in expanding idea, or sometimes in other forms. See the article on "Poetry" in *IDB* 3:829-838

6:6 בַּמָּה אֲקַדֵּם יְהוָה || אִכַּף לֵאלֹהֵי מָרוֹם[1]—The siglum || indicates parallel stichs. (a) b^e- + ma^h, BDB 553.4a. (b) *qdm* 'to go before' (v.6923), VDC–1. (d) *kpp* 'to bend, bow down' (3721 5x), N24. (f) *mārôm* 'height' (v.4791) = heaven, BDB 496. Isa. 33:5; 57:15. The first stich consists of p (prep.), v (verb), o (obj.); the 2d stich of v′ O′. The prep. phrase is omitted, and a noun-phrase is used. The 2d verb (v′) is synonymous with the 1st (v), and O′ is synonymous with o. This is parallelism.

הַאֲקַדְּמֶנּוּ בְעוֹלוֹת || בַּעֲגָלִים בְּנֵי שָׁנָה׃[2]—(a) *h*-interrog. *'ăqadd^{e}ménnû* has *nûn energ.* + s0 (§23.1221), cf. (b) in preceding distich. Who is the antecedent of *-énnû*? Verb and obj. are combined into one word. (b) b^e- 'with, by means of.' *'ôlā^h* 'holocaust' (v.5930), G51 of עלה. (c) *'ēgel* 'calf' (v.5695). (d-e) *bēn* + a number (of years) = age, here 'a year old.' Note that 'with year-old calves' is the entire 2d stich, paralleling 'with burnt offerings.' We might represent the distich as v-o p || P′.

6:7 הֲיִרְצֶה יְהוָה בְּאַלְפֵי אֵילִים || בְּרִבְבוֹת נַחֲלֵי־שָׁמֶן[1]—(a) Interrog. רצה 'to be pleased with, accept' (BVG-9). (c) *'élep̄* BVG-29. (d) *'áyil* 'ram' (v.352). This stich consists of v, s(ubj.), p. (e) *rib̲^{e}b̲ôt̲* 'myriad' (v.7233). (f) *náḥal* 'river' (v.5158) (g) *šémen* 'oil' (BVG-21). This stich consists of only a prep. phrase P′, which is synonymous with 'thousands of rams' (i.e. as an offering). We may therefore diagram the distich as: v s p || P′.

הַאֶתֵּן בְּכוֹרִי פִּשְׁעִי || פְּרִי בִטְנִי חַטַּאת נַפְשִׁי׃[2]—(a) *h*- interrog. Have you forgotten נתן? (b) *b^{e}k̲ôr* 'first-born' (v.1060) + s4. (c) *péša'* 'transgression, rebellion' (v.6587) + s4. 'Shall I give my first-born (for) my transgression?' (d) *p^{e}rî* 'fruit' (v.6529), cstr. (e) *béṭen* 'belly, womb, body' (v.990) + s4. (f) *ḥaṭṭa't̲* 'sin, sin-offering' (v.2403), cstr. But since the parallel word is *péša'*, which cannot mean 'tresspass-offering,' we must translate *ḥaṭṭa't̲* here as 'sin.' (g) BVG-35. Note that the verb is omitted in the 2d stich, 'fruit of my body' צצ 'my first-born' and 'sin of my soul' || 'my transgression.' v o_1 o_2 || O_1' O_2'.

6:8 ||הִגִּיד לְךָ אָדָם מַה־טּוֹב||[1]—(a) Est. 2:10[1]. Indef. subj. = passive (*Ges.* §144*d*, LXX ἀνηγγέλη); it is also possible to consider YHWH as the subj. (c) *'āḏām* 'man (generic, male and female)' (v.120), vocative. (d-e) Verbless cl., obj. of *higgîḏ*. I take this as a stich, parallel with the next.

וּמָה יְהוָה דּוֹרֵשׁ מִמְּךָ[2]—(a) Indef. pron. (§21.5), obj. of *dôrēš*. (b) Subj. of following ptcp. (c) *drš* 'to seek' (v.1875). (d) §23.1231. 'One made clear to you, O man, what is good || and what YHWH is seeking from you.' There are other ways of analyzing this portion.

|| כִּי אִם־עֲשׂוֹת מִשְׁפָּט[3]—(a-b) 'But, except.' This may indicate that the preceding *māʰ*-clause is interrog. (c) G65 in elliptical cl., 'He [is seeking from you] to do ....' (d) *mišpāṭ* 'judgment (the act, the sentence, the execution)' (v.4941, BDB 1048f, cf. Leon Morris, *The Biblical Doctrine of Judgment* [1960] 7-25).

|| וְאַהֲבַת חֶסֶד[4]—I understand this as the second stich in a tristich. (a) *'ăhāḇāʰ* 'love' (v.160), cstr. (b) *ḥésed* is a very important and rich word, which we shall study further in Lesson 60. 'Mercy' is too restricted a meaning; 'covenant loyalty, fidelity to the covenantal obligations' is closer. Cf. N. Glueck, Hesed *in the Bible* (1967).

וְהַצְנֵעַ לֶכֶת עִם־אֱלֹהֶיךָ׃[5]—(a) *ṣnʿ* 'to be modest, humble' (6800 1x), H60 used as adv. (b) We might expect לָלֶכֶת. (c) *'im* 'with' of accompaniment. 'Your God' could mean any god, but this is highly unlikely in a strong prophet of YHWH.

If I have analyzed this correctly, the tristich, as often, serves to bring the passage to a climax. The last word has not yet been written on Hebrew poetry. The discovery of Ugaritic poetry has made obsolete a number of former theories. The student should study the poetical passages in the Bible, rather than read about them in other books. Facts should always control theories.

For further study of poetry, cf. Stanley Gevirtz, *Patterns in the Early Poetry of Israel* (1963); Theodore H. Robinson, *The Poetry of the Old Testament* (1947); and G. Buchanan Gray, *The Forms of Hebrew Poetry* (1915). My study, "An Approach to Hebrew Poetry through the Masoretic Accents," is scheduled for publication in an early issue of *Jewish Quarterly Review*.

Learn the Words in Vocabulary Group 47.

שַׁאֲלוּ שְׁלוֹם יְרוּשָׁלִָם יִשְׁלָיוּ אֹהֲבָיִךְ׃

Pray for Jerusalem's peace; those that love thee shall have tranquillity.

Psalm 122:6

Purpose: To study conditional clauses
Materials: Esther 7:1-4

CAP. VII. ז

ז
א 2 וַיָּבֹא הַמֶּלֶךְ וְהָמָן לִשְׁתּוֹת עִם־אֶסְתֵּר הַמַּלְכָּה׃ וַיֹּאמֶר
הַמֶּלֶךְ לְאֶסְתֵּר גַּם בַּיּוֹם הַשֵּׁנִי בְּמִשְׁתֵּה הַיַּיִן מַה־שְּׁאֵלָתֵךְ
אֶסְתֵּר הַמַּלְכָּה וְתִנָּתֵן לָךְ וּמַה־בַּקָּשָׁתֵךְ עַד־חֲצִי הַמַּלְכוּת
3 וְתֵעָשׂ׃ וַתַּעַן אֶסְתֵּר הַמַּלְכָּה וַתֹּאמַר אִם־מָצָאתִי חֵן
בְּעֵינֶיךָ הַמֶּלֶךְ וְאִם־עַל־הַמֶּלֶךְ טוֹב תִּנָּתֶן־לִי נַפְשִׁי
4 בִּשְׁאֵלָתִי וְעַמִּי בְּבַקָּשָׁתִי׃ כִּי נִמְכַּרְנוּ אֲנִי וְעַמִּי לְהַשְׁמִיד
לַהֲרוֹג וּלְאַבֵּד וְאִלּוּ לַעֲבָדִים וְלִשְׁפָחוֹת נִמְכַּרְנוּ הֶחֱרַשְׁתִּי
ה כִּי אֵין הַצָּר שֹׁוֶה בְּנֵזֶק הַמֶּלֶךְ׃

7:1 לִשְׁתּוֹת[1]—Note *wayyāḇô'* with compound subj., and see §33.124. (a) Inf. of purpose, §35.423. VDC–6. 3:15[4].

עִם־אֶסְתֵּר[2]—(a) Note difference between *b*^{e}- 'with' (instrument) and *ʿim* 'with' (accompaniment). See BDB 767f.

7:2 גַּם בַּיּוֹם הַשֵּׁנִי[1]—(a) 1:9[1] (v.1571). (b-c) 2:14[3], 1:10[1]. For balance, cf. 5:6.

7:3 תִּנָּתֶן לִי נַפְשִׁי בִּשְׁאֵלָתִי[1]—For several parts of this verse, cf. 5:6-8. (a) 2:13[3]. What is the difference? (c) 4:13[2]. (d) Note suffix, cf. 5:7[2]. Various explanations of –בְּ: price, essence, instrument, etc. When we have a lot of repetition from a previous passage, it's a good time for careful review.

וְעַמִּי בְּבַקָּשָׁתִי׃[2]—(a) Second subj. of *tinnāṯen lî*; verb agrees with nearer, §33.123. (b) 7:3[1]. 5:7[2].

7:4 כִּי נִמְכַּרְנוּ אֲנִי וְעַמִּי[1]—(a) Causal, §38.53, BDB 473.3. (b) נִ—וּ: if *-nû* is sufformative, *ni-* must be stem-indicator. Why? *mkr* 'to sell' (v.4376). Parse first, then translate. (c-d) Compound subj., §33.1111 not applying. 7:1[1].

לְהַשְׁמִיד לַהֲרוֹג וּלְאַבֵּד[2]—Cf. 3:13[3]. Here we might expect passives, but the Heb. inf. cstr. is a verbal adj. and can be translated 'for destruction, etc.' §30.381

וְאִלּוּ לַעֲבָדִים וְלִשְׁפָחוֹת נִמְכַּרְנוּ[3]—(a) *'illû* (< *'in lû*) 'if indeed' (432 2/1), followed by perf. it represents a contrary-to-fact condition, §38.6112. (b) 'for, as.' 1:3[7]. (c) *šip̄ḥā*^{h} 'female slave' (v.8198). (d) §38.6112. 7:4[1].

הֶחֱרַשְׁתִּי[4]—R.10c. *ḥrš* 'to be silent, dumb' (v.2790a). Strong lists it under *ḥrš* 'to plow,' but one is from PS **ḥrθ*, the other from PS **ḫrš*. Study conditional clauses. This is contrary-to-fact, 'If we had been sold ...' (we weren't; we were condemned to death), 'I would have kept silent' (I didn't; I'm speaking out.' §32.514.

כִּי אֵין הַצָּר שֹׁוֶה[5]—(a) §38.53. (b) אֵין negates ptcp. (c) *ṣār* is usually translated 'enemy' (v.6862), but this is from *ṣrr*, and should be *ṣar* (R.14). *ṣār* could be from צוּר*, cf. Arab. *ḍâr* 'to injure, harm,' and if so, we could read it, 'the harm would not be equal to ....' RSV translates 'our affliction,' cf. v.6862b. (d) *šôwêʰ*, cf. 3:8[7]; 'worth' fits here and in 3:8 and 5:13

בְּנֵזֶק הַמֶּלֶךְ׃[6]—(a) *nḗzeq* 'damage, injury' (5143 1/1). 'Damage of the king' = that suffered by the king, objective genitive. Cf. RSV.

Memorize the meanings of the words in BVG–48.

Study the following pronominal suffixes:

בַּעֲלֵיהֶן	שְׁנֵיהֶם	עַמָּהּ	עַמּוֹ	מַלְכוּתֵךְ	עָלַי
בְּעֵינֵיהֶן	לָהֶם	לָהּ	לוֹ	לָךְ	לִי
תַּמְרֻקֵיהֶן	דָּתֵיהֶם	תַּמְרוּקֶיהָ	מַלְכוּתוֹ	בְּעֵינַיִךְ	מוֹלַדְתִּי
	בְּאָמְרָם	יְפֵיָהּ	לְמַלְכּוֹ	אָבִיךְ	נַעֲרֹתַי
	אוֹתָם	מִמֶּנָּה	מִמֶּנּוּ		מִמֶּנִּי
	עֲלֵיהֶם	מְנוֹתֶיהָ	גְּדוּלָּתוֹ	בַּקָּשָׁתֵךְ	בַּקָּשָׁתִי
	אֵינָם	מוֹלַדְתָּהּ	חֲמָתוֹ	שְׁאֵלָתֵךְ	שְׁאֵלָתִי

Note the following pronominal suffixes:

'ôṯî *me*
'ēlî to *me*
'ālay on *my* behalf
'āḥî my brother
'aḥay *my* brothers
šᵉlāḥánî he sent *me*
wayyišlāḥḗnî and he sent *me*
šᵉ'ēlāṯî *my* petition
na'ărôṯay *my* maids

מִצִּיּוֹן מִכְלַל־יֹפִי אֱלֹהִים הוֹפִיעַ׃
Out of Zion, the perfection of beauty, God shines forth.
Psalm 50:2

57

Purpose: To study the use of the converted imperfect
Materials: Esther 7:5-8

וַיֹּ֣אמֶר הַמֶּ֗לֶךְ
אֲחַשְׁוֵר֔וֹשׁ וַיֹּ֛אמֶר לְאֶסְתֵּ֥ר הַמַּלְכָּ֖ה מִ֣י ה֥וּא זֶה֙ וְאֵֽי־זֶ֣ה
6 ה֔וּא אֲשֶׁר־מְלָא֥וֹ לִבּ֖וֹ לַעֲשׂ֥וֹת כֵּֽן: וַתֹּ֣אמֶר אֶסְתֵּ֔ר אִ֚ישׁ
צַ֣ר וְאוֹיֵ֔ב הָמָ֥ן הָרָ֖ע הַזֶּ֑ה וְהָמָ֣ן נִבְעַ֔ת מִלִּפְנֵ֥י הַמֶּ֖לֶךְ
7 וְהַמַּלְכָּֽה: וְהַמֶּ֜לֶךְ קָ֤ם בַּחֲמָתוֹ֙ מִמִּשְׁתֵּ֣ה הַיַּ֔יִן אֶל־גִּנַּ֖ת
הַבִּיתָ֑ן וְהָמָ֣ן עָמַ֗ד לְבַקֵּ֤שׁ עַל־נַפְשׁוֹ֙ מֵֽאֶסְתֵּ֣ר הַמַּלְכָּ֔ה כִּ֣י
8 רָאָ֔ה כִּֽי־כָלְתָ֥ה אֵלָ֛יו הָרָעָ֖ה מֵאֵ֣ת הַמֶּֽלֶךְ: וְהַמֶּ֡לֶךְ שָׁב֩
מִגִּנַּ֨ת הַבִּיתָ֜ן אֶל־בֵּ֣ית ׀ מִשְׁתֵּ֣ה הַיַּ֗יִן וְהָמָן֙ נֹפֵ֔ל עַל־הַמִּטָּה֙
אֲשֶׁ֣ר אֶסְתֵּ֣ר עָלֶ֔יהָ וַיֹּ֣אמֶר הַמֶּ֔לֶךְ הֲ֠גַם לִכְבּ֧וֹשׁ אֶת־
הַמַּלְכָּ֛ה עִמִּ֖י בַּבָּ֑יִת הַדָּבָ֗ר יָצָא֙ מִפִּ֣י הַמֶּ֔לֶךְ וּפְנֵ֥י הָמָ֖ן חָפֽוּ:

7:5 מִי הוּא זֶה וְאֵי־זֶה הוּא¹—(a-c) Verbless, §31.224, §31.31. (d) 'Where?')v.335). In Mod. Heb. אֵיזֶהוּ means 'who/which is it?' but here, probably 'where is he?'

אֲשֶׁר־מְלָאוֹ לִבּוֹ לַעֲשׂוֹת כֵּן:²—(b) מלא is usually stative (§32.21), but here is fientive (§32.22), taking an obj. Ges. (§74g) suggests this is the reason for the *qāmāṣ* (normally *ṣērê*). Note suffix. (c) §36.6.

7:6 אִישׁ צַר וְאוֹיֵב הָמָן הָרָע הַזֶּה¹—This is direct discourse (§38.81). We can almost hear Esther biting off each word. (b) *ṣar* 'enemy' (v.6862). (c) G50 of איב, but a very common noun 'enemy' (v.340), and should be listed as such. (e) *ra'* 'evil, wicked' (v.7451).

וְהָמָן נִבְעַת²—(b) ־ת could be fsc, but this does not fit context (§33.11). נ־ could be what? ־ ־ נ is what pattern? §28.42. בעת (N) 'to be terrified' (v.1204). §32.51, .5111.

וְהַמֶּלֶךְ קָם בַּחֲמָתוֹ¹—(b) G10 or G50? §29.631. Which does context require? (c) 1:12⁶. Adv. phrase, §35.31, describing circumstances of the action.

אֶל־גִּנַּת הַבִּיתָן²—We would insert לבוא, but this could be looked upon as a "pregnant" construction. 'The king stood up into the garden.' *Ges.* §119ee. §36.54. (b) 1:5¹⁰.

וְהָמָן עָמַד³—(b) 3:4⁵. Note how the conv. impf. is avoided in this story. §32.533f.

לְבַקֵּשׁ עַל־נַפְשׁוֹ מֵאֶסְתֵּר⁴—(a) 2:15⁴, 4:8⁹. (b) 'on behalf of.' (c) 7:3¹. (d) What is the force of מִן? Purpose clause, §38.542, tells the purpose of the action of the main verb.

כִּי רָאָה כִּי־כָלְתָה אֵלָיו הָרָעָה מֵאֵת הַמֶּלֶךְ׃ [5]—(a) §38.53. (b) §29.71. (c) Introduces indirect discourse, §38.82. (d) §29.7131, VDC–6. כלה 'to finish,' but with רעה 'was determined' (v.3615). (f) f. of *ra'*, for **ra''āʰ*, 7:6[1]. (g) *min* + *'ēt*, 'from, by' (of author or composer).

7:8 וְהַמֶּלֶךְ שָׁב מִגִּנַּת הַבִּיתָן [1]—(b) 2:14[2], 6:12[1]. G10 or G50? (c-d) Cf. 7:7[2].

אֶל־בֵּית ׀ [2]—Cf. 7:7[1].

וְהָמָן נֹפֵל עַל־הַמִּטָּה אֲשֶׁר אֶסְתֵּר עָלֶיהָ [3]—(b) 6:13[5,7], 3:7[3]. Did Haman 'fall' *after* the king returned, or *before*? Read §32.5114. (d) 1:6[9]. (e-g) 6:8[2,3].

הֲגַם לִכְבּוֹשׁ אֶת־הַמַּלְכָּה עִמִּי בַּבָּיִת [4]—(a) Interrog. –הֲ, §35.23. (b) *kbš* 'to conquer, subdue' (v.3533), here 'to ravish.' (e-f) 'with me in the house,' §35.31. Note the ellipsis, 'Is (he) even (going) to rape the queen ...?'

הַדָּבָר יָצָא מִפִּי הַמֶּלֶךְ [5]—(a) Here, 'statement, words.' (b) YCC and CC', §29.8. (c) פֶּה 'mouth' (v.6310), with מִן of source. *pî* may be an old genitive ending, §25.3ff.

וּפְנֵי הָמָן חָפוּ׃ [6]—(a) 1:14[5]. (c) Two radicals – which is lacking? VDC–6 or VDC–10? If this is G15 of חפה 'to cover' (2645 12/2), 6:12[3], we would expect אֶת before the obj. (a-b). Some emend to read 'Haman's face grew red (*ḥammû*).'In vv. 6-7 there are seven main clauses with the noun preceding the verb. Don't let anyone tell you that the verb normally stands first in Hebrew. The conv. impf. is used in this part of the story only for the formula 'and ... said.' *Use your eyes!*

Learn the words in BVG–49.

Note the following pronominal suffixes:

bᵉnap̄šēḵ in *your* (f.s.) soul
lāḵ to *you* (f.s.)
'āḇîḵ *your* (f.s.) father
šᵉ'ēlāṯēḵ *your* (f.s.) petition
lᵉḵā to *you* (m.s.)
bᵉ'êʸnêʸḵā in *your* (m.s.) eyes
bᵉ'êʸnêʸḵem in *your* (m.p.) eyes
lāḵem to *you* (m.p.)

עַד־אָנָה מֵאַנְתֶּם לִשְׁמֹר מִצְוֹתַי וְתוֹרֹתָי

How long do you refuse to keep my commandments and my laws?

Exodus 16:28

Purpose: To learn something about relative clauses
Materials: Esther 7:9–8:2

וַיֹּ֣אמֶר חַ֠רְבוֹנָה אֶחָ֨ד מִן־הַסָּרִיסִ֜ים לִפְנֵ֣י הַמֶּ֗לֶךְ גַּ֣ם הִנֵּֽה־ 9
הָעֵ֣ץ אֲשֶׁר־עָשָׂ֪ה הָמָ֟ן לְֽמָרְדֳּכַ֡י אֲשֶׁ֣ר דִּבֶּר־ט֣וֹב עַל־הַמֶּ֗לֶךְ
עֹמֵד֙ בְּבֵ֣ית הָמָ֔ן גָּבֹ֖הַּ חֲמִשִּׁ֣ים אַמָּ֑ה וַיֹּ֥אמֶר הַמֶּ֖לֶךְ תְּלֻ֥הוּ
עָלָֽיו: וַיִּתְלוּ֙ אֶת־הָמָ֔ן עַל־הָעֵ֖ץ אֲשֶׁר־הֵכִ֣ין לְמָרְדֳּכָ֑י וַחֲמַ֥ת י
הַמֶּ֖לֶךְ שָׁכָֽכָה:

CAP. VIII. ח

בַּיּ֣וֹם הַה֗וּא נָתַ֞ן הַמֶּ֤לֶךְ אֲחַשְׁוֵרוֹשׁ֙ לְאֶסְתֵּ֣ר הַמַּלְכָּ֔ה אֶת־ א
בֵּ֥ית הָמָ֖ן צֹרֵ֣ר הַיְּהוּדִ֑ים וּמָרְדֳּכַ֗י בָּ֚א לִפְנֵ֣י הַמֶּ֔לֶךְ כִּֽי־
הִגִּ֥ידָה אֶסְתֵּ֖ר מַ֥ה הוּא־לָֽהּ: וַיָּ֨סַר הַמֶּ֜לֶךְ אֶת־טַבַּעְתּ֗וֹ 2
אֲשֶׁ֤ר הֶֽעֱבִיר֙ מֵֽהָמָ֔ן וַֽיִּתְּנָ֖הּ לְמָרְדֳּכָ֑י וַתָּ֧שֶׂם אֶסְתֵּ֛ר אֶת־
מָרְדֳּכַ֖י עַל־בֵּ֥ית הָמָֽן:

7:9 אֶחָד מִן־הַסָּרִיסִים¹—(b) *min* partitive, 'one from, one of (a larger group).'

גַּם הִנֵּה־הָעֵץ²—(a) This seems unusual to me (cf. BDB 169), possibly introducing a climax, 'Yea.' (b) *hinnêʰ* 'behold! here is!' (v.200⁹). (c) 2:23³. The sentence is broken with two relative clauses. After הנה we may expect a ptcp., which we find after the rel. cls.

אֲשֶׁר־עָשָׂה הָמָן³—Rel. cl., defining *hāʿēṣ*, §38.4

אֲשֶׁר דִּבֶּר־טוֹב⁴—(a) Introduces second rel. cl., this one describing Mordecai, §38.4. (b) Note accent and pointing. The D10 of this word often is closely joined to the next word. (c) This word can be an adj. 'good,' or an adv. 'well.'

עֹמֵד בְּבֵית הָמָן⁵—(a) The ptcp. resumes the main cl., after *hinnêʰ hāʿēṣ*. The cl. is verbless, cf. §31.24, although in Eng. we would consider 'the tree' as obj. of 'behold,' and 'standing' as describing 'the tree.' Learn to think in Heb. style. Does the following prep. phrase describe Haman, the house, or the tree?

תְּלֻהוּ עָלָיו⁶—(a) 5:14⁴. Defective writing, G37s0, note accent.

7:10 וַיִּתְלוּ אֶת־הָמָן¹—Take care! If ית– is HtD and ו– is ending, what is the root? Will it fit VDC–11? What is ו–, י– are afformatives? Parse and *then* translate. Who or what is/are subj. of verb? §32.114.

אֲשֶׁר־הֵכִין לְמָרְדֳּכַי²—(a) What is the antecedent? (b) 6:4⁵. Who or what is the subj. of this verb? Think out each phrase and clause.

וַחֲמַת הַמֶּלֶךְ שָׁכָכָה׃ [3]—(a) 2:1[2]. (c) 2:1[2] (7918 5/2), G11 with pausal accent.

8:1 צֹרֵר הַיְּהוּדִיִּים [1]—The first part of the verse consists of: prep. phr. (temporal), verb, subj., appositive, indir. obj., appositive, dir. obj with modifier. (a) 3:10[4].

כִּי־הִגִּידָה [2]—(a) Tells *why* Mordecai came, §38.53. (b) 2:10[1]. What did Esther make known?.

8:2 וַיָּסַר הַמֶּלֶךְ אֶת־טַבַּעְתּוֹ [1]—(a-d) 3:10[1] In contrast with 7:7-8, we now find eleven clauses starting with conv. impfs. in vv. 2-4. Read §§32.53, .5312, .533.

אֲשֶׁר הֶעֱבִיר מֵהָמָן [2]—Rel. cl. (a) What is the antecedent? (b) This word is translated in many ways. How does it fit best in this context? (c) If *to* indicates indir. obj. after verbs of *giving*, does *min* do the same after verbs of *taking*? In both cases, it is better to think of the prep. phrase as an adverbial modifier of the verb, cf. §35.11.

וַיִּתְּנָהּ לְמָרְדֳּכָי [3]—(a) What is the antecedent of ־ָהּ? Note *mēhāmān ... l^e mord^e kay* – do the preps. help us to translate *he'ĕḇîr*? Perhaps something like 'to cause to pass, to transfer.' Meanings are established by contexts.

וַתָּשֶׂם [4]—(a) 2:17[5]. What is subj. of this verb? What is obj.? How is the prep. phrase used?

Learn the words in Vocabulary Group 50.

Study the use of the accusative אֵת:

וַיִּקַּח הָמָן אֶת־הַלְּבוּשׁ
וְאֶת־הַסּוּס (6:11)

וַיְסַפֵּר לָהֶם הָמָן אֶת־כְּבוֹד עָשְׁרוֹ וְרֹב בָּנָיו
וְאֵת כָּל־אֲשֶׁר גִּדְּלוֹ הַמֶּלֶךְ
וְאֵת אֲשֶׁר נִשְּׂאוֹ עַל־הַשָּׂרִים וְעַבְדֵי הַמֶּלֶךְ
(5:11)

וְאֶת־פַּתְשֶׁגֶן כְּתָב־הַדָּת ... נָתַן לוֹ

מַצְרֵף לַכֶּסֶף וְכוּר לַזָּהָב
וּבֹחֵן לִבּוֹת יהוה׃
A crucible is for silver and a furnace for gold, but YHWH tries hearts.
Proverbs 17:3

Purpose: To observe phrases and clauses
Materials: Esther 8:3-6

3 וַתּוֹסֶף אֶסְתֵּר וַתְּדַבֵּר לִפְנֵי
הַמֶּלֶךְ וַתִּפֹּל לִפְנֵי רַגְלָיו וַתֵּבְךְּ וַתִּתְחַנֶּן־לוֹ לְהַֽעֲבִיר אֶת־
רָעַת הָמָן הָאֲגָגִי וְאֵת מַחֲשַׁבְתּוֹ אֲשֶׁר חָשַׁב עַל־הַיְּהוּדִֽים׃
4 וַיּוֹשֶׁט הַמֶּלֶךְ לְאֶסְתֵּר אֵת שַׁרְבִט הַזָּהָב וַתָּקָם אֶסְתֵּר
5 וַֽתַּעֲמֹד לִפְנֵי הַמֶּֽלֶךְ׃ וַתֹּאמֶר אִם־עַל־הַמֶּלֶךְ טוֹב וְאִם־
מָצָאתִי חֵן לְפָנָיו וְכָשֵׁר הַדָּבָר לִפְנֵי הַמֶּלֶךְ וְטוֹבָה אֲנִי
בְּעֵינָיו יִכָּתֵב לְהָשִׁיב אֶת־הַסְּפָרִים מַחֲשֶׁבֶת הָמָן בֶּֽן־
הַמְּדָתָא הָאֲגָגִי אֲשֶׁר כָּתַב לְאַבֵּד אֶת־הַיְּהוּדִים אֲשֶׁר
6 בְּכָל־מְדִינוֹת הַמֶּֽלֶךְ׃ כִּי אֵיכָכָה אוּכַל וְֽרָאִיתִי בָּרָעָה
אֲשֶׁר־יִמְצָא אֶת־עַמִּי וְאֵֽיכָכָה אוּכַל וְֽרָאִיתִי בְּאָבְדַן
מוֹלַדְתִּֽי׃

8:3 וַתּוֹסֶף אֶסְתֵּר וַתְּדַבֵּר[1]—(a) יסף 'to add' (v.3254), followed by another verb, 'to do ... again.' **tawsip*, §29.311. (c) 1:22[7].

וַתִּפֹּל לִפְנֵי רַגְלָיו[2]—(a) 3:7[3]. (c) *régel* 'foot' (v.7272), dual §25.423. (b-c) Prep. phrase, adverbial, modifying verb, telling *where* she fell.

וַתֵּבְךְּ וַתִּתְחַנֶּן־לוֹ[3]—(a) Note form, read §29.72 carefully, then read §29.721. בכה 'to weep' (v.1058). (b) 4:8[9]. VDC–1. (a-b) Note sequence of conv. impfs. Note §32.5333. Some of the statements in §§32.533ff. I have drawn from the standard grammars against my better judgment. There is still *very much to be done* in study of the conv. impf. and conv. perf.

לְהַֽעֲבִיר אֶת־רָעַת הָמָן[4]—(a) Cf. 8:2[2]. (c) Est. 7:6[1]. Here רָעָה 'evil' (v.7451), < **ra''at*. In this context, how translate העביר? §38.54.

מַחֲשַׁבְתּוֹ אֲשֶׁר חָשַׁב[5]—(a) *maḥăšéḇeṯ* 'device, plan' (v.4284), 2d of compound obj. of verb. (b) Introduces rel. cl.; what does it modify? (c) *ḥāšaḇ* 'he thought, devised' (v.2803). The verb is modified by the adverbial prep. phrase that follows.

8:4 וַיּוֹשֶׁט[1]—(a) 4:11[7]. For following words, 4:11.

וַתָּקָם[2]—(a) 5:9[4]. VDC–9. Note *qāmāṣ*'s. Note position of verb and subj.

וַתַּעֲמֹד[3]—(a) 3:4[5]. R.9c. The adverbial phrase that follows tells *where* she stood.

8:5 וְכָשֵׁר[1]—You should be able to read this verse to the *rᵉḇîaᶜ*. (a) *kāšēr* 'right, proper' (3787 3/1). In Ashkenazic pronunciation, this word > "kosher."

וְטוֹבָה אֲנִי[2]—(a-b) Verbless cl., §31. Pred. adj., §31.23. Word order, §31.43. Actually there are *four* "if" clauses (protases, §38.611), but *'im* is omitted before the last two, §30.14. §31.233.

יִכָּתֵב לְהָשִׁיב אֶת־הַסְּפָרִים[3]—(a) 1:19[4]. N20 or N40? §32.3511. (b) 4:13[1]. (d) 1:22[1]. (b-d) Indir. disc., §38.82. For use of inf. cstr., §32.3823. This is the main cl. (apodosis, §38.612) of the condition. The condition is "general" (it does not assume either alternative), hence the apodosis takes any kind of verb, here jussive. 'If I have found favor ... let it be written ... (and if not, then obviously it won't be written).'

מַחֲשֶׁבֶת הָמָן[4]—(a) 8:3[5]. Appositional cl. (§38.3, .45), explaining the "letters." This is further explained (defined) by the clauses which follow.

אֲשֶׁר כָּתַב לְאַבֵּד[5]—(a) What is the antecedent? (c) 3:9[2]. Indir. disc., cf. §32.3823, §38.82. It can also be taken as a purpose cl. Either 'which he wrote (saying) to destroy ...,' or 'which he wrote in order to destroy ....' To what does the following rel. cl. relate?

8:6 כִּי אֵיכָכָה אוּכַל[1]—(a) Causal, tells *why* Esther is so acting. (b) *'ê^y kāk̲ā* and *'ê^y k̲āk̲ā* (Eccl.), 'How?' (349 4/2). (c) 6:13[6]. §28.322.

וְרָאִיתִי בָּרָעָה[2]—(a) ָ is *ga'yâ* or grave metheg. According to *David Ḳimḥi's Hebrew Grammar* [Ḳimḥi 1160-1235 C. E.) §4d, it has a full vowel sound (ָ). It is not found in 8:6[4]. Since the penult is open, we cannot tell if *wāw* is conversive (§17.342), but after impf. it probably is (§32.5422). רָאָה בְּ‑ 'to gaze upon,' BDB 908.8a(3). (b) 8:3[4].

אֲשֶׁר־יִמְצָא[3]—Adj. cl., §38.4, defining which word? How should we translate (b) – 'which my people shall find' or 'which shall find my people'?

וְרָאִיתִי בְּאָבְדַן[4]—(a) Cf. 8:6[2]. (b) *'obd̲ān* 'destruction' (13 1/1), cstr., but *-ân* should not reduce. In effect, this is conditional, 'How can I endure if I shall have gazed upon ... ?'

Memorize the basic vocabulary in Group 51.

קְדֹשִׁים תִּהְיוּ כִּי קָדוֹשׁ אֲנִי יְהוָה אֱלֹהֵיכֶם׃
Holy shall you be, for holy am I YHWH your God.
Leviticus 19:2

60

Purpose: To study exegesis of poetry
Materials: Psalm 136:10-22

10 לְמַכֵּה מִצְרַיִם בִּבְכוֹרֵיהֶם כִּי לְעוֹלָם חַסְדּוֹ׃
11 וַיּוֹצֵא יִשְׂרָאֵל מִתּוֹכָם כִּי לְעוֹלָם חַסְדּוֹ׃
12 בְּיָד חֲזָקָה וּבִזְרוֹעַ נְטוּיָה כִּי לְעוֹלָם חַסְדּוֹ׃
13 לְגֹזֵר יַם־סוּף לִגְזָרִים כִּי לְעוֹלָם חַסְדּוֹ׃
14 וְהֶעֱבִיר יִשְׂרָאֵל בְּתוֹכוֹ כִּי לְעוֹלָם חַסְדּוֹ׃
15 וְנִעֵר פַּרְעֹה וְחֵילוֹ בְיַם־סוּף כִּי לְעוֹלָם חַסְדּוֹ׃
16 לְמוֹלִיךְ עַמּוֹ בַּמִּדְבָּר כִּי לְעוֹלָם חַסְדּוֹ׃
17 לְמַכֵּה מְלָכִים גְּדֹלִים כִּי לְעוֹלָם חַסְדּוֹ׃
18 וַיַּהֲרֹג מְלָכִים אַדִּירִים כִּי לְעוֹלָם חַסְדּוֹ׃
19 לְסִיחוֹן מֶלֶךְ הָאֱמֹרִי כִּי לְעוֹלָם חַסְדּוֹ׃
20 לְעוֹג מֶלֶךְ הַבָּשָׁן כִּי לְעוֹלָם חַסְדּוֹ׃
21 וְנָתַן אַרְצָם לְנַחֲלָה כִּי לְעוֹלָם חַסְדּוֹ׃
22 נַחֲלָה לְיִשְׂרָאֵל עַבְדּוֹ כִּי לְעוֹלָם חַסְדּוֹ׃

Psalm 136 This is an introduction to the rubric of the Israelite cult, namely an antiphonal psalm. The reader (or Group A) recited the words at the beginning of each verse, and the congregation (or Group B) recited the response, in this example, *kî l*^{e}*'ôlām ḥasdô*. I have set a portion of this Psalm in columns for visual help. Note that the right-hand column is a "recital of the great deeds of Yahweh." Much of Israel's worship was centered about the Lord's revelatory and redemptive activity, many portions of which are brought into liturgical passages of the Bible repeatedly. Look for this as you work in the Scriptures.

:10[1] (a) *l*^{e}*makkê*^{h} < *nky* H 'to smite' (v.5221), 'to the smiter of.' (b) *miṣráyim* pr.n. 'Egypt.' (c) *biḇ*^{e}*ḵôrêhem*: *b*^{e}*ḵôr* 'first-born' (v.1060, BVG-47. *b*^{e}- is perhaps the *beth essentiae*, specifying the part of Egypt that was smitten.

:10[2] (a) *kî* causal. The psalm opens with the words, *hôḏû la'ḏônāy kî ṭôḇ* 'Give thanks to YHWH for he is good.' The antiphonal gives the reason in a refrain repeated 26 times. (b) *l*^{e}*'ôlām*: *'ôlām* 'long duration (past or future)' (v.5769). The idea of 'eternity' is more Greek than Hebrew. (c) *ḥéseḏ* 'covenant obligation/loyalty' (v.2619). This psalm affords an outstanding definition of *ḥéseḏ*. While the mercy of YHWH is shown to Israel, the people of his covenant, there is no mercy to those who oppose him or his people.

:11 (a) *wayyôṣē'*: note long-*ô*, §29.311. 'He caused to come out, brought out.' (c) *mittôḵām: min* + *tôk* (v.8432) + s5.

:12 (b) *ḥăzāqā*^{h} 'strong, firm' (v.2389). *z*^{e}*rô*^{a}*'* 'arm, shoulder' (v.2220,BVG-46). (d) *nṭ*^{h}, V.5186, Gp51 'outstretched.' The words *b*^{e}*yāḏ ḥăzāqā*^{h} *ûḇizrô*^{a}*'* *n*^{e}*ṭûyā*^{h} are part of the Passover Seder. Cf. Exod. 6:1. 6; Deut. 4:34.

:13 (a) *l^e gôzēr*: *gzr* 'to cut, divide' (1504 13x), G52. (b-c) *yam-sûp̄* 'sea of reeds' (5488, BDB 693), a name given only to arms of the Red Sea; later the Greeks applied the name θάλασσα ἐρυθρά 'Red Sea' to the arms as well. Read a good article in *NBD, IDB, ISBE,* or another Bible encyclopedia. (d) *liḡzārîm*: *gézer* 'portion' (1506 2x).

:14 (a) *w^e he'ĕḇîr*: what stem? You certainly know עבר by now! (c) *b^e ṯôḵô*, cf. Ps. 136:11(c).

:15 (a) *w^e ni'ēr*: *n'r* 'to shake, shake out/off' (5287 12x). What stem? (b) *par'ō^h* 'Pharaoh.' (c) *ḥáyil* 'might, army' (v.2428). (d-e) Cf. 136:13(b-c).

:16 (a) *l^e môlîḵ*: הלך acts like WCC, BDB 236, 'the one who caused to walk.' (b) You should know *'am*. (c) *bammiḏbār*: *miḏbār* 'steppe, wilderness' (v.4057), with def. art. often = the wilderness of the wanderings (in the Sinai peninsula).

:17 (a) *l^e makkê^h*, 136:10. (b) *m^e lāḵîm*. pl. of *méleḵ*. *Is it definite? (c) g^e ḏôlîm*, v. 1419. Why pl.? Why not def.?

:18 (a) *wayyahărōḡ*, Est. 3:13[3]. Is it H or G?. (b) See 136:17. (c) *'addîrîm*: *'addîr* 'majestic' (v.117).

:19 (a) *l^e sîḥôn* pr.n. 'Sihon.' (e) *hā'ĕmôrî*, gentilic, 'the Amorite,' collective.

:20 (a) *ûl^e 'ôḡ*: *'ôḡ* pr.n. 'Og.' (c) *habbāšān*: pr.n. 'Bashan,' usually with def. art.

:21 (a) What various meanings does נתן have? (b) *'arṣām*: Do you recognize the word if you take off the s5?. 'Their land.' (c) *l^e naḥălā^h*: *naḥălā^h* 'possession, property, inheritance' (v.5159).

:22 With the help of the previous word, you should be able to do this portion.

Review what you have learned about poetry in Lesson 55. Then read the right-hand column of this psalm as printed at the top of this lesson. Now analyze the stichs as I have suggested them. Whether you agree with what I have done is beside the point – do you understand what I have tried to do? Start now to analyze every poetic passage that you see in the Hebrew Bible.

Know the basic vocabulary in Group 52.

A strophic analysis of Psalm 136

1 ‖ 2 ‖ 3	10 ‖ 11 ‖ 12	23 ‖ 24 ‖ 25
4	13 ‖ 14 ‖ 15	26
5 ‖ 6	16	
7 ‖ 8 ‖ 9	17 ‖ 18	
	19 ‖ 20	
	21 ‖ 22	

Purpose: More on phrases and clauses
Materials: Esther 8:7-9

7 וַיֹּאמֶר הַמֶּלֶךְ אֲחַשְׁוֵרֹשׁ לְאֶסְתֵּר הַמַּלְכָּה
וּלְמָרְדֳּכַי הַיְּהוּדִי הִנֵּה בֵית־הָמָן נָתַתִּי לְאֶסְתֵּר וְאֹתוֹ
8 תָּלוּ עַל־הָעֵץ עַל אֲשֶׁר־שָׁלַח יָדוֹ בַּיְּהוּדִיים׃ וְאַתֶּם
כִּתְבוּ עַל־הַיְּהוּדִים כַּטּוֹב בְּעֵינֵיכֶם בְּשֵׁם הַמֶּלֶךְ וְחִתְמוּ
בְּטַבַּעַת הַמֶּלֶךְ כִּי־כְתָב אֲשֶׁר־נִכְתָּב בְּשֵׁם־הַמֶּלֶךְ וְנַחְתּוֹם
9 בְּטַבַּעַת הַמֶּלֶךְ אֵין לְהָשִׁיב׃ וַיִּקָּרְאוּ סֹפְרֵי־הַמֶּלֶךְ בָּעֵת־
הַהִיא בַּחֹדֶשׁ הַשְּׁלִישִׁי הוּא־חֹדֶשׁ סִיוָן בִּשְׁלוֹשָׁה
וְעֶשְׂרִים בּוֹ וַיִּכָּתֵב כְּכָל־אֲשֶׁר־צִוָּה מָרְדֳּכַי אֶל־
הַיְּהוּדִים וְאֶל הָאֲחַשְׁדַּרְפְּנִים וְהַפַּחוֹת וְשָׂרֵי הַמְּדִינוֹת
אֲשֶׁר ׀ מֵהֹדּוּ וְעַד־כּוּשׁ שֶׁבַע וְעֶשְׂרִים וּמֵאָה מְדִינָה
מְדִינָה וּמְדִינָה כִּכְתָבָהּ וְעַם וָעָם כִּלְשֹׁנוֹ וְאֶל־הַיְּהוּדִים
י כִּכְתָבָם וְכִלְשׁוֹנָם׃

8:7 הִנֵּה בֵית־הָמָן נָתַתִּי[1]—(a) 'Behold!' (v.2009). Masoretic accents appear to make this an independent cl.; 'Behold Haman's house!' The absence of אֵת confirms this. (d) §13.1111.

וְאֹתוֹ תָּלוּ[2]—(a) §34.113. Note word order: emphasis. (b) VDC–10. The prep. phrase is adverbial; explain why.

עַל אֲשֶׁר־שָׁלַח יָדוֹ[3]—(a-b) 'on account of (the fact) that' = *because*. BDB 758.IIIa. §38.53. (c) 2:21[7].

8:8 וְאַתֶּם כִּתְבוּ[1]—(a) §21.1. To whom does this refer? (Note the number.) (b) §27.422. §32.32, §32.1121. 'Now *you* write ....'

כַּטּוֹב[2]—(a) Is there a def. art.? You should be able to do the rest of the clause.

וְחִתְמוּ[3]—(a) 3:12[10] §38.1. Does §32.324 apply here? Watch the context! You should be able to do the rest of the clause.

כִּי־כְתָב אֲשֶׁר־נִכְתָּב[4]—(a) *kî* causal, BDB 473. (b) 1:22[3], 3:14[1] (c) Introduces rel. cl., subj. of *nikṯāḇ*. (d) N10 or N50? VDC–3. §32.831. If ptcp., then we have a verbless cl., with *'ăšer* as subj., and *nikṯāḇ* as pred., §31.123, §31.24.

וְנַחְתּוֹם בְּטַבַּעַת הַמֶּלֶךְ[5]—Also a rel. cl., with *'ăšer* omitted. (a) VDC- 3. §28.42. §32.391. (b) 3:10[1]. In both clauses, there are prep. phrases used adverbially. Identify them.

אֵין לְהָשִׁיב׃[6]—(a-b) §32.3812. 'There is no recalling' = 'it cannot be recalled.'

8:9 וַיִּקָּרְאוּ[1]—(a) Vowel-pattern tells us what? 3:12[1]. For the following words, 3:12[1], 1:13[2]. §26.32. Does §33.13 apply?

בַּחֹדֶשׁ הַשְּׁלִישִׁי[2]—The main verb is modified by 3 adv. phrases, the 2d of which is modified by an appositional phr. Identify them. Cf. 3:12[2]. 3:12[3], 5:1[1], 1:1[10]. *Sîwân*, 3d month, is approximately May-June. §26.262. The word *yôm* is usually omitted in date-formulas.

וַיִּכָּתֵב[3]—Cf. 3:12[4]. Indefinite, 'let it be written,' §32.114. k^e- does not properly introduce a comparative clause (§38.7), but rather the noun (here *kōl*), the rest being a rel. cl., cf. *Ges.* §155*g*.

הָאֲחַשְׁדַּרְפְּנִים[4]—3:12[5]. For the rest of the verse, 3:12 and 1:1.

Learn the words in Vocabulary Group 53.

Note the following uses of אֲשֶׁר:

עִם־הַגֹּלָה אֲשֶׁר הָגְלְתָה עִם יְכָנְיָה 'with the captivity *which* was taken captive ...'
מִסָּרִיסֵי הַמֶּלֶךְ אֲשֶׁר הֶעֱמִיד לְפָנֶיהָ 'from the eunuchs *whom* he stationed before her'
הַשָּׂרִים אֲשֶׁר אִתּוֹ 'the princes *who* (were) with him'
הִגִּיד לָהֶם אֲשֶׁר־הוּא יְהוּדִי 'he told them *that* he (was) a Jew'
לְבוּשׁ אֲשֶׁר לָבַשׁ־בּוֹ הַמֶּלֶךְ 'clothing *in which* the king dressed'
וְסוּס אֲשֶׁר רָכַב עָלָיו הַמֶּלֶךְ 'and a horse *on which* the king rode'
עַל־הַמִּטָּה אֲשֶׁר אֶסְתֵּר עָלֶיהָ 'on the couch *on which* Esther (was)'
בְּכָל־עֵת אֲשֶׁר אֲנִי רֹאֶה 'every time *when* I see'
וְכַאֲשֶׁר אָבַדְתִּי אָבָדְתִּי 'and *when* I have perished, I have perished'
וּבְכֵן אָבוֹא אֶל־הַמֶּלֶךְ אֲשֶׁר לֹא־כַדָּת 'and thus I shall go in to the king, *which* (deed) is not according to custom'
כַּאֲשֶׁר דִּבַּרְתָּ 'according *as* you have spoken'

Be sure you understand the various different usages that are illustrated here.

It is better to hear the rebuke of a wise man than the song of fools.

טוֹב לִשְׁמֹעַ גַּעֲרַת חָכָם
מֵאִישׁ שֹׁמֵעַ שִׁיר כְּסִילִים׃

Ecclesiastes 7:5

Purpose: To observe the infinitives
Materials: Esther 8:10-13

וַיִּכְתֹּב בְּשֵׁם הַמֶּלֶךְ אֲחַשְׁוֵרֹשׁ וַיַּחְתֹּם
בְּטַבַּעַת הַמֶּלֶךְ וַיִּשְׁלַח סְפָרִים בְּיַד הָרָצִים בַּסּוּסִים
11 רֹכְבֵי הָרֶכֶשׁ הָאֲחַשְׁתְּרָנִים בְּנֵי הָרַמָּכִים׃ אֲשֶׁר נָתַן
הַמֶּלֶךְ לַיְּהוּדִים ׀ אֲשֶׁר בְּכָל־עִיר־וָעִיר לְהִקָּהֵל וְלַעֲמֹד
עַל־נַפְשָׁם לְהַשְׁמִיד לַהֲרֹג וּלְאַבֵּד אֶת־כָּל־חֵיל עַם
12 וּמְדִינָה הַצָּרִים אֹתָם טַף וְנָשִׁים וּשְׁלָלָם לָבוֹז׃ בְּיוֹם
אֶחָד בְּכָל־מְדִינוֹת הַמֶּלֶךְ אֲחַשְׁוֵרוֹשׁ בִּשְׁלוֹשָׁה עָשָׂר
13 לְחֹדֶשׁ שְׁנֵים־עָשָׂר הוּא־חֹדֶשׁ אֲדָר׃ פַּתְשֶׁגֶן הַכְּתָב
לְהִנָּתֵן דָּת בְּכָל־מְדִינָה וּמְדִינָה גָּלוּי לְכָל־הָעַמִּים וְלִהְיוֹת
11 הַיְּהוּדִיִּים עֲתִודִים לַיּוֹם הַזֶּה לְהִנָּקֵם מֵאֹיְבֵיהֶם׃

8:10 וַיִּכְתֹּב [1]—Cf. 3:12[9,10], 3:13[1]. Note the different G20 forms. For בַּסּוּסִים, 6:8[3].

רֹכְבֵי הָרֶכֶשׁ הָאֲחַשְׁתְּרָנִים בְּנֵי הָרַמָּכִים׃ [2]—(a) *rkb* ‘to ride’ (v.7392. What form? §27.611. (b) *rékeš* ‘courser, swift steed’ (7409 4/2). (c) *’ăhašt^{e}rānîm* ‘royal (steeds?),’ from Pers. adj. *ḫšatřa* ‘royal’ (BDB 31), taken to modify (b). However, the pl. seems to indicate that it modifies (a). (d) *ben* can mean ‘member of a class or guild.’ (e) *rammāḵ*, usually ‘mare’ or ‘dromedary’ (7424 1/1), but CaC^{2}āC suggests occupation or habit (§24.26), hence possibly ‘breeder’ or the like. Meanings are derived from contexts.

8:11 לְהִקָּהֵל וְלַעֲמֹד עַל־נַפְשָׁם [1]—The verse begins with *’ăšer*, and appears to be indir. disc., giving the content of the documents, ‘that the king has given to the Jews ....’ The second *’ăšer* introduces an adj. cl. Then follow 5 infs. cstr. (purpose) spelling out the king’s decree. (a) *qhl* ‘to assemble, gather’ (v.6950). §§28.42, .421, possibly reflexive (§32.83) ‘to gather themselves together. (b) 3:4[5]. (b-d) Idiom, ‘to stand for their lives,’ cf. 7:3[1]. What suffix? For the following words, 3:13[3].

אֶת־כָּל־חֵיל עַם וּמְדִינָה [2]—Possibly the dir. obj. of all three preceding infs. cstr. (b) *kol* before sg. ‘each, any.’ (c) 1:3[8]. Here, probably ‘force, (armed) power.’ ‘Any army of people or state.’

הַצָּרִים אֹתָם [3]—(a) Usually taken to be from *ṣrr*, but the form must be G55, and G55 of *ṣrr* should be *haṣṣôr^{e}rîm* (§29.522). G55 of *ṣûr* would be either *haṣṣārîm* or *haṣṣôrîm* (§29.631). צוּר ‘to besiege, assault’ (v.6696). For ptcp. with def. art., §36.2351.

טַף וְנָשִׁים וּשְׁלָלָם לָבוֹז׃ [4]—(a,b) 3:13[5]. (c,d) 3:13[9].

8:12 You should be able to do this verse. On what day of what month? §26.25.

8:13 לְהִנָּקֵם מֵאֹיְבֵיהֶם׃[1]—See 3:14 for first part of verse. *paṯšeḡen hakkᵉṯāḇ* is n. phr., subj. of the inf. cstr. (a) נקם 'to avenge' (v.5358). §28.42. (b) *'ôyēḇ* 7:6[1]. What morphemes can you identify? This verse sounds as if it might be the language of the document.

Learn the meanings of the words in BVG–54.

Study the following uses of the infinitive:

אָמַר ... לְהָבִיא אתושתי ... לְהַרְאוֹת הָעַמִּים ... אֶת־יָפְיָהּ He said, *Bring* Vashti ... *to show* the people her beauty.
וַתְּמָאֵן ... ושתי לָבוֹא and Vashti refused *to enter*.
מַה־לַּעֲשׂוֹת בַּמַּלְכָּה What *is to be done* with the queen?
כְּשֹׁךְ חמת המלך *When* the king's anger *was assuaged*.
לָדַעַת את־שלום אסרת *in order to know* Esther's welfare.
וּבְהַגִּיעַ תר נערה ונערה לָבוֹא אל־המלך and *when* each girl's turn *came to go in* to the king.
ויבקשו לִשְׁלֹחַ יד במלך and they sought *to stretch forth* their hand against the king.
יִכָּתֵב לְאַבְּדָם Let it be written, *Destroy them.*
כִּי אֵין לָבוֹא אל־שער המלך For it is not permitted *to enter* the king's gate.
ותשלח בגדים לְהַלְבִּישׁ את־מרדכי And she sent garments *to clothe* Mordecai.
אחת דתו לְהָמִית His law is clear: *Put (him) to death.*
אל־תדמי בנפשך לְהִמָּלֵט Don't suppose *that you will be delivered.*

I sought the Lord and He answered me, and from all my terrors He delivered me.	דָּרַשְׁתִּי אֶת־יהוה וְעָנָנִי וּמִכָּל־מְגוּרוֹתַי הִצִּילָנִי׃

Psalm 34:4 (MT 5)

63

Purpose: To observe participles
Materials: Esther 8:14-17

הָרָצִים
רֹכְבֵי הָרֶכֶשׁ הָאֲחַשְׁתְּרָנִים יָצְאוּ מְבֹהָלִים וּדְחוּפִים בִּדְבַר
הַמֶּלֶךְ וְהַדָּת נִתְּנָה בְּשׁוּשַׁן הַבִּירָה׃ וּמָרְדֳּכַי יָצָא ׀ טו
מִלִּפְנֵי הַמֶּלֶךְ בִּלְבוּשׁ מַלְכוּת תְּכֵלֶת וָחוּר וַעֲטֶרֶת זָהָב
גְּדוֹלָה וְתַכְרִיךְ בּוּץ וְאַרְגָּמָן וְהָעִיר שׁוּשָׁן צָהֲלָה וְשָׂמֵחָה׃
לַיְּהוּדִים הָיְתָה אוֹרָה וְשִׂמְחָה וְשָׂשֹׂן וִיקָר׃ וּבְכָל־ 16 17
מְדִינָה וּמְדִינָה וּבְכָל־עִיר וָעִיר מְקוֹם אֲשֶׁר דְּבַר־הַמֶּלֶךְ
וְדָתוֹ מַגִּיעַ שִׂמְחָה וְשָׂשׂוֹן לַיְּהוּדִים מִשְׁתֶּה וְיוֹם טוֹב
וְרַבִּים מֵעַמֵּי הָאָרֶץ מִתְיַהֲדִים כִּי־נָפַל פַּחַד־הַיְּהוּדִים
עֲלֵיהֶם׃

8:14 מְבֹהָלִים וּדְחוּפִים—For the first part, cf. 8:10[2]. (a) *m^{e}ḇōhālîm* 2:9[3], *u*-type vowel tells us what? §28.22, §32.81, .815. (b) 3:15[2]. §32.3712.

8:15 יָצָא׀[1]—Can you recognize 1st rad. י and preformative י in יָצָא and יֵצֵא? If not, learn it *now*.

בִּלְבוּשׁ מַלְכוּת תְּכֵלֶת וָחוּר[2]—(a) 4:2[3], cf. 1:11[3]. (c) 1:6[3] (v.8504). (d) 1:6[1] (2353 2/2). This verse is in contrast with 4:1[2].

וַעֲטֶרֶת זָהָב גְּדוֹלָה[3]—(a) *'ăṭārā^h* 'crown' (v.5850). (b) 1:6[9]. Does this modify (a)? §36.31. (c) 1:5[7]. What word does this modify? §36.11.

וְתַכְרִיךְ בּוּץ וְאַרְגָּמָן[4]—(a) *taḵrîḵ* 'garment' (8509 1/1). Since Sem. roots with the same 1st and 3d rads. are very rare, this appears to be a loan-word (*pace* BDB 501). (b) 1:5[5]. (c) 1:5[6].

וְהָעִיר שׁוּשָׁן צָהֲלָה וְשָׂמֵחָה׃[5]—This cl. is in contrast with 3:15[5]. (c) צהל 'to rejoice' (6670 9/1), G11, possibly inchoative, §32.5125. (d) Pausal G11 of stative verb; adj. would be *ś^{e}mēḥā^h*, nonpausal G11 *śām^{e}ḥā^h*. *śmḥ* 'to rejoice' (v.8056). Cf. §32.5125. Read §32.51.

8:16 לַיְּהוּדִים הָיְתָה אוֹרָה וְשִׂמְחָה וְשָׂשֹׂן וִיקָר׃—(a-b) There is no verb *to have* in Heb. One way to express possession is by the idiom הָיָה ל־ (which in certain other contexts means 'to become'); 'to the Jews was ....' (a) *'ôrā^h* 'light' (219 4/1). (e) *śāśōn* 'joy' (v.8342). (f) 1:4[5]. Note the concord: verb in fs with 4 subjs. §33.12, .122.

8:17 Cf. 4:3. Again, this is a planned contrast, a stylistic device of the author.

וְרַבִּים מֵעַמֵּי הָאָרֶץ מִתְיַהֲדִים[1]—(a) 1:4[8], here subsantival. (b) *min* partitive, 'many from' = 'many of.' (c) Gen. 1:1[2] (Lesson 45). The word can mean: the planet Earth, land, country, nation, or a small piece of land. (d) Denom. verb used in HtD 'to become Jews' (3054 1/1), §32.842.

פַּחַד־הַיְּהוּדִים[2]—(a) *páḥad* 'fear' (v.6343). Subj. of verb is a noun-phrase (§33.13).

Memorize the words in Group 55.

Note the following uses of the participle:
והמלך יוֹשֵׁב עַל־כִּסֵּא מַלְכוּתוֹ 'and the king (was) *sitting* on his royal throne'
וַיֵּצֵא הָמָן שָׂמֵחַ 'and Haman went out *rejoicing*'
וַיִּהְיוּ נִקְרָאִים לפני המלך 'and they were *being read* before the king'
עוֹדָם מְדַבְּרִים עִמּוֹ 'while they (were) still *speaking* with him'
לְכָל־אֹהֲבָיו 'to all his *friends*'
בְּשֹׂנְאֵיהֶם 'on *those who hate* them'
גָּלוּי לְכָל־הָעַמִּים '*revealed* to all the peoples'
מִסְפַּר הַהֲרוּגִים 'the number of *those who were killed*'
וְהַיָּמִים הָאֵלֶּה נִזְכָּרִים וְנַעֲשִׂים 'and those days (are) *being remembered* and *being observed*'
עַם־אֶחָד מְפֻזָּר וּמְפֹרָד 'one people *scattered* and *divided*'
הַיְּהוּדִים הַנִּמְצְאִים בְּשׁוּשָׁן 'the Jews *who were found* in Susa'
הָרָצִים 'the *couriers*'
רֹכְבֵי הָרֶכֶשׁ 'the *riders* of the swift horses'

Every time you come across a participle, note exactly how it used – as a verb, a noun, an adjective, a relative clause, or whatever.

Prove me, O Lord, and try me,
Refine my emotions and my intellect.
For Thy covenant love is before my eyes,
And I go about in Thy faithfulness.

בְּחָנֵנִי יהוה וְנַסֵּנִי
צָרְופָה כִלְיוֹתַי וְלִבִּי׃
כִּי־חַסְדְּךָ לְנֶגֶד עֵינָי
וְהִתְהַלַּכְתִּי בַּאֲמִתֶּךָ׃

Psalm 26:2-3

CAP. IX. ט

ט

וּבִשְׁנֵים עָשָׂר חֹדֶשׁ הוּא־חֹדֶשׁ אֲדָר בִּשְׁלוֹשָׁה עָשָׂר יוֹם א
בּוֹ אֲשֶׁר הִגִּיעַ דְּבַר־הַמֶּלֶךְ וְדָתוֹ לְהֵעָשׂוֹת בַּיּוֹם אֲשֶׁר
שִׂבְּרוּ אֹיְבֵי הַיְּהוּדִים לִשְׁלוֹט בָּהֶם וְנַהֲפוֹךְ הוּא אֲשֶׁר
יִשְׁלְטוּ הַיְּהוּדִים הֵמָּה בְּשֹׂנְאֵיהֶם׃ נִקְהֲלוּ הַיְּהוּדִים 2
בְּעָרֵיהֶם בְּכָל־מְדִינוֹת הַמֶּלֶךְ אֲחַשְׁוֵרוֹשׁ לִשְׁלֹחַ יָד
בִּמְבַקְשֵׁי רָעָתָם וְאִישׁ לֹא־עָמַד בִּפְנֵיהֶם כִּי־נָפַל פַּחְדָּם
עַל־כָּל־הָעַמִּים׃ וְכָל־שָׂרֵי הַמְּדִינוֹת וְהָאֲחַשְׁדַּרְפְּנִים 3
וְהַפַּחוֹת וְעֹשֵׂי הַמְּלָאכָה אֲשֶׁר לַמֶּלֶךְ מְנַשְּׂאִים אֶת־
הַיְּהוּדִים כִּי־נָפַל פַּחַד־מָרְדֳּכַי עֲלֵיהֶם׃ כִּי־גָדוֹל מָרְדֳּכַי 4
בְּבֵית הַמֶּלֶךְ וְשָׁמְעוֹ הוֹלֵךְ בְּכָל־הַמְּדִינוֹת כִּי־הָאִישׁ
מָרְדֳּכַי הוֹלֵךְ וְגָדוֹל׃

9:1 אֲשֶׁר הִגִּיעַ דְּבַר־הַמֶּלֶךְ וְדָתוֹ לְהֵעָשׂוֹת[1]—For the first part, cf. 8:12 (b) 2:12[1]. (f) If you have not learned how to recognize the N65, do it *now*. Two temporal cls. introduced with ב–, and an appositional cl. (verbless). *'ăšer* introduces another temporal clause, 'when.'

בַּיּוֹם אֲשֶׁר שִׂבְּרוּ אֹיְבֵי הַיְּהוּדִים לִשְׁלוֹט בָּהֶם[2]—(a-b) on the day that' = 'when.' §38.51. (c) *śbr* D 'to hope' (7663 8/1). Subj. follows (noun-phrase). (f) *šlṭ* 'to rule, domineer' (7980 9/2). 'Sultan' comes from this root, through Arabic. Inf. cstr. after verb of *thinking, hoping,* etc., §38.82.

וְנַהֲפוֹךְ הוּא[3]—(a) *hpk* 'to turn, overturn' (v.2015). §28.42. Verbless cl., 'and that (the hope expressed) [was] overturned.' §32.3925.

יִשְׁלְטוּ הַיְּהוּדִים הֵמָּה בְּשֹׂנְאֵיהֶם׃[4]—(a) 9:1[2]. Subj. follows. Cf. §32.524. (d) *śônē'* from *śn'* 'to hate' (v.8130). The sentence is hardly in classical style: "When the king's word and decree came to be done, when the enemies of the Jews hoped to domineer over them, and that was overturned, when the Jews themselves domineered over those who hated them."

9:2 נִקְהֲלוּ הַיְּהוּדִים בְּעָרֵיהֶם[1]—(a) 8:11[1]. (c) f.s. עִיר (3:15[5]), f.p. עָרִים, §25.6.

לִשְׁלֹחַ יָד בִּמְבַקְשֵׁי רָעָתָם[2]—(a-b) 2:21[7]. (c) Shewa under preform. *mêm* tells us what? Why no dagesh in ק? §13.41, .412. Why –בִּ? §15.651. Translate 'on those who were seeking.' (d) ־ָם is what? §23.121. Cf. 8:3[4] and 8:6[2]. Would *-ām* represent subjective or objective genitive? §36.323f.

וְאִישׁ לֹא־עָמַד בִּפְנֵיהֶם[3]—(a-b) = 'no man.' (d) בִּפְנֵי 'in the face of' BDB 816.II.3, here 'against them' reads better.

כִּי־נָפַל פַּחְדָּם[4]—(a) Causal, §38.53. (c) 8:17[2]. Explain form here.

9:3 וְכָל־שָׂרֵי הַמְּדִינוֹת וְהָאֲחַשְׁדַּרְפְּנִים וְהַפַּחוֹת וְעֹשֵׂי הַמְּלָאכָה[1]—(a) *'ăḥašdarpᵉnîm* 'pro-
tectors of the realm,' Pers. *ḫšatrapâvan.* 3:12[5], 8:9[4]. This is the longest word (incl. bound morphemes) that I have found in the Heb. Bible. (b) 3:12[6]. (c-d) 3:9[4].

מְנַשְּׂאִים[2]—(a) 3:1[4]. It is difficult to determine whether such a cl. is verbal or verbless. We could take the subj. as a compound n. cl., from the beginning of the verse, and the pred. as this ptcp. and its complement.

9:4 וְשָׁמְעוֹ הוֹלֵךְ[1]—(a) Caution! Not שָׁמְעוּ but *šom'ô* from *šōma'* 'report' (8089 4/1).
G65s0 of the verb would take the same form, cf. 29:18. (b) '[was] going, spreading.'

הוֹלֵךְ וְגָדוֹל׃[2]—(a-b) Idiom, G50 of *hlk* + adj., 'becoming continually greater,' cf. BDB 233 I.4d.

Learn the words in Vocabulary Group 56.

Note the following pronominal suffixes:

ba'ălêʸhen *their* husbands
mᵉrûqēʸhen *their* cleansers
bᵉ'ārēʸhem in *their* (m.p.) cities
bāhem in *them*
'ōṯām *them* (dir. obj.)
paḥdām the fear of *them*
yāḏām *their* hand
dâṯēʸhem *their* customs
šnêʸhem the two of *them*
lᵉhannîḥām to indulge *them*

Those who trust in YHWH:
Like Mount Zion he shall not be shaken,
For ever he shall dwell securely.

הַבֹּטְחִים בַּיהוָה
כְּהַר־צִיּוֹן לֹא־יִמּוֹט
לְעוֹלָם יֵשֵׁב׃

Psalm 125:1

65

Purpose: To continue the study of exegesis
Materials: Genesis 12:1-3; 15:4-7

Gen. ויאמר יְהוָה אֶל־אַבְרָם[1]—(b) יהוה is the covenant-name of the God of Israel
12:1 (6,518x as יְהוָה Q *'ăḏōnāy* and 305x as יֱהוִה Q *'ĕlôhîm*). The use of the name as a criterion for distinguishing J from E cannot be carried out satisfactorily. (d) Pr.n. 'Abram,' later changed to *'aḇrāhām* 'Abraham,' Gen. 17:5.

לֶךְ־לְךָ מֵאַרְצְךָ וּמִמּוֹלַדְתְּךָ וּמִבֵּית אָבִיךָ[2]—(a) G32 – do you recognize it? (b) "Ethical dative," like "get yourself out of ...." Translate (a-b) simply 'Go.' (c) ־אַרְצְ־ > ? (d) Est. 2:10[2]. (e) If you haven't learned to spot מִן as a bound morpheme (§22), do it *now*.

אֶל־הָאָרֶץ אשר אַרְאֶךָּ׃[3]—(b) Definite because defined by the following rel. cl. (d) *'ar'ekkā* < **'ar'enkā,* §23.1221. The root is ראה; what stem (vowel under preformative)? Cf. Est. 1:11[4].

12:2 וְאֶעֶשְׂךָ לְגוֹי גָּדוֹל[1]—(a) וְ|אֶ|עֶשְׂ|ךָ – what root? what stem? perf. or impf.? what PGN? (b) l^e- here something like 'into.' *gôy* 'nation, gentile' (v.1471). Indefinite, 'a great nation.'

וַאֲבָרֶכְךָ וַאֲגַדְּלָה שְׁמֶךָ[2]—(a) Break it into its parts. *brk* (D) 'to bless' (v.1288). Shewa under preformative, compensatory lengthening under 1st rad. = ? (b) Follow the same steps as for (a). Est. 3:1[2]. §27.531. §32.342. (c) Est. 2:5[3]. Obj. of (b).

וֶהְיֵה בְּרָכָה׃[3]—(a) G32 of hy^h. §32.325. RSV "so that you will be a blessing," is based on this principle, but the intent is stronger: 'so be a blessing!'

12:3 וַאֲבָרְכָה מְבָרְכֶיךָ[1]—(a) Cf. 12:2[2](b) and (c) – which is this? (b) Preformative ־מְ tells what? ־ֵי before s2 tells what? Is it 'the one who blesses' or 'those who bless'?

וּמְקַלֶּלְךָ אָאֹר[2]—(a) *qll* 'to be small, trifling; (D) to belittle, make contemptible' (v.7043). Stem? Sg. or pl.? (b) *'ā'ōr* for **'a'rōr*; *'rr* 'to curse' (v.779), G24 of CC^2, §§29.511, .5114.

וְנִבְרְכוּ בְךָ כֹּל מִשְׁפְּחֹת הָאֲדָמָה׃[3]—(a) Can נ—וּ be 29? N15? N37? What is the subj. of this verb? (b) Agent. (d) *mišpāḥā*^{h} 'clan, family' (v.4940). (e) *'ăḏāmā*^{h} 'ground, land, earth' (v.127). Possibly this word is used here rather than *'éreṣ* so there will be no tendency to limit the effect to the land promised to Abram. The obvious relationship of *'ăḏāmā*^{h} to *'āḏām* suggests that all mankind is in view.

15:4 וְהִנֵּה דְבַר־יְהוָה אֵלָיו לֵאמֹר[1]—You should be able to do this portion. דבר־יהוה is a much used expression in the Bible. The antecedent of *'ēlā*^{y}*w* is Abram, 15:3. לאמר = 'quote.'

לֹא יִירָשְׁךָ זֶה[2]—(c) 'This one' = Eliezer, 15:3, subj. of the negated verb. (b) *yrš* 'to take possession, inherit' (v.3423). Read §29.3211. Note use of suffix, 'he shall not inherit you' = 'he shall not be your heir.'

כִּי־אִם אֲשֶׁר יֵצֵא מִמֵּעֶיךָ הוּא יִירָשֶׁךָ׃[3]—(a-b) After neg. a strong adversative, 'but rather,' BDB 475.2b. (c) *'ăšer* 'the one who,' subj. of verbless cl. (e) **mēʿā^h*, only pl. cstr. and suf., 'internal parts, bowels, the source of procreation' (v.4578). (f) 'He' or 'that one.' (g) Cf. 15:4[2]; form here is pausal.

Gen. 15:5 וַיּוֹצֵא אֹתוֹ הַחוּצָה[1]—(a) G, N, or H? (c) *ḥûṣ* '(the) outside' (v.2399), + -*ā^h* loc. In Eng. 'outside' can be adverbial but in Heb. it must have ־ָה or a prep. to make it such.

וַיֹּאמֶר הַבֶּט־נָא הַשָּׁמַיְמָה[2]—(b) *nbṭ* (H) 'to look at, regard' (v.5027), H32 + *nâ'*, §32.327. Who is the subj. of (b)? of (a)? (c) Gen. 1:1[2]. Note unaccented ־ָה.

וּסְפֹר הַכּוֹכָבִים אִם־תּוּכַל לִסְפֹּר אֹתָם[3]—(a) Cf. Est. 3:12[1]. *spr* 'to count,' here G32. (b) *kôkāḇ* 'star' (v.3556); definite because well known. (c-f) Cond. cl., hence protasis, and (a-b) apodosis: 'If you're able, count the stars.' (d) Cf. Est. 6:13[6]. 'To be able' requires a complementary inf., (e). (e) Compare this with (a). What difference do you see? Don't overlook a dagesh!

וַיֹּאמֶר לוֹ כֹּה יִהְיֶה זַרְעֶךָ׃[5]—(a-b) Who said to whom? (c) Amos 7:11[1] (Lesson 50). (d) You should know it. (e) Est. 6:13[4]. Form here, + s2 pausal.

15:6 וְהֶאֱמִן בַּיהוָה[1]—(a) Cf. Est. 2:7[1] In H this word means 'to trust, believe,' and followed by ־בְּ 'to believe in, commit yourself to.'

וַיַּחְשְׁבֶהָ לּוֹ צְדָקָה׃[2]—(a) *ḥšb*, cf. Est. 8:3[5]. The word also means 'to reckon, account,' BDB 363.II.3. The s1 refers back to Abram's act of faith. (b) I.e. to Abram. (c) *ṣ^{e}ḏāqā^h* 'righteousness' (v.6666, cf. BDB 842).

15:7 וַיֹּאמֶר אֵלָיו אֲנִי יהוה אֲשֶׁר הוֹצֵאתִיךָ מֵאוּר כַּשְׂדִּים[1]—(a-e) You should be able to read this. (f) הוֹ—תִי suggests what stem, what type of verb, what person? VDC–9. Do you know יצא? Note that the verb agrees in PGN with the antecedent of אשר, viz. אני. (g) *'ûr* pr.n. 'Ur.' Look it up on a map of ancient Mesopotamia. (h) *kaśdîm* pr.n. 'Chaldees.' Look it up in a good Bible dictionary. Akk. *kašdu* later > *kaldu*; the Heb. reflects an earlier or dialectal form.

לָתֶת לְךָ אֶת־הָאָרֶץ הַזֹּאת לְרִשְׁתָּהּ׃[2]—(d-e) What land? (f) G65 of *yrš* is *réšeṯ*, §29.322. Can you work from *réšeṯ* to *l^{e}rištāh*? To whom or what does ־ָהּ refer? For *yrš*, Gen. 15:4[2].

These passages are foundational for the biblical concept of election. It has a purpose that extends far beyond the person or persons chosen. For an elementary discussion, cf. W. S. LaSor, *Israel, A Biblical View* (1976), 32-36. For fuller study, cf. H. H. Rowley, *The Biblical Doctrine of Election* (1950).

Learn the words in Vocabulary Group 57.

Purpose: To read with understanding
Materials: Esther 9:5-11

וַיַּכּוּ הַיְּהוּדִים בְּכָל־אֹיְבֵיהֶם מַכַּת־ ה
חֶרֶב וְהֶרֶג וְאַבְדָן וַיַּעֲשׂוּ בְשֹׂנְאֵיהֶם כִּרְצוֹנָם׃ וּבְשׁוּשַׁן 6
הַבִּירָה הָרְגוּ הַיְּהוּדִים וְאַבֵּד חֲמֵשׁ מֵאוֹת אִישׁ׃

וְאֵת | 7
פַּרְשַׁנְדָּתָא וְאֵת |
דַּלְפוֹן וְאֵת |
אַסְפָּתָא׃ וְאֵת | 8
פּוֹרָתָא וְאֵת |
אֲדַלְיָא וְאֵת |
אֲרִידָתָא׃ וְאֵת | 9
פַּרְמַשְׁתָּא וְאֵת |
אֲרִיסַי וְאֵת |
אֲרִדַי וְאֵת |
וַיְזָתָא׃ עֲשֶׂרֶת י

בְּנֵי הָמָן בֶּן־הַמְּדָתָא צֹרֵר הַיְּהוּדִים הָרָגוּ וּבַבִּזָּה לֹא
11 שָׁלְחוּ אֶת־יָדָם׃ בַּיּוֹם הַהוּא בָּא מִסְפַּר הַהֲרוּגִים בְּשׁוּשַׁן
12 הַבִּירָה לִפְנֵי הַמֶּלֶךְ׃

9:5 וַיַּכּוּ[1]—VDC–11. When there is *only one* radical, it has to be NCY, hence נכה H 'to smite' (v.5221). Note preform. with *pattāḥ*. The verb is followed by –בּ, cf. 'to beat up on.'

מַכַּת חֶרֶב וְהֶרֶג וְאַבְדָן[2]—(a) From root נכה, so try to guess the meaning. *makkā*^{h} 'plague, stroke, wound' (v.4347). It is defined by 3 nouns, unusual for cstr. to have more than one goverened noun. (b) *héreḇ* 'sword' (v.2719). (c) *héreḡ* 'slaughter' (2027 5/1). (d) Cf. 8:6[4]. Strong lists the words separately (12 1/1), but BDB 2 lists both as one entry – in my opinion, correctly.

כִּרְצוֹנָם׃[3]—Cf. 1:8[6].

9:6 הָרְגוּ הַיְּהוּדִים וְאַבֵּד חֲמֵשׁ מֵאוֹת אִישׁ׃ [1]—(a) 3:13[3]. (c) 3:13[3] Note sequence: *hār*^{e}*gû* G15, *w*^{e}*'abbēḏ* D60, §32.391, *Ges*. §113*z*. (d-e) §26.273. §36.14.

9:7-9 The 10 sons of Haman are "hanged" in the text layout. Reasons for the large and small letters, noted in marginal masorah, are not known to me. It is traditional to read these names as rapidly as possible.

9:10 עֲשֶׂרֶת בְּנֵי הָמָן[1]—(a) §26.24. (c) Definite, hence 'the 10 sons of Haman.'

וּבַבִּזָּה לֹא שָׁלְחוּ אֶת־יָדָם׃[2]—(a) *bizzā*ʰ 'spoil, booty' (961 10/3), cf. 3:13⁹, 8:11⁴. In this cl. the conj. *wāw* is better read 'but.'

9:11 You should be able to translate this entire verse.

Memorize the words in BVG–58.

Review the various vowel-patterns of the verb in G-impf.:

G20	yaqtul		yiqtal		yaqtil	
CCC	יִסְגֹּר	*yisgōr*	יִשְׁכַּב	*yiškab̲*		
GCC	תַּעֲבֹד	*ta'ăb̲ōd̲*	יֶחֱזַק	*yeḥĕzaq*	יַעֲלֶה	*ya'ălê*ʰ (?)
CGC	יִטְרֹף	*yiṭrōp̄*	יִשְׁחַט	*yišḥaṭ*		
CCG			יִשְׁלַח	*yišlaḥ*	יֹאמַר	*yō'mar*
'CC	יֶאֱסֹף	*ye'ĕsōp̄*	יֶאֱנַף	*ye'ĕnap̄*	יֹאבֵד	*yō'b̲ēd̲*
	יֶאְסֹר	*ye'sōr*				
CC'			יִמְצָא	*yimṣā'*		
WCC			יִירַד	*yî*ʸ*rad̲*	יֵצֵא	*yêṣē'*
YCC			יִיטַב	*yî*ʸ*ṭab̲*		
YṢC	יִצֹּק	*yiṣṣōq*	תִּצַּת	*tiṣṣat̲*		
NCC	יִפֹּל	*yippōl*	יִגַּשׁ	*yiggaš*	יִתֵּן	*yittēn*
CC²	יָסֹב	*yāsōb̲*	תֵּקַל	*tēqal*		
	יִדֹּם	*yiddōm*				
CWC	יָמוּת	*yāmût̲* (?)	יֵבוֹשׁ	*yēb̲ôš* (?)	יֵשֵׁב	*yêšēb̲*
CYC					יָדִין	*yād̲în* (?)
CCY			יִהְיֶה	*yihyê*ʰ	יֹאבֶה	*yō'b̲ê*ʰ (?)
hlk					יֵלֵךְ	*yêlēk̲*
lqḥ			יִקַּח	*yiqqaḥ*		

Wait eagerly for YHWH;
Be strong and be bold (in) your heart,
And wait eagerly for YHWH.

קַוֵּה אֶל־יהוה
חֲזַק וְיַאֲמֵץ לִבֶּךָ
וְקַוֵּה אֶל־יהוה׃

Psalm 27:14

67

Purpose: To examine the student's progress
Materials: Esther 6:1–9:4

With your Hebrew Bible open to Exodus 13:1-10 work over the following questions.

Which word(s) illustrate(s) the following:

Strong dagesh ("doubler")	קַדֶּשׁ־לִי	1
Weak dagesh ("hardener")	וּבַבְּהֵמָה	2
"Zero" shewa	בִּבְנֵי	3
Maqqeph	חָמֵץ׃	4
"Vocal" shewa	אֶתְכֶם	5
Silluq	וְהַחִוִּי	6
Geminate (doubled) *wāw*	מִמִּצְרַיִם	7
Nasog 'aḥor	הוּא	8
Shuruq	יְהוָה	9
Perpetual qᵉrê	וְהָיָה	10

Which word(s) illustrate(s) the following:

qāmāṣ ḥăṭûp̄	הוּא	1
Quiescent *ʾālep̄*	יֵאָכֵל	2
"Heavy" ending	הָעָם	3
Penultimate accent	לַאֲבֹתֶיךָ	4
Compensatory lengthening	כָּל־רֶחֶם	5
Pausal form	גְּבֻלֶךָ	6
Rule 19	הוֹצִאֲךָ	7
Rule 21	יְצָאתֶם	8
Connecting vowel with accent	אֵת	9
Defective writing of long vowel	בִּבְנֵי	10

Parse the following, giving stem, person, gender, number, any affixes, root, and meaning.

קַדֶּשׁ־לִי	v. 2	זָבַת	v. 5
זָכוֹר	v. 5	וְעָבַדְתָּ	v. 5
יְצָאתֶם	v. 3	תֵאָכֵל	v. 6
הוֹצִיא	v. 3	יֵרָאֶה	v. 7
יֵאָכֵל	v. 4	וְהִגַּדְתָּ	v. 8
יֹצְאִים	v. 5	בְּצֵאתִי	v. 8
יְבִיאֲךָ	v. 5	הוֹצִאֲךָ	v. 9
נִשְׁבַּע	v. 5	וְשָׁמַרְתָּ	v.10

Parse, giving gender, number, state, any affixes, lexical form, and meaning.

בָּאָדָם v. 2
וּבַבְּהֵמָה v. 2
הַזֶּה v. 3
מִבֵּית v. 3
עֲבָדִים v. 3
מִזֶּה v. 3
הָעֲבֹדָה v. 5
שִׁבְעַת v. 6

מַצֹּת v. 6
גְּבֻלֶךָ v. 7
לְבִנְךָ v. 8
לְאוֹת v. 9
עֵינֶיךָ v. 9
תּוֹרַת v. 9
לְמוֹעֲדָהּ v.10
יָמִימָה v.10

Parse the following verbs. Give stem, person, gender, number, any affixes, root, and meaning.

וַיִּקְרַע 4:1
וַיֵּצֵא 4:1
יֻצַּע 4:3
וַתָּבוֹאנָה 4:4
וַיַּגִּידוּ 4:4
וַתִּתְחַלְחַל 4:4
וַתְּצַוֵּהוּ 4:5
קָרָהוּ 4:7
לְאַבְּדָם 4:7
לְהִמָּלֵט 4:13
לֵךְ 4:16
וְצוּמוּ 4:16

אָצוּם 4:16
וַיּוֹשֶׁט 5:2
וַתִּגַּע 5:2
עָשִׂיתִי 5:4
מַהֲרוּ 5:5
וַיִּתְאַפַּק 5:10
וַיַּעַשׂ 5:14
נָדְדָה 6:1
נַעֲשָׂה 6:3
יָבִיאוּ 6:8
נָתוֹן 6:9
קַח 6:10

Parse the following substantives, giving gender, number, state, any affixes (including the def. art.), lexical form, and meaning.

גְּדוֹלָה 4:1
וְדָתוֹ 4:3
לָרַבִּים 4:4
נַעֲרוֹת 4:4
וְסָרִיסֶיהָ 4:4
הֲתָךְ 4:6
עִמָּהּ 4:8
וְנַעֲרֹתַי 4:16
בַּחֲצַר 5:1
פֶּתַח 5:1
בְּרֹאשׁ 5:2
בַּקָּשָׁתֵךְ 5:3
חֲצִי 5:3
בְּמִשְׁתֵּה 5:6
שְׁאֵלָתִי 5:7
לָהֶם 5:8

עַבְדֵי 4:11
יֹדְעִים 4:11
הֶחָצֵר 4:11
אַחַת 4:11
בְנַפְשֵׁךְ 4:13
אֲבִיךְ 4:14
שְׁלֹשֶׁת 4:16
שָׂמֵחַ 5:9
מִמֶּנּוּ 5:9
אֹהֲבָיו 5:10
אִשְׁתּוֹ 5:10
עָשְׁרוֹ 5:11
מִשְׁמְרֵי 6:2
מְשָׁרְתָיו 6:3
בְּלִבּוֹ 6:6
עוֹדָם 6:14

Know the words in vocabulary groups 46-58 and 12-33.

Purpose: To read with understanding
Materials: Esther 9:12-15

וַיֹּאמֶר הַמֶּלֶךְ לְאֶסְתֵּר הַמַּלְכָּה
בְּשׁוּשַׁן הַבִּירָה הָרְגוּ הַיְּהוּדִים וְאַבֵּד חֲמֵשׁ מֵאוֹת אִישׁ
וְאֵת עֲשֶׂרֶת בְּנֵי־הָמָן בִּשְׁאָר מְדִינוֹת הַמֶּלֶךְ מֶה עָשׂוּ
13 וּמַה־שְּׁאֵלָתֵךְ וְיִנָּתֵן לָךְ וּמַה־בַּקָּשָׁתֵךְ עוֹד וְתֵעָשׂ׃ וַתֹּאמֶר
אֶסְתֵּר אִם־עַל־הַמֶּלֶךְ טוֹב יִנָּתֵן גַּם־מָחָר לַיְּהוּדִים אֲשֶׁר
בְּשׁוּשָׁן לַעֲשׂוֹת כְּדָת הַיּוֹם וְאֵת עֲשֶׂרֶת בְּנֵי־הָמָן יִתְלוּ
14 עַל־הָעֵץ׃ וַיֹּאמֶר הַמֶּלֶךְ לְהֵעָשׂוֹת כֵּן וַתִּנָּתֵן דָּת בְּשׁוּשָׁן
טו וְאֵת עֲשֶׂרֶת בְּנֵי־הָמָן תָּלוּ׃ וַיִּקָּהֲלוּ הַיְּהוּדִיִּים אֲשֶׁר־
בְּשׁוּשָׁן גַּם בְּיוֹם אַרְבָּעָה עָשָׂר לְחֹדֶשׁ אֲדָר וַיַּהַרְגוּ
בְשׁוּשָׁן שְׁלֹשׁ מֵאוֹת אִישׁ וּבַבִּזָּה לֹא שָׁלְחוּ אֶת־יָדָם׃

9:12 בִּשְׁאָר מְדִינוֹת הַמֶּלֶךְ מֶה עָשׂוּ[1]—You should be able to read the first part. (a) *š^{e}'ār* 'rest, remainder' (v.7605). (a-c) Cstr. chain. (d) Note vowel, cf. Table G. The balance of the verse you should be able to do. Cf. 5:6, 7:2.

9:13 וַתֹּאמֶר אֶסְתֵּר[1]—(a) Can you explain this form? Learn it *now.* §32.5311, .5312, §32.533.

אִם־עַל־הַמֶּלֶךְ טוֹב[2]—Does this give you any trouble? Is it verbal or verbless? §31. Is it a protasis or an apodosis? §38.611, .612.

יִנָּתֵן גַּם־מָחָר[3]—(a) Note pattern yiC^2āCēC – do you recognize it? You should! §28.42. Master these basic patterns. (c) 5:8[5]. The story seems to deteriorate at this point.*

לַעֲשׂוֹת כְּדָת הַיּוֹם[4]—(a) Comp. inf., §34.8, after נתן 'to permit to ____.' (b-c) 'according to today's decree.' §38.71.

וְאֵת עֲשֶׂרֶת בְּנֵי־הָמָן יִתְלוּ[5]—(b) 9:10[1]. (e) Prob. G45. §32.352. There are two apodoseis in this sentence, §38.612, cf. §32.356. The sons of Haman were already killed, 9:7-10; does Esther want their dead bodies publicly hanged? Why?

9:14 This verse should be easy to translate. Note לְהֵעָשׂוֹת, and remember R.10a.

9:15 You should be able to do this. Cf. 9:2, 6.

---

*Those of us who believe in the doctrine of Inspiration need not be concerned by such a statement. Inspiration does not guarantee literary excellence, only doctrinal authority.

Memorize the words in Group 59.

Note the following uses of ־ל:

וְיִנָּתֵן לָךְ 'and let it be given *to* you'
וְהָמָן בָּא לַחֲצַר בית־המלך 'and Haman was coming in *to* the court ...'
שְׁלוֹשָׁה עָשָׂר לְחֹדֶשׁ שְׁנֵים עָשָׂר 'on the 13th *of* the 12th month'
ויאמר לָהּ המלך 'and the king said *to* her'
אֲנִי קָרוּא לָהּ 'I (was) called *by* her'
אַל־תְּדַמִּי בְנַפְשֵׁךְ לְהִמָּלֵט 'Don't imagine that you will be spared' (lit., *to* be delivered)
וַתִּשְׁלַח בְּגָדִים לְהַלְבִּישׁ מרדכי 'and she sent clothing *in order to* clothe Mordecai'
וַיְבַקֵּשׁ הָמָן לְהַשְׁמִיד אֶת־כָּל־הַיְּהוּדִים 'and Haman sought *to* destroy all the Jews'
אֵין לָבוֹא אֶל־שַׁעַר־המלך בִּלְבוּשׁ שָׂק 'It is forbidden to enter (lit. there is not *to* enter) the king's gate in sackcloth'
לאמר למלך לִתְלוֹת את־מרדכי '*to* say *to* the king *to* hang Mordecai'

זֹבֵחַ תּוֹדָה יְכַבְּדָנְנִי
וְשָׂם דֶּרֶךְ אַרְאֶנּוּ בְּיֵשַׁע אֱלֹהִים׃
The one who brings a sacrifice of thanksgiving
I will honor him,
And the one who establishes his manner of life
I will show him the salvation of God.
Psalm 50:23

Because of the repetitious and sometimes aimless nature of the next portion, students often become restless and fail to use their time well. I have therefore marked the material as three *supplementary* readings, to be omitted, read hastily, or used otherwise, as the teacher thinks best. Lesson 69 resumes the required material, and from there to the end there should be continuous effort to learn something new each day.

SR-1

Purpose: To complete the material in Esther
Materials: Esther 9:16-19

16 וּשְׁאָר הַיְּהוּדִים אֲשֶׁר בִּמְדִינוֹת הַמֶּלֶךְ נִקְהֲלוּ ׀ וְעָמֹד
עַל־נַפְשָׁם וְנוֹחַ מֵאֹיְבֵיהֶם וְהָרוֹג בְּשֹׂנְאֵיהֶם חֲמִשָּׁה
17 וְשִׁבְעִים אָלֶף וּבַבִּזָּה לֹא שָׁלְחוּ אֶת־יָדָם׃ בְּיוֹם־שְׁלוֹשָׁה
עָשָׂר לְחֹדֶשׁ אֲדָר וְנוֹחַ בְּאַרְבָּעָה עָשָׂר בּוֹ וְעָשֹׂה אֹתוֹ
18 יוֹם מִשְׁתֶּה וְשִׂמְחָה׃ וְהַיְּהוּדִיִּים אֲשֶׁר־בְּשׁוּשָׁן נִקְהֲלוּ
בִּשְׁלוֹשָׁה עָשָׂר בּוֹ וּבְאַרְבָּעָה עָשָׂר בּוֹ וְנוֹחַ בַּחֲמִשָּׁה
19 עָשָׂר בּוֹ וְעָשֹׂה אֹתוֹ יוֹם מִשְׁתֶּה וְשִׂמְחָה׃ עַל־כֵּן הַיְּהוּדִים
הַפְּרָוזִים הַיֹּשְׁבִים בְּעָרֵי הַפְּרָזוֹת עֹשִׂים אֵת יוֹם אַרְבָּעָה
עָשָׂר לְחֹדֶשׁ אֲדָר שִׂמְחָה וּמִשְׁתֶּה וְיוֹם טוֹב וּמִשְׁלֹחַ
כ מָנוֹת אִישׁ לְרֵעֵהוּ׃

9:16 וּשְׁאָר הַיְּהוּדִים אֲשֶׁר בִּמְדִינוֹת הַמֶּלֶךְ[1]—(a) 9:12[1], i.e. those *not* in Susa, cf. 3:8[2,3].

נִקְהֲלוּ ׀ וְעָמֹד עַל־נַפְשָׁם[2]—(a) 9:2[1]. (b) Defective writing, §11.3241; would you recognize עָמוֹד? Cf. 9:12. Read §32.391 again. (b-d) Cf. 8:11[1].

וְנוֹחַ מֵאֹיְבֵיהֶם וְהָרוֹג בְּשֹׂנְאֵיהֶם[3]—(a) נוח 'to rest' (v.5117), G60, §32.391. (c) Also G60. In this sentence we have N15 followed by 3 infs. abs.

חֲמִשָּׁה וְשִׁבְעִים אָלֶף[4]—(c) 3:9[3]. Note how this number is expressed, cf. §26.262, §26.28. For balance of verse, cf. 9:10[2].

9:17 בְּיוֹם־שְׁלוֹשָׁה עָשָׂר לְחֹדֶשׁ אֲדָר[1]—The text seems to be corrupt. We should expect an account of the death and destruction on the 13th day and the rest on the 14th.

וְעָשֹׂה אֹתוֹ יוֹם מִשְׁתֶּה וְשִׂמְחָה׃[2]—(a) §29.71. §32.3911. (c) Cstr. 'And to make it a day of drinking (or banquet) and joy.'

9:18 This verse summarizes the days for the Jews in Susa. Compare it with the previous verses.

9:19 עַל־כֵּן הַיְּהוּדִים הַפְּרָוזִים[1]—(a-b) 'Wherefore, on account of this.' (d) *pᵉrāzîm* (Q), pl. of *pᵉrāzî* 'dweller in a hamlet, rural population' (6521 3/1). Kt (§11.61) appears to be Gp55 of an unused verb *prz* 'to remove, separate,' BDB 826.

הַיֹּשְׁבִים בְּעָרֵי הַפְּרָזוֹת[2]—(a) 1:14[6], here 'dwellers, those who were dwelling.' (b) 3:15[5], 9:2[1]. (c) *pᵉrāzāʰ* 'open region, hamlet' (6519 3/1). This cl. modifies *hayyᵉhûḏîm happᵉrāzîm*.

עֹשִׂים אֵת יוֹם אַרְבָּעָה עָשָׂר לְחֹדֶשׁ אֲדָר שִׂמְחָה וּמִשְׁתֶּה וְיוֹם טוֹב[3]—This cl. should not be difficult for you.

וּמִשְׁלֹחַ מָנוֹת אִישׁ לְרֵעֵהוּ׃[4]—(a) *mišlō^{a}ḥ* 'outstretching, sending' (4916 3/2). *mānā^{h}* 2:9[4]. (c-d) Idiom, 'to one another.' (d) *rē^{ae}* 'neighbor' (v.7453).

SR-2

Purpose: To complete the material in Esther
Materials: Esther 9:20-25

וַיִּכְתֹּב מָרְדֳּכַי אֶת־הַדְּבָרִים הָאֵלֶּה
וַיִּשְׁלַח סְפָרִים אֶל־כָּל־הַיְּהוּדִים אֲשֶׁר בְּכָל־מְדִינוֹת
21 הַמֶּלֶךְ אֲחַשְׁוֵרוֹשׁ הַקְּרוֹבִים וְהָרְחוֹקִים׃ לְקַיֵּם עֲלֵיהֶם
לִהְיוֹת עֹשִׂים אֵת יוֹם אַרְבָּעָה עָשָׂר לְחֹדֶשׁ אֲדָר וְאֵת
22 יוֹם־חֲמִשָּׁה עָשָׂר בּוֹ בְּכָל־שָׁנָה וְשָׁנָה׃ כַּיָּמִים אֲשֶׁר־נָחוּ
בָהֶם הַיְּהוּדִים מֵאֹיְבֵיהֶם וְהַחֹדֶשׁ אֲשֶׁר נֶהְפַּךְ לָהֶם מִיָּגוֹן
לְשִׂמְחָה וּמֵאֵבֶל לְיוֹם טוֹב לַעֲשׂוֹת אוֹתָם יְמֵי מִשְׁתֶּה
וְשִׂמְחָה וּמִשְׁלֹחַ מָנוֹת אִישׁ לְרֵעֵהוּ וּמַתָּנוֹת לָאֶבְיֹנִים׃
וְקִבֵּל הַיְּהוּדִים אֵת אֲשֶׁר־הֵחֵלּוּ לַעֲשׂוֹת וְאֵת אֲשֶׁר־כָּתַב 23
מָרְדֳּכַי אֲלֵיהֶם׃ כִּי הָמָן בֶּן־הַמְּדָתָא הָאֲגָגִי צֹרֵר כָּל־ 24
הַיְּהוּדִים חָשַׁב עַל־הַיְּהוּדִים לְאַבְּדָם וְהִפִּל פּוּר הוּא
הַגּוֹרָל לְהֻמָּם וּלְאַבְּדָם׃ וּבְבֹאָהּ לִפְנֵי הַמֶּלֶךְ אָמַר עִם־ כה
הַסֵּפֶר יָשׁוּב מַחֲשַׁבְתּוֹ הָרָעָה אֲשֶׁר־חָשַׁב עַל־הַיְּהוּדִים
עַל־רֹאשׁוֹ וְתָלוּ אֹתוֹ וְאֶת־בָּנָיו עַל־הָעֵץ׃

9:20 הַקְּרֹבִים וְהָרְחוֹקִים׃[1]–The first part you should be able to do. (a) *haqq^{e}rôḇîm,* 1:14[1]. Note unusual קְ (R.1b). (b) *rāḥôq* 'far, distant' (v.7350). These two adjs. modify what word? §36.11.

9:21 לְקַיֵּם עֲלֵיהֶם[1]—(a) *qayyēm* appears to be a late and analogic formation, D65 of קום. For the normal form, §29.631. Read §29.6326. To establish, enjoin upon them.'

לִהְיוֹת עֹשִׂים[2]—'To be doing/making,' cf. §32.375.

בְּכָל־שָׁנָה וְשָׁנָה׃[3]–Cf. 3:14[2], 1:8[6]. For distributives, §33.125.

9:22 כַּיָּמִים אֲשֶׁר־נָחוּ בָהֶם[1]—(a) *kayyāmîm*, comparison, 'as the days.' (b-d) 'in which they rested' – explain the construction.

וְהַחֹדֶשׁ אֲשֶׁר נֶהְפַּךְ לָהֶם מִיָּגוֹן לְשִׂמְחָה[2]—(a) We might expect *kaḥōḏeš*. (c) niCCaC > neGcaC; is it G29 or N10? 9:1[3]. (e) *yāḡôn* 'sorrow' (3015 14/1).

וּמֵאֵבֶל לְיוֹם טוֹב[3]—(a) 4:3[2]. You should be able to do the next part.

וּמַתָּנוֹת לָאֶבְיוֹנִים׃[4]—(a) *mattānā*^{h} 'gift' (v.4979) < **mantanat* – do you recognize the root? *mattān* is collective 'gifts'; the fem. is *nomen unitatis*, a single unit of a class (e.g. m. *fleet*, f. *ship;* m. *hair* [of the head], f. *single hair*), *Ges.* §122*t*. (b) *'eḇyôn* 'poor, needy' (v.34). Why לְ–?

9:23 וְקִבֵּל הַיְּהוּדִים אֵת אֲשֶׁר־הֵחֵלּוּ לַעֲשׂוֹת[1]—(a) 4:4[7]. Note sg. followed by pl. subj., §33.1111. Two dir. objs. (§34.115) follow, in each instance a "that which" clause. (e) *ḥll* H 'to begin'; *hēḥēllû,* read §29.51 and note §29.511. (f) Complementary inf. after (e), 'to begin to do,' §34.8.

וְאֵת אֲשֶׁר־כָּתַב[2]—Second of compound obj. of לַעֲשׂוֹת, §34.115.

9:24 חָשַׁב עַל־הַיְּהוּדִים לְאַבְּדָם[1]—Causal cl. (a) *ḥāšaḇ*, 8:3[5]. (d) 3:9[2].

וְהִפִּל פּוּר הוּא הַגּוֹרָל[2]—(a) Is second *ḥîrîq* long-*î* or short-*i*? Know the Short-Vowel Chart! Cf. 3:7[3].

לְהֻמָּם[3]—(a) *hmm* 'to discomfit' (2000 13/1). G65s5, basic pattern CuC^2, §29.511, before dagesh ֻ.

9:25 וּבְבֹאָהּ[1]—Antecedent of the suffix is not clear: Esther? the plot? This part is a rehash of the story, and it is much inferior in style (see footnote on 9:12[3]).

יָשׁוּב מַחֲשַׁבְתּוֹ הָרָעָה [2]—(a) Gp50 of ישׁב or G20 of שׁוּב? (G40 would be יֵשֵׁב). (c) modifies (b). 'His evil plan shall return.'

עַל־רֹאשׁוֹ[3]—Adv. modifier of *yāšûḇ*, §35.31. You should be able to finish the sentence.

SR-3

Purpose: To complete the material in Esther
Materials: Esther 9:26-28

26 עַל־כֵּן קָרְאוּ
לַיָּמִים הָאֵלֶּה פוּרִים עַל־שֵׁם הַפּוּר עַל־כֵּן עַל־כָּל־דִּבְרֵי
הָאִגֶּרֶת הַזֹּאת וּמָה־רָאוּ עַל־כָּכָה וּמָה הִגִּיעַ אֲלֵיהֶם׃
27 קִיְּמוּ וְקִבְּלֻ הַיְּהוּדִים ׀ עֲלֵיהֶם ׀ וְעַל־זַרְעָם וְעַל כָּל־
הַנִּלְוִים עֲלֵיהֶם וְלֹא יַעֲבוֹר לִהְיוֹת עֹשִׂים אֶת־שְׁנֵי הַיָּמִים
28 הָאֵלֶּה כִּכְתָבָם וְכִזְמַנָּם בְּכָל־שָׁנָה וְשָׁנָה׃ וְהַיָּמִים הָאֵלֶּה
נִזְכָּרִים וְנַעֲשִׂים בְּכָל־דּוֹר וָדוֹר מִשְׁפָּחָה וּמִשְׁפָּחָה מְדִינָה
וּמְדִינָה וְעִיר וָעִיר וִימֵי הַפּוּרִים הָאֵלֶּה לֹא יַעַבְרוּ מִתּוֹךְ
הַיְּהוּדִים וְזִכְרָם לֹא־יָסוּף מִזַּרְעָם׃

9:26 This explains the name "Purim." The sentence should end with *happûr*.

עַל־כָּל־דִּבְרֵי הָאִגֶּרֶת הַזֹּאת[1]—(d) *'iggéreṯ* 'letter' (107 10/2) 'On account of all the words of this letter.' Has a portion of the letter become attached to the story? This could account for the change in style.

וּמָה־רָאוּ עַל־כָּכָה[2]—A second phrase governed by על, which is highly irregular. 'On account of what they had seen concerning this.'

וּמָה הִגִּיעַ אֲלֵיהֶם׃[3]—Yet a third phrase governered by *'al*. The prep. is usually repeated before each of its objects. 'On account of what had happened to them.' For this use of perf., §32.5114. The sentence continues into 9:27.

9:27 קִיְּמוּ וְקִבְּלֻ[1]—(a) Analogic D15 of קום, cf. §29.6326. (b) Kt D10, Q D15. Subj. follows, 'The Jews established and received upon them(selves).'

וְעַל־זַרְעָם וְעַל כָּל־הַנִּלְוִים עֲלֵיהֶם[2]—(b) *zéra'* 6:13[4]. (e) *lāwā*^{h} 'he joined, attached to' (v.3867), N reflexive, §32.83, 'upon all who were attached to them.' Note the repetition of the preps., cf. 9:26.

וְלֹא יַעֲבוֹר לִהְיוֹת עֹשִׂים[3]—(a) *lô'* + impf., §32.5215. (c) Comp. inf., §34.8. (c-d) 'to be doing, observing,' obj. (noun phrase) follows, 'these two days.'

כִּכְתָבָם וְכִזְמַנָּם[4]—(a) 1:22[3]. (b) *z^eman* 'time' (2165 4/2); why do I write it with *pattāḥ*? (R.14). Note dagesh.

9:28 נִזְכָּרִים וְנַעֲשִׂים[1]—(a) 2:1[3], 'being remembered and being done (observed).'

דּוֹר וָדוֹר מִשְׁפָּחָה וּמִשְׁפָּחָה[2]—(a) *dôr* 'generation' (v.1765); Akk. *dâru* was a 50-yr. cycle. (c) *mišpāḥā*^{h} 'family' (v.4940).

וִימֵי הַפּוּרִים הָאֵלֶּה לֹא יַעַבְרוּ[3]—(a) *$w^e y^e$mê > $wî^y$mê*, §15.652.

מִתּוֹךְ הַיְּהוּדִים[4]—(a) *min* + *tôḵ* 'midst,' 4:1[4]. 'From amongst the Jews.'

וְזִכְרָם לֹא־יָסוּף מִזַּרְעָם׃[5]—(a) *zēḵer* 'memorial, remembrance' (v.2143). (c) *sûp̄* 'to come to an end, perish' (5486 8/1).

I would praise the name of God with a song,
and I would magnify Him with thanksgiving.
This will please YHWH more than an ox
or a bull with horns and hooves.

אֲהַלְלָה שֵׁם־אֱלֹהִים בְּשִׁיר
וַאֲגַדְּלֶנּוּ בְתוֹדָה׃
וְתִיטַב לַיהוָה מִשּׁוֹר
פָּר מַקְרִן מַפְרִיס׃

Psalm 69:30-31

Purpose: To read with understanding
Materials: Esther 9:29-32

וַתִּכְתֹּב 29
אֶסְתֵּר הַמַּלְכָּה בַת־אֲבִיחַיִל וּמָרְדֳּכַי הַיְּהוּדִי אֶת־כָּל־
תֹּקֶף לְקַיֵּם אֵת אִגֶּרֶת הַפֻּרִים הַזֹּאת הַשֵּׁנִית׃ וַיִּשְׁלַח ל
סְפָרִים אֶל־כָּל־הַיְּהוּדִים אֶל־שֶׁבַע וְעֶשְׂרִים וּמֵאָה מְדִינָה
מַלְכוּת אֲחַשְׁוֵרוֹשׁ דִּבְרֵי שָׁלוֹם וֶאֱמֶת׃ לְקַיֵּם אֶת־יְמֵי 31
הַפֻּרִים הָאֵלֶּה בִּזְמַנֵּיהֶם כַּאֲשֶׁר קִיַּם עֲלֵיהֶם מָרְדֳּכַי הַיְּהוּדִי
וְאֶסְתֵּר הַמַּלְכָּה וְכַאֲשֶׁר קִיְּמוּ עַל־נַפְשָׁם וְעַל־זַרְעָם דִּבְרֵי
הַצּוֹמוֹת וְזַעֲקָתָם׃ וּמַאֲמַר אֶסְתֵּר קִיַּם דִּבְרֵי הַפֻּרִים 32
הָאֵלֶּה וְנִכְתָּב בַּסֵּפֶר׃

9:29 You should be able to read this verse with little help. תֹּקֶף 'authority' (8633 3/2). What do הַזֹּאת and הַשֵּׁנִית modify? For אִגֶּרֶת cf. 9:26[1]. I know of no explanation for the large ת.

9:30 You should be able to do this verse. שָׁלוֹם 2:11[4]. אֱמֶת 'truth' (v.571) < *'*imint*, root אמן.

9:31 Most of this verse is repetition of what we have covered several times. הַצּוֹמוֹת 4:3[3]. וְזַעֲקָתָם 4:1[5].

9:32 This verse, too, is familiar material. מאמר 1:15[6] (3882 3/3).

Learn the vocabulary in Group 60.

Note the following pronominal suffixes:

yāḏēnû *our* hand
bᵉśārēnû *our* flesh
'āḥînû *our* brother

בְּךָ־יְהוָה חָסִיתִי אַל־אֵבוֹשָׁה לְעוֹלָם׃
In Thee, O Lord, I have put my trust;
I would never be put to shame!
Psalm 71:1

אחרת לירחמאל ושמה
עטרה היא אם אונם:
ויהיו בני רם בכור
ירחמאל מעץ וימין ועקר:
ויהיו בני אונם שמי וידע
ובני שמי נדב ואבישור:
ושם אשת אבישור אביהיל
ותלד לו את אחבן ואת
מוליד: ובני נדב סלד ואפים
וימת סלד לא בנים: ובני
אפים ישעי ובני ישעי ששן
ובני ששן אחלי: ובני ידע
אחי שמי יתר ויונתן וימת
יתר לא בנים: ובני
יונתן פלת וזזא אלה היו בני
ירחמאל: ולא היה לששן
בנים כי אם בנות ולששן
עבד מצרי ושמו ירחע:
ויתן ששן את בתו לירחע
עבדו לאשה ותלד לו את
עתי: ועתי הוליד את נתן
ונתן הוליד את זבד: וזבד
הוליד את אפלל ואפלל
הוליד את עובד: ועובד
הוליד את יהוא: ויהוא
הוליד את עזריה: ועזריה
הוליד את חלץ וחלץ הוליד
את אלעשה: ואלעשה

הוליד את ססמי: וססמי
הוליד את שלום: ושלום
הוליד את יקמיה: ויקמיה
הוליד את אלישמע:
ובני כלב אחי ירחמאל
מישע בכרו הוא אבי זיף
ובני מרשה אבי חברון
ובני חברון קרח ותפח ורקם
ושמע: ושמע הוליד את
רחם אבי ירקעם ורקם
הוליד את שמי: ובן שמי
מעון ומעון אבי בית צור
ועיפה פילגש כלב ילדה
את חרן ואת מוצא ואת
גזז וחרן הוליד את גזז:
ובני יהדי רגם ויותם
וגישן ופלט ועיפה ושעף:
פילגש כלב מעכה ילד
שבר ואת תרחנה: ותלד
שעף אבי מדמנה את
שוא אבי מכבנה ואבי
גבעא ובת כלב עכסה:
אלה היו בני כלב
בן חור בכור אפרתה שובל
אבי קרית יערים: שלמא
אבי בית לחם חרף אבי
בית גדר: ויהיו בנים לשובל
אבי קרית יערים הראה

חצי המנחות: ומשפחות
קרית יערים היתרי
והפותי והשמתי והמשרעי
מאלה יצאו הצרעתי
והאשתאלי:
בני שלמא בית
לחם ונטופתי עטרות
בית יואב וחצי המנחתי
הצרעי: ומשפחות ספרים
ישבו יעבץ תרעתים
שמעתים שוכתים המה
הקינים הבאים מחמת
אבי בית רכב:
ואלה היו בני דויד
אשר נולד לו בחברון
הבכור אמנן לאחינעם
היזרעאלית שני דניאל
לאביגיל הכרמלית:
השלשי לאבשלום בן
מעכה בת תלמי מלך
גשור הרביעי אדניה בן
חגית: החמישי שפטיה
לאביטל השישי יתרעם
לעגלה אשתו: ששה
נולד לו בחברון וימלך
שם שבע שנים וששה
חדשים ושלשים ושלש
שנה מלך בירושלם:

THE ALEPPO CODEX (two-thirds of full size)

The page contains 1 Chr. 2:26–3:4. The Aleppo Codex is the oldest MS of the complete Hebrew Bible and is considered to be the most exact of all such codices.

Purpose: To note the Final Masorah
Materials: Esther 10:1-3 and Final Masorah

י CAP. X. י

וַיָּשֶׂם הַמֶּלֶךְ אֲחַשְׁרֹשׁ ׀ מַס עַל־הָאָרֶץ וְאִיֵּי הַיָּם׃ וְכָל־ א 2
מַעֲשֵׂה תָקְפּוֹ וּגְבוּרָתוֹ וּפָרָשַׁת גְּדֻלַּת מָרְדֳּכַי אֲשֶׁר גִּדְּלוֹ
הַמֶּלֶךְ הֲלוֹא־הֵם כְּתוּבִים עַל־סֵפֶר דִּבְרֵי הַיָּמִים לְמַלְכֵי
3 מָדַי וּפָרָס׃ כִּי ׀ מָרְדֳּכַי הַיְּהוּדִי מִשְׁנֶה לַמֶּלֶךְ אֲחַשְׁוֵרוֹשׁ
וְגָדוֹל לַיְּהוּדִים וְרָצוּי לְרֹב אֶחָיו דֹּרֵשׁ טוֹב לְעַמּוֹ וְדֹבֵר
שָׁלוֹם לְכָל־זַרְעוֹ׃

סכום פסוקי דמגלת אסתר מאה וששים ושבעה. וסימנו כבדני
נא נגד זקני עמי. וחציו ותען אסתר ותאמר. וסדריו חמשה.
וסימנו וזה גב המזבח׃

10:1 וַיָּשֶׂם הַמֶּלֶךְ אֲחַשְׁרֹשׁ ׀ מַס עַל־הָאָרֶץ וְאִיֵּי הַיָּם׃[1]—(a) 2:17[5]. (c) Note that Q adds a vowel where consonantal *wāw* is missing. (d) *mas* 'tribute' (v.4522). (g) *'î* 'isle, coastland' (v.336). (h) *yām* 'sea.'

10:2 וְכָל־מַעֲשֵׂה תָקְפּוֹ וּגְבוּרָתוֹ[1]—(b) *ma'ăśê*^{h} 'act, work, deed' (v.4639). Is ־ֵה abs. or cstr. Table F. (c) 9:29, note *qāmāṣ ḥāṭûp̄*. (d) *g*^{e}*b̲ûrā*^{h} 'might, strength' (v.1369).

וּפָרָשַׁת גְּדֻלַּת מָרְדֳּכַי[2]—(a) 4:7[3] (6575 2/2). Here, something like 'the account of.' (b) Written defectively, cf. 1:4[7], (1420 12/3).

הֲלוֹא־הֵם כְּתוּבִים[3]—(a) הֲ interrog., לוֹא neg. (c) Note pattern. Gp55, pres. state as result of past activity.

עַל־סֵפֶר דִּבְרֵי הַיָּמִים לְמַלְכֵי מָדַי וּפָרָס׃[4]—(a) 'Upon.' The title of the book follows, cf. the title of 1-2 Chronicles. (c-d) 'Affairs of the days' = journal, diary, the official record of events. (e) 'Of/for the kings of Media and Persia.'

10:3 מִשְׁנֶה[1]—Causal. *mišnê*^{h} 'second, next' (v.4932).

וְרָצוּי לְרֹב אֶחָיו[2]—(a) The ending וּי– is Gp50 of CCY, §29.71. רצה 'to like, please,' Gp 'to be liked by, acceptable to' (v.7521). (b) 5:11[2]. (e) *'āḥ* 'brother' (v.251); note *'eḥā*^{y}*w* as if from **'aḥḥ-* or **'iḥḥ-*.

דֹּרֵשׁ טוֹב לְעַמּוֹ וְדֹבֵר שָׁלוֹם לְכָל־זַרְעוֹ׃[3]—(a) *drš* 'to seek' (v.1875). (d) Unusual stem, for דבר is usually in D. It occurs in G mostly as ptcp.

סכום פסוקי דמגלת אסתר מאה וששים ושבעה. —(a) *s*[e]*k̲ûm* 'total of.' (b) *p*[e]*sûqê* 'verses.' (c) *d*[e]- Aram. 'of,' the the rest is in Heb.

וסימנו כבדני נא נגד זקני עמי. [2]—(a) *sîmânô* 'its sign,' followed by quotation of part of 1 Sam. 15:30, to get the word זִקְנֵי. ז = 7, ק = 100, נ = 50, י = 10, total 167, the number of verses in Esther. The use of a portion of a verse precludes any chance of error in the figure.

וחציו ותען אסתר ותאמר. [3]—(a) *w*[e]*ḥeṣyô* 'and its middle,' followed by a quotation from Est. 5:7, the middle verse of Esther, an additional check on the number of verses.

וסדריו חמשה. [4]—(a) *ûs*[e]*d̲ārā*[y]*w* 'and its *s*[e]*d̲ārîm*, sections, paragraphs,' (b) '5.' These are not marked in our text.

וסימנו וזה גַּב המזבח: [5]—(a) *w*[e]*sîmânô* 'and its sign,' followed by a quotation from Ezek. 43:13, to set out the word גַּב, ג = 3, ב = 2, total 5. All this was to ensure the accuracy of the count to protect the text from additions or losses.

Learn the words in BVG–61.

Analyze the following verbs (using VDC if it helps you):

יֵעוֹר	וַיְבַהֵל	וַיִּמָּצֵא	יֹאמַר	תָּבוֹא
יֵעָשֶׂה	וַיְבַקְשׁוּ	וַיִּוָּדַע	תֹּאמַר	תָּבֹא
וַיֶּאֱהַב	וַיְבַקֵּשׁ	וַתִּלָּקַח	תֹּאמַרְנָה	
וַיִּשְׁלַח	וַתְּמָאֵן	וַיִּתָּלוּ	וַיֹּאמֶר	וַיָּשֶׂם
וַיִּיטַב	וַיְשַׁנֶּהָ	יִנָּתֵן	וַיֹּאמְרוּ	וַיַּעַשׂ
וַיִּקְצֹף	וַתְּהִי	תַּגִּיד	וַתֹּאמֶר	תַּגִּיד
יִמָּלְאוּ	וַיְהִי	וַיִּכָּתֵב		

Blessed be the Lord day by day,
He bears us up, the God of our salvation.
Selah.

בָּרוּךְ אֲדֹנָי יוֹם יוֹם
יַעֲמָס־לָנוּ הָאֵל יְשׁוּעָתֵנוּ סֶלָה׃

Psalm 68:19

71

Purpose: To continue the study of exegesis
Materials: Hosea 1:2-5

Hosea 1:2 תְּחִלַּת דִּבֶּר־יְהוָה בְּהוֹשֵׁעַ[1]—(a) t^e*ḥillā*^{h} 'beginning' (v.8642), cstr. before a finite verb (§35.7) = dependent cl. There are enough examples of cstr. before a finite verb, both in the Heb. Bible and in comparative Sem. studies, that emendation should no longer be suggested. (b) D10. (c) Subj. (d) b^e- of agent. *hôšē*$^{a\text{ʿ}}$ pr.n. 'Hosea,' from *yšʿ* 'to save.'

לֵךְ קַח־לְךָ אֵשֶׁת זְנוּנִים וְיַלְדֵי זְנוּנִים[2]—(a) VDC–10. (b) VDC–10. (c) Cf. Gen. 12:1[2] (Lesson 65). (d) *'ēšeṯ* 'wife' (v.802b) < **'išt*, perhaps fem. of *'îš* but not cognate with *'iššā*^{h} (< **'nθ*). (e) z^e*nûnîm* 'harlotries' (2183 11x). (f) m.p.c. of *yéleḏ* 'child.'

כִּי־זָנֹה תִזְנֶה הָאָרֶץ מֵאַחֲרֵי יהוה׃[3]—(a) Causal. (b) CāCôC = ?. (b-d) §35.6. Translate something like, 'for the land has indeed gone into harlotry.' (d) To what does this refer? (e-f) To us, elliptical, but a common idiom in Heb., 'to commit adultery from (after)' = to be unfaithful to, cf. BDB 275.3.

1:3 וַיֵּלֶךְ וַיִּקַּח אֶת־גֹּמֶר בַּת־דִּבְלָיִם[1]—(a) Subj. is what? Remember the irregularities of הלך and לקח! (d) Pr.n. 'Gomer,' also a man's name (Gen. 10:2, etc.). (e-f) Patronymic, 'daughter of Diblaim.'

וַתַּהַר וַתֵּלֶד לוֹ בֵּן׃[2]—(a) הרה 'to conceive' (v.2029), CCY, §29.72. (b) *yld* 'to bear' (v.3205), WCC, §17.341, R.27. (c) "Dat. of advantage" – of course, there is no dative in Bib. Heb. (d) Indef., 'a son.'

1:4 ויאמר יהוה אליו[1]—You should have no trouble with this.

קְרָא שְׁמוֹ יִזְרְעֶאל[2]—(a) VDC–5. (b) Est. 2:5[3]. (c) Pr.n. 'Jezreel,' from *yizraʿ 'ēl* 'El will sow (sows).'

כִּי־עוֹד מְעַט וּפָקַדְתִּי אֶת־דְּמֵי יִזְרְעֶאל עַל־בֵּית יֵהוּא[3]—(a) Causal. (b-c) 'Yet a little, in a little while.' m^e*ʿaṭ* 'a little, a few' (v.4592). (d) BVG-16, v.6485, note accent, §17.342: conv. perf., §32.54. (f) *dām* in pl. = blood shed in quantity or by violence, BDB 196.2f. (g) Jezreel, a place-name; look it up in an atlas. (j) Pr.n. 'Jehu.' 'The house of Jehu' can mean the building he lives in, his family, or his dynasty. Which here? Look up "Jehu" in a Bible dictionary.

וְהִשְׁבַּתִּי מַמְלְכוּת בֵּית יִשְׂרָאֵל׃[4]—(a) תִ—תִי should immediately suggest stem, aspect, person, gender, number. *šbt* 'to cease, rest; (H) to cause to cease, destroy' (v.7673). Note accent, §17.342. (b) *maml^{e}k̲ût̲* 'kingdom' (4468 9x, cf. מַלְכוּת and מַמְלָכָה). (c-d) See note on Amos 7:10[2·3], Lesson 50.

1:5 וְהָיָה בַּיּוֹם הַהוּא וְשָׁבַרְתִּי אֶת־קֶשֶׁת יִשְׂרָאֵל בְּעֵמֶק יִזְרְעֶאל׃[1]—(a) Hc10 'and it shall be.' (b-c) 'In that day' often refers to a future time of judgment or blessing. (d) *šbr* 'to break' (v.7665). (f) *qéšet̲* 'bow (weapon or rainbow)' (v.7198), cstr., since after את and no def. art. (k) *'ēmeq* 'valley,' often a plain alongside a mountain (or half-valley) (v.6010). Look up the Valley of Jezreel in an atlas.

This is not an exercise in exegesis unless you attempt to ascertain the complete meaning. Simply identifying forms and meanings of words and translating is but the first step to exegesis.

Learn the words in Basic Vocabulary Group 62.

גַּם כִּי־אֵלֵךְ בְּגֵיא צַלְמָוֶת לֹא־אִירָא רָע
כִּי־אַתָּה עִמָּדִי
שִׁבְטְךָ וּמִשְׁעַנְתֶּךָ הֵמָּה יְנַחֲמֻנִי׃

Even if I should walk in a valley of deep darkness, I would not fear evil, for Thou art with me; Thy rod and Thy staff, they comfort me.

Psalm 23:4

72

Purpose: To continue the study of exegesis
Materials: Hosea 1:6-9

Hosea וַתַּהַר עוֹד וַתֵּלֶד בַּת[1]—(a,c) Cf. 1:3[1]. (d) Why no def. art.?
1:6 ויאמר לו קְרָא שְׁמָהּ לֹא רֻחָמָה[2]—(a-b) Who said to whom? (c-d) Cf. 1:4[2]. What is the difference? (e-f) Pr.n. 'Lo-ruhamah'; *rḥm* 'to have compassion' (v.7355). **ruḥḥā́mā*^{h} would be Dp11 paus., 'she has not received (or will not, §§32.513, .5132) compassion.'

כִּי לֹא אוֹסִיף עוֹד אֲרַחֵם אֶת־בֵּית יִשְׂרָאֵל[3]—(a) Causal. (c) Est. 8:3[1], here what PGN? (e) Note: shewa (compound) under preformative, ח in 2d rad. therefore no gemination and no compensatory lengthening, §15.1411. For *rḥm* see preceding note. Observe the idiom, 'I will not add again I will not have compassion on ....' Put it in proper English.

כִּי־נָשֹׂא אֶשָּׂא לָהֶם׃[4]—(b) Vowel pattern! (a-b) §35.6.1 (b) < **'enśā'* < **'inśa'* yiqtal, NC', §29.8. *nś'* has several meanings; which fits best here? Is RSV a good translation? Before you answer, look at BDB 670.1b(3), 671.3e. Use your large lexicon constantly.

1:7 וְאֶת־בֵּית יְהוּדָה אֲרַחֵם וְהוֹשַׁעְתִּים בַּיהוָה אֱלֹהֵיהֶם[1]—(a) w^{e}- 'but.' (d) See Hos. 1:6[3], above. (e) ו|הושעתי|ם – does חו—תִי suggest anything? *yš'* (H) 'to deliver, save' (v.3467); which suffix? §23.122. (f) b^{e} of agent, 'by means of YHWH their God.'

וְלֹא אוֹשִׁיעֵם בְּקֶשֶׁת וּבְחֶרֶב וּבְמִלְחָמָה בְּסוּסִים וּבְפָרָשִׁים׃[2]—(a) w^{e}- 'but.' (b) Analyze it; אוֹ–ִי– should tell you stem, WCC, and PGN of impf. Which suffix? For ישע see previous note. (c) Hos. 1:5[1]. b^{e}- 'by.' (d) Amos 7:11[2]. *û*- 'or.' (e) *milḥāmā*^{h} 'war, battle' (v.4421). (f) Est. 6:8[3]. (g) *pārāš* 'horseman' (v.6571). What does this statement mean?

1:8 וַתִּגְמֹל אֶת־לֹא רֻחָמָה וַתַּהַר וַתֵּלֶד בֵּן׃[1]—(a) *gml* 'to deal fully, bountifully; to wean' (v.1580, BDB 168.2). 'And she weaned Lo-ruhamah.' You should be able to finish the verse, cf. 1:3,6.

1:9 ויאמר קרא שמו לֹא־עַמִּי[1]—You should be able to read (a-c) even without the points, cf. 1:4,6. (d-e) Pr.n. 'Lo-ammi,' 'not my people.' Some commentators suggest that this son (and possibly the previous daughter) were not Hosea's children, but children of Gomer's harlotry.

כִּי אַתֶּם לֹא עַמִּי וְאָנֹכִי לֹא־אֶהְיֶה לָכֶם׃[2]—(a) Causal. (b) §21.1. To whom does this refer? Who is speaking? (c-d) Does this refer to the child or to whom? (e) Amos 7:14[2]. To whom does this refer? Does it add emphasis? (g) Do you associate this with יִהְיֶה? (g-h) 'To be to' = to belong to, hence 'I will not be yours,' i.e. 'your God.'

At this point, consult the commentaries – *after* you have gone carefully through the passage. There is much debate over the interpretation. For an excellent survey of the views, cf. H. H. Rowley, "The Marriage of Hosea," *Bulletin of the John Rylands Library*, 39,1 (Sept. 1956): 200-233, reprinted in *id., Men of God* (1963) 66-97. *Never read a commentary before you have worked over the text thoroughly!* To do so is to submit to brainwashing or the like. Don't let someone else tell you what to think. Let the text tell you. This should be the first rule of exegesis.

Note that Hos. 1:10-11 in the Eng. Bible is 2:1-2 in the Heb. Bible. Watch for such details, for references in your reading may be to one or the other system.

Learn the words in vocabulary Group 63.

Review the following sections on verb morphology:
§§27.11-.1172
§§27.13, .14
§§27.2, .21, .221,. 232, .233
§§27.31, .321, .333, .334
§§27.422, .423, .424
§27.6122
§§27.64, .651

Review the following sections on verb syntax:
§§30.12, .122, .22, .23, .33-.3395
§§30.381-.3821
§§32.-32.13
§§32.5-.524

אַךְ טוֹב וָחֶסֶד יִרְדְּפוּנִי כָּל־יְמֵי חַיָּי
וְשַׁבְתִּי בְּבֵית יהוה לְאֹרֶךְ יָמִים׃

Surely good and covenant loyalty shall pursue me all the days of my life,
And I shall return into the house of YHWH at length of days.

Psalm 23:6

73

Purpose: To read with understanding
Materials: Genesis 37:5-9

In this and the remaining lessons, you are reading for pleasure (I hope), with a minimum of help. Work from your biblical text and use the notes only as necessary.

37:5 וַיַּחֲלֹם יוֹסֵף חֲלוֹם וַיַּגֵּד לְאֶחָיו[1]—(a) *ḥlm* 'to dream' (v.2492). (b) Pr.n. 'Joseph,' *yôsēp̄* is G50 of *ysp* 'to add,' cf. Gen. 30:24. (c) Noun; cf. (a) and guess meaning (v.2472). Cognate acc., §34.2f. (d) Est. 2:22[2]. (e) *ʾāḥ* (v.251), pl. *ʾaḥîm*, note vowel changes.

וַיּוֹסִפוּ עוֹד שְׂנֹא אֹתוֹ׃[2]—(a) Est. 8:3[1]. (b) V.5750. (c) – – ָ tells us what? V.8130.

37:6 שִׁמְעוּ־נָא הַחֲלוֹם הַזֶּה אֲשֶׁר חָלָמְתִּי׃[1]—(a) V.8085. *ḥîrîq* under 1st rad. tells us what? VDC–1 or –5? (b) *nâʾ* 'I pray' (v.4994). (c-d) §36.54. (c,f) Cf. 37:5[1] (a,c).

37:7 הִנֵּה אֲנַחְנוּ מְאַלְּמִים אֲלֻמִּים בְּתוֹךְ הַשָּׂדֶה[1]— (a) V.2009, often (but not always) followed by ptcp. (b) §21.1. (c) *ʾlm* D 'to bind (sheaves)' (v.481). (d) *ʾălummîm* 'sheaves' (485 5x). §34.2. (e) V.8432. Est. 4:1[4]. (f) *śāḏê*^{h} '(open) field' (v.3704).

וְהִנֵּה קָמָה אֲלֻמָּתִי וְגַם־נִצָּבָה[2]—(b) Note accent, §29.6318 – is this G11 'stood' or G51 'were standing'? (c) F.s.s4, cf. 37:7[1]. (d) V.1571. (e) *nṣb* 'to stand upright/erect' (v.5324). Note vowels: is it D11 or N11?.

וְהִנֵּה תְסֻבֶּינָה אֲלֻמֹּתֵיכֶם וַתִּשְׁתַּחֲוֶיןָ לַאֲלֻמָּתִי׃[3]—(b) §§29.511, .5113. *sbb* 'to surround' (v.5437). (c) F.p.s7. (d) ןָ– – –ת or נָה– – –ת tell us what? §27.31. For this verb, §28.13, §28.9.

37:8 הֲמָלֹךְ תִּמְלֹךְ עָלֵינוּ[1]—(a) CāCôC, §27.64. What is –הֲ? §22.3. (a-b) §35.6. Translate something like, 'will you indeed reign over us?' (c) *ʿal* + s9, §23.121.

אִם־מָשׁוֹל תִּמְשֹׁל בָּנוּ[2]—(a) *ʾim* sometimes introduces a question (v.518, BDB 49f.). (b) *mšl* 'to rule, have dominion over' (v.4910). Note the prep. that follows.

עַל־חֲלֹמֹתָיו וְעַל־דְּבָרָיו׃[3]—(a) *ʿal* 'on account of.' (b) F.p.s0: (d) M.p.s0.

37:9 וַיַּחֲלֹם עוֹד חֲלוֹם אַחֵר וַיְסַפֵּר אֹתוֹ לְאֶחָיו[1]—(a-c) You should be able to do this, cf. 37:5. (d) *'āḥēr* 'another, different' (v.312). (e-g) You should be able to do this. (e) *spr* v.5608. (g) 37:5[1].

וְהִנֵּה הַשֶּׁמֶשׁ וְהַיָּרֵחַ וְאַחַד עָשָׂר כּוֹכָבִים[2]—(b) *šémeš* 'sun' (v.3121). (c) *yārēaḥ* 'moon' (v.3394). (d-e) §26.25. (f) *kôkāḇ* 'star' (v.3556).

Go over the story several times, until you can read it with comparative ease. Any language is enjoyable when you can read it without having to look up every word or parse every form.

Memorize the vocabulary in Group 64.

Review the use of *wāw* with the verb:
- §§32.53-.549
- §38.22

Review the following sections with regard to the D-stem:
- §§28.1, .2-.222
- §§29.523, .6326, .711
- §§32.222, .24
- §§32.81-815

Review the following sections with regard to the H-stem:
- §§28.3-.33
- §§29.311, .313, .332, .511
- §§29.632, .6322-.6325, .6412, .6413
- §29.711
- §§32.82-.824

God has ascended with a shout,
    YHWH, with the sound of a ram's horn.
Sing praises to God, sing praises!
    Sing praises to our king, sing praises!

עָלָה אֱלֹהִים בִּתְרוּעָה
יהוה בְּקוֹל שׁוֹפָר׃
זַמְּרוּ אֱלֹהִים זַמֵּרוּ
זַמְּרוּ לְמַלְכֵּנוּ זַמֵּרוּ׃

Psalm 47:6-7

37:10 וַיְסַפֵּר אֶל־אָבִיו וְאֶל־אֶחָיו וַיִּגְעַר־בּוֹ אָבִיו[1]—(c) *'āḇîw*, note that *'āḇ* always retains its final *-î* when adding a suffix, cf. §24.6. Pronounce it [ɑˈvi·v]. (f) *g'r* 'to rebuke' (1605 13x). Note that it does not take a dir. obj. (h) Subj. of (f).

מָה הַחֲלוֹם הַזֶּה אֲשֶׁר חָלָמְתָּ[2]—Verbless cl., §31.224. (e) *ḥālā́mtā*, pausal. How do you translate *-tā*? *-tî*?

הֲבוֹא נָבוֹא אֲנִי וְאִמְּךָ וְאַחֶיךָ לְהִשְׁתַּחֲוֹת לְךָ אָרְצָה׃[3]—(a) Note that –הֲ! G60 + G29 of בוא – how would you translate it? §35.6. (c-e) Compound subj. (3 subjs.) with pl. verb. §33.12. (f) Note that –וֹ– after a vowel is *-wô-*. ל– –וֹת tells us what? (h) *-āʰ* is directive (note accent), read §23.2, 'earthward, to(ward) the earth.'

37:11 וַיְקַנְאוּ־בוֹ אֶחָיו[1]—(a) R.1b! *qn'* (D) 'to be jealous, zealous, envious' (v.7065). Note use of prep., position of subj.

וְאָבִיו שָׁמַר אֶת־הַדָּבָר׃[2]—(b) *šmr* 'to keep, guard, watch over, protect' (v.8104). (d) *dāḇār* has many meanings besides 'word,' cf. BDB 182ff.

37:12 וַיֵּלְכוּ אֶחָיו לִרְעוֹת אֶת־צֹאן אֲבִיהֶם בִּשְׁכֶם׃[1]—(a) *hlk* is often formed like WCC, §29.321. Subj. follows. (c) *r'y* to tend, pasture, graze' (v.7462); ל– –וֹת tells us what? VDC–6. (e) *ṣô'n* (< *ṣa'n*, CaCC, with *a'* acting as quasi long-*â* > *ô*) 'sheep, goats, flock, small cattle' (v.6629). Is it definite? (f) s5. Pay attention to the pron. suffixes! (g) *šᵉḵem* pr.n. 'Shechem' – locate it in your Bible atlas. Use exegetical tools from now on.

37:13 ויאמר ישראל אל־יוסף[1]— Learn to read without vowel-points; it's faster. (b) Joseph's father was Jacob, also known as 'Israel,' cf. Gen. 32:29.

הֲלוֹא אַחֶיךָ רֹעִים בִּשְׁכֶם[2]—Verbless, ptcp. for predicate, §31.24. (c) 37:12[1](c). (d) 37:12[1](g).

לְכָה וְאֶשְׁלָחֲךָ אֲלֵיהֶם ויאמר לו הִנֵּנִי׃[3]—(a) G32 + *āʰ*, §27.43f., 'come, now,' or just 'come.' (b) *'eślāḥăḵā*, G24/44s2, *šlḥ* 'to send' (v.7971). Translate possibly 'I would like to send you,' cf. §32.5213. (f) *hinnēʰ* + s4, 'Here am I,' but in the context, more like 'OK, I'll go.'

37:14 לֶךְ־נָא רְאֵה אֶת־שְׁלוֹם אַחֶיךָ וְאֶת־שְׁלוֹם הַצֹּאן[1]—(a-b) G32 of *hlk* + *nâ'*, 'come/go, I pray.' (c) G32 of *r'y* 'to see,' here more like 'look into, find out about.' (e) *šālôm* 'peace, welfare,' cstr. 'the welfare of' = 'how they are.'

וַהֲשִׁבֵנִי דָּבָר[2]—(a) *wahăšîḇēnî*, H32s4; note that the pron. suf., in our way of speaking, is indir. obj., 'bring back word *to me*.' We can also say, 'Bring me word,' but *me* in such a sentence is not dir. obj.

וַיִּשְׁלָחֵהוּ מֵעֵמֶק חֶבְרוֹן וַיָּבֹא שְׁכֶמָה׃[3](a) *wayyišlāḥēhû*. In this and the preceding verb, note connecting vowel, §23.1321. What suf. here? §23.122. (b) *min* + *'ēmeq* 'valley' (v.6010). (c) *ḥeḇrôn*, pr.n. 'Hebron.' Find it on a map. (e) *šᵉḵémāʰ*, §23.2. Learn to spot the *hê*-directive/locative; note the accent. About how far was it from Hebron to Shechem?.

Learn the words in BVG 65.

Review the imperative (impv.) in the following:
§§27.42-.441, .74
§§28.21, .31, .41, .51
§§29.322, 7122, .93
§§32.32-.327
§32.543

Review the jussive (juss.) and cohortative (cohort.):
§§27.5-531
§§28.21, .31
§§29.7122, .72
§§32.34-.345
§§32.35-.357
§§32.544-.545

Review noun morphology; see pp. 23, 25.

A righteous man knows the rights of the poor;
a wicked man does not understand such knowledge.

יֹדֵעַ צַדִּיק דִּין דַּלִּים
רָשָׁע לֹא־יָבִין דָּעַת׃

Proverbs 29:7

Purpose: To read with understanding
Materials: Genesis 37:15-19

37:15 וַיִּמְצָאֵהוּ אִישׁ וְהִנֵּה תֹעֶה בַּשָּׂדֶה[1]—(a) *way|yimṣā'|ēhû*: do you understand each segment? *mṣ'* v.4672. (b) Indef., 'a man.' (d) תעה 'to err, wander about' (v.8582), parse. (e) 37:7[1]. (c-e) Verbless cl., ptcp. and modifier for pred., subj. omitted ('he').

וַיִּשְׁאָלֵהוּ הָאִישׁ לֵאמֹר מַה־תְּבַקֵּשׁ׃[2]—(a) *way|yiš'āl|ēhû*: *š'l* 'to ask' (v.7592). Who asked whom? (b) Definite, the aforementioned man. (c) = 'quote.' (d-e) 'What are you looking for?' §34.1.

37:16 אֶת־אַחַי אָנֹכִי מְבַקֵּשׁ[1]—(a-b) Dir. obj. Note s4 added to pl. אָחִי 'my brother,' אַחַי 'my brothers.' (c) *'ânôkî* 'I' (v.595). אני is used more often than אנכי in the later books of OT, but both *'ănî* and *'ânôkî* are found in the earliest and latest levels of Heb. (d) Almost a pres. tense, 'I am looking for.'

הַגִּידָה־נָּא לִי אֵיפֹה הֵם רֹעִים׃[2]—(a-b) *haggîdāʰ-nâ'*, note vowel under הַ: H11 would have הִ; H32/60/65 have הַ, VDC–7. With *-āʰ* and *nâ'* it must be impv., cf. §§32.326, .327. (d) *'êʸpōʰ* 'where?' (375 10x). (e-f) Verbless, 'they [are] shepherding,' with ptcp. for pred., modified by adv. of place.

37:17 נָסְעוּ מִזֶּה כִּי שָׁמַעְתִּי אֹמְרִים נֵלְכָה דֹּתָיְנָה[1]— (a) *nāsᵉ'û*: נסע 'to pull up stakes, set out, move on' (v.5265). (b) *min* + *zêʰ* 'from this [place].' (c) Causal or explicative, BDB 473. 3c. (d) *šm'* v.8085. (e) Ptcp., subj. not defined, 'I heard (them) saying.' (f) *nêlᵉkāʰ*, lengthened impf./juss., cf. §§32.34, .341, < *hlk*, 'Let us go.' (g) *dôṯāynāʰ*, pr.n. 'Dothan,' + loc. ה ָ-. Cf. 37:17[2](f).

וַיֵּלֶךְ יוֹסֵף אַחַר אֶחָיו וַיִּמְצָאֵם בְּדֹתָן׃[2]—(a-b) Verb, subj. (c-d) Modifier, tells where he went. (e) *way|yimṣā'|ēm*: what suf.? §23.122. (f) Adv. phr. telling where he found them. *dôṯān* is the more common form, cf. 37:17[1](g).

37:18 ויראו אתו מרחוק[1]—(a) From ראה. Can you point it?. (b) *'ittô* or *'ôṯô*? (c) *min* + *rāḥôq* 'far, distance' (v.7350). Who saw whom? Where?

וּבְטֶרֶם יִקְרַב אֲלֵיהֶם וַיִּתְנַכְּלוּ אתו לַהֲמִיתוֹ׃[2]—(a) *bᵉ* + *ṭérem* 'when not yet, before' (v.2962), generally with impf., BDB 382. (d) *yiṯ– – –û*, VDC–1. *nkl* 'to be crafty, deceitful,' HtD 'to deal deceitfully with' (5230 4x). (f) *lᵉ-* + inf. cstr., purpose, 'fo cause him to die.'

37:19 ויאמרו איש אל אחיו[1]—(b-d) §33.121. Can you point (or pronounce) the unpointed words? Keep trying! When you can read the consonants without looking at the vowels, you'll read much more rapidly.

הנה בַּעַל הַחֲלֹמוֹת הַלָּזֶה בָּא׃[2]—Direct quotation. (b) *bá'al* 'lord, owner, husband,' cstr., 'the lord of dreams.' (d) BDB 229, *hallāz* (1975 7x), *hallāzê*^{h} (1976 2x), *hallāzû* (1977 1x) 'this.' (g) G10 'has come,' or G50 'is coming'? After הנה which is more likely?

Learn the words in Basic Vocabulary Group 66.

Review the participle (ptcp.):
§§27.61-.632
§§28.21, .22, .31, .32, .42, .51, .61
§29.6318
§31.24
§§32.37-.376, .5363, .546

Review the infinitive absolute (inf.abs.):
§§27.64-6411
§§28.21, .22, .31, .32, .42, .51
§29.6319
§§32.39-.393

Review the verb forms on pp. 35, 51, 53, 55.

Be still and know that I am God;
I will be exalted among the nations,
I will be exalted in the earth.

הַרְפּוּ וּדְעוּ כִּי־אָנֹכִי אֱלֹהִים
אָרוּם בַּגּוֹיִם
אָרוּם בָּאָרֶץ׃

Psalm 46:10 (MT 11)

Purpose: To read with understanding
Materials: Genesis 37:20-24

37:20 וְעַתָּה לְכוּ וְנַהַרְגֵהוּ[1]—(a) *'attā*^{h} 'now' (v.6258). (b) *hlk* G37. (c) *w*^{e}|*naharg*|*ēhû*: G29/49s0 *hrg* 'to kill,' read §32.355.

וְנַשְׁלִכֵהוּ בְּאַחַד הַבֹּרוֹת וְאָמַרְנוּ חַיָּה רָעָה אֲכָלָתְהוּ[2]—(a) *šlk* (H) 'to throw, cast' (v.7993). You should now know ֵ־הוּ. Can you parse *našlîḵ*? Note vowels. VDC–3. (b) Cstr. (c) *bō'r* 'cistern, dug well, pit' (v.877). (d) Gc15. (e) *ḥayyā*^{h} 'beast, wild animal' (v.2416). (f) V.7453. (g) *'akālāt*|*hû*: note §27.221, §27.72, and the ת– on G11s0.

וְנִרְאֶה מַה־יִּהְיוּ חֲלֹמֹתָיו׃[3]—(a) ֶ־ה, VDC–6; if CCY, then –נ must be 29 (N10 would be ָ־ה), 'we shall see.' (b-d) N. cl., dir. obj. of verb, = indir. disc. (c) 'Be, come to be, become.' 'We shall see what his dreams will become' or 'what will become of his dreams.'

37:21 וַיִּשְׁמַע רְאוּבֵן וַיַּצִּלֵהוּ מִיָּדָם[1]—(b) Pr.n., 'Reuben,' < *r*^{e}*'û bēn* 'see, a son!' cf. Gen. 29:32. (c) *nṣl* 'to snatch, rescue, deliver' (v.5337), Hc20s0. (d) *min* + *yāḏ* + s5.

וַיֹּאמֶר לֹא נַכֶּנּוּ נָפֶשׁ׃[2]—(c) *nakkénnû* < **nankê*^{h} + *n* + *hû*, §27.714, prob. H49, for the energic would not apocopate; *nky* H 'to smite' (v.5221). (d) *Ges.* §117*ll* takes this as a 2d acc. to define the obj., 'Let us not smite him (in) the life.' It could also be taken as an appositive, 'a soul, a living being,' hence not be treated as an animal.

37:22 ויאמר אלהם | ראובן אַל־תִּשְׁפְּכוּ־דָם[1]—(b) Usually אליהם. Verb, obj., subj. (d-e) *'al* usually with juss. for neg. command, §32.353. (e) *špk* 'to pour out' (v.8210). (f) V.1818.

הַשְׁלִיכוּ אֹתוֹ אֶל־הַבּוֹר הַזֶּה אֲשֶׁר בַּמִּדְבָּר[2]—(a) *šlk* (H) 'to throw, fling' (v.7993), ־הַ– ִ־י–וּ must be H37 (VDC–3). (b) *bôr* 'pit, cistern, dug well' (v.953), cf. באר. (g) *midbār* 'steppe, wilderness' (v.4057). Since *midbār* is often used of pasture-land, it is not to be considered as 'desert,' and even 'wilderness' often conveys the wrong idea. Study words *in contexts*!

וְיָד אַל־תִּשְׁלְחוּ בוֹ[3]—Note word order. (a) 'A hand.' (b-c) §32.353. For *šlḥ yāḏ*, cf. Est. 2:21[6].

לְמַעַן הַצִּיל אֹתוֹ מִיָּדָם לַהֲשִׁיבוֹ אֶל־אָבִיו׃[4]—(a) *l*^{e}*má'an* 'for the sake of, in order that' (v.4616, see BDB 775). (b) *haṣṣîl*: note that *pattāḥ*! H65 of נצל after למען, 'in order to deliver him.' (d) *min* + *yāḏ* + s5. (e) *lahăšîḇô*: *l*^{e}- + H65s0 of *šûḇ*. Is this a second purpose cl., or a result cl.?

37:23 וַיְהִי כַּאֲשֶׁר־בָּא יוֹסֵף אֶל־אֶחָיו[1]—(a) Est. 1:1, και εγενετο. (b) Temporal cl. (c) G10 or G50? Try to read the clause without the pointing. Then check your results against the pointed text.

וַיַּפְשִׁיטוּ אֶת־יוֹסֵף אֶת־כֻּתָּנְתּוֹ[2]—(a) *pšṭ* 'to strip off, (H) to strip' (v.6584). (b,d) Unusual to have both objs. of H-stem indicated by את. (e) *kuttont* > *kuttōneṯ* 'tunic' (v.3801).

אֶת־כְּתֹנֶת הַפַּסִּים אֲשֶׁר עָלָיו׃[3]—This cl. is appositional, describing the tunic (§36.65). (b) *kᵉṯōneṯ*, a variant form of v.3801; the forms are used interchangeably. Cstr. (d) *pas* 'palm of hand, sole of foot' (6446 5x, always of a garment). We know this as 'a coat of many colors,' but *kᵉṯōneṯ happassîm* seems to mean a tunic with long sleeves (to the wrist) and skirt (to the feet), in contrast to the sleeveless, knee-length tunic.

37:24 וַיִּקָּחֻהוּ וַיַּשְׁלִכוּ אֹתוֹ הַבֹּרָה[1]—(a) *way|yiqqāḥû|hû*: remember that לקח often behaves as if NCC. Note obj. expressed here by s0, in next cl. by *'ōṯô*. (b) *wayyašlîḵû*: note the vowels, cf. with preceding word. Cf. 37:22[2]. (d) *habbōrāʰ*: note accent; when loc. ה־ָ is used, the def. art. may also be used, 'to the pit.'

וְהַבּוֹר רֵק אֵין בּוֹ מָיִם׃[2]—(a) *rêq*, also *rêʸq*, 'empty' (7386 14x). If you didn't know the meaning, could you figure it out from (c-e)? (e) *máyim* 'water' (v.4325).

Learn the words in Vocabulary Group 67.

Review the N-stem in the following sections:
§§28.4-.421
§§29.311, .312, .6322
§§32.83-.833

Review the HtD-stem in the following:
§§28.5-.53
§29.523
§§32.84-.843

וִיהִי נֹעַם אֲדֹנָי אֱלֹהֵינוּ עָלֵינוּ
וּמַעֲשֵׂה יָדֵינוּ כּוֹנְנָה עָלֵינוּ
וּמַעֲשֵׂה יָדֵינוּ כּוֹנְנֵהוּ׃

Let the favor of the Lord our God be upon us,
And the work of our hands establish Thou upon us,
Yea, the work of our hands, establish Thou it.

(Psalm 90:12)

77

Purpose: To read with understanding
Materials: Genesis 37:25-30

Gen. 37:25 וַיֵּשְׁבוּ לֶאֱכָל־לֶחֶם וַיִּשְׂאוּ עֵינֵיהֶם[1]—(a) Is this from ישב or שוב? Note *ṣērê*. (b) Is it *qāmāṣ* or *qāmāṣ-ḥăṭûp̄*? What difference does it make? (c) BVG-34. (d) If there were a dagesh in שׂ would it help? (e) עין can mean 'eye' or 'spring' – which is it here?

וַיִּרְאוּ וְהִנֵּה ארחת יִשְׁמְעֵאלִים בָּאָה מִגִּלְעָד[2]—(c) *ʾôr^{e}ḥā^{h}* 'caravan' (736 2x, G53 of *ʾrḥ* #731). (d) Pr.n. 'Ishmaelites.' (e) G11 or G51? Note accent! (f) Pr.n. 'Gilead.' Look it up on a map.

וּגְמַלֵּיהֶם נֹשְׂאִים נכאת וּצְרִי וָלֹט[3]—(a) BVG–63. Note geminate ל. (b) Note vowel pattern. Note various meanings of *nśʾ*. (c) *n^{e}ḵôʾṯ* 'spices' (5219 2x; Arab. *nakaʾat*). (d) *ṣ^{e}rî* or *ṣŏrî* 'balsam' (6875 6x). (e) *lōṭ* 'myrrh' (3910 2x, BDB 538).

הולכים לְהוֹרִיד מִצְרָיְמָה׃[4]—(a) Note vowel pattern: is it H of **wlk* or G of *hlk*? (b) *yrd* 'to go down, descend' (v.3881). (a-b) Note the expression, 'going to go down,' i.e., traveling for the purpose of going down to Egypt. It is not a compound verb like Eng. *going to do* – in Heb. that would be *ʿmd l^{e}-*. (c) Pr.n. *miṣráyim* 'Egypt.' What is the unaccented *-ā^{h}*?.

37:26 ויאמר יְהוּדָה אל־אחיו[1]—(b) *y^{e}hûḏā^{h}* 'Judah,' Gen. 29:35. Did you read אחיו *ʾeḥā^{y}w* or *ʾāḥi^{y}w*?

מַה־בֶּצַע כִּי נַהֲרֹג אֶת־אָחִינוּ וְכִסִּינוּ אֶת־דָּמוֹ׃[2]—(b) *béṣaʿ* 'unjust gain, profit' (v.1215). (c) Introduces a condition, BDB 473.2b, *Ges.* §159*aa, bb*. (d) N-stem or G29? BVG-30. (e) Sing. + s9. (f) *w^{e}kissînû*: note vowels; Dc19 of כסה 'to cover, conceal' (v.3680). Note ellipsis in apodosis: 'If we kill ... and conceal ..., what profit [is there for us]?'

37:27 לְכוּ וְנִמְכְּרֶנּוּ לישמעאלים וְיָדֵנוּ אַל־תְּהִי־בוֹ[1]—(a) G37 of *hlk*. Learn it! (b) Est. 7:4[1]. What is the difference between the forms? §32.342. (c) Gen. 37:25[2]. (d) s9. Subj. of following verb. The form could be f.d.s9 written defectively. 'Our hand(s), let it not be on him.'

כִּי־אָחִינוּ בְשָׂרֵנוּ הוּא[2]—(a) Causal. Verbless cl. with a pred. and an appositive. (c) *bāśār* 'flesh' (v.1320). s9 on a noun can be *-nû* or *-ḗnû*, §23.121.

וַיִּשְׁמְעוּ אחיו׃[3]—(a) Would you translate this 'they heard' or 'they agreed'? Why?

37:28 וַיַּעַבְרוּ אֲנָשִׁים מִדְיָנִים סֹחֲרִים[1]—(a) עבר is not easy to translate. Had the men 'passed by' or were they 'passing by' or 'about to pass by'? (c) Appositional. *midyānîm* 'Midianites.' Because both Reuben and Judah seek to rescue Joseph, and because both Ishmaelites and Midianites are mentioned, some scholars believe that two stories have been conflated. (d) Another appositive. *sḥr* 'to travel (as a merchant)' (v.5503), G55 'merchants.'

וַיִּמְשְׁכוּ וַיַּעֲלוּ את־יוסף מִן־הַבּוֹר[2]—(a) *mšk* 'to drag, draw, draw out' (v.4900). (b) This form could be Gc25 or Hc25 – which is it? (e-f) Cf. 37:20[2].

וימכרו את־יוסף לישמעאלים בְּעֶשְׂרִים כָּסֶף[3]—(a) 37:27[1]. Here see §32.533. (e) *bᵉ*- of measure, price, BDB 90.III.3b. *ʿeśrîm* v.6242. (f) *késep̄* 'silver,' but since coinage was unknown at this date, we should probably understand '20 [shekels of] silver,' BDB 494.8b. You should be able to finish the verse. For *miṣráymāʰ*, cf. 37:25[4].

37:29 וַיָּשָׁב ראובן אל־הַבּוֹר והנה אין־יוסף בַּבּוֹר[1]—(a) Is this from *šûḇ* or *yšb*? You should be able to do the rest of the clause.

ויקרע את־בגדיו׃[2]—Cf. Est. 4:1[2].

37:30 וישב אל־אחיו ויאמר[1]—You should be able to read this – even without pointing!

הַיֶּלֶד אֵינֶנּוּ וַאֲנִי אָנָה אֲנִי־בָא׃[2]—(a) BVG-20. Joseph was 17, but as next-to-youngest he was a *yéleḏ*. (b) §23.1221. (c,e) §21.1. (d) *ʾā̌nāʰ* < *ʾān* 'where?' (v.575) + ה-directive, BDB 33. (f) G10 and G50 of CWC can be confused – but what of G14 and G50?

Learn the words in Basic Vocabulary Group 68.

אַחַת דִּבֶּר אֱלֹהִים שְׁתַּיִם־זוּ שָׁמָעְתִּי
כִּי־עֹז לֵאלֹהִים׃
וּלְךָ־אֲדֹנָי חָסֶד
כִּי־אַתָּה תְשַׁלֵּם לְאִישׁ כְּמַעֲשֵׂהוּ׃

Once God has spoken, twice have I heard this,
That power belongs to God,
Even to You, my Lord, covenant loyalty,
For You will reward a man according to his work.

Psalm 62:11-12 (MT 12-13)

78

Purpose: To read with understanding
Materials: Genesis 37:31-36

37:31 וַיִּקְחוּ אֶת־כְּתֹנֶת יוֹסֵף וַיִּשְׁחֲטוּ שְׂעִיר עִזִּים[1]—(a) If you haven't learned to recognize forms of לקח yet, do it *now.* (c) 37:23. (e) *śḥṭ* 'to slaughter' (v.7819). (f) *śā‘îr* 'he-goat, buck' (v.8163); abs. or cstr.? (g) *‘ēz* 'she-goat' (v.5795).

וַיִּטְבְּלוּ אֶת־הַכֻּתֹּנֶת בַּדָּם׃[2]—(a) *ṭbl* 'to dip' (v.2881). (c) 37:23. (d) Is it 'in blood' or 'in the blood'?

37:32 וַיְשַׁלְּחוּ אֶת־כְּתֹנֶת הַפַּסִּים וַיָּבִיאוּ אֶל־אֲבִיהֶם[1]—(a) BVG-14. Is it G, D, or N? (c,d) 37:23. (e) What stem-indicators do you see at once? (g) 37:10. Note the rather strange juxtaposition of 'and they sent ... and they brought ....'

ויאמרו זאת מָצָאנוּ[2]—(b) §21.2. (c) נוּ– is what morpheme? §27.21.

הַכֶּר־נָא הַכְּתֹנֶת בִּנְךָ הִוא אִם־לֹא׃[3]—(a) D32 of *hkr* or H32 of *nkr*? *nkr* 'to observe, regard' (v.5234). (c) Since this word is in cstr., we must read –הַ as interrog. In a few instances, *hê*-interrog. takes *pattāḥ* and the strong dagesh, *Ges.* 101*l.* (d) *bēn* + s2; we should expect **benḵā* (Short Vowel Chart). (e) In Pentateuch (only!), *hî’* is always written הִוא – a fact which the theory of a Hexateuch does not satisfactorily explain. (f-g) 'Or not.' (c-g) Verbless correlative cls., '[Is] that the tunic of your son or [is it] not?'

37:33 וַיַּכִּירָהּ ויאמר כְּתֹנֶת בְּנִי[1]—(a) Hc20s1: if you don't understand that analysis, review your verb-forms. *nkr,* 37:32[3]. (d) *bēn* + s4. (c-d) Verbless, '[It is] my son's tunic.'

חַיָּה רָעָה אֲכָלָתְהוּ טָרֹף טֹרַף יוֹסֵף׃[2]—(a) *ḥayyā*^{h} BVG-30. (b) *rā‘ā*^{h} BVG-49, Est. 7:6[1]. (c) Remember that G11 preserves original ת– in suffixial forms. §27.721. This is G11s0 pausal. (d) *ṭrp* 'to tear, rend' (v.2963). CāCôC is what form? §27.64. (e) *Be careful!* The *ḥôlām* could be *ô* < *â* (R.2b), or it could be a *u*-vowel with compensatory lengthening before ר. What would **ṭurrap̄* be? VDC–1. 'Joseph has surely been torn to pieces!'

37:34 וַיִּקְרַע יַעֲקֹב שִׂמְלֹתָיו וַיָּשֶׂם שַׂק בְּמָתְנָיו[1]—(a) Est. 4:1[2]. (b) Gen. 37:1. (c) *śimlā*^{h} 'mantle, wrapper; pl. clothes' (v.8071). (d) Est. 2:17[5]. (e) Est. 4:1[3]. (f) *moṯnáyim* 'loins' (v.4975).

וַיִּתְאַבֵּל עַל־בְּנוֹ ימים רבים׃[2]—(a) Est. 6:12[3]. (b) 'On account of.' (d-e) Est. 1:4[8].

Gen. וַיָּקֻמוּ כָל־בָּנָיו וְכָל־בְּנֹתָיו לְנַחֲמוֹ[1]—(a) Would you recognize it better as וַיָּקוּמוּ? (b-
37:35 d) Two subjects, each a noun-phrase. (e) Est. 2:7[8]. Note that the pl. of *bat* is *bānôt*. (f) *nḥm* (d) 'to comfort' (v.5162). Parse it.

וַיְמָאֵן לְהִתְנַחֵם ויאמר כִּי־אֵרֵד אֶל־בְּנִי אָבֵל שְׁאֹלָה[2]—(a) Cf. Est. 1:12[1]. (b) Comp. inf. Cf. 37:35[1](f). (e) *'ērēd* < **'ayridu*, §29.321; cf. 37:25[4]. (h) *'ābēl*, Est. 6:12[3]. (i) *šᵉ'ôl* 'Sheol, the underworld, the realm of the dead' (v.7585). Note unaccented *-āʰ*. (d-i) Direct discourse, put in his own words: 'I shall go down to my son, to Sheol, weeping.'

וַיֵּבְךְּ אתו אָבִיו׃[3]—(a) Cf. Est. 8:3[3]. (b) Note that the Heb. verb takes a dir. obj.: we translate 'his father wept *for* him.'

37:36 וְהַמְּדָנִים מָכְרוּ אתו אֶל־מִצְרָיִם[1]—(a) *mᵉdānîm* variant form of *midyānîm* (37:28), the former attributed to E, the latter to JE – but the scant evidence is mixed, cf. BDB 193. (b) Gen. 37:27. (e) Gen. 37:25. 'They sold him into Egypt' is rather elliptical, and the following phrase is needed.

לְפוֹטִיפַר סְרִיס פַּרְעֹה שַׂר הַטַּבָּחִים׃[2]—(a) This is the indir. obj. of מכרו. Pr. n. 'Potiphar.' (b) You haven't forgotten this word, have you? (c) *par'ōʰ* 'Pharaoh' (Egypt. *pr-'ˀ* 'great house'). (e) *ṭabbāḥ* 'butcher, cook, bodyguard' (v.2876), but (d-e) always = 'captain of bodyguard.' To whom does it refer – Pharaoh or Potiphar?

Learn the words in Vocabulary Group 69.

Review the infinitive construct (inf. cstr.):
§§27.65-.654, .75, .752
§§28.21, .22, .31, .32
§§29.2213, .322, .93
§§31.141, .142
§§32.38-.386, .5364

Of the making of many books there is no end,
And much studying is a wearying of flesh.

עֲשׂוֹת סְפָרִים הַרְבֵּה אֵין קֵץ
וְלַהַג הַרְבֵּה יְגִעַת בָּשָׂר׃

Ecclesiastes 12:12

79

Purpose: To read with understanding
Materials: Genesis 45:4-10

Gen. ויאמר יוסף אל־אחיו גְּשׁוּ־נָא אֵלַי וַיִּגָּשׁוּ[1]—(a-d) No problem. (e) *ngš* 'to draw near,
45:4 approach' (v.5066), VDC–10. (h) Compare this form with (e). §32.533.

ויאמר אני יוסף אחיכם אשר־מְכַרְתֶּם אֹתִי מִצְרָֽיְמָה׃[2]—(a) Note *r^{e}bî$^{a‘}$*. (e) + s7. (b-e) You should be able to translate; verbless, subj., pred., appositive. (f) Gen. 37:27[1], Est. 7:4[1] ־תֶּם tells us what? (f-g) 'who you sold me' = 'whom you sold.' (h) Unaccented ־ָה. This is not indir. obj., 'you sold to Egypt,' but directional, 'Egyptward,' i.e. to be taken to Egypt. RSV 'sold into Egypt.'

45:5 ועתה אַל־תֵּעָצְבוּ וְאַל־יִחַר בְּעֵינֵיכֶם[1]—(a) *‘attā^h* 'now' (BVG-11). (c) תֵּ־ָ־וּ: what stem? PGN? *‘ṣb* 'to grieve; (N) to be grieved, full of grief' (v.6087). Read §32.353: what mood or aspect? §32.832. (e) חרה 'to be angry, burn with anger' (v.2734), G40, probably referring to the incident. RSV 'do not ... be angry with yourselves,' taken literally would require G47, but it gives the sense. (f) What does עין mean here? (v.5869).

כי־מכרתם אתי הֵנָּה[2]—(a) 'That you sold me,' n. cl., defining the subj. of *yiḥar*. (a-c) 45:4[2]. (d) *hḗnnā^h* 'hither, to this (place/time)' (v.2008, BDB 244).

כי לְמִחְיָה שְׁלָחַנִי אלהים לִפְנֵיכֶם׃[3]—(a) Causal. (b) *miḥyā^h* 'preservation of life' (4241 8x; cf. BDB 313). (c) ־ַנִי §17.32, §27.712. *šlḥ* BVG-14. (e) *lip̄nê* + s7.

45:6 כִּי־זֶה שְׁנָתַיִם הָרָעָב בְּקֶרֶב הָאָרֶץ[1]—(c) Dual, 'two years' (*šānā^h* BVG-3). 'This two years' = 'it is now the second year.' (d) *rā‘āb* 'famine, hunger' (v.7458). (e) *b^{e}qéreb* often = *b^e*- (BVG-11).

וְעוֹד חָמֵשׁ שָׁנִים אשר אֵין־חָרִישׁ וְקָצִיר׃[2]—(b) §26.23. (c) Both *šānîm* and *šānôt* are found; cf. 45:6[1]. (e) applies to the next two words as a unitary idea. (f) *ḥārîš* 'plowing, plowing-time' (2758 3x), cf. v.2790. (g) *qāṣîr* 'harvest, harvesting' (v.7105). '[There will be] yet five years where no plowing-and-harvesting' – put it in smooth Eng.

45:7 וַיִּשְׁלָחֵנִי אלהים לפניכם לָשׂוּם לָכֶם שְׁאֵרִית בָּאָרֶץ[1]—(a) §27.712. Gen. 45:5[3]. (d) *śûm*, v. 7760, here 'to establish,' BDB 963.3. (f) *š^e'ērîṯ* 'remnant, remainder' (v.7611). (g) To what does this refer?

ולְהַחֲיוֹת לָכֶם לִפְלֵיטָה גְּדֹלָה׃[2]—(a) לְהַ־ does not > ־לְ when ה is the stem-indicator. BVG-30, v.2421. (c) *p^{e}lîṭā^h* 'escape, deliverance' (v.6413). RSV 'to keep alive for you many survivors' – evaluate.

45:8 וְעַתָּה לֹא־אַתֶּם שְׁלַחְתֶּם אֹתִי הֵנָּה כִּי הָאֱלֹהִים[1]—(a) Gen. 45:5[1]. (b-c) The position of לֹא stresses 'it was not *you* ... but *God*.' 'You did not send me' fails to bring this out. (d) תֶּם–: you should know it! (f) 45:5[2]. (g) After neg., 'but.' (h) Def. = 'the (true) God),' i.e. YHWH.

וַיְשִׂימֵנִי לְאָב לְפַרְעֹה וּלְאָדוֹן לְכָל־בֵּיתוֹ וּמֹשֵׁל בְּכָל־אֶרֶץ מִצְרָיִם׃[2]—(b) §27.713, Gen. 45:7[1]. Who is the subj.? (c) 'For a father.' (d) Gen. 37:36[2]. (e) *'āḏôn* 'lord' (BVG-13). (f-g) Whose house? What does 'house' mean here? (h) *mšl* 'to rule, have dominion over' (v.4910), G50, followed by –בְּ.

45:9 מַהֲרוּ וַעֲלוּ אֶל־אָבִי וַאֲמַרְתֶּם אֵלָיו[1]—(a) Est. 5:5[1]. (b) What is the difference between וְעָלוּ and וַעֲלוּ? VDC–6 and –10. (d) Is there reason for using *'āḇî* rather than *'āḇînû?* (e) §32.543.

כֹּה אָמַר בִּנְךָ יוֹסֵף[2]—(a-b) The formula כֹּה אָמַר יְהוָה is used often in the prophets; here it is 'Thus says thy son.'

שָׂמַנִי אֱלֹהִים לְאָדוֹן לְכָל־מִצְרָיִם[3]—(a) CWC, G10s0, cf. 45:7[1], 8[2]. Who/what is the subj.? (d) 45:8[2].

רְדָה אֵלַי אַל־תַּעֲמֹד׃[4]—(a) *yrd*, Gen. 37:25[4]. §27.43. §29.322. §32.326. (d) *'md* 'to stand' (BVG-7), here 'to tarry, delay,' BDB 764.3c.

45:10 וְיָשַׁבְתָּ בְאֶרֶץ־גֹּשֶׁן וְהָיִיתָ קָרוֹב אֵלַי[1]—(a) Note pointing! וְ–ָ–ְ–תָּ should be c12 – but is it? of what verb? (c) Pr.n. 'Goshen.' Look it up! (d) Why no accent shift? §17.341. (e) BVG-11.

אַתָּה וּבָנֶיךָ וּבְנֵי בָנֶיךָ וְצֹאנְךָ וּבְקָרְךָ וְכָל־אֲשֶׁר־לָךְ׃[2]—You should be able to read this with little difficulty. (c-d) 'Grandsons.' (e) 'Small cattle, flocks' (BVG-65). (f) 'Large cattle, herds' (BVG-43).

Learn the words in BVG–70. At this point you should know at least half of the words in the Basic Vocabulary. Aim to learn the rest, until you can translate easily any word that occurs fifteen times or more (approximately 1,500 words).

טוֹב אַחֲרִית דָּבָר מֵרֵאשִׁיתוֹ
טוֹב אֶרֶךְ־רוּחַ מִגְּבַהּ רוּחַ׃
Better is the end of a matter than the beginning,
and the patient in spirit than the proud in spirit.

Ecclesiastes 7:8

Purpose: To prepare for the final examination
Materials: The work of the entire course

Use the following passage for review, with the help of the analytical notes.

1 וּלְכֹהֵן מִדְיָן שֶׁבַע בָּנוֹת וַתָּבֹאנָה
2 וַתִּדְלֶנָה וַתְּמַלֶּאנָה אֶת־הָרְהָטִים לְהַשְׁקוֹת צֹאן אֲבִיהֶן׃
3 וַיָּבֹאוּ הָרֹעִים וַיְגָרְשׁוּם וַיָּקָם מֹשֶׁה וַיּוֹשִׁעָן וַיַּשְׁקְ אֶת־
4 צֹאנָם׃ וַתָּבֹאנָה אֶל־רְעוּאֵל אֲבִיהֶן וַיֹּאמֶר מַדּוּעַ מִהַרְתֶּן
5 בֹּא הַיּוֹם׃ וַתֹּאמַרְןָ אִישׁ מִצְרִי הִצִּילָנוּ מִיַּד הָרֹעִים וְגַם־
6 דָּלֹה דָלָה לָנוּ וַיַּשְׁקְ אֶת־הַצֹּאן׃ וַיֹּאמֶר אֶל־בְּנֹתָיו וְאַיּוֹ
7 לָמָּה זֶּה עֲזַבְתֶּן אֶת־הָאִישׁ קִרְאֶן לוֹ וְיֹאכַל לָחֶם׃

Answer these questions (number refers to line of text):
(1) *ûlᵉḵôhēn*: Does §16.31 apply? Abs. or cstr.? *miḏyān* is pr.n. (2) *ʾeṯ-hārᵉhāṭîm*: Is *ʾeṯ* the prep. or sign of obj.? Is there a def. art.? How would you locate this word in lexicon? (2) *ʾăḇîhen*: What pron. suf.? Antecedent? (3) *wayᵉgārᵉšûm*: To whom/what does pron.suf. refer? (3) *wayyôšîʿān*: To whom/what does pron.suf. refer? (3) *wayyašq*: In context is this Gc20 or Hc20? (5) *bōʾ*: How is this inf.cstr. used? (5) *hiṣṣîlā́nû*: To whom does the pron.suf. refer? How is it related to the verb? (7) *wᵉyôʾḵal*: In context how is the *wāw* used? What kind of clause is it?

Identify the verb-forms (= parse them) from the morphological patterns:
(1) *wattaCōʾnā* §27.117 §29.6315
(2) *wattaCᵉCénā* §27.31 §29.7122
(2) *lᵉhaCCôṯ* §28.31 §29.71
(2) *wattᵉCaC^{2}éʾnā* §28.21 §29.2211
(3) *wayᵉCāGᵉCûm* §13.411 §29.122 §29.711
(3) *wayyāCōC* §29.631
(3) *wayyôCîCān* §27.712 §29.311
(3) *wayyaCC* §13.5332 §29.721
(4) *CiGaCten* §28.21 §29.12
(5) *hiC^{2}CîCā́nû* §27.712 §28.31 §29.4
(6) *CāCô^h* §27.64 §29.71
(7) *GăCaCten* §27.221 §29.11
(7) *CiCʾen* §27.42 *Ges.* §47*f*
(7) *wᵉyôʾCaC* §29.212 (§27.117?)

Review noun morphology, using the following words:
(1) *kôhēn* §15.223 §24.233
(1) *šéḇaʿ* §15.431 §17.11 §24.211

(2) *rᵉḥāṭîm* §15.611 §24.216 §24.211
(2) *ṣōʾn* §15.63
(2) *ʾăbîhen* §24.121
(3) *rōʿîm* §24.23
(5) *yôm* §15.7212 §24.212
(5) *ʾîš* §24.12
(5) *miṣrî* §24.55
(5) *yaḏ* §24.12
(7) *lāhem* §15.112 §15.131 §24.211

1 וַיְהִי בִּימֵי בִּלְקִים מַלְכַּת־שְׁבָא וּשְׁלֹמֹה יוֹשֵׁב עַל־כִּסֵּא
2 יְרוּשָׁלַיִם תַּחַת דָּוִד אָבִיו וּבִלְקִים יְפַת־תֹּאַר וְטוֹבַת־מַרְאֶה׃
3 וַתִּסַּע בִּלְקִים הַמַּלְכָּה לָלֶכֶת יְרוּשָׁלַיְמָה בְּחַיִל כָּבֵד מְאֹד
4 וַתָּבֹא אֶל־הָעִיר׃ וַיֵּצֵא לִקְרַאת אֹתָהּ אִישׁ הָאֱלֹהִים וּשְׁמוֹ
5 אֲחִיָּה הוּא נָבִיא יְהֹוָה׃ וַיֹּאמֶר אֵלֶיהָ לָמָּה בָּאתְ הֵנָּה
6 הָאִשָּׁה׃ וַתַּעַן אֵלָיו וַתֹּאמֶר שָׁמַעְתִּי אֶת־שֵׁמַע שְׁלֹמֹה הַמֶּלֶךְ וְלִלְמֹד
7 עַל־מְקוֹר חָכְמָתוֹ בָּאתִי הֵנָּה׃ וַיֹּאמֶר אֲחִיָּה הַנָּבִיא הִנֵּה
8 הַיָּמִים בָּאִים וַיָּקֶם יְהֹוָה גָּדוֹל מִשְּׁלֹמֹה וְחָכָם מִמֶּנּוּ
9 וּמְלָכִים יָבֹאוּ מֵאַפְסֵי־אָרֶץ וְיִשְׁתַּחֲווּ־לוֹ אַף־מַלְכֵי שְׁבָא
10 וּסְבָא יַקְרִיבוּ מִנְחָה אֵלָיו׃ וְכִרְאֹת בִּלְקִים אֵת כָּל־חָכְמַת
11 שְׁלֹמֹה וְהַבַּיִת אֲשֶׁר בָּנָה אָמְרָה אֵלָיו אֱמֶת הָיָה הַדָּבָר
12 אֲשֶׁר שָׁמַעְתִּי בְּאַרְצִי וְהִנֵּה לֹא־הֻגַּד־לִי הַחֵצִי׃ וַיֶּאֱהַב
13 שְׁלֹמֹה אֶת־בִּלְקִים וַתֵּשֶׁב לְאַרְצָהּ וַתֵּלֶד בֵּן וַתִּקְרָא אֶת־
14 שְׁמוֹ מְנֶלִיךְ כִּי אָמְרָה לְקַחְתִּיו מִן־הַמֶּלֶךְ שְׁלֹמֹה׃

Proper names: מְנֶלִיךְ, סְבָא, אֲחִיָּה, דָּוִד, יְרוּשָׁלַיִם, שְׁלֹמֹה, שְׁבָא, בִּלְקִים.
Difficult words: אֶפֶס BVG 64; מִנְחָה BVG 63; נָסַע BVG 66; שֶׁמַע report; מָקוֹר source.

Don't bother trying to look up this passage. It is composed of bits from various portions of the Old Testament, plus some legendary details, cast in "biblical" form by me. If you have problems, parse the verbs, work out the clauses, and do it bit by bit. You *may* get a sight-translation in the final exam.

If you plan to take Hebrew seriously, continue to read the Hebrew Bible in increasingly larger portions. Work your way through the *Handbook* again—better still, teach it to someone else. כָּל טוּב וּבְרָכוֹת.

יְבָרֶכְךָ יְהֹוָה וְיִשְׁמְרֶךָ׃
יָאֵר יְהֹוָה פָּנָיו אֵלֶיךָ וִיחֻנֶּךָּ׃
יִשָּׂא יְהֹוָה פָּנָיו אֵלֶיךָ וְיָשֵׂם לְךָ שָׁלוֹם׃

May YHWH bless you and protect you.
May YHWH cause his face to shine on you and may he show you grace.
May YHWH lift his face to you and appoint for you wholeness.

Numbers 6:24-25

BASIC VOCABULARY GROUPS

These groups have been selected on the following bases: (1) The word occurs at least 40x in the OT; (2) It is in the current lesson or close thereby; (3) It is cognate with such a word; (4) It is similar in sound or meaning to such a word. By grouping cognates, the student is able to learn two or more words with little more effort than it takes to learn one word.

Basic Vocabulary Group–1 Lesson 4

-בְּ *b*^{e}- in, with, by
-הַ *ha-* the
הוּא *hûʾ* he, that; הִיא *hîʾ* she, that (1931)
הָיָה *hāyā*^{h} he was (1961)
-וְ *w*^{e}- -וָ *wā-* and
יוֹם *yôm* day (3117); יוֹמָם *yômām* daily (3119)
מָלַךְ *mālaḵ* he ruled (4427); מַלְכוּת *malḵûṯ* kingdom (4438)
מֶלֶךְ *méleḵ* king (4428); מַלְכָּה *malkā*^{h} queen (4436)
מִן *min* from (4480)
עַד *ʿaḏ* up to, until (5704)

Basic Vocabulary Group–2 Lesson 5

הֵמָּה *hémmā*^{h} הֵם *hēm* they (m., 1992); הֵנָּה *hénnā*^{h} הֵן *hēn* they (f., 2004)
יָשַׁב *yāšaḇ* he sat (3427)
מוֹשָׁב *môšaḇ* seat, dwelling-place (4186)
עַל *ʿal* upon, unto (5921);
מַעַל *máʿal* upwards (4605)
עֶלְיוֹן *ʿelyôn* highest (5945)
מַעֲלָה *maʿălā*^{h} *ascent, stairs (4609)*
שֶׁבַע *šébaʿ* N he swore, sevened himself (7650)
שְׁבִיעִי *š*^{e}*ḇîʿî* 7th (7637); שִׁבְעִים *šiḇʿîm* 70 (7657)

Basic Vocabulary Group–3 Lesson 6

דִּין *dîn* דּוּן *dûn* he judged (1777); דִּין *dîn* legal case, judgment (1779)
-כְּ *k*^{e}- as, like
כִּסֵּא *kissēʾ* throne, seat of honor (3678)
מֵאָה *mēʾā*^{h} 100 (3967); מָאתַיִם *māʾtáyim* 200
מְדִינָה *m*^{e}*ḏînā*^{h} province (4082)
עָלָה *ʿālā*^{h} he climbed, it went up (5927); עֹלָה *ʿôlā*^{h} whole burnt offering (5930)
עֶשֶׂר *ʿéśer* עֲשָׂרָה *ʿăśārā*^{h} 10 (6235)
עָשָׂר *ʿāśār* עֶשְׂרֵה *ʿeśrē*^{h} -teen (6235-b)
עֲשִׂירִי *ʿăśîrî* 10th (6224); עֶשְׂרִים *ʿeśrîm* 20 (6242)
שָׁנָה *šānā*^{h} pl. שָׁנִים *šānîm* year (8141)

Basic Vocabulary Group–4 Lesson7

אֲשֶׁר *'ăšer* which, that (834)
וֹ– *-ô* הוּ– *-hû* his, him; הָ– *-āh* הָ– *-hā* her
כֹּל *kōl* all, every, each (3606); כָּלִיל *kālîl* entire, whole (3632)
–לְ *lᵉ-* to, for, in regard to
מִשְׁתֶּה *mištêʰ* feast, drink (4961); שָׁתָה *šāṯāʰ* he drank (8534)
עָשָׂה *ʿāśāʰ* he did, made (6213); מַעֲשֶׂה *maʿăśêʰ* deed, work (4639)
מַעֲשֵׂר *maʿăśēr* tithe, tenth (4643); עָשׂוֹר *ʿāśôr* 10, decade (6218)
עִשָּׂרוֹן *ʿiśśārôn* 1/10 ephah (6241)

Basic Vocabulary Group–5 Lesson 8

אֵת *'ēṯ*, אֶת־ *'eṯ*, –אֹת *'ōṯ-* sign of def. dir. obj. (857)
גָּדוֹל *gāḏôl* great (1419); גָּדַל *gāḏal* he was strong (1431); מִגְדָּל *miḡdāl* tower (4026)
חַיִל *ḥáyil* power, wealth, army (2428)
יָקָר *yāqār* rare, precious (3368)
מָצָא *māṣā'* he found (4672)
עַם *ʿam* people (5971)
לִפְנֵי *lip̄nê* before (6440)
רָאָה *rā'āʰ* he saw (7200); מַרְאֶה *mar'êʰ* sight, appearance (4758)
רַב *raḇ* many, great, chief (7227); רַבָּה *rabbāʰ* great; רָבָה *rāḇāʰ* he became great (7235)

Basic Vocabulary Group–6 Lesson 9

אֵלֶּה *'éllêʰ* these (428)
חָצֵר *ḥāṣēr* court, enclosure (2691)
כָּבוֹד *kāḇôḏ* might, glory, honor (3519); כָּבֵד *kāḇēḏ* to be heavy (3513); heavy (3515)
מָלֵא *mālē'* to be full (4390), full (4392); מְלֹא *mᵉlô'* fulness (4393)
עֹשֶׁר *ʿōšer* riches (6239)
קָטָן *qāṭān* small (6996); קָטֹן *qāṭōn* small (6994)
שְׁמֹנֶה *šᵉmōnêʰ* 8 (8083); שְׁמֹנִים *šᵉmōnîm* 80 (8084); שְׁמִינִי *šᵉmînî* 8th (8066)
תִּפְאֶרֶת *tip̄'éreṯ* beauty, glory (8597)

Basic Vocabulary Group–7 Lesson 10

אָחַז *'āḥaz* he held, seized (270); אֲחֻזָּה *'ăḥuzzāʰ* possession (272)
אַרְגָּמָן *'argāmān* purple (713)
זָהָב *zāhāḇ* gold (2091)
חֶבֶל *ḥéḇel* cord, rope (2256); כֶּסֶף *késep̄* silver, money (3701)
נָטָה *nāṭāʰ* he stretched out (5186); מַטֶּה *maṭṭêʰ* staff, rod (4294)
עָמַד *ʿāmaḏ* he stood (5975); עַמּוּד *ʿammûḏ* pillar, column (5982)
שֵׁשׁ *šēš* byssus, fine linen (8336)
כְּלִי *kᵉlî* vessel (3627); כְּלָיוֹת *kᵉlāyôṯ* kidneys (3629)

Basic Vocabulary Group–8 Lesson 11

אַיִן *'áyin*, אֵין *'ên* there is/was not, nonexistence of (369)
אִישׁ *'îš* man, male, husband (376); אִשָּׁה *'iššā*[h] woman, wife (802)
בַּיִת *báyit* house (1004)
גַּן *gan* garden, enclosure (1588)
יָד *yād* hand (3027); יָדָה *yādā*[h] (H) to give thanks (3034)
יַיִן *yáyin* wine (3196)
יָסַד *yāsad* he established, founded (3245)
כִּי *kî* that, for, when, because (3588); כִּי אִם *kî 'im* except
כֵּן *kēn* thus, so (3651); לָכֵן *lākēn* therefore

Basic Vocabulary Group–9 Lesson 14

אָמַר *'āmar* he said (559); אֹמֶר *'ómer* word, saying (561)
גַּם *gam* also, together with (1571)
טוֹב *ṭôb* he was good, pleasant (2895), good (2896); טוֹבָה *ṭôbā*[h] good (things), well-being
לֵב *lēb* heart, mind, will (3820); לֵבָב *lēbāb* heart, mind, will (3824)
נָשִׁים *nāšîm* women (802); אֲנָשִׁים *'ănāšîm* men (582)
סָרִיס *sârîs* eunuch (5631)
פָּנִים *pānîm* face (6440); פָּנָה *pānā*[h] he turned, faced (6437)
רָצוֹן *rāṣôn* good will, favor (7522); רָצָה *rāṣā*[h] he was pleased with, accepted (7521)
שָׁקָה *šāqā*[h] (H) to water, give to drink (8248)

Basic Vocabulary Group–10 Lesson 15

בּוֹא *bô'* to enter (935); תְּבוּאָה *t*[e]*bû'ā*[h] income, product (8393)
דָּבָר *dābār* word, thing (1697); דָּבַר *dābar* (d) to speak (1696)
חָכָם *ḥākām* wise, skillful, clever (2450); חָכְמָה *ḥokmā*[h] wisdom, experience (2451)
חֵמָה *ḥēmā*[h] heat, rage, poison (2534)
יָפֶה *yāpê*[h] beautiful, fair (3303)
מְאֹד *m*[e]*'ōd* very, exceedingly (3966)
מָאֵן *mā'ēn* (D) to refuse (3985)
קָצַף *qāṣap̄* he was angry, wroth (7107)
שָׁרַת *šārat* (D) to minister, serve (8334)

Basic Vocabulary Group–11 Lesson 16

אֶל *'ēl*, אֶל־ *'el* to, towards (413); אֵל *'ēl* God, god (410)
בָּעַר *bā'ar* it burned (1197)
יָדַע *yāda'* he knew (3045); דַּעַת *dá'at* knowledge (1847)
מַדּוּעַ *maddû*[a'] why? (4069)
לֹא *lô'*, לוֹא *lô'* not, no (3808)
מַה *ma*[h] what? (4100); לָמָה *lámā*[h] for what reason? why?
עֵת *'ēt* time (6256); עַתָּה *'attā*[h] now (6258)
קָרוֹב *qārôb* near (7138); קָרַב *qārab* he came near (7126)
קֶרֶב *qéreb* midst, inward part (7130); קָרְבָּן *qorbān* offering (7133)

Basic Vocabulary Group–12 Lesson 17

בָּזָה *bāzāʰ* he despised (959)
בַּעַל *báʿal* lord, owner, husband (1167)
דַּי *day* enough (1767)
זֶה *zêʰ* this (m.) (2088); **זאת** *zôʾṯ* this (f.) (2063)
יָצָא *yāṣāʾ* he went/came out, exited (3318)
לְבַד– *lᵉḇadd-* alone (+ pron. suf.) (905)
עָוֹן *ʿāwôn* iniquity, guilt, punishment (5771)
עַיִן *ʿáyin* eye, spring (5869)
רִאשׁוֹן *riʾšôn* former, first (7223); **רֹאשׁ** *rôʾš* head (7218); **רֵאשִׁית** *rēʾšîṯ* beginning (7225)
שָׁמַע *šāmaʿ* he heard (8085)

Basic Vocabulary Group–13 Lesson 18

אֶבֶן *ʾéḇen* stone, gem, weight (69)
אָדוֹן *ʾāḏôn* lord, master (113); **אֲדֹנָי** *ʾăḏônāy* (my) Lord **אִם** *ʾim* if (518)
כָּתַב *kāṯaḇ* he wrote (3789)
נָתַן *nāṯan* he gave, put, determined (5414)
עָבַר *ʿāḇar* he passed over/through/by (5674); **עֵבֶר** *ʿēḇer* region across/beyond (5676)
עוֹלָם *ʿôlām* long duration, eternity (5769); **בַּעֲבוּר** *baʿăḇûr* for, because of (5668)
רֵעַ *rēᵃʿ* friend, companion (7453); **רָעָה** *rāʿāʰ* **he tended, pastured, grazed (7462)**
שָׂרַף *śārap̄* he/it burned (8313)

Basic Vocabulary Group–14 Lesson 19

יָטַב *yāṭaḇ* it goes well with, (H) to do good to (3190)
יָרֵא *yārēʾ* he was afraid, feared, was in awe (3372); **יִרְאָה** *yirʾêʰ* reverence, fear (3374)
כְּסִיל *kᵉsîl* stupid, dull, fool (3684)
לָשׁוֹן *lāšôn* tongue (3956);
סָפַר *sāpar* he counted, (D) to recount, tell (5608); **סֵפֶר** *sēp̄er* writing, document (5612)
מִסְפָּר *mispār* number (4557)
פָּלַל *pālal* (HtD) to intercede, pray (6419); **תְּפִלָּה** *tᵉpillāʰ* prayer (8605)
קוֹל *qôl* voice, sound (6963)
שָׁלַח *šālaḥ* he sent, stretched out (hand) (7971)
שָׂבַע *śāḇaʿ* he was satisfied, sated (7646)

Basic Vocabulary Group– 15 Lesson 20

אָח *ʾaḥ* brother (251); **אָחוֹת** *ʾāḥôṯ* sister (269)
אֵשׁ *ʾēš* fire (784)
דֶּרֶךְ *dérek* way, road, manner (1870); **דָּרַךְ** *dārak* he marched, trod (1869)
הָלַךְ *hālak* he walked, came, went (1980)
הִנֵּה *hinnêʰ*, **הֵן** *hēn* behold! (2009)
הַר *har* mountain (2022)
יַחַד *yáḥaḏ* together in unison (3162); **יַחְדָּו** *yaḥdāw* together (3162)
יָסַר *yāsar* he admonished, disciplined; (D) to establish (3256)
מוּסָר *mûsār* chastening (4148)
מָאַס *māʾas* he rejected, refused (3988)

אַחַר *'aḥar,* אַחֲרֵי *'aḥărê* after (310); אָחוֹר *'āḥôr* the back part (268)
אַחֲרוֹן *'aḥărôn* last, latter, afterward (314); אַחֲרִית *'aḥărîṯ* end, latter time, posterity (319)
בִּקֵּשׁ *biqqēš* (D) he sought (1245)
בְּתוּלָה *bᵉṯûlāʰ* unmarried woman, virgin (1330)
דָּם *dām* blood; pl. shed blood (1818)
זָכַר *zāḵar* he remembered (2142)
נַעַר *náʿar* boy, youth, servant (5288); נַעֲרָה *naʿărāʰ* girl, damsel (5291)
נְעוּרִים *nᵉʿûrîm* youth, early life (5271)
פָּקַד *pāqaḏ* he visited, observed, mustered (*see* 6485)
פְּקֻדָּה *pᵉquddāʰ* oversight, visitation (6486)

Basic Vocabulary Group–17 Lesson 22

אוֹ *'ô* or, or if, except (176)
אַךְ *'āḵ* surely (389)
עֵד *ʿēḏ* witness, evidence (5707); עֵדוֹת *ʿēḏôṯ* testimonies (5713)
עֵדֻת, עֵדוּת *ʿēḏûṯ* testimony (5717)
עוּד *ʿûḏ* H to admonish, bear witness (5749)
עֵדָה *ʿēḏāʰ* congregation (5712); מוֹעֵד *môʿēḏ* place of meeting (4150)
שָׁמַר *šāmar* he kept, watched, preserved (8104)
מִשְׁמֶרֶת *mišméreṯ* guard, charge (4931)
קָבַץ *qāḇaṣ* he gathered, collected (6908)
תַּחַת *táḥaṯ* under, below, succeeding (8478)
קֶצֶף *qéṣep̄* wrath (7110)

Basic Vocabulary Group–18 Lesson 23

בֵּן *bēn* son, member of a group (1121); בַּת *baṯ* (< **bint*) daughter (1323)
בָּנָה *bānāʰ* he built (1129)
גָּלָה *gālāʰ* he uncovered, revealed, went into exile
גּוֹלָה *gôlāʰ* exile (1473)
יָמִין *yāmîn* right (hand/side), south (3225)
שְׂמֹאל *śᵉmō'l* left (hand/side), north (8040)
עִם *ʿim* with (5973)
עֻמָּה *ʿummāʰ* close by, parallel to, agreeing with (5980)
שֵׁם *šēm* name (8034)
שָׁמֵם *šāmēm* he was desolated, appalled (8074)
שְׁמָמָה *šᵉmāmāʰ* devastation, waste (8077)

Basic Vocabulary Group–19 Lesson 24

אָב *'āḇ* father, ancestor (1); אֵם *'ēm* mother (517)
אָבָה *'āḇāʰ* he was willing, consented (14)
אָמַן *'āman* he endured; H to trust, believe (539); אָמֵן *'āmēn* surely, Amen! (543)
אֱמוּנָה *'ĕmûnāʰ* faithfulness (530)
אֱמֶת *'ĕmeṯ* (< **'ĕment*) faithfulness, truth (5710)
דּוֹד *dôḏ* beloved, uncle (f. aunt) (1730)
לָקַח *lāqaḥ* he took, received (3947)
מוּת *mûṯ* to die (4191); מָוֶת *máweṯ* death (4194)
אֹרַח *'ōraḥ* way, path, traveler (734)
אֹרֶךְ *'ōreḵ* length (753)
אָרַךְ *'āraḵ* it was long, H to lengthen (748)

Basic Vocabulary Group–20 Lesson 25

בָּהַל *bāhal* N to be disturbed, D to hasten, terrify (926)
חֶסֶד *ḥésed* kindness, covenant loyalty/love (2618)
חָסִיד *ḥāsîd* loyal/pious one (2623)
יֶלֶד *yéled* boy, (f) girl; child (3206 ; יָלַד *yālad* G11 she bore; H to beget (3205)
מוֹלֶדֶת *môlédet* kindred (4137); תּוֹלְדוֹת *tôlᵉdôt* generations, history (8435)
נֶגֶד *néged* in front of, opposite (5048);' נָגִיד *nāgîd* leader, prince (5057)
נָגַד *nāgad* H to proclaim, declare (5046)
נָשָׂא *nāśā'* he lifted, carried (5375); נָשִׂיא *nāśî'* chief, prince (5387)
מַשָּׂא *maśśā'* load, burden (4853)
צִוָּה *ṣiwwāʰ* D he charged, commanded; מִצְוָה *miṣwāʰ*commandment (4687)

Basic Vocabulary Group–21 Lesson 27

בֶּשֶׂם *béśem,* בֹּשֶׂם *bóśem* spice, balsam (1314)
חֹדֶשׁ *ḥódeš* new moon, month (2320); חָדָשׁ *ḥādāš* new, rcent, fresh (2319)
מַר *mar(r)* bitter/-ness (4751)
נָגַע *nāgaʿ* he touched, reached, struck (5060) ; נֶגַע *négaʿ* stroke, plague, mak (5061)
קֵץ *qēṣ* end, extremity (7093); קָצֶה *qāṣêʰ* end, extremity (7097)
שָׁלוֹם *šālôm* welfare, completeness, peace (7965)
שֶׁלֶם *šélem* pl. peace-offering (8002)
שָׁלֵם *šālēm* he was complete, sound (7999)
שֶׁמֶן *šémen* fat, oil, olive oil (8081)
שֵׁשׁ *šēš,* שִׁשָּׁה *šiššāʰ* six (8337); שִׁשִּׁים *šiššîm* sixty

Basic Vocabulary Group–22 Lesson 28

בֹּקֶר *bóqer* morning (1242)
חֵן *ḥēn* favor, grace, charm (2580); חִנָּם *ḥinnām* for nothing, in vain (2600)
חָנַן *ḥānan* he was gracious (2603); תְּחִנָּה *tᵉḥinnāʰ* favor, supplication (8467)
חָפֵץ *ḥāpēṣ* he delighted in, desired (2654)
חֵפֶץ *ḥépeṣ* delight, pleasure (2656)
עֶרֶב *ʿéreb* evening (6153)
עֲרָבָה *ʿărābāʰ* desert-plain, Arabah (6160)
פִּילֶגֶשׁ *pîlégeš* concubine (6370)
שְׁנַיִם *šnáyim,* שְׁתַּיִם *štáyim* two (8147)
שֵׁנִי *šēnî* second (8145)
מִשְׁנֶה *mišnêʰ* double, copy, second (4932

Basic Vocabulary Group–23 Lesson 29

אָהֵב *'āhēb* he loved (157)
אַהֲבָה *'ahăbāʰ* love (160)
יָעַץ *yāʿaṣ* he advised, N to counsel together (3289); עֵצָה *ʿēṣāʰ* counsel, advice (6098)
עוֹד *ʿôd* still, yet, again (5750)
עַד *ʿad,* וָעֶד *wāʿed* forever (5704)
פַּעַם *páʿam* time, occurrence (6471)
קָרָא *qārā'* he called, named (7121);
קָרָה *qārāʰ* he met, it befell (7136)
שׁוּב *šûb* to turn back, return (7725)
שׂוּם *śûm,* שִׂים *śîm* to put, set, place, appoint (7760)
תֵּשַׁע *téšaʿ,* תִּשְׁעָה *tišʿāʰ* nine (8672)

Basic Vocabulary Group–24 Lesson 30

אֶדֶן *ʾéden* base, pedestal (134)
אֹהֶל *ʾōhel* tent, dwelling (168)
אֹת *ʾôṯ* sign, symbol, miracle (226, cf. #853)
אֵת *ʾēṯ*, –אִתּ *ʾitt-* with (854, cf. #853)
בָּמָה *bāmāʰ* high place (1116)
חֹק *ḥōq*, –חֻקּ *ḥuqq-* statute, decree (2706)
חֻקָּה *ḥuqqāʰ* statute (2708)
פֹּעַל *pṓʿal* deed, work (6467); פָּעַל *pāʿal* he did, made (6466)
שַׁעַר *šáʿar* gate (8179); שֹׁעֵר *šōʿēr* porter, door-tender (7778)
תָּלָה *tālāʰ* he hanged (8518)

Baasic Vocabulary Group–25 Lesson 31

אוּלַי *ʾûlay* if, perhaps (194)
אָז *ʾāz* then (227)
אֹזֶן *ʾṓzen* ear (241); אָזַן *ʾāzan* H to give ear, hear (238)
אָרוֹן *ʾārôn* ark (of covenant) (727)
הָלַל *hālal* D to praise, HtD to boast (1984)
תְּהִלָּה *tᵉhillāʰ* (song of) praise (8416)
מָגֵן *māḡēn* shield, buckler (4043)
נֶגֶב *néḡeḇ* southland, Negev (5045)
עֵץ *ʿēṣ* tree, pl. pieces/articles of wood (6086)
שֵׁן *šēn* tooth, ivory (8127)

Basic Vocabulary Group–26 Lesson 32

אַתָּה *ʾattāʰ* you (m.s.) (859); אַתֶּם *ʾattem* you (m.p.) (859)
אַתְּ *ʾatt* you (f.s.) (859)
זָבַח *zāḇaḥ* he slaughtered, sacrificed (2076)
זֶבַח *zéḇaḥ* sacrifice (2077)
מִזְבֵּחַ *mizbēᵃḥ* altar (place of sacrifice) (4196)
חָוָה *ḥāwāʰ* HtŠ to prostrate self, worship (7817)
חָנָה *ḥānāʰ* he encamped, retired (2853)
מַחֲנֶה *maḥănêʰ* camp (4264)
כָּרַע *kāraʿ* He bowed/knelt down (3766)
שָׁכַן *šāḵan* he settled down, dwelt (7931); מִשְׁכָּן *miškān* dwelling-place, tabernacle (4948)

Basic Vocabulary Group–27 Lesson 33

אָסַר *ʾāsar* he bound, imprisoned (631)
אֵצֶל *ʾḗṣel* beside (681)
–הֲ *hă-* interrogative particle (cf. §22.3ff.)
יָשָׁר *yāšār* straight, right, just (3477)
צָפוֹן *ṣāpôn* north (6828)
קָבַר *qāḇar* he buried (69120; קֶבֶר *qéḇer* grave (6913)
שָׁכַב *šāḵaḇ* he lay down (7901)
מִשְׁכָּב *miškāḇ* place/act of lying down, couch (4904)
שֻׁלְחָן *šulḥān* table (7979)
שָׁמַד *šāmaḏ* N to be exterminated; H to annihilate, destroy (8045)

Basic Vocabulary Group–28 Lesson 34

אֶחָד *'eḥād* one (259)
אַחֵר *'āḥēr* other, another, different (312)
אֵפוֹד *'ēpôd* Ephod (worn by priest) (646)
בִּין *bîn* to discern, perceive (995)
בִּינָה *bînāh* understanding (998); תְּבוּנָה *tᵉbûnāh* understanding (8394)
בֵּין *bên* between (996)
גּוֹרָל *gôrāl* lot, portion (1486)
יֵשׁ *yēš* there is/are (3426)
נָפַל *nāpal* he fell, lay (5307)
נָוֶה *nāwêh* abode of shepherd/sheep (5116)
נוּחַ *nûaḥ* to rest (5117)

Basic Vocabulary Group–29 Lesson 35

אֶלֶף *'élep* thousand (504)
אַלּוּף *'allûp* chief, chiliarch (441)
טַבַּעַת *ṭabbá'at* signet-ring, seal (2885)
כִּכָּר *kikkār* talent, round weight (3603)
מַלְאָךְ *mal'āk* messenger, angel (4379)
מְלָאכָה *mᵉlā'kāh* work, business (4399)
סוּר *sûr* to turn aside, H to take away (5490)
צַר *ṣar(r)* adversary, foe (6862); צָרַר *ṣārar* he was hostile toward (6887)
צָרָר *ṣārār* distress (6869)
שֶׁקֶל *šéqel* (a weight) (8255)
מִשְׁקָל *mišqāl* weight (4948)

Basic Vocabulary Group–30 Lesson 36

אָבַד *'ābad* he perished, was lost (7)
בָּזַז *bāzaz* he took as plunder (962)
הָרַג *hārag* he killed (2026)
זָקֵן *zāqēn* old (man), elder (2205)
חָיָה *ḥāyāh* he lived, was alive (2421); חַי *ḥay(y)* alive (2416)
חַיָּה *ḥayyāh* animal, beast (2416); חַיִּים *ḥayyîm* life (2416)
טַף *ṭap(p)* little children (coll.) (2945)
עָזַב *'āzab* he left, forsook (5860)
רוּץ *rûṣ* to run (7323)
שָׁלָל *šālāl* plundered, plunder, booty (7998)
תָּעָה *tā'āh* he erred, wandered about (8582)

Basic Vocabulary Group–31 Lesson 37

יָבֵשׁ *yābēš* it was dried up (3001)
יָרָה *yārāh* he threw; H to teach (3884)
תּוֹרָה *tôrāh* Torah, instruction, law (8451)
יָתַר *yātar* it remained, was left over (3498); יֶתֶר *yéter* remainder, excess (3499)
כֹּחַ *kōaḥ* strength, power (3581)
כָּנָף *kānāp* wing, extremity (3671)
כָּתֵף *kātēp* shoulder (-blade), side (3802)
עִיר *'îr* town, city (5892)
קָוָה *qāwāh* he waited for (6960)
תִּקְוָה *tiqwêh* hope (8615)

Basic Vocabulary Group–32 Lesson 38

אָבַל *ʾāḇal* he mourned, lamented (56)
בֶּגֶד *béḡeḏ* garment (899)
בָּגַד *bāḡaḏ* he acted treacherously (898)
בָּכָה *bāḵāʰ* he wept (1058); בְּכִי *bᵉḵí* weeping (1065)
זָעַק *zāʿaq* he cried (out), called (2199)
צָעַק *ṣāʿaq* he cried (out), called (6817)
לָבֵשׁ *lāḇēš* he put on clothing (3847); לְבוּשׁ *lᵉḇûš* clothing (3830)
סָפַד *sāp̄aḏ* he wailed, lamented (5594)
קָרַע *qāraʿ* he tore, rent (7167)
שַׂק *śaq(q)* sackcloth (8242)

Basic Vocabulary Group–33 Lesson 39

אָשָׁם *ʾāšām* guilt, guilt-offering (817)
חוּל *ḥûl*, חִיל *ḥîl* he twisted, writhed, danced (2342)
חֵיק *ḥêq*, חֵק *ḥêq* bosom (2436)
צָלַח *ṣālaḥ*, צָלֵחַ *ṣālēᵃḥ* he advanced, prospered (6743)
קוּם *qûm* to arise, stand (6965)
מָקוֹם *māqôm* (standing-) place (4725); קוֹמָה *qômāʰ* height (6667)
רֹחַב *rṓḥaḇ* breadth, width (7341)
רְחוֹב *rᵉḥôḇ* open place, plaza, street (7339)
רַק *raq* only, surely (7535)
תָּוֶךְ *táweḵ*, תּוֹךְ *tôḵ* midst (8432)

Basic Vocabulary Group–34 Lesson 41

בָּטַח *bāṭaḥ* he trusted, was secure (982); בֶּטַח *béṭaḥ* security, securely (983)
לֶחֶם *léḥem* bread, food (3899)
לָחַם *lāḥam* N to fight, do battle (3898); מִלְחָמָה *milḥāmāʰ* fight, battle, war (4421)
רָדַף *rāḏap̄* he pursued, chased, persecuted (7291)
רִיב *rîḇ* to strive, contend, conduct a law-suit (7378)
רִיב *rîḇ* strife, dispute, law-suit (7379)
שׁוֹר *šôr* a head of cattle, ox, bullock (7794)
שֶׂה *śêʰ* a sheep/goat (7716)
שָׂכַל *śāḵal* he was prudent; H to ponder, prosper (7919)
שָׂפָה *śāp̄āhʰ* lip, shore, speech (8193)

Basic Vocabulary Group–35 Lesson 42

אַל *ʾal* not (408)
אַלְמָנָה *ʾalmānāʰ* widow (490)
אֲנִי *ʾănî* I (589); אָנֹכִי *ʾānôḵî* I (595)
אֲרִי *ʾărî*; אַרְיֵה *ʾaryēʰ* lion (738)
בַּל *bal* not, nothing (1077); בְּלִי *bᵉlî* not, without (1097)
דָּמָה *dāmāʰ* he resembled, was like; D to liken, imagine (1819)
דָּמַם *dāmam* he was still, motionless, dumb (1826)
מָלַט *mālaṭ* N to slip away, escape; D to let escape, deliver (4422)
נֶפֶשׁ *nép̄eš* soul, person, self (5315)
פְּנִימִי *pᵉnîmî* inner (6442)

Basic Vocabulary Group–36 Lesson 43

אָכַל *ʾākal* he ate, fed (398); אֹכֶל *ʾṓkel* food (400)
מַאֲכָל *maʾăkāl* food (3978)
בּוֹשׁ *bôš* to be ashamed; H to shame (954)
בִּלְתִּי *biltî* only, beside, except;
לְבִלְתִּי *l^ebiltî* so as not to, in order not to (1115)
בְּעַד *b^eʿad*, בַּעַד *báʿad* away from, behind, about, in behalf of (1157)
חָרַשׁ *ḥāraš* H to be silent, dumb (2790 < **ḫrš*, Arab. *ḫarasa*)
חָרָשׁ *ḥārāš* artisan, engraver, artificer (2796 < **ḥrθ* Arab. *ḥarata*)
כַּאֲשֶׁר *kaʾăšer* according as, in so far as, when
לַיְלָה *láylāʰ*, לַיִל *láyil* night, at night (3915)
מִי *mî* who? (4310)

Basic Vocabulary Group–37 Lesson 44

גָּאַל *gāʾal* he redeemed, acted as kinsman (1350)
גְּבוּל *g^ebûl* border, boundary (1366)
גּוּר *gûr* to sojourn, dwell; גֵּר *gēr* stranger, sojourner (1616)
דָּבַק *dābaq* he kept close/clung to (1692)
דְּבַשׁ *d^ebaš* honey (1706)
דֶּלֶת *délet* door (1817)
חוֹמָה *ḥômāʰ* wall (of city) (2346)
נֹכַח *nōkaḥ* in front of (5227)
פָּתַח *pātaḥ* he opened (6605); פֶּתַח *pétaḥ* opening, doorway (6607)
שָׁמַיִם *šāmáyim* heaven(s), sky (8064)

Basic Vocabulary Group–38 Lesson 45

אוֹר *ʾôr* light, luminary (216)
אוֹר *ʾôr* to be/become light., H to give light, cause to shine (215)
אֱלוֹהַּ *ʾĕlôᵃh* God, god (433); אֱלֹהִים *ʾĕlōhîm* God, gods, judges, angels (430)
אֶרֶץ *ʾéreṣ* earth, land, country (776)
אֶרֶז *ʾérez* cedar (730)
בָּדַל *bādal* H to divide, separate; N to separate, withdraw (914)
בָּרָא *bārāʾ* he created, fashioned (1254)
חֹשֶׁךְ *ḥōšek* darkness (2822)
רוּחַ *rûᵃḥ* breath, wind, spirit (7307); רֵיחַ *rêᵃḥ* scent, odor (7381)
רוּעַ *rûᵃʿ* H to raise a shout, give a blast on horn (7321)
תְּרוּעָה *t^erûʿāʰ* shout of war/alarm/joy (8643)

Basic Vocabulary Group–39 Lesson 46

בְּהֵמָה *b^ehēmāʰ* animal, beast, cattle (999)
בָּחַר *bāḥar* he chose, tested (977); בָּחוּר *bāḥûr* young man (970)
בָּקַע *bāqaʿ* he cleft, split, broke open (1234)
זוּר *zûr* to be a stranger, G50 stranger (2114)
חֲצִי *ḥăṣî*, חֵצִי *ḥēṣî* half, middle (2677); חֵץ *ḥēṣ* arrow (2071)
יָכַח *yākaḥ* H to judge, convict, reprove, rebuke (3198)
לוּן *lûn*, לִין *lîn* to lodge, pass the night (3885)
מָהַר *māhar* D to hasten (4116)
שָׁאַל *šāʾal* he asked, inquired, asked for (7592)
שְׁאוֹל *š^eʾôl* Sheol, underworld (7585)

Basic Vocabulary Group–40 Lesson 47

אָדָם *ʾāḏām* man, mankind (120); אֲדָמָה *ʾăḏāmāʰ* ground, land, earth (127)
בַּרְזֶל *barzel* iron (1270)
גִּבְעָה *gibʿāʰ* hill (1398)
גֶּפֶן *gép̄en* vine (1612)
מָחָר *māḥār* tomorrow (4279); מָחֳרָת *moḥŏrāṯ* on the morrow (4283)
עָנָה *ʿānāʰ* he answered (6030)
עָנָה *ʿānāʰ* he was afflicted, bowed down (6031)
עֳנִי *ʿŏnî* affliction, poverty; עָנִי *ʿānî* poor, afflicted, weak (6041)
שָׂמַח *śāmaḥ* he rejoiced; D to gladden (8055)
שִׂמְחָה *śimḥāʰ* gladness, mirth, joy (8037)

Basic Vocabulary Group–41 Lesson 48

אַף *ʾap̄* also (637); אַף *ʾap̄* (< *ʾnp) nose, anger (639)
חָרֵב *ḥāreḇ* it was dry/dried up; H to dry up (tr.) (351)
חֵלֶב *ḥēleḇ* fat, choice (2459); חָלָב *ḥālāḇ* milk (2461)
חָלָה *ḥālāʰ* he became weak, was sick (2470)
חָלָל *ḥālāl* pierced, slain (2491)
עָמָל *ʿāmāl* labor, toil (5999)
יָחַל *yāḥal* N, D, H to wait, await (5176)
רָעָב *rāʿāḇ* famine, hunger (7858)
רָשָׁע *rāšāʿ* wicked, criminal (7563); רֶשַׁע *réšaʿ* wickedness (7562)

Basic Vocabulary Group–42 Lesson 49

אָמָה *ʾāmāʰ* handmaid (519)
אַמָּה *ʾammāʰ* forearm, cubit (length of forearm) (520)
גָּבַהּ *gāḇah* he/it was high, exalted (1361); גָּבֹהַּ *gāḇôᵃh* high, tall, proud (1364)
חָמָס *ḥāmās* violence, wrong (2555)
חָמֵשׁ *ḥāmēš,* חֲמִשָּׁה *ḥămiššāʰ* 5 (2568); חֲמִישִׁי *ḥămîšî* 5th (2549)
חֲמִשִּׁים *ḥămiššîm* 50 (2572)
לָכַד *lāḵaḏ* he captured, seized, took (3920)
קֹדֶשׁ *qōḏeš* sacredness, holiness (6944)
קָדַשׁ *qāḏaš* N to set apart, consecrate; H to sanctify (6942)
רָחַץ *rāḥaṣ* he washed, bathed (7364)

Basic Vocabulary Group–43 Lesson 50

בָּקָר *bāqār* herd, large cattle (1241)
בָּרַח *bāraḥ* he passed through, fled; H he chased (1272)
חָזָה *ḥāzāʰ* he saw, beheld (2372); חָזוֹן *ḥāzôn* vision, sight (2377)
חֶרֶב *ḥéreḇ* sword (2719)
כֹּהֵן *kôhēn* priest (3548)
כּוּן *kûn* it was established/proper/fixed; H to establish (3559)
מַמְלָכָה *mamlāḵāʰ* dominion, kingdom (4467)
נָבָא *nāḇāʾ* N to prophesy; HtD to act as a prophet (5012); נָבִיא *nāḇîʾ* prophet (5030)
שָׁם *šām* there, thither (8033)
קָדוֹשׁ *qāḏôš* sacred, holy (6918); מִקְדָּשׁ *miqdāš* sanctuary (4724)

Basic Vocabulary Group–44 Lesson 51

חוּץ *ḥûṣ* outside, abroad (2351)
מִגְרָשׁ *miḡrāš* common/open land, pasture (4054)
גָּרַשׁ *gāraš* he drove out/away, cast out (1644)
מָדַד *māḏaḏ* he measured (4058); מִדָּה *middā^h* measure (4060)
מִזְמוֹר *mizmôr* psalm, melody (4210); זָמַר *zāmar* D to sing, praise (2167)
מִקְנֶה *miqnê^h* cattle, possession (4735)
קָנָה *qānā^h* he got, acquired, bought (7069)
קָנֶה *qānê^h* reed, stalk, measuring-rod (7070)
שִׁיר *šîr* to sing (7891)
שִׁיר *šîr* song (7892)

Basic Vocabulary Group–45 Lesson 52

חָלַק *ḥālaq* he divided, apportioned (2505); חֵלֶק *ḥéleq* portion, share, territory (2507)
מַחֲלֹקֶת *maḥălṓqeṯ* share, division (4256)
יָצַב *yāṣaḇ* HtD to take one's stand (3320, cf. #5324)
מַצֵּבָה *maṣṣēḇā^h* pillar, sacred pillar (4676)
כֹּה *kō^h* here, now, thus (3541)
כָּכָה *kā́ḵā^h* thus (3602)
נֵר *nēr* lamp (5369); מְנוֹרָה *m^{e}nôrā^h* lampstand (4501)
סוּס *sûs* horse (5483)
רָכַב *rāḵaḇ* he (mounted and) rode (7392)
רֶכֶב *réḵeḇ* chariot(ry), rider, millstone (7393)
מֶרְכָּבָה *merkāḇā^h* chariot (4818)

Basic Vocabulary Group–46 Lesson 54

דַּל *dal(l)* poor, weak, oppressed (1800)
זֶרַע *zéra^c* seed, sowing, offspring (2233 < **zr*ʿ)
זָרַע *zāra^c* he scattered seed, sowed (2232)
זְרוֹעַ *z^{e}rô^{ac}* strength, arm (2220 < **δr*ʿ)
חָלַל *ḥālal* N to be defiled; D to defile, profane; H to begin (2490)
יָכֹל *yāḵōl* he was able (3201)
יָתוֹם *yāṯôm* orphan, fatherless (3490)
נְאֻם *n^{e}ʾûm* (cstr.) utterance of (a prophet or deity) (5002)
נָגַשׁ *nāḡaš* he drew near, approached (5066)
צָדֹק *ṣāḏōq* he was just, righteous (6663); צַדִּיק *ṣaddîq* just, righteous (6662)
קִיר *qîr* wall (7023)

Basic Vocabulary Group–47 Lesson 55

בֶּטֶן *béṭen* belly, womb, body (990)
בְּכוֹר *b^{e}ḵôr* first-born (1060)
דָּרַשׁ *dāraš* he sought, inquired, consulted (1875)
חָטָא *ḥāṭāʾ* he missed, went wrong, sinned; D to make a sin-offering (2398)
חַטָּאת *ḥaṭṭāʾṯ* sin, sin-offering (2403); חֵטְא *ḥēṭʾ* guilt, punishment, offence (2399)
פְּרִי *p^{e}rî* fruit (6529)
פֶּשַׁע *péša^c* transgression, rebellion (6587); פָּשַׁע *pāša^c* he rebelled, transgressed (6586)
רוּם *rûm* he was exalted, lifted; L, H to raise, erect (7311)
מָרוֹם *mārôm* height, elevation, high place (4791)
תְּרוּמָה *t^{e}rûmā^h* contribution, offering (8641)

Basic Vocabulary Group–48 — Lesson 56

אַיִל *ʾáyil* ram; leader, chief (352)
כֶּבֶשׂ *kéb̲eś* lamb, young ram (3532)
מָכַר *māk̲ar* he sold (4376)
נָהָר *nāhār* stream, river (5104)
נַחַל *náḥal* wady, torrent-bed (5158)
עֵגֶל *ʿḗgel* calf (5695)
קֶדֶם *qéd̲em* front, east, aforetime, beginning (6924); קָדִים *qād̲îm* east, east wind (6921)
שִׁפְחָה *šip̄ḥā^h^* maid, maid-servant (8198)
שָׁפַט *šāp̄aṭ* he judged, governed (8199); שׁוֹפֵט *šôp̄ēṭ* judge (8199)
מִשְׁפָּט *mišpāṭ* judgment (4941)

Basic Vocabulary Group–49 — Lesson 57

אִי *ʾê* where? (335); אַיֵּה *ʾayyê^h^* where? (346)
אָיַב *ʾāyab̲* he was hostile , אֹיֵב *ʾôyēb̲* enemy (340)
זָר *zār* strange, stranger (2114)
כָּלָה *kālā^h^* it was complete/finished; D to complete (3615)
כַּלָּה *kallā^h^* daughter-in-law, bride (3618)
כַּף *kap(p)* palm of hand, sole of foot (3709)
כֶּרֶם *kérem* vineyard (3754)
רַע *raʿ* evil, distress, calamity, bad(ness) (7453)
רָעַע *rāʿaʿ* he was evil, bad., H to hurt, do evil (7489)
רָעָה *rāʿā^h^* evil, misery, distress, injury (7451)
שָׁאַר *šāʾar* N to remain, be left over; H to leave over, spare (7604)
שְׁאֵרִית *š^eʾ^ērîṯ* rest, residue, remainder, remnant (7611)

Basic Vocabulary Group–50 — Lesson 58

חָרָה *ḥārā^h^* he was/became angry (2734)
חָרוֹן *ḥārôn* burning anger (2740)
עוֹר *ʿôr* skin, hide (5785)
עוּר *ʿûr* to rouse oneself, awake (5782)
עָרַךְ *ʿārak̲* he arranged, set in order (6186); עֵרֶךְ *ʿérek̲* order, row, estimate (6187)
פֹּה, פֹּו, פֹּא *pô(ʾ)* here, hither (6311)
פֶּה *pê^h^* mouth (6310); לְפִי *l^e^p̄î,* כְּפִי *k^e^p̄î* according to
קָטַר *qāṭar* D, H to burn sacrifices (6999); קְטֹרֶת *q^e^ṭṓreṯ* smoke, incense (7004)
קָצַר *qāṣar* he reaped, harvested (7114); קָצִיר *qāṣîr* harvest (-time) (7105)

Basic Vocabulary Group–51 — Lesson 59

אָסַף *ʾāsap̄* he gathered, collected
יָסַף *yāsap̄* he added H to add + inf. = to do again (3254)
אֵיךְ *ʾêk̲* how? how! (349); אֵיכָה *ʾêk̲ā^h^* how! (351)
חָשַׁב *ḥāšab̲* he thought, reckoned, regarded (2803)
מַחֲשָׁבָה *maḥăšāb̲ā^h^* thought, device (4284)
טָהֵר *ṭāhēr* he was clean, pure; D he cleansed (2891); טָהוֹר *ṭāhôr* clean, pure (2889)
כָּפַר *kāp̄ar* D to cover, atone for sin (3722)
כְּפִיר *k^e^p̄îr* young lion (3715)
כָּבַס *kāb̲as* D he washed, cleansed (3526)
כָּעַס *kāʿas* he was angry; H he provoked (3707)
רֶגֶל *régel* foot (7272)

Basic Vocabulary Group–52 Lesson 60

חָזַק *ḥāzaq* he grew strong, was firm, it was urgent; D he strengthened (2388)
חָזָק *ḥāzāq* hard, strong, firm, severe (2389)
טָמֵא *ṭāmēʾ* he was/became unclean; D he defiled (2930)
טָמֵא *ṭāmēʾ* unclean (2931); טֻמְאָה *ṭumʾāʰ* uncleanness (2932)
מִדְבָּר *midbār* steppe, wilderness (4057)
נָחַל *nāḥal* he took possession, inherited; H to cause to inherit, give as possession (5157)
נַחֲלָה *naḥălāʰ* possession, inheritance, property (5159)
נָכָה *nākāʰ* H to strike, smite (5221); מַכָּה *makkāʰ* blow, wound, plague (4347)
עָנָן *ʿānān* cloud (-mass) (6052
עוֹף *ʿôp̄* flying things, fowl (5776)

Basic Vocabulary Group–53 Lesson 61

אֲנַחְנוּ *ʾănáḥnû* we (587)
הֵיכָל *hêkāl* palace, temple (1964)
הָמָה *hāmāʰ* he murmured, roared (1993); הָמוֹן *hāmôn* sound, roar, tumult (1995)
חַג *ḥag(g)* feast, festival (2282)
חָרַף *ḥārap̄* he reproached, taunted (2778); חֶרְפָּה *ḥerpāʰ* reproach, contumely (2781)
יָצַק *yāṣaq* he poured, cast (3332)
יָצַר *yāṣar* he formed, shaped (3335)
לָמַד *lāmad* he studied, learned; D he taught (3925)
קֶרֶן *qéren* horn (7161)

Basic Vocabulary Group–54 Lesson 62

נָדַח *nādaḥ* H to thrust out, banish, impel; N pass. of same (5080)
נָדַר *nādar* he vowed (5087); נֶדֶר *néder* vow (5088)
נוּס *nûs* to flee, escape (5127)
נֶסֶךְ *nések* drink-offering (5262)
נָקָה *nāqāʰ* N to be cleaned, purged, free from obligation; D to acquit (5352)
נָקִי *nāqî* clean, innocent, exempt (5355)
צוּר *ṣûr* to confine, shut in, besiege (6696); מָצוֹר *māṣôr* siege (4692)
צוּר *ṣûr* rock, cliff (6697)
קָהַל *qāhal* N to assemble (intrans.); H to assemble (trans.) (6950)
קָהָל *qāhāl* assembly, convocation (6951)

Basic Vocabulary Group–55 Lesson 63

מִזְרָח *mizrāḥ* (place of) sunrise, east (4217)
מָשַׁח *māšaḥ* he anointed (4886); מָשִׁיחַ *māšîᵃḥ* anointed (-one), (later) messiah (4899)
נְחֹשֶׁת *nᵉḥōšet* copper, bronze, fetters (5178); נָחָשׁ *nāḥāš* serpent (5175)
פַּחַד *páḥad* dread (6343)
סָגַר *sāḡar* he shut, closed (5462)
עָזַר *ʿāzar* he helped, succored (5826)
עָפָר *ʿāp̄ār* dry earth, dust (6083)
עֶצֶם *ʿéṣem* bone, substance, self (6106)
עָצוּם *ʿāṣûm* mighty, numerous (6099)
צַוָּאר *ṣawwāʾr* (back of) neck (66770

Basic Vocabulary Group–56 Lesson 64

הָפַךְ *hāp̄ak̲* he overturned, turned (back) (2015)
פֵּאָה *pēʾāʰ* corner, side (6285)
פָּדָה *pāḏāʰ* he ransomed (6299)
פּוּץ *pûṣ* it was dispersed, scattered; N to be scattered (6327)
פָּלָא *pālāʾ* N to be extraordinary, hard to understand; H to do marvelous things (6381)
פֶּן *pen* lest (6435)
צָבָא *ṣāḇāʾ* army, host; pl. YHWH of hosts (6635)
שָׁבָה *šāḇāʰ* he took captive (7617)
שְׁבִי *šᵉḇî* captivity, captive (7628); שְׁבִית *šᵉḇît*, שְׁבוּת *šᵉḇûṯ* captivity (7622)
שֵׁבֶט *šēḇeṭ* staff, sceptre, tribe (7626)
שֶׁקֶר *šéqer* lie, falsehood, deception, deceit (8267)

Basic Vocabulary Group–57 Lesson 65

אָרַר *ʾārar* he cursed, called a curse upon (779)
בְּרִית *bᵉrîṯ* covenant, contract (1285)
בָּרַךְ *bārak̲* he knelt; D to bless (1288); בְּרָכָה *bᵉrāḵāʰ* blessing (1293)
גּוֹי *gôy* nation, people, pl. gentiles (1471)
יָרַשׁ *yāraš* he took possession, inherited (3423)
כּוֹכָב *kôḵāḇ* star (3556)
כָּרַת *kāraṯ* he cut off/down, made (a covenant) (3772)
צֶדֶק *ṣéḏeq* rightness, righteousness (6664)
צְדָקָה *ṣᵉḏāqāʰ* righteousness, justification (6666)
קָלַל *qālal* it was slight, trifling, swift (7043) קְלָלָה *qᵉlālāʰ* curse (7045)

Basic Vocabulary Group–58 Lesson 66

יָרֵךְ *yārēḵ* thigh, loins, side (3409)
כְּרוּב *kᵉrûḇ* cherub (3742)
מִשְׁפָּחָה *mišpāḥāʰ* clan, division of tribe (4940)
נָבַט *nāḇaṭ* H to look at, regard, show regard for (5027)
נָחַם *nāḥam* N to be sorry, repent; H to comfort (5162)
פַּר *par(r)* young bull, steer (6499)
שָׁחַת *šāḥaṯ* N to be marred, spoiled, corrupt; H active of same (7843)
שָׁכַח *šāḵaḥ* he forgot (7911)
שָׁכַם *šāḵam* H to rise/start early (7925)
תָּמִיד *tāmîḏ* continuously, continuity (8548)
תָּמִים *tāmîm* complete, sound (8549); תָּמַם *tāmam* it was complete, finished (8552)

Basic Vocabulary Group–59 Lesson 68

אֶבְיוֹן *ʾeḇyôn* poor, needy (34)
אַרְבַּע *ʾarbaʿ*, אַרְבָּעָה *ʾarbāʿāʰ* 4 (703)
אַרְבָּעִים *ʾarbāʿîm* 40 (705); רְבִיעִי *rᵉḇîʿî* 4th (7244)
דּוֹר *dôr* age, generation, life-time, dwelling-place (1755)
חֲמוֹר *ḥămôr* he-ass (2543)
רָחַק *rāḥaq* he was/became distant, it was far (7368)
רָחוֹק *rāḥôq* distant, far, distance (7350)
שָׁדַד *šāḏaḏ* he dealt violently with, despoiled (7703)
שׁוֹפָר *šôp̄ār* ram's horn, trumpet (7782)
שִׁית *šîṯ* to put, set, appoint (7896)
תּוֹעֵבָה *tôʿēḇāʰ* abomination (8441)

Basic Vocabulary Group–60 Lesson 69

הֶבֶל *hébel* vapor, breath, vanity (1892)
חָרַם *ḥāram* H to devote to a deity, ban, completely destroy (2763)
כָּשַׁל *kāšal* he stumbled, staggered (3782)
נָטַע *nāṭaʿ* he planted (5193)
נִצַּח *nāṣaḥ* D to act as overseer, conductor (5329)
נֵצַח *nēṣaḥ* eminence, perpetuity, everlastingness (5331)
נָצַר *nāṣar* he watched, guarded, kept (5341)
סֶלָה *séláʰ* Selah! lift up! exalt! (5542); סֶלַע *séla*ʿ crag, cliff, rock (5553)
סָלַח *sālaḥ* he forgave, pardoned (5545)
סֹלֶת *sṓlet̲* fine flour (5560)
עֶרְוָה *ʿerwāʰ* nakedness, pudenda (6172)

Basic Vocabulary Group–61 Lesson 70

אִי *ʾî* (*ʾyy*) island, coastland, region (339)
גֶּבֶר *gébẹr* man (not woman), male (1397); גִּבּוֹר *gibbôr* mighty man, hero (1368)
גְּבוּרָה *gᵉbûrāʰ* strength, might (1369)
חָתַת *ḥātat̲* it was shattered, he was dismayed (2865)
יָם *yām*, pl. *yamm-*, sea, west (3220)
נָשַׂג *nāśag̅* H to reach, overtake (5381)
פָּרַר *pārar* H to break, frustrate (6565)
פָּרַץ *pāraṣ* he broke through/into/down/in pieces (6555)
פָּרַשׂ *pāraś* he spread, spread out (6566)
רָנַן *rānan* he cried (in joy, exultation, distress) (7442); רִנָּה *rinnāʰ* ringing cry (7440)

Basic Hebrew Vocabulary–62 Lesson 71

הָרָה *hārāʰ* G11 she conceived, became pregnant (2029)
זָנָה *zānāʰ* he committed fornication; G11 she was a harlot; G51 harlot (2181)
יָשַׁע *yāšaʿ* H to deliver, save, give victory (3467); יֵשַׁע *yéšaʿ* deliverance, salvation (3468)
יְשׁוּעָה *yᵉšûʿāʰ* salvation, deliverance, victory (3744)
תְּשׁוּעָה *tᵉšûʿāʰ* deliverance, salvation (8668)
מְעַט *mᵉʿaṭ* a little, a few, fewness (4592)
רִחַם *rāḥam* D to have compassion, be compassionate (7355)
רַחֲמִים *raḥămîm* compassion, love (7356)
שָׁבַת *šābat̲* he ceased, rested; H to cause to cease, destroy (7673);
שַׁבָּת *šabbāt̲* Sabbath (7676)
תָּקַע *tāqaʿ* he thrust, gave a blow/blast, struck (8268)

Basic Hebrew Vocabulary–63 Lesson 72

גָּמָל *gāmāl* camel (1581)
מִנְחָה *minḥāʰ* gift, cereal offering
עֵמֶק *ʿēmeq* valley, deep place (6010) פָּרָשׁ *pārāš* horseman (6571)
קָשַׁב *qāšab̲* H to give attention, attend (7181)
קָשַׁר *qāšar* he bound, conspired (7194)
קֶשֶׁת *qéšet̲* bow (weapon, rainbow) (7198)
רָגַז *rāg̅az* he was agitated, excited, he quivered, quaked (7264)
רָפָא *rāpāʰ* he healed (7495)
רָפָה *rāpāʰ* it sank down, dropped, he relaxed; H to abandon (7503)
שָׁבַר *šābar* he broke; D to shatter (7665)
שֵׁבֶר *šēb̲er*, שֶׁבֶר *šéb̲er* breaking, fracture, breach (7667)

Basic Hebrew Vocabulary–64 Lesson 73

אָמֵץ *ʾāmēṣ* he was strong; D to strengthen, harden; H to exhibit strength; HtD to determine (553)
אֶפֶס *ʾép̄es* end, none at all, zero; *ʾép̄es kî* howbeit (657)
חֲלוֹם *ḥălôm* dream (2472)
יְאוֹר *yᵉʾôr* river (usually Nile) (2975) יַעַר *yáʿar* thicket, wood, forest (3293)
יְרִיעָה *yᵉrîʿāʰ* curtain, tent-coth (3407)
מָשַׁל *māšal* he ruled, had dominion over (4910) נָא *nāʾ* prithee, I pray (9994)
נָצַב *nāṣab̲* N to take one's stand; H to station, fix (5324)
סָבַב *sāb̲ab̲* he turned, turned around, surrounded (5437)
סָבִיב *sāb̲îb̲* round about, the surrounding region (5439)
תָּפַשׂ *tāp̄aś* he grasped, wielded (8610)

Basic Hebrew Vocabulary–65 Lesson 74

לְאֹם *lᵉʾōm* people, folk, nation (3816)
לוּחַ *lûaḥ* tablet, board (3871)
לִשְׁכָּה *liškāʰ* room, chamber, hall, cell (3957)
עֹל *ʿōl* (*ʿll*) yoke (5923)
צֵל *ṣēl* (*ṣll*) shadow (6738)
עָצַר *ʿāṣar* he restrained, retained (6113)
צֹאן *ṣōʾn* small cattle, flock (6629)
צָפָה *ṣāp̄āʰ* D to overlay, plate (6823)
צִפּוֹר *ṣippôr* bird (6833)
קָנָא *qānāʾ* D to be envious, excited to anger (7065); קִנְאָה *qinʾāʰ* jealousy, zeal (7068)
שָׂדֶה *śāḏêʰ* field, land (7704)

Basic Hebrew Vocabulary–66 Lesson 75

בָּלַל *bālal* he mixed, confounded, mingled (1101)
בָּלַע *bālaʿ* he swallowed, swallowed up (1104)
גִּיל *gîl,* גּוּל *gûl* he exulted rejoiced (1523)
גִּלּוּל *gillûl* pl. amulets, idols (1544)
טֶרֶם *ṭérem* not yet; בְּטֶרֶם *bᵉṭérem* before (when not yet) (2962)
מוֹל *môl,* מוּל *mûl* in front of, facing (4136)
מַצָּה *maṣṣāʰ* unleavened bread, matsah (4682)
מָתַי *māṯay* when? (4970)
נָסַע *nāsaʿ* he pulled up (tent-pegs). set out, journeyed (5265)
סָתַר *sāṯar* N to hide self, be concealed (5641)
רָצַח *rāṣaḥ* he murdered, slew (7523) שֶׁמֶשׁ *šémeš* sun (8121)

Basic Hebrew Vocabulary–67 Lesson 76

אָרַב *ʾārab̲* he lay in wait for, ambushed (693)
בְּאֵר *bᵉʾēr* dug-well, pit (875); בּוֹר *bôr,* בֹּאר *bôʾr* cistern, pit, well (953, 877)
בְּרִיחַ *bᵉrîaḥ* bar, bolt (1281)
גָּאוֹן *gāʾôn* exaltation, majesty, pride (1347)
חָגַר *ḥāḡar* he girded himself (2296)
לְמַעַן *lᵉmáʿan* for the sake of, on account of, in order that (4616)
מַיִם *máyim* water (4325)
נָכְרִי *nok̲rî* foreign, alien (5237)
נָצַל *nāṣal* H to snatch away, rescue, deliver (5337)
פָּגַע *pāḡaʿ* he reached, met, encountered (6293)
שָׁפַךְ *šāp̄ak̲* he poured, poured out (8230)

Basic Vocabulary Group–68 Lesson 77

דֶּבֶר *débe͟r* pestilence, plague (1698)
דָּגָן *dāgān* grain, corn (1715)
הָרַס *hāras* he threw down, broke down (2040); זוּב *zûb̠* to flow, gush (2100)
זָרָה *zārāʰ* he fanned, winnowed, scattered (2219)
חָלַץ *ḥālaṣ* he drew off; D he delivered, rescued (2502)
חָמַל *ḥāmal* he spared, had compassion (2550)
חֲנִית *ḥănît̠* spear (2595)
חָרְבָּה *ḥorbāʰ* waste, ruin, desolation (2723); מְעָרָה *mᵉʿārāʰ* cave (4631)
נָטַשׁ *nāṭaš* he left, forsook, abandoned (5203)
נָתַץ *nāt̠aṣ* he pulled down, broke down (5422)

Basic Vocabulary Group–69 Lesson 78

בָּשָׂר *bāśār* flesh (1320); יָרַד *yārad̠* he went down, descended (3381)
כָּסָה *kāsāʰ* D to cover, conceal, clothe (3680)
מוֹט *môṭ* to totter, slip, shake (4131); מָטָר *māṭār* rain (4306)
מֵעִים *mēʿîm* (pl.) bowels, inward parts (4578)
מָרָה *mārāʰ* he was disobedient, rebellious, stubborn; H to display (these qualities) (4784)
מָשַׁךְ *māšak̠* he drew, led, dragged, drew out, prolonged (4900)
מָשָׁל *māšāl* proverb, parable, similitude (4912)
סָמַךְ *sāmak̠* he leaned, supported, upheld, placed (hand) (5564)
פֶּסַח *pésaḥ* Passover (6453)
שָׁלַךְ *šālak̠* H to throw, fling, cast (7993)

Basic Vocabulary Group–70 Lesson 79

מָעוֹז *māʿôz* place/means of safety, protection, stronghold (4581)
מָתְנַיִם *mot̠náyim* loins (4975)
נָכַר *nāk̠ar* H to regard, observe, recognize, acknowledge (5234)
עֵז *ʿēz* (*ʿizz*) she-goat (5795)
פָּשַׁט *pāšaṭ* he stripped off, made a dash; D, H to strip (6584)
שָׁחַט *šāḥaṭ* he slaughtered; Gp50 hammered, beaten (7819)
שָׂחַק *śāḥaq* he laughed; D to play, jest, make sport (7832)
שִׂמְלָה *śimlāʰ* mantle, wrapper (8071)
שָׂעִיר *śāʿîr* he-goat, buck (8163); שֵׂעָר *śēʿār* hair (animal or human) (8181)
שְׂעֹרָה *śᵉʿōrāʰ* barley (8184)

RULES

RULES

1a. A *dagesh* in a *begadkepat* at the beginning of a word or following a shewa is a light dagesh, indicating stopped pronunciation (§11.44). A dagesh in any other letter, or in a begadkepat in any other position, is a strong dagesh, indicating a geminate (doubled) consonant (§11.43). A strong dagesh in a begadkepat both doubles and hardens it (§11.442).

1b. Consonants with shewa, except begadkepat and מּ, frequently lose the strong dagesh (§13.41). This particularly applies to יּ.

2a. *Pure-long vowels* do not reduce except in originally-closed syllables (§15.22), where they become the corresponding short vowel, subject to the short-vowel rules (§15.222)

2b. Long *â* became long *ô* in the Canaanite dialects (§14.11).

3. Words joined by maqqeph and words in construct have only one major accent (§17.12).

4. Original short vowels in final open syllables have generally vanished (§§15.51, ,52).

5. A doubly-closed syllable never occurs within a word and rarely occurs at word-end (§16.34).

6. When a doubly-closed syllable would result from the loss of a short vowel (Rule 4), one of the following occurs:
 a. If a geminate consonant would result, it loses gemination (§13.42);
 b. If a consonantal cluster would result, an anaptycitic vowel is inserted (§15.61);
 c. In a few cases, the doubly-closed syllable remains (§16.3423).

7. Syllables do not begin with consonantal clusters, except in forms of the word for 'two' (§16.35).

8. The conjunction —ו, when it occurs before labials (ב, מ, פ, called *bûmep̄*), or before consonants with shewa, develops to vocalic וּ *û*; before yod with shewa, however, long *î* is formed (§15.652).

9. At word-end, original *-cw > -*cû* and *-cy > -*cî* (§15.67).

10a. *Gutturals* reject dagesh (§11.432); before א, ע, and ר there is compensatory lengthening (§15.141*.
 b. Gutturals do not take simple vocal shewa (§15.42).
 c. Gutturals often vocalize a silent shewa (§15.421).
 d. Gutturals prefer *a*-class vowels, especially before them (§15.43).
 e. At word-end, ע, ח, or הּ (*he*[h] with mappiq) attract pattaḥ furtive after *i*- or *u*-class vowels (§15.4321).
 f. *i* > *e* (*ḥîrîq* > *s*[e]*ḡôl*) before nonfinal gutturals (§15.434).
 g. Initial א prefers *i*-class vowels when near the accent (§15.433).
 h. א at word-end and frequently at syllable-end is quiescent (§15.54).

11. Nun נ assimilates to a following consonant when no vowel separates (§13.111).

12. In HtD forms, when the first radical is a dental or a sibilant, metathesis, assimilation, or both occur (§13.112, §13.61)

13. Short vowels normally *lengthen* in accented or near-open syllables, and *reduce* in distant-open syllables (§15.11, §15.12, §15.23)
 b. Compensatory vowels do not reduce (§15.233).

c. The original vowel of a segolate does not reduce in sg. cstr. (§15.232). It does, however, reduce in pl. abs. forms.

d. In many forms, *ṣêrê* does not reduce (§15.223).

14. Short *a* does not lengthen in *erstwhile doubly-closed syllables* except in pause (§15.111, cf. §15.132).

15. Short *a* does not lengthen in accented-closed syllables in finite verbal forms, except in pause (§15.113).

16. In *near-open* syllables, *i-* or *u-*class short vowels *reduce* to shewa when preceded by a long *syllable* or by no syllable at all (§15.241).

17. In finite verbal forms *without sufformatives,* the accent is on the *ultima* (§17.21). In such forms *with sufformatives,* the following rules prevail:

a. If the *ultima* is *closed,* the accent is on the ultima, and the form follows the short-vowel chart (§17.221).

b. If the *ultima* is *open* and the *penult* is *long,* the accent is on the *penult,* and the form follows the short-vowel chart (§17.222).

c. If the *ultima* is open and the *penult* is *short,* in *nonpausal* forms the accent is on the *ultima,* the vowel of the *penult* reduces to shewa, and the vowel of the antepenult ha its pausal form (lengthened) and is marked by metheg (§17.223).

d. Under the same conditions (17c) but in *pausal form*, the accent is on the *penult,* and the form follows the short-vowel chart (§17.2231).

18. Short *a* frequently attenuates to short *i* in unaccented closed syllables (§15.32).

19. When two successive simple (vocal) shewas would occur, the first becomes *ḥîrîq* and the second becomes zero-shewa (§15.651).

20. In originally closed accented syllables, in certain forms original short *i* becomes short *a* (§15.33).

21. When *simple (vocal) shewa* would occur before *compound shewa,* the simple shewa is changed to the normal short vowel of the same vowel-class as the compound shewa (§15.653).

22. When *compound shewa* would occur before simple (vocal) shewa, the compound shewa develops to its corresponding normal short vowel, and the simple shewa becomes zero shewa (§15.2532).

23. The connecting vowel of a pronominal suffix, if any, takes the accent (§17.32). If a shewa precedes the suffix, it is zero shewa and the ך/כ of the suffix is spirantized.

24. In verbal forms, thematic *a* in G-perf. generally yields thematic *u* in G-impf., and thematic *i* or *u* in G-perf. yields thematic *a* in G-impf. (§27.331).

25. In G-impf., the vowell of the preformative is determined usually by the thematic vowel, as follows: thematic *a* preformative *i,* thematic *i* or *u* preformative *a* (§27.332).

26. When adding a consonantal sufformative (i.e. one which begins with a consoant) to a CC² verb which ends in a geminated consonant, the consonantal cluster which would occur is avoided by the insertion of a long vowel before the sufformative, namely וֹ (*ô*) in the perf. and ֵי (*ê^y^*) in the impf. (§15.64).

27. Nonpausal converted impf. forms which have a closed ultima and an open penult are accented on the *penult* (§17.341)

28. Nonpausal converted perf. forms ending in תָּ (*-tā*) or תִּי (*-tî*) generally are accented on the *ultima* (§17.342).

Part 2
GRAMMAR

§01. Hebrew is a member of the Semitic family of languages. Cognate languages include Akkadian (Assyrian and Babylonian), Arabic, Aramaic and Syriac, Ethiopic, Phoenician, Ugaritic, etc. Hebrew, Phoenician, and neighboring dialects are often referred to as *Canaanite dialects.* Cf. E. Kautzsch, ed., *Gesenius' Hebrew Grammar*, 2nd ed. rev. by A. E. Cowley (1909; repr. Oxford: Clarendon Press, 1963), §§1-2 (hereafter cited as *Ges.*).

§01.1 For information and literature on the Semitic languages see W. S. LaSor, *A Basic Semitic Bibliography (Annotated),* (Wheaton: Van Kampen, 1950), and J. H. Hospers, *Basic Bibliography of the Semitic Languages,* 2 vols. (Leiden: Brill, 1972-74).

§02. *Biblical Hebrew* is the name used for the Hebrew of the Old Testament. It includes some archaic forms, some late forms, and the stages of linguistic development between these extremes. This time-spread (at least as great as that between Chaucerian [14th cent.] and Modern English!) often causes the student difficulty with the so-called irregularities. Further complicating the problem is the fact that the vocalization of the Heb. Bible represents the pronunciation as of about the 7th cent. A. D., and includes several vocalic shifts that took place between the time of the Septuagint (3d cent. B. C.)—and in some cases even the time of the Vulgate (4th cent. A. D.)—and the Masoretes. The beginner should note these phenomena as he encounters them, but should not attempt to learn them during his introductory studies.

§03. The *Semitic Languages* are the languages spoken by the peoples of the Arabian peninsula and the adjacent regions to the north, west, and south, which have characteristics in common that can best be explained as deriving from a common origin (cf. §03.3).

§03.1 One characteristic of Semitic languages is the dominance of consonants that carry the basic idea, while the vowels (and certain consonant-and-vowel patterns) give the specific meanings of the words. Since the majority of words have three basic consonants, this feature is described as *Triconsonantalism.*

§03.11 The consonants that carry the basic idea are called the *Root.* In 3-consonant roots, the term "triliteral" is often used, but since some Semitic languages are written in syllabic rather than alphabetic form, this term is imprecise.

§03.12 It was an error of Semitists of former generations, sometimes repeated today, to attempt to force all words into original (hypothetical) 3-cons. roots. A number of basic words (such as 'hand,' 'back,' 'mouth,' 'father,' etc.) at the earliest known level are biconsonantal, and some are perhaps even monoconsonantal. A few are quadriconsonantal (cf. the word for 'four'). Cf. §24.1.

§03.2 Another characteristic of Semitic languages is the *verbal system.* Unlike the Indo-European languages known to most of us, Semitic languages do not have a three-tense system (past, present, future—although this in itself is a grave oversimplification). Rather, there is something like *aspect,* the verb-form describing an act or a state that is complete or incomplete in the time reference suggested by the context. Hence a "present" can be used for an action or state in the present or the future, or even one that is incomplete in past time.

§03.21 A second feature of the verbal system is the use of *derived stems* (wrongly called "conjugations"; the Heb. term *binyān* 'building' is preferable), to indicate simplicity, intensity or repetition, causation, etc., of the action. See §28.

§03.22 Aspect (tense, *Aktionsart*) and stem modification of the verb root are accomplished by alterations of the consonantal and vowel pattern, usually along with the addition of certain preformative (prefixed), sufformative (suffixed), and infixed elements. See §27.

§03.3 Since the similarities of phonology, morphology, syntax, and vocabulary of the Semitic languages are remarkably demonstrable, it is reasonable to assume that these languages had a common origin. *Proto-Semitic* (PS) is the name given to the hypothetical parent language. PS forms are hypothesized on principles that will explain the known derived forms. No actual PS forms exist except by coincidence or accident. There are no extant samples of "Proto-Semitic."

§03.4 There is no general agreement on the subgrouping of Semitic languages. They are often grouped geographically into *East Semitic* (Akkadian) and *West Semitic.* The latter is further subdivided into *Northwest Semitic* (Ugaritic, Hebrew, Phoenician, Aramaic, etc.) and *Southwest Semitic* (North Arabic, South Arabic, Ethiopic, etc.). The linguistic features, however, do not always fit the geographical distribution.

§03.41 Hebrew is one of the *H-languages.* in contrast with Babylonian which is an *Š-language.* This distinction is based on the causative stem (Hiphil/Shaphel) and the pronouns *hû/šû, hî/šî,* etc.

§03.5 It has been pointed out that the Semitic languages are more closely related to each other than are those classified as Indo-European. A larger group that would include certain languages of North Africa, frequently called *Hamito-Semitic languages*, is more comparable to the complex nature of the Indo-European family, whereas the Semitic languages are more comparable to a subfamily such as the Romance or the Germanic languages. Hamito-Semitic studies are still in their infancy due to the paucity of "Hamitic" materials other than those elements found in Egyptian and Berber.

§03.6 *Modern Hebrew* is a revival of late Biblical Hebrew after an interval of many centuries, during which time *Mishnaic Hebrew* developed. Except for many additions from Mishnaic Hebrew, Aramaic, and other (non-Semitic) languages, Modern Hebrew does not differ greatly from Biblical Hebrew. Since Hebrew is now a living language, an increasing number of Hebrew teachers are using the modern rules of pronunciation rather than the "classical" for Bib. Heb.

§04. In learning a language it is necessary to learn the grammar and its elements. This includes study of pronunciation, formation, and meaning of words in the language, and how words are joined to form meaningful statements. Thus language study involves *phonology, morphology, vocabulary,* and *syntax.* Part Two of this *Handbook* therefore contains the following divisions: (1) Phonology, (2) Morphology, (3) Syntax, and (4) Basic Vocabulary. Cf. Eugene A. Nida, *Learning a Foreign Language* (New York: Friendship Press, 1957), which is highly recommended.

§04.1 *Phonology* is the study of the elements of sound used to form words and phrases. We include "phrases" in this broad definition because in some languages some sounds occur in phrases which do not occur in words. *Division 1* of the grammar deals with Phonology. All sections in that division are numbered with 1 in the tens place (i.e. §10., §11., §11.1, §11.2, etc.).

§04.11 Strictly speaking the *sounds* of a language can only be studied in the spoken form. But in dealing with ancient languages, we have access only to written forms. Hence the study of *orthography* (the written form) is ancillary to the study of phonology. The student must always bear in mind the fact that orthography does not always exactly represent the sounds which the symbols are intended to convey (cf. *ough* in Eng. *tough, thought, though, through, slough,* etc.).

§04.12 When the orthography of a language is in a form not readily recognized by those who do not know the language, a system of transliteration is commonly used. For obvious reasons we use a system that can be produced by typewriter in a modified Roman alphabet.

§04.2 *Morphology,* also called *accidence,* is the study of the inflected forms of words, i.e. how they are modified to show grammatical elements. *Division 2* of the grammar deals with Morphology. The paragraphs in that division are numbered with numerals having 2 in the tens place (i.e. §20., §20.1, §21.2511, etc.).

§04.21 Languages are described as *isolating, agglutinating,* or *inflecting*, depending on the way they indicate the relationship between words. In an *isolating* language, such as Chinese and to a large extent Modern English, the relationship is shown purely by word order. Thus 'John hit Joe' means something quite different from 'Joe hit John.' In an *agglutinating* language such as Sumerian or Modern Turkish, the relationship is shown by elements that are added on to words. In an *inflecting* language the root or stem is modified by prefixes, infixes, suffixes, and other formative elements to build a word and to show the relationship between words. In Eng. the elements of inflection remain in words such as *he, him, his* and *ride, riding, rode, ridden,* etc.

§04.22 Hebrew, like all Semitic languages, is an *inflecting* language. Grammatical elements, such as gender, number, state, person, aspect (tense), etc., are indicated by morphological elements (changes in form).

§04.3 *Syntax* is the study of the means of joining words together so as to convey meaning. Knowing vocabulary is a necessary condition for understanding a language, but it is not a sufficient condition. Assigning Eng. equivalents to words in a Heb. sentence is merely an exercise in substitution of definitions. Without knowing the relationship of those words, i.e. the syntax of the language, the sentence has no meaning. The same is true in English. Note, e.g. that if the words of the first sentence in this paragraph were indiscriminately listed, the new "sentence" would have no meaning: convey is meaning means the of together to syntax study words the of joining. *Division 3* of this grammar deals with Syntax. All paragraphs in that division are numbered with numerals which have 3 in the tens place (i.e. §30., §30.1, §31.351, etc.).

§04.4 In spite of what we know about phonology, morphology, and syntax, we still cannot understand a language unless we know the meanings of the words. Thus *vocabulary control* is essential to language study.

§04.41 How much vocabulary should a student know in any given language? Clearly, the more words he knows, the more extensively and, perhaps, more rapidly he can read. But not all words are of equal importance. It is obviously more important to know those words which occur with high frequency than those which occur infrequently. Modern linguistic studies emphasize a *basic* vocabulary, and we have followed that approach in this *Handbook. Division 4* of the grammar contains a Basic Hebrew Vocabulary.

§04.42 There are approximately 1,100 words which occur with a frequency of 25 or more times in the Heb. Bible. If the student commits this basic vocabulary to memory, he should be able to read widely and fairly rapidly, especially in narrative literature. Then there are some low frequency words with considerable theological import. These also should be learned. In addition, there are words which, while of low frequency in the Heb. Bible may have relatively high frequency in any given book. Obviously, for purposes of reading with facility and understanding in that book the knowledge of such distinctive vocabulary is vital, but in terms of basic vocabulary acquisition these words are of secondary importance. Similarly, words which on the basis of word-count are of high frequency, but have the greatest number of occurrences in one book (e.g. *sélāh* 74x, 71x in Psalms) may be considered of secondary importance in terms of basic vocabulary.

§04.421 During the first year a student is expected to learn approximately 700 of the words in the basic vocabularly. He should make every effort to learn another 700 in the second year. Indeed, vocabulary acquisition and review is a process which must continue throughout our lifetime if we are to have ready access to the OT in the original languages.

§04.43 What about words not in the basic vocabulary? As indicated above (§04.42), the student must inform himself of the distinctive vocabulary, if any, for any book he may choose to read. Then, a good but brief lexicon will meet the need for the purpose of wide reading (e.g., William L. Holladay, ed., *A Concise Hebrew and Aramaic Lexicon of the Old Testament.*, Grand Rapids: Wm. B. Eerdmans, 1971). For careful study of a given passage a large lexicon which lists contexts and calls your attention to special usage of words is indispensible (e.g., Francis Brown, S. R. Driver, and Charles A. Briggs, *A Hebrew and English Lexicon of the Old Testament*; New York: Houghton-Mifflin Co., 1906). However, we probably ought not feel bound to seek the lexical meaning for every unfamiliar word that we encounter. We may frequently *guess* the meaning from context. This is especially the case, e.g., with low-frequency nouns. They may well be derived from a verbal root already familiar to the student. With the added advantage of knowing the several means of deverbal noun formation (see §§24, 24.2) the student should be able to make quite an intelligent guess.

§05. *Translation* is the process of transferring the thought expressed in one language to another language, preferably in equivalent words and equivalent syntax. "Equivalent" does not necessarily mean exact word-for-word transfer. The *idea* an author is seeking to impart in one language is what must be transferred to the second language. The words and syntax of the respective languages serve to control the idea in those languages. Thus translation is an attempt to put the *idea defined by the words and syntax of one language* into the *words and syntax of a second language so as to define the same idea.*

§06. The *numbering system* used in this *Handbook* is decimal and logical.

§06.1 Numbers are to be read as decimals, with "§10." (pronounced 'section ten") = §10.0000, "§11.1" ('section eleven point one') = §11.1000, and "§12.12" ('section twelve point one two') = §12.1200. Thus §04.421 is found after §04.42 but before §04.43, etc.

§06.2 The system is also logical, and subtopics are indicated by the addition of the next decimal. Accordingly, §27.41, §27.42, etc., are to be read as developments of (i.e. either expansions of or exceptions to) §27.4. Usually a subsection of 3 or 4 decimals must be read in the light of the section it is developing and must not be taken out of context.

§§07.—09. are arbitrarily omitted.

The Numbering System

Major divisions are indicted by the *tens:*
§10. Phonology
§20. Morphology
§30. Syntax
Primary subdivision of divisions is indicated by *units:*
§10. Phonology
§11. Orthography
§12. The Consonant
§13. Consonantal Phonetic Shifts
§14. The Vowels
§15. Vocalic Alteration
§16. The Syllable
§17. Stress Accent
Secondary subdivision is indicated by *first decimal:*
§27. Verb Morphology, G Stem
§27.1 Finite, inflected forms
§27.2 Perfect (completed aspect)
§27.3 Imperfect (incompleted aspect)
§27.4 Imperative
§27.5 Jussive and Cohortative
§27.6 Nonfinite, Participle and Infinitive
Tertiary subdivision is indicated by *second decimal:*
§32.3 Mood
§32.31 Indicative
§32.32 Imperative
§32.33 Subjunctive
§32.34 Precative
§32.35 Infinitive and Participle (not moods)
§32.36 Ventive and Permansive (not moods)
§32.37 Infinitive Absolute used as Finite Verb
Further subdivision is indicated by *third decimal:*
§36.32 Uses of the Genitive
§36.321 Attributive Genitive
§36.322 Possessive Genitive
§36.323 Subjective Genitive
§36.324 Objective Genitive
§36.325 *etc.*

§10. *Phonology* is that part of grammar that deals with the phonemic and phonetic elements of a language (roughly identifiable with the consonants and vowels by which they are represented), plus accent, syllabification, consonantal and vocalic alteration, and similar phenomena.

§10.1 *Phonetics* is the study of sounds. It includes the description of how the various sounds are produced, the classification of sounds, their relationship to one another, their influence on one another, and their shifts or alterations in the history of the language or language-group.

§10.11 In order to have a standard base for phonetic description, a system of phonetic transcription must be used. We use a modification of the International Phonetic Association (IPA) Alphabet whenever this is necessary.

§10.111 Phonetic description, when used, is represented within square brackets: [ʒ].

§10.112 The student should bear in mind, however, that the pronunciation of Hebrew (a) in the time of the writing of Esther, (b) in the time of the Masoretic punctuation, and (c) in modern speech—not to mention the artificial "classical" pronunciation—are entirely different. Much of our discussion will be based on comparative study and it is often hypothetical.

§10.2 *Phonemics* is the study of phonemes, which are the smallest meaningful units of sound in a given language. Phonemics also includes the study of the history of the individual phonemes and the phonetic alteration they have undergone.

§10.21 It is customary to represent phonemes between slant lines: /s/. Note that the actual phonetic value of the phoneme may be different from that suggested by the symbol used for the phoneme. Thus the PS phoneme /θ/ is reflectedby Arab. /ṯ/ phonetically described as [θ], whereas it is reflected by Heb. /š/ phonetically described as [ʃ] or [š].

§10.22 In some European languages there is no phonemic distinction between [ð] (like *th* in *these*) and [d]. Persons from such areas, learning English, have difficulty recognizing the difference between words such as *then* and *den*. Similarly, the English-speaking person has difficulty hearing the distinction between Arabic *kalb* [kɛlb] 'dog' and *qalb* [qɛlb] 'heart, mind.'

§10.23 A phoneme may occur in phonetically different forms in any given language. Such sounds are known as *allophones*. For example, the *p* in Eng. *spot* [spɔt] is different than the *p* in *pot* [p'ɔt]; the latter is aspirated, as can be felt if you hold the back of your hand close to your mouth when pronouncing each word. These allophones are never phonemic in Eng., i.e. no two words are differentiated simply by aspiration or lack thereof. On the other hand, aspiration is phonemic in Chinese, where many words are differentiated by nothing other than an aspirated or nonaspirated consonant.

§10.3 *Orthography* is the method of writing a language. The phenomena of orthography must not be confused with the data of phonetics and phonemics. However, since the written records are the only means we have of reconstructing the sounds which the writers were attempting to represent, we must work with the orthography.

§10.31 Most systems of orthography were not invented by the people using them and therefore do not fit the language either phonetically or phonemically. Our (Latin) alphabet, e.g., has 26 symbols, whereas our language has over 40 basic sounds. We have no symbols for [ʃ] (as in *sugar, nation, ship,* etc.), [č] (as in *church, match, nature,* etc.), [ð] (as in *those, then,* etc.), etc. At the same time, we often make one symbol do for sounds that could be represented by another symbol (e.g. *sends* [sɛnz], *judge* [ǧʌǧ], *since* [sɪns], etc. Needless to say, this greatly complicates the learning of writing a language or reproducing the sounds from the written form.

§10.311 It is at this point that orthography often confuses the study of phonetics. Because a certain phoneme is represented by /š/, we may uncritically assume that it has the sound [ʃ] (like *sh* in *ship*). This may be true for a later stage of the language, but not true for an earlier stage. For example, the Greeks borrowed the Phoenician *šîn* and not *sāmeḵ* for *sigma*; on the other hand they borrowed the *sāmeḵ* for *xi*. We must not ignore this and assume that the *sāmeḵ* was always and everywhere in the Semitic languages pronounced [s] (like *s* in *son*), or that *šîn* and its reflexes in Aramaic, Ugaritic, and Akkadian were all pronounced [š].

§10.32 When the orthography of a language is not readily recognized by a student, or it is not easily reproduced in written or typed form, a system of *transliteration* is generally employed. Such a system is neither phonemic nor phonetic, although at times it may closely approximate one or the other or even both. Thus *bêṯ with dagesh (*בּ*)* may be transliterated as *b* or as geminate *bb*, depending on its position in a word. In fact, transliteration is often used in this *Handbook* just to show whether the *dagesh* is a "hardener" or a "doubler." Transliteration is generally indicated by the use of *italic type.*

§10.4 *Speech* is communication by meaningful sounds, or the spoken form of a language. Writing is language in written form, or speech reduced to a system of symbols that are meaningful to a community using the language.

§10.41 The sounds that are used to produce speech are called *vowels* and *consonants*. The vowel is the basic sound, and the consonant is an interruption or restriction of that sound. The resulting component parts are *syllables*. One or more syllables forming a unit that conveys an idea is a *word*. We do not speak words, however, but *sentences*, which are thoughts expressed by one or more words.

§10.42 A *vowel* is the basic sound in speech, made by vibrating the vocal cords. The sound is modified by the angle of the jaw, the position of the tongue, and the shape of the mouth-opening. Any interruption or restriction of the sound, however, is considered as a consonant.

§10.421 There are several ways of describing the various vowels, but I find the "vowel triangle" the simplest. At one apex, the vowel [ɑ] (as in *father*) represents the vowel made with the jaw-angle open, the tongue flat. At the second apex, the vowel [i] (as in *machine*) represents the vowel made with the jaw-angle closed and the front of the tongue raised behind the teeth. At the third apex, the vowel [u] (as in Ger. *gut* or Eng. *boot*) is made with the jaw-angle closed, the lips rounded, and the back of the tongue raised. All other vowels are made at points between any two of these apices. See TABLE C.

§10.43 A *consonant* is an element in speech which interrupts or restricts the passage of breath, whether sound is being produced *at that instant* or not.

§10.431 Consonants are described by indicating (1) whether the voice is being used at the moment of articulation, (2) the point of articulation (i.e. the use of the lips, teeth, tongue, palate, uvula, or glottis to interrupt or restrict the sound), and (3) the nature of the interruption or restriction.

§10.4311 If the voice is used at the moment of articulation, the consonant is described as *voiced*. If the voice is not used at the moment of articulation, the consonant is described as *voiceless* or *surd*. Note that the voice *is used with the vowel* in either case. Compare the words *god, got, cod, cot,* for various combinations of voiced and surd consonants. Note also the immediate shift from surd [t] to voiced [d] in *Get down!*

§10.4312 Descriptors of the *point of articulation* include: (a) *labial* (or *bilabial*, the lips); (b) *labiodental* (the lower lip against the upper teeth); (c) *dental* (or *interdental*, the tongue between the teeth); (d) *alveolar* (or *dental*; the tongue against the alveolar ridge behind the upper teeth); (e) *palatal* (the region just behind the alveolar ridge); (f) *velar* (tongue against the velar arch at top of mouth); (g) *uvular* (back of tongue against the soft palate); (h) *glottal* (made by constricting the throat). Sometimes terms such as "alveopalatal," "back velar," "pharyngeal," etc., are used. See Figure 9.

§10.4313 The *nature of the interruption or restriction* is described as: (a) *stop* (or *plosive*; complete interruption of the sound), *spirant* (or *fricative, continuant;* the sound is restricted but not completely stopped at the point of articulation), (c) *nasal* (the sound is directed through the nasal cavity, (d) *sibilant* (a particular kind of spirant produced by placing the blade of the tongue in the alveolar or alveopalatal region), (e) *lateral* (a particular kind of spirant formed by stopping with the tip of the tongue against the alveolar ridge while allowing the sound to escape around the sides of the tongue), (f) *flap* (a particular kind of stop momentarily formed by placing the tip of the tongue against the alveolar ridge), (g) *semivowel* (a spirant formed by the lips or by the middle of the tongue in proximity to the alveolar ridge).

§10.44 A *syllable* is a vowel or diphthong set apart by a consonant or consonants from preceding or following vowels or diphthongs. This is sometimes defined as a *summit of sonority*.

§10.441 According to this definition, certain consonants have to be recognized as "vowels." For example, *bottle* [bɔ-tl̩], *chasm* [kæ-zm̩], *fighter* [fai-tr̩], *canon* [kæ-nn̩], and *houses* [hau-zz̩] are all disyllabic words, and [l̩, m̩, n̩, r̩, z̩] have to be considered as vocalic in nature.

§10.442 There may be consonants which are not indicated in writing. If two successive vowels form two summits or syllables, a consonant has divided them. E.g.: *idea* is a 3-syllable word, with either a semivowel [aɪ-di′jə] or a glottal stop [aɪ-di′ʔə] separating the last two vowels; likewise *coöperate* has either a bilabial semivowel [ko-wɔp′r̩-ret] or a glottal stop [ko-ʔɔp′r̩-ret] separating the *o*-vowels.

§11. *Orthography* is the term used to describe the method of writing or the study thereof. It includes not only the alphabet but also, in the case of Heb., the vowel points, other pointing, the accents, and the sentence indication or what we normally call "punctuation." Since vowels, etc., are indicated by points, the word *punctuation* is frequently used for these indicators as well as for sentence punctuation.

§11.1 Hebrew was originally written with an alphabet of 22 consonants. The writing was *from right to left* (←——).

§11.11 For the consonants and their phonetic equivalents, see Table B.

§11.111 The theory that the names of the letters were originally descriptive of the shapes of the letters, i.e. that the letters were originally pictograms, is far from certain.

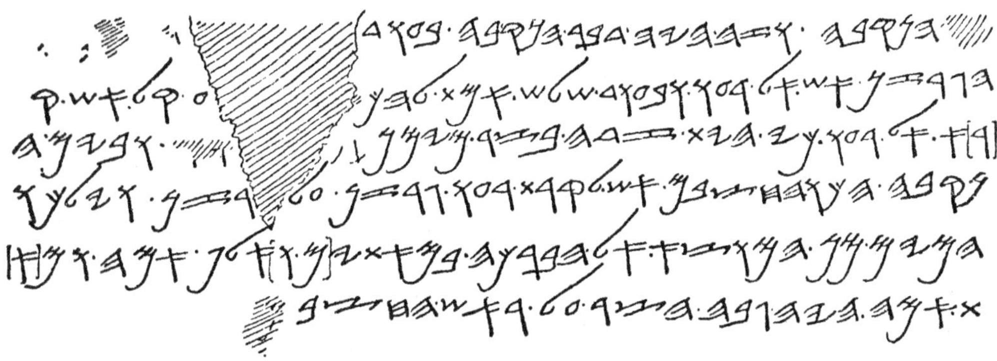

הנקבה . וזה . היה . דבר . הנקבה . בעוד

הגרזן . אש . אל . רעו . ובעוד . שלש . אמת . להנ ע . קל . אש . ק

רא . אל . רעו . כי . הית . זדה . בצר. מימן . ובים . ה

נקבה . הכו . החצבם . אש . לקרת . רעו . גרזן . על . גרזן . וילכו

המים . מן . המוצא . אל . הברכה . במאתים . ואלף. אמה. ומא

ת . אמה . היה . גבה . הצר . על . ראש . החצב[ם]

FIGURE 1. THE SILOAM INSCRIPTION

Written in the ancient "Phoenician" script, possibly in the days of Hezekiah (cf. 2 Kings 20:20), this is one of the earliest known inscriptions in "Biblical" Hebrew.

---

§11.12 This alphabet was borrowed from the Phoenicians, who either invented it or borrowed it from an unknown source. For the early forms of the letters, see TABLE A in Part Three of the *Handbook*.

§11.121 The earliest known Heb. writing is the Gezer Calendar, 10th cent. B. C. This calendar, the Siloam Inscription (8th cent.), and the Lachish ostraca (6th cent.) are all in the Phoenician or Canaanite type of writing. The *tetragrammaton* יהוה in the Habbakuk Commentary of the Dead Sea Scrolls likewise is in Phoenician script.

§11.122 The "square letters" (כְּתָב מְרֻבָּע) of our Heb. Bible, according to Jewish and Christian tradition, were introduced in the time of Ezra (5th cent. B. C.). It would seem that the Arameans (Syrians) had developed the Phoen. alphabet in a slightly different form which came to be known as כְּתָב אֲשׁוּרִי 'Syrian writing.' Cf Hans Jensen, *Die Schrift in Vergangenheit und Gegenwart* (Glückstadt: Verlag J. J. Augustin, n.d.), pp. 193-213); *Ges.* §5.

§11.13 At some point after adopting the Aramaic writing different forms were developed for five of the consonants, depending on whether they stood in final position (word-end) or nonfinal.

§11.131 The letters with final/nonfinal forms are: /k/ כ ך, /m/ מ ם, /n/ נ ן, /p/ פ ף, /ṣ/ צ ץ.

§11.1311 In pointed Hebrew, final *kap̄,* if it has no vowel, is always written with shewa in (not under) the letter: ךְ.

§11.132 Four of these, ץ ף ן ך, have "tails" that extend downward ("downward descenders"). It is likely that these were the earlier forms and that the descenders were turned in cursive writing except at word-end.

§11.133 No distinction between final and nonfinal forms is found before the 3d cent. B. C.

§11.14 The letters were *hung from the line,* as an examination of the scribed fragments of the Habakkuk Commentary of the Dead Sea Scrolls (lQpHab) clearly indicates. In other words, the scribe ruled his parchment, then placed the letters *below* the line, not above it as we do. The tops of all the letters excepd *lāmed* ל are even with this line. The bottoms are much less regular. See Fig. 3.

§11.15 The *lāmed* ל, which extends upwards above the line of writing, was generally written *from the bottom upward.* In Heb. script it is still so written.

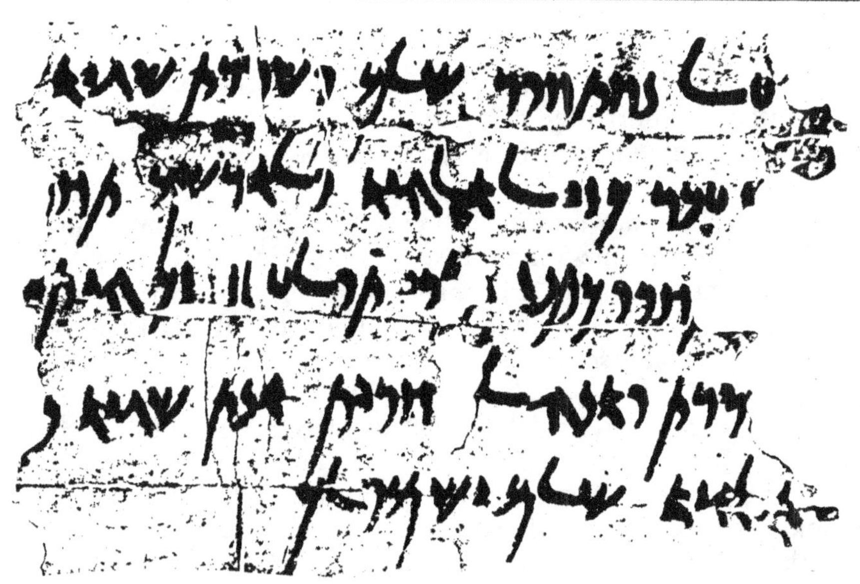

FIGURE 2. EGYPTIAN ARAMAIC PAPYRUS OF THE FIFTH CENTURY B.C.

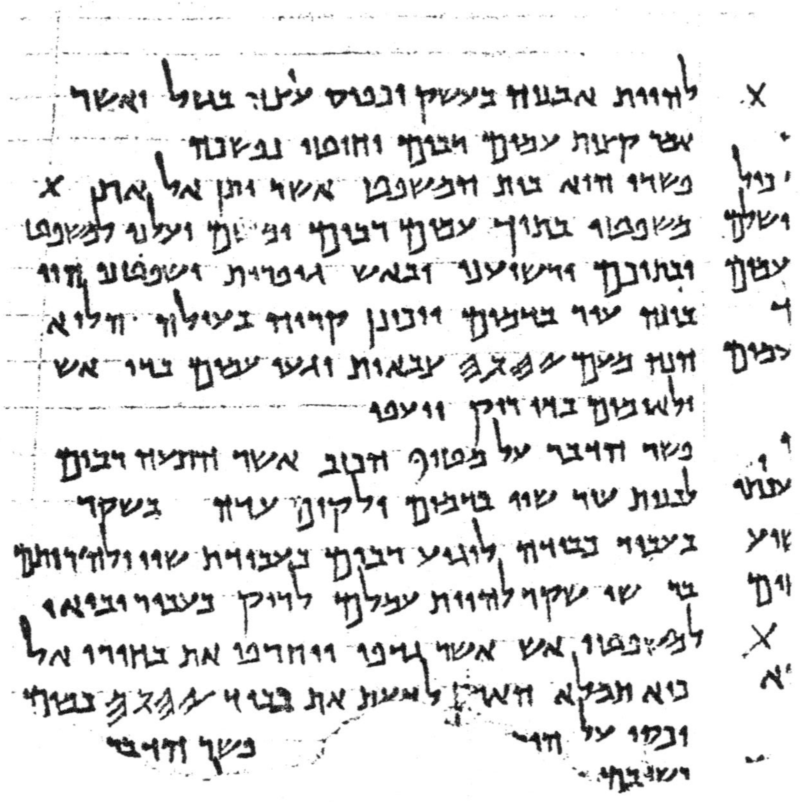

להיות אבניה בעשק וכפיס עֹצה בגזל ואשר
(2:10) אמר קצות עמים רבים וחוטי נפשכה
פשרו הוא בית המשפט אשר יתן אל את
משפטו בתוך עמים רבים ומשם יעלנו למשפט
(2:12) ובתוכם ירשיענו ובאש גופרית ישפטנו הוי
(2:13) בונה עיר בדמים ויכונן קריה בעולה הלוא
הנה מעם יהוה צבאות יגעו עמים בדי אש
ולאומים בדי ריק ייעפו
פשר הדבר על מטיף הכזב אשר התעה רבים
לבנות עיר שוו בדמים ולקום עדה בשקר
בעבור כבודה לוגיע רבים בעבודת שוו ולהרותם
ב[ ]שי שקר להיות עמלם לריק בעבור יבואו
למשפטי אש אשר גדפו ויחרפו את בחירי אל
(2:14) כיא תמלא הארץ ל.עת את כבוד יהוה כמים
יכסו על הי[ ] [פשר הדבר
.ש.בם]

FIGURE 3. COLUMN 10 OF THE HABAKKUK COMMENTARY

Written in "Syrian" script (square letters) around the end of the era (BC–AD), this is a *pešer* (commentary) on part of Habakkuk (1QpHab). Note the use of Phoenician script for the divine name יהוה in lines 7 and 14. Compare the original with the transcription into modern type.

§11.16 Other forms of the Heb. alphabet developed. One, the cursive script of most handwritten material (except manuscripts of the Scriptures), is used by most persons who write Hebrew. Unfortunately, it is not generally taught in Christian schools where Heb. is taught. Since it is cursive, it can be written much more readily than the square letters. See TABLE D. A second alphabet, used by Rashi (the acronym of Rabbi Solomon ben Isaac) in his commentaries on Scripture, will be of importance only to those wishing to read his works.

§11.17 Words are not divided at the end of a line. In some Heb. MSS and in some printed texts, certain consonants are extended to double their normal width (or even more) in order to fill up the line. In printed editions, these extended letters always come at the ends of lines, but in MSs they can be found anywhere except in the initial position.

§11.2 Possibly in the 10th cent. B.C. and among the Aramaic-speaking people, the use of certain consonant-signs to indicate vowels, first at word-end and then within the words, was developed. Cf. F. M. Cross and D. N. Freedman, *Early Hebrew Orthography* (New Haven: American Oriental Society, 1952).

§11.21 The vowel-letters (אִמּוֹת הַקְּרִיאָה, *matres lectionis*): א *'ālep̄,* rarely used as a vowel-letter in Bib. Heb.; ה *hê*, generally used at word-end to indicate *â*- and sometimes *ê*-sounds; ו *wāw*, used to indicate *ô*- and *u*-sounds, and י *yōd*, generally used to indicate *i*- and *e*-sounds.

§11.211 In the Renaissance the Heb. term was translated into Latin, and this term is widely used in Christian grammars today, even though Lat. is generally an unknown language. In this *Handbook* we shall use the term *vowel-letters* rather than *matres lectionis.*

§11.3 As Heb. became more and more a dead language, the reading of a text without vowels became increasingly difficult if not impossible. The traditional pronunciation was preserved by the Masoretes who added marks to the consonantal text to indicate the vowels.

§11.31 The Masoretes are generally dated c.500-1000 A. D. They were known as *ba'ălê hammasôrā*[h] 'lords of the tradition.' There were at least two schools of Masoretes, one in Babylonia which has given us the "Eastern Masorah," and the other in Palestine which has given us the "Western Masorah."

§11.311 We need not concern ourselves here with the work of the Masoretes other than the punctuation. For a good discussion, cf. B. J. Roberts,

הקהל הזה ברעב ויאמר
יהוה אל משה הנני ממטיר לכם לחם מן השמים
ויצא העם ולקטו דבר יום ביומו למען אנסנו
הילך בתורתי אם לא והיה ביום הששי והכינו
את אשר יביאו והיה משנה על אשר ילקטו
יום יום ויאמר משה ואהרן אל כל בני ישראל
ערב וידעתם כי יהוה הוציא אתכם מארץ
מצרים ובקר וראיתם את כבוד יהוה בשמעו
את תלנתיכם על יהוה ונחנו מה כי תלונו עלינו
ויאמר משה בתת יהוה לכם בערב בשר לאכל
ולחם בבקר לשבע בשמע יהוה את תלנתיכם
אשר אתם מלינם עליו ונחנו מה לא עלינו
תלנתיכם כי על יהוה ויאמר משה אל אהרן
אמר אל כל עדת בני ישראל קרבו לפני יהוה
כי שמע את תלנתיכם ויהי כדבר אהרן אל
כל עדת בני ישראל ויפנו אל המדבר והנה
כבוד יהוה נראה בענן

FIGURE 4. HAND-WRITTEN SCROLL OF COMPARATIVELY RECENT DATE

Beautifully written portion of Exodus (16:4-10). Note extended letters used to fill out lines. Note also the word-divisions, but no indication of verses. Compare the manuscript with the modern typography.

The Old Testament Text and Versions (Cardiff: University of Wales, 1951), pp. 40-63, and E. Würthwein, *The Text of the Old Testament* (New York: Macmillan, 1957), pp. 3-31.

§11.312 Nor need we concern ourselves with the long and continuing argument over the spelling Masorah—Masoretes as opposed to Massorah/Massoretes. In this *Handbook* I am following Webster for the Eng. and Eben-Shushan for the Heb. forms, both of which use single-*s*.

§11.313 Three systems of punctuation developed, two of them supralinear (i.e. above the line of consonants) and the third infralinear (below the letters). The infralinear or *Tiberian* system is that which we find in our Heb. Bible. See *Ges.* §8*g*, n.3.

§11.32 The vowel-points in the Tiberian system, their phonemic value, and their modern names are:

◌ַ	*a*	*pattāḥ*	◌ֻ	*u*	*qubbûṣ*
◌ָ	*ā*	*qāmāṣ gāḏôl*	וּ	*û*	*šûrûq*
◌ֶ	*e*	*s*[e]*gôl*	◌ֲ	*ă*	*ḥăṭap̄-paṭṭāḥ*
◌ֵ	*ē*	*ṣērē*	◌ֱ	*ĕ*	*ḥăṭap̄-s*[e]*gôl*
◌ִ	*i*	*ḥîrîq*	◌ֳ	*ŏ*	*ḥăṭap̄-qāmāṣ*
◌ָ	*o*	*qāmāṣ qāṭān (ḥāṭûp̄)*	◌ְ	*e*	*š*[e]*wâ*
◌ֹ	*ō*	*ḥōlām*			See TABLE C.

§11.321 Note that *qāmāṣ gāḏôl* (*ā*) and *qāmāṣ qāṭān* (*o*) are written alike. At one time they were probably pronounced alike, but today there is a distinct difference: [ɑ] and [ɔ], respectively.

§11.322 Note that *ṣêrê* and *ḥîrîq* are often written in a consonantal text that contains vowel-letters (§11.21) and are therefore found with *yōd*. This is called "full" writing (Lat. *plēnē*). In Mod. Heb. they are referred to as *ṣêrê mālē'* and *ḥîrîq mālē'* (*mālē'* = 'full').

§11.323 Note that *ḥōlām* is written *above* the consonants, and is the only exception to the infralinear system.

§11.3231 Note also that *ḥôlām* is often written with the vowel-letter (*wāw*), hence *ḥôlām wāw* or *ḥôlām mālē'*.

§11.324 The *šûrûq* is always written with *wāw* used as a vowel-letter. When the sound [u] was to be written and no *wāw* stood in the consonantal text, the Masoretes wrote *qubbûṣ* (◌ֻ). Such writing without the vowel-letter is called "defective" (Lat. *defectivē*, Heb. חָסֵר).

§11.3241 The common expressions "written fully (or *plēnē*)" and "written defectively" often lead to confusion in the student's mind. He asks, "Why didn't the Masoretes exercise some consistency when vocalizing the text?" The student should understand that the vowel-letters were there (or were absent) *before the Masoretes ever saw the consonantal text.* They only added the vowel-points to the existing consonantal text.

§11.3242 Another common expression that leads to confusion is the reference to the consonantal text (CT) as "the Masoretic Text." CT was determined possibly at the Council of Jamnia (Jabneh) towards the end of the first cent. A.D.. The Masoretes had no part in determining CT, which might better be called the "received text" (*textus receptus*) of the Heb. Bible.

§11.3243 That the CT was not the only recension of the Heb. Bible can clearly be demonstrated by several facts. There are numerous textual differences between the Heb. text of the biblical portions from Qumran (the "Dead Sea Scrolls"). Moreover there are numerous places where the Greek version (the Septuagint, LXX) can only be explained by assuming that a different text lay before the translators. Further, NT quotations of the OT often agree with neither MT nor LXX.

§11.325 Note that the three *ḥăṭap̄*-vowels are written as combinations of *šᵉwâ* with *pattāḥ, sᵉgôl,* or *qāmāṣ qāṭān.*

§11.4 The Masoretes added other points to the consonantal text, which are not to be confused with the vowel-points.

§11.41 At some point in time, either before or after the alphabet was borrowed from the Phoenicians, two different consonantal sounds were represented by the letter *šîn,* ש. As pronounced in recent and modern times, these are [š] and [s]. The Masoretes placed a dot on the upper right-hand corner for *šîn* שׁ, and on the upper left-hand corner for *śîn,* שׂ.

§11.411 When *ḥôlām* precedes *šîn,* only one dot is used to represent both facts: מֹשֶׁה *môšêʰ*. Likewise when *ḥôlām* follows *śîn,* only one dot is used: שׂ in conjunction with a following consonant עָשֹׂה *ʿāśōʰ*.

§11.412 When *ḥôlām* precedes *śîn* or follows *šîn*, both dots are placed on the corners of the consonant, שֹׁ *šō* or *ōś:* שֹׁסַע *šôsaʿ;* יִרְפֹּשׂ *yirpōś.*

§11.42 A consonantal *hê*, as distinguished from *hê* used as a vowel-letter, at the end of a word is indicated by a dot within the letter, called *mappîq:* הּ *hê-with-mappîq.*

§11.43 *Geminate consonants*, i.e. the same consonant repeated without an intervening vowel, were not represented in the orthography. The Masoretes indicated such gemination by placing a dot within the letter, called *dāgēsh*.

---

441 JUDICUM CAP. 21. כא

ארור נתן אשה לבנימן: ויאמרו הנה חג־יהוה בשלו 19
מימים ׀ ימימה אשר מצפונה לבית־אל מזרחה השמש
למסלה העלה מבית־אל שכמה ומנגב ללבונה: ויצו כ
את־בני בנימן לאמר לכו וארבתם בכרמים: וראיתם 21
והנה אם־יצאו בנות־שילו לחול במחלות ויצאתם מן־
הכרמים וחטפתם לכם איש אשתו מבנות שילו והלכתם
ארץ בנימן: והיה כי־יבאו אבותם או אחיהם לרוב ׀ אלינו 22
ואמרנו אליהם חנונו אותם כי לא לקחנו איש אשתו
במלחמה כי לא אתם נתתם להם כעת תאשמו: ויעשו־ 23
כן בני בנימן וישאו נשים למספרם מן־המחללות אשר
גזלו וילכו וישובו אל־נחלתם ויבנו את־הערים וישבו
בהם: ויתהלכו משם בני־ישראל בעת ההיא איש לשבטו 24
ולמשפחתו ויצאו משם איש לנחלתו: בימים ההם אין כה
מלך בישראל איש הישר בעיניו יעשה:

v. 20. ויצוו ק v. 22. לריב ק

חזק

סכום הפסוקים של ספר שופטים שש מאות ושמנה עשר. יראו
את יי' קדשיו סימן: וסדריו י"ד. דובב שפתי ישנים סימן:
וחציו. וירעצו וירצצו את בני ישראל:

FIGURE 5. PAGE OF LETTERIS BIBLE

Note the "final Masorah" at the end of the book of Judges. It records the fact that there are 618 verses in Judges, gives a mnemonic for this figure. It also notes that there are 14 *s*[e]*d̲ārîm*, gives a mnemonic, and records the middle words of the book (from Judg. 10:8).

§11.431 The dagesh that doubles a consonant is called *dāḡēš ḥāzāq* 'strong dagesh' (Lat. *dagesh fortē*) or *dāḡēš kaflān* 'doubling dagesh.'

§11.432 The strong dagesh is generally not found in the gutturals (א ה ח ע) and *rêš* (ר).

§11.433 In ordinary printed texts, there is no difference between *wāw* with *dāḡēš ḥāzāq* (*ww*) and *wāw* used as *šûrûq* (*û*). In careful writing, the dot in *šûrûq* stands higher in the *wāw* than does the dagesh.

§11.44 The consonants ב ג ד כ פ ת, known as *bᵉḡaḏkᵉp̄aṯ* or *beḡeḏkép̄eṯ*, at one time occurred in both stopped and spirantized forms (i.e. allophones, cf. §10.23). The Masoretes indicated the stopped forms by placing a dagesh in the midst of the letter: בּ גּ דּ כּ פּ תּ.

§11.441 The *dāgēsh* that "hardens" begadkepat letters is known as *dāgēsh qal* 'light dagesh' (Lat. *dagesh lēnē*) or *dāḡēš qašyān* 'hardening dagesh.'

§11.442 A begadkepat letter that is geminate (§11.43f) is also hardened. Hence one *dāgēsh* serves both purposes and is known as *dāgēsh ḥāzāq*.

§11.443 In MSs and in some printed texts, a horizontal stroke (like the macron) is placed over a begadkepat letter to show that it is *raphē* (רָפֶה), in other words, it does not have *dāgēsh*. In modern printed Bibles, *raphē* is rarely used.

§11.45 *Maqqēph* (מַקֵּף 'binder') is a horizontal stroke placed at the line of the upper parts of the letters, connecting two or more words: כָּל־יוֹם. Words connected with Maqqeph have only one major accent, on the last word of those bound. (§17.121).

§11.451 Certain prepositions and conjunctions of one syllable are usually written with Maqqeph.

§11.46 The only true mark of punctuation, i.e. sentence punctuation, is the *sôp̄ pāsûq* (סֹף פָּסוּק 'end of sentence'), which looks something like our colon (:). The versification of the Eng. Bible generally follows the division indicated by the use of the *sôph pāsûq*.

§11.5 The Masoretic Text (MT) contains many other marks, generally called *accents*. Originally these were introduced as an aid in reading. Then they became musical notations and serve as such to the modern Cantor. But for our purposes they are useful because (1) they divide the sentence into logical and grammatical segments, and (2) they generally indicate the accented syllable of a word or word-group.

§11.51 The accents are somewhat different in the books of Psalms, Job, and Proverbs (called in Heb. תא"ם *t*^{e}*'ôm*, from the initial letters. The student should learn the common accents first, then learn the distinctives in תא"ם.

§11.52 The accents can be distinguished as *conjunctive* (joining a word to the following word) and *disjunctive* (separating a word from the following). The student will find this distinction quite helpful.

§11.521 In general, *conjunctive* accents have shape that *leads toward the following word,* whereas *disjunctive* accents lead *away from* the following word or are vertical.

§11.53 The principal *disjunctive* accents are:

אֽ *sillûq*	א֗ *r*^{e}*b̲î*^{a}*'*	א֒ *s*^{e}*ḡôltâ*
א֫א֥ *'ôlê w*^{e}*yôrēd̲*	א֔ *zâqēp̄ qāṭôn*	א֓ *šalšélet̲*
א֑ *'at̲nāḥ*	א֖ *ṭip̄ḥâ*	

§11.531 *Sillûq* 'end' stands under the accented letter (i.e. syllable, since the letter also has its vowel) immediately before *sôp̄ pāsûq*. It is therefore the major *pausal* accent of the verse.

§11.532 *'ôlê w*^{e}*yôrēd* 'ascending and descending' is used only in the poetic books תא"ם. It is the main disjunctive in the verse, if used—even stronger than *'at̲nāḥ*. In shorter verses it is not used.

§11.533 a*t̲nāḥ* (֑) 'rest' stands under the accented syllable of the word that ends the first major portion of the verse.

§11.5331 If the sentence is compound, *'at̲nāḥ* may be equivalent to a semicolon. If the sentence is simple, *'at̲nāḥ* may be equivalent to a comma, or simply the place where you pause to take a breath or merely lower your voice.

§11.534 *R*^{e}*b̲î*^{a}*'* stands over the accented syllable of the word that ends the subdivision of the portion before or after the *'at̲nāḥ*. It is a strong disjunctive and requires at least a slight pause in reading.

§11.535 *Zāqēp̄ qāṭôn* 'little zaqeph' is a lesser disjunctive than revia' (however, see the order in *Ges.* §15*f.*). It is sometimes strong enough to require the pausal form of the word on which it stands.

§11.536 *Tip̄ḥā* is sometimes used instead of athnaḥ, especially where the verse consists of only two or three words.

§11.537 For other disjunctive accents, cf. *Ges.* §15*f,h*.

§11.54 The principal conjunctive (joining) accents are:

א֣ *muṇaḥ*	א֨ *'azlâ* (usually associated with *géreš*)
א֤ *m^ehuppāḵ*	א֥ *mêr^eḵâ*

§11.55 *Pause* is a term used with words immediately before a strong disjunctive accent. The form used when the word is *in pause* is called *pausal.*

§11.551 After *'ôlê w^eyôrēd,* athnaḥ is not necessarily pausal, cf. Ps. 45:6.

§11.56 In some instances, words otherwise exactly alike are distinguished by the position of the stress-accent. Note carefully: בָּאָ֫ה 'she is coming' and בָּ֫אָה 'she came'; בָּ֫נוּ 'they built' and בָּנ֫וּ 'in us.'

§11.57 In general, the accent is placed on the syllable bearing the stress-accent—often improperly called "tone"; hence such terms as "pretonic," "tonic," etc.

§11.571 Some accents, however, are not placed on the stressed syllable. The *prepositive* accents are placed on or under the first letter of the word, regardless of the stress. The *postpositive* accents are placed on or under the last letter of the word. In some instances, the accent is repeated on the stressed syllable. Cf. *Ges.* §15*e-p*. *'azlâ* (§11.54) is postpositive.

§11.58 *Metheg* (מֶֽתֶג 'bridle') is a small perpendicular stroke written under a consonant and left of the sublinear vowel (note מֶֽ above). In some situations the student will find it to be very significant. Cf. *Ges.* 16*c-g*.

§11.581 Metheg is used with long or lengthened short vowels in syllables where they might otherwise be expected to reduce (§15.ff.).

§11.582 **Metheg is used regularly with the vowel preceding a *ḥaṭap̄-š^ewâ* (§11.325).**

§11.583 Metheg is often used to indicate the secondary stress-accent of a word or of a word-group formed with Maqqeph.

§11.584 Of special importance is the use of metheg to distinguish *qāmāṣ gāḏôl* (*â*) from *qāmāṣ qāṭān* (*o*). Note the presence and absence of the metheg in the following examples:

אָֽכְלָה	*'āḵ^elā^h*	'she ate'	יִֽרְאוּ	*yîr^e'û*	'they fear' (<ירא)
אָכְלָה	*'oḵlā^h*	'food'	יִרְאוּ	*yir'û*	'they see' (<ראה)

I,14—2,4 ESTHER 1243

אליו כרשנא שתר אדמתא תרשיש מרס מרסנא ממוכן
שבעת שרי פרס ומדי ראי פני המלך הישבים ראשנה במלכות:
15 כדת מה־לעשות במלכה ושתי על ׀ אשר לא־עשתה את־מאמר
המלך אחשורוש ביד הסריסים: ס 16 ויאמר מומכן לפני
המלך והשרים לא על־המלך לבדו עותה ושתי המלכה כי על־
כל־השרים ועל־כל־העמים אשר בכל־מדינות המלך אחשורוש:
17 כי־יצא דבר־המלכה על־כל־הנשים להבזות בעליהן בעיניהן
באמרם המלך אחשורוש אמר להביא את־ושתי המלכה לפניו
ולא־באה: 18 והיום הזה תאמרנה ׀ שרות פרס־ומדי אשר שמעו
את־דבר המלכה לכל שרי המלך וכדי בזיון וקצף: 19 אם־על־
המלך טוב יצא דבר־מלכות מלפניו ויכתב בדתי פרס־ומדי ולא
יעבור אשר לא־תבוא ושתי לפני המלך אחשורוש ומלכותה יתן
המלך לרעותה הטובה ממנה: 20 ונשמע פתגם המלך אשר־יעשה
בכל־מלכותו כי רבה היא וכל־הנשים יתנו יקר לבעליהן
למגדול ועד־קטן: 21 וייטב הדבר בעיני המלך והשרים ויעש
המלך כדבר ממוכן: 22 וישלח ספרים אל־כל־מדינות המלך
אל־מדינה ומדינה ככתבה ואל־עם ועם כלשונו להיות כל־איש
שרר בביתו ומדבר כלשון עמו: ס
2 1 אחר הדברים האלה כשך חמת המלך אחשורוש זכר את־
ושתי ואת אשר־עשתה ואת אשר־נגזר עליה: 2 ויאמרו נערי
המלך משרתיו יבקשו למלך נערות בתולות טובות מראה:
3 ויפקד המלך פקידים בכל־מדינות מלכותו ויקבצו את־כל־
נערה־בתולה טובת מראה אל־שושן הבירה אל־בית הנשים
אל־יד הגא סריס המלך שמר הנשים ונתון תמרוקיהן: 4 והנערה

14 a-ℓ 𝔊 Αρκεσαιος, Σαρσαθαιος (Σαρεσθεος), Μαλησεαρ; 𝔏 *Mardochaeus, Soratheas, Pabat(h)aleus, Malesar (Malesath), Mucheas* ‖ β 𝔖 ברנשי, 𝔖^A ברשני ‖ γ Var^G שתר ‖ 𝔖 אשתר, 𝔖^A שתר ‖ 𝔖 ארמות, 𝔖^A ארמת ‖ 𝔖 רמוס, 𝔖^A מוס ‖ 𝔖 מסריא ‖ β L = non recte ‖ 16 a Q ממוכן cf 14; 𝔊 (Joseph. Arch. 11,193) Μουχαιος, 𝔊^L Βουγαιος, 𝔏 *Micheus (Mardochaeus)* ‖ β L non recte ‖ 17 a Var^M בעליהן ‖ 20 a ut 17 a ‖ Cp 2, 3 a Var^G נערה־ ‖ β Var^G הגא, 𝔖 הגי cf 8, 𝔊 (8) Γαι ‖ γ sic L Var^G; 𝔊 MSS L (Mas) תמרקיהן.

14 a >𝔖 ‖ b-b 𝔖 *qui sedebant coram rege et apparebant coram eo in porta regni* ‖ 15 a l: כדת ‖ 17 a frt mel ins אל־ ‖ 18 a prb l תמרינה ‖ b prps ובדי 20 a-a prps רב הוא ‖ 22 a-a >𝔊 et frt dl (l frt בלשון); prps מ׳ כל־שוה עמו, al כלשנו עמו ‖ Cp 2, 1 a 𝔊^{Bx} + οὐκέτι, l 𝔐.

Meg 4

FIGURE 6. PAGE OF "KITTEL BIBLE"

The 3d edition of *Biblia Hebraica* (*BH*³), popularly known as the "Kittel Bible," edited by R. Kittel and others and published in 1937, has been the accepted text of many scholars. It is being replaced by *BHS*. (See Figure 8).

§11.585 Some editors place metheg to the *right* of the vowel under conditions which they explain in their notes; thus Kittel *BH*.

§11.59 Two traditions of accent are found in the Decalogue (Exod. 20:2-17 and Deut. 5:6-18), and in Gen. 35:22. According to *Ges.* §15*p*, the second set in the Decalogue is to group the 12 verses into 10 commandments.

§11.6 At certain places the Masoretes preserved a tradition that differed from the consonantal text (CT). Since CT was considered sacred and inviolable, the Masoretes added the traditional reading in the margin, *and placed the vowels of the traditional reading,* together with a mark calling attention to the note, *on the consonantal text.*

§11.61 The consonantal text is called כְּתִיב *k*^{e}*ṯîḇ* 'written,' often spelled *kethibh* or *kethiv*). The Masoretic addition of vowel points and marginal consonants is called קְרִי *q*^{e}*rî* 'read' (impv.) or קְרֵי *q*^{e}*rê* 'read' (pass. ptcp.; in some works spelled *kere*). The abbreviations Q and K or Kt are found.

§11.62 In some places the consonantal text preserves a word or letters which are not found in the traditional pronunciation. These are left unpointed and are called *k*^{e}*ṯîḇ w*^{e}*lô' q*^{e}*rê'* 'written and not read.' Cf. *Ges.* §17*b*.

§11.63 Some common words are always read according to the *q*^{e}*rê'* which is not placed in the margin. This phenomenon is referred to as a "perpetual *q*^{e}*rê'*.

§11.631 The most common examples of perpetual Q. are: יְהוָה read אֲדֹנָי '(my) Lord,' יֱהוִה read אֱלֹהִים 'God'; הִוא read הִיא 'she' throughout the Pentateuch; and יְרוּשָׁלַםִ read יְרוּשָׁלַיִם 'Jerusalem.' *Ges.* §17*c*.

§11.7 The Masoretes also added marginal Masoroth at the tops and bottoms, at the sides and between the columns of the text. Other than the Q. readings mentioned above, these need not concern us. In *BH* some of the marginal Masoroth have been included; these are explained in the *Prolegomena* of *BH* (Fig. 6).

§11.71 At the end of the books in printed Bibles, portions of the final Masorah, giving the number of verses, the middle verse, and mnemonic devices for remembering these data, are included (cf. *Ges.* §17*d-e*, and Fig. 5).

§11.72 The *pâsēq* | is a thin vertical line found at numerous points in the Heb. OT. Its significance is uncertain. *Ges.* §15*f*, p.59, n.2.

§12. The *consonant* is the element that modifies sound into units to form meaningful patterns. There are 23 consonantal phonemes represented by the Heb. alphabet: /' b g d h w z ḥ ṭ y k l m n s ' p ṣ q r š ś t/. Cf. §11.1

§12.1 Consonants are described according to three characteristics: (1) the use or nonuse of the voice during production of the consonant, (2) the part of the mouth or throat used in making the consonant, and (3) the interruption or restriction of the breath by the consonant. See TABLE **B**.

§12.2 A consonant is either *voiced* or *surd.*

§12.21 A consonant is described as *voiced* (or *sonant*) when the voice is used *at the moment of its production.* Because the voice is used in producing vowels, some students have difficulty recognizing a voiced consonant. Try pronouncing pairs such as: *big—pig, die—tie, goo—coo, zee—see,* etc.

§12.211 In Heb. the following consonants are *voiced*: בּ /b/, גּ /g/, דּ /d/, ו /w/. ז /z/, י /y/, ל /l/, מ /m/, נ /n/, ר /r/.

§12.22 A consonant is described as *surd* (or *unvoiced, voiceless, silent*) when the voice is not used at the moment of production. Reread §12.21.

§12.221 In Heb. the following consonants are *surd*: א /'/. ה /h/, ח /ḥ/, ט /ṭ/, כּ /k/, ס /s/, ע /'/, פּ /p/, צ /ṣ/, ק /q/, שׁ /š/, שׂ /ś/. ת /t/.

§12.3 A consonant is described according to the point of articulation, or the part(s) of the body used in producing the consonant. Starting from the lips and moving inward, these points may be described as: *labial, dental, alveolar, palatal, velar, uvular, nasal, laryngeal, glottal.* Other terms are sometimes used, and in sounds requiring the use of several parts of the body, compound terms are sometimes used.

§12.31 A consonant is described as *labial* if the point of articulation is the lips. If both lips are used, the sound is bilabial; if the lower lip is pressed against the upper teeth, it is a *labiodental.*

§12.311 In Heb. the following consonants are *labials*: בּ /b/, ו /w/, מ /m/, פּ /p/. In their nonspirantized form the allophones /b p/, as well as /w m/ are *bilabials.* /b p/ are *stops*, /w/ is a *spirant*, and /m/ is a *nasal spirant.*

§12.32 A consonant is described as *alveolar* when it is pronounced by placing the tip of the tongue against or near the alveolar ridge behind the upper front teeth. The term is sometimes interchanged with *dental.*

§12.321 The following consonants are *alveolars* (or *dentals*): ד /d/, ט /ṭ/, ל /l/, נ /n/, ת /t/. In some dialects ר /r/ was probably an alveolar flap (the trilled or flap r). /d ṭ t/ are *stops.* /n/is a *nasal spirant.* /l/ is usually described as a *lateral spirant*, but the tip of the tongue is placed against the alveolar ridge.

§12.3211 The phonemes /l n r/ are difficult to describe and vary considerably from language to language. In Heb., /l/ was probably a voiced alveolar lateral spirant, the tip of the tongue being placed against the alveolar ridge and the sound coming out at the sides of the tongue (as in Italian, rather than English or Austrian).

§12.322 If the tongue is slightly grooved and the breath is allowed to pass through the groove, a *sibilant* [s] or [z] is produced. If the blade of the tongue is moved so that its point of articulation is a bit further back toward the roof of the mouth, and the breath is allowed to pass over the blade of the tongue, a compound sibilant, sometimes called an *alveopalatal sibilant* [š] or [ž] is produced.

§12.323 The following consonants are *alveolar sibilants*: ז /z/, ס /s/, צ /ṣ/, שׁ /š/, שׂ /ś/. All are *spirants*.

§12.33 If the middle of the tongue is raised toward the hard palate and the breath is stopped or restricted, the sound is a *velar*. The term *palatal* is sometimes used, and some scholars reserve the term "velar" for sounds produced further back in the mouth. (The word *key* begins with a palatal stop, whereas *coo* begins with a velar stop.) We shall use the term *velar* for both consonants.

§12.331 The following consonants are *velars*. גּ /g/, כּ /k/. Both are *stops*. י /y/ is made in approximately the same location, but is generally described as *alveopalatal*, i. e. using the alveolar ridge behind the teeth and the roof of the mouth. ח /ḥ/ when pronounced like the Ger. *Achlaut* (as by Ashkenazic Jews) is a *velar spirant*. The allophones ג /ḡ/ and ך כ /k̲/ are also *velar spirants*.

§12.34 If the back of the tongue is moved toward the back of the velum near the uvula or soft palate, a *uvular* stop or spirant is produced. This sound is not phonemic in Eng. Cf. §§10.2-.22.

§12.341 The following consonant is *uvular*: ק /q/. The Tiberian pronunciation of ר /r/ was probably a *uvular trill* (like the French *r grasseyé* [ʀ]). ח /ḥ/ *when pronounced like the Arab. ḥa* (as by Sephardic Jews) is a *laryngeal spirant*, made further back in the throat than the uvula.

§12.35 If the root of the tongue is moved back in the pharyngeal cavity, the consonant is a *pharyngeal*. If the articulation is produced in the glottis, it is a *glottal*. Since there is some question concerning the actual point of articulation of the Heb. consonants א /ʾ/, ה /h/, ח /ḥ/, and ע /ʿ/, we group them as *glottal stops* or *spirants*.

§12.351 The following consonants may be described as *glottals*: א /'/, ה /h/, ע /'/. The exact point of articulation of /h/ is not precise; it is sometimes made in the larynx, sometimes in the mouth, depending on the vowel that follows. In Mod. Heb. with some speakers it almost vanishes. א /'/ and ע /'/ are *glottal stops*. ח /ḥ/ when pronounced in Arab. fashion is a *laryngeal spirant*.

§12.36 Certain consonants are sometimes described as *emphatics*. In this category are placed some or all of the following: ח /ḥ/, ט /ṭ/, ע /'/, צ /ṣ/, and ק /q/ (in some works indicated as ḳ). They are sometimes described as the emphatic counterparts of /h/, /t/, /'/, /s/, and /k/, respectively, but this is phonetically questionable.

§12.361 Old Aramaic and Egyptian Arabic evidence may indicate that /q/ included some kind of glottal tightening at the moment of articulation, similar to *'áyin*.

§12.362 A number of scholars incline to the view that /ṭ/ *and* /ṣ/, as well as the Arab. phonemes /ḍ/ and /ẓ/ that have been absorbed in the two Heb. phonemes, originally included some kind of glottal tightening at the moment of articulation. If so, they might be phonetically represented as [t'] and [s'].

§12.4 A consonant is described as either a *stop* or a *spirant*. Certain intermediate sounds or phonetic developments are known as *affricates* or *aspirates*.

§12.41 A consonant is described as a *stop* (or *plosive*) when the passage of air from the lungs is stopped in some part of the throat or mouth when producing the sound. For the difference between a *stop* and a *spirant*, cf. such pairs as: *tree—three, bay—way, due—new, day—they,* etc. (In some languages air is also taken into the lungs while producing consonants, but this need not concern us here.)

§12.411 In Heb. the following consonants are *stops*: א /'/, בּ /b/, גּ /g/, דּ /d/, ט /ṭ/, כּ /k/, ע /'/, פּ /p/, ק /q/, תּ /t/.

§12.412 Allophonic forms of the phonemes /b g d k p t/ are *spirants*.

§12.42 A consonant is described as a *spirant* (or *fricative, continuant*) when the passage of air is not stopped. It is possible to continue the sound of such a consonant as long as breath holds out. Note that you can say *ho-m-m-m-me* but you cannot say *ho-p-p-p-pe*. Cf. §12.41.

§12.421 In Heb. the following consonants are *spirants*: ה /h/, ו /w/, ז /z/, ח /ḥ/, י /y/, ל /l/, מ /m/, נ /n/, ס /s/, צ /ṣ/, ר /r/, שׁ /š/, שׂ /ś/, plus the allophonic forms of /b g d k p t/.

§12.422 The phonetic development of a stop into a spirant is called *spirantization*. The spirant allophonic forms of the phonemes /b g d k p t/ are *spirantized* consonants.

§12.43 The exact phonetic nature of the emphatic צ /ṣ/ is unknown. On the basis of Arab. pronunciation, it is generally considered to be an emphatic surd sibilant /ṣ/, hence a spirant. In Mod. Heb. it is pronounced as the affricate [ts] (as in *hats* or *not so*). Some evidence that this may be a survival of an old prounuciation is found in the headings to chaps. 1, 2, 4, and 5 of the LXX of Lamentations, where the name of the letter is given as Τιαδε in some MSS.

§12.5 The phonetic nature of each of the Heb. consonants may therefore be described as follows:

א	/ʾ/	[ʔ]	surd glottal stop
ב	/b/	[b]	voiced bilabial stop; allophone spirantized [v]
ג	/g/	[g]	voiced velar stop; allophone once spirantized [γ]
ד	/d/	[d]	voiced alveolar stop; allophone once spirantized [ð]
ה	/h/	[h]	surd glottal spirant
ו	/w/	[w]	voiced bilabial spirant (semivowel), now [v]
ז	/z/	[z]	voiced alveolar sibilant
ח	/ḥ/	[x]	surd emphatic glottal/velar spirant
ט	/ṭ/	[tʿ]	surd emphatic alveolar stop, now [t]
י	/y/	[i]	voiced alveopalatal spirant (semivowel)
כ	/k/	[k]	surd velar stop; allophone spirantized [x]
ל	/l/	[l]	voiced alveolar lateral spirant
מ	/m/	[m]	voiced bilabial nasal spirant
נ	/n/	[n]	voiced alveolar nasal spirant
ס	/s/	[s]	surd alveolar sibilant spirant
ע	/ʿ/	[ʿ]	surd emphatic glottal stop, now [ʔ]
פ	/p/	[p]	surd bilabial stop; allophone spirantized [f]
צ	/ṣ/	[sʿ]	surd emphatic alveolar sibilant spirant, now [ts]
ק	/q/	[q]	surd uvular stop, now usually [k]
ר	/r/	[r]	voiced uvular (trilled) spirant, possibly [ʀ]
שׁ	/š/	[ʃ]	surd velar sibilant groove-spirant
שׂ	/ś/	[s]	surd alveolar sibilant split-spirant (?)
ת	/t/	[t]	surd alveolar stop; allophone once spirantized [θ]

§12.51 As in many languages, /w/ and /y/ may be classified as *semivowels*, i.e. they may serve both as consonants and vowels. Cf. Eng. *now—won* and *may—yam*. Cf. §11.21.

§12.52 On the pronunciation of ח /ḥ/, cf. §§12.341, .351.

§12.53 On the pronunciation of צ /ṣ/, cf. §12.43.

§12.6 Comparative Semitic studies indicate that the 23 Heb. consonantal phonemes developed from at least 29 PS phonemes. The student should carefully consider the following data when looking for cognate words.

§12.61 Heb. /z/ developed from two parent phonemes:

Heb. /z$_1$/	=	Arab. /z/	Aram. /z/	Akk. /z/	Ugar. /z/
Heb. /z$_2$/	=	Arab. /ḏ/	Aram. /d/	Akk. /z/	Ugar. /d/

§12.62 Heb. /ḥ/ developed from 2 parent phonemes:

Heb. /ḥ$_1$/	=	Arab. /ḥ/	Aram. /ḥ/	Akk. /'/	Ugar. /ḥ/
Heb. /ḥ$_2$/	=	Arab. /ḫ/	Aram. /ḥ/	Akk. /ḫ/	Ugar. /ḫ/

§12.63 Heb. /'/ developed from 2 parent phonemes:

Heb. /ʻ$_1$/	=	Arab. /ʻ/	Aram. /ʻ/	Akk. /'/	Ugar. /ʻ/
Heb. /ʻ$_2$/	=	Arab. /ġ/	Aram. /ʻ/	Akk. /'/	Ugar. /ġ/

§12.64 Heb. /ṣ/ developed from three parent phonemes:

Heb. /ṣ$_1$/	=	Arab./ṣ/	Aram. /ṣ/	Akk. /ṣ/	Ugar. /ṣ/
Heb. /ṣ$_2$/	=	Arab. /ḍ/	Aram. /ʻ/	Akk. /ṣ/	Ugar. /ṣ/ or /ẓ/
Heb. /ṣ$_3$/	=	Arab. /ẓ/	Aram. /ṭ/	Akk. /ṣ/	Ugar. /ẓ/

§12.641 In Old Aram. texts, /q/ is the reflex of Heb. /ṣ$_2$/ = Arab. /ḍ/. The same phenomenon is found in the Aram. of Jer. 10:11.

§12.65 Heb. /ś/ and /š/ developed from 3 parent phonemes:

Heb. /ś/	=	Arab. /š/	OSA /ś/	Aram. /s/	Akk. /š/
Heb /š$_1$/	=	Arab. /s/	OSA /s̀/	Aram. /š/	Akk. /š/
Heb. /š$_2$/	=	Arab. /ṯ/	OSA /θ/	Aram. /t/	Akk. /š/

§12.651 In a number of works, there is confusion over the relationship of Heb. /s/, /š/, and /ś/ with Arab. /s$_1$/ = OSA /s/, with Arab. /s$_2$/ = OSA /s̀/, and with Arab. /š/ = OSA /ś/. See my article, "The Sibilants in Old South Arabic," *JQR* 48 (1957-58): 161-173.

§12.66 PS *initial* /w/ > *y* י in Heb.: PS **waθaba* > Heb. *yāšab̲* יָשַׁב. In certain forms with preformatives, the original *w* is preserved (§29.31ff).

§13. In any given language or family of languages certain *phonetic shifts* may occur. When it can be demonstrated that any of these occurs only under certain conditions, it is called a *conditioned* shift. The most common consonantal changes are assimilation, dissimilation, lengthening, reduction, and metathesis. Occasionally the addition or loss of a consonant occurs.

§13.1 *Assimilation* is the conformation of one sound to another. If the similarity is in only one or two characteristics (review §12.1) it is *partial assimilation*; if it is in all three characteristics, it is *total assimilation*. If the two consonants are not separated by a vowel, it is *contiguous assimilation*, otherwise it is *distant*. If the first consonant is assimilated to the second, it is called *progressive assimilation*; if the second is assimilated to the first, it is *regressive assimilation*.

§13.11 Contiguous progressive total assimilation occurs under the following conditions.

§13.111 The consonant *nûn* regularly assimilates to the following consonant if no vowel intervenes. This is shown orthographically as *dāgēš ḥāzāq*, which indicates the gemination (doubling) of the following consonant. **yintēn* > *yittēn* יִתֵּן.

§13.1111 Third radical *nûn* does not assimilate to the following consonant except in the verb *nāt̲an*: **nāt̲ántā* > *nāt̲áttā* נָתַתָּ, but *šāk̲ántā* שָׁכַנְתָּ.

§13.1112 *nûn* drops out when it stands before a phoneme which rejects gemination (such as א ה ח ע ר). Compensatory lengthening of the vowel (15.14) may occur: *min* + *hṓddû* > *mēhṓddû* מֵהֹדּוּ.

§13.1113 If through assimilation and loss of an original final vowel, a geminate consonant would stand at word-end, simplification (§13.4) occurs. **'anpu* > **'appu* > **'app* > *'ap̄* אַף.

§13.112 In forms of the HtD stem (§28.5ff), the *t* of the preformative assimilates to a contiguous dental stop. Thus *td* > *dd* and *tṭ* > *ṭṭ*. This is shown orthographically by a strong dagesh in the following consonant. **mit̲dabbēr* > *middabbēr* מִדַּבֵּר; **yit̲ṭammā'* > *yiṭṭammā'* יִטַּמָּא. (*Ges.* §19*c*).

§13.113 In the numerals '1' and '6' *d* assimilates to the following alveolar stop or sibilant. **'aḥadtu* > **'aḥattu* > **'aḥatt* > *'aḥaṯ* אַחַת; **šidθu* > **šidšu* (cf. §12.65) > **šiššu* > **šišš* > *šēš* שֵׁשׁ; **šidθatu* > **šidšatu* > *šiššāʰ* שִׁשָּׁה.

§13.114 The writing of a geminate consonant by a single letter with dagesh should not be confused with assimilation. Thus *kāraṯ* + *tā* > *kārắttā*, written כָּרַתָּ.

§13.12 Contiguous progressive *partial* assimilation is found in forms of the HtD stem of roots with initial *z* or *ṣ*. Metathesis (§13.6) is also found in these forms. **niṯṣaddāq* > **niṣtaddāq* > *niṣṭaddāq* נִצְטַדָּק. Evidence for *z* is lacking in Bib. Heb. but is found in the Aram. of Dan. 2:9, **hiṯzammintûn* > **hiztammintûn* > *hizdammintûn* הִזְדְּמִנְתּוּן.

§13.13 Contiguous *regressive* total assimilation occurs when *nûn* stands before suffixes with *hê*: *-en* + *hû* > *-énnû* ־ֶנּוּ.

§13.2 *Arbitrarily omitted.*

§13.3 *Lengthening* (or *gemination*) is the prolongation of a consonant. With a fricative or spirant, the lengthening can readily be heard; with a stop there is somewhat more time between the contiguous vowels than with a single consonant. This is not heard within words in Eng., but it can be heard between words: note carefully the difference between *from any* and *from many*, or *take it* and *take Kit*.

§13.31 Gemination is not heard in Mod. Heb. We assume that it was heard at the time of the Masoretic punctuation, since the *dāgēš ḥāzāq* was used to indicate gemination. The consonant so lengthened is sometimes called "sharpened," and such gemination is "sharpening"—a term that is practically meaningless in modern linguistics.

§13.32 Gemination occurs as a result of total assimilation, cf. §13.11ff.

§13.33 Lengthening or gemination of a consonant is an element of morphology. We shall consider the formation of nouns with geminate 2d or 3d radicals (§§24.26, .27) and the formation of certain verb stems with gemination (e.g. the D-stem §28.2 and the HtD-stem §28.5) under Morphology.

§13.34 Gemination of the first consonant regularly occurs with the addition of the def.art., except with consonants which reject gemination (ח ע ר ה א). Hence *ha* + *yôm* > *hayyôm* הַיּוֹם, but *ha* + *'éreḇ* > *hā'éreḇ* הָעֶרֶב.

§13.341 The theory that the def. art. was originally **hal-*, cognate with Arab. *al-*, is probably to be rejected. The phoneme /l/ does not regularly assimilate to the following consonant in Heb., and even in Arab. it only assimilates to certain consonants (the "solar" letters, i.e. dentals and sibilants and *l*, *n*, and *r*). Moreover, such a morpheme is not found elsewhere in the Sem. languages.

§13.35 The first consonant of the impf. verbal form is lengthened when *wāw*-conversive is added to it, except when the consonant is א. *wa* + *yaḥălōm* > *wayyaḥălōm* וַיַּחֲלֹם.

§13.351 The theory that the converting *wāw* was originally **wan-* and that it is related to an Egyptian grammatical phenomenon deserves further exploration.

§13.36 The initial consonant is lengthened when it follows the interrogative/indefinite pronoun מָה: *ma*[h] + *la'ăśôṯ* > *ma*[h]*-lla'ăśôṯ* מַה־לַּעֲשׂוֹת (Est. 6:6).

§13.361 According to one theory, this gemination is a device to preserve the short-vowel in what would otherwise be a distant-open syllable and therefore require vowel reduction (cf. short-vowel rules).

§13.37 The initial consonant lengthens when the relative particle *še* is added to a word: *še* + *ya'ămōl* > *šeyya'ămōl* שֶׁיַּעֲמֹל.

§13.371 In some cases, this may be a device to preserve a short-vowel in a distant-open syllable (cf. §13.361). In other cases it may be the result of assimilation of the preposition –ל: *š*[e]+ *la* 'which (is/belongs) to,' cf. Mod. Heb. *šellāhem* 'which is theirs.' But evidence of assimilation of *l* is rare.

§13.38 The gutturals ע ח ה א and ר resist gemination.

§13.4 Long (geminate) consonants reduce (simplify) under certain conditions. Orthographically this is shown by writing the consonant without dagesh.

§13.41 Certain consonants when followed by a (vocal) *š*[e]*wâ* normally lose their gemination.

§13.411 Most common is the omission of dagesh in *yôḏ* with *š*[e]*wâ* which occurs in many forms of the imperfect acter *wāw*-conversive. **wayy*[e]*hî* > *way*[e]*hî* וַיְהִי.

§13.412 Other consonants that usually reduce before shewa are *w, l, m, n, q,* and the sibilants. Thus **wayy^{e}b̲aqq^{e}šû* > *way^{e}b̲aq^{e}šû* וַיְבַקְשׁוּ.

§13.413 This simplification is not apparent with /b g d k p t/. However it is possible that the *dagesh* was simply indicating the stop sound without gemination.

§13.414 Gemination, phonetically if not orthographically, is lost in Mod. Heb.

§13.42 When as a result of the loss of the original final short-vowel a geminate consonant would stand at word-end, that consonant reduces (simplifies): עַמִּי *ʿammî* but עַם *ʿam.*

§13.421 An apparent exception to this rule is the 2d pers. sg. fem. pron. (s3) אַתְּ *ʾatt.* Obviously the dagesh cannot be *dāḡēš qal* after a vowel, and cognates indicate that the word was originally **ʾanti.*

§13.5 Under certain conditions a consonant has been lost. Sometimes it is still represented orthographically.

§13.51 *Apheresis* is the loss of the initial sound or syllable of a word.

§13.511 Apheresis is found in certain forms of verbs that have *yōḏ* or *nûn* in the first radical (YCC, NCC verbs). In general, the loss occurs when the first radical would have been vocalized with shewa, such as the G-impv. (G32) and inf. cstr. (G65) forms: **y^{e}šēb̲* > *šēb̲* שֵׁב; **n^{e}ṯīn* > *tēn* תֵּן.

§13.5111 However, we cannot assume that it is the vocalization that has caused apheresis, since many other forms (e.g. the D-impf [D20]) regularly begin with *yôḏ* vocalized with shewa.

§13.5112 Not all YCC and NCC verbs are affected by apheresis. True YCC verbs (as opposed to those that were originally WCC) retain the *yôḏ*: *y^{e}ṭōb̲* יְטֹב (G65). Certain NCC verbs likewise retain the *nûn*: *n^{e}pōl* נְפֹל.

§13.512 The verbs לקח and הלך also lost the first syllable in G-impv. and inf.cstr. forms: **l^{e}qaḥ* > *qaḥ* קַח (G32); **hălēḵ* > *lēḵ* לֵךְ (G32).

§13.513 In the G-inf. cstr. (G65) forms where apheresis has taken place, a "ballast-*tāw*" is added: **y^{e}šēb̲* > **šēb̲+t* > *šéb̲eṯ* שֶׁבֶת; **n^{e}ṯēn* > **tēn+t* > *tett > *tēṯ* תֵּת.

§13.52 *Syncope* (or *syncopation*) is the loss of a sound or a syllable in the middle of a word.

§13.521 One of the most common occurrences is the syncopation of the h of the def. art. after a preposition: **bᵉhayyāmîm* > *bayyāmîm* בַּיָּמִים; **lᵉhammélek̲* > *lammélek̲* לַמֶּלֶךְ.

§13.5211 In poetic passages, syncopation is sometimes lacking, cf. *bᵉhaššāmáyim* בְּהַשָּׁמַיִם (Ps. 36:6 MT).

§13.522 Syncopation of /h/ in the impf., juss., and ptcp. forms of the H-, N-, HtD-, and HtŠ-stems is also found: **yᵉhap̄qēd̲* > *yap̄qēd̲* יַפְקֵד (H40); **tᵉhangîd̲* > *taggîd̲* תַּגִּיד (H21); **wayyᵉhinwāda'* > *wayyiwwād̲a'* וַיִּוָּדַע (Nc20); **wattᵉhiṯhalhal* > *wattiṯhalhal* וַתִּתְחַלְחַל (HtR [=HtD] c21); **mᵉhištaḥăwîm* > *mištaḥăwîm* מִשְׁתַּחֲוִים (HtŠ55); **mᵉhiṯlabbēš* > *miṯlabbēš* מִתְלַבֵּשׁ (HtD50).

§13.5221 Compare the inf. cstr. (65) forms without syncopation: *bᵉhiqqāb̲ēṣ* (N65), *lᵉhāb̲î'* (H65), *lᵉhar'ōṯ* (H65), *lᵉhiṯhannēn* (HtD65).

§13.523 /'/ is often syncopated after shewa, although it is preserved orthographically. In some instances, even the writing of א is omitted. **liqrᵉ'at* > *liqra'ṯ* לִקְרַאת (but cf. *lᵉhar'ōṯ* לְהַרְאוֹת); **tᵉ'ômîm* > *tômîm* תּוֹמִם (Gen. 25:24). Cf. §15.54.

§13.524 Syncopation is found in those forms of CCY verbs having vocalic sufformatives (i.e. commencing with a vowel): **galayu* > *gālû* גָּלוּ; cf. **gālaytā* > *gālîʸṯā* גָּלִיתָ.

§13.525 /h/ has syncopated in forms of 3ms pron. suf. (s0) added to words ending in a vowel or *-ay* diphthong: *-*a* + *hû* > *-*aw* > *-ô* וֹ—; *-*ay* + *hû* > *-*aʸhû* > *-aʸw* ־ָיו (pronounced [aw] or [av]).

§13.526 In the 1st sg. impf. of 'CC verbs, the second *'ālep̄* regularly drops out: **'ō'mar* > *'ōmar* אֹמַר. It sometimes drops in other forms, תֹּסֵף for תֹּאסֵף (Ps. 104:29), cf. *Ges.* §68*g-h*.

§13.53 *Apocope* (or *apocopation*) is the loss of the final sound or syllable of a word.

§13.531 Final /t/ of fem. substantives ending in *-*at* is lost except when preserved by a word in annexion (construct): **ḥemat* > *ḥēmāʰ* חֵמָה, cstr. *ḥămaṯ hammélek̲* חֲמַת הַמֶּלֶךְ.

§13.5311 The use of *hê* in absolute forms is an early use of vowel-letters (cf. §11.21). It is interesting to note that in Arab. such forms are written with *ha* with two dots over it (the sign of *ta*), called *tā' marbūṭaʰ* and pronounced as [t] when followed by a vowel (cf. W. Wright, *A Grammar of the Arabic Language:* Cambridge: University Press, 1896; vol. 1, p. 7 and footnote).

§13.5312 Note that fem. substantives ending in *-t* (in contrast with those ending in *-at*) preserve the *-t*, usually with anaptyxis (§15.61): **môladt* (cf. *môladtô* מוֹלַדְתּוֹ) > *môlédet* מוֹלֶדֶת.

§13.532 The loss of an original *-t* in 3fs forms of the perf. (G11, D11, etc.) is indicated by its preservation when suffixes are added: **qaṭalat* > *qāṭ^elā* קָטְלָה, but with suff. *q^eṭāláṯnî* קְטָלַתְנִי (G11s4).

§13.5321 The 3fs perf. (11) ending of CCY verbs pleonastically preserves the original final-*t* and also adds the customary *-a^h* ending: **ʿaśat* > *ʿāś^eṯā^h* עָשְׂתָה. This possibly developed to preserve the difference between the 3ms form **ʿaśay* > *ʿāśā^h* עָשָׂה and the 3fs form, which otherwise would also have been **ʿāśā^h*.

§13.533 Apocopation is a common feature of CCY verbs in the converted imperfect (c20), the jussive (40), and some imperative (32) forms. Note *taʿăśê^h* תַּעֲשֶׂה (G21) but *wattáʿaś* וַתַּעַשׂ (Gc21); *yihyê^h* יִהְיֶה (G20) but *y^ehî* יְהִי (G40); *yiḡlê^h* יִגְלֶה (G20) but *yíḡel* יִגֶל (G40).

§13.5331 Anaptyxis (§15.61) is commonly found in apocopated forms where doubly-closed syllables (§16.34) would have resulted: **wayyigl* > *wayyíḡel* וַיִּגֶל; **wattaʿś* > *wattáʿaś* וַתַּעַשׂ.

§13.5332 Anaptyxis does not occur in apocopated forms ending in /b d k t ṭ q/: *tiḇkê^h* but *watteḇk* וַתֵּבְךְּ, cf. also *wayyašq* וַיַּשְׁקְ, *wayyard* וַיֵּרְדְּ, *wayyišb* וַיִּשְׁבְּ. *Ges.* §28*d*.

§13.534 The loss of final /w/ and /y/ after an *i*-class vowel is due to the nature of the semivowels (§12.51) rather than apocopation: **y^ehîy* (cf. *yihyê^h*) > *y^ehî^y* יְהִי.

§13.54 The semivowels /w/ and /y/ are lost in those forms of CCW and CCY verbs (i.e. verbs originally with ו or י in the 3d rad.) where the semivowel would stand at word-end (i.e. not followed by any sufformative). The final vowel is represented orthographically by ה—. Cf. §13.524. For fuller discussion of this class of verb, see §29.7ff.

§13.55 א regularly loses its consonantal value at word-end (i.e. when not followed by any vowel); becoming *quiescent* (as it often does at syllable-end). In some cases it may not even be written.

§13.6 *Metathesis* is the transposition of sounds within a word.

§13.61 Metathesis is commonly found in forms of the HtD-stem of verbs which have an initial sibilant in the root; this metathesizes with the ת of the stem preformative: **hiṯšammēr* > *hištammēr* הִשְׁתַּמֵּר.

§13.62 Metathesis also occurs in the biblically-rare HtŠ-stem of *ḥāwāʰ*:**hiṯšaḥăwāʰ* > *hištaḥăwāʰ* הִשְׁתַּחֲוָה.

§13.621 This verb is often listed under שָׁחָה and identified as an HtD-stem. But the presence of /w/ in *all* forms occurring in Bib. Heb. requires that the *wāw* be included in the root. Moreover, the HtŠ-stem or its reflex is found in Arab., Aram., Akk., Ugar., and Eth., and hence it must be recognized as an indigenous PS verb-stem that cannot be ruled out of Bib. Heb.

§13.7 In some instances a consonant may be added by prothesis or epenthesis.

§13.71 *Prothesis* is the addition of a sound at the beginning of a word. Such a sound is *prothetic* (sometimes the term *prosthetic* is used).

§13.711 Prothetic א is possibly found in the words *ʼarbaʻ* אַרְבַּע, *ʼezrâḥ* אֶזְרָח, *ʼeṣbaʻ* אֶצְבַּע, and perhaps other words with 4 rads. that have initial א. The purpose may have been to avoid an initial cluster, as often in Arab.

§13.712 *Ges.* §19*m* suggests a prothetic ע in *ʻaqrāḇ* עַקְרָב, but there is little if any supporting evidence for prothetic ʻayin.

§13.713 Prothetic *hê* ה appears to be found in forms of the N stem with preformative *hin* —הִנ, cf. §28.421. Prothetic ה may also be found in forms of the HtD stem with preformative *hiṯ*- —הִת, cf. §28.51.

§13.72 *Epenthesis* is the addition of a sound within a word. Such a sound is *epenthetic.*

§13.721 An epenthetic *nûn,* commonly called *nûn energicum* (*Ges*. §58*i*), is added to some verb forms with pronominal suffixes, cf. §23.1221.

§13.73 The addition of a sound at the end of a word might be called *opisothesis,* and the sound could be termed *opisothetic*. However, the term *paragogic* is commonly used in Heb. grammars.

§13.731 *Nûn paragogicum* is found at the end of many verb forms otherwise ending in -*û* וּ– or -*î* ִי– (*Ges*. §47*m*). As Joüon correctly points out (J. §44*e,f*), the -*n* belongs to a primitive form and is attested by cognate languages. It does not add "energy" to the form.

§13.732 *Hê paragogicum* is found in cohortative and some imperative forms (§27.531, §27.43), cf. Joüon §45*a*. It is possible that the -*āʰ* of the juss. is to be related to the Arab. 2 energ. (§27.5).

§14. In all Semitic languages there were originally three vowels, each of which occurred in both long and short quantity. The difference between the long and the short vowels was phonemic (§10.2).

§14.1 The long vowels were /â î û/.

§14.11 In Heb., *â* > *ô* in what has come to be known as the *Canaanite shift*. *â* is found in words that came into Heb. after the Canaanite shift had occurred. On the basis of the Canaanite glosses in the Amarna letters (c.1365 B.C.) where the phoneme is written with syllabograms containing a *u*- (= *o*) vowel, we can assume that the Canaanite shift had occurred by the 15th cent. B.C.

§14.12 The long vowels *ê* and *ô* developed as a result of monophthongization (§15.7).

§14.13 We therefore find *five* long vowels in Bib. Heb.:

â generally written with *qāmāṣ* ◌ָ
ê written with ◌ֵי, ◌ֶה, and ◌ֵה
î written with *ḥîrîq,* generally with *yôḏ* (◌ִי)
ô written with *ḥôlām,* generally with *wāw* (וֹ)
û written with *šûrûq* (וּ) or *qubbûṣ* (◌ֻ)

§14.2 The short vowels were /a i u/.

§14.21 Evidence supporting this statement is found in Arab. where only 3 vowels are written orthographically (although others can be heard), in Akk. where the same 3 vowels are written (plus an *e*-vowel that developed secondarily), in Ugar. where 3 forms of *'aleph* occur (i.e. *'alif, 'ilif,* and *'ulif*), plus the fact that cognate words generally support the necessity of 3 and only 3 kinds of vowels in the parent word.

§14.22 In Heb. various colorations and quantities of these 3 vowels developed, depending on the location of the vowel with relation to the stress-accent (§17.), the type of syllable, the effect of certain consonants, analogy, and other factors. We shall consider these factors under Vocalic Change (§15.).

§14.23 Anticipating the discussion of vocalic alteration, we may summarize the results by saying that in Bib. Heb. we find five short vowels, *a, e, i, o,* and *u*, each of which may possibly occur in *normal, lengthened,* or *reduced* quantity. For the orthography cf. §11.32.

§14.231 When we analyze these vowels, however, we find again that the lengthened and reduced forms can be traced back to 3 and only 3 original short vowels in Heb.: *a, i, u.*

§14.2311 Lengthened *ā*–not to be confused with long *â*, since *ā* did not undergo the Canaanite shift (cf. the difference between the *â* and the *ā* in **'âlām* > *'ôlām*)— and reduced *ă* (with gutturals) are to be considered as allophonic varieties of /a/, and not as separate phonemes. (Note: since we do find a difference in meaning between words such as *dāḇar* 'he spoke' and *dāḇār* 'word, thing,' *a* and *ā* may appear to be phonemic. However this is a conditioned shift. The pausal form of the verb is exactly like the noun.)

§14.2312 Lengthened *ē* and reduced *ĕ* (with gutturals) can be shown to be allophonic varieties of /i/. Under certain conditions, *ĕ* is an allophone of /a/.

§14.2313 There is no evidence for lengthened *ī* or reduced *ĭ* apart from that given in §14.2312.

§14.2314 *Lengthened ō* develops from /u/ and is therefore to be carefully distinguished from long *ô* written defectively (cf. §11.322)—for *ô* developed from /â/ (§14.12). Reduced *ŏ* is likewise an allophone of /u/.

§14.2315 There is no evidence for lengthened *ū* or reduced *ŭ* apart from that given in §14.2314.

§14.232 The unmodified short vowels (i.e. neither lengthened nor reduced) are generally found only in unaccented closed syllables, and in the case of *i* and *u* only before strong dagesh.

§14.3 When a heterogeneous vowel occurs before the semivowels *w* and *y*, a *diphthong* generally develops. A diphthong is a *single sound* combining, but not losing or changing, the component sounds. Thus *ai* in *aisle* is [ɑɪ] and y in *boy* is [ɔɪ]. The term diphthong is sometimes used less properly for monophthongs (single sounds) that have developed from diphthongs.

§14.31 In Bib. Heb. the original /a i u/ vowels combined with /w/ or /y/ could only develop the following diphthongs: *aw* [ɑu]> [ɑv], *ay* [ɑɪ], *iu* [iu], and *uy* [uɪ]. Of these, only *aw, ay,* and *uy* actually occur. In many works, *uy* (found chiefly in passive participles of CCY verbs) is not considered to be a diphthong, and Masoretic pointing treats the *yōḏ* as a consonant.

§14.32 The secondary vowels *e* and *o* combined with /w/ or /y/ could develop only the following diphthongs: *ew* [ɛu] > [ɛv], *ey* [ɛɪ], and *oy* [ɔɪ]. Only *ey* and *oy* are found in Bib. Heb., and *ey* is generally treated as a monophthong *ê*[y] ֵי, while *oy* is considered to be a vowel followed by a consonant (cf. §14.31).

§14.33 In the light of the above discussion (§§14.31f.) we may state that only the diphthongs /aw/ and /ay/ occur in Bib. Heb.

§15. Vowels may *lengthen* or *reduce* (quantitative vowel gradation), undergo *phonetic change* (qualitative vowel gradation), *appear* (prothesis, epenthesis) or *disappear* (syncope, apheresis), *combine* (diphthongization, contraction, etc.), etc. In many languages, spelling is not affected by these phenomena (cf. *the ant* [ðiˈænt] with *the boy* [ðəˈbɔɪ]), but in Heb. the vowel-points attempt to reflect such *vocalic alteration.* It is extremely important for the student to learn these vocalic peculiarities.

§15.1 *Lengthening.* Under conditions that may be fairly well defined, *short vowels lengthened.* If this was to compensate for some other phenomenon (such as the refusal of a guttural to geminate) it is called *compensatory lengthening* (§15.14).

§15.11 A short vowel in an *accented syllable* (§16.f) is generally lengthened (§14.23). This is usually and incorrectly called "tone lengthening." Examples: דַּם־ *dam* but דָּם *dām;* עִתִּים *'ittîm* but עֵת *'ēṯ;* כָּל־ *kol* and כֻּלָּם *kullām* but כֹּל *kōl;* חֻקָּה *ḥuqqā*[h] but חֹק *ḥōq.* Exceptions noted below should be carefully studied.

§15.11 In syllables which would have been *doubly closed* (§16.12), short-*a* does not lengthen except in pause (§11.55). Note: עַם *'am,* cf. עַמִּי *'ammi* but pausal עָם *'ām,* contrasted with דָּם *dām,* דָּמִי *dāmî.*

§15.112 An *a-* vowel which was formerly in an originally-closed syllable that has opened as a result of anaptyxis (§16.3432, §15.6f) remains written as a short vowel, usually *s*[e]*gôl* but *pattāḥ* before a guttural. Such a vowel undergoes *neither lengthening nor reduction,* and may be looked upon essentially as remaining in a closed syllable. Note: **malku* > *mélek̲* מֶלֶךְ, with suffix *malkô* מַלְכּוֹ, but in construct *mélek̲ yiśrā'ēl* מֶלֶךְ יִשְׂרָאֵל.

§15.1121 Note, however, the effect of pause, §15.131.

§15.113 In finite verbal forms short-*a* does not lengthen under accent in closed syllables except in pause. Note: קָטַל *qāṭál,* pausal קָטָל *qāṭāl* where the syllable is closed, in contrast to יָצָא *yāṣā'* where the syllable is open because of quiescent 'aleph (§15.54).

§15.1131 This rule does not apply to *i-* or *u-*class vowels, or to nonfinite verbal forms (i.e. infinitives or participles), or to nouns., cf. *kāḇēḏ, qāṭōn* (finite verbal forms), *q*[e]*ṭōl* (inf. cstr.), *qôṭēl,* ptcp.), *miḏbār* (noun).

§15.114 *S*[e]*gôl* does not lengthen under accent in the "heavy suffixes" *-kem, ken, -hem, -hen* or in the "heavy endings" of verbs *-tem, -ten*: עֲלֵיהֶם, אֲכַלְתֶּם.

§15.115 The connecting vowel used with pronominal suffixes generally does not lengthen under accent: רְאִיתַנִי, יְכוֹנְנֶהָ.

§15.12 In an open syllable immediately before the stress-accent (called "near-open" in this *Handbook,* elsewhere often called "pretonic"), a short vowel is generally lengthened. As far as the short-vowel rules are concerned, the vowels in "accented" (open or closed) and "near-open" syllables can be treated as a single phenomenon. Cf. דָּבָר, מֵאָה, גּוֹרָל. The following exceptions should be carefully noted.

§15.121 In nouns and nonfinite verbal forms, *i-* or *u-class vowels* reduce (i.e. to shewa) in a near-open syllable when preceded by a long syllable or by no syllable at all (§15.241). **quṭul* > *qᵉṭōl* קְטֹל; **madabbērîm* > *mᵉḏabbᵉrîm* מְדַבְּרִים.

§15.122 For verbal forms, see §15.242, below.

§15.13 Certain peculiarities of short vowels in pausal forms (cf. §11.55) should be noted.

§15.131 The vowel of an *a-class* segholate may become *qāmāṣ* in pause. Cf. אֶרֶץ *ʼéreṣ* but pausal אָרֶץ *ʼāreṣ*. See *Ges.* §29*i-v* for full discussion.

§15.132 /a/ in an erstwhile doubly-closed syllable (i.e. a syllable that was doubly-closed before simplification occurred, §13.42) lengthens in pause. Cf. עַם *ʻam*, pausal עָם *ʻām*, רַב *raḇ*, pausal רָב *rāḇ*.

§15.133 Three words take their *pausal* form whenever they have the def. art.: הָאָרֶץ אֶרֶץ, הָעָם עַם, הָהָר הַר.

§15.134 When finite verbal forms are in pause, the short vowel lengthens under accent, in violation of the principles set down in §15.113 and §15.122: קָטַל, pausal קָטָל.

§15.135 The first vowel of CaYC > *CáyiC* nouns lengthens in pause, cf. בַּיִת *báyiṯ*, pausal בָּיִת *bāyiṯ*. In CaWC forms, the *a* is always lengthened: מָוֶת *māweṯ*.

§15.14 *Compensatory lengthening*. Possibly as a result of an effort (conscious or otherwise) to preserve a long syllable (§16.13), the vowel is generally lengthened when loss of a consonant (e.g. rejection of gemination) has caused a syllable to become open. Since the lengthening of the vowel is looked upon as compensation for the loss of the consonant, this is called compensatory lengthening.

§15.141 Before the gutturals א /ʼ/, ע /ʻ/, and ר /r/, a vowel is lengthened in lieu of gemination of the consonant: **haʻʻéḇeḏ* becomes הָעֶבֶד, the D-stem form **birrak* becomes בֵּרַךְ *bēraḵ*.

§15.1411 However, before the gutturals ה and ח there is *no* compensation: **haḥḥōḏeš* > *haḥōḏeš* הַחֹדֶשׁ; **tᵉḇahhēr* > *tᵉḇahēr* תְּבַהֵר. In some grammars this is called "implied dagesh forte" (*dagesh forte implicitum*).

§15.142 Certain consonants reject gemination when vocalized with "vocal shewa" (§13.41ff). In such cases there is no compensatory lengthening. Cf. *way(y)^{e}hî* וַיְהִי, *biq(q)^{e}šû* בִּקְשׁוּ.

§15.15 A short vowel before a semivowel (*w, y*) of the same class develops to a long vowel. Similarly, a short *a* before א may develop to a quasi-long *â*, then to *ô*.

§15.151 Short *a* before א > *ô: *â > ô* (cf. §29.212).

§15.152 Short *i* before י > *î: *w^{e}y^{e}hî > *wiy^{e}hî > wî^{y}hî* וִיהִי.

§15.153 Short *u* before ו > *û: *huwšaḇ > hûšaḇ* הוּשַׁב.

§15.2 *Reduction of vowels* has taken place under certain fairly well defined conditions.

§15.21 The student is cautioned to *distinguish carefully* between *long vowels* (i.e. those that are long by nature, sometimes called "pure long," cf. §14.1, §14.13), and *lengthened short vowels* (sometimes written with vowel-letters, called the "false plene," §14.23). There can be no doubt, as we observe the careful distinction in pointing, that there was a phonemic distinction between long vowels and lengthened short vowels.

§15.22 *Reduction of long vowels* (§14.1) has occurred only in originally-closed syllables. Under all other conditions the long vowel is irreducible.

§15.221 By "originally-closed" we mean a syllable that at no time in the historic development of the word (as far as we can determine) was open. For example, the form **hiq-ṭîl* (H10) once ended in a short vowel, **hiq-ṭî-lu*, hence the syllable *-ṭîl* is not originally-closed. On the other hand, in the form *hiq-ṭál-tā* (H12) the syllable *ṭal* was always closed by the consonantal sufformative. Likewise the form **yaq-ṭēl* (H40) was always closed, since the jussive did not end in a short vowel (cf. Arabic).

§15.222 When the long vowel reduced, it became subject to the rules governing the short vowel of the same class (i.e. *a-*, *i-*, or *u*-class). Hence, **yaqṭîl* (juss.) reduced to **yaq-ṭil* (§15.22), and then the short vowel lengthened according to §15.11, *yaq-ṭēl* יַקְטֵל.

§15.2221 This phenomenon is found in *jussive* and *converted imperfect* forms, and is an important factor in recognizing such forms (§27.51).

§15.223 Although ֵ *ṣērê* is a lengthened short vowel (§14.2312), in a number of instances it does not reduce, e.g.: לֵב הַמֶּלֶךְ *lēb ham-mé-leḵ* (cstr.), עַל כִּסֵּא מַלְכוּתוֹ *'al kis-sē' mal-ḵû-ṯô* (also cstr.). This phenomenon is to be particularly noted in the masc. sg. forms of G participles in construct (G52): שֹׁמֵר הַנָּשִׁים *šô-mēr han-nā-šîm.*

§15.23 *Reduction of short vowels.* In an open syllable that stands two or more syllables before the stress-accent (called a "distant-open syllable" in this *Handbook*, as distinct from the near-open syllable, §15.12), short vowels will reduce either (a) to shewa (§14.23) after nonguttural consonants, or (b) to compound shewa (a *ḥăṭap̄* vowel, §§11.32, .325) after gutturals: *dā-ḇā́r, dᵉ-ḇā-rîm* דְּבָרִים; *ḥṓ-deš, ḥŏ-ḏā-šîm* חֳדָשִׁים; *'ă-ḥaš-wē-rôš* אֲחַשְׁוֵרוֹשׁ.

§15.231 It is important to keep in mind the fact that words *in construct* (annexion, (§25.4) and words *joined by maqqeph* (§11.45) have only one major accent, hence the word(s) preceding the stressed word will have only unaccented-closed and distant-open syllables: פְּנֵי הַמֶּלֶךְ *pᵉ-nê ham-mé-leḵ*; note *ba-ḥă-ṣar bêṯ-ham-mé-leḵ* בַּחֲצַר בֵּית־הַמֶּלֶךְ.

§15.232 The vowels in originally doubly-closed syllables which have opened by anaptyxis i.e. the segolates, §15.61 and 15.611) *neither lengthen in near-open nor reduce in distant-open syllables.* They continue to act as if they were in a closed syllable. Note: מֶלֶךְ יְהוּדָה *me-leḵ yᵉ-hû-dāʰ;* בְּשַׁעַר הַמֶּלֶךְ *bᵉ-šá-ʿar ham-mé-leḵ;* הוּא־חֹדֶשׁ אֲדָר *hû'-ḥō-ḏeš 'a-ḏār.*

§15.233 Short vowels which have undergone compensatory lengthening (§15.14) do not reduce in distant-open syllables. The same is true of vowels before ה /h/ and ח /ḥ/, which have "implied doubling" (§15.1411): מַהֲרוּ אֶת־הָמָן *ma(h)-hărû 'eṯ-hā-mān;* וְשָׂרֵי הַמְּדִינוֹת *wᵉ-śā-rê ham-mᵉ-ḏî-nôṯ;* יֵעָשֶׂה *yē-'ā-śeʰ.*

§15.24 Short vowels in near-open syllables reduce under certain conditions, in apparent violation of §15.12.

§15.241 In a near-open syllable, *i-* and *u-class* short vowels (cf. §14.231) reduce to shewa when that syllable is preceded either by a long syllable (i.e. cvc or cv̂) or by no syllable at all, e.g.: בֵּן *bēn*, but בְּנִי *bᵉ-nî*; שֹׁמֵר *šô-mēr*, but שֹׁמְרִים *šô-mᵉ-rîm*; but cf. יִקְטְלֵנִי *yiq-tᵉ-lē-nî.*

§15.2411 Note that this rule applies to nouns, nonfinite verbal forms, and finite verbal forms with suffixes.

§15.2412 This rule does not apply to *a*-class vowels. However, an occasional participle (other than G-stem) seems to have followed the i/u-class rule by analogy. Note: יִשְׁמָעֵנִי *yiš-mā-'ē-nî* (cf. *yiq-ṭᵉ-lê-nî* in §15.241); מִשְׁפָּטִים *miš-pā-ṭîm* (cf. *šô-mᵉ-rîm*); but cf. נִמְצְאִים *nim-ṣᵉ-'îm* (where we would expect **nim-ṣā-'îm*).

§15.242 In nonpausal, finite verbal forms, any short vowel is reduced to shewa in an open, unaccented penult, and the vowel of the antepenult, if any, will be retained in its pausal form with metheg: קָֽטְלוּ, *qā-ṭᵉ-lû* (pausal קָטָ֫לוּ *qā-ṭā-lû*), cf. §17.2ff.

§15.2421 The description "open unaccented penult" is given here, rather than "near-open," because the phenomenon seems to be limited to a near-open penult.

§15.2422 This rule does not apply to forms in pause (§11.55) or to nonfinite forms, e.g.: יִקְטֹ֫לוּ *yiq-ṭō-lû*, נִדָּחִים *nid-dā-ḥîm.*

§15.2423 The difference in lengthening/reduction of short vowels will be of help to the student in distinguishing finite verbal forms as he gains a feeling for the language.

§15.243 A short vowel *cannot* reduce in a closed syllable.

§15.25 Under vocalic reduction, it may be useful to discuss the shews, since it often represents a reduced vowel.

§15.251 It is common to speak of two types of *šᵉwâ*, the "vocal shewa" (*šᵉwâ nā'* 'mobile shewa') and the "silent shewa" (*šᵉwâ nāḥ* 'resting shewa'). The silent shewa is sometimes called the "syllable divider," since it is found at the end of a closed syllable (except those closed with the strong dagesh, the so-called "sharpened syllables," §16.3613). However, since some "vocal" shewas are silent, and since not all syllables are divided by the "syllable divider," the distinction is often quite confusing.

§15.2511 Note that if *two successive shewas* are found in a Heb. word, the *first* must be a *silent* shewa (a syllable divider), and the *second* must be *vocal.* E.g. תִּכְתְּבוּ must be *tiḵ-tᵉ-ḇû*—it cannot possibly be *ti-ḵᵉt-ḇû,* since a short vowel cannot reduce in a closed syllable (§15.243), and it cannot possibly be *ti-ḵᵉ-tᵉ-ḇû* since the first of two vocal shewas always generated a short vowel (§15.651). Try pronouncing the word in these three different ways, and you'll see why it must be the first. In this particular example, the light dagesh in ת and its absence in ב should help you.

§15.252 The *vocal šᵉwâ* may be anything from a short vowel sound to no sound at all. It must be studied carefully.

§15.2521 Some grammarians call the consonant with vocal shewa a "half syllable" (cf. *Ges.* §28*a*). Others do not count it a syllable at all. According to phonetic rules, a distinct syllable can be heard in some cases and must therefore be counted as such. In other cases, we hear an initial consonantal cluster, cf. כְּתַבְתֶּם *k^e-tab-tém* [kə-tav'tɛm], but שְׁמֹנִים *š^e-mô-nîm* [ʃmo'nim]. If the preceding word ends in a vowel, the initial consonant with shewa often is joined to that vowel and the shewa becomes inaudible.

§15.2522 In some cases, the "vocal" shewa has reduced to zero (called "zero shewa" in this *Handbook*), and the following begadkepat letter will have *dāgēš qal (lenē): k^e-ṯōḇ* כְּתֹב, but *lik-tōḇ* לִכְתֹּב (note the *dāgēš* in the second instance).

§15.253 When a "vocal" shewa follows a guttural, it maintains somewhat more of the vowel sound, and it is written as a *ḥăṭap̄-š^ewâ* (§11.325). Thus *ḥā-ṣēr* חָצֵר becomes in cstr. *ḥă-ṣar* חֲצַר.

§15.2531 Usually the hateph-shewa is of the same vowel-class as the vowel which has been reduced. However, due to the influence of the guttural (§15.43), *i-class* vowels sometimes reduce to ḥaṭeph-pattaḥ

§15.2532 When secondary opening occurs (§15.421), a silent shewa develops into a vowel, first a hateph-vowel (**ya'-mōḏ* > *ya-'ă-mōḏ* יַעֲמֹד), and then to a full short vowel: **ya'-mō-ḏû* > *ya-'ă-mō-ḏû* > *ya-'a-m^e-ḏû* יַעַמְדוּ.

§15.254 It is obvious that the student who is conditioned to think only of "vocal" shewas and "syllable dividers" will be asking, "Where did that vowel come from?" or "What happened to that vowel?" We must rather learn to think of the process by which vowels reduced to zero and the process by which vowels developed from zero.

§15.3 *Qualitative vowel change* is the shift of a vowel of one class (a-, i-, or u-class) to a vowel of another class. Usually it is a conditioned shift, i.e., it occurs only under certain conditions.

§15.31 We have already noted the Canaanite shift of *â* to *ô* (§14.11). It does not appear to be a conditioned shift, and it occurred before the time of Bib. Heb.

§15.32 Short *a* > *i* in closed unaccented syllables: **yaq-ṭul* > *yiq-ṭōl* יִקְטֹל; cf. *ya-ḥă-lōm* יַחֲלֹם, where the syllable is not closed and the vowel-shift does not occur. This phenomenon has been called "attenuation" (thinning out). It is not always found, and is more often found near the beginning of a word, less often near the word-end. *Ges.* §27*s*.

§15.321 When secondary opening occurs (§15.421), attenuation is not found.

§15.322 Attenuation generally does not occur in the H impf. (H20), possibly because of the previous syncopation (§13.522).

§15.323 Attenuation does not occur with the def.art. or with prepositions that have syncopated with the def.art.

§15.33 Short *i* > *a* in originally-closed accented syllables (§15.221). This has come to be known as "Philippi's Law."

§15.331 Philippi's Law is particularly noticeable in forms of the D- and H-stems which have consonantal sufformatives (hence were originally closed; see illustrations in §15.221).

§15.332 In D12, 13, 14, and 19 forms, *i* regularly shifts to *a: *dib-bir-ta* > *dib-bár-tā* דִּבַּ֫רְתָּ.

§15.3321 In D17, 18 forms the shift is found, even though the syllable is not accented, possibly by analogy: **dib-bir-tem* > *dib-bar-tém* דִּבַּרְתֶּם.

§15.3322 The shift does not occur in D impf., impv., ptcp., or inf. cstr. (D20, D32, D50, D65).

§15.333 In H-perf. forms the shift *i* > *a* is found under the same conditions that govern the D forms (§15.331ff). **hiq-ṭîl-tî* > **hiq-ṭíl-tî* (§15.22) > *hiq-ṭál-tî* הִקְטַ֫לְתִּי; but *taq-ṭḗl-nā* תַּקְטֵ֫לְנָה.

§15.34 *Ges.* §27*w* notes dissimilation of vowels "in order to prevent two similar, or closely related vowels, from following one another in the same word." The phenomenon seems to be too uncommon to be established as a rule.

§15.35 The shift of *a* to *e* in a large number of segolates (§17.11) should be noted here. However there is a distinct possibility that *s*^{e}*ḡôl* was at one time pronounced [æ] like *a* in *man*), so that Heb. *méleḵ* may have sounded much like Arab. *malk* ([mælk] to rhyme with *talc* rather than [mɑlk] to rhyme with *chalk*). If so, there was no true vocalic shift.

§15.4 Because of the way the sounds are produced, the gutturals, especially /ḥ/ and /ʿ/, influence the neighboring vowels both quantitatively and qualitatively.

§15.41 Compensatory lengthening has been discussed in §15.14.

§15.42 A short vowel *in an open syllable beginning with a guttural* (Gv) does not fully reduce, but retains some of its quality and quantity as a ḥaṭeph-vowel (§15.253, §11.325).

§15.421 A syllable *closed with a guttural* (CvG) under certain conditions may open. (Cf. W. S . LaSor, "Secondary Opening of Syllables Originally Closed with Gutturals," *JNES* 15 1956: 246-250.) The guttural then generates a vowel which will be of the same nature as the preceding vowel. **yaḥ-lōm* > *ya-ḥă-lōm* יַהֲלֹם; **heʾ-mîn* > *he-ʾĕ-mîn* הֶאֱמִין; **yuʿ-mad* > *yo-ʿŏ-mad̲* יָעֳמַד.

§15.4211 This generated vowel can further develop into a normal short vowel, see §15.2532.

§15.4212 The vowel of the originally-closed syllable does not reduce in distant-open position but behaves as if it were still in an unaccented-closed syllable. Cf. §15.221.

§15.4213 The generated vowel (§15.4211, §15.2532) likewise behaves as it if were in a closed syllable when, by morphological development, the following vowel reduces: **yaʿ-mōd* > *ya-ʿă-mōd̲* + *û* > *ya-ʿa-mᵉ-d̲û* or *ya-ʿam-d̲u* יַעַמְדוּ, (note that the begadkepat letter is spirantized (§11.422)!

§15.43 Gutturals prefer *a*-class vowels about them, particularly before them. This is due to the way in which a guttural consonant is produced (§12.35) which in turn influences the production of the vowel sounds around it.

§15.431 Note that in the segolates (i.e. forms developed by anaptyxis from CvCC §15.61) the influence of a guttural is readily seen. Thus **malk* > *mélek̲* מֶלֶךְ, but **zibḥ* > *zéb̲aḥ* זֶבַח and **naʿr* > *náʿar* נַעַר. CiCG regularly > CéCaG, and CaGC/CiGC > CáGaC.

§15.4311 The *u*-class vowel in CuGC forms is not affected by the guttural: **puʿl* > *pṓ-ʿal* פֹּעַל.

§15.432 When an *i*- or *u*-class vowel precedes ח /ḥ/, ע /ʿ/, or הּ (*hê* with mappîq) /h/ *at word-end*, the influence of the guttural may be manifest in one of several ways.

§15.4321 If the vowel is long *î, ô,* or *û,* a slight *a*-sound (ᵃ) is inserted between the long vowel and the final guttural. Orthographically this is represented by a *pattaḥ* written *under* but pronounced *before* the final guttural, called *pattāḥ gᵉnûb̲āʰ* (*pattaḥ furtive*). **rûḥ* > *rûᵃḥ* רוּחַ, **hišlîḥ* > *hišlîᵃḥ* הִשְׁלִיחַ, **gab̲ôh* > *gāb̲ôᵃh* גָּבוֹהַּ. Note that the *pattaḥ* does *not* add a syllable to the word; it is [ruᵃx] and not [ru-ax] as often mispronounced.

§15.4322 If the vowel is a *lengthened short vowel*, not in pause, the *a*-sound generally supplants the short vowel: **šillēḥ* > *šillaḥ* שִׁלַּח, but the pausal form is *šillēᵃḥ* שִׁלֵּחַ.

§15.4323 Lengthened *ē* ֵ occasionally behaves as a long vowel (not a lengthened short vowel, cf. §15.11): **rēʿ* > *rēᵃʿ* רֵעַ.

§15.433 Initial א /ʾ/, *when in a closed or secondarily-opened syllable and near the stress-accent* will generally have an *i*-class vowel. Cf. *ʾešqōl* אֶשְׁקֹל, *ʾeʿĕśêʰ* אֶעֱשֶׂה (but *yaʿă-śêʰ* יַעֲשֶׂה). On the other hand, cf. *ʾaḇádtî* אָבַדְתִּי, *ʾānápt̄ā* אָנַפְתָּ, etc.

§15.4331 In H impf. (H24), however, the vowel with ʾaleph generally agrees with that of the other H impf. forms: *ʾašlíᵃḥ* אַשְׁלִיחַ.

§15.434 Short *i* ִ tends to develop to short *e* ֶ before nonfinal gutturals. This is particularly noticeable in 1cs impf. (24) forms: *yiqṭōl* יִקְטֹל *but ʾeqṭōl* אֶקְטֹל. Cf. also **ʾiḥḥad* > *ʾeḥāḏ*.

§15.5 *Loss of vowel.* Under certain conditions, a vowel may be lost.

§15.51 There is evidence that nouns at one time had a short-vowel indicator of case in the singular. Cognate evidence (Arab, Akk., Ugar.) suggests that the vowel was *-u* (nominative), *-i* (genitive), and *-a* (accusative). These original short-vowels have been lost in Heb.: **ʾarṣu* > **ʾarṣ* > *ʾéreṣ* אֶרֶץ; **šalâmu* > *šālôm* שָׁלוֹם.

§15.511 Loss of the final short vowel resulted sometimes in a doubly-closed syllable (i.e. a secondarily-, not an originally-closed syllable), and anaptyxis became necessary (§15.61).

§15.512 Presence of the original short vowel meant that certain syllables were not originally closed (§15.221), hence long vowels did not reduce (review §15.22).

§15.52 There is also evidence that finite verbal forms once ended in a short vowel, possibly *-a* for perfect indicative and imperfect subjunctive, and *-u* for imperfect indicative (cf. Arabic evidence).

§15.521 The original presence of the short vowel kept certain syllables from being "originally closed" (§15.221), hence preserved the long vowels (§15.22). Where the short vowel was not present (as in jussive and converted impf. forms), an originally-closed syllable provided the condition for reduction of an originally-long vowel.

§15.53 Under conditions not clearly defined, a reduced short vowel (i.e. a "vocal shewa" §15.252) may completely disappear when a prep. is added to the form. Note presence of dagesh when *lᵉ* + *kᵉṯōḇ* > *liḵtōḇ* לִכְתֹּב, but absence when *lᵉ* + *ṣᵉḇōʾ* > *liṣḇōʾ* לִצְבֹא.

§15.54 A reduced vowel (shewa) following 'aleph may disappear and the 'aleph become quiescent. The vowel preceding the 'aleph will then be subject to the conditions of an open syllable; cf. l^e + *'ĕmōr* > *lē'mōr* לֵאמֹר.

§15.6 *Generation of vowel.* Under certain conditions a vowel may be generated.

§15.61 In words which through loss of final short vowels (§15.51) have become doubly closed (excluding gemination), an *anaptyctic vowel* has been generated, usually a *s^egôl* but with gutturals a *pattaḥ* and with second-radical *yôḏ* (CYC) a *ḥîrîq*. Note carefully the following: **malku* >**malk* > *méleḵ* מֶלֶךְ; **ba'lu* > **ba'l* > *bá'al* בַּעַל; **maymu* > **maym* > **máyim* מַיִם.

§15.611 Nouns which have developed from CvCC forms with anaptyxis, particularly those which have two *s^egôls*, are generally called *segolates* (see §24.21ff).

§15.62 Through secondary opening of a syllable originally closed with a guttural, a ḥaṭeph-vowel may be generated, which in turn may develop into a short vowel (§15.2532).

§15.63 A short vowel before a quiescent 'aleph may generate a long (i.e. a *pure long* §14.1) vowel. Note: **ra'š* > **râ'š* > *rô'š* רֹאשׁ; **ṣa'n* > **ṣâ'n* > *ṣô'n* צֹאן. Because of the *â* > *ô* shift we assume that this phenomenon was very early (i.e. prior to the Canaanite shift, §14.11).

§15.631 In the impf. forms of five 'CC verbs (אפה, אמר, אכל, אבה, אבד) the short-*a* of the preformative combined with the following 'aleph to produce a quasi-long *â*-vowel which in turn shifted to long *ô*. *Ges.* §68*b*. **ya'kal* > **yâ'kal* > *yô'ḵal* יֹאכַל.

§15.64 In forms of CC² ('ayin-'ayin) verbs that have a consonantal sufformative, a vowel is inserted to prevent a sequence of three consonants, as follows:

§15.641 In the perf. (12, 13, 14, 17, 18, 19) the separating vowel is *ô*: **hasibbtā* > *hasibbôṯā* הֲסִבּוֹתָ.

§15.642 In the impf. (26, 28) the separating vowel is *ê*, orthographically represented by *s^egôl-yôḏ* ֶי . **tasibbnā^h* > *tasibbênā^h* תְּסִבֶּינָה.

§15.65 In a succession of reduced vowels (vocal shewas) a short vowel may be generated, as follows:

§15.651 The first of two successive vocal shewas will develop into a short vowel, usually a *ḥîrîq* but in some cases a *pattāḥ*: **d^eb^erê^yhem* > *diḇrêhem* דִּבְרֵיהֶם; **m^el^ekê^y qédem* (cf. *m^elāḵî^ym*) > *malḵê^y qéḏem* מַלְכֵי קֶדֶם.

§15.6511 If a sequence of three successive reduced vowels would have developed, it is the *second* which generated the short vowel: **l^{e}d^{e}b^{e}rê^{y}hem* > *l^{e}dib̲rê^{y}hem* לְדִבְרֵיהֶם.

§15.652 If the second shewa is with *yôd̲*, a long *î* is generated: **b^{e}y^{e}mê^{y} dāwîd̲* > *bî^{y}mê^{y} dāwîd̲* בִּימֵי דָוִד.

§15.653 If a simple vocal shewa stands before a ḥateph-vowel, the shewa generates a vowel of the same class as the ḥateph-vowel: **b^{e}ḥăṣar hammélek̲* > *baḥăṣar hammélek̲* בַּחֲצַר הַמֶּלֶךְ.

§15.654 If *wâw* with shewa stands before another consonant with vocal shewa, long *û* is generated: **w^{e}t̲^{e}k̲ḗlet̲* > *ût̲^{e}k̲ḗlet̲* וּתְכֵלֶת.

§15.66 The *pattāḥ g^{e}nûb̲ā^{h}* (cf. §15.4321) might be considered as a generated vowel, although the vowel is so weak that it is not considered to form a new syllable.

§15.67 The development of the *semivowels* (§12.51) into vowels at word-end and syllable-end (**-cw* > *-cû*, **-cy* > *-cî*) may be mentioned here, but is not properly the generation of a vowel, but rather the nature of the semivowel.

§15.7 A *diphthong* is a single sound made by combining two different vowel sounds without losing the component elements (§14.3). If either of the component parts is modified or if one sound is lost, the diphthong *monophthongizes*, and should be called a *monophthong*. Some discussions of diphthongs do not hold to this distinction.

§15.71 In Bib. Heb. diphthongs undergo vocalic alteration depending usually on the nature of the syllable in which they occur and its relation to the stress-accent.

§15.72 The diphthongs *aw* [ɑw] and *ay* [ɑɪ] normally are found only in closed accented syllables that have been formed by simplification of a geminate consonant at word-end: **ḥayy* > *ḥay* חַי (pl. חַיִּים); **gaww* > *gaw* גַּו (suffixial גֵּוֹו).

§15.721 If the syllable has been doubly closed by a semivowel and another consonant, anaptyxis (§15.61) generally is found: **mawt* > *mā́wet̲* מָוֶת; *bayt > *báyit̲* בַּיִת.

§15.7211 The original vowel in such a form is normally retained as if in an accented closed syllable (§15.112). *ay* lengthens in pause (§15.135).

§15.7212 The word **yawm* (cf. Arab. *yawm*) 'day' is always monophthongized in Bib. Heb. > *yôm* יוֹם. The form **yā́wem*, analogous to *mā́wet̲*, is not found.

§15.73 In all other conditions *aw* monophthongizes to *ô* and *ay* to *ê*.

§15.731 *aw* > *ô* except under the conditions in §15.72ff. **mawt* > *môṯ* (*ûḇᵉmôṯ ʾāḇîhā* וּבְמוֹת אָבִיהָ).

§15.732 *ay* > *ê* except under the conditions in §15.72ff. *However, the monophthong ê* is written in *four different ways*, which may at one time have represented four different phonetic shadings. At present all are pronounced [e:].

§15.7321 In an accented-open syllable in medial position, the monophthong is generally written *sᵉgôl yôḏ*: *ʿālêʸḵā* עָלֶיךָ.

§15.7322 In an accented open syllable at word-end the monophthong is generally written *sᵉgôl hê*: *mištêʰ* מִשְׁתֶּה.

§15.7323 In an unaccented (open) syllable at end of a sing. form the monophthong is generally written *ṣêrê hê*: *mištêʰ yáyin* מִשְׁתֵּה יַיִן.

§15.7324 In an unaccented syllable other than at the end of a sing. form, the monophthong is generally written *ṣêrê yôḏ*: *ʿêʸnôʷ* עֵינוֹ; *ʾêʸn šôwêʰ* אֵין שֹׁוֶה; *lip̄nêʸ hammélek̲* לִפְנֵי הַמֶּלֶךְ.

§15.74 There are residual cases which apparently cannot be included in general rules. These must be observed as they are encountered.

§16. A *syllable* may be defined as the sounds producing a summit of sonority, see §10.44. Scholars have difficulty defining a syllable, but there is usually no problem in recognizing one. In Bib. Heb. the study of syllabification is important because of the relationship between *vowel quantity* and the syllable.

§16.1 The last syllable of a word is called the *ultima*. The next-to-last syllable is the *penult*. The syllable before the penult is the *antepenult*.

§16.11 A syllable ending in a vowel, whether V (vowel) or CV (consonant-vowel) is an *open* syllable. A syllable ending in a consonant, whether VC or CVC, is a *closed* syllable.

§16.12 If a syllable begins with two or more consonants (CCV, CCVC) the combination of consonants is called a *consonantal cluster*. A syllable ending with two consonants (VCC, CVCC) is a *doubly-closed* syllable.

§16.13 A *syllable* is considered to be *long* (a) if it contains a long or a lengthened short-vowel, or (b) if it is closed (i.e. cv̂, cv̄, cvc).

§16.2 A Hebrew word has as many syllables as it has separate vowels or diphthongs.

§16.21 There is difference of agreement among Heb. scholars in counting syllables with "vocal shewa" (§15.2521) or syllables with secondary opening (§15.421). In this *Handbook* we shall count it a syllable if a summit of sonority is present, i.e. if we hear a vowel, however faintly, except in the case of pattaḥ furtive (§15.4321).

§16.3 In Bib. Heb. *every syllable* (with one exception) *must begin with a consonant*, and (with 2 exceptions) *with only one consonant*. (The student is reminded that 'aleph א and 'ayin ע are consonants.) A syllable may be open, closed, or doubly-closed (§§16.11f). Hence we find the following syllables:

V	open syllable, vowel only (§16.31)
CV	open syllable (§16.32)
CVC	closed syllable (§16.33)
CVCC	doubly-closed syllable (§16.34)
CCV(C)	syllable beginning with a cluster (§16.35)

§16.31 The only syllable beginning with a vowel in Bib. Heb. is the conjunction **wa-*, which, when it comes before a consonant with shewa or before one of the labials *b, m, p* undergoes a shift to the long vowel *û-*: *ûṯᵉḵélet*, *ûḇimlôṯ*.

§16.32 An *open syllable* is composed of a consonant and the vowel that follows it. (Orthographically the vowel is usually written *under* the consonant, §11.32ff). It may be *accented* (cv́) or *unaccented* (cv).

§16.321 Because of the effect upon vowel quantity we must further distinguish between a *near-open* unaccented syllable and a *distant-open* unaccented syllable, as described in the following sections.

§16.3211 A *near-open syllable* is an open syllable *immediately before* the syllable with the stress-accent (§11.56). The penult of דָּבָר *dā-ḇā́r* (CV-cv́c) is near-open.

§16.3212 A *distant-open syllable* is an open syllable that stands two or more syllables before the stress-accent. The antepenult of מְלָכִים *mᵉ-lā-ḵîm* (CV-cv-cv́c) is distant-open. The fourth syllable from the end of אֲחַשְׁוֵרוֹשׁ *'ă-ḥaš-wē-rôš* (CV-cvc-cv-cv́c) is also distant-open. In other words, any unaccented open syllable which is not near-open is distant-open.

§16.3213 Open syllables that *follow* the stress-accent are generally not included in the rules for accent. They usually behave as near-open syllables (unless they are monophthongs), cf. קָטַלְתָּ *qā-ṭál-tā*, אֵלֶּה *'él-lêʰ*.

§16.33 A *closed syllable* consists of two (or more) consonants plus an invervening vowel. Usually the closed syllable in Bib. Heb. is consonant-vowel-consonant (CVC). It may be *accented* or *unaccented.*

§16.331 Certain vocalic alterations differ according to whether the syllable is originally-closed or closed by secondary development; review §15.221.

§16.3311 Syllables *not originally closed* may have become closed by a secondary development such as the loss of a final short-vowel (§15.511) or the reduction of a vowel to zero shewa (§15.53).

§16.3312 A syllable may have been originally closed by the morphology of the word (e.g. *hiḵ-táḇ-tā,* where the penult was originally closed by the addition of the consonantal sufformative *-tā*), or by the fact that the form was always closed (e.g. *yap̄-qēḏ,* where the jussive never had a final short vowel, as confirmed by Arab. evidence.

§16.34 The *doubly-closed syllable* is comparatively rare in Bib. Heb. It occurs only at word-end and (with very few exceptions) only with nongeminate consonants (cf. §13.42).

§16.341 A doubly-closed syllable is found in the 2fs pers. pron.: אַתְּ *'att.*

§16.342 It is also found in 2fs perf. (13) verbal forms, קָטַלְתְּ *qā-ṭalt.*

§16.3421 In CCG verbs anaptyxis occurs, but the light dagesh remains as if the syllable were doubly-closed: שָׁלַחַתְּ *šā-lá-ḥatt.*

§16.3422 In CCY verbs the semivowel becomes a full vowel and the doubly-closed syllable simplifies, גָּלַיְתְּ* > גָּלִית *gā-lîṯ.*

§16.3423 Some apocopated verbal forms (§13.53) remain doubly-closed: וַתֵּבְךְּ *wat-tēḇk* (however, this is generally pronounced [wa'tɛv-kə]).

§16.343 Through the loss of the final short-vowel (§15.51f), apocopation (§13.53), the addition of a "ballast-t" (§13.513), or the addition of a feminine morpheme (§25.13), a doubly-closed syllable may have resulted. In such instances, one of three things subsequently occurred:

§16.3431 If the syllable would have been doubly-closed by a geminate consonant (§13.3), gemination is lost: *'*immu* > *'imm* > *'ēm* אֵם (but cf. the suffixial *'immo*= אִמּוֹ). Such a syllable may be called "erstwhile doubly-closed." Cf. §15.111.

§16.3432 If the syllable would have been doubly-closed by different (i.e. nongeminate) consonants, *anaptyxis* generally resulted (§15.61): **malku* > **malk* > *méleḵ* מֶלֶךְ (cf. suffixial *malko*= מַלְכּוֹ).

§16.3433 In a few instances the doubly-closed syllable remains, cf. §16.3423.

§16.35 Initial *clusters* are almost nonexistent in Bib. Heb., and indeed in all Semitic languages. Syllables such as CCV or CCVC are extremely rare, and because of this fact are sometimes not recognized.

§16.351 The words for '2' begin with clusters, as the dagesh in the fem. form clearly indicates: שְׁנַיִם *šná-yim*, שְׁתַּיִם *štá-yim*. It is impossible for the shewa to represent a vowel before dagesh (§16.3622).

§16.352 In a very few instances it is possible that a *prothetic* א has been added to avoid a cluster.

§16.353 In this *Handbook* we do not consider words that have shewa after the first consonant (except the words for '2') to have an initial cluster, since it can be demonstrated that the shewa is a reduced vowel. Thus we read *kᵉ-lî* and not *klî* for כְּלִי (even though the word is often pronounced [kli]), since the plur. is *kē-lîm* כֵּלִים.

§16.354 It is possible that a prothetic *hê* is found in certain forms of the N- and HtD-stems. Arab. evidence suggests that the N-stem indicator was **an/in*, developing in Heb. to *han-*. Aram. evidence suggests an original **it-* for the HtD-stem, which likewise developed in Heb. to *hiṯ-*.

§16.36 Since the student may have difficulty recognizing syllables in Heb. orthography, the following observations may be helpful.

§16.361 The end of a syllable *within a word* is marked either by *dāḡēš ḥāzāq* (the "doubling dagesh," §11.431) or by *šᵉwâ naḥ* (the "silent shewa," see §15.251).

§16.3611 In *all consonants except bᵉgadkᵉpat* a dagesh is the "doubler," and therefore closes the syllable: דַּמִּים *dam-mîm*.

§16.3612 A dagesh in a begadkepat *preceded by a vowel* must be the strong dagesh, hence a syllable divider: מְדַבֵּר *mᵉ-ḏab-bēr*.

§16.3613 A syllable closed by the strong dagesh is sometimes said to be a "sharpened" syllable. The term is linguistically meaningless, and probably was derived from the Aram. description that the letter was "pointed" (i.e. with dagesh). The term should be discarded.

§16.362 Recognizing the silent shewa is somewhat more difficult.

§16.3621 If two *successive* shewas occur in a word, the *first* must be *silent shewa*, cf. §15.2511.

§16.3622 If shewa stands *before a begadkepat letter with dagesh* the shewa must be *silent*, hence a syllable-divider: לִכְתֹּב *lik̲-tōb̲*. If the shewa were a vowel, the only dagesh permissible in the begadkepat would be the doubler (§16.3612), which would put the shewa in a closed syllable contrary to §15.243.

§16.3623 A simple shewa *under a guttural* must be silent shewa, since otherwise the guttural would require a ḥaṭeph-vowel, §15.42.

§16.3624 In some cases, a vowel has reduced to zero and the shewa becomes a syllable-divider, even though a following begadkepat letter may be spirantized, cf. the cstr. מַלְכֵי *mal-kê*. The short-vowel, normally indicating a closed syllable, may be of help.

§16.363 The final syllable of a word is not marked except (a) when *kap̄ sôp̄ît̲* stands at word-end and shewa is inserted in it ךְ, or (b) when two different consonants stand at word-end (i.e. a doubly-closed syllable) and shewas are written with both of them: קָטַלְתְּ *qā-ṭalt*. אַתְּ *'att* is an exception.

§17. *Accent*, as considered in this *Handbook*, deals only with *stress-accent*, i.e. the syllable(s) on which stress is placed. It can usually be determined by the Masoretic accents, cf. §11.5ff. Tone-accent, which has to do with rising, level, and falling intonation, cannot be positively determined and need not concern us for a reading knowledge of Bib. Heb. (In older grammars stress-accent is often referred to as "tone.") Because of the influence of stress upon vowel quality and quantity, the student is advised to learn well the rules of accent.

§17.01 The Aram. terms *milra'* (properly *millᵉra'* מִלְּרַע)'below' = 'after,' i.e. on the final syllable) and *mil'ēl* (properly *millᵉ'ēl* מִלְּעֵיל 'above' = 'before,' i.e. on the next-to-last syllable) are used by some Heb. grammarians. *Ges.* §15*c*.

§17.1 Nouns *in the absolute state* are generally accented on the *ultima* (§16.1). Originally this accent was on the penult, prior to the loss of the final short-vowel (§15.51): *da-bá-ru* > *dā-b̲ār* דָּבָר.

§17.11 *Segolates*, i.e. nouns that have developed from forms that would have been doubly-closed after loss of the final short-vowel (§16.3432), are accented on the *penult* (§15.61). In the original form with the final vowel, the accent would likewise have been on the penult: **mál-ku* > **malk* > *mé-lek̲*.

§17.12 Nouns (and other words) *in the construct state* or *joined to the following word by maqqeph* (§11.45) have no primary stress-accent.

§17.121 The student should note that the vowels of words in construct and the vowels of words joined to a following word by maqqeph *will always be those of unaccented syllables*, i.e. unaccented closed (u.c.), near-open (n.o.), or distant-open (d.o.). THIS IS EXTREMELY IMPORTANT!

§17.122 Secondary stress-accent will be found on such "bound" words under certain circumstances, but these have no effect on the rules of accent.

§17.2 *Verbs* are accented according to the following rules.

§17.21 In *finite verbal forms without sufformatives*, the accent is on the *ultima*: *qā-ṭál* קָטַל; *yiq-ṭṓl* יִקְטֹל.

§17.22 In finite verbal forms *with* sufformatives, the following conditions prevail:

§17.221 If the ultima is *closed*, the accent is on the *ultima*: *qā-ṭál* קָטַל, *qᵉ-ṭal-tém* קְטַלְתֶּם.

§17.222 If the ultima is *open* and the penult is *long*, the accent is on the *penult*: *qā-ṭál-nû* קָטַלְנוּ; *hiq-ṭî́-lā* הִקְטִילָה.

§17.2221 *Note that a syllable is long if it contains a long or lengthened vowel or if it is closed* (see §16.13).

§17.223 If the ultima is open and the penult is *short*, the accent is on the *ultima* in nonpausal forms (§11.55): *qā-ṭᵉ-lû* קָטְלוּ; *ʿā-wᵉ-ṯā́ʰ* עָוְתָה.

§17.2231 In pausal forms (cf. §17.223) the accent is on the *penult*: *qā-ṭā́-lāʰ* קָטָלָה; *ʿā-śā́-ṯā* עָשָׂתָה.

§17.3 *Accent shift* occurred under certain conditions:

§17.31 At some stage the accent shifted toward the *end* of a number of words. It is believed that the pausal form preserves the earlier accentuation: *ʾā-nô-ḵî́*, pausal *ʾā-nṓ-ḵî* (Akk. *a-nā́-ku); ʾat-tā́,* pausal *ʾát-tā* (Arab. *ʾán-ta*); *ʿā-śᵉ-ṯā.* pausal *ʿā-śā́-ṯā*; and note the pron. suf. *-ḵā́,* pausal *é-ḵā.*

§17.311 For a full discussion see F. W. Bush, "Evidence from Milḥama and the Masoretic Text for a Penultimate Accent in Hebrew Verbal Forms," *Revue de Qumrâ* 8 (Nov. 1960): 501-514. Israeli proper names, likewise, preserve the penultimate accent–and proper names generally preserve earlier elements in a language.

§17.32 Forms with suffixes that have a connecting vowel take the accent *on the connecting vowel*: *wîʸ-ḥun-nék-kā* וִיחֻנֶּךָּ.

§17.33 The "heavy" sufformatives are accented, cf. §17.221.

§17.34 The addition of *wāw*-conversive (§22.13) may cause an accent shift:

§17.341 In the imperf. with waw conversive, the accent is on the *penult* when the ultima is closed and the penult is open: *yāqṓm* יָקֹם, but *wayyā́qom* וַיָּקָם (*Ges.* §49*d*).

§17.342 In nonpausal perf. 2ms (12) and 1cs (14) forms the addition of *wāw*-conv. causes the accent to shift from the penult to the ultima if the penult is closed: *dib-bár-tā* but *wᵉ-ḏib-bar-tā́* וְדִבַּרְתָּ֫. This is the only way a conv.-perf. can be recognized other than by context.

§17.41 Secondary stress accents can be placed on any closed syllable, or on any open syllable with a long- or lengthened short-vowel or with a short-vowel with metheg that precedes the primary accent, or on any closed syllable or open syllable with a long- or lengthened short-vowel that follows the primary accent. This applies also to the bound words in construct or joined by maqqeph.

§17.35 Under conditions not fully defined, a succession of two stressed syllables (i.e. two successive words that would juxtapose stressed syllables) is avoided by moving the first stressed syllable away (i.e. forward) from the second. This is called *nāsôḡ 'āḥôr* 'moving backwards.' Hence **lā-ṯḗṯ lāh* > *lā́-ṯeṯ lāh* לָ֫תֶת לָהּ (Est. 2: 9).

§17.4 The primary accent is never placed on a syllable further from the end of the word than the penult. There is no antepenultimate accent in Bib. Heb. (in some instances, the addition of locative ה ָ- to a word with penultimate accent may appear to put the stress on the antepenult, but a "closed" syllable has developed).

§17.41 Secondary stress accents can be placed on any closed syllable, or on any open syllable with a long- or lengthened short-vowel or with a short-vowel with metheg that precedes the primary accent, or on any closed syllable or open syllable with a long- or lengthened short-vowel that follows the primary accent. This applies also to the bound words in construct or joined by maqqeph.

§§18, 19 are arbitrarily omitted.

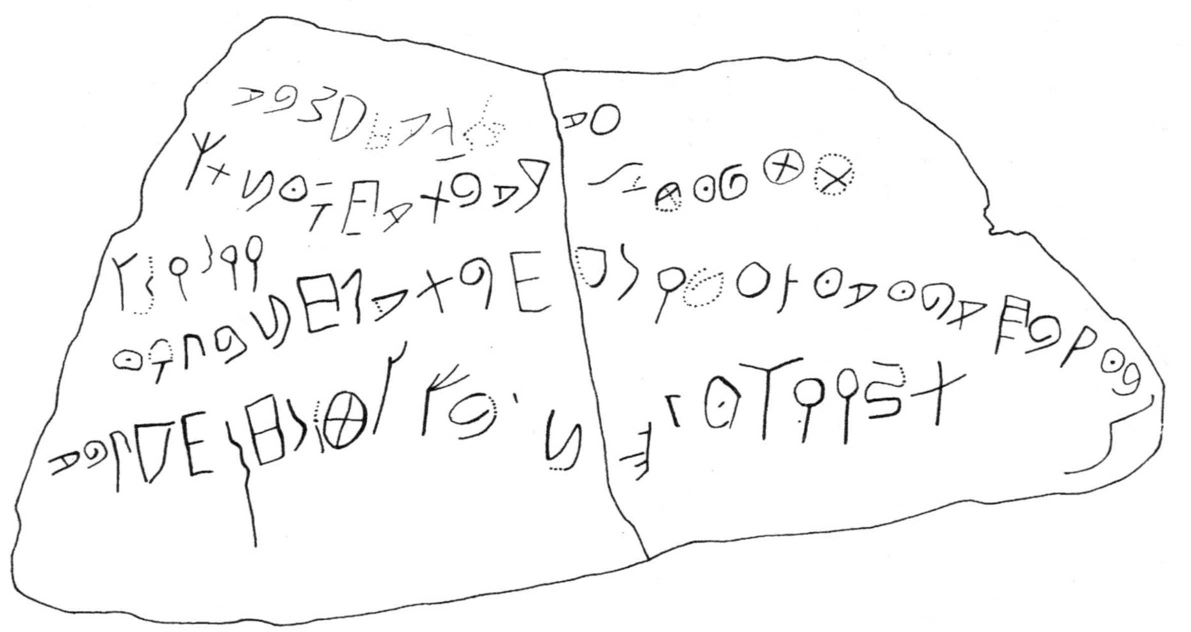

FIGURE 7. 12th CENTURY HEBREW FROM IZBET SARTAH

The Izbet Sartah sherd has been identified as "Proto-Canaanite," but might better be left unclassified for the present,since "Proto-Canaanite" has also been used for the Eblean tablets. The sherd comes from an Israelite settlement, but is obviously written from *left to right*. The bottom line is clearly the alphabet, with *mêm* and *rêš* missing and *qôp̄* written twice; *pê* and *ʿáyin* are reversed, as in the acrostic verses in Lamentations. (Photo by Moshe Weinberg; courtesy *Biblical Archaeology Review*)

§20. *Morphology* is the study of changes in form of the words in a language. It includes *inflection, derivation,* and *composition* of words. The term *morphology*, however, is often used as equivalent to *inflection*, which is the change in form made to express the relationship of the inflected word to other words in the phrase, clause, or sentence.

§20.1 A *morpheme* is the smallest meaningful grammatical unit of a language. It may be a word, such as 'a' or 'more.' or it may be an inflectional element of a word, such as '-ed' or '-ing.' In learning a language it is necessary to be able to recognize the morphemes quickly and accurately.

§20.11 An *allomorph* is an alternate morpheme, or alternate form of a morpheme of equivalent significance; e.g. the plural morpheme in spoken Eng. is [s] in *hats*, [z] in *boys*, [z̧] in *houses* [hauz-z̧], vowel umlaut in *feet* or *mice*, and [n̥] in *oxen*. In written Eng. the plural allomorphs are generally given as /-s/ and /-es/, plus the irregular forms.

§20.12 A morpheme which can stand alone is called a *free form*. A morpheme which cannot stand alone is called a *bound form*. We are principally concerned with bound forms in this study.

§20.2 A bound form which is added at the beginning of a free form is called a *prefix* or *preformative*. One which is added at the end is called a *suffix* or *sufformative*. One which is inserted into the free form is called an *infix*.

§20.21 In this *Handbook* we distinguish between *prefixes* and *preformatives* and between *suffixes* and *sufformatives*:

§20.211 Morphemes whose removal would still leave a word intact we call *prefixes* and *suffixes*. Thus the def.art., the conj. **wa-*, and the prepositional morphemes are prefixes. Likewise, the pronominal morphemes are suffixes. (Note that the vowel-pointing may be altered when a morpheme is added or removed, but the essential word remains.)

§20.212 Morphemes whose removal would destroy the word we call *afformatives,* whether *preformatives* or *sufformatives*. Thus the inflectional morphemes of the verb are termed afformatives. For obvious reasons we have chosen to retain the term "infix" rather than use the term "informative" for a morphological element that occurs within the word.

§20.3 In the Semitic languages, most words exhibit a triconsonantal structure, called by many grammarians the *root*. (But cf. *Ges.* §30*c* where "root" is used for the hypothetical 2-consonantal expansion in Heb.) The basic consonants of the root are called the radicals (because they pertain to the *radix* or root). Other consonants may be added before, within, or after the root, hence it is necessary to be able to distinguish the radicals that form the root in order to ascertain the essential meaning of a word.

§20.31 Hebrew, like the other Semitic languages, uses the consonantal structure to carry the essential idea. The vowels and other morphological elements give the specific meaning, as well as the indication of relationship to other words in the clause.

§20.32 Many lexicons list all words under their roots–which is of little help to the beginner (or even to advanced students, in the case of unusual forms). Moreover, in some cases these are hypothetical 3-consonant roots, and comparative studies indicate that there were a number of biconsonantal (and perhaps even some uniconsonantal) roots in the Sem. languages. Four- and 5-cons. roots appear to be chiefly borrowings. Some multiconsonantal roots have been formed by reduplication (e.g. *qalqal* and *q^{e}taltal* forms).

§20.4 *Classification of words* in the Semitic languages is somewhat subjective. In this *Handbook* we shall distinguish particles, pronouns, nouns and adjectives, and verbs.

§20.41 The term *particle* is generally used to describe parts of speech that are uninflected, such as prepositions, conjunctions, etc. Cf. *Ges.* §§31, 99. More properly, these are free-form morphemes (§20.12). For our purposes we shall include bound particles, such as prefixed or suffixed particles, as well as free-forms that undergo inflection. The use of these and other particles (i.e. uninflected free-forms) will be discussed under the general heading of Syntax.

§20.42 *Pronouns* (§30.312) may be free-form (independent) or bound (suffixed); some are inflected, some are not. Independent, inflected pronouns are considered under §21.1. Pronominal suffixes are discussed under §23.1. The use of pronouns will be considered under Syntax.

§20.43 *Nouns* and *adjectives* are often considered together, for two reasons. (1) They are inflected in similar ways. (2) More important, nouns are often used in annexion (construct) as adjectives, and adjectives are frequently used substantivally (as nouns). The problem is further complicated by the fact that some verbal forms are essentially nouns and/or adjectives.

§20.431 Noun formation will be considered under §24. Noun inflection will be considered under §25. Most nouns and adjectives are inflected to show gender, number, and state.

§20.432 Adjectives, particularly the numeral adjectives, will be considered under §26.

§20.433 Verbal nouns and verbal adjectives will be considered under the treatment of the verb, §§27–29.

§20.434 The use of substantives, including pronouns, nouns, adjectives, and verbal substantives, will be treated under Syntax.

§20.44 *Verbs* (i.e. those forms excluding verbal nouns/adjectives) are generally inflected to indicate person, gender, and number. In addition, all verbal forms (including verbal nouns/adjectives) are inflected to indicate one or more of the following: aspect ("tense"), voice, mood, completion of the predication, persistency of the predication, intensity, causation, reflexivity, and occasionally other elements. These subjects will be considered in §§27–29.

§20.441 Verbs may take pronominal suffixes. With finite verbal forms, the suffix generally indicates the direct object of the verb; with the participle and the infinitive construct, the suffix stands in something like a genitive relationship to the verb. The forms of the suffixes will be considered under §23; the uses of the suffixes will be considered under Syntax.

§20.5 Since morphology deals with those elements of a language which indicate relationships within the word-group or clause it is often confused with syntax. In this *Handbook* we shall attempt to deal only with the morphological elements under Morphology, whereas the significance of the morphemes will be considered under Syntax.

§21. The *free-form morpheme*, whether a pronoun, a preposition, or a conjunction, is one of the means used in Heb. to indicate the relationship(s) between words in a clause.

§21.1 Independent *personal pronouns* distinguishing person, gender, and number (*Ges.* §32) are as follows:

PGN	CODE	HEBREW		MEANING
3ms	(p0)	הוּא		he, it
3fs	(p1)	(הִיא	הִוא	she, it
2ms	(p2)	אַתָּה	אָתָּה	you (m.s.)
2fs	(p3)	אַתְּ	אַתְּי	you (f.s.)
1cs	(p4)	אָנֹכִי	אָנֹכִי	I
"		אֲנִי	אָנִי	"
3mp	(p5)	הֵם	הֵמָּה	they (m.)
3fp	(p6)	הֵן	הֵנָּה	they (f.)
2mp	(p7)	אַתֶּם		you (m.p.)
2fp	(p8)	אַתֶּן	אַתֵּנָה	you (f.p.)
"			אַתֵּנָּה	"
1cp	(p9)	אֲנַחְנוּ	אֲנָחְנוּ	we
"		נַחְנוּ	נָחְנוּ	"

§21.2 *Demonstrative pronouns*, categorized as "near" or "distant" (*Ges*. §34), are inflected to indicate gender and number.

NEAR			DISTANT		
ms	זֶה	this (m.)	ms	הוּא	that (m.)
fs	זֹאת	this (f.)	fs	הִיא	that (f.)
mp	אֵלֶּה	these (m.)	mp	הֵמָּה, הֵם	those (m.)
fp	אֵלֶּה	these (f.)	fp	הֵנָּה, הֵן	those (f.)

The demonstrative pronouns may take prefixed particles.

§21.3 The *relative pronoun* ('who, which') is usually אֲשֶׁר. The pointing suggests that this originally may have been a substantive in construct (cf. Aram. אֲתַר, Arab. *'aṯar*, and note 2 Sam. 7:7). It is not declinable, and stands for m. or f., sing. or plur., personal or impersonal. In the later writings, ·שֶׁ (or more rarely ·שַׁ followed by the doubling dagesh) is found. Cf. *Ges*. §37.

§21.4 The *interrogative pronoun* occurs in a *personal* form מִי 'who?' and an *impersonal* form מַה 'what?' with no indication of gender. Cf. *Ges*. §37.

§21.41 Note the following combinations: with a preposition לְמִי 'to whom?'; annexed to a noun בַּת־מִי 'whose daughter?' (lit. 'daughter of whom'); with the sign of definite direct object אֶת־מִי 'whom?'

§21.42 מַה is usually joined to the following word by maqqeph (cf. §§11.45, 13.36).

§21.421 The vowel of מַה varies, following the pointing of the definite article (§22.2ff): מַה־לַּעֲשׂוֹת, מָה־אֶעֱשֶׂה, and מֶה־עָשִׂיתָ.

§21.43 The constructions אֵי־זֶה and אֵי־זֹאת are also used as impersonal interrogatives 'which, what?': וְאֵי־זֶה הוּא 'and what is he?'

§21.5 The *indefinite pronouns* are morphologically identical with the interrogative pronouns (§21.4ff): personal מִי 'whoever'; impersonal מַה 'whatever.' Gender is not indicated morphologically.

§21.6 The *partitive* מִן may be mentioned here although, strictly speaking, it is a preposition. Originally it was possibly a substantive in construct meaning 'separation.' Cf. *Ges*. §§119*w*, 101*a*.

§21.61 מִן as a free form is usually found only before the def. art., in which case it is always joined by maqqeph: מִן־הָאָרֶץ.

§21.62 In most other instances, מִן is bound or prefixed to the word it governs, with assimilation of the *nûn*, resulting in dagesh or compensatory lengthening according to phonetic rules (§§13.32, 15.14ff). Cf. §22.42.

§22. Certain particles are bound morphemes, prefixed to the word they govern. See *Ges.* §§101-104.

§22.1 The *conjunction* is always prefixed. Originally it was **wa-*, but it is found in a variety of forms. Cf. *Ges.* §104*d-g*.

§22.11 In near-open syllables (§16.3211), the vowel of the conjunction sometimes reduces to shewa וְ contrary to short-vowel rules (§15.12). In other cases it lengthens to *qāmāṣ* וָ. Accordingly we find both וְאִם (2 Sam. 20:19) and וָאֵם (Est. 2:7).

§22.12 In distant-open syllables (§16.3212) the vowel of the conjunctions normally reduces to shewa וְ: e.g. וְעֶשְׂרִים *wᵉ-ʿeś-rîm*. However, there are noteworthy exceptions as follows:

§22.121 Before בּ, מ, or פּ (called בּוּמַף) or before any consonant with shewa the conjunction develops to the long vowel *šûrûq* וּ: וּבִמְלֹאוֹת, וּמֵאָה, וּפָנִים, וּתְכֵלֶת. Cf. §15.654.

§22.122 Before *yôḏ* with *šᵉwâ* the conjunction becomes וִי *wî*, וְיְ *wᵉyᵉ* > וִי *wî*: וְיְהִי* > וִיהִי. Cf. §15.652.

§22.123 Before a consonant with compound shewa the conjunction is vocalized with a short-vowel of the same class as the compound shewa: וַעֲבָדָיו. Cf. §15.653.

§22.13 The conjunction normally has the form וַ· (with the doubling dagesh) when it has *conversive* force with the verb in the *imperfect* (§§27.00, 13.35): וַיָּבוֹא. Review §§15.14, 13.41 for exceptions.

§22.2 The *definite article* is *always* prefixed and is vocalized in several ways. The basic form is הַ· (*ha-* with dagesh): מֶלֶךְ + הַ· > הַמֶּלֶךְ. Cf. *Ges.* §35. Note carefully the following alternate vocalizations:

§22.21 Before א, ע, or ר the dagesh is rejected, usually with compensatory lengthening of *pattāḥ* to *qāmāṣ* (cf. §§13.38, 15.14f): הָעַמִּים, הָרְגָּמָן, הָרָצִים.

§22.22 Before חָ (*ḥā*, not *ḥo*) and before ע or ה in a near-open syllable with *qāmāṣ*, the def. art. has the form הֶ without dagesh: הֶחָלָב *heḥālāḇ*: הֶעָמָל *heʿāmāl*; הֶהָמוֹן *hehāmôn*.

§22.23 Before ה, ח, and occasionally ע the form of the def.art. is הַ (*dāgēš* rejected but no compensation, §15.1411): הַהוּא, הַחָכְמָה *hahokmāʰ*, הַעִוְרִים.

§22.231 For a summary of the preceding sections, see Table G. It is essential that the student be able easily to recognize the various forms of the definite article, in order to avoid confusion with other preformative ה-elements.

§22.24 When the inseparable prepositions -בּ, -כּ, and -ל are added to a word having a def. art., the ה is syncopated along with the shewa of the preposition; the vowel (and dagesh if any) of the def. art., however, remain (cf. §13.521): הַיּוֹם + בְּ > בַּיּוֹם; בְּהֶחָצֵר > בֶּחָצֵר.

§22.241 Note that syncopation does not occur when the conjunction is prefixed to a word having the def. art.: וְהָעִיר.

§22.25 The words אֶרֶץ, הַר, and עַם always take their pausal forms when written with the def. art. (§15.133).

§22.3 The interrogative particle is always prefixed. Before nongutturals (including ר) with a vowel that has not been reduced, it is pointed with *ḥăṭap̄-pattāḥ* הֲ: הֲגַם. *Ges.* §100*k-n*. Note carefully the following exceptional forms:

§22.31 Before gutturals with *qāmāṣ* or *ḥăṭap̄-qāmāṣ* the interrogative particle is הֶ: הֶאָמוּר, הֶחֳדַלְתִּי.

§22.32 Before gutturals not pointed with *qāmāṣ* or *ḥăṭap̄-qāmāṣ* and before consonants with shewa the interrog. part. is pointed with *pattāḥ*: הַאֵלֵךְ, הַבְרָכָה. Sometimes the doubling dagesh is inserted in the consonant following the interrog. part.: הַבְּדֶרֶךְ.

§22.33 The interrog. part. can nearly always be distinguished from the def. art. by its *different* pointing. The student should first master the pointing of the def. art., and then study the differences with the interrog. part.

§22.4 Certain prepositions occur regularly as bound morphemes.

§22.41 The prepositions -בּ, -כּ, and -ל are always prefixed to the word they govern and are therefore known as the *inseparable prepositions*. They were originally vocalized with short-*a* (or possibly short-*i*), which reduces to shewa in distant-open syllables (§16.3212), e.g. בְּמִדְבַּר־סִינַי, and frequently in near-open syllables (§16.3211), e.g. בְּשֵׁם. Sometimes, lengthening of the vowel occurs in near-open syllables, לָכֶם.

§22.411 The pointing of the inseparable prepositions varies in accordance with §§15.651, .653.

§22.412 The def. art. syncopates when an inseparable preposition is prefixed, cf. §22.24 and TABLE G.

§22.42 The prep. מִן is usually prefixed to the word it governs unless that word has the def. art., cf. §21.61.

§22.421 In accordance with §13.111 the *nûn* of the prep. מִן may assimilate: קֶדֶם + מִן > מִקֶּדֶם. With gutturals §§15.14ff apply: עַם + מִן > מֵעַם; חוּץ + מִן > מִחוּץ.

§23. Certain bound morphemes are suffixed to words they modify.

§23.1 The most common of these are the *pronominal suffixes*. Cf. *Ges.* §§33, 103.

§23.11 Like the independent pers. pron. (§21.1) the pron. suf. distinguish person, gender, and number.

§23.12 The pron. suf. may be added to nouns (genitival), to verbs (objective), or to particles (indirect object with לְ, direct object with אֵת, partitive with מִן, agency with בְּ, etc.).

§23.121 The forms of the pron. suf. genitival (added to nouns, participles, infinitives construct, and prepositions) are:

PGN		SUFFIX before sg.		SUFFIX before pl.		MEANING
3ms	s0	־הוּ	־וֹ	ָ־יו	ָ־ו	of him, his
3fs	s1	־הָ	ָ־הּ	ֶ־יהָ		of her, hers
2ms	s2	־ךָ	ְ־ךָ	ֶ־יךָ		of you (m.), your
2fs	s3	־ךְ	ֵ־ךְ	ַ־יִךְ	ַ־יִךְ	of you (f.), your
1cs	s4	־י	ִ־י	ַ־י	ָ־י	of me, my
3mp	s5	־הֶם	ָ־ם	ֵ־יהֶם		of them (m.), their
3fp	s6	־הֶן	ָ־ן	ֵ־יהֶן		of them (f.), their
2mp	s7	־כֶם	ְ־כֶם	ֵ־יכֶם		of you (m.), your
2fp	s8	־כֶן	ְ־כֶן	ֵ־יכֶן		of you (f.), your
1cp	s9	־נוּ	ֵ־נוּ	ֵ־ינוּ		of us, our

§23.122 The forms of the pron. suf. objective (added to finite verbs) are:

PGN		SUFFIX			MEANING
3ms	s0	הוּ -			him
3fs	s1	הָ -	or	הּ ֶ -	her
2ms	s2	ךָ -			you (m.)
2fs	s3	ךְ -			you (f.)
1cs	s4	נִי -			me
3mp	s5	הֶם -	or	ם ָ -	them (m.)
3fp	s6	ן ָ -			them (f.)
2mp	s7	כֶם -			you (m.)
2fp	s8				you (f.) unattested
1cp	s9	נוּ -			us

§23.1221 To add emphasis, or sometimes, apparently, just for a stylistic device, a *nûn* is inserted between the verb and the suffix (§13.721). This is often called *nûn energicum,* even when it has no energic value.) Usually this nûn assimilates to the following consonant, if any, but in the case of *-hû* or *-hā* the ה assimilates to the nûn (§13.13):

-a + n + nî	> *-ánnî*	ַ-נִּי		תְּבַעֲתַנִּי
-e + n + kā	> *-ékkā*	ֶ-ךָּ	or ֶ-כָּה	וַיֶּאֱהָבֶךָּ
-e + n + hû	> *énnû*	ֶ-נּוּ		יְכַסֶּנּוּ
-e + n + hā	> *-énnā*	ֶ-נָּה		תְּכַלֶּנָּה

§23.123 The addition of a pronominal suffix to a particle often results in an unusual form of the particle which the student must learn to recognize.

§23.1231 When a pron.suf. is added to the prep. מִן, a reduplicated form of the prep. is used (except with the "heavy" suffixes s5, s6, s7, s8): **minminhû* > *mimménnû* מִמֶּנּוּ 'from him.'

§23.1232 When a pron. suf. is added to the prep. -כְּ, a long form -כְּמוֹ is used: כָּמֹוהָ. A similar form of -בְּ is sometimes used for "ballast" in poetical passages: בְּמוֹ־אֵשׁ (Isa. 43:2).

§23.1233 When a pron. suf. is added to the sign of the definite direct object (commonly vocalized ־אֶת)it is vocalized ־את *'ōt*, except with s7: + s0 אתוֹ, + s4 אתִי, but + s7 אֶתְכֶם. Occasionally for s5 we find אֶתְהֶם, and for s8 אֶתְהֶן. Cf. *Ges.* §103*b*.

§23.13 Certain phenomena may occur when adding a pronominal suffix, which must be understood for proper identification of the suffix and/or the attached form.

§23.131 Due to elision (§13.52) forms arise which may not be immediately recognized.

§23.1311 Resulting from syncopation of ה, the 3ms suf. (s0) often develops: *-áhû* > *-aw* > *-ô* (either ו— or ה—). *Ges.* §58*d.*

§23.1312 Similarly, *-tî* + *-hû* > *-tîhû* > *-tî^y^w* תִּיו—. *Ges.* §58*d.*

§23.1313 By apocopation (§13.53) of the final short-*a* of its normal form *-ā̆hā* (or *-éhā*), the 3fs (s1) sometimes develops: **-āhā* > *-āh* ־ָהּ. *Ges.* §58*e.*

§23.132 The addition of a pron. suf. may disturb syllabification and accent.

§23.1321 The connecting vowel, when present, will normally take the accent: נִי- + קָטַל > קְטָלַנִי.

§23.1322 The "heavy suffixes" ־הֶם, ־הֶן, ־כֶם, and ־כֶן always take the accent, whether preceded by a connecting vowel or not.

§23.1323 When no connecting vowel is present, the suffix takes the accent: ךָ— + קָטַל > קְטָלְךָ.

§23.1324 When the connecting vowel has developed to shewa, it is a "zero" shewa (see §15.2522), and the following kāph of a suffix is spirantized: ךָ- + לֵבָב > לְבָבְךָ.

§23.1325 After the addition of a pron. suf., the form with suffix will be vocalized according to the short-vowel rules. Note the illustrations in the preceding sections.

§23.14 For a summary of pronominal suffixes, see TABLE H.

§23.2 The old accusative ending *-a* is preserved in the suffixed particle ־ָה. The particle has locative or directive force and is often called *hê-locative* or *hê-directive*: שָׁמָּה 'there,' הֵנָּה 'here'; מִדְבָּרָה 'to the desert.' *Ges.* §90*c-i.*

§23.21 Since the locative particle rarely takes the accent, it can be distinguished from the normal feminine ending *-ā^h^* ־ָה (with accent). Furthermore, there is usually no alteration of the vowel pattern: צָפוֹן 'north,' צָפוֹנָה 'northward.'

§23.22 In some circumstances the vocalic pattern is altered by the addition of *hê-locative*. Of particular note are the segolates which are affected in the following ways:

§23.221 With the addition of the vocalic locative particle *-ā* a doubly-closed syllable no longer exists and an anaptyctic vowel is not required (review §15.61). The original form is preserved. Note the following carefully: **'arṣ* > *'éreṣ* אֶרֶץ but אַרְצָה; **bayt* > *báyiṯ* בַּיִת but בַּיְתָה; **qidm* > *qéḏem* קֶדֶם but קֵדְמָה, **nagb* > *néḡeḇ* נֶגֶב but נֶגְבָּה.

§23.222 When the 2d rad. of the segolate is ח or ע, a ḥaṭeph-vowel is often found, causing the accent to fall on an apparent antepenult (contrary to §§17.4). Thus הָאֹהֱלָה *hā-'ō-hĕ-lāʰ*; הַיַּעְרָה *hay-yá-'ă-rāʰ*. To avoid placing the accent on the antepenult, some scholars use the term "half-open" for the originally-closed syllable and consider such words as having only 3 syllables.

§23.23 It is possible that the locative morpheme is to be found in לַיְלָה 'night,' a noun always construed as masculine and with penultimate accent. Possibly the word originally meant 'at night,' and was later taken to mean simply 'night; cf. *Ges.* §90*f*, n.1.

§23.3 The *cohortative* particle, sometimes called the lengthened imperfect/imperative, is a suffixed morpheme added to the verb. It resembles the locative particle ָה– in form but it differs in that it may take the accent. Note אֶשְׁמְרָה, לְכָה, but אָשׁוּבָה, and נֵלְכָה.

§23.4 The suffixed adverbial particle *-ām* ָם–, when added to nouns, yields an adverbial form: יוֹם 'day,' יוֹמָם 'daily.' Cf. C. H. Gordon, *Ugaritic Textbook* (1965), §11.4.

§24. *Noun formation.* Nouns are formed in three ways: (a) original nouns, not derived from other words, called "primitive" nouns; (b) those formed from verbs, "deverbal" nouns; and (c) those formed from other nouns, "denominal" nouns. To these may be added (d) loan-words. Within these general classes, there are further morphological classifications, depending upon the internal vowel pattern, the use of pre- or sufformative elements, doubling or reduplication of certain radicals, etc. Cf. *Ges.* §§79-86.

§24.1 *Primitive nouns* are original noun forms that are *not* derived from a verbal root or from another noun. Cf. *Ges.* §§81, 82. Many such primitive nouns are biconsonantal and a few are even monoconsonantal. Formerly, Hebrew grammarians found very few such nouns, and often tried to trace these to 3-consonant roots (cf. אָב 'father,' listed in BDB under אבה 'to decide'). It seems highly improbable that early man moved from abstract to concrete ideas. Far more probable is the view that many verbal roots are really denominal, having been developed from primitive concrete words.

§24.11 Monoconsonantal primitive nouns (cv) are very rare; cf. *pê* פֶּה 'mouth,' and *śê* שֶׂה 'sheep, goat,' as possibilities.

§24.12 A number of primitive nouns have two consonants, with either a short vowel (CvC) or a long vowel (Cv̂C). Cf. the following: *dām* דָּם 'blood,' *yād* יָד 'hand,' *bēn* בֵּן 'son,' *'ēl* אֵל 'god,' *koᵃḥ* כֹּחַ 'strength,' *ṭôḇ* טוֹב 'good,' *qôl* קוֹל 'voice,' *šîr* שִׁיר 'song,' *rûᵃḥ* רוּחַ 'wind,' *lûᵃḥ* לוּחַ 'tablet.' See PARADIGM N-1.

§24.121 Certain 2-cons. words such as אָב 'father,' אָח 'brother,' etc., exhibit **peculiarities in morphology (e.g. cstr. אֲבִי, אֲחִי pl. אָבוֹת, אַחִים, Akk.** *'aḫḫû*). These have to be learned individually, for they conform to no general rule. Cf. *Ges.* §96 for tables. Memorize these words when you first come across them in reading. They are of very high frequency.

§24.122 Fem. nouns develop either CvCat or CvCt, cf. **dagat* > *dāgāʰ* דָּגָה, **bint* > *baṯ* בַּת (§15.33), pl. *bānôṯ* בָּנוֹת.

§24.1221 Fem. forms from Cv̂C are regular, but not common, cf. *dôḏāʰ* דּוֹדָה, and the pl. abs. and cstr. forms of *dôr, dôrôṯ* דּוֹרוֹת. Fem. forms of the G ptcp. (G51, 53, etc.) of Cv̂C verbs fall into this category, but they are not primitive nouns.

§24.13 There are also certain 3-cons. nouns which must be considered as "primitive," since they stand for things which are basic to the earliest conceivable stage of language, e.g. קֶרֶן 'horn,' אֶרֶץ 'earth,' שֶׁמֶשׁ 'sun,' יָרֵחַ 'moon,' רֶגֶל 'foot,' etc.

§24.2 *Deverbal nouns* are derived from verbal roots. In many cases it is difficult to determine whether the noun came first (in which case the verb is denominal) or the verb. Various classes of nouns are distinguished by internal vocalic pattern, or by the derivation of the noun from one of the derived verbal stems.

§24.21 A large number of nouns are formed with one short vowel (CvCC): **malk* > *mélek̲* מֶלֶךְ, *sipr > *sēper* סֵפֶר, **qudš* > *qōḏesᵉ* קֹדֶשׁ. See PARADIGM N-2. See §15.61.

§24.211 **If there is a guttural in the root (GCC, CGC, CCG), the vocalic pattern may be altered, particularly when the guttural is in the 2d or 3d** radical. **na'r* > *ná'ar* נַעַר, **pu'l* > *pṓ'al* פֹּעַל, **zar'* > *zéra'* זֶרַע, **niṣḥ* > *nḗṣaḥ* נֵצַח. See PARADIGM N-2.

§24.212 If the root has a medial *wāw* or *yôḏ* (CWC, CYC), monophthongization occurs (§15.72ff.) **mawt* > *mā́weṯ*, cstr. *môṯ* מוֹת, **zayt* > *záyiṯ*, cstr. *zêṯ* זֵית.

§24.213 If the root ends in *yōḏ* (CCY), the basic CvCY form may be distorted almost beyond recognition. **gady* > *gᵉḏî* גְּדִי; **ḥiṣy* > *ḥắṣî* חֲצִי, *ḥuly > *ḥŏlî* חֳלִי. See PARADIGM N-2.

§24.214 If the second radical is repeated for the third (CC²), the basic pattern is no longer apparent. CaC² *'amm > 'am עַם, 'ammî עַמִּי CiC² *'izz > 'ēz עֵז, 'izzîm עִזִּים CuC² *ḥuqq > ḥōq חֹק, ḥuqqî חֻקִּי.

§24.215 The originally monosyllabic forms developed fem. forms quite regularly. *malk + at > *malkat > malkāʰ מַלְכָּה, *šipḥat > šip̄ḥāʰ שִׁפְחָה, *ḥurbat > ḥorbāʰ חָרְבָּה. For cstr., suf., and pl. forms, see PARADIGM N-3.

§24.216 The pl. of CvCC nouns is irregular in that it takes the form of the pl. of CvCvC nouns in fpa: *mélek̲*, mpa *mᵉlāk̲îm* מְלָכִים, mpc *malk̲ê* מַלְכֵי; *malkāʰ*, fpa *mᵉlāk̲ôt̲* מְלָכוֹת, fpc *malk̲ôt̲* מַלְכוֹת.

§24.22 Many nouns are formed with two short vowels (CvCvC). Theoretically, any combination of vowels is possible CaCaC, CaCiC, CaCuC, CiCaC, CiCiC, CiCuC, CuCaC, CuCiC, CuCuC. Not all are attested. Cf. *dabar > dāb̲ār דָּבָר, *zaqin > zāqēn זָקֵן, *'amuq > 'āmōq עָמֹק, *libab > lēb̲āb̲ לֵבָב, *bi'ir (?) > bᵉ'ēr בְּאֵר, *bi'uš (?) > *bᵉ'ōš > bō'š בֹּאשׁ, *muluk > mᵉlōk̲ מְלֹךְ. See PARADIGM N-4.

§24.221 Feminine nouns on this pattern generally add *at > -āʰ ָה to the basic (masc.) form. The normal short-vowel rules apply. *ṣadaqat > ṣᵉd̲āqāʰ צְדָקָה, *bahimat > bᵉhēmāʰ בְּהֵמָה. See PARADIGM N-5.

§24.222 If there were originally nouns of the pattern CvWvC or CvYvC, they are no longer distinguishable. Forms such as *báyit̲* בַּיִת, and *mā́wet̲* מָוֶת are properly identified as CvCC type, as the accent indicates (§24.212).

§24.223 Nouns built on this pattern from roots with a weak 3d rad. (CvCvY) are fairly common, and regularly end in -êʰ ֶה in m.s.a.: *śaday > śād̲êʰ שָׂדֶה.

§24.224 Nouns built on this pattern from CC² roots generally fall together with those of the CvC² pattern. A notable exception is *libab > lēb̲āb̲ לֵבָב, which also develops *libb > lēb̲ לֵב (suf. libbî לִבִּי).

§24.225 Nouns with two short vowels form feminine nouns in two ways, with the addition of *-at > -āʰ, or with the addition of -t with anaptyxis as applicable. Normal application of the short-vowel rules occurs.

§24.2251 With the addition of -at we get forms such as CaCaCat, *ṣadaqat > ṣᵉd̲āqāʰ צְדָקָה, CaCiCat, *bahimat > bᵉhēmāʰ בְּהֵמָה, etc.

§24.2252 The f.s.c. forms develop regularly., *ṣadaqat > ṣᵉd̲ᵉdat̲ > ṣidqat̲ צִדְקַת (R.19), *bahimat > behĕmat̲ בֶּהֱמַת (R.10b, R.21).

§24.2253 With the addition of -t we get forms such as : CaCiCt *ḥabirt > ḥāb̲éret̲ חֲבֶרֶת, *'amint > 'ĕmet̲ אֱמֶת (R.11; probably the original form was *'amant with application of R.20), CiCuCt *niḥušt > nᵉḥōšet̲ נְחֹשֶׁת.

§24.2254 The f.s.c. forms, since they can reduce no further, are like the f.s.a.

§24.2255 The f.p.a. and f.p.c. forms are regular, with application of short-vowel rules.

§24.23 Many Heb. nouns are formed with one long and one short vowel (cv̂cvc). The long vowel is often *â > ô (R.2b). CâCaC, *'âlam > 'ôlām עוֹלָם, CâCiC, *'âyib > 'ôyēḇ אוֹיֵב, CâCaY, *ḥâzay > ḥôzē^h חוֹזֶה, CûCaC, *'ûgab > 'ûgāḇ עוּגָב. See PARADIGM N-6.

§24.231 The introduction of gutturals and other "weak" consonants can cause "irregularities" in the vowel pattern, following the phonetic rules.

§24.232 Fem. nouns are formed either by adding *-at > -ā^h or by adding -t.

§24.233 The G ptcp of the CaCaC verb (CôCēC, קוֹטֵל) is formed in this manner. See §§27.62ff. In m.s.c., the ṣêrê does not reduce.

§24.24 Other Heb. nouns are formed with one short and one long vowel (cvcv̂c). The distinction between Cv̂CvC and CvCv̂C is to be noted carefully, for the nuance of meaning of words is given by the vowel pattern (and also by consonantal pattern). CaCâC, *gadâl > gāḏôl גָּדוֹל, CaCîC, *paqid > pāqîḏ פָּקִיד, CaCûC, *'amûn > 'āmûn אָמוּן, CiCâC, *ḥimâr > ḥămôr חֲמוֹר, CiCîC, *kisîl > k^esîl כְּסִיל, CiCûC, *gibûl > g^eḇûl גְּבוּל. See PARADIGM N-7.

§24.241 Since both i- and u-vowels reduce in near-open syllables under the same conditions (§15.241), it is quite possible that CiCv̂C and CuCv̂C forms have fallen together.

§24.242 Fem. nouns in general are built regularly, usually with the addition of *-at > -ā^h. In a number of cases, however, particularly when the long vowel is û, the 3d rad. is geminate. We should perhaps consider such forms as built on a cvcv̂c² pattern.

§24.243 The addition of the fem. morpheme -t causes reduction of the long vowel (R.2a). Thus gibîr (גְּבִיר) + -t > *gibirt > g^eḇéreṯ גְּבֶרֶת.

§24.244 The G-pass. ptcp. (Gp50) is formed on the pattern CaCûC: qāṭôl קָטוֹל.

§24.2441 The "Aramaic-type" G-pass. ptcp. is formed on the pattern CaCîC. A large number of adjectives used as substantives, built on this pattern, are found in Bib. Heb., cf. māšî^aḥ 'anointed (one),' pāqîḏ 'one appointed,' nāśî' 'one lifted up, prince,' nāḡîḏ 'one set in front, ruler,' nāḇî' 'one called by a deity, prophet.'

§24.245 The G inf. abs. (G60) is formed on the pattern CaCôC: qāṭôl קָטוֹל.

§24.25 There are some nouns with two long vowels, Cv̂Cv̂C, usually *CîCôC*: *qîṭôr* קִיטוֹר, *šîḥôr* שִׁיחוֹר, *qîmôš* קִימוֹשׁ. It has been suggested that these have developed by compensation for CiC^{2}v̂C, *Ges.* §84*u*. See PARADIGM N-8.

§24.26 A large number of nouns are formed with geminate middle radical (CvC^{2}vC). The idea of the D-stem is suggested in words of habit, occupation, quality, etc. *šabbāt* שַׁבָּת, *kikkār* כִּכָּר, *qaddēš* קַדֵּשׁ, *'iwwēr* עִוֵּר, *ṭabbâḥ* טַבָּח, *šikkôr* שִׁכּוֹר, *'addîr* אַדִּיר, *'ammûḏ* עַמּוּד, *šiqqûṣ* שִׁקּוּץ. PARADIGM N-9.

§24.261 Fem. forms built on this pattern develop with *-at* > *-ā*^{h} or with *-t*. **yabbašat* > *yabbāšā*^{h} יַבָּשָׁה, **'iwwalt* > *'iwwéleṯ* אִוֶּלֶת, **kuttunt* > *kuttōneṯ* כֻּתֹּנֶת.

§24.27 Nouns with geminate third radical (*qatall* or *qatlal*, with other vocalizations) usually indicate inherent qualities, colors, etc. **qaṭânn* > *qāṭôn*, pl. *q*^{e}*ṭannîm* קְטַנִּים, **ḥamišš* > *ḥāmêš*, cstr. *ḥămêš*, pl. *ḥămiššîm* חֲמִשִּׁים, **na'ṣûṣ* > **na'ăṣûṣ*, pl. *na'ăṣûṣîm* נַעֲצוּצִים, see PARADIGM N-10.

§24.271 Fem. nouns built on this pattern are readily distinguishable because the gemination is preserved by the *-ā*^{h} ending. *g*^{e}*ḏullā*^{h} גְּדֻלָּה, *'ăniyyā*^{h} עֲנִיָּה, but cf. ^{8}*ḥamîššat* > *ḥămiššā*^{h} חֲמִשָּׁה, cstr. **ḥamîšt* > *ḥămēšeṯ* חֲמֵשֶׁת.

§24.28 Nouns formed by reduplication often denote colors and conditions. The reduplication may involve the last two radicals (*q*^{e}*ṭalṭal*), or in the case of a biconsonantal or hollow root, it may involve both radicals (*qalqal*, with other vocalizations). See PARADIGM N-11.

§24.281 For the form *q*^{e}*ṭalṭal*, cf. *y*^{e}*raqraq* יְרַקְרַק, *p*^{e}*ṯaltōl* פְּתַלְתֹּל.

§24.282 For the form *qalqal*, cf. *gilgal* גִּלְגָּל, *kalkēl* כַּלְכֵּל, *kaḏkōḏ* כַּדְכֹּד, **qudqud* > *qoḏqōḏ* קָדְקֹד.

§24.283 Fem. nouns built on this pattern may add *-ā*^{h} or *-t*. **ḥaparparat* > **ḥăp̄arpārā*^{h} חֲפַרְפָּרָה*, pl. *ḥăp̄arpārôṯ* חֲפַרְפָּרוֹת, *y*^{e}*raqraqqā*^{h} יְרַקְרַקָּה, **'ăḏamdamt* > *'ăḏamdémeṯ* אֲדַמְדֶּמֶת, **gulgult* > *gulgōleṯ* גֻּלְגֹּלֶת.

§24.284 The D inf. cstr. (D65) of CC^2 and CWC verbs is built on this pattern: **sabbēb* > *sôḇēḇ* סוֹבֵב, **qawwēm* > *qômēm* קוֹמֵם.

§24.3 Many deverbal nouns are formed with *preformative* elements. The student will readily understand this method of noun formation when he has studied verb morphology. See PARADIGM N-12.

§24.31 Preformative *hê* is used for the formation of infinitives (verbal nouns) of the H-, N-, and HtDstems. Many H60 forms have become adverbs (cf. *Ges.* §113*k*): הַשְׁכֵּם; cf. הַמְלֵט,, fem. הֵנָּפָה, הַכָּרָה.

§24.32 Preformative *yôḏ* is common in names, less common in ordinary noun forms: יְקוּם, יָרִיב.

§24.33 Preformative *mêm* is extremely common. D-, H-, and HtD-ptcps., places, instruments, agents, actions, qualities, etc., are nouns of such formation. Several vocalizations are found. Cstr. and pl. forms are regular. Cf. *malqôaḥ* מַלְקוֹחַ, *maḇdîl* מַבְדִּיל, *malbûš* מַלְבּוּשׁ, *mistôr* מִסְתּוֹר,

§24.34 Preformative *nûn* is found in N ptcp. forms: נוֹלָד, נִמְצָאִים.

§24.35 Preformative *šîn* is found occasionally, perhaps with a causative significance: *šaCCaCt*, **šalhabt* > שַׁלְהֶבֶת. Cf. *Ges.* §§55*i*, 85*o*.

§24.36 Preformative *tāw* is frequently found, particularly with original *WCC ("Pe Waw") and CWC stems, supposedly for the purpose of "strengthening" them. In some cases, at least, it suggests a possible relationship with the T-causative element of Coptic, and may be an Egypto-Semitic survival. Vocalizations include the following: **tawšab* > *tôšāḇ* תּוֹשָׁב, **tayman* > *têmān* תֵּימָן, *tašbēṣ* תַּשְׁבֵּץ, *talmîḏ* תַּלְמִיד, *tağmûl* תַּגְמוּל.

§24.361 Fem. forms with *tāw* preformative include the following vocalizations: **tawḥalt* > *tôḥéleṯ* תּוֹחֶלֶת, **tip'arat* > *tip̄'ārāh* תִּפְאָרָה, **tahpûkât* > *tahpûḵôṯ* תַּהְפֻּכוֹת.

§24.37 Preformative *'ālep̄* common in Arab. and other Sem. languages, frequently indicates an adjectival function, e.g. אַכְזָב 'deceitful,' אַכְזָר 'cruel,' אֵיתָן 'perennial.' *Ges.* §19*m*.

§24.4 Some nouns are formed with sufformatives. See PARADIGM N-13.

§24.41 Sufformative *lāmeḏ*, in my opinion, is very dubious. Cf. *Ges.* §85*t*.

§24.42 Sufformative *mêm* is perhaps related to the adverbial particle (§23.4): אוּלָם. Cf. *Ges.* §85*t*.

§24.43 Sufformative *nûn* is often found: גָּאוֹן, הָמוֹן, חָזוֹן. Cf. *Ges.* §585*u*. Some nouns commonly classified in this category are probably original quadriconsonantals.

§24.431 The ending **-ân* > וֹן- in some cases suggests the superlative degree: רִאשׁוֹן 'foremost,' אַחֲרוֹן 'last,' אֶלְיוֹן 'highest.' This may be related to the so-called *nûn energicum* found in certain verbs.

§24.44 To form the verbal noun, *-t* is added to certain roots that undergo apheresis (§13.511). This is sometimes called a "ballast *t*" (§13.513).

§24.5 *Denominal nouns* are those formed from other nouns. See PARADIGM N-13.

§24.51 Some nouns are formed on the G-ptcp. pattern from other nouns: שֹׁעֵר 'porter' < שַׁעַר 'gate'; בֹּקֵר 'herdsman' < בָּקָר 'herd.' Cf. *Ges.* §86*c*.

§24.52 Some nouns are formed on the CaC²âC-pattern from other nouns: קַשָּׁת 'archer' < קֶשֶׁת 'bow.' Cf *Ges.* §86*d*.

§24.53 Some nouns are formed from other nouns by the addition of preformative *mêm*, indicating place: מַעְיָן 'place of fountain' < עַיִן 'fountain,' מַרְגְּלוֹת 'place about the feet' < רֶגֶל 'foot.' Cf. *Ges.* §86*e*.

§24.54 Sufformative *-ân* or *-ôn* with an adjectival force (cf. §24.431) is sometimes used to form denominal nouns: קַדְמוֹן 'eastern' < קֶדֶם 'east'; חִיצוֹן 'outer, external' < חוּץ 'outside.' Cf. *Ges.* §86*f*.

§24.55 Sufformative *-î* (*ḥîrîq mālē'* ִי-) is used to form ordinal numbers, patronymics, tribal names, etc.: שְׁלִישִׁי 'third' < שָׁלוֹשׁ 'three'; מוֹאָבִי 'Moabite' < מוֹאָב 'Moab.' Note especially בֶּן יְמִינִי or simply יְמִינִי 'Benjamite' < בִּנְיָמִן 'Benjamin.' Cf. *Ges.* §86*h*.

§24.551 Notice the pl. and fem. formations of such denominal nouns: מוֹאָבִיָּה/מוֹאָבִית 'Moabitess'; עִבְרִיּוֹת, עִבְרִיִּים 'Hebrews.'

§24.56 Sufformative *šûrûq tāw* (וּת-) is added to a noun to form an abstract noun: יַלְדוּת 'youth' < יֶלֶד 'child'; עַלְמָנוּת 'widowhood' < עַלְמָנָה 'widow'; מַלְכוּת 'royalty, kingship/-dom' < מֶלֶךְ. Cf *Ges.* §86*k*.

§24.561 Sufformative *-îṯ* (ִית-) may be related to the abstract *-ûṯ* ending, cf. שְׁאֵרִית 'remainder, remnant.' Cf. *Ges.* §86*l*.

§24.57 Multiple afformatives are occasionally found. Note the following: קוּם 'to stand,' קוֹמְמִי 'upright,' קוֹמְמִיּוּת 'in an upright position'; כזר 'to be cruel,' אַכְזָר 'cruel,' אַכְזָרִי 'merciless,' אַכְזְרִיּוּת 'cruelty.' Cf. *Ges.* §86*k*.

§24.6 There are a number of nouns of peculiar formation which cannot be included in any rule. They must be learned as they are encountered. See PARADIGM N-14.

§24.7 *Loan words*, or words of foreign derivation, must likewise be learned as they are encountered.

§25. *Noun inflection.* Inflection is the change in form which is made to show the relationship of the inflected word to other words in a phrase, clause, or sentence. In Heb., inflection includes those changes of form which serve to indicate *case, gender, number,* and often *comparison.* Cf. *Ges.* §§87-96.

§25.1 *Gender.* In Heb. only *masculine* and *feminine* gender are distinguished. There is normally no *neuter.* (In some words, *personal* and *impersonal* forms are distinguished, cf. §21.4.) The m. and f. morphemes were not originally sex-indicators, as can be seen from the primitive nouns אָבוֹת 'fathers,' which has a f.p. morpheme, and נָשִׁים 'women,' which has a m.p. morpheme. It is not correct to call the *impersonal* forms "neuter," since the word neuter implies a third something, being *neither* the first nor the second.

§25.11 The *masc. sg.* form is generally the *basic* form of the word, with no morphological change in the absolute state (§25.4). We sometimes refer to it as the "zero morpheme" (∅). *dāḇār* דָּבָר 'a word, thing'; *dôḏ* דּוֹד 'uncle.'

§25.12 The *masc. pl.* is formed by adding *-îm* ־ִים to the basic word, cf. §25.231.

§25.13 The *fem. sg.* form generally adds **at* > *-āʰ* ־ָה to the basic word. There may be vowel alteration due to accent shift. **dôḏ* + *aṯ* > **dôdat* > *dôḏāʰ* דּוֹדָה; **malk* + *-at* > **malkat* > *malkāʰ* מַלְכָּה.

§25.131 Less often the fem. sg. adds *-t* ־ת to the basic word. If a doubly-closed syllable would result, anaptyxis occurs (§15.61). *šēnî* + *-t* > *šēnîṯ* שֵׁנִית; *maggēd* + *-t* > **maggēdt* > *maggéḏeṯ* מַגֶּדֶת.

§25.14 The *fem. pl.* form generally adds **-ât* > *-ôṯ* ־וֹת to the basic word, i.e. *in place of* the fem. sg. ending: *bᵉṯûlāʰ, bᵉṯûlôṯ* בְּתוּלוֹת 'virgins.'

§25.15 There are a number of irregular nouns which do not follow the above patterns. They must be learned as they are encountered.

§25.2 *Number.* Originally, 3 numbers were indicated, *singular* (one), *dual* (two), and *plural* (three or more).

§25.21 The *sing.* has been discussed, §§25.11, .12.

§25.22 The du. remains only in certain nouns referring to parts of the body that occur in pairs (עֵינַיִם 'eyes,' אָזְנַיִם 'ears,' רַגְלַיִם 'feet,' etc.), and a few other nouns.

§25.221 The du. ending is ־ַיִם -*áyim* in the absolute state. This ending is added directly to the ground-form of masc. nouns and to the original *-*at* or *-*t* of fem. nouns (cf. §25.13f): (m.) יוֹם 'day,' יוֹמַיִם 'two days'; רֶגֶל 'foot,' רַגְלַיִם '(two) feet'; (f.) שָׂפָה 'lip,' שְׂפָתַיִם 'lips'; נְחֹשֶׁת 'copper, bronze,' נְחֻשְׁתַּיִם 'bronze chains.'

§25.23 The *plural* is formed by adding pl. morphemes to the basic word, as follows:

§25.231 The *masc. pl.* is formed by adding -*îm* ־ִים to the basic word. Vocalic alteration may result. **dabar* + -*îm* > *d*ᵉ*b̲ārîm* דְּבָרִים; **malk* + -*î* > *m*ᵉ*lāk̲îm* מְלָכִים; **šamônay* + *îm* > *š*ᵉ*mônîm* שְׁמוֹנִים.

§25.232 The *fem. pl.* is formed by adding -*ôt̲* ־וֹת to the basic word (not to the f. sg.!). **dôd̲* + -*ā*ʰ > *dôd̲ā*ʰ דּוֹדָה (sing.), but note *dôd̲* + -*ôt̲* > *dôd̲ôt̲* דּוֹדוֹת (plur.).

§25.3 *Case.* Judging from comparative study and from a few residual morphemes, we assume that Heb. originally differentiated 3 cases morphologically: *nominative* in -*u* (subject of sentence) *genitive* in -*i* (object of preps. and the second word [*nomen rectum*] in construct [annexion, §25.42]), and *accusative* in -*a* (obj. of transitive verbs and certain adverbial uses). Except for residual examples, these case-endings have become lost in Bib. Heb. Cf. *Ges.* §90.

§25.31 The nom. is rarely found in Bib. Heb. It is possibly preserved in פְּנוּ אֵל (in contrast with פְּנֵי אֵל), and in some rare forms, mostly found in poetic passages.

§25.32 The gen. -*i* (in some cases -*a*, cf. the Arab. diptote gen. -*a*) is probably preserved in some words with suffixed endings (see the long discussion in *Ges.* §90*l*-*n*), and survives as the "zero-shewa" (§15.2522) before suffixes (witness the spirantized *kap̄* in the endings -*k̲a* ־ְךָ and -*k̲em* ־ְכֶם).

§25.33 From cognate studies we assume that Heb. once had an acc. case ending in -*a*, but it is debatable whether there is surviving evidence.

§25.331 The locative particle -*ā*ʰ ־ָה is possibly a survival of the acc. case-ending, cf. §23.2, *Ges.* §90*c*-*i*.

§25.4 *State* is a concept foreign to our language system, and therefore difficult to explain in meaningful terms. It is best understood as we see it (see discussion under Syntax). Among the Sem. languages in general, we find the following: *absolute state, construct state, emphatic state,* and *indeterminate state.* Only the first two are normally identified in Heb. (a) *Absolute state* (abs.;

sometimes *status absolutus, st. abs.*) describes a noun or substantive which is *not* bound to the following word by annexion. (b) *Construct state* (cstr., *status constructus, st. cstr.*) describes a noun or substantive which *is* bound to the following word by annexion.

§25.41 In the *absolute* state, a word bears a major stress-accent, hence the vowels are in the normal form for that word. A word in abs. may take def. art.

§25.411 A noun with pron. suf. also bears a major stress-accent, but it is not in abs. (cf. §25.5ff.).

§25.42 In the *construct* state, a noun has no major stress-accent, hence the vowels may undergo qualitative alteration, and other differences may occur.

§25.421 The *masc. sg. cstr.* (msc) will have reduced vowels wherever the rules apply: abs. *dāḇār* דָּבָר, cstr. *dᵉḇar 'esṯer* דְּבַר אֶסְתֵּר.

§25.4211 Segolates do not undergo vocalic reduction: abs. *méleḵ*, cstr. *méleḵ yᵉhûḏāʰ* מֶלֶךְ יְהוּדָה.

§25.4212 The *ṣêrê* in a number of words does not reduce: *lēḇ*, cstr. *lēḇ hamméleḵ* לֵב הַמֶּלֶךְ; all G52s of the *CôCēC* type.

§25.4213 Substantives ending in *–êʰ* ־ֶה take the ending *–ēʰ* ־ֵה in cstr.: abs. *mištêʰ* מִשְׁתֶּה, cstr. *mištēʰ nāšîm* מִשְׁתֵּה נָשִׁים.

§25.422 The *fem. sg. cstr.* (fsc) preserves the original *-at* ending. Vowel reduction occurs where applicable: abs. *ḥēmāʰ*, cstr. *ḥămaṯ hamméleḵ* חֲמַת הַמֶּלֶךְ; abs. *ṭôḇāʰ*, cstr. *ṭôḇaṯ mar'êʰ* טוֹבַת מַרְאֶה.

§25.4221 The f.s.c. of nouns formed by adding *-t* (§25.131) undergo vowel reduction if applicable.

§25.423 The du. cstr. ending was originally an **ay* diphthong which has monophthongized to *ê* (§15.732) written *ṣêrê yôḏ* ־ֵי. (m.) רַגְלֵי, (f.) שִׂפְתֵי. Note the similarity to the m.p.c. morpheme (§§25.424).

§25.424 The *masc. pl. cstr.* (mpc) is formed by adding **-ay* > *-êʸ* ־ֵי (§15.732) to the basic word. Vowel reduction will occur wherever the rules apply: **malk* + *-ay* > **malkay* > *malḵê qéḏem* מַלְכֵי קֶדֶם 'kings of east' = 'eastern kings'; **rô'êʰ* + *-ay* > **rô'ay* > *rô'êʸ pᵉnêʸ hamméleḵ* רֹאֵי פְּנֵי הַמֶּלֶךְ.

§25.425 The *fem. pl. cstr.* (fpc) is formed by adding **-ât* > *-ôṯ* וֹת– to the basic word. Vowel reduction occurs where applicable. Where it does not occur, the fpa and fpc forms are identical: abs. *šānôṯ* שָׁנוֹת, cstr. *šᵉnôṯ* שְׁנוֹת; abs. *ṭôḇôṯ* טוֹבוֹת, cstr. *ṭôḇôṯ* טוֹבוֹת.

§25.43 Because of the loss of stress-accent, words in cstr. undergo morphological change.

§25.431 Forms in masc. sg. have reduced vowels wherever possible: *dᵉ-ḇar ham-mélek̲* shows the reduction of vowels in the word *dā-ḇār*, abs. דָּבָר, cstr. דְּבַר.

§25.432 Forms in fem. sg. preserve the original *-at* ending (§25.13): *malkaṯ šéḇā'* 'the Queen of Sheba,' abs. מַלְכָּה, cstr. מַלְכַּת.

§25.433 Forms in *masc. pl. cstr.* (mpc) add **-ay* to the basic word, which diphthongizes in accordance with §15.732: **malk* + *ay* > **malkay* > *malk̲ê* מַלְכֵי קֶדֶם 'kings of east' = 'eastern kings.'

§25.434 Forms in *fem. pl. cstr.* (fpc) add **-ât* > *-ôṯ* וֹת– to the basic word (cf. fpa, §25.14); however, since a word in cstr. has no major stress-accent, the vowels will reduce according to the short-vowel rules (§§15.ff), cf. fpa *šānôṯ*, fpc *šᵉnôṯ*.

§25.5 A substantive may be inflected by adding a *pronominal suffix*. Grammatically this is equivalent to a noun in cstr., but since the suffixed word has a primary accent, we must treat *suffixial* forms separately. The pron. suf. or the connecting vowel takes the primary accent, hence there will be vocalic alteration in most of these forms.

§25.51 The *masc. sg. suf.* (mss) forms generally undergo accent shift and resulting vocalic alteration: *dāḇār* + *-ô* > *dᵉḇārô* דְּבָרוֹ.

§25.511 Nouns of CvCC type usually revert to the basic form **malk*, abs. *méleḵ*, suf. *malkḗnû* מַלְכֵּנוּ **sipr*, abs. *sép̄er*, suf. *sip̄rî* סִפְרִי **qudš*, abs. *qṓḏeš*, suf. *qoḏšᵉḵem* קָדְשְׁכֶם.

§25.512 Nouns of CCY type drop the final radical and add suf.: **śaday* > abs. *śāḏêʰ* שָׂדֶה, suf. *śāḏᵉḵā* שָׂדְךָ; **rô'ay* > abs. *rô'êʰ* רֹאֶה, suf. *rô'î* רֹאִי.

§25.513 Nouns of CvCY type, which develop to *-êʰ* ֶה– revert to the consonantal form of the 3d rad.: **piry* > abs. *pᵉrî*, suf. *piryô* פִּרְיוֹ; **yupy* > *yᵉp̄î*, suf. *yop̄yāʰ* יָפְיָהּ.

§25.52 *Fem. sg. suf.* (fss) forms revert to the original form with *-at* and add suf.: **malkat*, abs. *malkāʰ*, suf. *malkāṯî* מַלְכָּתִי, מַלְכַּתְכֶם; **ṣadaqat*, abs. *ṣᵉḏāqāʰ*, suf. *ṣiḏqāṯî* צִדְקָתִי; **gibirt*, abs. *gᵉḇéreṯ*, suf. *gᵉḇirtî* גְּבִרְתִּי.

§25.53 The *masc. pl. suf.* (mps) forms add *-ay* > *-ê*^{y} ־ֵי to the basic word. This becomes the connecting vowel except with s0 and s4 (3ms and 1cs), and takes the accent except with "heavy" suffixes (s5, s6, s7, s8): **malk* + *-ay* > *malkê* + s9 > *malkênû* מַלְכֵּינוּ; **dabar* + *-ay* > *dib̲rê* + s2 > *d*^{e}*b̲ārê*^{y}*k̲ā* דְּבָרֶיךָ.

§25.531 Words from CCY roots drop the last radical before adding *-ay*: **ḥôzay* + *-ay* > *ḥôzê*^{y} + s2 > *ḥôzé*^{y}*k̲ā* חֹזֶיךָ.

§25.532 With s0 (3ms) and s4 (1cs) a different pattern develops in the vocalic alteration: *dāb̲ār* + *-ay* > *dib̲rê* + s4 > *d*^{e}*b̲ārî* דְּבָרַי; *ʿéb̲ed̲* + *-ay* > *ʿab̲d̲ê* + s0 > *ʿăb̲āḏā*^{y}*w* עֲבָדָיו.

§25.533 The "heavy suffixes" always bear the major stress-accent, with resulting vowel reduction: *dāb̲ār* + *-ay* + *kem* (s7) > *dib̲rê*^{y}*k̲ém* דִּבְרֵיכֶם; *ḥāk̲ām* + *-ay* + *-kem* > *ḥak̲mê*^{y}*k̲ém* חַכְמֵיכֶם.

§25.54 *Fem. pl. suf.* (fps) forms add *-ay* > *-ê* to the *plural* form, resulting in a form that appears to have both fem. and masc. pl. morphemes. Vocalic alteration usually occurs: *š*^{e}*d̲āqôt̲* + *-ay* + s4 > *šid̲qôt̲ay* צִדְקֹתַי; *naʿărôt̲* + *-ay* + s1 > *naʿărôt̲éhā* נַעֲרוֹתֶיהָ.

§25.6 Certain nouns of very common occurrence form their construct and plural forms irregularly. These must be learned by observation. See PARADIGM N-15., *Ges.* §96.

§26. *Adjectives.* We are concerned here only with the morphology of adjs.; the syntax of adjs. will be discussed in §36.

§26.1 Most "adjectives" in Bib. Heb. are either nouns or stative verbs. To serve adjectivally, substantives may be placed in cstr. ('a hill of holiness' = 'a holy hill'), or the modifier may be inflected to agree with its substantive.

§26.11 The inflection of adjs. or of words used adjectivally is completely regular. The masc., fem., sg., and pl. forms will be formed regularly according to the consonant-and-vowel pattern for the word in question. There will be no irregular plur. forms.

§26.2 The *numerals* were originally substantives, and often occur in construct with their nouns. *Cardinal numbers* are used for counting or telling *how many.* Cf. *Ges.* §97. Because the numerals are less regular than other words used adjectivally, we shall study them in detail.

§26.21 The word for '1' occurs in the following forms:

m.s.a.	אֶחָד	*'eḥād*	m.s.c.	אַחַד	*'aḥad*
f.s.a.	אַחַת	*'aḥat*	f.s.c.	אַחַת	*'aḥat*

§26.211 The original form, based on the vocalization, would appear to be **'aḥḥadu,* but the Arab. cognate *'aḥadu* does not support this.

§26.212 Fem. **'aḥadtu* > **'aḥatt* > *'aḥat* אַחַת.

§26.213 The plur. אֲחָדִים means 'some.'

§26.22 The word for '2' has the dual ending: m.d.a. *šnáyim* שְׁנַיִם, m.d.c. *šnê* שְׁנֵי, f.d.a. *štáyim* שְׁתַּיִם, f.d.c. *štê* שְׁתֵּי.

§26.221 The words for '2' begin with an initial cluster (§16.12, §16.351), but whether this was original in PS is not certain; on the one hand, Arab. *iθnân* (without *ḥamzā*) suggests that it was original, but Arab. *θintân* may suggest just the opposite.

§26.23 The numbers '3' through '9' are declined as follows. *Note that the forms with the* fem. *endings are used with* masc. *nouns!*

	WITH MASCULINE				WITH FEMININE			
	ABS.		CSTR.		ABS.		CSTR.	
'3'	שְׁלשָׁה	*š^{e}lôšā^h*	שְׁלשֶׁת	*š^{e}lôšet*	שָׁלשׁ	*šālôš*	שְׁלשׁ	*š^{e}lôš*
'4'	אַרְבָּעָה	*'arbā'ā^h*	אַרְבַּעַת	*'arbá'at*	אַרְבַּע	*'arba'*	אַרְבַּע	*'arba'*
'5'	חֲמִשָּׁה	*ḥămiššā^h*	חֲמֵשֶׁת	*ḥăméšet*	חָמֵשׁ	*ḥāmēš*	חֲמֵשׁ	*ḥămēš*
'6'	שִׁשָּׁה	*šiššā^h*	שֵׁשֶׁת	*šéšet*	שֵׁשׁ	*šēš*	שֵׁשׁ	*šēš*
'7'	שִׁבְעָה	*šib'ā^h*	שִׁבְעַת	*šib'at*	שֶׁבַע	*šéba'*	שֶׁבַע	*šéba'*
'8'	שְׁמֹנָה	*š^{e}mônā^h*	שְׁמֹנַת	*š^{e}mônat*	שְׁמֹנֶה	*š^{e}mônê^h*	שְׁמֹנֶה	*š^{e}mônê^h*
'9'	תִּשְׁעָה	*tiš'ā^h*	תִּשְׁעַת	*tiš'at*	תֵּשַׁע	*téša'*	תְּשַׁע	*téša'*

§26.231 The word *šālôš* developed from **θalâθ* (§12.65).

§26.2311 The fem. developed from **šalašt* > *šālôšet*, with application of Rules 2a, 6b. The suf. form is *š^{e}loštām* שְׁלָשְׁתָּם (note the *qāmāṣ ḥāṭûp*). With *maqqēp* we find both שְׁלֹשׁ־ and שְׁלָשׁ־.

§26.232 *'arba'* may have been a 4-cons. word, as cognates suggest (Arab. *'arba'u* has *hamza*). The ordinal, however, seems to suggest an original **rba'* to which prothetic *alif* has been added.

§26.233 *ḥāmēš* developed from **ḫamiš,* although Arab. *ḫamsu* suggests **ḫamš* (§12.62, §12.65).

§26.2331 The fem. *ḥămiššā^h* may have developed by analogy with *šiššā^h*.

§26.234 *šiššā*ʰ developed from **θdś* (cf. OSA), **θadšā* > **šadšā* (§12.65) > *šiššā* (§13.113, Rule 18).

§26.235 *šeḇaʿ* developed from **šabʿ* (Arab. *sabʿu,* §12.65), with anaptyxis (§15.61).

§26.2351 The form *šᵉḇaʿ* is found in שְׁבַע עֶשְׂרֵה '17' and שְׁבַע מֵאוֹת '700.'

§26.236 *šᵉmônê*ʰ developed from **θamânay* (Arab. *θamâni, θamâniyä*, §12.65, §14.11).

§26.237 *tēšaʿ* developed from **tišʿ* (Arab. *tisʿu,* §12.65), with anaptyxis (§15.61).

§26.2371 The form *tᵉšaʿ* is found in תְּשַׁע עֶשְׂרֵה '19' and תְּשַׁע מֵאוֹת '900.'

§26.24 The words for '10' are:

'10' עֲשָׂרָה *ʿăśārā*ʰ   עֲשֶׂרֶת *ʿăśereṯ*   עֶשֶׂר *ʿéśer*   עֶשֶׂר *ʿéśer*

§26.241 The masc. form developed from CaCC, Arab. *ʿašru,* while the fem. form developed from CaCaCat, Arab. *ʿašarä.*

§26.2411 The masc. from CaCaC עָשָׂר is found in the compound numbers 11-19.

§26.242 A fem. pl. form עֲשָׂרוֹת is found, meaning 'tens.'

§26.25 The numbers '11' to '19' are composed of the words for the units (§26.23) and special forms of the word for '10.' Note that whereas the fem. form of the unit is used with a masc. noun, just the reverse is true of the word for '10.'

	WITH MASC. NOUNS		WITH FEM. NOUNS	
'11'	אַחַד עָשָׂר	*ʾaḥaḏ ʿāśār*	אַחַת עֶשְׂרֵה	*ʾaḥaṯ ʿeśrē*ʰ
or	עַשְׁתֵּה עָשָׂר	*ʿaštê*ʰ *ʿāśār*	עַשְׁתֵּה עֶשְׂרֵה	*ʿaštê*ʰ *ʿeśrē*ʰ
'12'	שְׁנֵים עָשָׂר	*šnêʸm ʿāśār*	שְׁתֵּים עֶשְׂרֵה	*štêʸm ʿeśrē*ʰ
'13'	שְׁלֹשָׁה עָשָׂר	*šᵉlôšā*ʰ *ʿāśār*	שְׁלֹשׁ עֶשְׂרֵה	*šᵉlôš ʿeśrē*ʰ
'14'	אַרְבָּעָה עָשָׂר	*ʾarbāʿā*ʰ *ʿāśār*	אַרְבַּע עֶשְׂרֵה	*ʾarbaʿ ʿeśrē*ʰ
'15'	חֲמִשָּׁה עָשָׂר	*ḥămiššā*ʰ *ʿāśār*	חֲמֵשׁ עֶשְׂרֵה	*ḥămēš ʿeśrē*ʰ
'16'	שִׁשָּׁה עָשָׂר	*šiššā*ʰ *ʿāśār*	שֵׁשׁ עֶשְׂרֵה	*šēš ʿeśrē*ʰ
'17'	שִׁבְעָה עָשָׂר	*šiḇʿā*ʰ *ʿāśār*	שְׁבַע עֶשְׂרֵה	*šᵉḇaʿ ʿeśrē*ʰ
'18'	שְׁמֹנָה עָשָׂר	*šᵉmônā*ʰ *ʿāśār*	שְׁמֹנֶה עֶשְׂרֵה	*šᵉmônê*ʰ *ʿeśrē*ʰ
'19'	תִּשְׁעָה עָשָׂר	*tišʿā*ʰ *ʿāśār*	תְּשַׁע עֶשְׂרֵה	*tᵉšaʿ ʿeśrē*ʰ

§26.251 The form *ʿaštêʸ* in the alternate for '11' is cognate with Akk. *ištēn.* It appears to be cstr., as do all the unit words in the forms of '11'-'19' used with the fem.

§26.252 The forms for '12' *šnê*^{y} *'āśār* and *štê*^{y} *'eśrē*^{h} are also found.

§26.253 For the numbers '17' and '19,' see §§26.2351, .2371.

§26.26 The words for '20' to '90' (in the tens) are all plurals:

'20'	עֶשְׂרִים	*'eśrîm*
'30'	שְׁלוֹשִׁים	*š*^{e}*lôšîm*
'40'	אַרְבָּעִים	*'arbā'îm*
'50'	חֲמִשִּׁים	*ḥămiššîm*
'60'	שִׁשִּׁים	*šiššîm*
'70'	שִׁבְעִים	*šib̲'îm*
'80'	שְׁמֹנִים	*š*^{e}*mônîm*
'90'	תִּשְׁעִים	*tiš'îm*

§26.261 The number '20' is the pl. of '10.' It is not inflected.

§26.2611 This may have developed from the dual of '10,' **'eśráyim,* cf. Joüon §100*i*.

§26.2612 For '20,' '70,' and '90,' we should expect the normal pl. for segolates: **'ĕśārîm,* etc. *Ges.* §97*f,* n.2 asks whether the forms we have might be survivals of older pl. forms of segolates.

§26.262 Compound numbers are formed in various ways. Note the following:

'23'	20 + 3	עֶשְׂרִים וּשְׁלֹשָׁה	*'eśrîm ûš*^{e}*lôšā*^{h}
'32'	2 + 30	שְׁנַיִם וּשְׁלֹשִׁים	*šnáyim ûš*^{e}*lôšîm*
'127'	7 + 20 + 100	שֶׁבַע וְעֶשְׂרִים וּמֵאָה	*šéba' w*^{e}*'eśrîm ûmē'ā*^{h}
'675'	600 + 5 + 70	שֵׁשׁ מֵאוֹת חָמֵשׁ וְשִׁבְעִים	*šēš mē'ôt̲ ḥāmēš w*^{e}*šib̲'îm*
'1,254'	1,000 +200 +50 + 4	אֶלֶף מָאתַיִם חֲמִשִּׁים וְאַרְבָּעָה	*'élep̄ mā't̲áyim ḥămiššîm w*^{e}*'arbā'ā*^{h}

§26.2621 According to S. Herner, *Syntax der Zahlwörter im AT* (1893), 71ff., the smaller number more commonly precedes in Ezekiel and the Priestly Code, the larger elsewhere.

§26.27 The forms for the hundreds are as follows:

§26.271 The word for '100' is inflected: *mē'ā*^{h} מֵאָה, cstr. *m*^{e}*'at̲* מְאַת, pl. *mē'ôt̲* מֵאוֹת.

§26.2711 The form מאיות is found in 2 Kgs. 11:4,9,10,15 Kt, usually read מֵאָיוֹת 'hundreds.'

§26.272 The du. מָאתַיִם (*m^e'āṯáyim) means '200.'

§26.273 The words for '300' to '900' are composed of the units (in cstr.) and *mē'ōṯ*: *š^{e}lōš^e mē'ōṯ* שְׁלֹשׁ מֵאוֹת 'three of hundreds.'

§26.2731 For '700' and '900' cf. §§26.2351, .2371.

§26.2732 Note the pointing in '800': שְׁמֹנֶה מֵאוֹת.

§26.28 The numbers from '1,000' and up are formed as follows:

§26.281 '1,000' *'élep̄* אֶלֶף, pl. אֲלָפִים, cstr. אַלְפֵי, '2,000' du. אַלְפַּיִם.

§26.282 '3,000' *š^{e}lōšeṯ 'ălāp̄îm* שְׁלֹשֶׁת אֲלָפִים.

§26.283 Numbers above 10,000 may be formed in two ways, either using multiples of the word for '1,000' or using a word meaning 'myriad' (cf. *μυριας*).

§26.2831 '10,000' *'ăśéreṯ 'ălāp̄îm* עֲשֶׂרֶת אֲלָפִים, '18,000' *š^{e}mo^{h}nā^h 'āśār 'élep̄* שְׁמוֹנָה עָשָׂר אֶלֶף.

§26.2832 '10,000' *r^{e}ḇāḇā^h* רְבָבָה, or *ribbô* רִבּוֹ. '20,000' *ribboṯáyim* רִבֹּתַיִם (Ps. 68:18), probably 'myriads, tens of thousands'; also שְׁתֵּי רִבּוֹת (Neh. 7:70) and שְׁתֵּי רִבּוֹא (Neh. 7:71). '40,000' אַרְבַּע רִבּוֹא (Neh. 7:66).

§26.2833 '100,000' מְאַת אֶלֶף (Num. 2:9), מֵאָה אֶלֶף (2 Kg. 3:4).
§26.2833

§26.2834 אַלְפֵי רְבָבָה 'thousands of myriads' (Gen. 24:60).

§26.3 *Ordinal numbers* are used to express order or succession. *Ges.* §98.

§26.31 As in many languages, 'first' is not a numeral, but the word for 'head, chief' רִאשׁוֹן. It is declined as a noun ending in ־וֹן (§24.431).

§26.32 The ordinals '2d' to '9th' are formed by suffixing *-î*, fem. *-îṯ*, and, except for '2d' and '6th,' long *î* is infixed after the 2d rad.

'2d'	שֵׁנִי		*šēnî*	שֵׁנִית	שְׁנִיָּה	*šēnîṯ*	*š^{e}nîyā*
'3d'	שְׁלִישִׁי		*š^{e}lîšî*	שְׁלִישִׁית	שְׁלִישִׁיָּה	*š^{e}lîšîṯ*	*š^{e}lîšîyā^h*
'4th'	רְבִיעִי		*r^{e}ḇî'î*	רְבִיעִית		*r^{e}ḇî'îṯ*	
'5th'	חֲמִישִׁי	חֲמִשִׁי	*ḥămîšî*	חֲמִישִׁית		*ḥămîšîṯ*	
'6th'	שִׁשִּׁי		*šiššî*	שִׁשִּׁית		*šiššîṯ*	
'7th'	שְׁבִיעִי		*š^{e}ḇî'î*	שְׁבִיעִית		*š^{e}ḇî'îṯ*	
'8th'	שְׁמִינִי		*š^{e}mînî*	שְׁמִינִית		*šînîṯ*	
'9th'	תְּשִׁיעִי		*t^{e}šî'î*	תְּשִׁיעִית		*t^{e}šî'îṯ*	
'10th'	עֲשִׂירִי		*'ăśîrî*	עֲשִׂירִית	עֲשִׂירִיָּה	*'ăśîrîṯ*	*'ăśîrîyā^h*

§26.4 *Multiplicatives* are generally formed by using the dual: *'arba'táyim* אַרְבַּעְתָּיִם 'quadruple, fourfold' (2 Sam. 12:6), *šiḇ'āṯáyim* שִׁבְעָתַיִם 'sevenfold' (Gen. 4:15).

§26.41 Possibly the final *-m* was originally an adverbial ending (§Joüon §100*o*), but this fails to account for the diphthong.

§26.42 We also find שָׁלֹשׁ פְּעָמִים '3 times,' חָמֵשׁ יָדוֹת '5 hands (= times).'

§26.43 Note also the following: שֵׁנִית 'a second time' (Gen. 22:15), בַּשְּׁלִישִׁית 'the third time' (1 Sam. 3:8), בַּשְּׁבִיעִית 'the 7th time' (1 Kg. 18:44), פַּעַם חֲמִישִׁית 'a 5th time' (Neh. 6:5).

§26.44 For adverbial use, the following forms occur: אַחַת 'once,' שְׁתַּיִם 'twice,' שָׁלֹשׁ 'thrice.' Joüon §102f. suggests that פַּעַם 'time(s)' is to be understood.

§26.5 *Distributives* are formed in three ways.

§26.51 The repetition of the cardinal may be used: שְׁנַיִם שְׁנַיִם 'two by two,' שֵׁשׁ וָשֵׁשׁ 'six each,' אִישׁ־אֶחָד אִישׁ־אֶחָד לַשָּׁבֶט 'one man for each tribe' (Josh. 3:12).

§26.52 Periphrasis may be used: אֶחָד לְ– 'one for ...' (Num. 17:18).

§26.53 Or simply לְ– may be used: לְמֵאוֹת וְלַאֲלָפִים 'by hundreds and by thousands.' Ges. §134*q*.

§26.6 *Fractions* can be expressed by use of the ordinals (as in Eng.). In addition, we find the following:

½	חֲצִי	*ḥăṣî*		
⅓	שָׁלִישׁ	*šālîš*		
¼	רֶבַע	*réḇa'*	רֹבַע	*rṓḇa'*
⅕	חֹמֶשׁ	*ḥṓmeš*		
⅔	פִּי שְׁנַיִם	*pî šnáyim*		
⅒	עִשָּׂרוֹן	*'iśśārôn*	עֶשְׂרֹנִים	*'eśrônîm*

§26.7 The following special uses should be noted: שָׁבוּעַ pl. שָׁבוּעוֹת 'week'; עָשׂוֹר '10 days, 10th day,' עֲשָׂרוֹת 'groups of 10.'

§26.71 The *x*, *x* + 1 formula, the *x*, 11*x* formula, and similar, are not to be taken literally, but serve as rhetorical or stylistic devices: '3 ... 4 ... ' (Am. 1:3, etc., cf. Prov. 30:18,29); '2 ... 3 ... 4 ...' (Prov. 30:15), '6 ... 7 ...' (Prov. 6:16; Job 5:19), '7-fold ... 77 fold' (Gen.4:24). These devices are quite common in Ugar., cf. Gordon, *Ugar. Gram.* §7.46, §7.60.

§26.8 *Word order* with numerals is complex and often confusing.

§26.81 The numeral *one* is placed after its noun and in condord with it.

§26.82 The numerals 2 to 10 are placed before the noun, often in a cstr. form, and the noun is in the plur. *Ges.* §134*o*, n.2 explains the form not as *nomen regens* but as a connective form, the *gen. explicativus* or *epexegeticus* (*Ges.* §128*k*).

§26.83 The numerals 11 to 19 are placed before the noun which (usually) is in the sing.

§26.84 The numerals from 20 up may either precede or follow the noun. When they precede the noun, it is usually in the sing.; when the noun stands first it is in the plur.

§26.85 The numeral 100 is sometimes in the abs. when it precedes the noun.

§26.86 Numerals ending with 'thousands' generally precede and the word for 'thousands' is in cstr.

§26.87 The *ordinals* are adjectives and therefore follow the noun. Ordinal numerals which can be inflected are in concord. All ordinals agree in definiteness.

§26.871 In numbering the days of the month or the year, the cardinal is often used instead of the ordinal, and is sometimes in cstr.: בִּשְׁנַת שָׁלֹשׁ 'in year of 3' = 'in the 3d year.'

§26.872 Since there are no special forms for ordinals above 10, the cardinal is used, and may stand before or after the noun. *Ges.* §134*o*.

§26.9 Probably the best way to learn the peculiarities of the numbers is to read extensively in passages where many numbers are used, e.g. Gen. 5, Num. 29, 1 Kgs. 10, Ezra 2, etc.

§27. *Verb morphology* is probably the major stumbling-block for students trying to learn Hebrew. THE STUDENT MUST DETERMINE TO MASTER THE MAJOR PRINCIPLES AT ONCE, AND TO ADD TO THESE FAITHFULLY. The Semitic verbal system is *unlike* systems with which most of us are familiar. We must seek to understand the Semitic pattern. Many of the terms are the same, but what they represent are not like our English equivalents. We must learn what the terms mean as they are used with reference to Hebrew.

§27.1 The Heb. verb occurs in both *finite* and *nonfinite* forms. The forms in both categories can be inflected, although the inflections differ.

§27.11 The *finite* Heb. verb (§30.3321) may be inflected to show any or all of the following:
aspect (tense) (§30.333), §§27.2, .3
voice (§30.334),
mood (§30.335)
person (§30.336)
number (§30.337)
gender (§30.339)
derived stems
accusative suffixes

§27.111 The finite verb in the indicative (and subjunctive) may be inflected to show:
completed action, §27.2
incompleted action, §27.3

§27.1111 *Completed action* is generally past tense, hence this inflection is called *perfect, preterite, telic,* etc. In Heb. the tense (time of the action or state predicated by the verb) must be learned from context. Completed action may be *in the future!*

§27.1112 *Incompleted action* may be either some action or state that is occurring at the present or will occur in the future, hence this inflection is called *imperfect, present, future, atelic,* etc. Again, tense must be determined from context.

§27.1113 In Mod. Heb., a three-tense system has developed, with the perf. serving as past, the impf. as future, and the participle serving as present. This system was already developing in late Aramaic and Syriac.

§27.112 The verb may be inflected to show voice:
active voice
passive voice

§27.1121 *Active* voice means that the grammatical subject of the verb is achieving what is stated by the verb. Since many verbs are not verbs of action, but rather express state or condition, the term is sometimes misleading. See §30.38ff.

§27.1122 *Passive* voice means that the grammatical subject receives the action stated by the verb. In general, stative and intransitive verbs cannot be put in the passive. In Heb., however, verbs which are identified as "intransitive" sometimes do take a direct object and can be made into passive verbs.

§27.1123 In Heb., as in most Sem. langs., voice is indicated by the vowel pattern (hence the term "internal passives"). In general, the passive has a *u*-vowel after the first radical (*quṭal, quṭṭal*) or after the stem preformative (*hoqṭal*). The so-called conjugations Pu'al and Hoph'al are internal passives of the Pi'ēl and Hiph'îl, respectively.

§27.1124 In the G-stem, the internal passive was lost, except for the G pass. ptcp. (Gp50). A number of G pass. finite verbal forms occur in the Heb. Bible, but they have been pointed by the Masoretes as D pass. or H pass., depending on the consonants. When a verb occurs only in G act. and D pass., or G act. and H pass., we can be reasonably sure that the pre-Masoretic forms were G pass.

§27.113 A verb may be inflected to show mood:
indicative mood, §§27.2, .3
subjunctive mood,
imperative mood, §27.5
jussive mood, §27.6
cohortative mood, §27.6

§27.1131 The *indicative* (§30.3351) is the basic form of the perf. and impf., hence we do not look for any morphological indicators.

§27.1132 The *subjunctive* (§30.3352), with the loss of final short vowels (§15.51), is no longer identifiable. Since it occurs in Akk., Arab., and Eth., we assume that it was once found in Heb. We must now identify it by the context.

§27.1133 The *imperative,* since it can only refer to an incompleted action, is formed in a manner similar to the impf.

§27.1134 The *jussive,* likewise, can only refer to an incompleted action and is formed in a manner similar to the impf.

§27.1135 The *cohortative* can only refer to an incompleted action and is formed from the impf. In fact, it is often called the "lengthened imperfect."

§27.114 The verb may be inflected to show person (§30.336) and number (§30.337). In the Sem. system, gender (§30.339) is also indicated for 2d and 3d pers.

§27.1141 Since the base form in the Sem. languages is 3 m.s., it is customary to "turn the paradigm around," as follows:

Singular	Plural
3 m.s.	3 m.p.
3 f.s.	3 f.p.
2 m.s.	2 m.p.
2 f.s.	2 f.p.
1 c.s.	1 c.p.

§27.115 A verb may be modified to show that it is built on a *derived stem*. It is a characteristic feature of Semitic languages to build derived verbal stems to indicate some modification of the idea inherent in the root and thereby indicate repetition, extension (in time or space), intensity, causation, forensic declaration, causation, pretension, reciprocity, reflexivity, attempt, and even such unusual ideas as partaking of the color of. These derived stems are often called "conjugations"–but this is entirely different than what we mean when we speak of conjugations in Latin, French, or German.

§27.1151 Using the root *gdl*, we list here some of the stems that are found in various Sem. languages:

gadala	*gaddala*	*gâdala*	*gadalla*	*(i)gdâlla*
hagdala				
'agdala	*'agaddala*	*'agâdala*	*šagdala*	*šagaddala*
tagadala	*tagaddala*	*tagâdala*		
(i)gtadala	*(i)gtaddala*			
(i)ngadala	*(i)ntagdala*	*(i)ntanagdala*		
(i)ngadala	*(i)ntagdala*	*(i)ntanagdala*		
(i)štagdala	*(i)štagaddala*	*(i)štagâdala*		
(i)gdawwala	*(i)gtawdala*			

§27.1152 No known Sem. language contains all of these derived stems. Wright lists 15 for Arab., but only about 10 are in common use. Eth. has 12, not all of which are commonly used.

§27.1153 Early Heb. grammarians used the verb פעל for the paradigm word, and the names of the stems or conjugations (the Hebrews used the word *buildings*) are derived therefrom. We find the following stems in Bib. Heb.:

G	קַל	*Qal*	Ground-form, simple stem
D	פִּעֵל	*Pi'ēl*	Doubled stem, intensive
H	הִפְעִיל	*Hiph'îl*	Causative stem
N	נִפְעַל	*Niph'al*	N-stem, passive stem
HtD	הִתְפָּעֵל	*Hithpa'ēl*	HtD-stem, reflexive stem
HtŠ		*Hishtaph'ēl*	(found in only one verb)
Š	שַׁפְעֵל	*Shaph'ēl*	(rare; frequent in Syr.)
T	תִּפְעֵל	*Tiph'ēl*	(rare)

Other stems mentioned in grammars are usually those substituted for the above in certain types of "weak" verbs, to be discussed below.

§27.116 A transitive verb may also add on accusative suffixes to indicate the dir. obj. Since these suffixes modify the syllabic and accent patterns, the verb forms undergo alteration, to be discussed below. Cf. §23.122.

§27.117 The addition of ·וַ to an *imperfect* converts the verb aspect so that it has the force of the perfect. The addition of וְ to a *perfect* in many instances converts the aspect to the force of the imperfect. When parsing, identify such a verb as a *converted (inverted) imperfect* or a *converted perfect.*

§27.1171 In many grammars such a *wāw* is described as "*wāw* consecutive" (cf. *Ges.*§49*a*,n.1).The name was based on the theory that such a form must always be preceded by a verb without an inverting *wāw*. This theory will not hold up, in view of the fact that such books as Ruth, Esther, 1 Samuel, etc., *begin* with *wāw* conversive. In Heb., the term used is *wāw hahippûḵ* 'the inverting *wāw*.'

§27.1172 Moreover, comparative studies of the Sem. verb show that the conv. impf. is not the impf., but a *yqtl* perf. (cf. Akk. *iprus* with no final vowel), while the conv. perf. is possibly related to the Akk. permansive.

§27.12 The Heb. verbal adjective or *participle* (§30.382) may be inflected to show one or more of the following:

gender (§30.3141)
number (§30.3142)
state (§36.3)
derived stem (§27.115)
genitive suffixes (§23.121)

§27.13 The *infinitive construct* is a verbal noun, sometimes similar to the Eng. gerund and sometimes similar to the Eng. infinitive. It may be inflected to show:

the derived stem (§27.115)
genitive or accusative pron. suf. (§23.121f.)

§27.131 The addition of a pron. suf. to an inf. cstr. may alter the vocalic pattern markedly, due to the addition of a primary stress-accent, cf. *limlōḵ* לִמְלֹךְ, *lᵉmolḵô* לְמָלְכוֹ, basic form **muluk*.

§27.14 The *infinitive absolute* is very difficult to describe. At times it is a verbal noun (gerund), at times an adverb, and at times unlike any Eng. equivalent. It cannot be inflected and it does not accept any bound morpheme (§20.12) except the conj. וְ. (In two disputed instances we find the prep. לְ, cf. Joüon §123*c*.)

§27.15 To *parse* a Heb. verb is to identify the stem, aspect (tense), voice, mood, person, gender, number, and any bound morphemes that appear in the word, to give the root (or the lexical form) and the meaning.

the stem (conjugation), §27.115
the aspect (tense) if applicable, §27.111
the voice (unless stem indicates it), §27.112
the mood, §27.113
the person, gender, and number, if applicable, §27.114
if a participle, gender, number, and state, §27.12
pronominal suffixes, if any, §23.122f.
conversive *wāw,* if any, §27.117
prefixes, if any, §22.4
the root or lexical form of the word, §20.32
the meaning of the form

§§27.151 To make sure that the student includes all necessary information, and to eliminate the need of writing all these data, the following *Table of Indicators* may be used. It need not be memorized, as a copy is included in every examination. However, once the logic of the system is understood, it can be memorized in 15 minutes or less.

TABLE OF INDICATORS

Stem Conjugation		PGN	Perf.	Impf.	Impv.	Juss./ Cohort.	Ptcp.	Inf.	Pron. Suf.	PGN
G	qtl	3 ms	10	20	--	40	50 m.s.a.	60 inf.abs.	s0	3 ms
Gp	qtl pass.	3 fs	11	21	--	41	51 f.s.a.		s1	3 fs
N	nqtl	2 ms	12	22	32	42	52 m.s.c.		s2	2 ms
D	qttl	2 fs	13	23	33	43	53 f.s.c.		s3	2 fs
Dp	qttl pass.	1 cs	14	24		44			s4	1 cs
HtD	htqttl									
HtDp	" pass.	3 mp	15	25	--	45	55 m.p.a.	65 inf.cstr.	s5	3 mp
H	hqtl	3 fp	16	26	--	46	56 f.p.a.		s6	3 fp
Hp	hqtl pass.	2 mp	17	27	37	47	57 m.p.c.		s7	2 mp
HtŠ		2 fp	18	28	38	48	58 f.p.c.		s8	2 fp
		1 cp	19	29	--	49			s9	1 cp

c *after stem indicator and before the number,* indicates *wāw* conversive; *wāw* conj. not indicated.
s *after the number* plus suffix indicator indicates pron. suf.
e.g. וַיִּתְּנָהּ is identified as Gc20s1 of נתן, which is much simpler than writing 'third masculine singular, imperfect, of נתן, with 3 fem. sing. suf. and *wāw* conversive.'

§27.2 The *perfect* is indicated morphologically by (a) the addition of sufformatives to show person, gender, and number, and (b) by a vowel-pattern in the resulting form. Since the G-perf. is the simplest form, this is the starting-point for the study of the Sem. verb.

§27.21 The *sufformatives* for the perf. in all stems are the following:

3 ms	(10)	כככ	'he did ...'
3 fs	(11)	כככָ ה	'she did ...'
2 ms	(12)	כככ תָּ	'you (m.s.) did ...'
2 fs	(13)	כככ תְּ	'you (f.s.) did ...'
1 cs	(14)	כככ תִּי	'I did ...'
3 mp	(15)	כככ וּ	'they did ...'
3 fp	(16)	כככ וּ	'they (f.) did ...'
2 mp	(17)	כככ תֶּם	'you (pl.) did ...'
2 fp	(18)	כככ תֶּן	you (f.p.) did ...'
1 cp	(19)	כככ נוּ	'we did ...'

The כככ represent the 3 radicals of the root, cf. *Ges.* §44.

§27.211 The sufformatives should be learned as recognition elements: תֶּם—— 'you did ... ,' תִּי—— 'I did ... ,' etc. To "go to the paradigm" for this is to introduce an unnecessary step.

§27.212 The perf. sufformatives are constant for all stems, thus אָמַרְתִּי is G14, דִּבַּרְתִּי D14, הֵבַנְתִּי H14, etc. Learn to spot the sufformative and identify it at once. That is what happens when you speak the language!

§27.22 There is a *vocalic pattern* in addition to the sufformative. We can indicate this by using C for the consonant and adding the proper vowels. The pattern for the G-perf. of transitive verbs is CaCaC, which, of course, is subject to the rules of vocalic alteration, depending on stress-accent, influence of gutturals, type of syllable, etc.

§27.221 Adding the sufformatives (§27.21) to the vocalic pattern, we get the following:

G10	CaCaCa	*qāṭal*	קָטַל
G11	CaCaCat	*qāṭ^{e}lā^h*	קָטְלָה
G12	CaCaCtā	*qāṭáltā*	קָטַלְתָּ
G13	CaCaCti	*qāṭalt*	קָטַלְתְּ
G14	CaCaCtî	*qāṭáltî*	קָטַלְתִּי
G15	CaCaCû	*qāṭ^{e}lû*	קָטְלוּ
G16	" " "	" " "	
G17	CaCaCtém	*q^{e}ṭaltém*	קְטַלְתֶּם
G18	CaCaCtén	*q^{e}ṭaltén*	קְטַלְתֶּן
G19	CaCaCnû	*qāṭálnû*	קָטַלְנוּ

§27.2211 Note the application of Rule 4 throughout the verb paradigm. Note especially the application of Rules 15 and 17 to the forms we have just seen.

§27.2212 It should be obvious that the knowledge of the short-vowel chart (TABLE E) and the rules of vocalic alteration will greatly reduce the amount of memorization.

§27.23 There are two other vocalic patterns for the G-perf., generally found in *stative* verbs (§30.3393). Such verbs are usually, but not always, intransitive (§30.339). The patterns are CaCiCa and CaCuCa.

§27.231 The *thematic vowel* is the vowel after the second radical (or a 3-radical root). In the paradigms it is indicated CCCa, CGCi, GCCu, etc.–which is to identify the vowel and not to locate it. The thematic vowel always stands before the last radical. Of course, it undergoes the required vocalic alterations.

§27.232 Adding the perf. sufformatives to *thematic-i,* we get the following forms:

G10	CaCiCa	*kāḇēḏ*	כָּבֵד	G15	CaCiCû	*kāḇᵉḏû*	כָּבְדוּ
G11	CaCiCat	*kāḇᵉḏāʰ*	כָּבְדָה	G16	”	”	
G12	CaCiCtā	*kāḇáḏtā*	כָּבַדְתָּ	G17	CaCiCtem	*kᵉḇaḏtém*	כְּבַדְתֶּם
G13	CaCiCti	*kāḇadt*	כָּבַדְתְּ	G18	CaCiCten	*kᵉḇaḏtén*	כְּבַדְתֶּן
G14	CaCiCtî	*kāḇáḏtî*	כָּבַדְתִּי	G19	CaCiCnû	*kāḇáḏnû*	כָּבַדְנוּ

§27.2321 Note that Rule 15 does not apply here. On the other hand, Rule 20 does apply, causing the G12, 13, 14, and 19 forms to undergo the *i* > *a* shift. The G17, 18 forms undergo the same shift, apparently by analogic formation.

§27.233 Adding the perf. sufformatives to *thematic-u,* we get the following forms:

G10	CaCuCa	*qāṭōn*	קָטֹן	G15	CaCuCû	*qāṭᵉnû*	קָטְנוּ
G11	CaCuCat	*qāṭᵉnāʰ*	קָטְנָה	G16		”	”
G12	CaCuCtā	*qāṭṓntā*	קָטֹנְתָּ	G17	CaCuCtem	*qᵉṭontém*	קְטָנְתֶּם
G13	CaCuCti	*qāṭṓnt*	קָטֹנְתְּ	G18	CaCuCten	*qᵉṭontén*	קְטָנְתֶּן
G14	CaCuCtî	*qāṭṓntî*	קָטֹנְתִּי	G19	CaCuCnû	*qāṭṓnnû*	קָטֹנּוּ

§27.2331 Note that Rule 20 does not apply here, hence the G12, 13, 14, 17, 18, 19 forms retain their thematic vowel. Note the *qāmāṣ ḥāṭûp̄* in the G17, 18 forms. Rule 17 applies to all thematic vowels.

§27.3 The *imperfect* is indicated morphologically by (a) the addition of preformatives and (in some instances) sufformatives to indicate person, gender, and number, and (b) by a vowel pattern in the resulting form.

§27.31 The afformatives (pre- and suf-) for the impf. in all stems are as follows:

3 ms	(20)	י ככב	'he will ...'
3 fs	(21)	ת ככב	'she will ...'
2 ms	(22)	ת ככב	'you (m.s.) will ...'
2 fs	(23	ת ככב י	'you (f.s.) will ...'
1 cs	(24)	א ככב	'I will ...'
3 mp	(25)	י ככב וּ	'they will ...'
3 fp	(26)	ת ככב נָה	'they (f.) will ...'
2 mp	(27)	ת ככב וּ	'you (pl.) will ...'
2 fp	(28)	ת ככב נָה	'you (f.p.) will ...'
1 cp	(29)	נ ככב	'we will ...'

§27.311 The impf. afformatives should be learned as recognition elements: —ת 'you (m.s.) will ...,' ת—וּ 'you (pl.) will ..., —נ 'we will ...,' etc.

§27.312 The impf. afformatives are constant for all stems of the verb: תַּעַמְדוּ G27, תֵּעָמְדוּ N27, תִּתְבָּרְכוּ HtD27, etc.

§27.32 In addition to the preformatives and sufformatives, there is a *vowel pattern* for the G-impf. The normal pattern for the transitive verb is yaCCuCu, which is subject to the rules for short-vowels.

§27.321 Adding the preformatives and sufformatives we get the following:

G20	yaCCuCu	*yiqṭōl*	יִקְטֹל
G21	taCCuCu	*tiqṭōl*	תִּקְטֹל
G22	taCCuCu	*tiqṭōl*	תִּקְטֹל
G23	taCCuCî	*tiqṭ[e]lî*	תִּקְטְלִי
G24	'aCCuCu	*'eqṭōl*	אֶקְטֹל
G25	yaCCuCû	*yiqṭ[e]lû*	יִקְטְלוּ
G26	taCCúCnā	*tiqṭṓlnā[h]*	תִּקְטֹלְנָה
G27	taCCuCû	*tiqṭ[e]lû*	תִּקְטְלוּ
G28	taCCúCnā	*tiqṭṓlnā[h]*	תִּקְטֹלְנָה
G29	naCCuCu	*niqṭōl*	נִקְטֹל

§27.3211 Note the application of Rules 4, 13, 17, 18.

§27.33 There are two other vowel patterns for the G-impf.: yiCCaCu, commonly found with *stative* verbs, and yaCCiCu, found with certain verbs of the types GCC, 'CC, YCC, CC^2, and the verb נתן.

§27.331 The thematic vowel of the impf. is related to that of the perf. according to the following scheme:

Perf.	Impf.
CaCaCa	yaCCuCu
CaCiCa	yiCCaCu
CaCuCa	yiCCaCu

This is sometimes described as *Barth's Law.*

§27.332 The vowel of the preformative of the impf. is in turn determined by the thematic vowel of the impf.

Thematic a	yiCCaC
Thematic i	yaCCiC
Thematic u	yaCCuC

§27.3321 From the above discussions it is apparent that the G-impf. will take one of three vocalizations: **yaqtul* > *yiqtōl, yiqtal,* and *yaqtil.* We may tabularize the relationship of the perf. and impf. vocalizations as follows.

§27.333 Adding the impf. afformatives to *thematic a,* we get the following:

G20	yiCCaCu	*yik̲bad̲*	יִכְבַּד	G25	yiCCaCû	*yik̲b*^{e}*d̲û*	יִכְבְּדוּ
G21	tiCCaCu	*tik̲bad̲*	תִּכְבַּד	G26	tiCCáCnā	*tik̲bád̲nā*^{h}	תִּכְבַּדְנָה
G22	tiCCaCu	*tik̲bad̲*	תִּכְבַּד	G27	tiCCaCû	*tik̲b*^{e}*d̲û*	תִּכְבְּדוּ
G23	tiCCaCî	*tik̲b*^{e}*d̲î*	תִּכְבְּדִי	G28	tiCCáCnā	*tik̲bád̲nā*^{h}	תִּכְבַּדְנָה
G24	'iCCaCu	*'ek̲bad̲*	אֶכְבַּד	G29	niCCaCû	*nik̲bad̲*	נִכְבַּד

§27.3331 Note the application of Rules 4, 13, 18, and 20.

§27.334 Adding the impf. afformatives to thematic *i* we get the following:

G20	yaCCiCu	*yittēn*	יִתֵּן	G25	yaCCiCû	*yitt*^{e}*nû*	יִתְּנוּ
G21	taCCiCu	*tittēn*	תִּתֵּן	G26	taCCiCnā	*tittánnā*	תִּתֵּנָּה
G22	taCCiCu	*tittēn*	תִּתֵּן	G27	taCCiCû	*titt*^{e}*nû*	תִּתְּנוּ
G23	taCCiCî	*titt*^{e}*nî*	תִּתְּנִי	G28	taCCíCnā	*tittánnā*^{h}	תִּתֵּנָּה
G24	'aCCiCu	*'ettēn*	אֶתֵּן	G29	naCCiCu	*nittēn*	נִתֵּן

§27.3341 Note the application of Rules 4, 13, 18, 20.

§27.3342 Evidence for *yaqtil* pattern often has to be taken from pausal forms. יֹאכֵלוּן Dt. 18:1; תֹּאמֵר 1 Kgs. 5:20; יֹאמֵרוּ Jer. 5:2, etc. This is not dissimilation from original **o, pace Ges.* §68*c* n.2. Cf. *Ges.* §42*i*, and J. Barth, 'Das ĭ-Imperfekt im Nordsemitischen,' *ZDMG* (1889) 177f. Cf. also *Ges.* §68*c*.

§27.4 The form of the *imperative* is sometimes described as "the impf. with the preformative ת– removed." This may be helpful in a general way, but the vocalic pattern is not the same. Compare the following: impf. *tiqṭᵉlû*, impv. *qiṭlû; impf. tik̲bă̊dnāʰ*, impv. *kᵉb̲ă̊d̲nāʰ*. It is better to learn the impv. as a separate inflection, consisting of (a) the addition of sufformatives for 2fs, 2mp, and 2fp, and (b) a characteristic vowel pattern. *Ges.* §46.

§27.41 The impv. sufformatives are:

2ms (32)	——	2mp (37)	וּ——
2fs (33)	ִי——	2fp (38)	נָה——

§27.411 These are the same as the sufformatives of the 22, 23, 27, and 28 forms—but without the preformative.

§27.412 These sufformatives are used for the impv. in all derived stems.

§27.42 The *vowel pattern* of the G impv. takes three different forms (cf. §§27.32, .33): CCuC, CCaC, and CCiC. Since a word cannot begin with a consonantal cluster (§16.3), a vowel is inserted after the first radical, usually of the same type as the thematic vowel. This vowel has reduced to shewa: **qṭul* > **quṭul* > *qᵉṭōl* קְטֹל. Arab., on the other hand, adds a prosthetic vowel (without *hamzā*): *uqtul*.

§27.421 Originally the G impv. did not have a final short vowel. Arab. distinguishes the following imperatives:

impv.	*uqtul* < *qtul*
impv. 1 energ.	*uqtulanna*
impv. 2 energ.	*uqtulan*, p. *uqtulā*

In Heb. the "shortened impv." does occur, but most impv. forms are formed with an original short vowel (possibly by analogy with the impf.).

§27.422 The G impv. with thematic *u* develops as follows:

G32	CCuCu	*qᵉṭōl*	קְטֹל
G33	CCuCî	*qiṭlî*	קִטְלִי
G37	CCuCuw	*qiṭlû*	קִטְלוּ
G38	CCuCnā	*qᵉṭŏ̊lnāʰ*	קְטֹלְנָה

§27.423 The G impv. with thematic *i* develops as follows:

G32	CCaCu	*ḥăzaq*	חֲזַק
G33	CCaCî	*ḥizqî*	חִזְקִי
G37	CCaCû	*ḥizqû*	חִזְקוּ
G38	CCaCnā	*ḥăzáqnā*[h]	חֲזַקְנָה

§27.424 Most verbs with thematic *i* in impf. are "weak," and many of them have apheresis (§13.511) in impv. Weak verbs will be studied in §29. The verb *yāšaḇ* יָשַׁב is inflected as follows:

G32	CCiCu	*šēḇ* < *y*[e]*šēḇ*	שֵׁב
G33	CCiCî	*š*[e]*ḇî*	שְׁבִי
G37	CCiCû	*š*[e]*ḇû*	שְׁבוּ
G38	CCiCnā	*šēḇnā*[h]	שֵׁבְנָה

§27.425 Rule 19 applies in G33 and G37 forms. This sometimes results in a closed syllable, cf. שִׁמְכוּ (without dagesh) and אִסְפִּי (with dagesh).

§27.43 The impv. can add an הָ־ ending, perhaps adding a bit of emphasis, but sometimes only a stylistic variant. G32 שְׁמַע with ה שִׁמְעָה.

§27.431 The impv. with *–ā*[h] is probably derived from the same form as the Arab. impv. 2 energ.: **uqtula* > Arab. *uqtulan*, pausal *uqtulā*, Heb. *qiṭlā*[h] קָטְלָה.

§27.44 CCY verbs ("*lāmeḏ hê*") can take a shortened impv., similar to the apocopated juss. forms (§13.533) but without the preformative. These will be discussed more fully in §29.72.

§27.441 This form is derived from the original impv. without a final short vowel (§27.421).

§27.5 The *jussive* (shortened impf.) and the *cohortative* (lengthened impf.) are properly moods (§30.335ff.). In Arab. we find the evidence for this statement in the following moods:

impf. ind.	*yaqtulu*
impf. sbjtv.	*yaqtula*
impf. juss.	*yaqtul*
impf. 1 energ.	*yaqtulanna*
impf. 2 energ.	*yaqtulan*, p. *yaqtulā*

§27.51 The *juss.* originally differed from the impf. in morphology by the absence of the final short vowel. Cf. Arab. impf. *yaqtulu*, juss. *yaqtul*. Because of the loss of final short vowels in Heb. (§15.52), the two forms have fallen together, and, with a few important exceptions, the vowel pattern of the juss. is exactly like that of the impf.

§27.511 The G40 forms are regularly the same as the G20 (§27.321).
G20 *yaCCuCu > *yiCCōC* יִקְטֹל
G40 *yaCCuC > *yiCCōC* יִקְטֹל

§27.512 The G40 forms of verbs that had pure-long vowels in originally-closed syllables, where Rule 2 applies, will be discussed in §29.

§27.513 The juss. forms of derived stems, where the juss. and impf. are formally different, will be discussed in §28.

§27.52 Because of the nature of the juss. (§30.3355), we generally think of it as applying only to verbs in the third person ("Let him speak!" "Let them be silent!"). However, in Arab. we find the juss. in all persons, hence we assume that the same once applied to Heb.

§27.521 In Bib. Heb. the juss. is almost exclusively limited to the 2d and 3d persons. *Ges.* §48*h*.

§27.53 The *cohortative* is likewise a mood (§30.3354). It is perhaps related to the Arab. second energic (2 energ.) *yaqtulan,* pronounced in pause *yaqtulā*. We normally think of the cohort. as limited to 1st pers. ("Let us go into the field"). However, since the 2 energ. in Arab. occurs in all persons, we could assume the same for Heb. In Bib. Heb., however, the cohort. is almost exclusively limited to 1st pers. *Ges.* §48*b-e*. W. Wright, *A Grammar of the Arabic Language* (1896), p.61D.

§27.531 The cohort. is formed by adding ־ָה to the impf. 1cs or 1cp, with the shift in accent causing vocalic alteration according to vowel rules.

G24 *'eqṭōl* אֶקְטֹל
G44 *'eqṭ*ᵉ*lā*ʰ אֶקְטְלָה.

§27.6 The *nonfinite* verbal forms follow the rules for nouns and adjectives in their inflection. However, we shall consider them here, since they are usually included in verb conjugation.

§27.61 The *participle* (ptcp.) in the G stem is formed by vowel-pattern only. In the derived stems (§28.), there is a preformative *m-* ־מְ. In the G stem, there is a formal difference between the ptcp. of the trans. and the ptcp. of the intrans. verbs. *Ges.* §50.

§27.611 The G ptcp. of trans. verbs (verbs with thematic *a*) is formed as follows: *CâCiCu > *CôCēC qôṭēl* קוֹטֵל.

§27.6111 The first vowel (*ô*) is pure-long, and therefore unchangeable (§14.11, §15.22). Because it is often written defectively (§11.3241) the student may fail to note that it is a long vowel.

§27.6112 The *ṣêrê* is a short vowel and subject to the rules governing short vowels. However, it generally does not reduce in sg. cstr. (§15.223).

§27.612 The G ptcp. of intrans. verbs (verbs with thematic *i* or *u*) is formed exactly like the G10 (perf. 3ms) forms of those verbs:

Perf. (G10)			Ptcp. (G50)		
CaCiCa >	*CāCēC*	כָּבֵד	CaCiCu >	*CāCēC*	כָּבֵד
CaCuCa >	*CāCōC*	קָטֹן	CaCuCu >	*CāCōC*	קָטֹן

§27.6121 According to some grammarians, these forms of the stative verb are not ptcps. but are verbal adjectives (cf. Joüon §50*b*). Since all ptcps. are verbal adjs., this distinction is confusing.

§27.6122 Both vowels in the ptcps. of statives are short vowels, and therefore can reduce in accordance with the short-vowel rules. Study the following carefully:

	m.s.a.	m.s.c.	m.p.a.	m.p.c.
CâCiC	*qôṭēl*	*qôṭēl*	but *qôṭ^{e}lîm*	*qôṭ^{e}lê^y*
CaCiCu	*kāḇēḏ*	*k^{e}ḇēḏ*	*k^{e}ḇēḏîm*	*kiḇ^{e}ḏê^y*
CaCuCu	*qāṭōn*	*q^{e}ṭōn*	*q^{e}ṭannîm*	*q^{e}ṭannê^y*
CaCuCu	*nāqōḏ*	*n^{e}qōḏ*	*n^{e}quddîm*	*n^{e}quddê^y*

§27.6123 The *ḥōlām,* like the *ṣêrê,* does not reduce in sg. cstr. Both vowels, however, reduce in the pl. forms where the rule applies.

§27.6124 The form with thematic *u* (CaCuCu) often geminates the 3d rad. in the pl. forms: נָקֹד, נְקֻדִּים. The usual paradigm word קָטֹן borrows the pl. forms from the adj. קָטָן.

§27.62 The *fem.* ptcp. of the type CôCēC is found in two forms, the one adding the fem. ending *-at* > *-ā^h*, and the other adding the fem. *-t*, as follows:

CâCiCat	> CôC^{e}Cā	*'ôm^{e}rā^h*
CâCiCt	> CôCéCet	*'ôméreṯ*

§27.621 The fem. ptcp. of the trans. verb is inflected as follows:

f.s.a.	f.s.c.	f.p.a.	f.p.c.
'ôméreṯ, 'ôm^{e}rā^h	*'ôméreṯ*	*'ôm^{e}rôṯ*	*'ôm^{e}rôṯ*
אֹמְרָה, אֹמֶרֶת	אֹמֶרֶת	אֹמְרוֹת	אֹמְרוֹת

§27.622 The fem. ptcp. of the stative verb (see §27.612) is inflected exactly like the fem. adjs. of the same types:

b^{e}rēk̲ā^h	*b^{e}rēk̲at̲*	*b^{e}rēk̲ôt̲*	*b^{e}rēk̲ôt̲*
n^{e}b̲ēlā^h	*nib̲lat̲*	*n^{e}b̲ēlôt̲*	*nib̲lôt̲*
š^{e}k̲ēnā^h	*š^{e}k̲énet̲*	*š^{e}k̲ēnôt̲*	*š^{e}k̲ēnôt̲*
ʿămuqqā^h			

§27.6221 As can be seen, there are several ways in which this ptcp. (adj.) can develop. The student who has the short-vowel rules well in hand should have no difficulty understanding the various developments.

§27.63 The G *passive ptcp.* (Gp50) develops from the following vowel pattern: CaCûCu > *qāṭûl* קָטוּל.

§27.631 This form is inflected as an adj., following the rules for short and long vowels.

bārûk̲ *b^{e}rûk̲* *b^{e}rûk̲îm* *b^{e}rûk̲ê^y*

§27.6311 There is normally no pass. for stative verbs. However, the CaCûC form is sometimes found in stative verbs, denoting an inherent quality. אָמוּן 'faithful,' בָּטוּחַ 'trustful.' *Ges.*§50

§27.632 In a few instances, the pass. ptcp. has what appears to be an active sense, e.g. אֲחֻזֵי חֶרֶב 'handling the sword' (Cant. 3:8). BDB 28 identifies the form as an act. ptcp. Likewise, זָכוּר 'he remembers' (Ps. 103:14). Cf. Joüon §50*e*. The latter might be a mispointing of an inf. abs. Cf. *Ges.* §50*f.*

§27.64 The G infinitive absolute (inf. abs.) is formed by the following vowel pattern: CaCâCu. This develops to CāCôC (§14.11, §15.12), קָטוֹל.

§27.641 It is very important for the student to note that the infinitive *construct* (§27.65) is NOT an inf. abs. in the cstr. state. The terms *absolute* and *construct*, used of the infinitives, are unfortunate. The two infinitives are entirely different, and are derived from entirely different vowel patterns.

§27.6411 The basic difference between inf. abs. and inf. cstr. is often obscured by the use of full writing for the inf. cstr. and defective writing for the inf. abs. (§11.3241). However, the *ô* of the inf. abs. (קָטֹל) is *irreducible,* whereas the *ō* of the inf. cstr. regularly reduces before a fem. ending or a pron. suf.

§27.65 The *G infinitive construct* (inf. cstr., G65) is formed quite often by the vocalic pattern CuCuCu; however, other vowel patterns are found, CiCiCu and CiCaCu being attested, and yet others being suggested.

§27.651 The development of these G65 patterns is as follows:
*CuCuCu > *CeCōC* קְטֹל
*CiCiCu > *C^eCēC n^eṯēn* > *tent* > *tēṯ* תֵּת
*CiCaCu > *C^eCaC* שְׁכַב
Cf. *Ges.* §45*c-e*.

§27.6511 When the prep. ל־ is prefixed to an inf. cstr., the vocal shewa sometimes reduces to zero, and a closed syllable develops. Study the following: *n^epōl* נְפֹל, with ב־ בִּנְפֹל (Job 4:13), with כ־ כִּנְפֹל (2 Sam. 3:34), but with ל־ לִנְפֹּל *note dagesh* (Ps. 118:13), likewise לִשְׁכַּב (Gen. 34:7), etc.

§27.6512 The G65 of אמר with ל־ develops as follows: **l^e'ĕmōr* > *lē'mōr* לֵאמֹר. But note בֶּאֱמֹר. Joüon §49*f* n.1.

§27.652 G65 forms with fem. ending or with suffixes develop as follows:
*CuCuCatu > *CuC^eCā^h* חֶמְלָה or *CoC^eCā* אָכְלָה
*CiCiCatu > *CiC^eCā^h* שִׂנְאָה, רִבְעָה
*CiCaCatu > *CiC^eCā^h*
*CaCiCatu > *CaC^eCā^h* אַהֲבָה
Cf. *Ges.* §65*c*.

§27.653 A few inf. cstr. forms are found that have developed like the Aram. inf.:
*maCCaCu > *miCCaC* מִקְטַל
Cf. מִקְרָא (Num. 10:2), מַסַּע (Num. 10:2), מִקַּח (2 Chr. 19:7), מַשָּׂא (Num. 4:24). The form מִשְׁלוֹחַ (Est. 9:19) has developed from a form *maCCâCu > *miCCôC* (*Ges.* §45*e*).

§27.654 The warning implicit in §27.6411 needs to be repeated here.

§27.7 *Pronominal suffixes* may be added to verb forms (except inf. abs.). The pron. suf. may be accusative or genitive.

§27.71 The pron. suf. added to a finite verb is acc., indicating the direct object of the verb. The pron. suf. may have one of three forms. (*Ges.* §57)

§27.711 The acc. pron. suf. added to a verb-form ending in a vowel, takes the following forms:

s0	3ms	־ֹה ־וֹ ־ֵהוּ	*-hû, -ô^w, -ô^h*
s1	3fs	־ָהּ	*-hā*
s2	2ms	־ְךָ	*-ḵā*
s3	2fs	־ָךְ	*-āḵ*
s4	1cs	־ֵנִי	*-nî*

s5	3mp	־הֶם ־ם ־֫מוֹ	*–hem, –m, ´–mô*
s6	3fp	־ן	*–n*
s7	2mp	־כֶם	*–ḵem*
s8	2fp	(lacking)	(lacking)
s9	1cp	־֫נוּ	*´–nû*

§27.712 The acc. pron. suf. added to a perf. ending in a consonant takes the following forms:

s0	3ms	־ָ֫הוּ ־וֹ ־הֹ	*—áhû, —ô^{w}, —ô^{h}*
s1	3fs	־ָהּ	*—āh*
s2	2ms	־ךָ ־ֶ֫ךָ ־ָךְ	*—kā, —éḵā, —āḵ*
s3	2fs	־ֵךְ ־ֶ֫ךְ	*—ēḵ, —éḵ*
s4	1cs	־ַ֫נִי ־ָ֫נִי	*—ánî, —ā́nî*
s5	3mp	־ָם ־ָ֫מוֹ	*—ām, —ām, —ā́mô*
s6	3fp	־ָן	*—ān*
s7	2mp	־כֶם	*—ḵem*
s8	2fp		*(lacking)*
s9	1cp	־ָ֫נוּ	*—ā́nû*

§27.713 The acc. pron. suf. added to an impf. ending in a consonant takes the following forms:

s0	3ms	־ֵ֫הוּ	*—ḗhû*
s1	3fs	־ֶ֫הָ	*—éhā*
s2	2ms	־ךָ ־ֶ֫ךָ ־ָךְ	*—ḵā, —éḵā, —āḵ*
s3	2fs	־ֵךְ	*—ēḵ*
s4	1cs	־ֵ֫נִי	*—ḗnî*
s5	3mp	־ֵם ־ֵ֫מוֹ	*—ēm, —ḗmô*
s6	3fp		*lacking*
s7	2mp	־כֶם	*—ḵem*
s8	2fp		*lacking*
s9	1cp	־ֵ֫נוּ	*—ḗnû*

§27.714 The pron. suf. is sometimes added to a form to which *nûn energicum* has been added.

3ms	־ֶ֫נּוּ	**-énhû > -énnû*
2ms	־ֶ֫ךָּ ־ֶ֫כָּה	**-enkā > -ékkā*
1cs	־ַ֫נִּי ־ֶ֫נִּי	*-ánnî, -énnî*

These are the only PGN in which the *n* occurs (*Ges.*§58*j-k*).

§27.72 The G perf. verb to which a suffix is added has to be revocalized because of the accent shift. Study the following:

G10	*qāṭal*	+ suf. > *q^{e}ṭal-*	קְטָלַ֫נִי קְטָלָ֫הוּ
G11	*qāṭ^{e}lát*	+ suf. > *q^{e}ṭālaṯ-*	קְטָלַ֫תְךָ קְטָלָ֫תַם
G12	*qāṭáltā*	+ suf. > *q^{e}ṭalt-*	קְטַלְתַּ֫נִי קְטַלְתּוֹ

G13	*qāṭalt*	+ suf. > *qᵉṭaltî-*	קְטַלְתִּינִי
G14	*qāṭáltî*	+ suf. > *qᵉṭaltî-*	קְטַלְתִּיךָ
G15	*qāṭᵉlû*	+ suf. > *qᵉṭālû-*	קְטָלוּהוּ
G17	*qᵉṭaltem*	+ suf. > *qᵉṭaltû-*	קְטַלְתּוּהוּ
G19	*qāṭálnû*	+ suf. > *qᵉṭalnû-*	קְטַלְנוּכֶם

§27.721 The 3 fs + suf. preserves the old *-t* ending:
CaCaCat > *CāCᵉCāʰ*, but + *-ḵā* + *CeCāCaṯḵā* קְטָלַתְךָ.

§27.722 The 2fs + suf. preserves the old *-ti* ending (cf. Arab. *qatalti*):
CaCaCti > *CāCáCt*, but + *-nî* > *CᵉCaCtînî* קְטַלְתִּינִי.
The *i* is regularly written *plēnē* ִי־, but historically it is a *short* vowel.

§27.723 The 2mp + suf. preserves the earlier *-u*, which is still seen in Arab. *qataltum*, but the *-m* is lost:
*CaCaCtum > *CᵉCaCtém* but + *-hû* + *CᵉCaCtúhû* קְטַלְתּוּהוּ.
The *u* is regularly written fully וּ–, but historically it is a short vowel.

§27.73 The G impf. verb to which a suffix is added is revocalized as follows:
(a) with a vocalic suffix (-v) or a connecting vowel, the thematic vowel reduces to shewa:,
yiqṭōl + *-ēnî* > *yiqṭᵉlēnî* יִקְטְלֵנִי;
(b) with a consonantal suffix (-cv) the thematic vowel takes the form for an unaccented closed syllable:,
yiqṭōl + *-kā* > *yiqṭolḵā* יִקְטָלְךָ (*qāmāṣ ḥăṭûp̄*).

§27.74 The G impv. forms to which a pron. suf. is added follow the vocalization of the impf.

§27.75 The pron. suf. added to a nonfinite verb form is genitive. It may be either subjective or objective genitive (§36.323f).

§27.751 The pron. suf. added to the ptcp. follows noun rules for vocalization.

§27.752 The inf. cstr. with pron. suf. regularly preserves the vowel after the *first* radical and the other vowel reduces to shewa. Note carefully:
*CuCuCu > *CᵉCōC, qᵉṭōl*, but *qoṭlô* קָטְלוֹ, *qoṭlᵉḵā* קָטְלְךָ.

§28. *Derived stems* ("conjugations," Heb. *binyānîm* 'buildings') are formed by (a) alterations in the root, such as gemination of the second or third radical, reduplication of the radicals, and the like, (b) the addition of pre- or infixed stem indicators (or both), and (c) a vowel pattern. For the effect upon the root meaning and some of the derived stems, cf. §§27.115-.1153.

§28.1 The most common stems in Bib. Heb. may be conveniently presented as follows:

THE DERIVED VERBAL STEMS

	Simple	Intensive	Causative
Active	G (qtl) Qal ('light') *qāṭal* קָטַל	D (qttl) Pi'ēl *qiṭṭēl* קִטֵּל	H (hqtl) Hiph'îl *hiqṭîl* הִקְטִיל
Passive	Gp (qtl) Qal passive *qōṭal* קֹטַל*	Dp (qttl) Pu'al *quṭṭal* קֻטַּל	Hp (hqtl) Hoph'al *hoqṭal* הָקְטַל
Reflexive	N (nqtl) Niph'al *niqṭal* נִקְטַל	HtD (htqttl) Hithpa'ēl *hiṯqaṭṭēl* הִתְקַטֵּל	HtŠ (hštqtl) Hishtaph'ēl *hištaḥăwāʰ* הִשְׁתַּחֲוָה

§28.11 The names *Pi'ēl, Hiph'îl,* etc., came from early Heb. grammarians who used the verb *p'l* פעל for the paradigm. However, the presence of ע in the verb, because of its influence on vowels and its rejection of gemination, plus the presence of פ, which is a *begadkepat* letter, make the verb unsuitable for clear paradigms. Modern grammarians generally use the verb *qṭl* קטל.

§28.12 We advocate using the system which is widely used in recent Akk., Ugar., and some Heb. grammars, which is self-explanatory. See §27.1153. The symbols are explained as follows:

G ground stem, §27.
D doubled stem, §28.2
H preformative *h,* §28.3
N preformative *n,* §28.4
HtD preformative *hiṯ*- and doubled 2d rad., §28.5
HtŠ preformative *hiṯ*- and *š,* §28.9

Internal passives are indicated by adding the symbol p: Dp = D-pass.

§28.121 This system can be expanded to include other, less-common stems, such as:

L Pôlēl (long vowel after 1st rad.), §28.6
R Pilpēl (reduplication), §28.7

This can be further expanded to include HtR, HtL, Lp, etc.

§28.122 The great advantage of using this system is readily apparent in comparative Sem. studies. The N-stem, for example, is called "VII" in Arab., "IV 1" in Akk., and "Niph'al" in Heb., while the D-stem is "II" in Arab.,

"I 2" in Eth., "II 1" in Akk., and "Pi'ēl" in Heb. The stem *ištaqattala,* Eth. IV 2, in Akk. is "II III 2"!

§28.13 The HtŠ-stem, which is very common in Arab. and Akk., is found in Bib. Heb. only in the verb הִשְׁתַּחֲוָה 'to bow down.' This is listed in most lexicons under the root שחה, but should be listed as חוה, since the verb occurs about 170x in the Heb. Bible, almost always with *consonantal wāw.*

§28.14 The schematic table in §28.1 includes only the perf. (10) forms. For the other forms, see PARADIGM V-1, The Verb Synopsis.

§28.2 The *D-stem* is characterized by the gemination of the middle radical (if possible) and the vowel pattern. The fundamental idea in this stem seems to be *intensification, strengthening,* or *repetition.* It may also indicate *urging, causing* (approximating the H-stem), *permitting, declaring* (a forensic use), and similar ideas. Nouns formed from the D-stem (§24.26) often have the sense of *occupation* or *habitual activity.*

§28.21 The *basic patterns* for the D-stem are as follows:

D10	CiC²iCa	Rules 4, 13	מִלֵּא	גִּבַּרְתִּי
	CiC²aCa	Rules 2, 13, 15	יִסַּד	
D20	yaCaC²iCu	Rules 4, 13, 17, 20	יְדַבֵּר	
D32	CaC²iCu	Rules 4, 13, 17, 20	דַּבֵּר	
D40	yaCaC²iC	Rules 13, 17, 20	יְגַל	
D50	maCaC²iCu	Rules 4, 13, 20	מְדַבֵּר	
D60	CaC²âCu	Rules 2b, 4	יַסֹּר	
	CaC²iCu	Rules 4, 13	אַבֵּד	
D65	CaC²iCu	Rules 4, 13	אַבֵּד	יַסְּרָה

§28.211 The basic form of Dl0 is usually given as **qattala* (following Arab.) or **qattila* (following Aram). The evidence for an *i*-vowel following the 1st rad. is found in CGC verbs, where *ē* (rarely *ā*) is found in near-open syllables (e.g. קֵרַבְתִּי, וּפֵרֵשׂ, עֵרָה, גֵּרַשְׁתָּ, בֵּרֵךְ, בֵּאֵר, etc.). Had the vowel been originally *a,* it would have lengthened to *ā,* since there is no reason for attenuation in CGC (see Rule 18).

§28.212 The evidence for two basic vocalizations of D10 is copious. CiC²iCa: מִלֵּא, בִּקֵּשׁ, בֵּאֵר, דִּבֵּר, and many others; CiC²aCa: דִּכָּא, לִמַּד, אִבַּד, גִּדַּל, קִדַּשׁ, all CCG and all CCY verbs.

§28.213 The evidence for the preformative vowel in D20 *ya-* and D50 *ma-* (contrary to *yu-* and *mu-*, suggested by Arab. and Akk.) is found in such forms as: אֲבַקְשָׁה, אֲבָרְכָה, אֲלַמְּדָה, אֲצַוֶּה (hence אֲקַטֵּל. not אֻקַטֵּל, which the *u*-vowel would require) and is substantiated by Ugar. evidence (cf. C. H. Gordon, *Ugaritic Textbook,* §9.35 and Note [2]).

§28.22 The basic patterns for *D-passive* forms are as follows:

Dp10	CuC^{2}aCa	Rules 4, 13, 15	נֻתַּץ	
Dp20	yaCuC^{2}aCu	Rules 4, 13, 15	יְבֻקַּשׁ	
Dp32	*lacking*			
Dp50	maCuC^{2}aCu	Rules 4, 13, 15	מְפֻזָּר	מְלֻמָּדָה
Dp60	CuC^{2}âCu	Rules 2b, 4, 13, 15	גֻּנֹּב	
Dp65	CuC^{2}aCu	Rules 2b, 4, 13, 15	עֻנּוֹתוֹ	

§28.221 Note that the vowel *following the first radical* in Dp-stem establishes the passive voice.

§28.222 Masoretic pointing has identified numerous forms as D-pass. which were originally G-pass. (which later fell into disuse, except for Gp-ptcp., and was replaced by the N-stem). If the verb does not occur in D-act., or if the D-pass. meaning parallels the G-act. meaning, the form is doubtless an original G-pass. Cf. *Ges.* §52*e*. Note Dp10 יֻלַּד 'be born,' must be Gp10, probably vocalized יֻלַד*.

§28.3 The *H-stem* is indicated by a preformative *h*- (־ה), which is syncopated in the impf. (H20) and ptcp. (H50) forms, together with the basic vowel pattern. Cf. §13.52, .522. The fundamental idea of the H-stem is *causative,* but it often has a *declarative* sense (to pronounce just or guilty). If the G-stem of a verb has a transitive meaning, the H-stem normally takes two objects (§34.35)–'to cause *x* to do *y*.' If the G-stem is intransitive, the H-stem is often transitive (e.g. G 'to rise,' H 'to raise, cause to rise'; G 'to lie,' H 'to lay, cause to lie; G 'to see,' H 'to show, cause to see'). The H-pass. is usually the passive of the H-act., but cf. §28.322.

§28.31 The basic patterns of the H-stem are as follows:

H10	hiCCîCa	Rules 2a, 4, 13	הִקְדִּישׁ	הִקְדַּשְׁתִּי
H20	yahaCCîCu			
	> yaCCîCu	Rules 2a, 4, 13	יַצְדִּיק	
Hc20	wayaCCîC	Rule 2a	וַיַּלְבֵּשׁ	
H40	yaCCîC	Rule 2a	יַבְדֵּל	
H32	haCCîC	Rules 2a, 13	הַרְחֵק	
H50	mahaCCîCu			
	> maCCîCu	Rules 2a, 4, 13	מַזְכֶּרֶת	
H60	haCCiCu	Rules 2a, 13	הַקְדֵּשׁ	
H65	haCCîCu		הַקְדִּישׁ	

Cf *Ges.* §53.

§28.311 Evidence for H10 with preformative *i* (hiCCîCa or hiCCiCa) rather than with preformative *a* (as usually given, haCCîCa) is found in 'CC, GCC, CWC, and CC² verbs, all of which show a primary *i*-vowel in the preformative (e.g. הֶאֱבִיד, הֶעֱבִיר, הֵבִיא, הֵסֵב). The only contraindication is found in H10 of WCC verbs (e.g. הוֹצִיא), which are probably to be explained as analogic to H20 (e.g. יוֹלִיד).

§28.312 My former colleague, Dr. Gleason L. Archer, Jr., suggested the possibility that the *î* thematic vowel belonged originally only to the H20, and invaded the H10 through analogy. This would explain the *i* > *a* shift in perf. (e.g. הִמְלַכְתִּי) as well as the *î* > *ē* shift in the impf. (e.g. תַּקְטֵלְנָה).

§28.313 The *h*-preformative has syncopated in H20/50 (§13.522), e.g. **m^{e}hamlîḵ* > *mamlîḵ* מַמְלִיךְ, **t^{e}hašbîʿû* > *tašbîʿû* תַּשְׁבִּיעוּ. A few forms retain the *h* in Bib. Heb., e.g. *y^{e}hôšî^{aʿ}* (1 Sam. 17:47), *y^{e}hôdê^{h}* (Ps. 28:7), and *m^{e}huqṣāʿôṯ* (Ezek. 46:22). The H32 form likewise suggests that the H20 originally was formed with *h*.

§28.314 The H conv. impf. (Hc20) and the H juss. (H40) end in originally-closed syllables, which accounts for the short-vowel (*e*) before the final radical.

§28.32 The basic patterns for *H-passives* are as follows:

Hp10	huCCaCa	Rules 4, 13, 15	הָמְלַךְ	
Hp20	yahuCCaCu			
	> yuCCaCu	Rules 4, 13, 15	יָעֳמַד	
Hp32	*lacking*			
Hp50	mahuCCaCu			
	muCCaCu	Rules 4, 13	מָשְׁבָּת	מֻרְבָּק
Hp60	huCCîC (?)			
Hp65	huCCaCu			

§28.321 Note that the *u*-vowel in the preformative establishes the passive voice.

§28.322 In some verbs, the H-pass. is the passive of the G-stem (cf. *Ges.* §53*h*). However, Hp20's of this category are probably Gp20's that have been altered by Masoretic pointing, cf. §28.222 and *Ges.* §53*u*.

§28.33 The Š-stem (*Shaph'ēl*) is probably a survival of the original *h/š* causative. The two forms are attested in OSA, where the H-causative is found in Sabean and the Š-causative is found in Minean and Qatabanian. Cf. *Ges.* §55*i*.

§28.4 The *N-stem* is characterized by a preformative *hin* (> *n*- in some forms, and the *h* syncopates in others (§13.522) plus a basic vowel pattern. Originally, the N-stem was the reflexive of the G-stem, and is still such in many verbs. In Bib. Heb., the N-stem came to replace the G-pass. (which disappeared, except for the Gp ptcp. and for some forms pointed as Dp's or Hp's, cf. §28.222, §28.322). The N-stem can also be *reciprocal,* and as such it becomes almost *active!* The student should observe this stem carefully in context.

§28.41 It is incorrect to speak of the N-stem as "the passive of the G-stem."

§28.42 The basic patterns for the N-stem are as follows:

N10	naCCaCa	Rules 4, 13, 15, 18	נִלְצַם	
N20	yahanCaCiCu			
	> yanCaCiCu	Rules 4, 11, 13, 18	יִלָּצֵם	תִּשָּׁגַלְנָה
N32	hanCaCiCu	Rules 4, 11, 13, 18	הִלָּחֵם	
N50	naCCaCu	Rules 4, 13, 18	נִלְחָם	
N60	naCCâCu	Rules 4, 13, 18	נִלְחֹם	
N60	hanCaCâCu	Rules 4, 11, 13, 18	הִנָּתוֹ	
N65	hanCaCiCu	Rules 4, 11, 13, 18	הִלָּחֵם	הִקָּדְשִׁי

Cf. *Ges.* §51.

§28.421 The original **han-* is postulated on the N32/60/65 forms. This is supported by Arab. *inqatala* (note that *'alif* is without *ḥamzā*). We should probably suppose an original **an-* to which has been added a prothetic *hê* (§16.354).

§28.5 The *HtD-stem* is formed by prefixing the stem indicator *hiṯ-* (or *tiṯ-*, *'eṯ-*, *miṯ-*, as required), geminating the middle radical, and using the proper vowel-pattern. The HtD-stem often has the significance of the *reflexive of the D-stem.* Sometimes it approximates the G-stem in meaning or is *reciprocal.* It may even have an active force ('to do/act for oneself'), in which case it takes a direct object.it rarely has a *passive* significance.

§28.51 The basic patterns for the HtD are as follows:

HtD10	hitCaC^{2}iCa	Rules 4, 13	הִתְהַלֵּךְ	הִתְהַלַּכְתָּ
	hitCaC^{2}aCa	Rules 4, 13, 15	הִתְאַנַּף	
HtD20	yahitCaC^{2}iCu			
	> yitCaC^{2}iCu	Rules 4, 13	יִתְהַלֵּךְ	תִּתְהַלַּכְנָה
HtD32	hitCaC^{2}iCu	Rules 4, 13	הִתְהַלֵּךְ	
HtD50	mahitCaC^{2}iCu			
	> mitCaC^{2}iCu	Rules 4, 13	מִתְהַלֵּךְ	
HtD60	hitCaC^{2}iCu	Rules 4, 13	הִתְהַלֵּךְ	

Cf. *Ges.* §54

§28.511 The preformative *y^ehiṯ- in HtD20/50 is suggested by the HtD32 form.

§28.512 Evidence for a second vocalic pattern with thematic *a* in HtD10 is found in seven verbs: יהטמא, הִתְאחטא, הִתְעַנַּג, הִתְנַפַּל, הִתְאַפַּק, הִתְאַנַּף, and הִתְפַּלָּא. Cf. Joüon §53*b*.

§28.52 HtD passives occur infrequently, and only in perf. and inf. cstr. in Bib. Heb. The basic patterns are:

HtDp10	hutCuC²aCa	Rules 4, 13, 15	הָתְקָטַל
HtDp65	hutCaC²iCu	Rules 4, 13	הָתְקַטֵּל

Note the following forms: הֻדַּשְּׁנָה for *hoṯdašš^{e}nā^h (§13.112, Rules 1b, 12), Is. 34:6; הֻטַּמָּאָה for *hoṯṭammā'ā^h (pausal, Rule 12), Dt. 24:4; הָתְפָּקְדוּ for *hoṯpaqq^{e}dû (Rule 1b), Num. 1:47, etc.; הֻכַּבֵּס for *hoṯkabbēs, Lev. 13:55f., cf. *Ges.* §54*h,l*.

§28.53 In the HtD- and HtDp-stems, when the 1st rad. is a *dental* or a *sibilant,* metathesis (§13.61) or assimilation (§13.112), or both, may occur. See Rule 12, and note illustrations in §28.52.

§28.54 The tG, tD (probably equivalent to HtD), and tA stems occur regularly in Aram., and have been replaced by internal passives (Gp, Dp, and Ap/Hp) in Heb. Their relationship to Arab. V (*taqattala*) and to Eth. III 1 (*taqatĕla*), III 2 (*taqattala*), and III 3 (*taqâtĕla*) is apparent. The force of the stems, however, varies from language to language.

§28.541 The *Tiph'ēl*, or *Taph'ēl,* may possibly be a survival of the tA-stem, although it generally has an *active* causative meaning. Cf. תִּרְגַּלְתִּי 'to teach to walk' (Hos. 11:3), יְתַחֲרֶה 'to contend with' (Jer. 12:5). Cf. also the deverbal nouns with preformative ת.

§28.6 The L-stem (*Pô'ēl*) is formed by a vowel pattern with a long *ô* < *â* after the 1st rad. It expresses an aim or endeavor to perform an action, sometimes with hostile intent. Cf. *Ges.* §55*b,c*.

§28.61 The basic patterns of the L-stem are as follows:

L10	CâCiCa	*qôṭēl*	שֹׁרֵשׁ	Isa. 40:24
Lp10	CâCaCa	*qôṭal*	שֹׁרָשׁוּ	Jer. 12:2
L20	yaCâCiCu	*y^{e}qôṭēl*	יְסֹעֵר	Hos. 13:3
L50	maCâCiCu	*hiṯqôṭēl*	מְלוֹשְׁנִי	Ps. 101:5 *Kt.*
HtL10	hitCâCiCa	*yiṯqôṭēl*	הִתְגֹּעֲשׁוּ	Jer. 26:16
HtL20	yitCâCiCu	*yiṯqôṭēl*	יִתְגֹּעֲשׁוּ	Jer. 46:8

Cf. *Ges.* §55*b*.

§28.62 The L-stem is the reflex of Arab. III *qâtala* and Eth. I 3 *qâtĕla.* The HtL-stem is the reflex of Arab. VI *taqâtala* and Eth. III 3 *taqâtĕla.*

§28.63 The form of the L-stem is generally used in place of the D-stem for CWC and CC² verbs. In such cases, the stem has the normal force of the D-stem. *Ges.* §55*c.*

§28.7 Some derived stems are formed by reduplicating the 2d and 3d rads. (*qᵉṭalṭal*) or by repeating the 3d rad. (*qiṭlal*). The former has been designated as the R-stem (for reduplication), and the HtR. No satisfactory symbol has been suggested for the second form.

§28.71 The R-stem, or *qᵉṭalṭal,* is used mainly to indicate movements repeated in quick succession: סְחַרְחַר 'to go about quickly, to palpitate (heart)' (Ps. 38:11); pass. חֳמַרְמַר 'to be heated, to be red' (Job 16:16; Lam. 1:20). *Ges.* §55*e.*

§28.72 The *qaṭlēl* (or *paʿlēl*) is the reflex of Arab. IX *iqtalla* which generally suggests permanent conditions, colors, and the like. The vowel in the 1st syllable generally attenuates (Rule 18). Note: שַׁאֲנַן 'to be at rest,' רַעֲנַן 'to be green, pass. אֻמְלַל 'to be withered.' *Ges.* §55*d.*

§28.73 The *qilqēl* (or *pilpēl*) is not truly a derived stem, but is used for the D-stem in roots that are basically biconsonantal (Cv̂C, i.e. CWC and CYC) and, by analogy, in CC² roots. These will be discussed in §29. Cf. *Ges.* §55*f.*

§28.8 Verbs with four consonantal radicals are very rare in Bib. Heb. They develop either on the pattern of the D-stem (*qirsēm,* pass. *ruṭpaš*) or on the pattern of the H-stem (*hiśmîʾl* < **hiśmᵉʾîl*). Cf. *Ges.* §56.

§28.9 *Compound stems,* quite common in Akk., Arab., and Eth., are extremely rare in Bib. Heb. The NtD (which is common in Mishnaic Heb.) occurs in Ezek. 23:48, וְנִוַּסְּרוּ (developed from **niṯwassᵉrû*). The HtŠ (common in Akk., Arab., Ugar.) may be placed here, but it is basically a tŠ, like the tG, tD, and tA mentioned in §28.54. It occurs many times, but only in the verb הִשְׁתַּחֲוָה from חוה.

§29. *Weak verbs* are generally learned as separate paradigms. Due to the presence of certain types of consonants ('weak' consonants), there are certain alterations in the 'strong' verb pattern. These types of verbs need to be analyzed.

§29.01 In the Middle Ages, Heb. grammarians used פעל as the paradigm word. The first radical was called פ, the 2d rad. ע, and the 3d rad. ל, hence the names "Pê Aleph" (i.e. *ʾālep̄* in the "*pê*" radical), " 'Ayin Wāw" (*wāw* in the *ʿáyin* radical), etc. In a day when פעל is no longer used as the paradigm word, and in Sem. languages where these names are incongruous (such as Arab., Eth., and especially Akk.), there is little reason to continue to use this terminology.

§29.02 With very few exceptions, the "weak verbs" are entirely regular, provided the student knows the rules for short-vowels, long-vowels, and diphthongs, and the phenomena associated with certain consonants: *nûn* assimilates, *'ā́lep̄* may quiesce, gutturals effect the neighboring vowels and reject *dāḡēš*, *wāw* and *yôḏ* form diphthongs and monophthongize, etc..We shall therefore analyze the "weak" verbs as regular, noting the laws that have affected the forms.

FIRST RADICAL WEAK

'CC	Pê Aleph	א in 1st radical, §§29.14, .22
GCC	Pê Guttural	guttural in 1st radical, §29.11
NCC	Pê Nûn	נ in 1st radical, §29.4
WCC	Pê Wāw	י (originally ו) in 1st radical, §29.31
YCC	Pê Yôd	י in lst radical, §§29.33, .34

SECOND RADICAL WEAK

CGC	'Ayin guttural	guttural in 2d radical, §29.12
CWC	'Ayin Wāw	ו in 2d radical, §29.61
CYC	'Ayin Yôd	ע in 2d radical, §§29.62, .64
CC^2	'Ayin-'ayin	2d and 3d radicals same, §29.5

THIRD RADICAL WEAK

CC'	Lamed 'Aleph	א in 3d radical, §§29.14, .21
CCG	Lamed Guttural	guttural in 3d radical, §29.13
CCY	Lamed Hê	original י in 3d radical, §29.7
CCW	Lamed Hê	original ו in 3d radical, §29.7

DOUBLY WEAK

NC'		ן in 1st, א in 3d radical, §29.8
NCY		נ in 1st, orig. י in 3d
YC'		etc.
etc.		

§29.1 For verbs with a guttural in the root (GCC, CGC, CCG), review thoroughly §15.4, and look at §12.35, §13.38, §15.321. Review Rule 10.

§29.11 GCC verbs are regular with one exception. Before certain consonants, secondary opening may occur (§15.421ff). This affects G20, N10, N50, H10, H20, H50, and H60/65–in other words, any form where the first radical normally closes a syllable. For a full study, cf. LaSor's article noted in §15.421. The following is typical: **yaqtul* > *yiqtōl*, but *yaḥălōm* יַחֲלֹם.

§29.111 The vowel generated by secondary opening may become a full short vowel: *yiqt^{e}lû* but *ya'am^{e}d̲û* יַעַמְדוּ, cf. §15.4213.

§29.112 Accent seems to have some effect on the vowel quality:

G20	יֶחְסַר	but	יַחְסְרוּ
H10	הֶעֱבַרְתִּי	but	וְהַעֲבַרְתִּי
H10	הֶעֱמַדְתָּ	but	וְהַעֲמַדְתָּ

§29.113 The student should be alerted to the fact that *pattāḥ under the preformative*–which is the first clue in recognizing an H20/50—may occur in G20 of GCC.

§29.114 Note also that *dāḡēš* in the 1st rad.–the first clue in recognizing an N20/32/65–is rejected by GCC, and when the first radical is ה or ח, there is no compensatory lengthening (§13.38, §15.14).

§29.12 CGC verbs are entirely regular, if we bear in mind the influence of a guttural (§15.4). The most noteworthy effects are in the D and HtD stems, where normal gemination is rejected (§13.38). Study the following:

D10	מִהַר	implied doubling	בֵּרֵךְ	compensatory lengthening
D20	יְמַהֵר	implied doubling	תְּבָרֵךְ	compensatory lengthening
HtD20	יִתְכַּחֲשׁוּ	implied doubling	יִתְבָּרֵךְ	compensatory lengthening

Cf. *Ges.* 564.

§29.121 In all forms where a vocal *š^{e}wâ* is found with the 2d rad. of a regular verb, it is replaced by *ḥāṭap̄ š^{e}wâ* in CGC verbs (§11.325, §15.253, §15.42).

§29.122 Note that *rêš* often behaves as a guttural in CRC verbs, both in its refusal to accept *dāḡēš* and in its influence on vowels.

§29.13 CCG verbs often distort the vowel-pattern, due to the preference of the guttural for an *a*-class vowel (§15.4322). This is particularly noteworthy in reference to Barth's Law (§27.331). The student will find *yiqtal forms where he should expect *yaqtul forms. Often the pausal forms will display the "correct" vowel-pattern (cf. D10 *šillaḥ,* paus. *šillē^{a}ḥ*). Cf. *Ges.*§65.

§29.131 In the 2fs (13) forms an anaptyctic vowel is generated (§15.61): *qāṭalt* but *šāláḥatt* (note that the *dāḡēš* remains), שָׁלַחַתְּ. This occurs in all stems.

§29.14 'CC and CC' verbs must be considered separately, rather than as GCC or CCG, due to the fact that *'ālep̄* often quiesces (§13.523); see §29.2.

14 כַּאֲשֶׁר שָׁמְמוּ עָלֶיךָ[a] רַבִּים
[b]כֵּן־מִשְׁחַת[c] מֵאִישׁ מַרְאֵהוּ וְתֹאֲרוֹ מִבְּנֵי אָדָם׃[b] ל
15 כֵּן יַזֶּה[a] גּוֹיִם רַבִּים עָלָיו יִקְפְּצוּ מְלָכִים פִּיהֶם ב[18]
כִּי אֲשֶׁר לֹא־סֻפַּר לָהֶם רָאוּ וַאֲשֶׁר לֹא־שָׁמְעוּ הִתְבּוֹנָנוּ׃ ח[19]
53 1 מִי הֶאֱמִין לִשְׁמֻעָתֵנוּ וּזְרוֹעַ יְהוָה עַל־מִי נִגְלָתָה׃ ג חס בליש[1]
2 וַיַּעַל כַּיּוֹנֵק לְפָנָיו[a] וְכַשֹּׁרֶשׁ מֵאֶרֶץ צִיָּה ל
לֹא־תֹאַר לוֹ וְלֹא הָדָר וְנִרְאֵהוּ[b] וְלֹא־מַרְאֶה וְנֶחְמְדֵהוּ׃ לד פסוק לא ולא ולא[2]. ל. ל
3 נִבְזֶה וַחֲדַל אִישִׁים אִישׁ מַכְאֹבוֹת וִידוּעַ[a] חֹלִי ג. ל
וּכְמַסְתֵּר פָּנִים מִמֶּנּוּ נִבְזֶה[b] וְלֹא חֲשַׁבְנֻהוּ׃ ב
4 אָכֵן חֳלָיֵנוּ הוּא נָשָׂא וּמַכְאֹבֵינוּ[a] סְבָלָם יח[3]
וַאֲנַחְנוּ חֲשַׁבְנֻהוּ נָגוּעַ מֻכֵּה אֱלֹהִים וּמְעֻנֶּה׃ ב. ב ומל[4]. ב חד כת ה וחד כת י[5]
5 וְהוּא מְחֹלָל[a] מִפְּשָׁעֵנוּ מְדֻכָּא מֵעֲוֺנֹתֵינוּ לג ר״פ. ל חס
מוּסַר שְׁלוֹמֵנוּ עָלָיו וּבַחֲבֻרָתוֹ נִרְפָּא־לָנוּ׃ יב פת[6]
6 כֻּלָּנוּ כַּצֹּאן תָּעִינוּ אִישׁ לְדַרְכּוֹ פָּנִינוּ ל
וַיהוָה הִפְגִּיעַ בּוֹ אֵת עֲוֺן כֻּלָּנוּ׃
7 נִגַּשׂ [a]וְהוּא נַעֲנֶה[a] וְלֹא יִפְתַּח־פִּיו ד[7]. ב[8]
כַּשֶּׂה לַטֶּבַח יוּבָל וּכְרָחֵל לִפְנֵי גֹזְזֶיהָ נֶאֱלָמָה ב זקף קמ
[b]וְלֹא יִפְתַּח פִּיו׃[b]
8 מֵעֹצֶר וּמִמִּשְׁפָּט לֻקָּח וְאֶת־דּוֹרוֹ מִי יְשׂוֹחֵחַ ה[9]
כִּי נִגְזַר מֵאֶרֶץ חַיִּים [a]מִפֶּשַׁע עַמִּי[ab] נֶגַע[c] לָמוֹ׃[d] ג[10]
9 וַיִּתֵּן[a] אֶת־רְשָׁעִים קִבְרוֹ וְאֶת־עָשִׁיר[b] בְּמֹתָיו[c] ג[11]
עַל לֹא־חָמָס עָשָׂה וְלֹא מִרְמָה בְּפִיו׃ ג[12]

[18]Lv 16,14. [19]Mm 3985. Cp 53 [1]Mm 1727. [2]Mm 771. [3]Mm 1941. [4]Mm 2403. [5]Mm 2404. [6]Mm 2405. [7]Mm 1598. [8]Mm 2824. [9]Mm 1496. [10]Mm 2406. [11]Mm 2283. [12]Mp sub loco.

14 [a] l c 2 Mss 𝔖𝔗 עָלָיו ‖ [b–b] frt tr ad fin 53,2 ‖ [c] 𝔔[a] משחתי Ms מושׁ׳ traditio bab מָשְׁ׳ 𝔖 *mḥbl* cf 𝔗𝔙, l מָשְׁחָת ‖ **15** [a] 𝔊 *θαυμάσονται*; prp יֶהֱזוּ vel יֶחֱזוּ, al יִרְגְּזוּ, יִבְזָהוּ ‖ **Cp 53,2** [a] prp לְפָנֵינוּ ‖ [b] tr huc ‸ cf σ′ ‖ **3** [a] 𝔔[a]𝔊𝔖𝔙 וְיֹדֵעַ 𝔔[b] וידע; l וזג ‖ [b] 𝔔[a] ונבוזהו; 𝔖 *wšṭnjhj*, prp וַנִּבְזֵהוּ ‖ **4** [a] ins c nonn Mss 𝔖𝔙 הוּא ‖ **5** [a] prp מְחֻלָּל ‖ **7** [a–a] prp הוּא וְנ׳ ‖ [b–b] prb dl ‖ **8** [a–a] prp מִפְּשָׁעֵם ‖ [b] 𝔔[a] עמו ‖ [c] l נֻגַּע vel נֻגַּע cf 𝔔[a] 𝔊 ‖ [d] 𝔊 *εἰς θάνατον*, l לַמָּוֶת ‖ **9** [a] 𝔔[a] ויתנו; prp וַיֻּתַּן ‖ [b] prp שְׂעִירִים ‖ [c] 𝔔[a] בומתו 𝔊(𝔖𝔙) *ἀντὶ τοῦ θανάτου αὐτοῦ* = בְּמוֹתוֹ cf 𝔗; prp בָּמָתוֹ sepulchrum suum.

FIGURE 8. THE "STUTTGART BIBLE"

Biblia Hebraica Stuttgartensia is the successor to the "Kittel Bible." Like *BH*[3] it is based on the Leningrad MS (L), dated 1009 or 1008 A.D.. It is characterized by its clarity of text, expanded Masoretic notes, and simplified apparatus.

§29.141 C'C verbs can be treated as CGC verbs.

§29.15 CCH verbs, i.e. verbs ending in *hê* with *mappîq*, are CCG verbs and can be treated as such. They should *not* be confused with "Lamed Hê" (CCY, CCW) verbs. CCH verbs are comparatively rare. Note: G10 גָּבַהּ, G20 יִגְבַּהּ, G65 גְּבֹהַּ.

§29.151 The so-called "Lamed Hê" verbs are *not* CCH, and the student should never consider them as such. They are developed from CCY or CCW roots. The 3d rad. ה is only an orthographic representation. See §29.72.

§29.2 'CC and CC' verbs are usually similar to GCC and CCG, but the student is cautioned to observe carefully the behavior of the *'ắlep̄*.

§29.21 'CC verbs display the following peculiarities.

§29.211 The א is a normal guttural in **yiqtal*-type impfs. and in some **yaqtul*-type variants of **yaqtil* (cf. §27.321, §27.333, §27.334). Note **ti'balu* > **te'ĕḇal* תֶּאֱבַל; **ya'ḥuzu* > *ya'ăḥōz* יֶאֱחֹז.

§29.212 In six 'CC verbs (אפה אמר אכל אחז אבה אבד), the א quiesces at the end of a syllable and the vowel of the preformative is lengthened to a quasi-long vowel, **a'* > *â'* > *ô'*, §15.151. Note the G20 forms: **ya'ḥizu* > **yâ'ḥiz* > *yô'ḥēz* יֹאחֵז. Ges. §68.

§29.213 In the impf. 1cs (24) forms of these verbs, the preform. א and the א of the 1st rad. coalesce, and only one א is written: **'a'ḥizu* > **'aḥiz* > *'ôḥēz* אֹחֵז.

§29.214 In some cases, the quiescent א falls out orthographically, תֹּאסֵף* > תֹּסֵף.

§29.22 CC' verbs differ from CCC verbs in one point: the א quiesces at the end of a syllable, which results in an open syllable and affects the application of Rule 15 (§15.113) and Rule 20 (§15.33). Cf. קָטַל and בָּרָא, כָּבַדְתָּ and מָצָאתָ, הִקְדַּשְׁתִּי and הִמְצֵאתָ. Cf. *Ges.* §75.

§29.221 The following points should be carefully noted.

§29.2211 In 26, 28, 38 forms, ֶ-אנָה (ֶ instead of ַ or ֵ) occurs: תִּקְרֶאנָה.

§29.2212 Before s2, s7, s8 suffixes, א is consonantal and takes compound shewa: יִמְצָאֲהוּ.

§29.2213 G65 of CC' sometimes adds ת (analogy to CCY verbs), מְלֹאת.

§29.2214 In G51 forms of the pattern קוֹטֶלֶת quiescent א results in forms without anaptyxis: מוֹצֵאת.

§29.2215 In Hc20, H32, H40 forms we sometimes find *ḥîrîq 'ā̊lep̄*. Since א has left the syllable open, the *ḥîrîq* must be long *î* written defectively (§15.22): וַיַּחֲטִא.

§29.2216 א is often elided and omitted orthographically: מָצָתִי for מָצָאתִי.

§29.3 Because of the initial *w* > *y* shift in many Sem. languages, including Heb. (§13.7), original WCC and YCC verbs have fallen together as YCC. However, in several points, they are distinct, hence it is necessary to study them separately. We shall use the symbol WCC to mean those 'Pê Yôd' verbs which originally had *wāw* in the 1st rad.

§29.31 WCC verbs can be readily distinguished from YCC verbs in the N and H stems.

§29.311 In N10, N50, and all H-act. forms, the original *wāw* appears as long *ô* written fully (§11.3231), monophthongized from an **aw* diphthong. Study the following:

N10	**nawsapa*	>	*nôsap̄*	נוֹסַף
N50	**nawsapu*	>	*nôsāp̄*	נוֹסָף
H10	**hawṣî'*	>	*hôṣî'*	הוֹצִיא
H20	**yawṣî'u*	>	*yôṣî'*	עוֹצִיא
H50	**mawṣî'u*	>	*môṣî'*	מוֹצִיא
H60	**hawlidu*	>	*hôlēḏ*	הוֹלֵד
H65	**hawšîbu*	>	*hôšîḇ*	הוֹשִׁיב

§29.312 In N20, N32, and in some HtD forms, ו is a strong consonant capable of gemination:

N20	**yinwasiru*	>	*yiwwāsēr*	יִוָּסֵר
N33	**hinwasirî*	>	*hiwwās^{e}rî*	הִוָּסְרִי
HtD20	**y^{e}hitwakkaḥu*	>	*yiṯwakkaḥ*	יִתְוַכָּח

§29.313 In H-pass., **-uw* at syllable-end > *û* (§15.153):

Hp10	**huwrada*	>	*hûraḏ*	הוּרַד
Hp22	**tuwšabu*	>	*tûšaḇ*	תּוּשַׁב

§29.32 Peculiarities in G-stem of WCC verbs to be noted (*Ges.* §69) are:

§29.321 WCC G20's of the *yaqtil type have *ṣêrê* (**ay* > *ê*) in the preformative. It is almost always written defectively, but is irreducible:

G20	**yayšibu*	>	*yêšēḇ*	יֵשֵׁב
G25	**yayšibû*	>	*yêš^{e}ḇû*	יֵשְׁבוּ

§29.3211 G20's of the **yiqtal* type have long *î*, rarely written defectively: **yiyraš* > *yî^{y}raš* יִירַשׁ.

§29.3212 The unusual forms, יִצֹּק and אֶצָּרְךָ seem to be *yaqtul-type impfs.

§29.322 In G32, G65 WCC verbs of *yaqtil-type, apheresis (§13.51ff.) is found. In addition, in the G65 forms, a ballast-*t* (§13.513) is added. Because of the resultant doubly-closed syllable, anaptyxis usually is found (§15.61).

G32	**yišibu*	>	*šēḇ*	שֵׁב
G65	**yišibu*	>	*šéḇeṯ*	שֶׁבֶת
G65	**yadaʿu*	>	*dáʿaṯ*	דַּעַת

§29.3221 There is no apheresis in WCC verbs of the *yiqtal type: G32 *yᵉraš* יְרַשׁ.

§29.33 The only true YCC verbs (i.e. with original 1st rad. *yôḏ*) in the Heb. Bib. are: יטב, ינק, יקץ, ילל, ישר, and יבשׁ (?), cf. *Ges.*§70. Some observations will be helpful.

§29.331 There is no apheresis or elision in true YCC verbs, e.g.: יִיטַב, יִינַק (G20), בִּיבֹשׁ (< יְבֹשׁ + בְּ, G65).

§29.332 In the H-stem, monophthongization occurs, but the *yôḏ* is written:

H20	**yayṭîbu*	>	*yêʸṭîḇ*	יֵיטִיב
H10	**hiyṭîba*	>	*hêʸṭîḇ*	הֵיטִיב

The H10 form seems to be formed by analogy with the H20 (cf. §28.311).

§29.34 Some YṢC verbs (i.e. verbs beginning with -יצ) form a special class of YCC verbs. In this class, *yôḏ* is consonantal and assimilates as if it were a *nûn*. Sometimes YṢC verbs are listed as NCC, with confusion in lexical arrangement. Holladay, *Lexicon,* p.243, lists נצב, which occurs in N, H, and Hp stems and means 'stand, station, establish, be set up'; on p.140 he lists יצב, which occurs only in HtD and means 'take one's stand.' Obviously, all entries could be listed under יצב. Cf. Joüon §77.

§29.341 The six YṢC verbs in Bib. Heb. are: יצב, יצג, יצע, יצק, יצר, and (?) יצת. The verb יצא is an exception.

§29.3411 Note the following forms:
יצג H10 הִצִּיב, H50 מַצִּיב, H65 הַצִּיב;
יצג H20 יַצִּיג, Hp20 יֻצַּג;
יצע H20 יַצִּיעַ, Hp20 הֻצַּע;
יצק G24 אֶצֹּק, H25 יַצִּיקוּ;
יצר G24s2 אֶצָּרְךָ, but Gc20 וַיִּיצֶר;
יצת Gc21 וַתִּצַּת, G25 יִצָּתוּ, H10 הִצִּית, H27 תַּצִּיתוּ.

§29.4 NCC verbs, in addition to assimilation (§13.111), have two other noteworthy features.

§29.41 In G32 and G65 forms there is apheresis (§13.511), and the G65 then adds a "ballast" ת (§13.513), usually with resulting anaptyxis (§15.61). Note: G32 *n^{e}ḡaš > gaš גַּשׁ, G65 *n^{e}ḡaš > géše<u>t</u> גֶּשֶׁת.

§29.411 Apheresis is permitted but not required in G65's of *yiqtal-type verbs, and required in G32's of this type. Note: G20 יִגַּע, G32 גַּע, G65 לָגַעַת or נְגוֹעַ.

§29.412 Apheresis does not occur in *yaqtul-type of NCC verbs: G20 יִפֹּל, G65 נְפֹל.

§29.42 In NGC verbs (i.e. NCC with guttural in 2d rad.), the *nûn* does *not* assimilate. These verbs behave as CCC verbs: יִנְהַג, יִנְאָקוּ, יִנְעַץ, יִנְאַף, יִנְחַל, וָאֶנְעָלֵךְ, יִנְעַם. One exception is יֵחַת (< יִנְחַת).

§29.43 In H-pass. of NCC's, *qubbûṣ* normally is found before the *dāḡēš*: מֻגָּשׁ.

§29.44 The verb *ntn* נתן is especially noteworthy because the 3d rad.-ן assimilates to consonantal sufformatives (§13.1111): *natantî > *nāṯáttî* נָתַתִּי. This is the *only* verb that behaves in this manner.

§29.45 The verb *lqḥ* לקח follows the pattern of NCC verbs except in the N-stem. Note: G20 יִקַּח, G32 קַח, G65 קַחַת, but N10 נִלְקַח.

§29.5 CC² verbs were probably originally biconsonantal (cf. *Ges.* §67*a*), and have been expanded, probably by analogy, into triconsonantals in certain forms.

§29.51 The simplest development of the CC² is by gemination (§13.3) of the 2d rad. Some observations may be helpful. However, this is not intended as an exhaustive treatment; it is an aid to, not a substitute for, the student's observation. By faithfully observing these and other forms, the student will gradually master this difficult verb type.

§29.511 Some basic patterns for CC² verbs which develop by gemination of the 2d rad. include:

	CCC	CC²	EXAMPLES		
G10	CaCaCa	CaC²a	*tam*	תַּם	§29.5111,.5114
G11	CaCaCat	CaC²at	*támmā^{h}*	תַּמָּה	§29.5112
G14	CaCaCtî	CaC²ôtî	*sabbôṯî*	סַבּוֹתִי	§29.5113
G20	yaCCuCu	yaCuC²u	*yāsōḇ*	יָסֹב	§29.5111,.5114
G26	taCCuCnā	taCuC²ênā	*t^{e}subbênā^{h}*	תְּסֻבֶּינָה	§29.5113
G20	yaCCuCu	yaC²uCu	*yissōḇ*	יִסֹּב	§29.5115
G20	yiCCaCu	yiCaC²u	*tēqal*	תֵּקַל	§29.5111
G20	yiCCaCu	yiC²aCu	*yimmal*	יִמַּל	§29.5115
G65	CuCuCu	CuC²u	*sōḇ*	סֹב	§29.5111

H10	hiCCîCa	hiCiC^{2}a	*hēsēḇ*	הֵסֵב	§29.5111
H15	hiCCîCû	hiCiC^{2}û	*hēsábbû*	הֵסַבּוּ	§29.5112
H12	hiCCîCtā	hiCiC^{2}ôtā	*hăsibbôṯā*	הֲסִבּוֹתָ	§29.5113
H20	yaCCîCu	yaCiC^{2}u	*yāsēḇ*	יָסֵב	§29.5111
H25	yaCCîCû	yaCiC^{2}û	*yāsḗbbû*	יָסֵבּוּ	§29.5112
H20	yaCCîCu	yaC^{2}iCu	*yassēḇ*	יַסֵּב	§29.5115

§29.5111 When the geminate consonant stands at word-end, it simplfies (§13.42); the short-*a,* however, does not lengthen under accent (§15.111). **tamma* > **tamm* (§15.51) > *tam* תַּם.

§29.5112 The geminate consonant is preserved in forms having vocalic sufformatives: **tamm* + *û* > *tammû* תַּמּוּ.

§29.5113 The succession of 3 consonants is avoided by epenthesis (§15.64) before consonantal sufformatives. The epenthetic vowel is *ô* in perf. and *ê* in impf. and impv. Study the following examples.

G14	CaC^2 + tî	CaC^{2}ôtî	*sabbṓṯî*	סַבּוֹתִי
H12	hiCiC^2 + tā	hiCiC^{2}ôtā	*hăsibbôṯā*	הֲסִבּוֹתָ
G26	taCuC^2 + nā	taCuC^{2}ênā	*t^{e}subbê^{y}nā^{h}*	תְּסֻבֶּינָה
H26	taCiC^2 + nā	taCiC^{2}ênā	*t^{e}sibbḗ^{y}nā^{h}*	תְּסִבֶּינָה

§29.5114 By necessity, the thematic vowel (§27.231) of CC^2 verbs follows the *first* radical, except in N20 forms and in some H-stem forms. Note the following:

G20	CCC	יִקְטֹל	CC^2	יָסֹב
G65	CCC	קְטֹל	CC^2	שֹׁד
N20	CCC	יִקָּטֵל	CC^2	יִסַּבּוּ

§29.5115 In some verbs, the *first* radical, rather than the second, is doubled. This is called "Aramaic doubling," since the phenomenon is fairly common in Aram. Note: G20 יִסֹּב, יִמַּל; H20 יַסֵּב.

§29.52 A second CC^2 pattern developed by analogy to the "strong verb"; note the following three sections.

§29.521 In some G10 and G11 forms, particularly of transitive verbs:

	normal CC^2	analogic CCC	*Examples*	
G10	CaC^{2}a	CaCaCa	*tam*	*sāḇaḇ*
G11	CaC^{2}at	CaCaCat	*tammā^{h}*	*sāḇ^{e}ḇā^{h}*

§29.522 In forms which have a pure-long vowel preceding or following what would be the 2d rad.:

	CCC	CC²	EXAMPLES			
G50	CâCiCu	CâCiCu	*sôḇēḇ*	סוֹבֵב	*sôḇᵉḇîm*	סוֹבְבִים
G60	CaCâCu	CaCâCu	*šāḏôḏ*	שָׁדוֹד		
Gp50	CaCûCu	CaCûCu	*sāḏûḏ*	שָׁדוּד	*šᵉḏûḏāʰ*	שְׁדוּדָה

§29.523 In forms which require a geminate middle radical:

D10	CiC²iCa	CiC²iCa	*hillēl*	חִלֵּל
Dp10	CuC²aCa	CuC²aCa	*šuddad*	שֻׁדַּד
HtD10	hitCaC²iCa	hitCaC²iCa	*tittammēm*	תִּתַּמֵּם

§29.53 In addition to the formation of D- and HtD-stems by expansion of CC² to CCC (§29.523), the intensive of CC² verbs is frequently formed by the L-, Lp-, and HtL- stems (§28.6). In rare cases, the R-stem (§28.7) is used. These forms are probably analogic with CWC and CYC verbs (§29.6). Note carefully the following:

L10	CâCiCa	CôCēC	*dômēm*	דּוֹמֵם
Lp20	CâCaCa	CôCaC	*nôḏaḏ*	נֹדַד
L20	yaCâCiCu	yᵉCôCēC	*yᵉšôḏēḏ*	יְשׁוֹדֵד
HtL20	yitCâCiCu	yitCôCēC	*yiṯhôlēl*	יִתְהוֹלֵל
R10	CiCCiCa	CiCCēC	*gilgēl*	גִּלְגֵּל
			gilgáltî	גִּלְגַּלְתִּי
			šiʿăsaʿ	שִׁעֲשַׁע

§29.54 It is quite possible that some biconsonantal roots also expanded by the insertion of a long-vowel, thus yielding CWC and CYC verbs, or by the addition of a long-vowel, thus yielding CCW and CCY verbs. These will be discussed below.

§29.6 The descriptions ע״ו and ע״י ('Ayin-Wāw and 'Ayin-Yôd) are somewhat imprecise. Some grammarians prefer to speak of "hollow verbs." The student should be alerted to the fact that there are at least four types of verbs that may be included in these terms:

CWC, with consonantal *wāw* in 2d rad.
CYC, with consonantal *yôḏ* in 2d rad.
CûC, with long-*û* within a biconsonantal root
CîC, with long-*î* within a biconsonantal root

A certain amount of analogic levelling has further complicated the problem.

§29.61 True CWC verbs are: רַוַח, גָּוַע, חָוַר, עָוָה, עִוֵּת, צָוַח, צָוָה, קִוָּה, רָוָה. In all of these the *wāw* is a strong consonant, and the verb is treated accordingly as CCG, GCC, CCY, etc. In this *Handbook,* we shall not normally refer to such verbs as CWC, reserving this *siglum* for hollow verbs.

§29.62 True CYC verbs are: אָיַב, חָיָה, חָיָה, עָיַף. These verbs likewise can be treated as GCC or CCY verbs. In this *Handbook,* CYC will normally not refer to such verbs, but will be reserved for CîC verbs.

§29.63 "CWC" (i.e. CûC) verbs were probably originally 2-cons. roots which expanded by the insertion of a long-vowel.

§29.631 Some basic patterns for the G-stem of CûC verbs are as follows:

	CCC	CûC	EXAMPLES		
G65	C^{e}CôC	CâC > CôC	*bô'*	בּוֹא	§29.6311
		CûC	*qûm*	קוּם	
G10	CaCaCa	CâCa	*qâm*	קָם	§29.6312
	CaCiCa	CiCa	*mēṯ*	מֵת	
	CaCuCa	CuCa > CôC	*'ôr*	אוֹר	(?)
G11	CaCaCat	CaCat	*qâmā^h*	קָמָה	§29.2613
	CaCiCat	CiCat	*mēṯā^h*	מֵתָה	
G12	CaCaCta	CaCtā	*qamtā*	קַמְתָּ	
	CaCiCta	CiCtā	*máttā*	מַתָּ	
G20	yaCCuCu	yaCûCu	*yāqûm*	יָקוּם	§29.6314
			t^{e}qûmê^{y}nā^h	תְּקוּמֶינָה	§29.6315
	yiCCaCu	yiCâCu	*yēḇôš*	יֵבוֹשׁ	§29.6314
			yē'ôr	יֵאוֹר	
			yāmûṯ	יָמוּת	§29.6314
G50	CâCiCu	CâCu	*qâm*	קָם	§29.6313
			'ôr	אוֹר	
		CêCu	*mêṯ*	מֵת	
G60	CaCôCu	CôC	*qôm*	קוֹם	§29.6319
			môṯ	מוֹת	
			bôš	בּוֹשׁ	
G40	yaCCuC	yaCōC	*yāšōḇ*	יָשֹׁב	§29.6317

§29.6311 The lexical form of Cv̂C verbs is the inf. cstr. (G65), since this form preserves the long vowel. The thematic vowel occurs between the two radicals in most forms of these verbs.

§29.6312 The G10 of almost all CûC/CôC verbs is CāC: בָּא, קָם, אָץ, גָּר, כָּל, מָל, מָשׁ, נָם, סָר, רָם, רָץ, שָׂשׂ, שָׁב, etc. Thematic *i* or *u* is quite rare, cf. §29.6317.

§29.6313 Whether the *a* in the G10 form is *long â* or lengthened *short ā* is debatable. If it had been long *â*, it should have undergone the Canaanite shift to *ô* (§14.11); however, the same could be said for the G50 form, where the basic pattern would seem to require *â*. If it is *â*, §15.221 would account for the short vowel in קַמְתָּ. The verb מֵת almost certainly has a short-vowel *i* > *ē* due to accent. It undergoes the *i* > *a* shift in מַתָּה (§15.33). The verb בּוֹשׁ appears to have a long *ô* in G10. It is possible that originally there were CaC, CiC, CuC (?), as well as CâC and CîC verbs.

§29.6314 Except for the "Heavy endings," the stress accent remains on the root in finite forms: קָמָה, קָמוּ. Note §29.6318.

§29.6315 Almost all impfs. of CôC/CûC verbs are of the form yāCûC. Two exceptions are יֵאוֹר and יֵבוֹשׁ, both intransitive (thematic *u* in perf.), developing possibly **yiCāCu* > **yiCâC* > *yēCôC*. A similar development would be expected for מֵת, but here the G20 is יָמוּת.

§29.6316 Before consonantal sufformatives, an epenthetic vowel is used, *ô* וֹ in the perf., and *ê* ֵי in impf., impv., and juss., possibly by analogy to CC² verbs, cf. §29.5.

§29.6317 The characteristic long-vowel of CûC/CôC verbs stands in an originally-closed syllable in G40 and Gc20 forms. In accordance with §15.221, such vowels reduce and then behave as short-vowels. Note carefully: G20 יָשׁוּב, G40 יָשֹׁב, Gc20 וַיָּשָׁב. Cf. 29.6324, .6412.

§29.6318 The ptcp. forms (G50/51) can easily be confused with the perf. (G10/11), hence the student must observe the accent and the context.

G10	*šāb*	שָׁב		
G50	*šā́b*	שָׁב		
G11	*šā́bāʰ*	שָׁבָה		
G51	*šābā́ʰ*	שָׁבָה	*mētā́ʰ*	מֵתָה
G55	*šābî*	שָׁבִים	*mētîm*	מֵתִים
G57	*šābêʸ*	שָׁבֵי	*mētêʸ*	מֵתֵי

§29.6319 The G60 has characteristic long *ô* regardless of the perf. thematic vowel.

§29.632 The basic patterns for other stems of CûC/CôC verbs include the following:

	CCC	CvC	EXAMPLES		NOTES
N10	naCCaCa	naCôCa	*nādôš*	נָדוֹשׁ	§29.6321
N10		naC²ôCa	*nimmôl*	נִמּוֹל	§29.6322
N20	yanCaCiCu	yanCôCu	*yikkôn*	יִכּוֹן	R. 4, 11, 18
N50	naCCaCu	naCôCu	*nākôn*	נָכוֹן	§29.6323

H10	hiCCîCa	hiCîCa	*hēqîm*	הֵקִים	§29.6324
H14	hiCCîCtî	h^{e}CîCôtî	*hăqîmôṯî*	הֲקִימוֹתִי	§29.6316
H20	yaCCîCu	yaCîCu	*yāqîm*	יָקִים	§29.6323f.
H40	yaCCîC	yaCîC>yāCēC	*yāqēm*	יָקֵם	§29.6325
H32	haCCîC	haCîC>haCēC	*hāqēm*	הָקֵם	§29.6325
H60	haCCîC	haCîC>haCēC	*hāqēm*	הָקֵם	§29.6325
H65	haCCîCu	haCîCu	*hāqîm*	הָקִים	
L10		CôCiCa	*kônēn*	כּוֹנֵן	§29.6326
L20		y^{e}CôCiCu	*y^{e}ḵônēn*	יְכוֹנֵן	
L32		CôCiC	*kônēn*	כּוֹנֵן	
L50		m^{e}CôCiCu	*m^{e}šôḇēḇ*	מְשׁוֹבֵב	
HtL10	hitCôCiCa	hitCôCiCa	*hiṯmôṭ^{e}ṭā^h*	הִתְמוֹטְטָה	§29.6326
HtL20		yitCôCiCu	*yiṯkônēn*	יִתְכּוֹנֵן	
			tikkônēn	תִּכּוֹנֵן	
R10		***kilkala**	*kilkel*	כִּלְכֵּל	§29.6327
R20		***y^{e}kalkilu**	*y^{e}ḵalkēl*	יְכַלְכֵּל	
R50		***m^{e}kalkilu**	*m^{e}ḵalkēl*	מְכַלְכֵּל	
R65		***kalkilu**	*kalkēl*	כַּלְכֵּל	
HtR20		***tiṯḥalḥalu**	*tiṯḥalḥal*	תִּתְחַלְחַל	§29.6327

§29.6321 The characteristic long-vowel of the G-stem is replaced by *ô* וֹ in the N-stem; whether this developed from a thematic *u* is not clear. This vowel shows up in all N forms: N10 נָכוֹן, N20 יִכּוֹן, N32 הִכּוֹן, N50 נָכוֹן, N60 נָסוֹג, N65 הִטּוֹחַ.

§29.6322 CûC/CôC verbs sometimes have "Aramaic doubling" of the 1st rad. in N-perf. and H-stem. Cf. נִמּוֹל with נְמַלְתֶּם, הִסִּיתוּךָ with הֵסִית, יַסִּית with וַיָּסֶת, מַסִּית with מֵקִים. Cf. §29.5115.

§29.6323 Note that because of the monosyllabic nature of Cv̂C roots, the preformative vowel frequently stands in an open syllable and lengthens or reduces according to its relation to the stress-accent.

§29.6324 The characteristic long-vowel of CûC/CôC verbs is replaced in the H-stem by the customary long *î* of that stem: H10 הֵקִים, H20 יָקִים, H50 מֵקִים, H65 הָקִים.

§29.6325 Because the juss., inf. cstr., and some impv. forms were originally closed (§15.221), the long vowel of the H-stem reduces in those forms and is subject to the short-vowel rules. Note H20 יָקִים but H40 יָקֵם, Hc20 וַיָּקֶם, H32 הָקֵם, H60 הָקֵם (but we also find הָכִין and הָקִים). Cf. §§29.6316, .6412.

§29.6326 Since there is no middle radical to double, Cv̂C verbs properly have no D-, Dp-, or HtD-stems. They are normally replaced by the L- Pôlēl), Lp- (Pôlal), and HtL- (Hithpôlēl) stems. However, probably by analogic formation, some D- and HtD-stems are found in some Cv̂C stems, particularly in late Heb., e.g.: D10 קִיֵּם, Dc24 וַאֲקַיְּמָה, D32s4 קַיְּמֵנִי, D65 קַיֵּם.

§29.6327 Instead of the L- and HtL-stems, the reduplicated forms (R and HtR, §28.7) are found in some Cv̂C verbs.

§29.633 CWC and CC² verbs are alike in formation in Gc20, Hc20, Hp forms, and the L forms. Therefore CWC verbs often develop other forms by analogy that appear to be CC² forms. Note: G10 בַּז is from בּוּז, but the form appears to be from בָּזַז; N10 נָמַר (for נָמוֹר*) is from מוּר, but it appears to be from מָרַר. The student will only learn these analogic formations through much careful observation. Every time he comes across a form which he cannot explain, he should seek every possible solution. In this way, a high degree of mastery will ultimately be gained.

§29.64 The CYC (ʿAyin-Yôd) verbs, actually CîC, differ from CWC (CûC/CôC) only in the impf. (20), impv. (32), and inf. cstr. (65) forms. It is possible, therefore, that these were yaqtil formations of Cv̂C verbs and should be treated as such.

§29.641 Some basic patterns for CîC verbs are:

	CCC	CîC	mples		NOTES
G65	CiCiC	CîCu	*śîm*	שִׂים	§29.6411
G20	yaCCiCu	yaCîCu	*yāśîm*	יָשִׂים	§29.6323
G40	yaCCiC	yaCîC>yaCiC	*yāśēm*	יָשֵׂם	§29.6412
G32	CCiC	CîC	*śîm*	שִׂים	
H20	yaCCîCu	yaCîCu	*yāḇîn*	יָבִין	§29.6413

§29.6411 The G65 form of CîC verbs is the lexical form, since the characteristic long-*î* is preserved in that form. Cf. §29.6311.

§29.6412 In the G- and H-juss. and conv. impf. forms of CîC verbs, the thematic vowel (long-*î*) occurs in an originally-closed syllable and therefore reduces to a short-vowel, subject to the short-vowel rules. Note: G20 יָבִין but G40 יָבֵן, Gc20 וַיָּבֶן. Cf. §§29.6316, .6325.

§29.6413 Because the characteristic long-*î* replaces the thematic vowel, the G and H forms of impf. and juss. fall together. The student must depend on context and lexical indications of usage to determine the stem in such cases.

§29.642 Some verbs occur as both CûC/CôC and CîC verbs; note שִׂים and שׂוּם, לִין and לוּן, etc.

§29.7 The so-called "Lamed-Hê" verbs (i.e. those with ה in the 3d rad. in the lexical form), are in fact CCW and CCY verbs. (For true CCH verbs, see §29.15). In those forms where the semivowel *w* or *y* (§12.51) would stand at word-end they have been lost (§13.54). Since only isolated forms of CCW verbs occur in OT, we shall use CCY to designate all ל״ה verbs. *Ges.* §75.

§29.71 The following CCY endings should be *memorized:*

ָה– the perf. 3 ms (10) forms in all stems, not having suffixes:
G10 בָּנָה, D10 צִוָּה, N10 נִבְנָה, H10 הִפְנָה, etc.;

ֶה– all impf. forms without sufformatives (20, 21, 22, 24, 29) and the ptcp. m.s.a. (50) in all stems:
G20 יִבְנֶה, D21 תְּכַלֶּה, N24 אִבָּנֶה, H50 מַרְאֶה, etc.;

ֵה– impv. 2 m.s. (32) forms in all stems:
G32 פְּנֵה, D32 צַוֵּה, N32 הֵרָאֵה, H32 הַקְרֵה, etc.;

ֹה– all G60 and N60 and some D60 forms:
G60 עָלֹה, N60 הֵרָאֹה, D60 קַוֹּה;

וֹת– all inf. cstr. (65) forms in all stems:
G65 בְּנוֹת, N65 הִבָּנוֹת, D65 צַוּוֹת, etc.;

וּי– Gp50 of true CCY:
3 בָּנוּי

וּו– Gp50 of CCW, often simply וּ–

§29.711 Note that the normal indicators of D, H-, and other stems may be partially or completely obscured in CCY verbs. At this point the student should make a careful comparison of CCY with CCC forms in the synoptic paradigms.

§29.712 In the perf. before consonantal sufformatives, the 3d rad. develops to *-ay* in the passive and to *-î* in the active (suggesting a basic CaCiCa type): G12 גָּלִיתָ, Dp12 צֻוֵּיתָ.

§29.7121 Note that ִי– is consistently found in G-perfs. with consonantal sufformatives, but in H-, D-, N-, and HtD-stems, there is alternation between ִי– and ֵי– in the perf. In Hp- and Dp- perf., ֵי– is consistently found. N14 נִגְלֵיתִי, N19 נִגְלִינוּ, H12 הִגְלִיתָ, H14 הִגְלֵיתִי; Dp12 צֻוֵּיתָ, Dp14 צֻוֵּיתִי.

§29.7122 Before consonantal sufformatives in the impf. (26,28), impv. (38), and juss. (46,48), the original *y* develops to *-ay*. With monophthongization, this results in the ending ֶינָה–, similar to CC' verbs (§29.2): G26/28 תַּעֲלֶינָה.

§29.713 Before vocalic sufformatives, the original *-y* usually elides: G15 **galayû* > *gālû* גָּלוּ. Similarly, there is elision of *yôḏ* before suffixes: D10s5 **ṣiwwayām* > *ṣiwwām* צִוָּם.

§29.7131 Note especially the perf. 3 fs (11) form. After elision of the original *-y*, the fem. sufformative *-at* was added directly to the firm radicals, and then (possibly at a later date) the *-āʰ* ending was added, resulting in a pleonastic form ־ָתָה: עָשָׂתָה. In nonpausal forms, the penultimate vowel is reduced, עָשְׂתָה, Rule 17.

§29.72 An important phenomenon in CCY verbs is *apocopation* (§13.53) in the conv. impf. (c20), juss. (40), and, in some stems, even in impv. (32) forms. Anaptyxis may or may not follow (§15.61). Note the following examples:

G20 **yiglayu* > **yiglay* > *yiglêʸ* יִגְלֶה
G40 **yiglay* > *yigl* > *yíḡel* יִגֶל
Gc20 **way* + *yiglay* > *wayyigl* > *wayyíḡel* וַיִּגֶל
Gc21 **wat* + *tiklay* > *wattikl* > *wattḗḵel* וַתֵּכֶל
Gc21 **wat* + *tibkay* > *wattibk* > *wattēḇk* וַתֵּבְךְּ

Note that the preformative *i* usually develops to *ē* ֵ after *tāw*.

§29.721 Anaptyxis does not occur in apocopated forms ending in ב, ד, כ, ת, ט, or ק. Note: וַתֵּבְךְּ, וַיַּשְׁקְ, וַיֵּרְדְּ, וַיִּשְׁבְּ. Cf. *Ges.* §28*d*.

§29.723 The very common verbs הָיָה and חָיָה are subject to the action of Rules 9 and 16 after apocopation: G20 *yihyêʰ* יִהְיֶה, G40 **yihy* > **yihî* > *yᵉhî* יְהִי, pausal יֶהִי.

§29.723 Apocopated forms of GCY verbs, yaqtil-type, are identical in Gc20 and Hc20. In such cases only context will show whether the verb is simple or causative—and sometimes even context does not help. Note: וַיִּחַץ, וַיַּעַן, וַיַּעַשׂ. The *yiqtal* types, however, are different: Gc20 וַיִּפֶן, Hc20 וַיֶּפֶן.

§29.8 *Doubly-weak verbs.* Some verbs have 2 or even 3 "weak" radicals: NC', NCY, NWG, 'CY, YC', CW', GC², etc. Cf. *Ges.* §76. *The student will have to observe such roots with extreme care.* For example, the verb חָיַי occurs as an alternate for חָיָה, and, developing as a CC² verb, its G10 is חַי. Such forms will only be learned through wide reading and careful observation.

§29.81 Grammarians occasionally speak of "defective" verbs, cf. *Ges.* §78. These verbs, in reality, take some stems from one root, and some from another, usually combining such types as CC² with CWC, or CWC with CYC.

§29.9 Certain alterations (or perhaps restorations) are made in the verbal form to which suffixes are added (review §20.21).

§29.91 In the perf. with pron. sufs., several points are noteworthy:

§29.911 The *-t* of 3 fs (11) is preserved by the suffix: אֲהֵבַתְהוּ.

§29.912 The original *-tî* of 2 fs (13) is preserved, making the form identical with 1cs (14): יְלִדְתִּנִי.

§29.913 In 2 mp (17), *-tû* replaces *-tem* before suffixes. The *-u* is probably original, cf. Arab. *qataltum*. הֶעֱלִיתֻנוּ.

§29.914 In forms ending with a consonant, a connecting vowel (*a* ַ) is found: אֲכָלַנִי.

§29.92 In the impf., in forms ending with a consonant, a connecting vowel, *-ē* ֵ, is found: תִּגְמְלֵנִי.

§29.93 With G32 and G65 forms, the suffix is added to the basic form but with different reduction of the vowels in the pattern. Note carefully the following:

G32 **kutub* > *kᵉṯōḇ* כְּתֹב
G32s1 **kutub* + *āh* > *koṯbāh* כָּתְבָה (*qāmāṣ ḥăṭûp̄!*)
G65 **muluk* > *mᵉlōḵ* מְלֹךְ
G65s0 **muluk* + *ô* > *molḵô* מָלְכוֹ
G65 **zaʿap̄* + *ô* > *zaʿpô* זַעְפּוֹ
G65s4 **šibir* + *î* > *šibrî* שִׁבְרִי
G65s7 *ʾ*akul* + *kem* > *ʾăḵolḵem* אֲכָלְכֶם. Cf *Ges.* §61.

§29.931 In yiqtal-type verbs, however, the penultimate vowel remains, with near-open lengthening: G32 שְׁלַח, G32s4 שְׁלָחֵנִי.

§29.94 For discussion of suffixes added to verbal forms, see §§23.12f., 23.13f.

DIVISION THREE. SYNTAX

§30. *Syntax* is the joining together of words to convey meaning. In grammar, syntax is the study of such patterns or structures and the synthesizing of rules defining the various elements of syntax for any given language. The native speaker learns from childhood by constant trial and error how to express his thoughts so as to convey meaning and how to understand what another speaker is saying to him. The foreigner must analyze many sentences and formulate rules, whether from the spoken or written language itself or from grammars that contain such analyses. Syntax is the most important part of language study.

§30.1 A *sentence* is the simplest communication of a complete idea. (In modern studies, the term *clause* is often used.) A sentence is a word or group of words that conveys an idea. "Run!" "Sit down!" "Fire burns." "John threw a stone." "While I was running, I tripped and fell." In traditional terms, a sentence consists of a *subject* and a *predicate.*

§30.11 The *subject* is that about which something is stated. It is the person, place, or thing that is, or acts, or is acted upon. It is that which the sentence is about—hence the name subject. The term *topic* is sometimes used.

§30.111 The *simple subject* is a noun or other substantive. "*Vashti* refused to come." "*He* had raised Hadassah." "The *righteous* will be rewarded." "*Swimming* is good exercise."

§30.112 The *complete subject* is composed of the simple subject and the words that explain or define or complete its meaning. "*Vashti the queen* refused to come." "*The quick, brown fox* jumped . . . ." "*Lifting a heavy box* may cause an injury."

§30.113 A *compound subject* consists of two or more subjects that have a common predicate. They are usually joined with a conjunction. "*The man and his wife* were killed." "*Rain or snow* is predicted for tonight."

§30.12 The *predicate* is that which is stated about the subject, or that which is *predicated.* When the term "topic" is used in lieu of "subject," then the term "comment" is used for "predicate."

§30.121 The *simple predicate,* in English, is a verb or verb-phrase. "God *is* (= exists)." "Mordecai *had brought* Hadassah *up.*" In Hebrew, a simple predication may be made without a verb. *ṭôḇaṯ mar'ēʰ hîʾ* 'good of appearance [was] she.'

§30.122 The *complete predicate* is composed of the simple predicate and the word or words that explain or complete the meaning. "The king *appointed officers in all the provinces of his kingdom.*" In Hebrew, a complete predication may be made without a verb, cf. F. I. Anderson, *The Hebrew Verbless Clause in the Pentateuch*, 1970.

§30.123 A *compound predicate* consists of two or more predicates joined to the same subject. "Mary *climbed the stairs, undressed, turned out the light, and climbed into bed.*"

§30.1231 A compound predicate may have a compound subject (30.113). "Jim and Jane got in the car and drove to Lake Gregory."

§30.13 A sentence may be *declaratory* (declaring a fact), *interrogative* (asking a question), *imperative* (expressing a command or request), or *exclamatory* (expressing surprise, grief, or some other emotion as an exclamation). "Abraham believed God." "Where is the lamb?" "Turn and be saved!" "Hallelujah!"

§30.14 *Ellipsis* is the omission or a word or group of words that would be necessary for grammatical completeness of a sentence or clause. Such a clause is *elliptical.*

§30.141 If there is no possibility of confusion or misunderstanding, the subject may be omitted, as in imperative sentences spoken directly to the subject, or in replies to questions. "Run!" (The subject is "you.") "Screamed, would be more accurate" (in reply to the question, "Did she sing?").

§30.142 If there is no ambiguity, the predicate may be omitted. "Harry" is perfectly clear as a reply to the question, "Who met you?"

§30.143 In replies to specific questions, both subject and predicate are commonly omitted when the answer is "Yes," "No," "Maybe," or the like. In fact, such replies can be conveyed in silence by a shrug of the shoulders, a nod of the head, or by some other means. In studying a written language, we have no means of recognizing such methods of communicating ideas.

§30.144 In an inflecting language (§04.21), such as Hebrew, the verb inflection may indicate the subject. It is not correct to consider this as ellipsis. *lô' biqᵉšāʰ dāḇār* 'she did not ask anything' ("she" is in the verb form).

§30.2 Most statements are not simple, therefore other elements are present in the sentence. Some are used to modify either the subject or the predicate, hence are known as *modifiers.* Some are used to complete the predicate, hence are known as *complements.* Some are outside the main thread of subject-and-predicate and are therefore *independent elements.*

§30.21 The *modifier of the subject* may be one or more of the following:

the definite article, "*the* queen," §36.2
a possessive pronoun, "*his* daughter," §36.521
an interrogative pronoun, "*which* book?" §36.55

an indefinite pronoun, "*whatever* place," §30.3124
a demonstrative pronoun, "*this* year," §36.54
an attributive adjective, "*big* box," §36.1
an adjectival participle, "*speeding* car," §36.7
an adjectival infinitive, "a night *to remember*," §36.8
an adjectival phrase, "the Jews *in Susa*," §36.4
an adjectival clause, "a word *which speaks to us*," §38.4
an appositional word or phrase, "Mordecai *the Jew*," §36.6

§30.211 Some of the above can be placed in other categories, such as the relative clause ("which speaks to us," §38.4), or the independent element ("the Jew," §36.6). We are attempting to describe the elements functionally. Furthermore, we are attempting here to describe the elements of syntax *as they are found in English,* in order to have a basis for discussing the elements of syntax as they are found in Hebrew.

§30.22 The *complement of the verb* may be one or more of the following:
a direct object, "he hit *John*," §34.1
a predicate nominative, "this is *he*," §31.2
a predicate adjective, "John is *tall*," §34.5
an infinitive or infinitival clause, "she wants *to sing*," §34.6
a cognate accusative, "he ran *a race*," §34.2
a predicate objective, "they crowned him *king*," §34.3
a predicate genitive, "the book was *John's*," §§34.3, .5
an indirect object, "he gave the book *to John*," §35.1
a supplementary participle, "he came *running*," §34.9
a direct quotation, "he said, '*Go!*'" §38.81
an indirect quotation, "he said *he would go*," §38.82

§30.221 The complement of the verb when a substantive (§30.31) may in turn be modified by any of the types of modifiers listed in §30.21.

§30.222 We repeat that this is a description of elements found in English, and is not to be considered as a description of the elements in Hebrew. It will serve as a basis for analysis and comparison when we turn to Hebrew syntax.

§30.23 The *modifier of the predicate* may be one or more of the following:
an indirect object, "he gave it *to him*," §35.11
an adverb, "he ran *quickly*," §35.2
an adverbial phrase, "he fell *through the window*," §35.3
an adverbial clause, "she talked *while she was working*," §35.4
the nominative absolute, "*the matter having been settled*, we shook hands,"
an adverbial accusative, "I have waited *hours*," §35.5

§30.24 Modifiers can be used *to modify other modifiers* (§37). For example, the adverb often modifies the adjective which is modifying a noun or other substantive. "A *very* tall building."

§30.25 *Independent elements* include interjections, vocatives, parenthetical statements, and the like. "*Behold,* three men stood at the door of the tent." "*John,* how are you?" "He brought up Hadassah (*that is Esther*), the daughter of his uncle."

§30.251 *Apposition* is the setting of a word, phrase, or clause alongside another without a connective, usually to define or limit the latter. It is a specific kind of independent element, since the sentence would be *grammatically* complete without it. At the same time, it is an essential part of the statement, since the communication would be incomplete without it. A noun or pronoun so used is an *appositive,* and a phrase or clause so used is *appositional.* "A bus, *Number 6,* runs to Babylon."

§30.2511 In Hebrew, the use of words, phrases, and clauses without a connective is a very common feature. Cf. F. I. Anderson, *The Sentence in Biblical Hebrew,* 1974, Chapter 3.

§30.3 The *words* in a sentence have rather well-defined duties in the expression of the thought. We classify them according to their use in the sentence as *parts of speech*: nouns, pronouns, adjectives, articles, verbs, adverbs, prepositions, conjunctions, and interjections.

§30.31 A *substantive* is a noun or any word serving as a noun. A word or group of words so used is employed *substantivally.*

§30.311 A *noun* is the name of a person, place, or thing. It can serve as:
a defined subject, "the *jar* leaked," §33.1
a direct object, "I offended the *boy*," §34.1
a cognate accusative, "he sailed the *sea*," §34.2
a predicate nominative, "that was *Jim*," §31.21
a predicate genitive, "the book was *John's*," §34.5
an objective complement, "they crowned him *king*," §34.3
an indirect object, "I gave it to the *girl*," §35.11
the object of a preposition, "take it from my *share*," §36.4
an adverbial accusative, "we walked *miles,*" *35.5*
a modifier of a noun, "the mammon of *unrighteousness*," §36.3
the object of a participle, "leaving *Rome,* we turned north," §35.41
the subject of a nominative absolute, "*morning* having come, I awoke"
object of an infinitive, "to know *John* is to love *him*"
subject accusative of an infinitive, "I want *him* to go"

§30.312 A *pronoun* is a word which stands for a noun. It designates a person, place, or thing (or the plurals), without naming it. A pronoun can serve in any of the ways a noun does. Cf. §30.311.

§30.3121 A *personal pronoun* indicates a person: "I," "we," "you," "he," "she," "they." "It" is an impersonal pronoun.

§30.3122 A *possessive pronoun* is a personal pronoun inflected to show possession. "*My* wife," "*her* book," "*their* child."

§30.3123 A *demonstrative pronoun* is a pronoun that indicates or singles out the person(s) or thing(s) referred to. "*This* is my book." "*These* are your keys." "*That* is her car." "*Those* are good seats." A demon. pron. can serve as an adj.: "*Those* books."

§30.3124 An *interrogative pronoun* is a pronoun that asks "who?," "what?," etc. "*Who* are you?" "*What* is that?" "*To whom* does this belong?" "*Which* is yours?" Some interrog. prons. can serve as adjs. "*Whose* book is this?" "*Which* car shall we use?"

§30.3125 An *indefinite pronoun* is a pronoun that does not identify the referent. "*Anybody* can do it." "*Some* are visitors." An indef. pron. may serve as an adj. "*Some* men are born free."

§30.3126 A *reflexive pronoun* is a compound pronoun used as the object of a verb or preposition when the object denotes the same person or thing as the subject. "I hurt *myself.*" "They deceive *themselves.*"

§30.3127 An *adjective pronoun* is a word that can be used either as an adjective or as a pronoun, such as the demonstrative pronoun and the indefinite pronoun.

§30.3128 A *relative pronoun* is a pronoun used to *relate* a clause to a substantive or a substantival clause. "The crown *which* Vashti wore was gold." "He objected to a woman being president, *which* was, in his view, unconstitutional."

§30.313 The *antecedent* of a pronoun is the substantive to which it refers.

§30.314 In inflecting languages, a substantive may be inflected to indicate gender, number, and case. In English, most nouns are inflected to show number, and some pronouns also have morphological indicators of gender and case (cf. *he, she, him, her*).

§30.3141 *Gender* (in grammar) is the morphological indication of membership in a class, often defined by one of the terms *masculine, feminine,* and *neuter.* These terms are usually, but not always, related to the sex of the person, place, or thing named. (Many neuter objects are personalized, such as "she" for a ship.) In Eng., certain prons. are inflected to show gender: masc. "he," fem. "she," neut. "it."

§30.3142 *Number* (gram.) is the morphological indication of whether there is one (singular), two (dual), three (trial), or more (plural) of the referent. The trial is not found in languages with which most of us are familiar. The dual is comparatively rare. Accordingly, "plural" generally means "more than one." Sing. "house," "I," "it"; plur. "houses," "we," "they."

§30.3143 *Case* (gram.) is the morphological indication of the syntactical relationship of the word to other words in the sentence. In Eng. we generally indicate the nominative, possessive, and objective cases. Nom. "I," "he," "they"; poss. "my," "his," "their"; obj. "me," "him," "them." In the familiar inflecting languages, we find the following cases: nominative, genitive, dative, accusative, ablative, locative, instrumental.

§30.3144 *Definiteness* is the morphological indication that the word is *definite* or *defined.* In Eng. we simply use the def. or indef. art. (§30.3223), but in some languages (cf. Swedish) an inflectional morpheme serves this purpose. The term *state* is used to describe such inflection in Sem. languages.

§30.32 An *adjective* is a word which describes or defines (limits) a substantive. An adjective can serve as a substantive (§30.311), but *as an adjective* it serves either as a predicate adjective (§31.22) or as an attributive adjective (§36.1).

§30.321 A *predicate adjective* is an adjective used in the predicate, generally after a copulative verb. "They are *sick.*" Normally the predicate adjective modifies the subject, but in certain expressions, it may modify the object. "It made him *ill.*"

§30.322 An *attributive adjective* is an adjective that expresses an attribute, serving to define, describe, particularize, supplement, or otherwise limit the substantive or substantival word-group with which it is constructed.

§30.3221 A *descriptive adjective* describes a substantive by stating a characteristic that sets the substantive apart from other substantives of the same name. "A *small* house." "A *wooden* box."

§30.3222 A *definitive adjective* defines or limits a substantive by designating or pointing out one specific member of the class to which the substantive refers. "*The* book." "*That* man." "*One* woman." "*What* city?"

§30.3223 The definite article and the demonstrative pronouns are specific kinds of definitive adjectives

§30.323 *Adjectives of comparison* are used to express a comparison or relative degree of an attribute. Such an adjective may be in the *positive* degree ("warm"), the *comparative* degree ("warmer"), or the *superlative* degree ("warmest").

§30.324 A group of words may serve as an *adjectival phrase* or an *adjectival clause.*

§30.33 A *verb* is a word which can assert something – usually an action – concerning a person, place, or thing. Since some verbs express state or condition, it is imprecise to define a verb as "an action word." "He *runs.*" "It *stands* there." "They *were hit* by the car." "*Wait!*"

§30.331 A *verb phrase* is a group of words used as a verb, generally consisting of a verb and its auxiliaries. In inflecting languages, the verb form is often a single word that requires a verb-phrase in English translation. "It *shall be given* to you."

§30.332 Verbs may be *inflected* or otherwise qualified to indicate any or all of the following categories: *tense, voice, mood, person, number.*

§30.3321 A *finite* verb is one which can be inflected to show tense, voice, mood, and the person and number of the subject, or any combination of these elements.

§30.3322 A *nonfinite* verb is any verb that it not finite. In Heb. this category includes the verbal adjective (participle) and the two verbal nouns (infinitive construct, infinitive absolute).

§30.333 *Tense* (gram.) is a category of verb inflection signifying time and/or duration. In Eng. it is usually expressed by verb-phrases, such as "I *was running,*" "he *will run,*" "you *used to run,*" etc. In inflecting languages, tense is generally indicated by verb morphology: *je suis* 'I am,' *je serai* 'I will be,' *j'étais* 'I was.'

§30.3331 We generally categorize tenses as *past, present,* or *future.* "He *ran.*" "I *say.*" "They *will fall.*" We also have compound tenses, such as "I *have* already *voted.*" "She *will be leaving.*" "They *will have been gone* three weeks."

§30.3332 In the Sem. languages, the verb is inflected to show *aspect* or *kind of action* (*Aktionsart*), rather than tense. The verb predication is either *completed* or *incomplete.*

§30.334 *Voice* is a set of categories in verb inflection which indicate the relation of the verbal predication to the subject.

§30.3341 In the *active voice,* the subj. is the agent, the doer, and the action or predication of the verb is directed to another object (person, place, or thing). "The car *struck* Joe." Stative verbs are considered to be active: "The village smithy *stands.*"

§30.3342 In the *passive voice,* the subj. is the recipient of the action or predication expressed by the verb. "Joe *was hit* by a car." The passive can be turned around to form an active, by reversing the subj. and the verb modifier: "The car *hit* Joe."

§30.3343 In the *reflexive voice*, the subj. is both the agent and in some way the recipient of the predication of the verb. "I *cut myself.*" וְהִתְגַּדִּלְתִּי "I will magnify myself" (Ezek. 38:23). *lā́mmā tiṯrā'û* "Why do you look at one another?" (Gen. 42:1).

§30.335 *Mood* (in grammar) is the expression of the relation of a verb to reality, the attitude of the speaker toward what he is saying, such as certainty, uncertainty, command, wish, and the like. In Eng. mood is often expressed by the auxiliary verbs *can, may, might,* etc. In inflecting langs. it can be expressed by the verb morphology.

§30.3351 The *indicative mood* (indic.) is the mood of the verb used for ordinary statements, whether declaratory or interrogative. "That *is* treason." "Where *are* you?"

§30.3352 The *subjunctive mood* (sbjtv.) is used for doubtful, hypothetical, or subordinate statements, whether declaratory or interrogative. "If this *be* treason." "If I *were* you."

§30.3353 The *imperative mood* (impv.) is used for commands. "*Take* this and *go.*" Sometimes a modified form is used for requests: "Please *take* a letter." The impv., strictly speaking, is limited to 2d pers. sg. or pl.

§30.3354 The *cohortative mood* (cohort.), which is often subsumed under the sbjtv. or the impv., is a mood expressing exhortation, encouragement, entreaty, and the like. "*Let us go* now even unto Bethlehem." Strictly speaking, the cohort. is limited to 1st pers. pl.

§30.3355 The *jussive mood* (juss.) is used to express a suggestion or a mild command. It is often subsumed under the sbjtv. "*Let* the king *write* a letter." Strictly speaking, the juss. is limited to the 3d pers. sg. or pl. In some verbal systems, however, a "jussive" is found in all three persons sg. and pl.

§30.3356 The *optative mood* (opt.) expresses a wish or desire. It is often subsumed under the sbjtv., and sometimes under the impv., cohort., or juss. "*Would* that he were here."

§30.3357 The *precative mood* (prec.) expresses entreaty or supplication. It is often subsumed under the sbjtv. or opt. "*Let* no one *defile* this tomb." Strictly speaking, it is limited to the 3d pers. sg. or pl.

§30.336 A verb may be inflected to show the *person* of the subj. In Eng. we use independent pers. prons., since the verb inflection does not convey this information.

§30.3361 The *first person* is the speaker of the utterance. "*I* did it." "*We* plan to leave early." πιστεύω 'I believe,' שָׁמַעְנוּ 'we heard.'

§30.3362 The *second person* is the person (or persons) addressed. "*Thou* art our Father." "*Ye* are my brethren." "*You* can't go." πιστεύεις 'you (sg.) believe.' שְׁמַעְתֶּם 'you (pl.) heard.'

§30.3363 The *third person* is the person(s) or thing(s) spoken about. "*He* grew suddenly." "*She* is very pretty." "*It* is too large." "*They* are all through." πιστεύει 'he/she believes.' שָׁמְעוּ 'they heard.'

§30.337 The *gender of the subject* is often indicated by the verb form, cf. §30.3141.

§30.338 A verb may be inflected to show the *number* of the subj. It may be *singular* ("he *runs*") or *plural* ("they *run*").

§30.339 Several terms are in more or less common use to describe other characteristics of a verb.

§30.3391 A *transitive verb* is a verb which expresses an action that extends beyond the subj. It is capable of taking a direct object, and it can be made into a passive.

§30.3392 An *intransitive verb* is a verb which indicates a complete action or other predication without the need of a direct object. "The dog just *lies* in his bed.' Normally an intrans. verb cannot be put in the passive.

§30.3393 A *stative verb* is a verb expressing a state or condition. It does not take a dir.obj. "The tree *stands* in the garden." (Contrast the transitive verb, "He *stands* the plants in a row.")

§30.3394 A *factitive verb* is a verb which takes both a dir. obj. and an object complement indicating consequence. It is usually a verb expressing the idea of *making*. "They *made* him king."

§30.3395 To avoid the confusion caused by the terms *active* (= not *stative*) and *active* (= not *passive*), the term *fientive* is used by some grammarians for the former (active, not stative).

§30.34 An *adverb* is a word which modifies a verb, an adjective, or another adverb. Most adverbs answer one of these questions: "How?" "When?" "Where?" or "By how much?" Note these examples. "They grow *tall.*" "He was here *yesterday.*" "I went *home.*" "It is *very* far."

§30.341 A group of words may serve as an *adverbial phrase* or an *adverbial clause.*

§30.342 *Adverbs of comparison* are similar to adjs. of comparison (cf. §30.323). Note the following degrees: pos. "he threw the ball *far*"; comp. "Sue drives *better* than Eileen"; super. "Steve carried the ball *farthest.*"

§30.35 A *preposition* is a word placed before a substantive (§30.31) to indicate the relationship of that substantive to some other word in the sentence or clause. The substantive is called the *object* of the preposition, and the preposition is said to *govern* its object. "I got it *from her.*" "I gave it *to Fred.*"

§30.351 The object of a preposition is usually in some grammatical case. In English, it is the objective case. "I gave it to *him.*" In Semitic languages where case-endings are preserved, the object of a preposition is in usually in the genitive case. (In Akkadian, some pronouns also distinguish a dative case.)

§30.352 A preposition may be used before other parts of speech than nouns and pronouns (such as infinitives, participles, adjectives, etc.). In such instances, we should think of the object of the preposition as acting substantivally (§30.311).

§30.353 A preposition sometimes governs more than one object. "We went *to London* and *Paris.*" In Hebrew, the preposition is usually repeated.

§30.354 The prepositional phrase (i.e. the preposition and the word or words it governs) may be used as an adverbial phrase (§30.341) or as an adjectival phrase (§30.323). "I have found favor *in his sight*" (the phrase modifies the verb). "The man *from Mars* had three eyes" (the phrase modifies the noun).

§30.36 A *conjunction* is a word used to connect words or groups of words. Unlike the preposition, it has no grammatical object, and the connection indicated is much less definite than that which is indicated by a preposition. "Esther rose *and* stood." "Take the robes *and* the horse." "Tea *or* coffee?" "I saw *where* it was." "*If* you go, I'll go."

§30.361 *Coördinating conjunctions* join words or statements that are equal in rank, or coördinate. They may be copulative ("and") or adversative ("but"). "Take the robes *and* the horse." "My wife went, *but* I stayed home."

§30.362 *Subordinating conjunctions* are used to introduce subordinate (dependent) clauses, i.e. clauses that are dependent on the main clause, and are principally temporal, local, causal, final, or result clauses.

§30.3621 A *temporal* clause (§38.51) modifies the main predication by telling *when* it occurred. "*When Esther's maids came and told her*, she was distressed."

§30.3622 A *local* clause (§38.52) tells *where* it occurred. "He took her to the house *where the women lived.*"

§30.3623 A *causal* clause (§38.53) tells *why* (as a result of what cause) the predication occurred. "I told you *because I thought you should know.*"

§30.3624 A *final* or *purpose* clause (§38.54) tells *why* (for what purpose or objective) it occurred. "He gave it to me *so that I could read it.*"

§30.3625 A *result* clause (§38.55) tells the *result* of the main predication. "I taught him carefully *so that he was able to hold the job.*" Sometimes the line between result and purpose is very fine.

§30.363 *Correlative conjunctions* are generally used in pairs to relate two otherwise independent statements (*either . . . or, not only . . . but also,* etc.).

§30.3631 Ellipsis (§30.14) is frequently found in correlative statements. "Either you take it or I shall be angry" (= "either you take it and I shall be pleased, or you refuse it and I shall be angry"). "You or I will have to go" (= "either you will have to go or I will have to go"). "Either one" (= either of two alternatives presented in the context).

§30.364 *Asyndeton* is the juxtaposition of clauses without a conjunction. "I came, I saw, I conquered."

§30.37 An *interjection* is a cry or other exclamatory sound, expressing some emotion or feeling. It has no grammatical connection with the word or group of words in which it stands, strictly speaking, hence its name. "*Oh well,* I guess I can do it." "She saw, *alas!,* that she could not make it." Many of our ordinary interjections are not used in literary language, and some are unprintable (such as the labiolingual trill called the "razzberry").

§30.38 *Infinitives* and *participles* are unique in their ability to serve in a dual capacity in a sentence, in contrast to other words which are used as a particular part of speech in any given sentence. It therefore is extremely important that we learn to recognize the dual usage of these parts of speech. In English we use the terms "gerund" for a verbal noun and "gerundive" for a verbal adjective. In Hebrew, the participles, and especially the infinitives, are not exact counterparts of what we understand by the English terms.

§30.381 An *infinitive* is a verb-form which serves as both verb and noun. As a verb, it can perform many of the functions of a verb, in a main clause (§30.4221) or in a subordinate clause (§30.43). As a noun, it can perform many of the functions of a noun (§30.311).

§30.3811 The infinitive may be used:

as a verbal complement, §32.222
in a noun clause, §33.5
in an adverbial clause, §35.42
as an appositive, §36.63
as a noun modifier, §36.8
as a modifier of a modifier, §37.43
in a substantival clause, §38.312
in an adjectival clause, §38.44
in an adverbial clause, §38.5ff.

§30.3812 In Hebrew we must distinguish further between the *infinitive absolute* and the *infinitive construct* (§32.38f).

§30.382 A *participle* is a verb-form that is both verb and adjective. Like the infinitive, it can serve in a dual capacity in a sentence. It can serve as a verb ("The king saw Queen Esther *standing* in the court"). It can also serve as an adjective (§30.32ff.). In the example just given, "standing" describes "Esther." The participle may be used substantivally (§§30.31, .311). It may also be used adverbially ("*Lifting* his hand, he began to speak"). In English the participle is most frequently used to form compound verb forms: "I *was waiting* for hours."

§30.3821 The participle may be used:

as subject of a nominal sentence, §31.133
as a substantive in the predicate of a nom. sent., §31.24
as a substantive to define the subj. of a verb, §33.4
in an adverbial clause to modify the verb, §35.41
as a noun in construct, §36.7
as an appositive, §36.64
as a noun modifier, §37.41
as a modifier of a modifier, §37.4
in an adjectival clause, §38.421

§30.39 A word may serve in various ways: it may be a noun in one sentence and a verb in another, a verb in one sentence and an interjection in another, etc. "He clouted the ball." "You've got to have clout." "Shoot him." "Shoot! I missed it."

§30.391 For such reasons, some scholars object to the idea of "parts of speech." Nevertheless, *in any given clause* each word has its own peculiar usage and can be defined *for that clause* as a specific part of speech.

§30.392 In the Semitic languages, where many types of words have multiple usage, some grammarians distinguish only the verb, the substantive, and the particle. It is my opinion that the student learns a strange language better if he retains some of the familiar categories of his own language while attempting to master the idiosyncracies of the new language.

§30.4 A *group of connected words* in a sentence may serve as a part of speech. If the group does *not* contain a subject and a predicate, it is called a *phrase.* If it *does* contain a subject and a predicate, or a word which implies or replaces a predicate, it is called a *clause.*

§30.41 A *phrase* can be used as a noun, an adjective, an adverb, or a verb. In some instances a phrase may also serve as one of the other parts of speech.

§30.411 A phrase used as a noun is a *noun-phrase*; one used as a verb is a *verb-phrase.* A phrase used as an adjective is an *adjective-phrase,* and a phrase used as an adverb is an *adverbial phrase.* A verb-phrase is sometimes called a *periphrastic,* and the use of a periphrastic is *periphrasis.*

§30.4111 The use of the verb *to be* and a participle ("I was speaking"), although quite common in English, is found in the Bible generally only in later Hebrew. In Modern Hebrew it is more common, especially with the verb in the perfect (past) to form a past-continuous tense.

§30.412 Many adjectival and adverbial phrases consist of a preposition and its object with or without other words.

§30.413 An *appositional* phrase is a phrase used in apposition to a substantive or another substantival phrase. "Jeremiah, *a man of deep emotion,* was never married."

§30.42 A *clause* is a group of words that forms part of a sentence and that contains a subject and a predicate (cf. §30.4). In some modern grammars, the term "clause" is used where "sentence" is used in this grammar.

§30.421 A *compound sentence* contains two or more clauses, each of which is able to stand independently as a simple sentence. The clauses are called "coördinate" (cf. §30.361). "He is going and I am staying home."

§30.422 A *complex sentence* consists of two or more clauses, one or more of which cannot stand independently, and at least one of which *can* stand independently.

§30.4221 The clause which *can* stand alone is the *main clause* (or the *independent clause*). "If he goes, *I shall go with him.*"

§30.4222 The clause which *cannot* stand alone is the *dependent* or *subordinate clause.* "*If he goes,* I shall go with him."

§30.423 An *appositional clause* is a clause used in apposition to a substantive or substantival clause. "Jeremiah, *who urged submission to Babylon,* was taken to Egypt."

§30.43 A *subordinate clause,* like a phrase, can be used as a part of speech. If it is used as a noun, it is a *noun* or *substantive clause.* If it modifies a substantive, it is an *adjectival clause.* If it serves as an adverb, it is an *adverbial clause.*

§30.431 Subordinate clauses are generally introduced by *subordinating words.* Relative pronouns (*who, to whom, whose,* etc.) are used for adjectival clauses. Adverbial conjunctions (§30.362) or relative adverbs (*so that, where, while, for,* etc.) are used for adverbial clauses.

§30.44 It is possible to build a sentence with an unlimited number of dependent and independent clauses (like the way Aunt Maggie talks on the telephone – all one sentence). Only the inability of the hearer/reader to comprehend the entire sentence limits the complexity with which the speaker/writer may construct his sentence.

§30.5 The *study of syntax* usually begins with the basic elements of the sentence. Each part of speech is analyzed in its usage. In my opinion, this results in a knowledge of the parts but a corresponding loss of the sense of the whole. In this *Handbook,* I propose to consider the verb of the predicate (or the verbless predicate, in verbless sentences) as central, and the other parts of the sentence are then studied in their relationship to the main predication.

§30.6 In my *Handbook of New Testament Greek* (1973), I used the portion numbered §30.6ff. to present sentence diagrams. While I believe that this is an excellent way of seeing the structure of the sentence and getting into the meaning of the text, I have been unable to come up with any way of diagramming Hebrew sentences. We could, of course, diagram the English translation – but that would not help us visualize the structure of the Hebrew. How, for example, could we diagram the clause *lāmā ʿāzab̲tā́nî* 'Why did you leave me'? How can we put this in the standard sentence diagram? The student who wishes to diagram the English translation may consult my *Handbook of New Testament Greek.*

§31. *The verbless predication.* In the Semitic languages, a predication expressing a constant condition is often formed by the juxtaposition of the subject with a verbless predicate. To translate it into English, we must add a copula.

§31.01 Arab grammarians consider any clause that begins with a noun to be a *nominal sentence.* Since the subject is in the verb morphology, a sentence such as "Maḥmud loves Maryam" is described as a subject (Maḥmud) and a predicate (he loves Maryam). In Hebrew syntax, we sometimes find sentences where the predicate contains a verb, but where the sentence structure seems to indicate a nominal or verbless sentence.

§31.1 The *subject* of a verbless (nominal) clause can be a noun or any word or word-group serving as a noun (§30.4).

§31.11 The subj. may be a *noun.* וְהַנַּעֲרָה יְפַת־תֹּאַר וְטוֹבַת מַרְאֶה 'The *girl* was shapely and comely' (Est. 2:7).

§31.111 It may be a compound subject (§30.113). *ûḵᵉḏay bizzāyôn wāqā́ṣep̄* 'and like enough [will be] (the) *scorn and anger* (= scorn and anger will be plenty)' (Est. 1:18).

§31.112 Repetition of the noun gives the subj. distributive force. *ûḇᵉḵol-mᵉḏînāʰ ûmᵉḏînāʰ* 'and in every last city' (Est. 4:3).

§31.12 The subject may be any kind of pronoun.

§31.121 The subject may be a *personal pronoun.* אֲנִי יהוה 'I [am] YHWH' (Exod. 6:2) *hîʾ ʾestēr* 'she [is] Esther' (Est. 2:7).

§31.122 The subj. may be a *demonstrative pronoun.* מַה־זֶּה 'What is *this* ?'

§31.123 The subj. may be a *relative pronoun.* אֲשֶׁר לַמֶּלֶךְ '*which* [belonged] to the king' (Est. 1:9).

§31.124 The subj. may be an *interrogative pronoun. māʰ-llaʿăśôṯ bammalkāʰ* '*what* [is one] to do with the queen?' (Est. 1:15).

§31.125 The subj. may be an *indefinite pronoun.* מִי־בַעַל דְּבָרִים '*whoever* is lord of words (= has a complaint) (Exod. 24:14).

§31.13 The subject of a nominal sentence may be a *noun-phrase* (§30.411).

§31.131 The noun-phrase may be two or more nouns in annexion (cstr.). כְּטוֹב לֶב־הַמֶּלֶךְ 'when good [was] *the heart of the king*' (Est. 1:10).

§31.132 The noun-phrase may be a noun modified by an adjective. אֵבֶל גָּדוֹל לַיְּהוּדִים '*Great mourning* [was] to the Jews' (Est. 4:30).

§31.133 The noun-phrase may be a prep. phrase. וּלְנָגִיד מִמֶּנּוּ 'and for a prince [was one] from him' (= of his descendants, one became a prince) (1 Chr. 5:2).

§31.14 The subj. of a nom. sent. may be a *noun-clause* (an infinitive + any words connected with it).

§31.141 The noun-clause generally is formed with an inf. cstr. לֹא טוֹב הֱיוֹת הָאָדָם לְבַדּוֹ 'not good [is] *man's being by himself*' (Gen. 2:18).

§31.142 The use of the inf. abs. in such a sentence is rare. אָכֹל דְּבַשׁ הַרְבּוֹת לֹא־טוֹב '*to eat* much honey [is] not good' (Prov. 25:27).

§31.2 The *predicate* of a nom. sent. may be a noun or an adjective or any word or group of words serving in either of these capacities.

§31.21 The pred. may be a *noun.* הַמִּזְבֵּחַ עֵץ 'the altar [was] *wood.*' (Ezek. 41:22). הֲלֹא בֹעַז מֹדַעְתָּנוּ '[is] not Boaz our *acquaintance*?' (Ruth 3:2).

§31.211 The pred. may be a compound noun: *wᵉʼanšê sᵉḏōm rāʻîm wᵉḥaṭṭāʼîm* 'and the men of Sodom [were] *wicked and sinners*' (Gen 13:13).

§31.22 The predicate may be a *pronoun.*

§31.221 The pred. may be a *personal pronoun.* אָנֹכִי הוּא 'I [am] *he*' (Isa. 43:25).

§31.222 The pred. may be a pronoun object of a preposition. פֶּה־לָהֶם 'a mouth [is] *to them*' (= they have a mouth) (Psa. 115:5); *lî hakkésep̄* 'to me (= mine) [is] the silver' (Hag. 2:8); *wᵉlô štê nāšîm* 'to him (= he had) two wives' (1 Sam. 1:2).

§31.223 The pred. may be an *indefinite pronoun*: מַה־שְּׁאֵלָתֵךְ ... וְתִנָּתֵן לָךְ *Whatever* [is] thy request ... let it be done for thee' (Est. 7:2).

§31.224 The pred. may be an interrogative pronoun. מִי־אֲבִימֶלֶךְ '*who* [is] Abimelech?' (Judg. 9:28).

§31.23 The pred. may be an *adjective.* וּזֲהַב הָאָרֶץ הַהִוא טוֹב 'and the gold of that land [was] *good*' (Gen. 2:12).

§31.231 The pred. may be a phrase used adjectivally. *mēhem ʻal-kᵉlê hāʻăḇōḏāʰ* '(some) of them [were] *over the vessels of the cult*' (1 Chr. 9:28).

§31.232 The pred. may be an adjective of number: *šnêm ʻāśār ʻăḇāḏéʸḵā* '(we) *twelve* [are] thy servants' (Gen. 42:13).

§31.233 The predicate adjective agrees with the noun to which it refers in gender and number, but it is *without* the definite article (cf. examples in §31.23 above).

§31.24 The pred. may be a *participle* (cf. §30.382). וְנָהָר יֹצֵא מֵעֵדֶן 'and a river [was] *going out* from Eden' (Gen. 2:10).

§31.25 The pred. may be an *adverb*. Since the nom. cl. juxtaposes a subj. and a pred., it is questionable whether the adverbial force is not the product of English translation. *ûp̄ᵉnêhem ʾaḥōrannîṯ* 'and their faces [were] *backward* (= turned away)' (Gen. 9:23); *šām habbᵉḏōlaḥ* '*there* [is] the bdellium' (Gen. 2:12); לְעוֹלָם חַסְדּוֹ '*for ever* [is] his covenant love' (Ps. 136:1). *ʾêʸ hébel* '*where* [is] Abel?' (Gen. 4:9). *ʿōšer bᵉḇêṯô* 'wealth [is] *in his house*' (Ps. 100:3). הֲשָׁלוֹם בֹּאֶךָ '*peacably* (lit. peace) [is] your coming?' (1 Kgs. 2:13).

§31.251 The pred. may be an *adverbial phrase*. אֲשֶׁר לִפְנֵי שַׁעַר הַמֶּלֶךְ 'which [was] *before the king's gate*' (Est. 4:6).

§31.26 The pred. may be a *noun-phrase*: *mᵉlōʾ kol-hāʾāreṣ kᵉḇōḏô* '*the fullness of all the earth* [is] his glory' (Isa. 6:3).

§31.27 The pred. may be a *noun-clause*. וַאֲנִי הִנְנִי מֵקִים אֶת־בְּרִיתִי אִתְּכֶם 'I – I indeed [am] raising my covenant with you' (Gen. 9:9).

§31.3 In some nominal sentences, a *copula* is used to tie the subj. to the pred. The copula may be (1) the 3d pers. pron., (2) a form of the verb היה, or (3) either of the particles יֵשׁ or אֵין.

§31.31 The pron. may be a simple copula. *ʾaḥaṯ hîʾ yônāṯî* 'one she (= is) my dove' (Cant. 6:9). אֵלֶּה הֵם מִשְׁפְּחֹת הַקְּהָתִי 'these they (= are) the families of the Qohathites' (Num. 3:27).

§31.311 The demon. pron. may serve also as a copula or as both pron. and copula. הוּא אֲחַשְׁוֵרוֹשׁ הַמֹּלֵךְ 'that [was the] Ahasuerus who [was] ruling' (Est. 1:1).

§31.32 The pron. may add emphasis to the subj. *wᵉyôsēp̄ hûʾ haššallîṭ ʿal-hāʾāreṣ* 'Joseph, *he* (= was) the governor over the land' (Gen. 42:6). אַתָּה הוּא הָאֱלֹהִים 'You [are] he, the (true) God (= it is you who are God)' (1 Kgs. 18:39).

§31.321 Often the pron. is not truly a copula, but rather the subj. of a nom. cl. which is in apposition to another word or group of words. In addition to the two examples just given, consider these: זֹאת מַתַּת אֱלֹהִים הִיא 'this – the gift of God [is] it' (Eccl. 5:18). *wᵉšébaʿ haššibbŏlîm haṭṭôḇōṯ šéḇaʿ šānîm hēnnāʰ* 'and the seven good ears – seven years [are] they' (Gen. 41:26).

§31.33 The particle יֵשׁ 'existence of' is used as a copula. אָכֵן יֵשׁ יהוה בַּמָּקוֹם הַזֶּה 'surely existence of YHWH (= Y. was) in this place' (Gen. 28:16).

§31.331 Likewise, the part. אֵין 'nonexistence of' is used as a copula. *kî 'ēn lāh 'āḇ wa'ēm* 'for nonexistence to her (= she had no) father and mother' (Est. 2:8). אֵין יוֹסֵף בַּבּוֹר 'nonexistence of Joseph (= J. was not) in the pit' (Gen. 37:29). *wᵉ'ânēḵ 'aḏ-'ôlām* 'and nonexistence of you for ever (= you will be no more)' (Ezek. 27:36).

§31.34 Forms of הָיָה are often used as a copula in a noun clause, especially for a more exact specification of time. *wᵉhā'āreṣ* הָיְתָה *ṯōhû wāḇōhû* 'and the earth *was* waste and emptiness' (Gen. 1:2). The distinction between a verbless clause and a verbal clause in such sentences is not clear-cut. *Ges.* §141*g*.

§31.4 *Word-order* in the nominal sentence is significant. Since the subj. is generally the important item, the order is normally *subj.–pred.* If emphasis is on the pred., it stands first. Joüon §154*f-j*. (C. Albrecht, "Die Wortstellung im hebräischen Nominalsätze," *ZAW* 7: 218ff., 8: 249ff.)

§31.41 The interrog. pron. stands first, and the reply is usually in the same order, *pred.–subj.* מֵאַיִן אַתֶּם 'Where are you from?' מֵחָרָן אֲנַחְנוּ 'We are from Haran' (Gen. 29:4 cf. Gen. 24:23-24).

§31.42 After a relative particle, the order is *pred.–subj.* אֲשֶׁר זַרְעוֹ בוֹ 'which its seed [is] in it' (Gen. 1:11). הָעָם שֶׁיהוה אֱלֹהָיו 'the people who YHWH [is] its God' (Ps. 144:15).

§31.43 After certain conjunctions the order is normally *pred.–subj.* כִּי עֵרֹם אָנֹכִי 'for naked [am] I' (Gen. 3:10, cf. 3:19). *'im lôqēᵃḥ ya'ăqōḇ 'iššāʰ* 'if Jacob [is] taking a wife' (Gen. 27:46). If the subj. is emphatic, it stands first. אִם יהוה הָאֱלֹהִים 'if *YHWH* [is] the (true) God' (1 Kgs. 18:21).

§31.44 The student should note carefully the various examples of word-order in verbless clauses. For example: *subj.—adv.—pred.* Gen 26:29b; 12:6b; *adv.—subj.—pred.* Gen. 4:7; 37:16; *pred.—subj.—adv.* Gen. 43:2b; *adv.—pred.—subj.* Gen. 41:2, etc.

§31.5 The *tense* of a verbless clause can only be determined by context. A verbless cl. may be used for past, present, or future time, or it may predicate a timeless condition. *Ges.* §140*e*.

§31.51 The context may require translation in *past* tense. וְלוֹט יוֹשֵׁב 'and Lot [was] sitting' (Gen. 19:1).

§31.52 The context may require *present* tense. מַדּוּעַ אַתָּה עוֹבֵר אֵת־מִצְוַת הַמֶּלֶךְ 'Why [are] you transgressing the king's command?' (Est. 3:3).

§31.53 The context may even require translation in *future* tense. 'For after seven days אָנֹכִי מַמְטִיר I [will be] causing (it to) rain' (Gen. 7:4).

§31.54 In many expressions, the verbless predication is *timeless*. אָנֹכִי יהוה 'I [am essentially and timelessly] YHWH.'

§31.6 The verbless clause may be used in several ways in addition to simple copular predications. Note the following.

§31.61 The nominal sentence may be optative or jussive. עָלַי קִלְלָתְךָ 'upon me [be] thy curse' (Gen. 27:13). *ri'šôn hû' lāḵem lᵉḥoḏšê haššānāʰ* 'first [let this become] to you with reference to the months of the year'' (= make this the first month of the year; Exod. 12:2) *Ges.* §141*f*.

§31.62 The verbless clause may be used in a condition. אִם יהוה הָאֱלֹהִים 'if YHWH [is] the (true) God' (1 Kgs. 18:21).

§31.63 Note the following: כָמוֹךָ כְּפַרְעֹה 'like you like Pharaoh' (lit. 'as you [are] so Pharaoh [is]; (Gen. 44:18).

§31.64 It becomes obvious that the statement in *Ges.* §140*e* (''Noun-clauses with a substantive as predicate, represent something *fixed, a state* or in short, *a being* so and so'') leaves something more to be said. For further study, cf. F. I. Anderson, *The Hebrew Verbless Clause in the Pentateuch*, 1970.

§31.7 Ellipsis (§30.14ff) is often found in the verbless clause.

§31.71 After הִנֵּה the subj. is often omitted. *hinnēʰ šip̄ḥāṯēḵ* 'Behold, [I am] thy handmaid' (Gen. 16:6). וְהִנֵּה עֹמֵד 'and behold, [he was] standing' (Gen. 24:30)

§31.72 The subj. may be omitted. אִם־עַל־הַמֶּלֶךְ טוֹב 'If [it seems] good to the king' (Est. 1:19). *wᵉḡam hôlēḵ liqrā'ṯᵉḵā* 'and indeed [he is] coming to meet you' (Gen. 32:7 [ET 6]).

§31.8 Of special noteworthiness is the ''dangling'' construction (something like a *nominative absolute*), where a verbless clause is placed in apposition with a noun or a noun-clause. הָאֵל תָּמִים דַּרְכּוֹ 'God – his way [is] perfect' (Ps. 18:31). *bᵉnî šᵉḵem ḥāšᵉqāʰ nap̄šô bᵉḇittᵉḵem* 'My son Shechem – his soul longs for your daughter' (Gen. 34:8). *hā'ănāšîm hā'ēllêʰ šᵉlēmîm hēm 'ittānû* 'These men – peaceful [are they] with us?' (Gen. 34:21). *YHWH 'ĕlôhêḵā 'ēš 'ôḵᵉlāʰ hû'* 'YHWH your God – a consuming fire [is] he' (Deut. 4:24).

§31.9 Concord in the verbless cl. at times seems unusual.

§31.91 A collective subj. may have a plur. pred. וְכָל־הָאָרֶץ בּוֹכִים 'and the whole land [was] weeping' (2 Sam. 15.23). *ûḇêʸṯ šā'ûl hôlᵉḵîm wᵉḏallîm* 'and the house of Saul [was] going and weak (= becoming steadily weaker)' (2 Sam. 3:1). Note the following: הוּא אַהֲרֹן וּמֹשֶׁה 'that [was] Aaron and Moses' (Exod. 6:26).

§32. A *verbal* predication (§30.121)—as distinguished from the verbless predication (§31.)—states more than an equivalence between subject and predicate. If the verb is transitive (§30.3391), the action of the subj. on the obj. of the verb is indicated. If the verb is intransitive (§30.3392), some change in state, or some effect of the state, is generally indicated. In some sentences where the subj. precedes the verb, it is possible that a nominal sentence is intended (cf. §31.01). *Ges.* §142*a-e.* נַעֲשֶׂה אָדָם בְּצַלְמֵנוּ 'let us make man in our image' (Gen. 1:26). In contrast, note: *ûmord*^{e}*k̲ay yāḏa‘ ’eṯ-kol-’ăšer na‘ăśā*^{h} 'And (as for) Mordecai, [note *r*^{e}*ḇî*^{a}*‘*] he knew all that was done' (Est. 4:1).

§32.1 By its morphology, the verb indicates person, gender, and number of the subj. (§30.144), as well as other elements, such as aspect (tense), voice, mood, etc.

§32.11 The subj. indicated morphologically may be 1st pers. (the one speaking), 2d pers. (the one spoken to), or 3d pers. (the one spoken about.

§32.111 In the 1st pers., there is no need to define the subj. more closely; the hearer/reader knows that it is the speaker/writer (or the one represented as such in the context) who is making the predication. *’ăšer ‘āśîṯî lô* 'which I have made for him' (Est. 5:4).

§32.1111 The pron. may be used for emphasis. *wa’ănî zāqántî wāśáḇtî* 'and *I* am old and grey' (1 Sam. 12:2).

§32.1112 In letters or inscriptions the author often inserts his name to define the subject, since he is not visible. וְרָאִיתִי אֲנִי דָנִיֵּאל 'and I *Daniel* saw' (Dan. 12:5).

§32.112 In the 2d pers. there is no need to define the subj., since the hearer/reader(s) know(s) that he/she/they is/are the person(s) addressed by the speaker/writer. מַה־זֹּאת עָשִׂית 'What is this thou hast done?' (Gen. 3:13).

§32.1121 For the sake of emphasis, the subj. may be defined. הֲלֹא אַתֶּם שְׂנֵאתֶם אוֹתִי 'Did *you* not hate me?' (Jud. 11:7).

§32.113 When the subj. is 3d pers., it must be more closely defined, except when it is clear from the immediate context. *wayyō’m*^{e}*rû na‘ărê hammélek̲* 'and they said, i.e. the servants of the king, ... ' (Est. 2:2). *wayyaggeḏ-lô mord*^{e}*k̲ay* 'and he (i.e. Mordecai) told him' (Est. 4:7).

§32.1131 If the subj. is clear from context, it may be omitted. *zāk̲ar ’eṯ-wašti* 'he remembered Vashti' (Ahasuerus is the subj., just mentioned: Est. 2:1).

wattišlaḥ bᵉgāḏîm 'and she sent clothes' (i.e. the queen, mentioned in the previous clause, Est. 4:4).

§32.1132 Sometimes the subj. is not specified, even though it has not been mentioned for several sentences/lines. *nāṯan lô* 'he gave to him' (Est. 4:8; Mordecai, mentioned in 4:7 gave to Hatach, mentioned in 4:6).

§32.1133 Even when it is clear from context, the subj. may be defined. *wattáʿan ʾestēr* 'and Esther answered'. (Since the conversation is between Esther and Mordecai, and since the verb forms distinguish masc. from fem., it is perfectly clear that Esther is the subj. Nevertheless, possibly for stylistic reasons, she is named.)

§32.114 The *impersonal subject* is often expressed by the 3d sing.: וַיְהִי 'and *it* came to pass'; וַיֵּאוֹר 'and *it* became light'; וַתֵּצֶר לְדָוִד 'and *it* was narrow for David' (= he was in a jam). *Ges.* §144*b-c*.

§32.115 The *indefinite subject* is often expressed by the 3mp. יַשְׁקוּ '*they* [= people in general] watered (the flocks at that well; Gen. 29:2); *yᵉḇaqᵉšû lammélek̲* 'let *them* seek on behalf of the king ...' (Est. 2:2).

§32.1151 The 3d sing. (m. or f.) is also used for an indef. subj. *Ges.* §144*d*.

§32.1152 The ptcp. pl. is often used in this manner. *Ges.* §144*i*.

§32.1153 The indef. subj. is often best rendered by a passive, cf. Est. 2:2.

§32.12 The verb morphology also distinguishes the *gender* of the subj., either *masculine* or *feminine*. There is no *neuter*, and inanimate things have either masc. or fem. grammatical gender. In some verb forms, masc. and fem. are not distinguished. *ʿāśāʰ hammélek̲ ... mištêʰ* 'the king made a banquet' (Est. 1:5). *gam wašti hammalkāʰ ʿāśᵉṯāʰ mištēʰ nāšîm* 'Vashti the queen also made a banquet for the women' (Est. 1:5). *wᵉʾēḏ yaʿălêʰ min-hāʾāreṣ* 'and a mist (m.) used to go up from the earth' (Gen. 2:6). *wᵉhāʾāreṣ hāyᵉṯāʰ ṯōhû wāḇōhû* 'and the earth (f.) was *tohu* and *bohu*' (Gen. 1:2).

§32.13 The verb morphology generally distinguishes the *number* of the subj., either *singular* or *plural*. The dual, if it ever existed in Heb. verb morphology, has disappeared. *wayyṓʾmer hāmān* 'and Haman said (sg.)' (Est. 3:8). *wayyōʾmᵉrû ʿaḇḏêʸ hammélek̲* 'and the king's servants said (pl.)' (Est. 3:3).

§32.2 Some verbs predicate a state or condition, and are called *stative* verbs (§30.3393). Other verbs predicate an act, and are called *active* (or *fientive*) verbs. Verbs of the latter category may confine the activity to the agent (*intransitive*, §30.3392), or the activity may extend to a person or thing other than the agent (*transitive*, §30.3391). However, in Heb. these distinctions are not always equivalent to our Western system.

§32.21 The G-stem of some verbs predicates a state or condition (§§27.23, .233): כָּבֵד 'he is heavy,' קָטְנָה 'she is small,' יָכֹלְתִּי 'I am able,' זָקַנְתִּי 'I am old.'

§32.211 The predication of a stative verb in Heb. may be complete, כָּבֵד 'he is heavy,' or it may be incomplete, חָפֵץ 'he is delighted with, takes pleasure in.'

§32.2111 If the stative verb makes an incomplete predication, this may be completed by: (1) a substantive in the accusative, (§34.1), (2) a prepositional phrase (§34.112), or (3) a complementary infinitive (§34.82). In some instances, the verb appears to be transitive. יְכָלְתִּיו 'I have prevailed over him' (Ps. 13:5); *hammélek̲ ḥāp̄ēṣ bîʸqārô* 'the king delights in his honor' (Est. 6:7); חָפַצְתִּי צַדְּקֶךָּ 'I desire thy justification' (Job 33:32).

§33.212 Verbs which are *stative* in the G-stem may be *fientive* or *transitive* in the D or H-stem: לָבַשׁ 'he dressed, put on clothing,' הִלְבִּישׁ 'he clothed [another person].'

§32.22 The G-stem of other verbs predicates an action. These verbs are usually called *active*, but because of the confusion between "active = not passive" and "active = not stative," some grammars use the term *fientive.*

§32.221 The predication of a fientive (active) verb may be complete ("he lied") or incomplete ("he made").

§32.2211 If the fientive verb makes an incomplete predication, this is generally completed by a substantive in the accusaive, or its equivalent (§34), and the verb is considered to be *transitive. bᵉrēšît̲ bārā' 'ĕlōhîm 'ēt̲ haššāmáyim wᵉ'ēt̲ hā'āreṣ* 'when in the beginning God created the heavens and the earth ... ' (Gen. 1:1).

§32.222 Verbs which are simply transitive (i.e. take only *one* object) in the G-stem, may take two objects in the D- or H-stem; רָאָה 'he saw *x*,' הֶרְאָה 'he caused *y* to see *x*,' or 'he showed *y x*.'

§32.23 It becomes apparent that we cannot hold to a simple distinction between *transitive* and *intransitive* verbs. יָכֹל *stative* 'he is able,' may take an obj.: *yādá'tî kî-k̲ōl tûk̲āl* (pausal) 'I know that you shall prevail over all' (Job 42:2). Likewise, *šāk̲ab̲* (stat.) 'he lay down,' may be used transitively, וְאִם שָׁכוֹב יִשְׁכַּב אִישׁ אֹתָהּ 'and if a man shall indeed lie (with) her ...' (Lev. 15:24).

§32.24 Certain verbs may take *two* objects. Most common are *factitive* verbs (§30.3394). The objects may be *act and consequence, material and result*, etc. See §34.3ff. This is not to be confused with a compound object. *Object of act and consequence:* 'they crowned *him king*.' *Compound object:* 'the car struck *John* and *Mary*.

§32.3 For *mood,* review §30.335ff. In Heb., the loss of final short vowels (§15.51) has made it impossible to identify certain moods, such as the subjunctive, the energic, and, in most instances, the jussive. If Heb. was like Akk. in the use of the sbjtv., the verb in every dependent clause should be in the sbjtv. On the other hand, if it was like Arab., the use of the sbjtv. would be much more restricted.

§32.31 The *indicative* is the mood used for ordinary predications (§30.3351). In the absence of final short vowels, we assume that all finite verbs not in the impv., juss., or cohort. are indicative – which may be quite wrong.

§32.311 The indic. is used in a *declaratory* statement (§30.13): *wayy^{e}k̲ullû haššāmáyim w^{e}hāʾáreṣ w^{e}k̲ol-ṣ^{e}b̲āʾām* 'and the heavens and the earth and all their host were finished' (Gen. 2:1).

§32.3111 A *negative* declaratory predication is indicated by the use of לֹא with the indic. The neg. adv. is almost invariably placed immediately before the verb. כִּי לֹא הִמְטִיר יהוה אֱלֹהִים עַל־הָאָרֶץ 'for the Lord God had not caused it to rain on the earth' (Gen. 2:5). Cf. *Ges.* §152*a*.

§32.3112 For the use of לֹא and impf. for negative commands, see §32.3211.

§32.312 The indic. is used in an *interrogatory* predication. *mî higgîd̲ l^{e}k̲ā kî ʿê^{y}rōm ʾáttā^h* 'who told you that you (were) naked?' (Gen. 3:11).

§32.32 The *imperative* mood is found only in the 2d pers. (§27.4ff.). It is used for commands, and in some instances for permission, assurance, consequence, and the like (*Ges.* §110).

§32.321 The impv. generally expresses real *commands*: תְּלֻוהוּ עָלָיו 'Hang him on it!' (Est. 7:9).

§32.3211 A *negative command* is not expressed in the impv. It is generally expressed either by לֹא + impf. or by אַל + juss.

§32.322 The impv., especially after a previous attempt to dissuade, may express *permission*: וַיֹּאמֶר לוֹ רוּץ 'so he said to him, "(O.K.), run!" ' (2 Sam. 18:23).

§32.323 The impv. may express *certainty* or *assurance: kî-ʾim-śîśû w^{e}gîlû ʿădê^y-ʿad̲* 'but rejoice and be glad forever' (Isa. 65:18) – i.e. in the new heavens and the new earth which YHWY promises to create (65:17). וּדְעִי וּרְאִי כִּי־רַע וָמָר עָזְבֵךְ אֶת יהוה 'then know and see that your forsaking YHWH is evil and bitter' (Jer. 2:19) – after a reproval for their wickedness.

§32.3231 The impv. of the N-stem is used with this force. *w^{e}'attem hē'ās^{e}rû* 'and you shall be bound' (Gen. 42:16; lit., 'and you, be bound!'). 'Ascend this mountain ... and die ... וְהֵאָסֵף אֶל־עַמֶּיךָ and be gathered to your people' (Deut. 32:48-50).

§32.324 An impv. which follows another impv. (with conjunctive *wāw*) may express the consequence of complying with the first command: *zō't 'ăśû wî^{y}ḥ^{e}yû* 'do this and live' (Gen. 42:16). פְּנוּ אֵלַי וְהִוָּשְׁעוּ 'turn to me and be saved' (Isa. 45:22). *Ges.* §110*f.*

§32.325 An impv. which follows a juss., a cohort., or an interrog. sentence (with conj. *wāw*) may express a consequence which is intended or which is certain. *w^{e}hiṯpallēl ba'aḏkā weḥ^{e}yē^{h}* 'and he will pray for you, and you shall live' (lit., so live!; Gen. 20:7). *wa'ăḇāreḵ^{e}ḵā wa'ăgadd^{e}lā^{h} š^{e}méḵā weh^{e}yē^{h} b^{e}rāḵā^{h}* 'and I would bless you and make your name great, so be a blessing' (Gen. 12:2). וּבַמָּה אֲכַפֵּר וּבָרְכוּ 'and with what shall I make atonement that you may bless (lit. and bless, *impv.*) the inheritance of YHWH?' (2 Sam. 21:3).

§32.326 The impv. with ָה (the "lengthened impv.") seems to be merely a stylistic variant, not perceptibly different from the normal impv. *g^{e}šā^{h}-nnā ûšăqā^{h}-llî* 'come here and kiss me!' (Gen. 27:26). Note especially: *mol^{e}ḵā^{h} 'ālē^{y}nû* 'reign over us' (Judg. 9:8) and *m^{e}lōḵ-'ālē^{y}nû* 'reign over us' (Judg. 9:14).

§32.327 נָא 'please' may be added to either the normal or the lengthened impv. Sometimes it seems to be little more than a stylistic variant. גְּשָׁה־נָּא 'come here' (Gen. 27.26). הַגִּידִי נָא לִי 'tell me, pray' (Gen. 24:23).

§32.34 The *cohortative* (sometimes called the "lengthened impf.," §27.53) occurs usually in 1st pers., and expresses the intention or desire of the speaker to accomplish that which is predicated by the verb. נֵלְכָה וְנַעַבְדָה אֱלֹהִים אֲחֵרִים 'we would go and serve other gods' (Dt. 13:7). *ûḇ^{e}yaḏ 'āḏām 'al-'eppōlā^{h}* 'but into the hand of man (*vice* YHWH) let me (lit, I would) not fall' (2 Sam. 24:12).

§32.341 In general, when the speaker is free to act, the cohort. expresses intention, determination, or desire. *n^{e}natt^{e}qā^{h}* 'let us break asunder' (Ps. 2:3). When the speaker is bound by or dependent upon others, the cohort. expresses a wish or request. *na'b^{e}rā^{h}-nnā^{h}* 'we would like to pass through, please' (Num. 20:17).

§32.342 The cohort. following an impv. or juss. (with conj. *wāw*) expresses an intention or intended consequence. וְהָבִיאָה־לִּי (leng. impv., §32.326) וְאֹכֵלָה 'so bring it to me and I would eat (= that I may eat)' (Gen. 27:4). *wᵉṯiqrab̲ wᵉṯāb̲ôʼāʰ* ... *wᵉnēḏā́ʻāʰ* 'and let (the counsel of the Holy One of Israel) draw near and enter, and we would (= that we may) know' (Isa. 5:19). *Ges.* §108*d.*

§32.343 The cohort. may express a contingent intention in the protasis or apodosis of a conditional sentence. *ʼim-ʼăḏabbᵉrāʰ lôʼ-yēḥāśēḵ kᵉʼāb̲î wᵉaḥdᵉlāʰ maʰ-minnî yahălōḵ* (unusual G65 form) 'if I would speak, my grief is not assuaged, and would I forbear, what has gone from me?' (Job 16:6). כִּי לֹא־ תַחְפֹּץ זֶבַח וְאֶתֵּנָה 'for you do not delight (in) sacrifice, else would I give (it)' (= if you did, I would give) (Ps. 51:15). *Ges.* §108*e-f.*

§32.344 The cohort. on rare occasion occurs in 3d pers. *yᵉmahēr yāḥîšāʰ maʻăśēhû* 'let him hasten, let him speed his work' (Isa. 5:19). וְעוֹלָתְךָ יְדַשְּׁנֶה־סֶּלָה 'and your burnt offering may he regard favorably (selah)' (lit., may he make fat = acceptable) (Ps. 20:4).

§32.345 The cohort. may be followed by נָא 'I pray, please, would you': נַעְבְּרָה־נָּא 'let us pass through, we pray' (Num. 20:17).

§32.35 The *jussive* (sometimes called the "shortened imperfect," §27.51) occurs generally in the 3d pers., and expresses the intention of the speaker that another person might accomplish the predication of the verb. *Ges.* §109.

§32.351 The juss. may express a *wish, request,* or *restraint.* יָקֵם יהוה דְּבָרוֹ 'may YHWH establish (filfill) his word!' (1 Sam. 1:23). *tāšob̲-nāʼ népeš-hayyéleḏ hazzêʰ* 'let the life of this child return!' (1 Kg. 17:21).

§32.3511 The subj. of the juss. may be impersonal or indefinite. יְהִי אוֹר 'let there be light!' (Gen. 1:6).

§32.3512 The addition of נָא seems to strengthen a request, making it like an optative or precative. *yēšeb̲-nāʼ ʻab̲dᵉḵā...wᵉhannáʻal yáʻal* 'let thy servant stay ... and let the boy go up' (Gen. 44:33).

§32.352 The juss. may express *advice* or *recommendation.* הֲלֹא אֲחוֹתָהּ הַקְּטַנָּה טוֹבָה מִמֶּנָּה תְּהִי־נָא לְךָ תַּחְתֶּיהָ 'Is not her little sister better (prettier) than she? Let her be yours, I pray, instead of her (the older sister)' (Judg. 15:2).

§32.353 The juss. occurs in the 2d pers., generally with אַל to indicate a lighter form of the *negative command, dissuasion,* or *deprecation.* רְדָה אֵלַי אַל־תַּעֲמֹד 'come down to me; don't delay' (Gen. 45:9). *zᵉḵōr ʼal-tiškaḥ* 'remember; don't forget' (Dt. 9:7).

§32.354 The juss. occurs occasionally in 1st pers. In this usage, it approaches the cohort. in force. וְלֹא־נַשְׁאֵת בָּהֶם אִישׁ 'and let us not leave a man of them' (1 Sam. 14:36). *w*^{e}*lô'-nôṯar bô* ... *gam-'eḥāḏ* 'and let us not leave in it ... even one' (2 Sam. 17:21).

§32.355 The juss. (with conj. *wāw*) following an impv., cohort., or an interrog. clause may express an intention or an assurance of a contingent occurrence. *qaḥ wālēḵ ûṯ*^{e}*hî*^{y} *'išā*^{h} *l*^{e}*ḇen-;ăḏônê*^{y}*ḵā* 'take (her) and go, and let her be (= she shall be) a wife for the son of your lord' (Gen. 24:51). *'immāl*^{e}*ṭā*^{h} *nnā' šāmmā*^{h} ... *ûṯ*^{e}*ḥî*^{y} *napšî* 'let me escape thither, I pray, ... and let my soul live (= and I shall be safe)' (Gen. 19:20). וּמַה בַּקָּשָׁתֵךְ ... וְיִנָּתֶן לָךְ 'What is your petition ... and let it be given to you' (= and it shall be given to you)' (Est. 5:3). *Ges.* §109*f*.

§32.356 The juss. may be used in either protasis or apodosis of conditional sentences. תָּשֶׁת־חֹשֶׁךְ וִיהִי לָיְלָה 'let you make darkness, then let it be dark' (= if you make darkness, then it is night, Ps. 104:20). *w*^{e}*'im šāḵôḇ yiškaḇ 'îš 'ôṯāh ûṯ*^{e}*hî*^{y} *niddāṯā*^{h} *'ālā*^{y}*w w*^{e}*ṭāmē' šiḇ'aṯ yāmîm* 'and if a man shall indeed lie with her (lit., bed her), and let her uncleanness be upon him, then he shall be unclean seven days' (Lev. 15:24). *Ges.* §109*h*.

§32.357 In a number of passages the H-juss. (H40) יוֹסֵף occurs where it has no jussive force. Possibly this is a G20 *yaqtil* form **yawsip*. Num. 22:19; Dt. 18:16; Hos. 9:15; Jon. 2:2; Ezek. 5:16; Gen. 4:12.

32.36 Omitted arbitrarily.

§32.37 The *participle* is not a mood. It is a verbal noun, often serving adjectivally, and may be used as a noun

- as subj. of a verb, §33.4
- as obj. of a verb, §34.112
- as a governing noun in annexion, §36.311
- as a modifier of a noun, §36.1

The ptcp. may also be used as a verb, and as such it is considered here.

§32.371 General observations about the verbal nature of the ptcp. include the following.

§32.3711 The act. ptcp. has various shades of meaning and is sometimes difficult to translate. Thus מֵת may mean 'dying' (Zech. 11:9), 'dead' (often, and *hammēṯ* is always 'the dead'); נֹפֵל may mean 'falling' (often), 'fallen' (Judg. 3:25, 1 Sam. 5:3), 'ready to fall' (Isa. 30:13, Amos 9:11); and עֹשֶׂה may mean 'will be doing, is about to do' (Gen. 41:25).

§32.3712 The *pass. ptcp.* generally describes a state or condition as the result of activity, but we must observe certain features. Gp50 כָּתוּב 'written,' Np50 *nôrā'* 'to be feared,' *neḥmāḏ* 'to be desired, desirable,' Dp50 *m*^{e}*hullāl* 'worthy to be praised' (Ps. 18:4).

§32.3713 The stative verb (§32.21) properly does not form a ptcp., but rather an adj. of the form CāCēC or CāCōC: *kāḇēḏ* 'heavy,' *qāṭōn* 'small.' Some verbs which are stative in form (i.e. CaCiCa) are transitive, e.g. *śānē'* 'he hated,' and have true ptcps.: *śônē', śānû'*. *Ges.* §116*b*.

§32.3714 If a verb has *both* ptcp. CôCēC and adj. CāCēC forms, they are notably different. לָעֵן *bᵉlaʿănê śāp̄āʰ* 'by (men) of stammering lips' (Isa. 28:11), but cf. לוֹעֵן *kullô lôʿēn lî* 'everyone mocks me' (Jer. 21:7).

§32.372 The ptcp. may take an obj. in the acc., or, if the verb from which it is derived takes a prepositional obj., the ptcp. will do the same. *'ôhēḇ 'eṯ-dāwîḏ* 'hating David' (1 Sam. 18:29). עֹשֵׂנִי 'who made me' (Job 31:15). מִי רֹאֵנוּ 'who sees us?' (Isa. 29:15). *hārôḏîm bāʿām* 'who rule over the people' (1 Kg. 9:23). *hinᵉnî rôp̄ē' lāḵ* 'behold, I will heal you' (2 Kg. 20:5).

§32.3721 The verbal adj. CāCēC may take an acc. of the person or thing if the verb from which it is derived does so. *mālē' rûᵃḥ ḥoḵmāʰ* 'full of the spirit of wisdom' (Dt. 34:9).

§32.3722 The pass. ptcp may take an acc. after the abs. form, or a gen. after the cstr. form. לָבוּשׁ בַּדִּים 'clothed (in) linen' (Ezek. 9:2). *qārûʿêʸ bᵉgāḏîm* 'torn of (= in respect to) clothes' (2 Sam. 13:31). *śᵉrûp̄ôṯ 'ēš* 'burnt with fire' (Is. 1:7).

§32.373 The ptcp. sometimes stands in a "dangling" construction (*casus pendens*), which may be considered as subj. of a compound noun-clause. *šôp̄ēḵ dam hā'āḏām bā'āḏām dāmô yiššāp̄ēḵ* 'the one who sheds man's blood, by man shall his blood be shed' (Gen. 9:6). *kol-'îš zôḇēᵃḥ zéḇaḥ ûḇā' náʿar hakkôhēn* ... 'if any one sacrificed a sacrifice, then the priest's servant came ...' (1 Sam. 2:13). *Ges.* §116*w*.

§32.374 A ptcp. may be followed by a finite verb. שָׂם תֵּבֵל כַּמִּדְבָּר וְעָרָיו הָרָס 'who made the world like a wilderness, and its cities he overthrew' (Is. 14:17). *maṣdîqê rāšāʿ ʿéqeḇ šôḥaḏ wᵉṣiḏqaṯ ṣaddîqîm yāsîrû mimménnû* 'who acquit the guilty for a bribe, and the right of the righteous they take from him' (Is. 5:23).

§32.3741 According to Driver *Tenses* §117, a ptcp. followed by perf. with conj. *wāw* asserts something indefinite or undetermined and may generally be translated, 'whoever, whenever, if ever.' מַכֵּה אִישׁ וָמֵת מוֹת יוּמָת 'whoever smites a man and he dies shall surely be put to death' (Exod. 21:12).

§32.3742 A ptcp. followed by impf. with conv. *wāw*, on the other hand, asserts an actual concrete event. It is generally translated by a clause introduced by 'who, that.' *lā'ēl hāʿônêʰ 'ōṯî bᵉyôm ṣārāṯî wayᵉhî ʿimmāḏî* 'to the God who answered me in the day of my distress and was with me' (Gen. 35:3).

§32.375 In some passages we seem to see the ptcp. developing as a historical tense (continuous past, continuous present, etc.) in Bib. Heb. Such usage is fairly common in Aram. and Syr., and fully developed in Mod. Heb. הַבָּקָר הָיוּ חֹרְשׁוֹת 'the cattle were plowing' (Job. 1:14). *wayyihyû niqrā'îm lip̄nê hammélek̲* 'and they were being read in the presence of the king' (Est. 6:1).

§32.376 According to E. Sellin, *Über die verbal-nominale Doppelnatur der hebräischen Participien und Infinitive, usw.*, p.40ff., the ptcp. when construed as a verb expresses a single and comparatively transitory act, or relates to particular cases, historical facts, and the like, while the ptcp. construed as a noun indicates repeated, enduring, or commonly occuring acts, occupations, or thoughts. *Ges.* §116*f.*

§32.38 The *infinitive construct* is not a mood, but a verbal noun. As such, it may be used:

as subj. of a verb, §33.5
as obj. of a verb, §34.12
as gen. after a cstr., §36.312
as obj. of a prep., §35.42

As a verb, the inf. cstr. can be used in the following ways.

§32.381 The inf. cstr. may be used after יֵשׁ, אֵין, or לֹא, as follows:

§32.3811 After *yeš*, it indicates possibility or permission. הֲיֵשׁ לְדַבֶּר־לָךְ אֶל־הַמֶּלֶךְ 'Is it OK to speak to the king on your behalf?' (2 Kg. 4:13). *'im 'iš* (= *yēš*) *l^e^hēmîn* 'if it is possible (= it is not possible) to go to the right ...' (2 Sam. 14:19).

§32.3812 After אֵין *'ên* it indicates impossibility or prohibition. כִּי אֵין לָבוֹא אֶל־שַׁעַר הַמֶּלֶךְ 'for it is not permitted to enter the king's gate' (Est. 4:2).

§32.3813 After לֹא it indicates a more absolute or categorical impossibility. . *kî lô' l^e^hôrîš 'et̲-yôš^e^b̲ê^y^ hā'ēmeq* 'for he could not dispossess the inhabitants of the plain' (Judg. 1:19). לֹא לְהַזְכִּיר בְּשֵׁם יהוה 'Don't mention the name of YHWH' (Amos 6:10).

§32.382 In some instances, the inf. cstr. by itself serves as a finite verb. אִם אָמְרִי 'if I say' (Job 9:27). מַה לַּעֲשׂוֹת 'What shall we do?' (Est. 1:15). *'aḥat̲ dāt̲ô l^e^hāmît̲* 'his law is single (= clear): put (him) to death!' (Est. 4:11).

§32.3821 In a sequence of clauses, the inf. cstr. is usually followed by a finite verb. כַּהֲרִימִי קוֹלִי וָאֶקְרָא 'when I lifted my voice and cried' (Gen. 39:18). *'ad̲ bô'î w^e^lāqaḥtî 'et̲kem* 'until I come and take you' (2 Kg. 18:32).

§32.3822 An inf. cstr. may be used in a clause following one with a finite verb. כִּי לֹא־אֶשָּׂא אֲשֶׁר־לָךְ לַיהוה וְהַעֲלוֹת עֹלָה חִנָּם 'for I will not lift up to YHWH what is yours and offer up a burnt-offering free (= what cost me nothing)' (1 Chr. 21:24).

§32.3823 The inf. cstr. often serves in indirect discourse (cf. §38.824).

§32.383 Especially to be noted is the use of the inf. cstr. with ל as a periphrastic future. *wᵉ'eprāyim lᵉhôṣî' 'el-hôrēḡ bānāʸw* 'and Ephraim is for bringing forth his sons to the slayer' (= his sons are destined to be slain, Hos. 9:13).

§32.384 The inf. cstr. puts its obj. in the same case as the verb from which it is derived, and if the verb can take two objs., so can the inf. cstr. *lᵉhāmîṯ 'eṯ-dāwîḏ* 'to kill David' (1 Sam. 19:1). *lᵉhillāḥem bô* 'to fight with him' (Num. 22:11). *'aḥărê hôḏîᵃ' 'ĕlôhîm 'ôṯkā 'eṯ-kol-zō'ṯ* 'since God has caused you to know all this' (Gen 41:39). לְהוֹצִיאָנוּ מִמִּצְרָיִם 'to bring us forth from Egypt' (Exod. 14:11).

§32.385 The inf. cstr. (except as described in §§32.3812f.) is generally negated by לְבִלְתִּי. *ṣiwwîṯîkā lᵉḇiltî 'ăḵol-mimménnû* 'I commanded you not to eat any of it' (Gen. 3:11).

§32.386 In a number of instances, the inf. cstr. appears to be used as an inf. abs. (Cf. Joüon §123*q*). *wᵉhašqôṯ biḵlê zāhāḇ* 'and they drank from gold vessels' (Est. 1:7). הַכּוֹת אֶת־מוֹאָב 'and they smote Moab' (2Kg. 3:24). But cf. §32.3822.

§32.39 The *infinitive absolute* is not a mood. However, since it is sometimes used as a finite verb, this usage may be listed here. *Ges.* §113.

§32.391 After a clause with a finite verb, the inf. abs. may be used to predicate action by the same subject. *wayyiṯqᵉ'û baššôpārôṯ wᵉnāpôṣ hakkaddîm* 'and they sounded with the rams-horns and broke the pitchers' (Judg. 7:19). שָׂדוֹת יִקְנוּ וְכָתוֹב בַּסֵּפֶר וְחָתוֹם וְהָעֵד עֵדִים 'and they shall buy fields and write deeds (lit., in the documents) and seal (them) and cause witnesses to witness (them)' (Jer. 32:44).

§32.3911 The inf. abs. may follow a perf. (Hag. 1:6), a conv. perf. (Zech. 12:10), an impf. (Jer. 32:44), a conv. impf. (Gen. 41:43), a cohort. (Josh. 9:20), an impv. (Isa. 37:30), or a ptcp. (Hab. 2:15). *Ges.* §113*z*.

§32.392 The inf. abs. may be used at the beginning of a narration, in which case its use must be determined from context.

§32.3921 The inf.abs. may be used as an impv.: שָׁמוֹר אֶת־יוֹם הַשַּׁבָּת לְקַדְּשׁוֹ 'keep the day of the Sabbath to hallow it' (Dt. 5:12). *Ges.* §113*bb*.

§32.3922 It may be used for the juss.: הַקְרֵב אֹתָהּ בְּנֵי־אַהֲרֹן לִפְנֵי יהוה 'let the sons of Aaron offer it before Y.' (Lev. 6:7, ET 14). *Ges.* §113*cc.*

§39.3923 It may be used for the cohort.: *'āḵôl wᵉšāṯô* 'let us eat and drink' (Isa. 22:13).

§32.3924 It may be used for an impf. in emphatic promises: אָכוֹל וְהוֹתֵר 'you/they shall eat and some left over' (2 Kg. 4:43). *Ges.* §113*ee.*

§32.3925 The inf. abs. may be used for any historical tense. *Ges.* §113*ff.*

§32.3926 In some instances, the inf. abs. seems to have the force of the passive, cf. עָשֹׂה אֵלֶּה לָךְ 'these things have been done to you' (Ezek. 23:30, but see RSV). *Ges.* §113*ff.*

§32.393 The subj. may be added when the inf. abs. takes the place of a finite verb. הַקְרֵב אֹתָהּ בְּנֵי־אַהֲרֹן לִפְנֵי יהוה 'The sons of Aaron [are] to offer it before YHWH' (Lev. 6:7 [ET 14]).

§32.4 The *voice* of the verb is indicated by verb morphology (§27.112). In Western languages, we think of *active* and *passive* as rather clearly defined terms. In Heb. there is some degree of confusion of which the student must be aware.

§32.41 In the term *active voice,* the word "active" may be misleading. It defines the relationship of the subj. to the predication of the verb (§30.3341), and may, with some verbs, indicate no *action* at all. Note these different actives: *kātáḇtî* 'I wrote,' *qāṭṓntî* 'I am (have become) small,' *mālᵉ'û* 'they were full.'

§32.411 Be careful not to confuse the auxiliary *was/were* of a pass. verb with the copular verb *was/were.* "The pitcher *was broken*" is pass.; "the pitcher *was full*" is act.

§32.42 The *passive* in general identifies the subj. as the recipient of the action predicated by its verb (§30.3342). Thus intransitive and stative verbs cannot be passive. The intr. 'I rise' will not form a pass. 'I was rised,' nor will the stat. 'I am heavy' form a pass. 'I was heavied.' In Heb., however, we find several noteworthy points about the passive that run counter to our understanding of the pass. in Eng. *Ges.* §121.

§32.421 A trans. verb can, of course, be made passive. וַתָּמָת רָחֵל וַתִּקָּבֵר 'and Rachel died and was buried' (Gen. 35:19).

§32.4211 The personal agent or efficient cause is usually expressed by the prep. ל–. וַיֵּעָתֶר לוֹ יהוה 'and YHWH was entreated by him' (Gen. 25:21). בָּרוּךְ הוּא לַיהוה 'blessed be he by YHWH' (Ruth 2:20).

§32.4212 The agent may be expressed by ־בּ: בָּאָדָם דָּמוֹ יִשָּׁפֵךְ 'by man his blood shall be poured out' (Gen. 9:6).

§32.4213 The agent may be expressed by מִן: *w*^{e}*lô'-yikkārēṯ kol-bāśār 'ôḏ mimmê*^{y} *hammabbûl* 'and all flesh shall not again be cut off by the waters of the flood' (Gen. 9:11).

§32.422 The pass. may be impersonal or indefinite. עֶגְלַת בָּקָר אֲשֶׁר לֹא־עֻבַּד 'a heifer which has not been worked' (Deut. 21:3 – the act. would be 'one had not worked the heifer,' a very unlikely construction in Eng.).

§32.423 Verbs which take two objects in the active (§32.24) may retain one (the second or more remote obj.) in the pass., while the nearer obj. becomes the subj. *Ges.* §121*c*. Compare the following: *'ăšer 'ar'ékkā* 'which I will show you' (act.) (Gen. 12:1); *'ăšer 'attā*^{h} *mor'ē*^{h} 'which you have been shown' (pass.) (Exod. 25:40). In both clauses, *which* stands for the 2d obj.

§32.4231 Both objs. are retained with the pass. in an unusual clause: וְיִמָּלֵא כְבוֹד־יהוה אֶת־כָּל־הָאָרֶץ 'and the earth will be covered (with) the glory of YHWH' (Num. 14:21).

§32.424 The sign of the acc. אֶת sometimes is used with a pass. *wayyuggaḏ l*^{e}*riḇqā*^{h} *'eṯ-diḇrê 'ēśāw* 'and there were told to Rebecca the words of Esau' (Gen. 27:42). *wayyiwwālēḏ laḥănôḵ 'eṯ-'îrāḏ* 'and Irad was born to Enoch' (Gen. 4:18). Grammatically, we would have to assume that the speaker was thinking of an active verb, 'one told the words ...,' 'his wife bore Irad ....' But there are enough examples of this phenomenon that we must consider it as acceptable grammatically. *Ges.* §121*b*.

§32.5 The *aspect* or *tense* (*Aktionsart*) of the predication is indicated by verb morphology (§27.111). It is extremely important to understand how these forms are to be translated. Cf. S. R. Driver, *The Use of the Tenses in Hebrew* (3d ed. 1892), F. R. Blake, *A Resurvey of Hebrew Tenses* (1951), C. Brockelmann, *Hebräische Syntax* (1956), §§40-42.

§32.51 The Heb. *perfect* (CaCaCa, CaCiCa, CaCuCa) predicates actions, states, or events which, from the viewpoint of the speaker, are portrayed as *completed,* whether in the past (was completed), the present (is complete), or the future (will have been completed). This also holds true when simple (conjunctive) *wāw* is added, but it does not hold true with *conversive wāw,* see §32.54.

§32.511 The perf. may be used to predicate action or state in past time.

§32.5111 The perf. may indicate action or state as simple past. וּלְאָדָם אָמַר 'and to Adam he said ...' (Gen. 3:17). *gam waštî hammalkā*^{h} *'āś*^{e}*ṯā*^{h} *mištē*^{h} *nāšîm* 'also, Esther made a women's banquet' (Est. 1:9).

§32.5112 The perf. may indicate continuous past action or condition. *šālôš šānîm mālak̠ bî^{y}rûšālāim* 'he reigned for three years in Jerusalem' (1 Kg. 15:2).

§32.5113 The perf. may indicate repeated action in the past. *wayyēṣ^{e}'û śārê p̄^{e}lištîm way^{e}hî middê ṣē'ṯām śāk̠al dāwîḏ mikkōl 'aḇḏê šā'ûl* 'and the chiefs of the Philistines used to go forth, and as often as they went forth, David was more successful than all the servants of Saul' (1 Sam. 18:30).

§32.5114 The perf. may be used as a *pluperfect* or *past anterior.* וַיִּנָּחֶם יהוה כִּי עָשָׂה אֶת־הָאָדָם 'and YHWH repented that he had made man' (Gen. 6:6). *w^{e}lāḇān hālak̠ liḡzōz 'eṯ-ṣō'nô wattiḡnōḇ rāḥēl 'eṯ-hatt^{e}rāp̄îm* 'for Laban had gone to shear his sheep, so Rachel stole the terraphim' (Gen. 31:19).

§32.512 The perf. may be used to predicate action or state occurring in the present.

§32.5121 This may be a present condition that results from completed action. לָמָּה נָפְלוּ פָנֶיךָ 'why is your face fallen?' (Gen. 4:6). עָזְבוּ אֶת־יהוה 'they have forsaken YHWH (and still are in that condition)' (Is. 1:4). *lā́mmā^{h} rāḡ^{e}šû gôyim* 'why do (the) nations rage?' (Ps. 2:1).

§32.5122 With certain verbs, present activity is the result of action that has just been completed, hence the perf. is used. *higgáḏtî hayyôm* 'I declare today' (Dt. 26:3). כִּי יָעַצְתִּי 'for I advise' (2 Sam. 17:11). בַּיהוה נִשְׁבַּעְתִּי 'I swear by YHWH' (2 Sam. 19:8).

§32.5123 With certain verbs, present state or achievement is the result of past activity. This is sometimes called the *perf. of experience. gam-ḥăsîḏā^{h} baššāmáyim yāḏ^{e}'ā^{h} mô'ăḏêhā w^{e}ṯôr w^{e}sîs w^{e}'āḡûr šām^{e}rû 'eṯ-bō'ānā^{h}* 'even (the) stork in the heavens knows her appointed times, and (the) turtledove, swallow, and crane observe the time of their coming' (Jer. 8:7).

§32.5124 Such verbs may also be used to describe a past event. *'āk̠ēn yēš YHWH bammāqôm hazzê^{h} w^{e}'ānôk̠î lô' yāḏá'tî* 'therefore YHWH was in this place and I didn't know (it)' (Gen. 28:16).

§32.5125 Only slightly different is the *inchoative perf.,* which expresses a condition that is viewed as having just begun. יהוה מָלָךְ 'YHWH has become (and is now) king!' (Ps. 97:1).

§32.5126 With stative verbs, the perf. very often expresses a present state which obtains because of completed activity. *zāk̠ántî lô' yāḏá'tî yôm môṯî* 'I am old; I don't know when I will die' (Gen. 27:2). רַק שְׂנֵאתַנִי וְלֹא אֲהַבְתָּנִי 'you only hate me; you don't love me' (Judg. 14:16).

§32.513 The perf. may even be used of future time. Context will determine this.

§32.5131 The perf. is used to describe graphically an event that is to take place. *ḥelqat haśśāḏêʰ māḵᵉrā noʿŏmî* 'Naomi is selling (is going to sell) the portion of the field' (Ruth 4:3). הֵן עַבְדִּי נָתַתִּי רוּחִי עָלָיו 'behold my servant! I will put my spirit on him' (Is. 42:1).

§32.5132 Quite similar, but usually put in a separate category, is the *prophetic perfect.* גָּלָה עַמִּי מִבְּלִי־דָעַת 'my people will go into captivity for lack of knowledge' (Is. 5:13). (This could be put in §32.5131.) *kî yéleḏ yullaḏ-lā́nû* 'for to us a child is (= will be) born' (Isa. 9:5). *hahôlᵉḵîm baḥṓšeḵ rā'û 'ôr gāḏôl* 'those who walk in darkness will see a great light' (Isa. 9:1).

§32.5133 The perf. may serve as a *future perf. ʿaḏ 'im-killû lištôṯ* 'until they shall have finished drinking' (Gen. 24:19). *kî ʿāz yāṣā' YHWH lipānéḵā* 'for then YHWH shall have gone before you' (2 Sam. 5:24).

§32.514 The perf. may be used to express hypothetical situations.

§32.5141 The perf. may express a simple hypothetical statement or question. כִּמְעַט שָׁכַב אַחַד הָעָם אֶת־אִשְׁתֶּךָ 'one of the people might have bedded your wife' (Gen. 26:10). *wᵉḵa'ăšer 'āḇáḏtî 'āḇā́ḏtî* 'and when (if) I perish, I perish' (Est. 4:16).

§32.5142 The perf. is regularly used in *unreal* or *contrary-to-fact* statements, and if conditional, in both protasis and apodosis. *lo'-ʿāśiṯî mᵉ'ûmāʰ kî-śāmû 'ôṯî babbôr* 'I did nothing that they should have put me in the pit' (Gen. 40:15). לוּ חָפֵץ לַהֲמִיתֵנוּ לֹא לָקַח עֹלָה 'If he had wanted to kill us, he would not have received a burnt-offering' (Judg. 13:23).

§32.5143 The perf. may be used to express an unfulfilled desire. לוּ מַתְנוּ 'would we had died!' (Num. 14:2).

§32.5144 The use of the perf. as a precative is debatable. The following sentences may be precatives. *hēḇḗ'ṯā yôm-qārā́'ṯā wᵉyihyû kᵉmônî* 'bring in the day which thou hast announced, and they shall be (let them be) like me!' (Lam. 1:21). עֲצַת רְשָׁעִם רָחֲקָה מֶנִּי 'far be the counsel of evildoers from me!' (Job 21:16). But cf. Driver, *Tenses,* §20.

§32.515 In some instances, the perf. appears to serve as a past ptcp., which is lacking in Heb. *wayᵉḥappēś baggāḏôl hēḥēl ûbaqqāṭôn killāʰ* 'and he searched, beginning with the oldest and ending with the youngest' (Gen. 44:12).

§32.52 The *imperfect* (yaCCuCu, yiCCaCu, yaCCiCu) predicates an action, condition, or event which from the viewpoint of the speaker is seen as *incomplete,* whether in past time, present, or future. This description holds true when simple (conjunctive) *wāw* is added, but it does not apply with conversive *wāw.* Cf. §32.53.

§32.521 The impf. predicates an action or state viewed as not complete but which is to be completed (in contrast to the ptcp., which views the action as always continuous), hence the impf. is often similar to the *future tense.*

§32.5211 The impf. may sometimes be translated by a simple future. יָדַעְתִּי כִּי מָלוֹךְ תִּמְלוֹךְ 'I know that you shall certainly be king' (1 Sam. 24:21). *w^e^hēn lô'-ya'ămînû lî w^e^lô' yišm^e^'û b^e^qôlî* 'Look, they won't believe me and they won't listen to me!' (Exod. 4:1).

§32.5212 The impf. may portray a future event from a past or future viewpoint, thus requiring a compound tense for translation. *'ăšer lô yiqqārē'* 'who shall not have been called' (the context requires action anterior to the clause which precedes; we would probably say 'who has not been called,' Est. 4:11). *w^e^'et-d^e^mê y^e^rûšāláyim yādî^a^ḥ miqqirbāh* 'and the blood of Jerusalem he shall have cleansed from her midst.' (Is. 4:4). וַיִּקַּח אֶת־בְּנוֹ אֲשֶׁר יִמְלֹךְ תַּחְתָּיו 'and he took his son who was to reign in his stead' (2 Kg. 3:27).

§32.5213 The impf. often portrays an event that has some contingency or uncertainty, or one that is hypothetical or unrealized. In such instances, it is generally translated with a modal auxiliary. מִפְּרִי עֵץ־הַגָּן נֹאכֵל 'from the fruit of (any) tree of the garden we may eat' (= 'we are permitted to eat,' Gen. 3:2). *kol 'îš w^e^'iššā^h^ 'ăšer-yāḇô' 'el-hammélek̲* ... 'any man or woman who may enter (by chance enters) into the king ...' (Est. 4:11). *hăyādôa^a^' nēda' kî yô'mar* 'should we indeed have known what he would say?' (Gen. 43:7).

§32.5214 The impf. sometimes expresses obligations or commands, and is translated by 'should' or 'shall' or the like. *'al-g^e^ḥōk̲ā tēlēk̲ w^e^'āpār tô'k̲al* 'on your belly you shall walk, and dust you shall eat' (Gen. 3:14). מַעֲשִׂים אֲשֶׁר לֹא־יֵעָשׂוּ עָשִׂיתָ עִמָּדִי 'deeds which should not be done you have done to me' (Gen. 20:9).

§32.5215 The impf. with לֹא is used in strong prohibitions. *lô' tô'k̲^e^lû mimménnû* 'you shall not eat (any) of it' (Gen. 3:3). *lô' tirṣaḥ, lô' tin'ap̄, lô' tiḡnōḇ* 'you shall not murder; you shall not commit adultery; you shall not steal' (Exod. 20:13-15).

§32.5216 The impf. is used in conditional statements, real or hypothetical. *'im-'ōt̲āh tiqqaḥ-l^e^k̲ā qāḥ* 'if you want to take it, take it' (1 Sam. 21:10, ET 9). כִּי־אֵלֵךְ בְּגֵיא צַלְמָוֶת לֹא־אִירָא רָע 'if I should walk in the valley of deep darkness, I would not fear evil' (Ps. 23:4).

§32.5217 The impf. is often used after final (telic) conjunctions. לְמַעַן יַאֲמִינוּ 'in order that they might believe' (Exod. 4:5). *'ăšer yî^y^ṭōḇ l^e^k̲ā* 'that it might be well with you' (Deut. 4:40). פֶּן־תְּמֻתוּן 'lest you die' (Gen. 3:3).

§32.5218 The impf. is often found in indirect discourse (*oratio obliqua*), in which case we must follow Eng. rules for translation. *lirʼôṯ māʰ-yyiqrāʼ lôʷ* 'to see what he would call it' (Gen. 2:19). שָׁמְעוּ כִּי־שָׁם יֹאכְלוּ לָחֶם 'they heard that they would (be able to) eat bread there' (Gen. 43:25).

§32.522 The impf. often resembles the *present tense.*

§32.5221 The impf. is used to portray continuing activity in the present. מַה־תְּבַקֵּשׁ 'what are you looking for?' (Note the reply, אָנֹכִי מְבַקֵּשׁ, Gen. 37:15f.). On the other hand, note *mēʼáyin yāḇṓʼû* 'where did they come from?'; reply, *bāʼû* 'they came from,' 2 Kg. 20:14).

§32.5222 The impf. is often used for actions of general occurrence, universal truth, habit, etc. *ʿal-kēn yēʼāmar* 'therefore it is said (as a proverb) ...' (Gen. 10:9). *mikkol-maʾăḵāl ʾăšer yēʾāḵēl* 'of all food which may be eaten (= is edible)' (Gen. 6:21). *bē ḥāḵām yᵉśammaḥ-ʾāḇ* 'a wise son makes a father happy' (Prov. 10:1). *kaʾăšer yālōq hakkéleḇ* 'as a dog laps' (Judg. 7:5). *kol ʾăšer yᵉḏabber bôʼ yāḇôʼ* 'whatever he speaks surely comes (true)' (1 Sam. 9:6). *lôʼ yiṯrabbēʼ ʿālay ṭôḇ* 'he never prophesies good about me' (1 Kg. 22:8).

§32.5223 The impf. is sometimes used for potentiality. This appears to be somewhat weaker than the use of יָכֹל with an inf. אֵיכָה אֶשָּׂא לְבַדִּי 'how shall (= can) I bear the burden by myself?' (Dt. 1:12, cf. 1:9). *ʾăšer lôʼ-yôʼmᵉrû zôʼṯ ʾîzāḇel* 'so that no one will be able to say (= can say), "This is Jezebel" ' (2 Kg. 9:37).

§32.5224 The impf. is sometimes used like an adjective. *binyāmîn zᵉʾēḇ yiṭrāp̄* 'Benjamin is a wolf that devours (a devouring wolf)' (Gen. 49:27). *ʿēṣ lôʼ yiqraḇ* 'a tree that does not rot' (Is. 40:20). *ʿām lôʼ-yāḇîn* 'an undiscerning people' (Hos. 4:14).

§32.523 The impf. sometimes has the force of a *past tense.* This is usually in connection with actions that were customary or general in the past.

§32.5231 The impf. is used of events that occurred regularly. וְאֵד יַעֲלֶה 'and a mist used to go up' (Gen. 2:6). *ûmᵉʿîl qāṭōn taʿăśêʰ-llô ʾimmô* 'and his mother used to make a little robe for him every year' (1 Sam. 2:19). *ʾaḥaṯ lᵉšālôš šānîm tāḇṓnāʰ ʾŏniyyôṯ taršîš* 'once every 3 years the ships of Tarshish came' (2 Chr. 9:21). *wᵉlôʼ yiṯbôšāšû* 'and they were not (at any time) ashamed' (Gen. 2:25).

§32.5232 Similar is the use of the impf. to describe continuous state in past time. כָּכָה יַעֲשֶׂה אִיּוֹב כָּל־הַיָּמִים 'this is the way Job was always doing' (Job 1:5).

§32.5233 The impf. is regularly used of past time after certain conjunctions. *ʾāz yāšîr môšêh* 'then Moses sang' (Exod. 15:1). *wᵉḵol-ʿēśeḇ haśśāḏêʰ ṭérem yiṣmāḥ* 'and no herb of the field had yet sprouted' (Gen. 2:5). *wāʾôḵal bᵉṭérem tāḇôʼ* 'and I had already eaten before you came' (Gen. 27:33).

§32.524 In a fairly large number of cases, the impf. appears to be a *perfect* in everything except form, suggesting that a *yqtl* perf. (like Akk. *iprus*) may have been present at one time in Heb. תִּבְלָעֵמוֹ אָרֶץ 'earth swallowed them' (Exod. 15:12, and often in that chapter). *kî 'ăḏabbēr 'el-nāḇôṯ* 'for I spoke to Naboth' (1 Kg. 21:6). *wᵉ'eṯ pōʻal* YHWH *lô' yabbîṭû ûmaʻăśēʰ yāḏāʸw lô' rā'û* 'and the work of YHWH they did not contemplate and the deed of his hands they did not see' (Is. 5:12; in the prophets, the impf. often interchanges with the perf.). *'aʻălêʰ 'eṯ-ḵem mimmiṣráyim* 'I brought you up from Egypt' (Judg. 2:1).

§32.53 The *converted imperfect* is formed by the addition of *wāw, pattāḥ*, and *dāḡēš ḥāzāq* (§27.311). If the verb is 1cs (with preform. א), *dāḡēš* is rejected and *pattāḥ* is lengthened to *qāmāṣ* (§15.14). The conv. impf. can be used in many of the situations where the simple perf. is used (cf. §32.51). Note that the *wāw* can*not* be separated from the verb, and the verb *must* stand *first* in its clause.

§32.531 Some preliminary observations may be helpful.

§32.5311 The name "*wāw* consecutive" was based on the theory that such forms were always preceded by a perf. or some other verb form, and therefore followed in consecution. This is *not* supported by biblical data. The Heb. term וָו הַהִפּוּךְ 'the *wāw* of the reversal,' or Eng. "*wāw* conversive" or "*wāw inversive*" is to be preferred. See Joüon §117*a*, n.1.

§32.5312 It should be noted that the conv. impf. is not an impf. at all. In every instance where the Heb. juss. is formally distinguished from the impf. (§§29.6317, .6325, .6412), the conv. impf. has the form of the juss., except that in some forms there is also an accent shift (G40 יָקֹם, Gc20 וַיָּקָם, paus. וַיָּקֹם). For the theory of a *yqtl* perf., cf. §32.524.

§32.5313 Driver *Tenses* §70 explains the accent-shift in the conv. impf. as due to the "*heavy prefix* -וַ." This is not convincing, for every word with -הַ, -בַּ, etc., has the same kind of "prefix" – and the accent never shifts. Further, Driver notes forms with the same accent shift but without the -וַ, which leaves the reason for the shift unexplained (*Tenses* §83, Obs.).

§32.5314 Joüon compares the Heb. conv. impf. with Arab. *lam yaqtul* and Akk. *iqtul*, §117*c*, n.1.

§32.532 The conv. impf. of statives in general is equivalent to the perf. of statives. *wayyimmālē' hoḵmāʰ* 'and he was full of wisdom' (1 Kg. 7:14). וַיְהִי 'and it was, καὶ ἐγένετο' (often).

§32.533 The conv. impf. of fientive verbs very often conveys the idea of past time together with some notion of succession with the preceding verb (if any). *ûḇᵉ'arbaʻ ʻeśrēʰ šānāʰ bā' kᵉḏorlā'ōmer ... wayyakkû 'eṯ-rᵉpā'îm* 'and in the 14th year came Chedorlaomer *et al.* and they smote the Rephaim' (Gen.

14:5). כִּי שָׁמַעְתָּ לְקוֹל אִשְׁתֶּךָ וַתֹּאכַל 'for you listened to the voice of your wife and you ate' (Gen. 3:17). *hăšāma' 'ām qôl* YHWH *wayyéḥî* 'has a people ever heard the voice of YHWH and lived?' (Dt. 4:33). *weᵉlāmmāʰ lô'-šāmá'tā bᵉqôl* YHWH *wattá'aṭ 'el-haššālāl* 'why did you not obey the voice of YHWH, but you swooped on the plunder' (1 Sam. 15:19).

§32.5331 When the succession is absent, conv. impf. is avoided. *wayyêṣē'* ... *wayyāḇô'* ... *wᵉrāḥēl lāqᵉḥāʰ wattᵉśîmēm* 'and he went out ... and he entered ...; now Rachel had taken and had put them ...' (Gen. 31:33f.).

§32.5332 The conv. impf. is avoided if the action, though actually subsequent, is not presented as such. וְהוּא קִלְלַנִי ... וְהוּא־יָרַד לִקְרָאתִי 'and he cursed me ... but when he went down to meet me ...' (1 Kg. 2:8).

§32.5333 The conv. impf. is avoided when the second action is simultaneous with the first. *wattᵉhî lāhem hallᵉḇēnāʰ lᵉ'āḇen wᵉhaḥēmār hāyāʰ lāhem laḥōmer* 'and they had brick for stone and bitumen for mortar' (Gen. 11:3).

§32.5334 The conv. impf. is avoided when repeating an account. וְיוֹאָב וְכָל־הַצָּבָא אֲשֶׁר־אִתּוֹ בָּאוּ 'and Joab and all the army that was with him came' (they had already come in the previous verse, 1 Sam. 3:22f.).

§32.534 The conv. impf. is used to express logical sequence. *lāmāʰ 'āmártā 'ăḥôṯî hîʷ' wā'eqqaḥ 'ōṯāh lî lᵉ'iššāʰ* 'why did you say "she is my sister" so that I took her for my wife?' (Gen. 12:19).

§32.5341 The c20 may be used to "recap" an account. *wayᵉḵullû haššāmáyim wᵉhā'áreṣ wᵉkol-ṣᵉḇā'ām* 'so the heavens and the earth and all their host were finished' (Gen. 2:1).

§32.5342 The c20 may be used for explanation. *wattiqrā' šᵉmô môšêʰ wattō'mer kî min-hammáyim mᵉšîṯihû* 'and she called his name Moses, for she said, "Because I drew him from the water"' (Exod. 2:10).

§32.5343 The conv. impf. is often used in a narrative when no sequence at all is intended. וַיֹּאכַל וַיֵּשְׁתְּ וַיָּשָׁב וַיִּשְׁכָּב 'and he ate and he drank (no sequence intended), and he returned and he lay down' (1 Kg. 19:6).

§32.535 The conv. impf. may serve as an instantaneous present. עֲבָדֶיךָ נָשְׂאוּ ... וַנַּקְרֵב אֶת־קָרְבַּן יהוה 'your servants have taken up ... and we now present YHWH's offering' (Num. 32:49-50).

§32.536 There are a number of relatively rare usages that are noteworthy.

§32.5361 The conv. impf. may be used after a perf. of a stative verb with a pres. meaning. יַעַן כִּי גָבְהוּ בְּנוֹת צִיּוֹן וַתֵּלַכְנָה נְטוּיוֹת גָּרוֹן 'because the daughters of Zion are haughty and they walk with outstretched necks' (Is. 3:16).

'āhāḇtā ṣéḏeq wattiśnā' réša' 'you love righteousness and hate wickedness' (Ps. 45:7).

§32.5362 The conv. impf. following a simple impf. is relatively rare. וְהִנֵּה
תְּסֻבֶּינָה אֲלֻמֹּתֵיכֶם וַתִּשְׁתַּחֲוֶיןָ, לַאֲלֻמָּתִי 'and behold your sheaves were gathering around and bowing down to my sheaf' (Gen. 37:7). *wᵉrā'āʰ šā'ûl kol-'îš gibbôr wᵉḵol-ben-ḥáyil wayya'asᵉpēhû* 'and any time Saul saw a strong man or a valiant man, he attached him (to himself)' (1 Sam. 14:52).

§32.5363 The conv. impf. may follow a ptcp. הַקֹּרֵא לְמֵי הַיָּם וַיִּשְׁפְּכֵם 'the one who calls the waters of the sea and pours them out' (Amos 5:8).

§32.5364 The conv. impf. may follow an inf. cstr. *kahărîmî qôlî wā'eqrā'* 'when I lifted my voice and cried' (Gen. 39:18).

§32.5365 The conv. impf. may follow a prophetic perf. and have the same force. *kî-yéleḏ yullaḏ-lā́nû bēn nittan-lā́nû wattᵉhî hammiśrāʰ 'al-šiḵmô* 'for a child has been (= will be) born to us, a son has been given to us, and the government shall be on his shoulder' (Is. 9:5).

§32.5366 The conv. impf. may be used in a conditional sentence. לוּלֵי מִהַרְתְּ
וַתָּבוֹת לִקְרָאתִי 'unless you had hastened and had come to meet me' (1 Sam. 25:34).

§32.54 The *converted perfect* can be formed by the addition of וְ– to a verb in the perf. There is a shift of stress-accent in verbs which have a closed penult and an open ultima, resulting in an accented ultima. If the verb form is incapable of accent-shift, we must identify the conv. perf. by context alone. The effect of the *wāw* (and the accent shift) is to give the verb the force of the impf. Cf. Driver, *Tenses,* §105ff.

§32.541 The conv. perf. may be used without any preceding verb (cf. §32.5311). *'ănî* YHWH *wᵉhôṣē'ṯî 'eṯḵem* 'I am YHWH and I will bring you forth' (Exod. 6:6). וְהָיָה בְּתֵת יהוה לָנוּ אֶת־הָאָרֶץ 'and it shall be, when YHWH gives us the land' (Josh. 2:14). *wᵉ'āhaḇtem 'eṯ-haggēr* 'you shall love the sojourner' (Dt. 10:19). *hēn-rabbî 'attāʰ 'am hā'āreṣ wᵉhišbattem 'ōṯām missiḇlōṯām* 'Behold the people of the land are now many, and do you want to give them rest from their labors?' (Exod. 5:5).

§32.542 The conv. perf. may be used after an impf. It often serves as a future tense. וְאַבְרָהָם הָיוֹ יִהְיֶה לְגוֹי גָּדוֹל וְעָצוּם וְנִבְרְכוּ בוֹ כֹּל גּוֹיֵי הָאָרֶץ and Abraham shall surely become a great and mighty nation and in him all the nations of the earth shall be blessed' (Gen. 18:18).

§32.5421 The conv. perf. may follow an impf. denoting frequent or customary action. *'al-kēn ya'ăzoḇ-'îš 'eṯ-'āḇîw wᵉ'eṯ-'immô wᵉḏāḇaq bᵉ'ištô wᵉhāyû lᵉḇāśār 'eḥāḏ* 'therefore man shall leave his father and mother and he shall cleave to his wife and they shall become one flesh' (Gen. 2:24 – this is a general statement about any man). וְאֵד יַעֲלֶה מִן־הָאָרֶץ וְהִשְׁקָה אֶת־כָּל־פְּנֵי הָאֲדָמָה 'and a mist used to go up from the land and water all the face of the ground' (Gen. 2:6).

§32.5422 The conv. perf. may follow an impf. used with hypothetical or modal force. *wᵉ'im-yēḥāḇᵉ'û bᵉrô'š hakkarmel miššām 'ăḥappēś ûlᵉqaḥtîm* 'and though they would hide themselves in the top of Carmel, from there I would seek and I would take them' (Amos 9:3).

§32.543 The conv. perf. may be used after an impv. ... עֲשֵׂה לְךָ תֵּבַת עֲצֵי־גֹפֶר וְכָפַרְתָּ אֹתָהּ 'make yourself an ark of gopher wood ... and cover it' (Gen. 6:14).

§32.544 The conv. perf. may be used after a juss. יְהִי מְאֹרוֹת ... וְהָיוּ לְאוֹתוֹת 'let there be luminaries ... and let them become signs' (Gen. 1:14f.). *'al-nā' tiqbᵉrēnî bᵉmiṣráyim wᵉšāḵaḇtî 'im-'ăḇôṯay* 'please don't bury me in Egypt, but I shall (= let me) lie down with my ancestors' (Gen. 47:29f.).

§32.545 The conv. perf. may be used after a cohort. *wᵉ'attāʰ lᵉḵāʰ niḵrᵉṯāʰ bᵉrîṯ ... wᵉhāyāʰ lᵉ'ēḏ* 'and now, come, let us make a covenant ... and let it become a witness' (Gen. 31:44). *'ălaqŏṭāʰ-nnā' wᵉ'āsap̄tî bā'ŏmārîm* 'please let me glean and I will (= let me) gather with the reapers' (Ruth 2:7).

§32.546 The conv. perf. may be used after a ptcp. *hinᵉnî mēḇî' 'eṯ-hammabbûl máyim 'al-hā'āreṣ ... wᵉhăqîmôṯî 'eṯ-bᵉrîṯî 'ittāḵ* 'behold I am bringing (= will bring) the flood waters upon the earth ... and I will raise up my covenant with you' (Gen. 6:17f.).

§32.547 The conv. perf. may follow a perf. *mānáʿtî mikkem 'eṯ-haggéšem ... wᵉhimṭartî 'al-'îr 'aḥāṯ wᵉ'al-'îr 'aḥaṯ lô' 'amṭîr* 'I withheld the rain from you ... and I would cause it to rain (Hc14) on one city, while on another city I would not cause rain (H24)' (Amos 4:7); note interchange of conv. perf. and simple impf.

§32.5471 The conv. perf. may follow a prophetic perf. *hinnēʰ bēráḵtî 'ōṯô wᵉhip̄rēʸṯî 'ōṯô wᵉhirbēʸṯî 'ōṯô* 'behold I have blessed (= will bless) him, and I will make him fruitful and multiply him' (Gen. 17:20 – note accent on the perf. forms).

§32.548 The conv. perf. is used following an impf. which is preceded by certain particles and conjunctions. In fact, it is rare in such instances to find an impf. repeated; the preference seems to favor the conv. perf. Cf. Driver *Tenses* §§115f.

§32.549 *Simple* or *conjunctive wāw* may be used with the perfect. There is *no* accent shift and *no* inversion of meaning. *wa'ănî zāqántî wᵉśáḇtî* 'and as for me, I am old and grey' (1 Sam. 12:2).

§32.6 [*Permansive.* Omitted in Heb.]

§32.7 [*Ventive.* Omitted in Heb.]

§32.8 From the basic root of the verb, a number of *derived stems* (§28) may be formed. It is essential to understand the significance of these stems for translation and exegesis.

§32.81 The D-stem (cf. §28.2) basically predicates an action that involves *repetition* or *continuity* of activity. בִּקַּשְׁתִּי 'I sought,' שִׁבֵּר 'he broke in pieces, smashed,' דִּבֵּר 'he spoke,' לִמַּדְתָּ 'you taught.' *Ges.* §52*f.*

§32.811 The D of an active (fientive) verb often has *causative* force. Compare *lāmad̲* 'he learned,' and *limmēd̲* 'he caused to learn, he taught.' *ûlᵉmad̲tem 'ōṯām* 'and you shall learn them' (Deut. 5:1); *limmad̲tî 'eṯkem ḥuqqîm ûmišpāṭîm* 'I have taught you statutes and ordinances' (Deut. 4:5).

§32.812 The D of stative verbs is often *factitive* or *causative.* מָלֵא 'it was full'; מִלֵּאתִי 'I filled.' אֲשֶׁר מִלֵּאתִיו רוּחַ חָכְמָה 'whom I filled (with) a spirit of wisdom' (Exod. 28:3).

§32.813 The D often has *forensic* meaning, especially with certain verbs. צִדְּקָה נַפְשָׁהּ מְשֻׁבָה יִשְׂרָאֵל מִבֹּגֵדָה יְהוּדָה 'backslidden Israel has justified herself more than false Judah' (Jer. 3:11) *kî-ḥāp̄áṣtî ṣaddᵉqékkā* 'for I desire to justify you (= to declare you just)' (Job 33:22).

§32.814 The D-stem is used to form certain denominal verbs (i.e. verbs formed from nouns), e.g. שֵׁרֵשׁ 'he rooted out, extirpated,' שִׁלֵּשׁ 'he did three times, tripled, divided into three parts, did for the third time,' כִּהֵן 'he acted as a priest.' *Ges.* §52*h.*

§32.815 The Dp (*pu'al*), as the passive of the D-stem, regularly expresses the passive of the various nuances of the D-active.

§32.82 The H-stem (cf. §28.3) basically expresses the idea of *causation.* בּוֹא 'to enter,' הֵבִיא 'he caused to enter, brought in,' יָצָא 'he went out,' הוֹצִיא 'he caused to go out, sent out.'

§32.821 The H of an intransitive or stative verb generally becomes transitive. שׁוּב 'to turn, return,' הֵשִׁיב 'to turn (tr.), cause to return.' נגד (unused in G, but prob. 'to be conspicuous,' cf. נֶגֶד), הִגִּיד 'to make conspicuous, report, announce.' Note the following: הִקְרִיב 'he brought near,' הֶעֱמִיק 'he made deep,' הֶחֱיָה 'he made alive' BDB 616f.

§32.8211 The H of a stative verb may indicate *entry into* a state or *the exhibiting of* a state. הִזְקַנְתִּי 'I have become old,' הִשְׂכִּיל 'he acted wisely.'

§32.8212 The H of a stative may simply make it *fientive*. הֵיטִיב 'he did good,' הִשְׁחִית 'he did evil,' הִרְבָּה 'he made many, magnified,' הִמְעִיט 'he made little.'

§32.8213 The H of of some words is intransitive, but only in translation. הִקְשִׁיב 'he listened' (= caused to extend [the ear]), הֵשִׁיב 'he replied' (= caused to return [a word]). Joüon §54*e*.

§32.822 The H-stem expresses a *forensic* meaning, especially with the verbs צדק and רשׁע. *wᵉhiṣdîqû 'et-haṣṣaddîq wᵉhiršî'û 'et-hārāšā'* 'and they (the judges) acquit (declare just) the righteous and condemn (declare guilty) the wicked' (Deut. 25:1).

§32.8221 The H may suggest the idea of *thinking* or *estimating* a state or condition. הֵקַל 'he belittled, despised' (2 Sam. 19:44).

§32.8222 Note these unusual meanings: הִשְׁאִיל 'he consented (= permitted to be asked)', לָוָה 'he borrowed,' הִלְוָה 'he loaned (= permitted to borrow).'

§32.823 The H-stem is used to form certain denominal verbs. הֵימִין 'he turned to the right,' הִשְׂמְאִיל 'he went to the left'; *maqrîn maprîs* 'growing horns (and) hooves' (Ps. 69:32).

§32.824 The H-passive (*hoph'al*) is generally the passive of the H-stem.

§32.83 The N-stem (cf. §28.4) may originally have been *reflexive* (cf. Arab.) or *passive* (cf. Akk.). The earliest Heb. N-stem forms appear to have been *reflexive*. נִשְׁמַר 'he kept/guarded himself,' נִסְתַּרְתִּי 'I hid myself,' and possibly נִשְׁבַּעְתִּי 'I swore, performed an oath (= sevened myself [?]).'

§32.831 The N-stem has replaced the G-pass. in Bib. Heb., and is often translated by the passive. וּמָרְדֳּכַי יָדַע אֶת־כָּל־אֲשֶׁר נַעֲשָׂה 'and Mordecai knew all that *was done*' (Est. 4:1).

§32.832 The N is sometimes similar to the Gk. middle. נִשְׁאַל 'he asked permission (for himself)' (1 Sam. 20:6).

§32.833 The N is sometimes *reciprocal*. נִלְחֲמוּ 'they fought (with one another).'

§32.834 The N may express a *permissive* or *tolerative* idea. הַאִדָּרֹשׁ אִדָּרֵשׁ לָהֶם 'Shall I indeed let myself be asked by them?' (Ezek. 14:3).

§32.84 The HtD-stem (cf. §28.5) is basically *reflexive* (Ht-) and and *iterative* (D-). הִתְהַלַּכְתִּי 'I walked about,' הִתְחַבֵּא 'he hid himself.'

§32.841 The HtD may be *reciprocal*. לָמָּה תִּתְרָאוּ 'Why do you look at one another?' (Gen. 42:1).

§32.842 The HtD may be *reflexive* and *forensic* or *putative*. וְהִתְחָל 'and feign (impv.) illness' (2 Sam. 13:5). מִתְיַהֲדִים 'pretending to be Jews' (or possibly 'becoming Jews').

§32.843 The HtD may be *reflexive* and *factitive*. הִתְגַּדֵּל 'he made himself great, acted arrogantly.'

§32.844 The HtR-stem (§28.121, §28.7) expresses action that involves twisting, turning, etc., for the subj. of the verb. *wattiṯḥalḥal hammalkāʰ mᵉʾōḏ* 'and the queen *writhed in anguish* exceedingly' (Est. 4:4).

§33. The subj. of a verb is indicated by the verb morphology (§27. ff.). However, for emphasis or for greater clarity (especially in 3d pers.), the subj may be more closely defined. The *defined subject* of a verb may be:

a noun, §33.1
a noun group (a compound subject), §33.12
a noun-phrase, §33.13
a noun-clause, §33.6
a pronoun, §33.2
an adjective used substantivally, §33.3
a participle, §33.4
an infinitive construct, §33.5
an infinitive absolute, §33.7

For a noun in construct with a finite verb, cf. §35.7.

§33.1 The defined subj. may be a *noun*, which we assume (from comparative studies) to be in the nominative case (§25.3). *wayyeʾĕhaḇ* הַמֶּלֶךְ *ʾeṯ-ʾestēr* 'and he, *viz. the king*, loved Esther' (Est. 2:17). We simply translate a defined subj. as the subject, 'The *king* loved ....'

§33.11 The verb and its defined subj. are generally *in concord* (i.e., they agree in person, gender, and number). וַיֹּאמֶר הַמֶּלֶךְ לְאֶסְתֵּר 'and the *king* said to Esther' (Est. 9:12). וַתֹּאמֶר אֶסְתֵּר 'and *Esther* said' (Est. 9:13). וַיֹּאמְרוּ נַעֲרֵי הַמֶּלֶךְ 'and *the king's servants* said' (Est. 2:2). תֹּאמַרְנָה שָׂרוֹת '(the) *princesses* said' (Est. 1:18).

§33.111 Under certain conditions concord may be lacking.

§33.1111 A plural subject may be expressed by a verb in the singular, particularly if the verb stands first and is separated from its subj. וַיָּבוֹא אֵלַי אֲנָשִׁים 'and men came to me' (Ezek. 14:1). *wayyippōl miyyiśrāʾēl šᵉlōšîm ʾéleṗ raḡlî* 'and of Israel 30,000 infantry fell' (1 Sam. 4:10). *wᵉʿānāʰ ʾiyyîm* 'and islands shall answer' (Isa. 2:17)

§33.1112 A feminine subj. often is found with a verb in the masc. וַיֶּחֱמוּ הַצֹּאן 'and the flocks bred' (Gen. 30:39; cf. *wattēláḵnā haṣṣōʾn* in the same verse). *hāʾéḇen hazzōʾṯ ... yihyêʰ bêʸṯ ʾĕlôhîm* 'this stone ... shall be the house of

God' (Gen. 28:22). עָרֵיכֶם יִהְיוּ חָרְבָּה 'your cities will be waste' (Lev. 26:33). *w^e^kol-hannāšîm yitt^e^nû y^e^qār l^e^ba'ălê^y^hen* 'Let all the women give honor to their husbands' (Est. 1:20).

§33.1113 If the subj. is morphologically masc. or fem., but the opposite in meaning, concord will be in meaning. הָיָה קֹהֶלֶת חָכָם 'the preacher [f. in form, m. in meaning] was wise' (Eccl. 12:9).

§33.1114 If the defined subj. is a surrogate for the 1st pers., the verb may be in 1st pers. נַפְשִׁי אִוִּיתִךָ בַּלַּיְלָה אַף־רוּחִי בְקִרְבִּי אֲשַׁחֲרֶךָּ (note verbs in 1st pers.) 'My soul (= I) longs for thee in the night, yea, my spirit within me seeks thee (lit., I seek thee)' (Isa. 26:9). *qôlî 'el-YHWH 'eqrā'* 'My soul (= I) cries (G24) unto YHWH' (Ps. 3:5). These are not to be considered as "dangling" constructions.

§33.1115 Concord is sometimes lacking with the idiom היוה ל– 'to belong to, to have.' תּוֹרָה אַחַת יִהְיֶה לָאֶזְרָח 'One law shall be for the native ...' (Exod. 12:49). *'arba' yādôt yihyê^h^ lākem* 'You shall have four-fifths (lit. hands)' (Gen. 47:24).

§33.1116 The noun אֱלֹהִים generally is used with a sing. verb when it means "God" (*vice* "gods"), except when spoken by or to a pagan. וַיֹּאמֶר אֱלֹהִים 'and God said' (Gen. 1:3 and often). *'ĕlôhîm 'ăšer yêl^e^kû lipānê^y^nû* 'gods who shall go before us' (Exod. 32:1). Note the words of Jezebel, *kō^h^ ya'ăśûn 'ĕlôhîm* 'Thus may (your) God do...' (1 Kgs. 19:2), or Abram's words to Abimelech, *ka'ăšer hit'û 'ōtî 'ĕlôhîm mibbê^y^t 'ābî* 'when God caused me to wander from my father's house' (Gen. 20:13).

§33.112 If the subj. is collective, a plur. verb may be used with a sing. noun. אֲשֶׁר תָּבֹאןָ הַצֹּאן לִשְׁתּוֹת 'where the flock comes to drink' (Gen. 30:38). *w^e^hā'ām nāsû* 'and the people fled' (1 Chr. 11:13, but cf. *w^e^hā'ām nās* 2 Sam. 23:11). וַיַּרְא כָּל־הָעָם וַיִּפְּלוּ 'and all the people saw (sg.), and they fell (pl.)' (1 Kgs. 18:39).

§33.12 The defined subj. may be a *group of nouns* (i.e. a compound subj., §30.113). וְהַמֶּלֶךְ וְהָמָן יָשְׁבוּ לִשְׁתּוֹת 'And *the king and Haman* sat down to drink' (Est. 3:15). *kî nimkárnû 'ănî w^e^'ammî* 'for I and my people are sold' (Est. 7:4). וְאַתְּ וּבֵית אָבִיךְ תֹּאבֵדוּ 'and you and your father's house shall perish' (Est. 4:14).

§33.121 If the compound subj. is regarded as separate entities, the verb is generally in the plural. מֹשֶׁה אַהֲרֹן וְחוּר עָלוּ 'Moses, Aaron, and Hur went up (pl.)' (each one went up) (Exod. 17:10).

§33.122 If the compound subj. forms a unitary idea, the verb is generally in the singular. *śaq wā'ēper yuṣṣa' lārabbîm* 'sackcloth and ashes [both, not one or the other] was spread for the many' (Est. 4:3). *réwaḥ w^e^haṣṣālā^h^ ya'ămōd* 'relief and deliverance will arise' (Est. 4:14). *késep̄ wᵉzāhāḇ yirbêʰ-llāḵ* 'silver and gold [= wealth] will be multiplied for you' (Deut. 8:13).

§33.123 When the compound subj. is mixed in gender or number, the verb often agrees with the nearer subj. וַתְּדַבֵּר מִרְיָם וְאַהֲרֹן 'and Miriam and Aaron spoke' (Num. 12:1, but *wayyō'mᵉrû* in 12:2). *wattiggaš gam lē'āʰ wîʸlādéʸhā* 'Likewise Leah and her children drew near (f.s.)' (Gen. 33:7, the following word is m.p. *wayyištaḥăwû*).

§33.124 If the compound subj. is considered as one subj. accompanied by another, the verb agrees with the principal subj. וַתִּשָּׁאֵר הִיא וּשְׁנֵי בָנֶיהָ 'and she was left and her two sons [along with her]' (Ruth 1:3). *gam-'ănî wᵉna'ărôṯay 'āṣûm* 'I too shall fast and (together with) my maidservants' (Est. 4:16). *yāḇô' hammélek̲ wᵉhāmān ... 'el-hammištêʰ* 'Let the king along with Haman come to the banquet' (Est. 5:4).

§33.125 If the subj. is distributive, the verb is generally plural. וַיֹּאמְרוּ אִישׁ אֶל־אָחִיו 'and *each* said *to his brothers*' (Gen. 37:19). *'ăšer lô' yišmᵉ'û 'îš śᵉp̄aṯ rēyēhû* 'that they may not hear (= understand) *each the language of his fellowman*' (Gen. 11:7). *ḥiḡrû 'îš 'eṯ-ḥarbô* 'Gird on, each of you, his sword!' (1 Sam. 25:13).

§33.126 When the subj. is *dual*, concord is irregular. יִרְפּוּ יָדָיו 'his hands fell (= his courage failed)' (2 Sam. 4:1). יָדַיִם תִּרְפֶּינָה 'all hands shall fall' (Isa. 13:7). *'êʸnay tir'éʸnāʰ* 'my eyes will see' (Mic. 7:10). *wᵉṯáḥaz bᵉṣiyyôn 'êʸneʸnû* 'and let our eyes gaze upon Zion' (Mic. 4:11).

§33.13 The subj. may be a *modified noun*, i.e. a noun with a pron. suf., or a noun in annexion (cstr.). נָדְדָה שְׁנַת הַמֶּלֶךְ '*the king's sleep* fled' (Est. 6:1). *wayyō'mᵉrû 'aḇḏêʸ hammélek̲* 'and *the king's servants* said' (Est. 3:3). וְהִנֵּה תְסֻבֶּינָה אֲלֻמֹּתֵיכֶם 'and behold, *your sheaves* gathered around ...' (Gen. 37:7).

§33.131 The verb may agree with either of the nouns in cstr., and the observations in §§33.111ff. apply also. *kaḏ* (f.) *haqqémaḥ* (m.) *lô' k̲ālāṯā* (f.), *wᵉṣap̄áḥaṯ* (f.) *haššémen* (m.) *lô' ḥāsēr* (m.), 'The jar of meal was not finished and the pitcher of oil did not decrease' (1 Kgs. 17:16). בַּהֲמוֹת שָׂדֶה תַּעֲרוֹג 'beasts (f.p.) of the field (m.s.) shall crave (f.s.) ...' (Joel 1:20).

§33.133 When the defined subj. consists of a noun in cstr. with כֹּל, the verb is generally in concord with the governed noun (*nomen rectum*). וַתֵּצֶאןָ כָל־הַנָּשִׁים 'and all the women went out' (Exod. 15:20). *kōl hannᵉšāmāʰ tᵉhallēl yāh* 'Let all breath praise Yah!' (Ps. 150:6). Exod. 12:12 offers a rare exception, *kol-mᵉlā'k̲āʰ lô'-yē'āśêʰ* 'no work shall be done.'

§33.134 The subj. may be a substantive modified by partitive מִן. יָצְאוּ מִן־הָעָם לִלְקֹט '*some of the people* went out to gather' (Exod. 16:27).

§33.2 The defined subj. may be a *pronoun*. For the use of personal pronouns see §§32.111-.113.

§33.21 The subj. may be a *personal pronoun*. הִוא נָתְנָה־לִּי '*she* gave me' (Gen. 3:12). הוּא יְשׁוּפְךָ רֹאשׁ וְאַתָּה תְּשׁוּפֶנּוּ עָקֵב '*he* shall bruise your head and *you* shall bruise his heel' (Gen. 3:15).

§33.211 The use of the pers. pron. as the defined subject is not very common. Frequently it indicates some particular emphasis. Review §§32.111-.113.

§33.212 Note the following: וַיִּתָּלוּ שְׁנֵיהֶם 'and they two were hanged' (Est. 2:23).

§33.23 The defined subj. may be an *interrogative pronoun*. מִי הִגִּיד לְךָ '*who* told you?' (Gen. 3:11). מַה־נַּעֲשָׂה '*what* was done?' (Est. 6:3).

§33.24 The defined subj. may be an *indefinite pronoun*. לָדַעַת ... וּמַה־יֵּעָשֶׂה בָּהּ 'to know ... and *whatever* would be done with her' (Est. 2:11).

§33.25 The defined subj. may be a *demonstrative pronoun*. וְנַהֲפוֹךְ הוּא 'and *that* was overturned' (Est. 9:1).

§33.26 The defined subj. may be a *relative pronoun*. This is extremely common in relative clauses. אֲשֶׁר הָגְלָה '*who* was taken captive' (Est. 2:7). *m^{e}la'ḵtô 'ăšer 'āśā^h* 'the work *which* he did' (Gen. 2:2).

§33.261 The rel. pron. often serves for both antecedent and relator (e.g. *he who, that which,* etc.), and occasionally does so as subj. of a verb. אֲשֶׁר־עֻשֵּׂיתִי בַסֵּתֶר '*I who* was made (Dp14, prob. originally Gp14) in secret' (Ps. 139:15)

§33.4 The defined subj. may be a *participle*. Such usage generally indicates a general or vague subj. לֹא יָנוּס נָס 'no one could flee' (Amos 9:1). הַשֹּׁמֵעַ 'and anyone who hears' (Ezek. 33:4). *kî 'im-b^{e}zō'ṯ yiṯhallēl hammiṯhallēl* 'but let the one who glories glory in this' (Jer. 9:23).

§33.41 A ptcp. serving as a verb generally has its own subject defined. מִי יוֹדֵעַ 'Who knows?' (Est. 4:14). *'ê^{y}n 'estēr maggéḏeṯ môlaḏtāh* 'Esther was not telling her kinship' (Est. 2:20). *w^{e}ḵol-'aḇḏê^y hammélek̲ ... kôr^e'îm* 'and all the king's men were bowing' (Est. 3:2).

§33.5 The defined subj. may be an *infinitive construct*. Usually this is part of a noun-clause (cf. §33.6). אָז הוּחַל לִקְרֹא בְּשֵׁם יהוה 'then *calling* on YHWH's name was begun' (Gen. 4:26). According to Davidson, *Hebrew Syntax*, §90, Rem. 1, the inf. cstr. in such usage always is prefixed with –ל.

§33.51 The inf. cstr. may have a defined subject. either in the nominative (accusative?) or in the genitive.

§33.511 The subj. is clearly not in cstr., hence in the nom. (or acc.) in numerous texts. בְּהָנִיחַ יהוה אֱלֹהֶיךָ לְךָ (note *b*ᵉ*hā-*) 'when YHWH your God gives you rest' (Deut. 25:19). *l*ᵉ*biltî hakkôt-'ôtô kol-môṣ*ᵉ*'ô* 'so that no one finding him shall smite him' (Gen. 4:15). לָנֻס שָׁמָּה הָרֹצֵחַ 'the manslayer to flee thither' (Num. 35:6).

§33.512 In other passages, the subj. of the inf. cstr. must be in the genitive (i.e. construct, or with pronom. suf.). בְּמָלְכוֹ 'when he ruled' (1 Sam. 13:1). *biś*ᵉ*na't* YHWH *'ôtānû* 'in the Lord's hating us' (Deut. 1:27).

§33.513 In many instances it is impossible to determine either by pointing or by word-order whether the subj. of the inf. cstr. is nominative (accusative) or genitive. Cf. Joüon §124*h*. Obviously, the terminology of cases is taken from our Latin-Greek background.

§33.6 The defined subj. may be a *noun-clause* (i.e. a clause serving as a noun; we distinguish this from a verbless clause, §31.). לֹא־יֵעָשֶׂה כֵן בִּמְקוֹמֵנוּ לָתֵת הַצְּעִירָה לִפְנֵי הַבְּכִירָה '*Giving the younger before the older (daughter)* is not done in our place' (Gen. 29:26).

§33.61 Frequently such noun-clauses are hidden in a sentence where the impersonal *it* or *there* is used with the verb, e.g. 'It is pleasant to dwell in unity.' Ask *who?* or *what?* is pleasant; and the noun-clause will answer the question. Study these examples: *w*ᵉ*lô' yûkal lirō't 'et-hā'āreṣ* 'and it was not possible *to see the earth*' (Exod. 10:5). *'ēt kol-'ăšer tō'mar yinnāten lāh* 'There would be given to her *all that she would ask*' (Est. 2:13). יְהִי אוֹר 'Let there be *light*' (Gen. 1:6).

§33.7 The defined subj. may be an *infinitive asbolute*. This usage is quite rare. וּמַה־יּוֹכִיחַ הוֹכֵחַ מִכֶּם 'What does *reproving* from you reprove?' (Job 6:25).

§34. *Complement of the verb.* Some verbs require a word or words to complete the predication, cf. §30.122, §30.22. "She *fainted*" is a complete predication, but "he *threw*" leaves us waiting to hear the rest of the statement.

§34.1 The complement may be the *direct object* of a transitive verb (§30.3391). From comparative Sem. studies, we assume that it is in the accusative case.

§34.11 The dir. obj. is generally a noun or pronoun. *gam vaštî 'āś*ᵉ*tāʰ mištēʰ nāšîm* 'Also Vashti made *a women's banquet*' (Est. 1:9). וַיַּעַשׂ אֱלֹהִים

אֶת־הָרָקִיעַ 'And God made *the firmament*' (Gen. 1:7). לֹא נְגַעֲנוּךָ 'We did not touch *you*' (Gen. 26:29).

§34.111 The dir.obj. may be an *adjective* used substantivally. אֲשֶׁר־עָשָׂה אִתְּךָ אֶת־הַגְּדֹלֹת וְאֶת־הַנּוֹרָאֹת הָאֵלֶּה 'who has done with you *these great and fearsome (things)*' (Deut. 10:21)

§34.112 The dir.obj. may be a *participle* used substantivally, cf. *hannôrāʾôṯ* in the previous example.

§34.113 The particle אֵת\אֶת־\–אֹת is used, as a general rule, when the dir. obj. is *definite* (§30.3144). Note the examples in §34.11.

§34.1131 A word is considered to be *definite* if it is one of the following:
a proper noun (name) or an expression standing for such;
a substantive with a definite article;
a substantive with a pronimal suffix;
a substantive in construct with a word that is definite;
a noun preceded by כֹּל 'every';
a demonstrative pronoun;
the interrogative pronoun מִי 'who(m)?' (but not מָה);
אֲשֶׁר when it means 'that which, the one who';
in certain instances a noun with a number

§34.1132 The particle *ʾēṯ* is sometimes called the *nota accusativi* 'sign of the accusative.' The name is not well chosen, since *ʾēṯ* sometimes stands before words which are clearly the subject of the sentence, cf. *Ges.* §117*i*.

§34.1133 The very complex use of *ʾēṯ* should be studied carefully in *Ges.* §117*a-m*, and Joüon §125*e-i*.

§34.1134 In a number of instances, particularly in later books, –לְ is used much as אֵת, cf. *Ges.*§117*n*, Joüon §125*k-l*. Since *l-* is regularly the sign of the object in Aramaic, this may be due to Aramaic influence.

§34.114 Many verbs which are stative (§30.3393) in the G-stem, and which normally would not require a complement, become factitive (§30.3395) in D or H and require a complement. Cf. §32.812, §32.821ff.

§34.1141 Some verbs which are intransitive in Eng. take direct objects in Heb., and therefore may require a complement. לְבַשׁ בְּגָדֶיךָ 'Be clothed (with) *your garments*' (1 Kgs. 22:30). *wattimmālēʾ hāʾāreṣ ʾōṯām* 'and the land was full (of) *them*' (Exod. 1:7). *yāṣᵉʾû ʾeṯ-hāʿîr* 'they went out (of) *the city*' (Gen. 44:4).

§34.1142 Likewise the dir. obj. may be found with the N- and HtD-stems of certain verbs, such as נִלְחַם (Ps. 190:3) and הִתְהַלֵּךְ (Isa. 14:2). *Ges.* §117*w*.

§§34.115 A verb may be completed by a *compound object* (i.e. two or more objects). This is not to be confused with the two objects discussed in §34.3, below. In the compound object, the predication of the verb affects two *different* objects. *qaḥ ʾet-hallᵉbûš wᵉʾet-hassûs* 'take *the clothing* and *the horse*' (Est. 6:10).

§34.12 The complement may be a *noun-phrase* or *noun-clause*. לָדַעַת אֶת־שְׁלוֹם אֶסְתֵּר 'to know *Esther's welfare*' (Est. 2:11). *wayyā́śem ʾet-kissᵉʾô* 'and he placed *his throne*' (Est. 3:1). זָכַר ... אֲשֶׁר־עָשָׂתָה 'he remembered . . . *what she had done*' (Est. 2:1).

§34.13 After verbs of *saying* and the like, a *direct quotation* may serve as verbal complement. This is generally considered under *direct discourse*, §38.31. ויאמר לה המלך מַה־לָּךְ אֶסְתֵּר 'And the king said to her, "*What's with you, Esther?*" (Est. 5:3)

§34.14 After verbs of *saying, thinking, feeling*, and other sensory actions, a clause may serve as complement. This is often discussed under *indirect discourse*, §38.82.

§34.141 The clause may be introduced with אֵת. *wayyagged-lô mordᵉkay ʾēt kol ʾăšer qārā́hû* 'And Mordecai told him *all that had befallen him*' (Est. 4:7). וְאֵת אֲשֶׁר נִשְּׂאוֹ 'and *how he had elevated him*' (Est. 5:11).

§34.142 The clause may be introduced with כִּי. וַיַּרְא יהוה כִּי רַבָּה רָעַת הָאָדָם 'And YHWH saw *that the wickedness of man (was) great*' (Gen. 6:5).

§34.143 The clause may be introduced with אֲשֶׁר. *kî higgîḏ lāhem ʾăšer hûʾ yᵉhûḏāʰ* 'for he had told them *that he (was) a Jew*' (Est. 3:4)

§34.144 There may be no introductory word. אִמְרִי־נָא אֲחֹתִי אָתְּ 'Say, indeed, *you are my sister*' (Gen. 12:13). וַתֹּאמֶר אֶסְתֵּר לְהָשִׁיב אֶל־מָרְדֳּכָי 'And Esther said *to take back (this reply) to Mordecai*' (Est. 4:15).

§34.16 A participle in its verbal force may require a complement, which can be either in the accusative or in the genitive. אֹיֵב אֶת־דָּוִד "hating *David*" (1 Sam. 18:29). אֹהֲבֵי שְׁמֶךָ "those that love *thy name*" (Ps. 5:12). It is doubtful whether the ancient Hebrew thought of the one as a verb and the other as a noun, *vice Ges.* §116*f-g*.

§34.161 Verbal adjectives of the pattern CāCēC (distinguished by context from stative verbs) may take a complement if the verb of the same root requires one. *kî lôʾ ʾēl ḥāpēṣ résaʿ ʾáttāʰ* "For Thou (art) not a god delighting *(in) wickedness*" (Ps. 5:5 EV 4). *Ges.* §116*f*.

§34.19 The object may be omitted if understood from context. In translation it is necessary to add "it" or "them" for acceptable English. *wᵉlōʾ qibbēl* 'and he would not receive [*them*, i.e. the garments]' (Est. 4:4).

§34.2 The *cognate accusative.* An intransitive verb sometimes takes as its object a word that is cognate with it, or whose meaning closely resembles that of the verb. The terms "internal object" and "absolute object" are also used, but "cognate accusative," which was taken over from the classical languages, is not entirely inappropriate. זֹרֵעַ זֶרַע 'seeding *seed*' (Gen. 1:29). *qᵉḇûraṯ ḥămôr yiqqāḇēr* 'he shall be buried (with) *the burial of an ass*' (Jer. 22:19). (*Ges.* §117*p-r.*)

§34.21 The complement may not be a cognate word. *wāʾezʿaq qôl-gāḏôl* 'and I cried (with) *a great voice*' (Ezek. 11:13, cf. Est. 4:1).

§34.22 In many instances the "cognate acc." seems to be an adverbial acc. (cf. §35.5), especially when a similar clause is found with a prep. obj. rather than a dir. obj. *kî-hālaḵ šimʿî mîrûšāláyim gat* "that Shimei had gone from Jerusalem (to) *Gath*" (1 Kgs. 2:41, cf. 2:40, *wayyēleḵ gáttāʰ* 'and he went *Gathward*').

§34.23 The use of the inf. abs. with a finite verb (§35.6) is a specialized use of the cognate acc., cf. *Ges.* p.367, n.1. מוֹת תָּמוּת 'you shall die *dying*' (Gen. 2:17).

§34.3 Factitive verbs (§30.3394) require both a *direct object* and an *objective complement* (or *predicate objective*) to complete the predication. These are often called "verbs with two objects," which can lead to confusion with the the compound object (§34.115).

§34.31 Verbs of *calling, naming, choosing,* and the like, require an obj. comp. The dir. obj. ("nearer object") can be distinguished by putting the predication in the passive, e.g. "They called *him* (dir. obj.) *John* (obj. comp.); in passive, the dir. obj. becomes the subject, "*He* was called John). *qārᵉʾāʰ šᵉmô dān* 'She called *his name Dan*' (Gen. 30:6). נָשִׂיא אֲשִׁתֶנּוּ 'I exalted *him prince*' (1 Kgs. 11:34)

§34.32 Verbs of *asking, answering, desiring, demanding* and the like often require an obj. comp. שְׁאֵלוּנוּ שׁוֹבֵינוּ דִּבְרֵי־שִׁיר 'Our captors asked *us words of song*' (Ps. 137:3). *ûmeʰ-ʿānāʰ ʾōṯô bilʿām* 'and *what* Balaam answered *him*' (Mic. 6:5)

§34.33 Verbs of *making, fashioning,* and the like require an obj. comp. עַמּוּדָיו עָשָׂה כֶסֶף 'He made *its columns silver*' (Cant. 3:10). *wayyiḇnêʰ ʾeṯ-hāʾăḇānîm mizbēᵃḥ* 'He built *the stones (into) an altar*' (1 Kgs. 18:22)

§34.34 In some instances, the obj. comp. is a cognate accusative (§34.2, subject to the observations there). אִֽיעָצֵךְ נָא עֵצָה "I would counsel *you*, pray, *a counsel*" (1 Kgs. 1:12).

§34.35 Transitive verbs in the D- or H-stem require an obj. comp. The object of the causation is the dir. obj. ("he caused *me* to see *them*"). הַרְאֵנִי נָא אֶת־כְּבֹדֶךָ "Show *me*, pray, *thy glory*"(Exod. 33:18). *l^e har'ōṯ hā'ammîm . . . 'eṯ-yop̄yāh* "to cause *the peoples* to see *her beauty*" (Est. 1:11).

§34.351 An intransitive verb becomes transitive in the H-stem, requiring an object (§34.114). In some cases it may take a "cognate acc." as an obj. comp. *wayyalbēš 'ōṯô biḡḏê-šēš* "And he clothed *him* (with) *garments of fine linen*" (Gen. 41:42).

§34.4 The verbal object may be a pronoun suffixed to the verb. *watt^e ṣawwēhû* "And she commanded *him*" (Est. 4:5).

§34.41 If the pronoun cannot be suffixed, the particle אֵת must be used. See §34.11.

§34.42 If both the dir. obj. and the obj. comp. are pronouns, one is suffixed and the other is joined to אֵת. וְהִרְאַנִי אֹתוֹ "and He will cause *me* to see *it*" (2 Sam. 15:25).

§34.43 Great care must be taken with the inf. cstr. plus suffix (65s-). The suffix is often *subject* of the predication of the inf. cstr.: *b^e har'ōṯô 'eṯ-'ōšer k^e ḇôḏ malḵûṯô* "when *he* showed (them) the wealth of the glory of his kingdom" (Est. 1:4). However, it may be the *object* of the inf. cstr.: לְהָרְגֵנִי "to kill *me*" (Exod. 2:14).

§34.5 The verb היה requires a complement when it has the meaning "to become." On the basis of Arab., we may assume that the predicate is in the accusative (Wright, *Arabic Grammar*, 2 §§41, 44, 74). וְהִוא הָיְתָה אֵם כָּל־חָי 'And she became *mother of all life*' (Gen. 3:20).

§34.6 (Arbitrarily omitted.)

§34.7 The *infinitive absolute* may serve as dir. obj. of the verb. לִמְדוּ הֵיטֵב "Learn *to do well*" (Isa. 1:17)

§34.8 The dir. obj. may be an inf. cstr. used substantivally. לֹא אֵדַע צֵאת וָבֹא "I do not know *going out* and *coming in*" (1 Kgs. 3:7).

§34.81 The inf. cstr. in a noun-clause may require its own verbal complement. וְהַמֶּלֶךְ אָמַר לְהָשִׁיב אֶת־וַשְׁתִּי "The king said to bring back *Vashti*" (Est. 1:17). *way^e ḇaq^e šû lišlō^a ḥ yaḏ bammélek̠* "And they sought to lay *a hand* on the king" (Est. 2:21). Cf. §38.82.

§34.82 Certain verbs require another verb (in the infinitive) to complete the predication. Such an infinitive is usually called a *complementary infinitive.* וַתְּמָאֵן הַמַּלְכָּה וַשְׁתִּי לָבוֹא 'But Queen Vashti refused *to enter*' (Est. 1:12).

§34.821 It is a common mistake to consider an inf. cl. as a comp. inf. when in fact it is the subject of the verb in an inverted clause. Cf. *w^a^lammélek ʾên šôwêʰ lᵉhanníḥām* 'To be gracious to them is not fitting for the king.' (Est. 3:8) This error generally occurs when the subj. is anticipated by "it" ("it is not fitting to . . . ").

§34.822 Verbs commonly requiring a comp. inf. are *to begin to, to cease to, to continue to, to hasten to, to want to, to refuse to,* and the like. Cf. BDB 517.7.b.(c).

§34.823 Quite commonly the inf. cstr. לֵאמֹר is used after verbs of *saying* and the like. It serves no function in the syntax and is best omitted in translation or represented by quotation marks. *wayᵉḇā́reḵ ʾôṯām ʾĕlôhîm lēʾmōr* 'And God blessed them, *quote*' (Gen. 1:22).

§34.9 The *supplementary participle* may be found in Hebrew (*Ges.* §117*h*), especially with verbs of feeling. *wayyišmaʿ môšêʰ ʾeṯ-hāʿām bôḵêʰ* 'and Moses heard the people *weeping*' (Num. 11:10). This might better be looked upon as an adj. modifying the noun "people."

§35. The *modifier of the verb.* The predication of the verb may be modified or defined more precisely in a number of ways (§30.23). Since such a modifier applies to the verb it is called an *adverb* or *adverbial modifier.*

§35.1 The *indirect object* is used to define more precisely the predication of verbs of *giving, telling, teaching, throwing,* and the like. Since it is possible in Eng. to use such expressions as "throw me the ball," "teach her Latin," "give them cake," etc., it is not always recognized that the pronouns following the verbs are essentially adverbial modifiers. The *direct* action of the verb is on the *thing* and the *indirect* action is on the person, which could be rephrased in a prepositional phrase, "throw the ball *to me*," "teach Latin *to her*," "give cake *to them*."

§35.11 The indir. obj. is generally indicated by the prep. -לְ. וַיַּגִּידוּ לָהּ 'And they told *her*' (Est. 4:4). *wattiqrāʾ ʾestēr lahăṯāḵ* 'And Esther called *to Hatach*' (Est. 4:5)

§35.111 The prep. אֶל *ʾel* is also used. *bᵉʾomrām ʾēlāʸw yôm wāyôm* 'in their saying *to him* day by day' (Est. 3:4).

§35.112 Occasionally the indir. obj. is expressed by the acc. suffix. *kî ʾéreṣ hannéḡeḇ nᵉṯattā́nî* "for the land of the Negev thou hast given *me*" (Josh. 15:19). *Ges.* §117*x*.

§35.113 It is obvious that wherever the indir. obj. is indicated by a prep. it could be included in §35.3 under adverbial phrases.

§35.2 The verb may be modified by an *adverb* (§30.34). In addition to negative (§35.22) and interrogative (§35.23) adverbs, there are a number of primitive adverbs: of place, שָׁם 'there,' הֵן and פֹּה 'here'; of time, אָז 'then'; of manner, כֵּן and כָּכָה 'thus'; and of extent, גַּם and אַף 'also,' אַךְ 'surely, only,' דַּי 'enough.'

§35.21 Besides primitive adverbs there are adverbs formed from nouns or adjectives, with or without afformative elements, such as מְאֹד 'very,' יַחְדָּו 'together,' נֶגְבָּה 'southward,' יוֹמָם 'daily,' etc. Cf. §§23.2, .4.

§35.211 Some fem. adjectives are used as adverbs. רִאשֹׁנָה 'formerly,' נִפְלָאוֹת 'wonderfully,' יְהוּדִית 'in the Jewish language.' *Ges.* §100*d*.

§35.212 A number of H60 forms are used as adverbs. הַרְבֵּה 'much,,' הַשְׁכֵּם 'early,' הַעֲרֵב 'at evening.' *Ges.* §100*e*.

§35.213 Numerals can serve as adverbs. שְׁתַּיִם 'twice,' שֵׁנִית 'for the second time,' שֶׁבַע 'sevenfold.' *Ges.* §100*f*.

§35.22 Negative particles can serve as adverbs. The most common are לֹא, אַל, לְבִלְתִּי אֵין.

§35.221 לֹא with a verb (to be distinguished from its other uses) negates the verb. With the perf., and sometimes with the impf., (cf. §35.2212), it is a simple negative. *lôʾ higgîḏāʰ ʾestēr ʾeṯ-ʿammāʰ* 'Esther had not made known her people' (Est. 2:10).

§35.2211 If לֹא is not immediately before the verb, it changes the meaning of the predication. This is important for exegesis. *lôʾ ʿal-hammélek̠ lᵉḇaddô ʿāwᵉṯāʰ waštî* . . . does not deny that Vashti had done evil, but rather denies that it affected only the king (Est. 1:16). Study BDB 518-520

§35.2212 לֹא before the imperfect, especially 2ms (22), expresses a strong prohibition, cf. §32.5215.

§35.2213 Before nouns or adjectives, לֹא negates the word or expresses the opposite, often in litotes. לֹא by itself is simply "no" or "not so."

§35.222 אַל expresses negation as a wish, rather than a reality, and is used with the jussive or cohortative. It is milder than לֹא + the impf. (cf. §35.221). BDB 39.

§35.223 לְבִלְתִּי is used to negate the inf. cstr., expressing purpose or result (§§38.54, .55). *ʾăšer ṣiwwîṯîkā lᵉḇiltî ʾăḵol-mimménnû* 'which I commanded you not to eat from it' (Gen. 3:11). לְבִלְתִּי הַכּוֹת־אֹתוֹ 'so that no one should smite him' (Gen. 4:15).

§35.224 אֵין can be used as a neg. addv. to negate the ptcp. אֵין שֹׁוֶה 'it is not fitting' (Est. 3:8). *ʾên ʾestēr maggéḏeṯ môlaḏtāʰ* 'Esther was not making known her kinfolk' (Est. 2:20).

§35.2241 אֵין before the inf. cstr. expresses impossibility. *ʾên lāḇôʾ ʾel-šáʿar hamméleḵ bilᵉḇûš śāq* 'it's impossible to enter the king's gate in sackcloth' (Est. 4:2).

§35.2242 To consider יֵשׁ and אֵין plus pron. suf. as adverbs (*Ges.* §100*o*) is probably based more on translation than on Hebrew thought-pattern. The particles are basically substantives (cf. *Ges.* §§141*k*, 152*i-p*).

§35.229 It is important to observe the *position* of the negative particle. As a general rule, it negates the word, phrase, or clause which it immediately precedes

§35.23 *Interrogative adverbs* raise a question about the time, place, manner, or extent of the predication. The most common are: מָתַי 'when?,' אֵי or אַיֵּה 'where?,' אָנָה 'whither?,' אֵיךְ or אֵיכָה 'how?,' מַדּוּעַ 'why?,' עַד־מָתַי 'how long?'

§35.231 The interrogative particle הֲ- *hă-* (§22.3ff.) may with some degree of doubt be considered as an adverb, cf. *Ges.* §100*i-n.*

§35.3 An *adverbial phrase* consists of a preposition and its object, either a pron. suf. or a substantive (cf. §§30.35, .354), used to modify or define the predication.

§35.31 The adverbial phrase may limit the word(s) to which it refers in *place, time, manner,* or *extent.*Since prepositions can be used in various ways *the student must study the uses of each one!* Note the following: בּ- *bîmê* (1:1) temporal, *bᵉšûšān* (1:2) local, *bᵉḥaḇlê-ḇûṣ* (1:6) manner; כּ- *kᵉšéḇeṯ* (1:2) temporal, *kᵉyaḏ hamméleḵ* (1:7) manner – and these are from just the first seven verses of Esther!

§35.32 In some sentences, the verb appears to be modified by a ptcp. or by a noun in construct. וַיֵּצֵא ... הָמָן שָׂמֵחַ וְטוֹב לֵב 'and Haman went out *rejoicing* and *good of heart*' (Est. 5:9). It is possible that the Hebrew thought of these terms as modifying "Haman" rather than describing how he went out. The line between an adjective and an adverb in such sentences is not easy to define.

§35.4 The verb may be modified by an *adverbial clause*, see also §38.5. Here we are considering only those adverbial clauses which do not have coördinating conjunctions (hence do not form complex sentences).

§35.41 A ptcp. may form an adverbial clause. וַיְהִי שָׁאוּל אֹיֵב אֶת־דָּוִד 'and Saul was *hating David*' (1 Sam. 18:29). If the ptcp. cl. were simply a predicate, the verb would not be used, but see remarks in §35.32.

§35.42 The inf. cstr. is often used in adverbial clauses. וַתִּכְהֶיןָ עֵינָיו מֵרְאֹת 'and his eyes were so dim *he couldn't see* (lit. 'from seeing'; Gen. 27:1).

§35.421 The inf. cstr. + בְּ– *b–* can form a *temporal* adv. cl., usually translated 'when.' *bᵉhiqqāḇēṣ nᵉʿārôṯ* '*when* maidens *were gathered*' (lit., 'in the being gathered of maidens'; Est. 2:8).

§35.422 The inf. cstr. + כְּ– *k–* can form a temporal or circumstantial adverbial clause, usually translated 'when,' but sometimes more properly 'while.' *kᵉšéḇeṯ hamméleḵ . . . ʿal kissēʾ malḵûṯô* '*when*/while the king was sitting on his royal throne' (lit., 'as the sitting of the king'; Est. 1:2).

§35.423 The inf. cstr. + לְ– *l-* is commonly used adverbially in a purpose clause. *lᵉḏáʿaṯ ʾeṯ-šᵉlôm ʾestēr* '*to know* Esther's welfare' (lit., 'toward the knowing of'; Est. 2:11). לִרְאֹת אֶת־הָעִיר '*to see* the city' (Gen. 11:5).

§35.4231 The inf. cstr. + ל may also suggest incipiency. וַיְהִי הַשֶּׁמֶשׁ לָבוֹא 'and *when* the sun was *about to go down*' (Gen. 15:12).

§35.4232 The inf. cstr. + ל may suggest appointing or compelling to do something. וַיְהִי הַשַּׁעַר לִסְגּוֹר 'and the gate was (= had) *to be shut*' (Josh. 2:5). כִּי אֵין לָבוֹא 'for no one *may enter*' (Est. 4:2). *ʿālay lāṯeṯ lᵉḵā* '*it was incumbent* upon me *to give* you' (2 Sam. 18:11).

§35.4233 The inf. cstr. + ל is often used as a complementary infinitive, cf. §34.82.

§35.43 An *infinitive absolute* may be used in an adverbial clause. הָלֹךְ עָרוֹם וְיָחֵף '*walking* naked and barefoot' (Isa. 20:2). *ʾāqîm ʾel-ʿēlî . . . hāḥēl wᵉḵallēʰ* 'I will raise against Eli all I have spoken . . . *from beginning to end*' (1 Sam. 3:12).

§35.5 An *adverbial accusative* may be used to modify a verb (cf. §35.211). Since case-endings have all but vanished in Heb., the *hê*-directive is one of the few clear examples of this usage. נֵלְכָה דֹּתָיְנָה 'let's go *to Dothan*' (Gen. 37:17). *wayyissaʿ ʾaḇrām hālôḵ wᵉnāsôaʿ hannégbāʰ* 'and Abram set out, going and traveling (= traveling continuously, *Ges.* §113*s-t*) *toward the Negev*' (Gen. 12:9).

§35.6 An *infinitive absolute* is often used to modify a verb of the same root (and generally the same stem) by lending great strength to the predication. It is most difficult to translate into Eng. הֲמָלֹךְ תִּמְלֹךְ עָלֵינוּ 'will you *indeed* reign over us?' (Gen. 37:8). *ʾim ʿannēh^{h} ṯ^{e}ʿannēh^{h} ʾōṯô kî ʾim-ṣāʿōq yiṣʿaq ʾēlî ṣāmôa^{c} ʾešmaʿ ṣaʿăqāṯô* 'If you *do* afflict him, *indeed* if *for any reason* he should cry out to me, I will *certainly* hear his cry' (Exod. 22:22 MT; supporting the injunction, 'You shall not afflict a widow or an orphan').

§35.7 A verb may be modified by a *substantive in construct* with the verb. Such a construction, common in Akk. (with sbjtv.) and found in Arab. but generally not recognized in Heb., puts the verb in a subordinate clause. תְּחִלַּת דִּבֶּר־יהוה 'the beginning of YHWH spoke' (Hos. 1:2, = 'when YHWH first spoke [by Hosea]'). *b^{e}rēʾšîṯ bārāʾ ʾĕlôhîm* 'in the beginning of (= when) God created' (Gen. 1:1)

§35.71 Very common is the use of אֲשֶׁר (cstr. of אֲשֶׁר 'place') in cstr. with a finite verb. בְּכֹל אֲשֶׁר־הִתְהַלַּכְתִּי 'in every place of (= where) I walked about' (2 Sam. 7:7)

§35.711 As *ʾăšer* came to be used more as a conj., it lost the meaning 'place of,' and מְקוֹם was added to express the idea. *b^{e}ḵol-m^{e}ḏînā^{h} ûm^{e}ḏînā^{h} m^{e}qôm* (cstr.!) *ʾăšer d^{e}ḇar-hammélek̲ . . . maggîa^{c}* 'in each city where the word of the king reached' (Est. 4:3).

§36. The *modifier of the noun.* A substantive quite often does not stand alone in a clause, but is modified or defined in some way, cf. §§30.2, .21.

§36.1 A noun may be modified by an *attributive adjective* (§30.322f). לְגוֹי גָּדוֹל 'into a *great* nation' (Gen. 12:2). Cf. *Ges.* §132.

§36.11 The adj. is in *concord* with the noun (i.e. it agrees with the noun in gender, number, and definiteness). Note that agreement in *gender* refers to the *grammatical* gender and not to the morphology. זְעָקָה גְּדוֹלָה 'a *great* cry' (Est. 4:1). *m^{e}lāḵîm ʾaddîrîm 'majestic* kings' (Ps. 136:18). *n^{e}ʿārôṯ rabbôṯ* '*many* maidens' (Est. 2:8). הֶחָצֵר הַפְּנִימִית 'the *inner* court' (Est. 4:11). *nāšîm nokrîyôt* '*strange* women' (1 Kgs. 11:1). *bayyôm hašš^{e}lîšî* 'on the *third* day' (Est. 5:1).

§36.111 It is unusual in Heb. to modify two substantives with a single adj.; where two substantives are modified by the same modifier, the adj. is usually repeated. *l^{e}šallaḥ ʾîš ʾet-ʿabdô w^{e}ʾîš ʾet šip̄ḥātô hāʿibrî w^{e}hāʿiḇrîṯ ḥop̄šîm* 'and each man shall send away free his *Hebrew* manservant or maidservant' (Jer. 34:9).

§36.1111 If a single adj. is used, it will agree with a masc. substantive. *ûr^{e}ḥôbôt hāʿîr yimmāl^{e}ʾû y^{e}lādî wî^{y}lādôt m^{e}śaḥaqîm bir^{e}ḥôbôtéhā* 'and the city's streets shall be filled with boys and girls *playing* in its streets' (Zech. 8:5). חֻקִּים וּמִצְוֹת טוֹבִים '*good* statutes and commandments' (Neh. 9:13).

§36.1112 When two substantives form a unitary idea, a single adjective may be used. צֹאן וּבָקָר הַרְבֵּה מְאֹד 'very *many* flocks and herds' (2 Sam. 12:2). Deut. 31:21, *rāʿôṯ rabbôṯ wᵉṣārôṯ* may contain two nouns ('many evils and troubles'), or it may have two adjectives, 'evils *many* and *sore*').

§36.112 With a *collective* noun a plur. adj. may be used. צֹאן רַבּוֹת '*many* sheep' (Gen. 30:43). *hāʿām hahôlᵉḵîm baḥōšeḵ* 'the people *walking* in darkness' (Isa. 9:1). נֶפֶשׁ שְׁנָיִם '*two* souls' (Gen. 46.27).

§36.113 When אֱלֹהִים stands for the God of Israel, it generally takes a sing. adj. (and verb) אֱלֹהִים צַדִּיק O *righteous* God' (Ps. 7:10).

§36.1131 When referring to false gods, אֱלֹהִים takes pl. adjs. (and verbs) אֱלֹהִים אֲחֵרִים '*other* gods' (Exod. 20:3).

§36.1132 When a Hebrew speaks to a gentile or vice versa about the God of Israel, the pl. adj. may be used. Cf. 1 Sam. 28:13, אֱלֹהִים רָאִיתִי עֹלִים מִן־הָאָרֶץ 'I saw God *going up* from the earth.' The use of pl. verbs in such instances is more common than the use of adjs.

§36.1133 This distinction is not consistently made, cf. אֱלֹהִים חַיִּים (Deut. 5:23, EV 26) and אֱלֹהִים חָי (2 Kgs. 19:16) '(the) *living* God.' Note pl. adj. and sg. pron. in the following: *kî ʾĕlôhîm qᵉḏôšîm hûʾ* 'for He is a *holy* God' (Josh. 24:19).

§36.114 A subst. in the *dual* is modified by a *plural* adj. עֵינַיִם רָמוֹת '*haughty* eyes' (Ps. 18:28).

§36.115 A substantive may have more than one modifier. הָאֵל הַגָּדֹל הַגִּבֹּר וְהַנּוֹרָא 'the *great, mighty,* and *terrible* God' (Deut. 10:17).

§36.1151 When two adjs. follow a fem. subst., sometimes only the nearer agrees in gender. רוּחַ גְּדֹלָה וְחָזָק 'a *great* and *strong* wind' (1 Kgs. 19:11).

§36.12 The adj. regularly stands *after* the substantive it qualifies. See examples in preceding sections.

§36.121 If the subst. is in *construct* the modifying adj. stands after the annexion. אִישׁ אֱלֹהִים קָדוֹשׁ 'a *holy* man of God' (2 Kgs. 4:9). *ʿăṭéreṯ zāhāḇ gᵉḏôlāʰ* 'a *great* crown of gold' (Est. 8:15).

§36.122 The pl. adj. רַבּוֹת\רַבִּים when it means 'many' (but not when it means 'great') may precede the noun. רַבִּים צַיָּדִים '*many* hunters' (Jer. 16:16). But cf. יָמִים רַבִּים '*many* days' (Gen. 21:34 and often).

§36.13 The distinction between "adjective" and "substantive" in the Semitic languages is not clearly defined. Accordingly we find adjs. serving as substantives, modifying substantives by annexion (§36.3), and substantives modifying substantives by annexion (§36.3) or apposition (§36.6). Many times our confusion arises from translation and failure to understand the Hebrew idiom.

§36.14 Because of the complex nature of numeral modifiers, we shall treat them separately, cf. §36.9.

§36.15 The substantive כֹּל 'completeness, wholeness, whole' requires special attention. Like Gk. πᾶς, it does not follow the noun it modifies, but precedes it. In Heb., however, it is considered to be in construct (§36.31) with the following substantive (which is therefore in the gen.). Study carefully BDB 481f.

§36.151 *kōl* before a determinate (definite, cf. §34.1131) substantive means 'all, every, the whole of.' כָּל־הָאָרֶץ 'all the earth' (Gen. 11:1). *wᵉkol-yēṣer maḥšᵉbōṯ libbô* 'and every imagination of the thoughts of his heart' (Gen. 6:5). *kol-yᵉmê ʾāḏām* 'all the days of Adam' (Gen. 5:5). *Ges.* §127*b*.

§36.152 *kōl* before an indeterminate (not definite) substantive means 'any, each.' כָּל־דָּבָר 'anything' (Judg. 19:19). *bᵉḵōl-yôm* 'in any day, every day' (Ps. 7:12). *kol-ʿēṣ* 'every (kind of) tree, any tree' (Gen. 2:9).

§36.1521 Before indeterminate collectives or in poetry before any indeterminate substantive, *kōl* may mean 'all, every.' כָּל־בָּשָׂר 'all flesh' (Gen. 6:12). *kol-yāḏáyim* 'all hands, every hand' (Isa. 13:7).

§36.2 The *definite article* modifies a noun or other substantive by indicating a specific member or group of a category (§30.3223).

§36.21 From several lines of evidence we conclude that the def. art. was a late development in language. Not all Sem. languages have a def. art. (cf. Akk. and Ugar.). Those that do have a def. art. do not have a common element that can be traced to a common ancestor (Heb. *ha–*, Arab. *al–*, Aram. postpositive *–â*, OSA postpositive *–n*). Accordingly we find the def. art. omitted in the oldest portions of Bib. Heb. (e.g. the Song of Moses, Song of Deborah, etc.).

§36.22 Since the usage of the def. art. does not exactly coincide with our English usage, we should study it carefully for exegetical purposes (cf. *Ges.* §126).

§36.221 The def. art. is used for a person or thing previously mentioned (anaphoric). הַמֶּלֶךְ '*the* king' (previously mentioned, Est. 1:9-10).

§36.222 The def. art. is used for a person or thing that is well known. הָאַלּוֹן '*the* oak' (RSV 'an oak' fails to bring out the force of the Heb., Gen. 35:8).

§36.2221 The def. art. may denote a substantive that is unique. הָאָרֶץ '*The* earth,' הַשֶּׁמֶשׁ '*the* sun').

§36.2222 The def. art. is used when a class-term stands for an individual. *śāṭān* 'adversary,' *haśśāṭān* '*the* Adversary, ὁ διάβολος, Satan'; likewise הַמָּשִׁיחַ 'the Anointed, ὁ χριστός, Messiah.'

§36.2223 The def. art. is used with stock expressions. הַיּוֹם '*to*day,' הַשָּׁנָה '*this* year.'

§36.2224 Sometimes the def. art. is used where we would use a possessive pronoun. *wattiqqaḥ haṣṣāʿîp̄* 'and she took *her* veil' (Gen. 24:65).

§36.223 The def. art. may denote a class. *hāʾaryêʰ* the lion' (as a class), hence 'a lion.'

§36.2231 The def. art. may be used when an indefinite member of a class is thought of in a definite situation. In Eng. we would generally use an indef. art. in translation. Cf. Amos 5:19, 'A man fled from a lion (הָאֲרִי) and a bear (הַדֹּב) met him.'

§36.2232 The def. art. is used in comparison. Cf. Isa. 1:18, 'white as (the) snow (*kaššéleḡ*), red as (the) crimson (*kattôlāʿ*).

§36.2233 The def. art. may be used on a substantive in the sing. when it is equivalent to a collective. *ʾeṯ haṣṣāḏîq wᵉʾeṯ-hārāšʿ yišpōṭ hāʾelōhîm* 'God will judge *the* righteous and *the* wicked' (Eccl. 3:17). (*Ges.* §126*m*).

§36.224 The def. art. may be used to designate the vocative. הַמֶּלֶךְ '*O* king.'

§36.225 The def. art. may be used to express the superlative degree (§30.323). הַצְּעִרָה 'the *smallest, least*' (1 Sam. 9:21). *bᵉnô haqqāṭān* 'his *youngest* son' (Gen. 9:24).

§36.226 The def. art. is used on any attributive that modifies a substantive that is definite. *hāʿîr haggᵉḏôlāʰ* 'the great city,' *ʾestēr hammalkāʰ* 'Esther the queen,' cf. §36.11.

§36.23 Omission of the def. art. should also be noted carefully.

§36.231 The def. art. is often omitted in poetry. This is partly due to the late emergence of the def. art. (§36.21), and partly due, perhaps, to conscious imitation of such poetry. אֶרֶץ 'the earth' (Ps. 2:2). מְלָכִים 'O kings' (Ps. 2:10). *šimḵā gāḏôl wᵉnôrāʾ* 'thy great and fearsome name' (Ps. 99:3; cf. §36.11).

§36.2311 In poetry, a prefixed prep. is often pointed with the def. art. This may be due to the Masoretes (cf. *Ges.* §126*h*). *baššāmáyîm* (Ps. 2:4).

§36.232 The def. is usually omitted with proper nouns of *places.* סְדֹם 'Sodom,' כְּנַעַן 'Canaan,' etc.

§36.2321 However, certain place names usually have the def. art. הַכַּרְמֶל Carmel,' הַלְּבָנוֹן 'Lebanon,' הַיַּרְדֵּן 'the Jordan,' הָעַי 'Ai' (lit., 'the Ruins'), etc.

§36.2322 The def. art. may be omitted from the modifier of an anarthrous proper noun. *ṣîḏôn rabbāʰ* 'Great Sidon' (Josh. 11:8), אֵל אֶלְיוֹן 'God most high.' This is contrary to §36.11; cf. *Ges.* §126*y*.

§36.2323 Some once-common nouns that became proper nouns (with the def. art.) have subsequently been treated as proper nouns and omit the def. art. Cf. אָדָם 'man > Adam,' שָׂטָן 'adversary > Satan,' אֱלֹהִים 'gods > God,' אֹהֶל מוֹעֵד 'tent of meeting > Tabernacle,' etc.

§36.233 The def. art. is regularly omitted when a word is in construct with a following substantive. וְסָרִיסֵי הַמֶּלֶךְ 'and *the* eunuchs of the king' (Est. 6:14). *ʾeṯ-ṣōʾn ʾaḇîhem* '*the* flock of their father' (Gen 37:12). The student should note carefully that *if the governed noun is definite, the governing noun is also definite*.

§36.2331 There are a number of instances where the def. art. is used on a construct. *haqqéḇer ʾîš-hāʾĕlōhîm* 'the tomb of the man of God' (2 Kgs. 23:17). הָאָרוֹן הַבְּרִית 'the ark of the covenant' (Josh. 3:14). *ʾeṯ-hayᵉṯaḏ hāʾéreḡ* 'the peg of the loom' (Judg. 16:16). Because of the number of such examples, it seems somewhat capricious to try to explain them away or (worse!) to speak of "syntactically impossible additions" (*Ges.* §127*g*, cf. *Ges.* §127*f-h*). A grammarian derives *rules* from *data,* he does not try to conform data to rules.

§36.234 The def. art. is regularly omitted with the names of persons. יהוה, מֹשֶׁה, דָּוִד, etc. The student should note that since a personal name is *definite*, a noun in construct with it will be definite. *dᵉḇar-YHWH* '*the* word of the Lord' (Hos. 1:1, etc.).

§36.2341 Gentilics, however, usually take the def. art. הַכְּנַעֲנִי 'the Canaanite,' *hāʿiḇrî* 'the Hebrew' (*Ges.* §125*e*).

§36.235 The def. art. is omitted if the word has a pron. suf. since the suffix makes the word definite. אַמָּהּ '*her* people' (Est. 2:10).

§36.2351 A ptcp. with acc. suf. can take the def. art. הַמַּכֵּהוּ 'the one smiting him' (Is. 9:12), cf. *Ges.* §127*i*.

§36.2352 In a number of instances, gen. suff. are found on words with the def. art. הָעֶרְכְּךָ 'thy value' (Lev. 27:23; since the word occurs in this form twice in one sentence, it is unreasonable to delete the *hê, cf.* BDB 790). *kol-hehārôṯêʸhā* 'all its pregnant women' (2 Kgs. 15:16; since the Masoretes clearly noted the form, we cannot simply say "dittography of the ה" *pace Ges.* §127*i*).

§36.236 The def. art. is omitted from a substantive which is indefinite or so far unknown, cf. §36.221, note §36.2231.

§36.2361 In a few instances, אֶחָד is used as an indefinite article. קַח צִנְצֶנֶת אַחַת 'take *a* jar' (Exod. 16:33). *wattašlēḵ ʾiššāʰ ʾaḥaṯ* 'and *a* woman threw' (Judg. 9:53). This usage is similar to Gk. *τις*. *Ges.* §125*b*.

§36.2362 The omission of the def. art. sometimes serves as an "indefinite for amplification" (*Ges.* §125*c*). מִפְּנֵי־חֶרֶב 'from a sword' (Isa. 35:8; *ḥéreḇ* occurs 3x in this verse, hence we should expect the def. art. on at least two of the forms). אִשָּׁה 'a woman' (Hos. 3:1, apparently meaning the woman of Hos. 1, hence 'such a woman,' *Ges.* §125*c*).

§36.237 The def. art. is regularly omitted from a predicate noun or adjective, §§31.21, .23. The student should learn to distinguish between the attributive adj. (with the def. art.) and the predicate adj. (without the def. art., see §31.233.

§36.2371 An important exception to this rule is the ptcp. with def. art. used as a relative clause and serving as predicate. *hûʾ hassôḇēḇ* 'that (is) the one encircling' (Gen. 2:11). *Ges.* §126*k*.

§36.238 The def. art. is often omitted from the word יוֹם when it is modified by a numeral adj. יוֹם הַשִּׁשִּׁי 'the sixth day' (Gen. 1:31). *miyyôm hāriʾšôn* 'from the first day' (Exod. 12:15). *Ges.* §126*w*.

§36.2381 However, when the prep. -בְּ is added to יוֹם in such a construction, the def. art. is used. *bayyôm hašš*ᵉ*ḇîʿî* 'on the seventh day' (Gen. 2:1).

§36.24 Certain observations should be made.

§36.241 If a def. art. is added to the last element of a construct, it makes each element in the construct *definite*. עַל־יְדֵי עֹשֵׂי הַמְּלָאכָה 'into *the* hands of *the* doers of *the* deed' (Est. 3:9).

§36.2411 The entire construction is definite if the def. art. has been omitted from the last element for any of the reasons described in §§36.232, .234, or .235.

§36.242 If a substantive is modified by two or more adjectives or demonstratives, the def. art. is generally used on *each* modifier. *wᵉʾerʾêʰ ʾeṯ-hammarʾêʰ haggāḏôl hazzêʰ* 'and I shall see this great sight' (Exod. 3:3).

§36.243 If the governing noun (*nomen regens*, §36.311) is defined for any reason, its modifier regularly takes the def. art. Exceptions are noted in preceding sections.

§36.244 A circumlocution is necessary to indicate indefiniteness when the governing noun would otherwise be definite. *mizmōr lᵉḏāwîḏ* 'a psalm of David'; *mizmor-dāwîḏ* would be 'the (only or well-known) psalm of David.'

§36.3 A *substantive in the genitive* may be used to modify another substantive, cf. §30.311. In the Sem. languages this is generally indicated by *annexion* or the *construct state*. It may also be indicated by the addition of a pron. suf., to be discussed below, §36.52.

§36.31 *Annexion* (סְמִיכוּת) is the juxtaposing of two substantives to indicate a genitival relationship. The first element regularly loses its major accent (§17.121) with resulting vocalic alteration (R.3), and is said to be *in construct* with the word that follows.

§36.311 The first substantive in annexion is called the *governing noun* (*nomen regens*).

§36.3111 Since the governing noun is only part of the idea being expressed (*the house of* means nothing), it is indefinite. It becomes definite only if the governed noun is definite.

§36.3112 The governing noun is indefinite if the governed noun is indefinite. *bilᵉḇûš śāq* 'in *a* garment of sackcloth' (Est. 4:2)

§36.3113 The governing noun is definite if the governed noun is definite. *mᵉğillaṯ ʾestēr* '*the* scroll of Esther.' *ʾel-rᵉḥôḇ hāʿîr* 'to *the* plaza of *the* city' (Est. 4:6). *ʿal kissēʾ malḵûṯô* 'on *the* throne of *his* royalty' (Est. 1:2).

§36.3114 The same rule holds for a chain of constructs. *ʿṓšer kᵉḇôḏ malḵûṯô* '*the* splendor of *the* glory of *his* kingdom' (Est. 1:4). *ʿal pᵉrî-gṓḏel lᵉḇaḇ mélek-ʾaššûr* 'against *the* fruit of *the* greatness (= pride) of *the* heart of *the* king of *Asshur*' (Isa. 10:12). *ûšᵉʾār mispar qéšeṯ gibbôrê bᵉnê-qēḏār* 'and *the* rest of *the* number of *the* archer(s) of *the* mighty-men of *the* sons of *Kedar*' (Isa. 21:17).

§36.312 The second word in annexion is the *governed noun* (*nomen rectum*). In inflected Sem. languages, it is in the genitive case, and is regularly translated as such in Heb. It is often called "the genitive," and the governing noun is sometime said to be "in construct with its genitive." The case of the *first* noun in annexion is determined by its position in its clause. It can be nom., gen., or acc.–but its case-ending, even in inflected languaages, normally does not appear.

§36.3121 A *governed* noun may be annexed in turn to another noun, and thus become also a governing noun. See the examples in the chains of constructs in §36.3114.

§36.3122 If the *final* word in a chain of constructs is definite, each of the words in the chain will be definite, cf. §36.3113f.

§36.313 As a general rule, there is only *one* governing noun and *one* governed noun in annexion. It is irregular in Hebrew to have expressions such as "the men and women of Jerusalem" or "houses of brick and stone." (This rule does not concern the formation of chains of constructs, discussed in §36.3114.) *Ges.* §128*g*.

§36.3131 Where two governing nouns would occur, the second is put in a separate phrase with a suffix. דְּבַר־הַמֶּלֶךְ וְדָתוֹ 'the king's word and decree' (lit. 'the word of the king and his decree,' Est. 4:3). *naʿărôṯ ʾestēr wᵉsârîséʸhā* 'Esther's maids and eunuchs' (lit. 'the maids of Esther and her eunuchs,' Est. 4:4).

§36.3132 A *single* governing noun may be placed in construct with two governed nouns if the two can be thought of as a single category. קֹנֵה שָׁמַיִם וָאָרֶץ 'creator of *heaven and earth*' (= everything, Gen. 14:19). *bᵉʿîr dᵉlāṯáyîm ûbᵉrîᵃḥ* 'in a city of *a pair of door-panels and a bar*' (i.e. a gate that could be closed and barred, 1 Sam. 23:7).

§36.3133 Thus *ʾĕlôhê ʾaḇrāhām wᵉyiṣḥāq wᵉyaʿăqōḇ* is to be understood in the sense of 'the God of the Patriarchs,' whereas *ʾĕlôhê ʾaḇrāhām ʾĕlôhê yiṣḥāq wēʾlôhê yaʿăqōḇ* may suggest the God of each of the Patriarchs individually.

§36.3134 In some clauses, כֹּל seems to modify two phrases. *kol-ʿaḇḏê hammélek̠ wᵉʿam mᵉḏînôṯ hammélek̠* 'all the king's slaves and (all) the people of the king's province' (Est. 4:11).

§36.314 With few exceptions, nothing may be interposed between a governing noun and a governed noun. In other words, the construct or annexion may not be broken.

§36.3141 If the governing noun is modified by an adjective, this adj. must be placed *after the governed noun* (§36.122). It will of course be in concord with the noun it modifies. וַעֲטֶרֶת זָהָב גְּדוֹלָה 'and a great crown of gold' (Est. 8:15; note gender of the adj.).

§36.3142 The locative ־ָה *-āʰ* may be interposed between the governing and governed nouns. *ʾărṣāʰ kᵉnáʿan* '*to* the land of Canaan' (Gen. 12:5).

§36.315 Annexion is sometimes deliberately avoided.

§36.3151 To preserve the indefiniteness of the governing noun when the governed noun is definite, –ל may be used, cf. §36.244.

§36.3152 When there would be two (or more) governing nouns and a single genitive, a pron. suf. is used, cf. §36.3131.

§36.3153 In later (?) Heb. שֶׁל (*ša* 'which' [cf. Akk.] + *l*) is used for the gen. כַּרְמִי שֶׁלִּי 'my vineyard' (Cant. 1:6). *bᵉšellᵉmî* 'on account of whom?' (Jon. 1:7). Cf. BDB 980.4d. This use of *šel* is very common in Mod. Heb.

§36.32 Annexion may be used for just about any of the uses of the genitive familiar to us in our western languages. In a chain of constructs (§36.3114), each gen. may serve a different use.

§36.321 The *adjectival genitive* serves to define a subst. much as an attrib. adj. (§36.1) would do. It includes the attributive gen., the gen. of reference, and the gen. of apposition.

§36.3211 The *attributive gen.* defines a subst. by giving an attribute. It is similar to the gen. of material, the gen. of quality, and other genitives. גִּבּוֹר חַיִל 'a man *of wealth*' (Ruth 2:1).

§36.3212 The *gen. of reference* defines a subst. by reference to another subst. בִּימֵי עֻזִּיָּהוּ 'in the days *of Uzziah*' (Isa. 1:1).

§36.3213 The *gen. of apposition* defines a subst. by another subst. which is an appositive. עִיר נָחוֹר 'the city *of Nahor*' (= 'the city, Nahor,' Gen. 24:10). *ben-ʾāḏām* 'son *of man* ' (= 'human being,' Ezek. 33:2).

§36.322 The *possessive gen.* defines a subst. by associating it with the one who possesses it. *ʾel-yāḏ šaʿašgaz* 'into the hand *of Shaashgaz*' (Est. 2:14). לֵב־הַמֶּלֶךְ the heart *of the king*' (Est. 1:10).

§36.3221 The *gen. of close relationship*, which is a possessive gen., defines a substantive by relating it to a son, a father, or other relative, whether real or ideal. בְּנֵי־נֹחַ 'the sons *of Noah*' (Gen. 10:1). *baṯ-dôḏô* 'the daughter *of his uncle*' (Est. 2:7).

§36.323 The *subjective gen.* defines a subst. of action or feeling by relating it to the one from whom that action or feeling is derived. *bᵉʾahăḇaṯ* YHWH *ʾeṯ-yiśrāʾēl* 'in the love *of* YHWH for Israel' (1 Kgs. 10:9).

§36.3231 Sometimes the *gen. of the author* is distinguished from the subj. gen. מַשְׂאַת מֹשֶׁה 'the tax *of* (imposed by) *Moses*' (2 Chr. 24:6).

§36.324 The *objective gen.* defines a subst. by relating it to the object of its action or feeling. אֵימַת הַמֶּלֶךְ 'the dread *of* (for) *the king*' (Prov. 20:2). *niqmat hêʸkālô* 'the vengeance *of his temple*' (Jer. 50:28).

§36.325 The *gen. of description* defines a subst. by giving its quality, material, contents, or by comparing it with another subst. It can easily be confused with the gen. of reference.

§36.3251 The *gen. of quality*: *bigdê haqqṓdeš* 'the garments *of holiness*' (Exod. 29:29). מֹאזְנֵי צֶדֶק '*just* balances' (Lev. 19:36).

§36.3252 The *gen. of material*: מִזְבַּח אֲדָמָה 'an altar *of earth*' (Exod. 20:24). *bᵉḥablê-bûṣ* 'with cords *of byssus*' (Est. 1:6).

§36.3253 The *gen. of contents*: *ʾéreṣ zâbat ḥālāb ûdᵉbāš* 'a land flowing *of milk and honey*' (Exod. 33:3). נֹאד הֶחָלָב 'the skin (bottle) *of milk*' (Judg. 4:19).

§36.3254 A peculiar Heb. idiom is found in expressions such as *bimᵉqôm qodšô* 'the place *of his holiness*' (= 'his holy place,' Ps. 24:3 MT). הַר קָדְשִׁי 'the hill *of my holiness*' (= 'my holy hill,' Ps. 2:6 MT).

§36.326 The *gen. of measure* defines a subst. by giving a measure of space, time, or value. גָּבְהֵי שָׁמַיִם 'heights *of heaven*' (= heaven-high, Job 11:8). Heb. tends to use other constructions, such as "6 cubit its height."

§36.3261 Closely related to the gen. of measure is the *gen. of comparison.* אִישׁ־דְּבָרִים 'an eloquent man' (Exod. 4:10). *báʿal-haḥălômôt* 'dreamer' (Gen. 37:19). *ben-šānāʰ* 'a year old' (Exod. 12:5).

§36.3262 A noteworthy use of the gen. is to express the *superlative degree* (§30.23). לְטוֹב בֵּית הַנָּשִׁים 'to the best (part) *of the house* of the women' (Est. 2:10). *qṓdeš qŏdāšîm mēʾiššêʸ YHWH* '*it is the holiest* of the Lord's fire-offerings' (Lev. 2:3). קוֹמַת אֲרָזָיו 'the *highest* of its cedars' (Isa. 37:24). *mibḥar qᵉrābḗnû* 'the *choicest* of our tombs' (Gen. 23:6).

§36.3263 Also closely related is the *gen. of limit.* יְפֵה תֹאַר 'beauty *of form*' (Gen. 39:6). *happārôt rāʿôt hammarʾêʰ* 'the cows evil *of appearance*' (Gen. 41:4).

§36.327 The *gen. of source, cause, origin* defines a subst. by giving its source. חַסְדֵי יהוה 'the mercies *of YHWH*' (Ps. 89:2 MT). פְּרִי־בָטֶן 'fruit *of womb*' (Gen. 30:2). *ṭᵉmēʾ-népeš* 'unclean *of* (because of) *a corpse*' (Lev. 22:4). *ḥălal ḥéreb* 'pierced *of* (by means of) *a sword*' (Num. 19:16).

§36.328 The *partitive gen.* (*gen. of the whole*) defines a subst. by relating it to the whole of which it is a part. כַּף־רַגְלָהּ 'the sole *of her foot*' (Gen. 8:9).

This usage is particularly common with numbers in cstr. שִׁבְעַת יָמִים 'seven *of days*' (Est. 1:5). *ʿaḏ-ḥăṣî hammalḵûṯ* 'unto half *of my kingdom*' (Est. 5:6).

§36.3281 Note that a numeral in cstr. before a determinate noun is *not* partitive. שֶׁבַע הַנְּעָרוֹת means 'the 7 maids,' not '7 of the maids' (Est. 2:7).

§36.329 Other uses of the genitive can be named, and the placing of a genitive in one or another category is somewhat subjective. The distinctions are made by grammarians; the Semites, obviously, made no *formal* distinction but lumped all these categories in a single case, which we call *genitive.*

§36.4 A *prepositional phrase* (i.e. a subst. with a preposition) may be used to modify another substantive. It is important for careful exegesis to distinguish between this *adjectival* prepositional phrase, and the *adverbial* phrase discussed in §35.31. I have found, in my reading, that the adv. phrase is far more common than the adj. phrase.

§36.41 The proper, bound-form prepositions (§22.4) are: בּ–, כּ–, ל– (with compound forms בְּמוֹ– and כְּמוֹ–), and מִן > מִ–. These must be studied carefully in many contexts, and the student should make extensive use of BDB for each preposition.

§36.411 The prep. בּ–, originally *bi-, but through analogy > *ba-*, acc. *bā́nû*, near-open *bᵉḵā* and *bāhém*, basically means 'in.' This may be position, proximity, or assistance. BDB 88-91, *Ges.* §119*h-q*.

§36.4111 The ב of position (בֵּית הַכְּלִי) can be used to indicate: position, *bᵉšûšan* '*in* Susa' (Est. 1:2), הַיָּפָה בַּנָּשִׁים 'the fairest *among* the women' (Cant. 1:8), *bišʿārêʸḵā* '*within* thy gates' (Exod. 20:10); time, *bišnaṯ-šéḇaʿ lᵉmalḵûṯô* '*in* the seventh year of his reign' (Est. 2:12).

§36.4112 The ב of proximity (בֵּית הַדִּיבּוּק וְהַנְּגִיעָה) is used as follows: *binᵉhar kᵉḇār* '*at/by* the river Chebar' (Ezek. 10:20, if it modifies the pronoun); *yāḏô bakkōl wᵉyaḏ kōl bô* 'his hand *against* everyone and the hand of everyone *against* him' (Gen. 16:12). This usage is much more common in adverbial phrases.

§36.4113 The ב of instrument or accompaniment (בֵּית הָעֵזֶר) is usually found in adv. phrases. As adj.: עֵץ בְּלַחְמוֹ 'a tree *with* its sap' (Jer. 11:19); בְּעַם כָּבֵד '*with* many people' (Num. 20:20, if it modifies 'Edom').

§36.4114 In some contexts, ב must mean 'from' (cf. C. H. Gordon, *Ugaritic Handbook*, §§10.1, .4, .5, and OSA *bn* 'from'). *wayyišʾal šāʾûl ba-YHWH* 'and Saul asked *from* YHWH' (1 Sam. 28:6, adverbial).

§36.4115 After -כְּ the prep. -בְּ is usually omitted. כְּהַר־פְּרָצִים 'as *on* Mt. Perazim' (Isa. 28:21). Cf. Joüon §133*h*.

— —

§36.412 The prep. -לְ, originally **la-* (but cf. Arab. *li-*), accented *lā́nû*, near-open *lāšéḇeṯ*, also *lᵉḵā*, basically has the idea of *direction/location with reference to*. Its usage is mostly adverbial. Cf BDB 510-518, *Ges.* §119*r-u*, §114*f-s*.

§36.4121 The ל of reference: מִחוּץ לָעִיר 'outside *with reference to* (= of, from) the city' (1 Kgs. 21:14). *ʾîš ʾîš lᵉmaṭṭêʰ* 'a man *for* a tribe (Num. 1:4); *népeš ḥayyāʰ lᵉmînāh* 'a living being *according to* its kind' (Gen. 1:24); *hălôʾ ʾânōḵî ṭôḇ lāḵ mēʿăśārāʰ bānîm* 'Am I not better *for* you than 7 sons?' (1 Sam. 1:8), *bišnaṯ-šéḇaʿ lᵉmalḵûṯô* 'in the 7th year *of* his reign' (Est. 2:16).

§36.4122 The ל of direction (not properly motion, which generally requires אֶל) suggests the idea of *becoming* or *adding to*: צַו לָצָו 'precept *upon* precept' (Isa. 28:10); *lāḵem yihyêʰ lᵉʾoˌ:lāʰ* 'it shall be to you *for* food' (Gen. 1:29, approaching an adverbial function); *wayyíḇen ʾeṯ-haṣṣēlāʿ' lᵉʾiššāʰ* 'and He fashioned . . . the rib . . . *into* a woman' (Gen. 2:22, quite adverbial). By its nature, this usage is almost always advebial.

§36.4123 The ל of possession is principally used as a periphrasis for the co construct. בֵּן לְיִשַׁי 'a son *of* Jesse' (1 Sam. 16:18); *diḇrêʸ hayyāmîm lᵉmalḵêʸ yiśrāʾēl* 'the affairs of the days *of* the kings of Israel' (2 Kgs. 15:11); *wᵉlô štêʸ nāšîm* 'and he *had* two wives' (1 Sam. 1:2); *maḥšᵉḇôṯ šālôm wᵉlôʾ lᵉrāʿāʰ* 'plans of welfare and not *of* evil' (Jer. 29:11).

§36.4124 Of special noteworthiness is the use of -הָיָה ל which often conveys the idea of 'he/it became,' approaching an adverbial function. 'I have set my bow in the cloud, *wᵉhāyᵉṯāʰ lᵉʾôṯ bᵉrîṯ* and it shall *become* a covenant-sign' (Gen. 9:13).

§36.413 The prep. -כְּ, originally **ka-* (but possibly **ki-*), near-open *kāʾéllêʰ*, was originally a substantive (*Ges.* §118*s*; Joüon §133*g* says it seems to have a demonstrative origin), with the idea of *resemblance, similitude*. Cf. BDB 453-455, *Ges.* §118*s-x*.

§36.4131 The כ of quality serves to modify a substantive by describing it *as* or *like* another substantive. אִם לָעֵת כָּזֹאת 'if for a time *like* this' (Est. 4:14). *mᵉšawwêʰ raḡlay kāʿayyālôṯ* 'making my feet *like* (the feet of) hinds' (Ps. 18:34 MT). *kî hûʾ kᵉʾîš ʾĕmeṯ* 'for he (was) *like* a man of truth' (Neh. 7:2).

§36.4132 The כ of quantity is used with numbers to modify a substantive with approximation, translated 'about.' כִּשְׁלֹשֶׁת אַלְפֵי אִישׁ '*about* 3,000 men' (Exod. 32:28). כְּיוֹם תָּמִים '*about* a whole day' (Josh. 10:13, adverbial in context). *kámmāʰ* '*like* what, how many?' (Gen. 47:8).

§36.4133 The כ of mode or limitation expresses conformity to a standard, comparison, etc. אִישׁ כִּלְבָבוֹ 'each one *according to* his heart' (1 Sam. 13:14). *daq kakkᵉpôr* 'as fine *as* hoar-frost' (Exod. 16:14).

§36.4134 Sometimes כ is repeated to express complete correspondence. כָּמוֹךָ כְּפַרְעֹה 'you are *like* Pharoah himself' (Gen. 44:18). *kaḥăšêḵāʰ kāʾôrāʰ* 'darkness and light are *both alike*' (Ps. 139:12).

§36.414 The prep. מִן expresses the idea of separation or withdrawal, hence it can be used for separation, source or origin, partition, comparison, and similar ideas. Cf. BDB 577-583, *Ges.* §119*v-z*, §133*a-e*.

§36.4141 The מִן of separation is generally used with verbs in adverbial phrases, translated 'from,' 'down from,' 'away from,' etc.

§36.4142 The מִן of source or origin has broad usage, material, personal, temporal, etc. עָפָר מִן הָאֲדָמָה 'dust *from* the ground' (Gen. 2:7). *ʾim mizzéraᶜ hayyᵉhûḏîm* 'if *from* the seed of the Jews' (Est. 6:13). מִיּוֹם דַּעְתִּי אֶתְכֶם '*from* the day I (first) knew you' (Deut. 9:24). *ḥămaṯ* (cstr.!) *miyyáyin* 'heat *from* (because of, arising from) wine' (Hos. 7:5). *miyyāmîm rabbîm* '*after* many days' (Josh. 23:1). *haggibbôrîm ʾăšer mēᶜôlām* 'the mighty men who (were) *of* old' (i.e. living in antiquity, not necessarily continuing to live from that time on, Gen. 6:4).

§36.4143 An extension of this use is the juxtaposition of a *min*-phrase with an *ᶜaḏ* or other similar prep. phrase to express limits. לְמִגָּדוֹל וְעַד־קָטָן '*from* great *to* small' (Est. 1:20). *minnᵉhar miṣráyim ᶜaḏ-hannāhār haggāḏôl* '*from* the river of Egypt *to* the great river' (Gen. 15:18).

§36.4144 The מִן partitive is used to express one or some *from* the category named. אֶחָד מִן־הַסָּרִיסִים 'one *of* (i.e. *from among*) the eunuchs' (Est. 7:9). שְׁנַיִם מִכֹּל 'two *from* all (every kind)' (Gen. 6:19). Without a numeral, *meʾaḇnê hammāqôm* '(one) *of* the stones of the place' (Gen. 28:11). וְלֹא יָלִין מִן־הַבָּשָׂר '*None of* the flesh shall remain overnight' (Deut. 16:4). *mēʾaḥaḏ ʾaḥêʸḵā* '*any* one *of* your brothers' (Deut. 15:7).

§36.4145 Especially noteworthy is the מִן of comparison. מַה־מָּתוֹק מִדְּבַשׁ 'What (is) sweeter *than* honey?' (Judg. 14:18). *ᶜārûm mikkōl ḥayyaṯ haśśāḏêʰ* '*more* subtle *than* any beast of the field' (Gen. 3:1). *gāḏôl ᶜăwônî minnᵉśōʾ* 'my iniquity (is) *too* great to bear' (lit. 'great my iniquity *from* bearing, Gen. 4:13).

§36.42 Certain particles are generally identified as proper, free-form prepositions. According to competent scholars, most or all of these were originally substantives. They must be studied carefully in many contexts.

§36.421 The prep. אֶל (אֶל־, אֱלֵי, אֱלֵי–) means basically 'to,' hence 'towards,' 'unto,' 'in addition to,' ''according to,' 'against,' 'at,' etc. It is principally used in adv. phrases. It is often used for עַל, especially in Sam., Kgs., Jer., and Ezek. Cf. BDB 39-41.

§36.422 The prep. אֵת (אֶת־, אִתּ־; also אוֹת־ in Josh., Sam., Kgs., Jer., Ezek.), conveys the idea of proximity, hence 'with,' 'together with,' 'near,' etc. It suggests closer association than does עִם. Its usage is generally in adv. phrases, but cf. *pᵉšᶜêʸnû ʾittā̂nû* 'our sins (are) *with* us' (Isa. 59:12), *ʾăšer ʾet̲-qéd̲eš* 'which (is) *near/by* Qadesh' (Judg. 4:11). *ḥōq mēʾēt̲ parᶜōʰ* 'a prescribed portion *from* (*with*) Pharaoh' (Gen. 47:22). Cf. BDB 85-87.

§36.423 The prep. בֵּין (fem. בֵּית) conveys the idea of an interval between, whether space, time, or concept. בֵּין הַגְּזָרִים '*between* the pieces' (Gen. 15:17). *bên bêt̲ʾēl ûb̲ên hāᶜāy* '*between* Bethel *and* Ai (note repetition of בֵּין)' (Gen. 13:3). הַאֵדַע בֵּין טוֹב לְרָע 'Can I know (the difference) *between* good *and* (ל־) evil?' (2 Sam. 19:36 MT). Cf. BDB 107-108.

§36.424 The prep. עַד (עֲדֵי, עָדַי־) conveys the idea of direction toward, hence 'as far as,' 'even to,' 'up to, 'until,' 'while,' etc. It is usually found in adv. phrases. Cf. BDB 723-724.

§36.425 The prep. עַל (עֲלֵי,עָלַי־) basically means height, hence 'upon,' 'above,' 'according to,' 'on account of,' 'beyond,' and many other meanings. It is usually found in adv. phrases. Cf. BDB 752-758.

§36.426 The prep. עִם (עִמּ־, עִמָּד־) expresses the idea of companionship, hence 'with.' It is used mostly in adv. phrases. Cf. BDB 767f.

§36.427 Most of these preps. can be compounded with other preps., and the resulting meanings should be carefully studied in contexts and in BDB.

§36.428 There are quite a few "improper" prepositions, so-called because they are recognizably substantives in cstr. with a following genitive. Some are compounded with other preps. The more common are:

אַחַר, אַחֲרֵי 'after' (BDB 29-30)
בְּלִי with ב־, ל־, מ־, 'without' (BDB115f)
מוּל 'in front of' (BDB 557)
עֻמָּה + ל 'close by, alongside' (BDB 769)
יַעַן 'because of' (BDB 774)
מַעַן + ל 'for the sake of, in view of' (BDB 775)
נֶגֶד + ל 'in front of, before' (BDB 617)
סָבִיב + preps. 'around' (BDB 687)
פְּנֵי + preps. 'before' (BDB 816-819)
תּוֹךְ + בּ 'in the midst of' (BDB 1063)
תַּחַת 'under, beneath, instead of' (BDB 1065f)

§36.43 A prep. generally stands before only one object, and must be repeated when two or more words are governed by the same idea. However, when a closely joined phrase occurs, a single prep. is sometimes found. *millip̄nê hammélek̲ wᵉhammalkāʰ* 'before *the king and queen*' (Est. 7:6). *ʿal-gᵉlîlê k̲ésep̄ wᵉʿammûd̲ê šēš* 'upon *rings of silver and columns of alabaster*' (the rings and the columns considered together as holding the hangings, Est. 1:6).

§36.5 A substantive may be modified by a *pronoun* (§§30.312-.3128).

§36.51 Since Heb. does not decline pers. prons., the pron. in the gen. does not occur.

§36.52 The subst. may be modified by a *pronominal suffix*. In inflected Sem. languages, this suf. is in gen., and is regularly translated as such in Heb., either by 'of' or by a possessive pronoun.

§36.521 The pron. suf. is usually possessive. בְּעֵינָיו 'in *his* eyes' (Est. 2:9).

§36.522 The pron. suf. may be a subjective genitive. שְׁאֵלָתִי וּבַקָּשָׁתִי '*my* petition and request' (Est. 5:7).

§36.523 The pron. suf. may be an objective genitive. וּמוֹרַאֲכֶם וְחִתְּכֶם 'the fear and dread *of you*' (Gen. 9:2).

§36.524 The pron. suf. may be a genitive of reference. תַּמְרֻקֵיהֶן *their* unguents' (i.e. intended for their use; Est. 2:3).

§36.525 The pron. suf. may be a genitive of origin. כֹּה יִהְיֶה זַרְעֶךָ 'so shall *your* progeny be' (i.e. those who trace their origin to you,' Gen. 15:5).

§36.526 Doubtless other categories of the genitive could be identified in the pron. sufs., since they are very common. If we include the infinitive construct as a substantive, then we must also identify some pron. sufs. as accusatives of the object.

§36.53 A substantive may be modified by a pers. pron. for the sake of clarity or emphasis. כִּרְאֹתִי אֲנִי דָנִיֵּאל 'when I saw, *I* Daniel' (Dan 8:15). אֲדֹנָי הוּא 'the Lord *himself*' (Isa. 7:14). *hayyᵉhûd̲îm hēmmāʰ* 'the Jews *themselves*' (Est. 9:1).

§36.531 Closely related to the use of the pron. is the use of נֶפֶשׁ or עֶצֶם for 'self.' לֹא־אֵדַע נַפְשִׁי 'I *myself* do not know' (Job 9:21). וּכְעֶצֶם הַשָּׁמַיִם 'and like heaven *itself*' (Exod. 24:10).

§36.54 A subst. may be modified by a *demonstrative pronoun* (§30.3123). בָּעֵת הַזֹּאת 'in *this* time' (Est. 4:14). *bayyôm hahûʾ* 'on *that* day' (Est. 5:9). On הוּא and זֶה cf. BDB 214-216, 260-262; Joüon pp. 443-446.

§36.541 The demon. pron. זֶה is used with words denoting number or time in noteworthy ways. זֶה שְׁלוֹשִׁים יוֹם *'for* 30 days *now'* (Est. 4:11). *ʿattāʰ zêʰ yāḏáʿtî 'Now/this time* I know' (1 Kgs. 17:24).

§36.542 זֶה (and less often זֹאת) is used in ways that should be studied carefully, cf. BDB 260ff.

§§36.55, .56 *omitted arbitrarily.*

§36.57 A subst. may be modified by a *relative clause* used adjectivally, cf. §38.4.

§36.6 A subst. may be modified by another subst. or substantival clause *in apposition* (cf. §30.251).

§36.61 The appositive may be a *noun. hammélek̠ ʾăḥašwērôš* 'the king *Ahasuerus*' (Est. 1:5). נַעֲרָה בְתוּלָה 'a maiden *a virgin*' (2 Kgs. 9:4). אִישׁ כֹּהֵן 'a man *a priest*' (Lev. 21:9).

§36.62 The appositive may be a *phrase.* מָרְדֳּכַי בֶּן יָאִיר 'Mordecai *the son of Jair*' (Est. 2:5). *mištêʰ šiḇaṯ yāmîm* 'a banquet, *7 days*' (Est. 1:5).

§36.63 The appositive may be an *infinitive construct.*

§36.64 The appositive may be a *participle.* כַּדָּת אֵין אֹנֵס 'according to the law "No *compelling*' " (Est. 1:7).

§36.65 The appositive may be a *clause.* הוּא אֲחַשְׁוֵרוֹשׁ הַמֹּלֵךְ מֵהֹדּוּ וְעַד־כּוּשׁ 'that was Ahasuerus *who ruled from India to Nubia*' (Est. 1:1). *bik̠lê zāhāḇ wᵉk̠ēlîm mikkēlîm šônîm* 'in vessels of gold, *each differing from the other*' (Est. 1:7).

§36.651 The identification of an appositional clause is somewhat subjective, since it is an adjectival clause that is descriptive (not restrictive). In Eng., the absence of a rel. conj. would probably indicate an appos. cl., but in Heb. the def. art. and the demon. pron. may serve a similar purpose.

§36.66 The *vocative* is an appositive. מַה־לָּךְ אֶסְתֵּר 'What's bothering you, *Esther*?' (Est. 5:3). חֹזֶה לֵךְ 'Go, *seer* . . . !' (Amos 7:12).

§36.7 A substantive may be modified by a *participle* or a *ptcp. clause. hayyᵉhûḏîm hannimṣᵉʾîm bᵉšûšān* 'the Jews *who were found in Susa*' (Est. 4:16). *kirʾôṯ hammélek̠ ʾeṯ-ʾestēr hammalkāʰ ʿômeḏeṯ beḥāṣēr* 'When the king saw Esther the queen *standing in the court*' (Est. 5:2).

§36.9 A subst. may be modified by a *numeral.* Because of the complexities of the numeral system, the student should read §§26.2-.9 carefully, and review the more important sections frequently. *Ges.* §134.

§36.91 The numeral '1' as an adj. follows its noun and is in concord with it. וְהָיוּ לְבָשָׂר אֶחָד 'and they shall become *one* flesh' (Gen. 2:24). וְשָׂפָה אֶחָת 'and *one* language' (Gen. 11:6). וּדְבָרִים אֲחָדִים 'and *few* words' (Gen. 11:1).

§36.92 The numerals '2' to '10' can be used in any of three ways: in cstr. *before* the subst., in abs. *before* the subst., and in abs. *after* the subst. The subst. is in the plural. *Ges.* §134*a-c*.

§36.921 The num. acting as a subst. may stand in cstr. before another subst., cf. §26.23, .82. שְׁלֹשֶׁת יָמִים '*three* days' (Est. 4:16). *šᵉlôš sᵉʾîm qémaḥ sōlet̲* '*three* measures (f.) of fine flour' (Gen. 18:6). Cf. §36.3f.

§36.922 The num. in the absolute as a subst. may stand before another subst. which in effect is in apposition (§36.61), cf. *Ges.* §131*d*, 134*b*. וְהָיָה לְאַרְבָּעָה רָאשִׁים 'and it became *four* heads' (Gen. 2:10). וְשָׁלֹשׁ אַמּוֹת קֹמָתוֹ 'and *three* cubits its height' (Exod. 27:1).

§36.923 The num. in the abs. as an adj. may stand after a subst. in the abs. וּפָרִים עֲשָׂרָה 'and *ten* bulls' (Lev. 32:16).

§36.924 The num. '2' may take a pron. suf. (cf. §36.52). שְׁנֵיוּ אֲנַחְנוּ 'we *two*' (1 Sam. 20:42). שְׁנֵיהֶם (Gen. 2:25), שְׁתֵּיהֶן (1 Sam. 25:43), שְׁתֵּיהֶם (Ruth 1:19; 4:11) 'they *two*.'

§36.93 The numerals '11'–'19' generally have the numbered object in the *singular* with the following nouns: יוֹם 'day,' שָׁנָה 'year,' אִישׁ 'man,' נֶפֶשׁ 'soul,' שֵׁבֶט 'tribe,' and מַצֵּבָה 'pillar,' and sometimes with אַמָּה 'cubit,' חֹדֶשׁ 'month,' עִיר 'city,' and שֶׁקֶל 'shekel.' Other substantives are in the plural. *Ges.* §134*f*.

§36.931 The nouns listed in §36.93, in the sing. *follow* the num. and are without the article. שְׁנֵי עָשָׂר אִישׁ '*twelve* men' (Josh. 3:12). חֲמֵשׁ עֶשְׂרֵה אַמָּה '*fifteen* cubits' (Gen. 7:20). On inflection of the numerals, cf. §26.25.

§36.932 Nouns in the plur. likewise follow the noun and are without the article. לְאַרְבָּעָה עָשָׂר כְּבָשִׂים 'the *fourteen* lambs' (Num. 29:15). וְשֵׁשׁ עֶשְׂרֵה בָּנוֹת 'and *sixteen* daughters'(2 Chron. 13:21). Cf. §26.25.

§36.94 The even *tens* (20, 30, 40, etc.) may precede or follow the noun they modify. If the num. precedes, certain common items may be in the sing. אַרְבָּעִים שָׁנָה '*forty* years' (Judg. 3:11). עֶשְׂרִים אֶלֶף '20,000' (1 Chron. 18:4). עֶשְׂרִים קְרָשִׁים '20 boards' (Exod. 36:23). וְאֵילִים עֶשְׂרִים 'and 20 rams' (Gen. 32:15 MT).

§36.941 Numerals consisting of *tens and units* (21, 42, 75, etc.) can be used in several ways. Note the following:

שְׁתַּיִם וְשִׁשִּׁים שָׁנָה '62 years' (Gen. 5:20),
שְׁלֹשִׁים וּשְׁמֹנֶה שָׁנָה '38 years' (Deut. 2:14),
חָמֵשׁ שָׁנִים וְשִׁבְעִים שָׁנָה '75 years' (Gen. 12:4),
הַשָּׁבֻעִים שִׁשִּׁים וּשְׁנַיִם 'the 62 weeks' (Dan. 9:26).

Cf. BDB 797.2a-c.

§36.95 With the nums. מֵאָה '100' and אֶלֶף '1,000' there is considerable variety, and the student is advised to note the various methods in BDB 547f and 48f, respectively. Cf. §26.271 and §26.281, and *Ges.* §134*g*.

§36.96 After the num. certain units of measure or weight are commonly omitted. אֶלֶף כֶּסֶף '1,000 (shekels of) silver' (Gen. 20:16), מֵאָה אֹרֶךְ '100 (cubits) length' (Exod. 27:11), שְׁתֵּי־לֶחֶם 'two (כִּכָּר loaves) of bread' (1 Sam. 10:4), שֵׁשׁ שְׂעֹרוֹת '6 (ephas of) barley' (Ruth 3:15). *Ges.* §134*n*. With days of the month, יוֹם is usually omitted, בְּאֶחָד לַחֹדֶשׁ 'on the first (day) of the month' (Gen. 8:5).

§36.97 *Ordinal* numerals (only 1-10 are morphologically indicated as such, cf. §26.3ff) act as true adjectives and are subject to the principles set forth in §36.1f. Usually the def. art. is omitted with numerals above 10.

§36.971 In numbering years and days of the month, the cardinals are used (usually even for 1-10). בִּשְׁנַת שָׁלֹשׁ 'in the third year' (1 Kgs. 15:25). בְּאַרְבַּע עֶשְׂרֵה שָׁנָה 'in the 14th year' (1 Kgs. 6:1). בְּיוֹם אֶחָד 'on the first day' (Ezra 10:16).

§36.972 In numbering the months, the ordinals are always used. עַד הַחֹדֶשׁ הָעֲשִׂירִי 'until the tenth month' (Gen. 8:5). בַּחֹדֶשׁ הַשִּׁשִּׁי 'in the sixth month' (Hag. 1:1).

§36.973 It should be noted that 'the first month' is always Nisan, whether the year began in Nisan or Tishri. Cf. Jer. 36:23, which indicates that the ninth month (36:9) was in the winter, even though the calendration was Tishri-Elul.

§37. A *modifier* may be used *to modify another modifier*. In Eng. if the first modifier is a possessive noun or one in apposition, its modifier is *adjectival*; if the first modifier is an adjective or adjectival phrase/clause, its modifier is *adverbial*. Cf. G. L. Kittredge and F. E. Farley, *An Advanced English Grammar* (1913, repr. 1972), Part Three, Chap V. In Heb. the distinction between adverbs and adjectives is not always clear.

§37.1 An *adjective* or any adjectival modifier can be modified by an *adverb* or *adverbial phrase/clause.* וְהִנֵּה־טוֹב מְאֹד 'and behold (it was) *very* good' (Gen. 1:31). *kî ṭôḇ hāʿēṣ l^{e}maʾăḵāl* 'that the tree (was) good *for food*' . . . *w^{e}neḥmāḏ hāʿēṣ l^{e}haśkîl* 'and the tree (was) desirable *to make wise*' (Gen. 3:6). *raq raʿ kol-hayyôm* '*only* evil *continually*' (Gen. 6:5). כַּטּוֹב בְּעֵינֵיכֶם 'whatever (is) good *in your eyes*' (Est. 8:8).

§37.12 Very common is the use of לֹא with an adj. to form an adj. of opposite meaning (like the *a*[*ν*]-privative of Greek). בֵּן לֹא־חָכָם 'an *unwise* son' (Hos. 13:13). Cf. BDB 519.2.a. The result in translation is adjectival.

§37.2 An *adjectival genitive* can be modified by another *adjective* or *adjectival phrase.*

§37.21 This is found very often in annexion, where a pron. suf. modifies the genitive. כֹּל יְמֵי חַיֶּיךָ 'all the days of *your* life' (Gen. 3:17).

§37.22 It is also found in a chain of constructs. לִפְנֵי חֲצַר בֵּית־הַנָּשִׁים 'before the court *of the women's house*' (Est. 2:11).

§37.3 An *appositional modifier* may be modified. בְּשׁוּשַׁן הַבִּירָה 'in Susa *the citadel*' (Est. 2:5). אֶסְתֵּר בַּת־דּוֹדוֹ 'Esther the daughter *of his uncle*' (Est. 2:7). *qaḥ-nāʾ ʾeṯ-binḵā ʾeṯ-y^{e}ḥîḏḵā* 'Take now thy son, *thine only son*' (Gen. 22:2).

§37.4 An *adverbial phrase* can be modified. *kî gēr yihyê^{h} zarʿăḵā b^{e}ʾéreṣ lôʾ lāhem* 'for your seed shall be a sojourner in a land *not theirs*' (Gen. 15:13).

§38. *Compound and complex sentences.* For stylistic reasons, most sentences are not limited to a single clause, but are compounded of two or more clauses. These are *compound* or *complex* sentences, or both.

§38.1 The *compound* sentence (§30.421) is composed of two or more *independent or correlative* clauses. In Heb. either or both (or all) may be verbless clauses (§31.). In Eng. the clauses are usually joined by a coördinating conjunction (§30.361). *wattôsep̄ ʾestēr watt^{e}ḏabbēr wattippōl lip̄nê hamméleḵ wattēḇk^{e}* 'And Esther added *and* she spoke before the king *and* she fell before his feet *and* she wept' (Est. 8:3). אָרוּר כְּנָעַן עֶבֶד עֲבָדִים יִהְיֶה לְאֶחָיו 'Cursed (be Canaan; he shall be the lowliest slave to his brothers' (Gen. 9:25).

§38.11 *Conjunctive* clauses are independent clauses placed in juxtaposition to make a complete statement. In Eng. they are usually joined with a coördinating conjunction (§30.361) and frequently so in Heb. *wattōʾmár š^{e}ʾēlāṯî ûḇaqqāšāṯî* 'And she said, "(This is) my request *and* (this is) my petition" ' (Est. 5:7). וּבְנֵי יִשְׂרָאֵל פָּרוּ וַיִּשְׁרְצוּ וַיִּרְבּוּ וַיַּעַצְמוּ and the Israelites were fruitful and grew numerous and multiplied and grew strong' (Exod. 1:7).

§38.111 The statements may be interrogative. הַאֵלֵךְ וְקָרָאתִי 'Shall I go and call?' (Exod. 2:7).

§38.112 Sometimes the use of this form is for emphasis. מִי שָׂם פֶּה לָאָדָם אוֹ מִי־יָשׂוּם אִלֵּם אוֹ חֵרֵשׁ אוֹ פִקֵּחַ אוֹ עִוֵּר 'Who made man's mouth, or who appointed them dumb or deaf or seeing or blind?' (Exod. 4:11). Obviously, both clauses refer to the same God.

§38.12 *Adversative* or *disjunctive* clauses are placed in contrast to form a statement. In Eng. they are commonly joined with a conjunction such as *but*, whereas in Heb. the conj. ־ו *and* is frequently used. The conjunctive and disjunctive correlative clauses, therefore, must be distinguished by context. וְהֹכַחְתִּיו בְּשֵׁבֶט אֲנָשִׁים . . . וְחַסְדִּי לֹא־יָסוּר מִמֶּנּוּ 'and I will chasten him with the rod of men . . . but my covenant-loyalty I will not remove from him' (2 Sam. 7:13-14).

§38.13 The use of coördinate clauses is called *parataxis,* in contrast with *hypotaxis* or the use of subordinate clauses. Heb. seems to prefer parataxis, whereas Greek (and to a lesser extent English) prefers hypotaxis.

§38.14 *Correlative* clauses are independent clauses which are juxtaposed either for contrast *(either . . . or)* or for cumulative effect (*not only . . . but also*). They are usually joined by correlative conjunctions (§30.363). גַּם־קֹב לֹא תִקֳּבֶנּוּ גַּם־בָּרֵךְ לֹא תְבָרֲכֶנּוּ 'Neither curse them at all nor bless them at all' (Num. 23:25).

§38.141 In correlative clauses *ellipsis* is fairly common (§30.3631). *w*ᵉ*lôʾ-yāmuṯû ḡam-hēm gam-ʾattem* 'Neither they shall die nor you' (Num. 18:3). רֹעֵה צֹאן עֲבָדֶיךָ גַּם־אֲנַחְנוּ גַּם־אֲבוֹתֵינוּ 'Your servants are shepherds, *both* we *and* our fathers' (Gen. 47:3).

§38.142 The clauses may be interrogative. הֲנֵלֵךְ אֶל־רָמֹת גִּלְעָד לַמִּלְחָמָה אִם־נֶחְדָּל 'Shall we go to Ramoth-Gilead to fight *or* forbear?' (1 Kgs. 22:15). *haʾĕnôš mēʾlôᵃh yiṣdāq ʾim mēʿôśēhû yiṭhar-gāḇer* 'Can mortal be more righteous than God, or a strong man cleaner than his Maker?' (Job 4:17).

§38.143 The clauses may be correlative conditional clauses. אוֹ־בֵן יִגָּח אוֹ־בַת יִגָּח כַּמִּשְׁפָּט הַזֶּה יֵעָשֶׂה לּוֹ 'If it [the ox] gores a son or if it gores a daughter, it shall be done to it according to this sentence' (Exod. 21:31).

§38.2 A *complex* sentence (§30.422) is composed of two or more clauses, at least one of which is *independent* (§30.4221), and at least one is *dependent* or *subordinate* (§30.4222). In Hebrew it is possible to use a verbless clause in either or both positions. More important, subordination in Heb. may be indicated *by context* (and therefore apparent in translation) even though the Heb. text contains only coördinate clauses.

§38.21 The *subordinate* clause in effect is a modifier, modifying the main clause. It can therefore be *substantival, adjectival,* or *adverbial* (cf. §30.411).

§38.22 A subordinate cl. in Eng. is generally introduced by a *subordinating conjunction* (§30.362). In Heb. וְ– may introduce a clause which in context must be translated by a subord. conj. Note Est. 5:9-10. The clauses begin with the words *wayyēṣēʾ* . . . *wᵉkirʾôṯ hāmān* . . . *wᵉlôʾ-qām, wᵉlôʾ zā* . . . *wayyimmālēʾ* . . . *wayyiṯʾappēq* . . . *wayyāḇôʾ* . . . *wayyišlaḥ, wayyāḇēʾ*. RSV translates these 'And Haman went out . . . But when Haman saw . . . that he neither rose nor trembled . . . he was filled . . . Nevertheless Haman restrained himself . . . and he went home; and he sent and fetched . . . .'

§38.23 A noun or other substantive may be placed *in construct with a finite verb* with the effect of putting the verb in subordination. Some grammarians have rejected this idea, but the fact has been well established. See numerous examples in *Ges.* §130*d.* The same grammatical phenomenon is found in Akk., Arab. (cf. Wright, *Arabic Grammar,* II 222A), and probably Ugar. קִרְיַת חָנָה דָוִד 'the city of (where) David camped (Isa. 29:1). שְׁלַח־נָא בְּיַד תִּשְׁלָח 'Send, pray, by the hand of (whomever) Thou wilt send' (Exod. 4:13).

§38.3 A *substantival clause* (or *noun clause*) is a clause serving as a noun, whether as the subject or direct object of a verb, or in apposition with a substantive, or as predicate in a verbless clause, and whether in a main clause or in a subordinate clause.

§38.31 The subst. cl. may serve as *subject* of a verb (§33.6) or of a verbless predication (§31.141). תּוֹעֵבָה יִבְחַר בָּכֶם '*He who chooses you* (is) an abomination' (Isa. 41:24).

§38.32 The subst. cl. may serve as *direct object* of a verb. וַיַּרְא אֱלֹהִים אֶת־כָּל־אֲשֶׁר עָשָׂה 'And God saw *all that He had made*' (Gen. 1:31).

§38.321 With verbs of *saying, thinking, seeing,* and the like (*verba cordis*), the object is generally a clause which is called *indirect discourse* (§38.82). The clause may be introduced by כִּי, אֲשֶׁר, simple וְ–, or by no conj. at all. 'And Mordecai told him אֵת כָּל־אֲשֶׁר קָרָהוּ *all that had befallen him*' (Est. 4:7).

§38.4 The subst. cl. may serve as an *adjectival clause*, modifying any other substantive (cf. §36., .1, .3, .4).

§38.41 It may modify the subj. or the pred. of a verbless clause. אַשְׁרֵי הָאִישׁ יֶחֱסֶה־בּוֹ 'Happy (is) the man *he* (= who) *trusts in him*' (Ps. 34:9). 'I am YHWH אֲשֶׁר הוֹצֵאתִיךָ מֵאוּר כַּשְׂדִּים *who brought you out from Ur of the Chaldees*' (Gen. 15:6). 'Thou art my Rock, אֶחֱסֶה־בּוֹ *in whom I take refuge*' (Ps. 18:3).

§38.42 It may modify the subj. or dir. obj. of a verb. 'And the maiden אֲשֶׁר תִּיטַב בְּעֵינֵי הַמֶּלֶךְ *who pleases the king* shall become queen' (Est. 2:21). 'And He placed there the Adam אֲשֶׁר יָצָר *whom He had fashioned*' (Gen. 2:8).

§38.421 Often the modifying clause is *participial*. 'For all the men are dead הַמְבַקְשִׁים אֶת־נַפְשֶׁךָ *who (were) seeking your life*' (Exod. 4:19). 'I have given to you every plant זֹרֵעַ זֶרַע *which yields seed*' (Gen. 1:29).

§38.422 Ellipsis is often found. 'And God saw אֶת־כָּל־אֲשֶׁר עָשָׂה every (thing) *which He had made*' (Gen. 1:31). It is easy to take the entire clause as object after אֶת.

§38.43 It may modify an indirect obj. or the obj. of a preposition. 'Look to the rock חֻצַּבְתֶּם *from which you were hewn,* and to the hole of the pit נֻקַּרְתֶּם *from which you were digged*' (Isa. 51:1). 'to the banquet אֲשֶׁר־עָשִׂיתִי לוֹ *which I have made for him*' (Est. 5:4).

§38.44 It may modify another modifier. 'And I will smite Egypt with all my wonders אֲשֶׁר אֶעֱשֶׂה בְּקִרְבּוֹ *which I will do in its midst*' (Exod. 3:20). 'And Esther called to Hatach, one of the king's eunuchs אֲשֶׁר הֶעֱמִיד לְפָנֶיהָ *whom he* [the king) *stationed before her*' (Est. 4:5). 'I have seen the affliction of my people אֲשֶׁר בְּמִצְרָיִם *who (are) in Egypt*' (Exod. 3:7).

§38.45 It may serve as an appositive. 'Mordecai אֲשֶׁר הַחִלּוֹתָ לִנְפֹּל לְפָנָיו *before whom you have begun to fall*' (Est. 6:13).

§38.46 In many instances, as a matter of style or of necessity, we find the use of a "resumptive" or "retrospective" pronoun. 'For the place אֲשֶׁר אַתָּה עוֹמֵד עָלָיו *on which you are standing*' (lit., 'which you are standing on it') (Exod. 3:5). 'Thus shall be done to the man אֲשֶׁר הַמֶּלֶךְ חָפֵץ בִּיקָרוֹ *in whose honor the king delights*' (Est. 6:11).

§38.5 An *adverbial clause* modifies the main clause by defining the *time, place, cause, purpose, result,* or *circumstance* of the main predication. Cf. §30.13, §35.4ff.

§38.51 A *temporal* clause modifies the main clause by referring it to an action or state that is prior to, contemporary with, or subsequent to the main predication. The most common conjunctions in Eng. are 'before,' 'when/while,' and 'after,' respectively. In Heb. there are many different ways of expressing a temporal modifier, and the student should observe them carefully.

§38.511 To indicate time *before* the main predication, טֶרֶם, לִפְנֵי, or עַל־פְּנֵי may be used, or coördinate clauses with no indication of subordination.

§38.5111 טֶרֶם means 'not yet,' hence stands before the imperfect. בְּטֶרֶם תָּבוֹא אֲלֵהֶן הַמְיַלֶּדֶת '*Before the midwife comes to them,* they give birth' (Exod. 1:19). 'I would go and see him בְּטֶרֶם אָמוּת *before I die*' (Gen. 45:28, lit. 'when I shall not yet have died').

§38.5112 לִפְנֵי or עַל־פְּנֵי means 'before.' 'Your father commanded לִפְנֵי מוֹתוֹ *before his dying*' (Gen. 50:15). לִפְנֵי שַׁחֵת יהוה אֶת־סְדֹם 'Before YHWH destroyed Sodom . . . , it was like the garden of YHWH' (Gen. 13:10). 'And Haran died עַל־פְּנֵי תֶּרַח אָבִיו *before Terah* his father (died)' (Gen. 11:29). פְּנֵי is used before the inf. cstr. and nouns, as a general rule.

§38.512 To indicate time *contemporary with* the main predication ־בְ, ־כְ, or compounds with these preps. are frequently used with the inf. cstr. עוֹד and compounds may also be used in nonverbal clauses, or coördinate clauses may express the idea of contemporaneity.

§38.5121 Quite common is the use of ־בְ with the inf. cstr. 'And it shall be בַּעֲבֹר כְּבֹדִי *while my glory is passing by,* that I will place you in the cleft of the rock' (Exod. 33:22). Cf. §35.421.

§38.5122 Compounds with ב also are used. בְּיוֹם עֲשׂוֹת '*When* the Lord God *made* earth and heaven' (Gen. 2:5). בְּכָל־עֵת אֲשֶׁר '*every time that* I see Mordecai . . . (Est. 5:13).

§38.5123 כ is used, alone or with compounds, often with the inf. cstr., to express the idea of 'as, while, when.' 'In those days, כְּשֶׁבֶת הַמֶּלֶךְ *when the king was sitting* on his throne' (Est. 1:2).'And I, כַּאֲשֶׁר שָׁכֹלְתִּי שָׁכָלְתִּי *when I am bereaved* I'm bereaved' (Gen. 43:14, indicating resignation).

§38.5124 עוֹד 'while' is used in verbless clauses and with ptcps. עוֹדָם מְדַבְּרִים עִמּוֹ '*while they (were) speaking with him*, the king's eunuchs arrived' (Est. 6:14, the main cl. is conjunctive: 'they were still speaking . . . and the eunuchs arrived'). 'And he sent them away from Isaac his son בְּעוֹדֶנּוּ חַי *while he (was) still alive*' (Gen. 25:6).

§38.5125 Coördinate cls. may be used. וַיִּהְיוּ בְנֵי־יִשְׂרָאֵל בַּמִּדְבָּר '*While the Israelites were in the wilderness*, they found (וַיִּמְצְאוּ) a man gathering wood on the Sabbath' (Num. 15:32).

§38.513 To indicate time *subsequent* to the main predication אַחֲרֵי, אַחַר, מִקֵּץ, and other expressions are used.

§38.5131 אַחֲרֵי + the inf. cstr. is often used. 'And the days of Adam were אַחֲרֵי הוֹלִידוֹ אֶת־שֵׁת *after his begetting Seth* . . . '(Gen. 5:4). אַחַר is sometimes used. 'If the leprosy breaks out again in the house אַחַר חִלֵּץ הָאֲבָנִים *after he has scraped the stones*' (Lev. 14:43).

§38.5132 מִקֵּץ also is used. 'And they returned from spying out the land מִקֵּץ אַרְבָּעִים יוֹם *at the end of 40 days*' (Num. 13:25). Likewise the cognate מִקְצֵה: 'And so מִקְצֵה שְׁלֹשֶׁת יָמִים *after 3 days* the officers went through the camp' (Josh. 3:2).

§38.5133 כַּאֲשֶׁר is sometimes used ('when' = 'after'). 'And the hair of his head began to grow כַּאֲשֶׁר גֻּלָּח *after he had been shaved*' (Judg. 16:22 – it certainly didn't grow back when, i.e. at the same time, he was shaved!).

§38.5134 Other idioms are found. וַיְהִי לְשִׁבְעַת הַיָּמִים 'and after 7 days (הָיָה ל– = 'became' ?) the waters of the flood were on the earth' (Gen. 7:10). וַיְהִי יָמִים רַבִּים 'And so *after many days* the word of the Lord came (הָיָה) to Elijah' (1 Kgs. 18:1).

§38.514 Since Heb. lacks an elaborate tense-system, such as is found in Greek, we must pay careful attention to context when translating temporal clauses. The *perf.* (action completed) may be translated as simple past ('did'), past perfect ('had done'), or future perfect ('will have done'), while the *impf.* (action not completed) may be translated as present ('does'), future ('will do'), past ('was doing, began to do'), or subjunctive ('would do') – and other translations are possible.

§38.52 A *local clause* modifies the main clause by referring it to the place of the predication of the main clause. The most common Eng. conjs. are 'where,' 'whence' (= from where), and 'whither' (= to where).

§38.521 אֲשֶׁר, usually with some prep. or adv., is used to introduce a local clause. 'And in every city מְקוֹם אֲשֶׁר דְּבַר הַמֶּלֶךְ מַגִּיעַ *where the king's word was reaching*' (Est. 4:3). בַּאֲשֶׁר כָּרַע '*Where he staggered*, there he fell' (Judg. 5:27). אֶל כָּל־הַמָּקוֹם אֲשֶׁר נָבוֹא שָׁמָּה '*Wherever we come* (lit. into every place where we shall enter there), say that you are my sister' (Gen. 20:13).

§38.53 A *causal clause* modifies the main cl. by giving the reason for the main predication. It answers the question 'Why; because of what?' In Eng. the common conjs. are 'because,' 'since,' 'as,' 'inasmuch as,' and sometimes simply 'that.'

§38.531 יַעַן, often followed by אֲשֶׁר or כִּי, is commonly used in a causal clause. יַעַן לֹא־הֶאֱמַנְתֶּם בִּי '*Because you did not believe in me* . . . therefore you shall not . . . ' (Num. 20:12). 'For יַעַן אֲשֶׁר עָשִׂיתָ אֶת־הַדָּבָר הַזֶּה *because you have done this thing* . . . ' (Gen. 22:15). יַעַן כִּי גָבְהוּ בְּנוֹת צִיּוֹן '*Because the daughters of Zion are haughty* . . . '(Isa. 3:11).

§38.532 כִּי is often used without יַעַן. כִּי רָאָה כִּי־כָלְתָה אֵלָיו הָרָעָה '*for he saw that evil was determined against him*' (Est. 7:7; the second כִּי introduces indirect discourse, §38.82).

§38.533 אֲשֶׁר may be used without יַעַן. 'God has given me my wages אֲשֶׁר־נָתַתִּי שִׁפְחָתִי לְאִישִׁי *because I gave my handmaid to my husband*' (Gen. 30:18).

§38.534 With verbless clauses other expressions are found. 'Behold I am judging you עַל־אָמְרֵךְ *because you said* . . .' (Jer. 2:35). כִּי אֵין לָבוֹא '*for entering is forbidden* . . .' (Est. 4:2).

§38.54 A *purpose clause* (also called a *final clause*) modifies the main cl. by giving the purpose of the main predication. It answers the question 'Why; for what purpose?' In Eng. the purpose clause is introduced by 'that,' 'so that,' 'in order to,' 'to the end that,' 'to,' etc., and the negative purpose cl. by 'that not,' 'lest.'

§38.541 לְמַעַן, sometimes followed by אֲשֶׁר, is used with the impf. meaning 'in order that.' 'Say that you are my sister לְמַעַן יִיטַב־לִי בַעֲבוּרֵךְ *in order that it may be well for me for your sake*' (Gen. 12:13). 'For I have chosen him לְמַעַן אֲשֶׁר יְצַוֶּה אֶת־בָּנָיו *in order that he might charge his children* . . .' (Gen. 18:19).

§38.542 בַּעֲבוּר, sometimes followed by אֲשֶׁר, is used: 'Prepare for me the food בַּעֲבוּר תְּבָרֶכְךָ נַפְשִׁי *so that my soul may bless you* before I die' (Gen. 27:4). 'You shall bring it to your father בַּעֲבֻר אֲשֶׁר יְבָרֶכְךָ *that he may bless you before his dying*' (Gen. 27:10).

§38.543 Very often ל + inf. cstr. is used to express purpose (cf. §35.423). 'And she commanded (him to go) to Mordecai לָדַעַת מַה־זֶּה *to know what this was all about*' (Est. 4:5). 'And she sent clothes לְהַלְבִּישׁ אֶת־מָרְדֳּכַי *to clothe Mordecai*' (Est. 4:4; followed by another purpose cl.).

§38.5431 The neg. is introduced by לְבִלְתִּי: 'I have made a humble plea to the king לְבִלְתִּי הֲשִׁיבֵנִי *that he would not send me back* . . .' (Jer. 38:26).

§38.544 אֲשֶׁר may introduce a purpose clause. 'Gather the people, and I will cause them to hear my words, אֲשֶׁר יִלְמְדוּן לְיִרְאָה אֹתִי *so that they may learn to fear me*' (Deut. 4:10). The negative adds לֹא: 'Come, let's go down and confuse their language there אֲשֶׁר לֹא יִשְׁמְעוּ אִישׁ שְׂפַת רֵעֵהוּ *so that they may not understand each other*' (Gen. 11:7).

§38.545 Purpose may be expressed by coördinate clauses with no indication of subordination. 'Let me turn aside, וְאֶרְאֶה אֶת־הַמַּרְאֶה הַגָּדֹל הַזֶּה *that I might see this great sight*' (Exod. 3:3).

§38.55 A *result clause* modifies the main cl. by giving the result of the predication. It answers the question, 'So what happened as a result?,' and is therefore sometimes called a *consecutive clause*. In Eng. such cls. are introduced by 'that' or 'so that.' The line between purpose and result is not always clear.

§38.551 In Heb., result cls. may be introduced by כִּי or אֲשֶׁר. 'And Aaron, what is he כִּי תַלִּונוּ עָלָיו *that you murmur against him*?' (Num. 16:11). 'I will make your seed like the dust of the earth אֲשֶׁר אִם־יוּכַל אִישׁ לִמְנוֹת עֲפַר הָאָרֶץ גַּם־זַרְעֲךָ יִמָּנֶה '*so that if anyone is able to count the dust of the earth, so also can your seed be counted*' (Gen. 13:16 – the result clause is in turn a conditional clause, cf. §38.6).

§38.552 Sometimes result is indicated simply by coördinate cls. '. . . except the one to whom the king shall extend the golden scepter, וְחָיָה *and he shall live*' (Est. 4:11, or is this purpose?). 'A mist used to go up from the land וְהִשְׁקָה *and it watered* all the face of the ground' (Gen. 2:6; the "*wāw*-consecutive" was so named because it often introduces a *consecutive* clause).

§38.56 A *circumstantial clause* modifies the main cl. by giving a circumstance of the predication, such as manner or comparison. It answers the question 'How?' Since the adverbial cls. already discussed (§§38.51-.55) also give circumstances, this category tends to become a catch-all. Do not place a clause in this category if it fits one of the others.

§38.561 The circumstance is often expressed in a coördinate clause. 'And the Philistine princes came out, וַיְהִי מִדֵּי צֵאתָם *and as often as they came forth*, David was more successful than Saul's servants' (1 Sam. 18:30). 'When Haman saw Mordecai וְלֹא קָם וְלֹא זָע מִמֶּנּוּ *and he didn't stand up and he didn't tremble before him* . . . ' (Est. 5:9).

§38.562 Sometimes asyndetic clauses are used. 'He shall tear it by its wings לֹא יַבְדִּיל *without dividing it in two*' (Lev. 1:17). 'Woe to them that tarry late in the evening יַיִן יַדְלִיקֵם *while wine inflames them*' (Isa. 5:11).

§38.563 Sometimes the structure of the clause suggests some other adverbial concept. אַחֲרֵי הוֹדִיעַ אֱלֹהִים אוֹתְךָ אֶת־כָּל־זֹאת '*Since God caused you to know all this*, there is none so discreet and wise as you are' (Gen. 41:39 – obviously this is not *temporal*; but could it be *causal*?).

§38.6 *Clauses of condition or concession* form a special category, for the main cl. is conditioned by the subordinate cl. and may therefore express unreality as well as reality. Accordingly, we *may* have to use the subjunctive in the main cl. There are also other variables to be discussed.

§38.61 The conditional sentence contains two parts, the *conditional clause* and the *conclusion*. They may be affirmative or negative. "If you study, you learn." "If you don't study, you won't learn." "If you don't eat, you'll be sick." "If you quit, you won't get your pension."

§38.611 The *subordinate* or *conditional* cl. is called the *protasis*, sometimes referred to as the "if-clause." It expresses a *condition* ("if") or *concession* ("though"), although the conjunctions may be omitted or expressed by other means, such as "provided," "granted that," "supposing," "whoever," etc.

§38.6111 The protasis may be noncommittal (*general*), more or less probable in the speaker's mind (*more vivid, less vivid*), or contrary to fact (*unreal*). "If you are hungry, eat" (I have not expressed an opinion about your hunger). "If it does rain tomorrow, we'll stay home" (it seems more probable to the speaker). "If it should clear by noon, we'll go" (it seems less probable to the speaker). "If I were Superman, I could do it" (contrary to fact). Since the difference is in the mind of the speaker, the terms "more vivid" and "less vivid" are preferred to "more probable" and "less probable."

§38.6112 The protasis may stand before, after, or within the apodosis. "If it's Tuesday, this must be Brussels." "Stay in line, if you want a seat." "Shoot, if you must, this old, grey head."

§38.6113 There may be two or more protases with one apodosis, and they may be conjunctive ("if . . . and if . . . then . . . ") or disjunctive ("if . . . or if . . . then . . . "). The time of the protases may be different ("if you ever did . . . or if you should ever do . . . "; "if you had . . . and [if you] now have . . . ").

§38.6114 The protasis may not be expressed in the form of a condition. "Only you shall not draw near to the vessels of the sanctuary and to the altar, lest you die' (Num. 18:3 = 'if you draw near, you will die').

§38.612 The *conclusion* of the conditional sentence is called the *apodosis*. It expresses the result of the condition, or what is true if the condition is true. However, this is sometimes obscured by the structure.

§38.6121 The aposodis may be declaratory, interrogative, imperative, or exclamatory (§30.13). "If you are hungry, you should eat." "If you are hungry, why aren't you eating?" "If you are hungry, eat." "If you are hungry, good! That means you're getting well."

§38.62 There are a number of *variables* in a conditional sentence. In careful exegesis, each one must be noted.

§38.621 Variables of *time*: each part of the sentence may be expressed in past, present, or future, and almost any combination is possible. "If I was there, I paid to get in." "If he left her there, she's still there." "If you wrote, you'll get a reply." The same can be done with the present condition. The future condition, however, can only be probable, and the apodosis cannot take a tense that has no probability (such as the past).

§38.6211 Some conditions are expressed in past or present but have no true time significance. These are called *simple* or *general* conditions. "If you study, you learn." "If the moon was full, the house was visible" (not indicating a specific occasion, but a general observation).

§38.622 Variables of *degree of reality*: The sentence may be noncommittal, more or less probable, or contrary to fact, cf. §38.6111. The degree of reality in the protasis determines the degree of reality in the apodosis, as a general rule – this is what makes it a conditional sentence.

§38.6221 *Present conditions* are generally noncommittal, i.e. the speaker does not express an opinion. The present condition may be *simple* ("If you do this, I'll pay you" – a simple agreement) or *general* (If you work well, I'll praise you" = "whenever you work well," a general statement).

§38.6222 *Past conditions* can be *noncommittal* ("If he started it, he finished it" – I have not stated or implied either that he did or did not start) or *contrary-to-fact* ("If he had started it, he would be finished how" – I imply that he did not start). Past conditions can also be simple or general, cf. §38.6211.

§38.6223 *Future conditions* can only be *probable*, since the future to us is still uncertain, but the degree of probability in the speaker's mind is variable. Hence, a fut. cond. can be *more vivid* (more probable) or *less vivid* (less probable), cf. §38.6111.

§38.63 Since *mood* (§30.335) is essential in forming conditional clauses in our Indo-European language-family, and since Heb. does not distinguish subjunctive and optative moods morphologically, we must use other features in analyzing a Heb. cond. cl. The principal elements are: the presence or absence of a conjunction, the aspect of the verb in a verbal clause, context.

§38.631 Conditions may be expressed by *juxtaposition of clauses* (without any conj. or with *wāw*). This is also possible in Eng. and Ger., but here mood is important ("*Were* I you, I *would* do it"). With such juxtaposition in Heb. it is possible to look upon each clause as independent.

§38.6311 There is a close relationship between *temporal*, *causal*, and *result* cls., on the one hand, and *conditional* cls., on the other. "*When* he eats this, he will die" = "*If* he eats . . . ." It is therefore not easy, or even possible, to make a clear-cut distinction between the cond. cl. and these other modifying cls.

§38.6312 Joüon observes (§167*a*) that usually there is some grammatical modification, such as the use of juss. or cohort., to indicate that there is a condition implied in the juxtaposition.

§38.632 The *conditional particles* (conjunctions) are:
אִם, neg. אִם לֹא, used with simple and general conds.;
כִּי, used somewhat as אִם, cf. BDB 473 2.b;
לוּ (לוּא), neg. לוּלֵא (לוּלֵי), used in unreal conds.;
אֲשֶׁר (rarely), cf. BDB 83 8.d;
וְ– in prot. and apod. or only in apod., cf. BDB 254 5, cf. Joüon §167*b*.

§38.633 *Verb aspect* (tense) is important, but not always decisive, in analyzing a cond. cl.

§38.6331 The *perfect*, with the implication of action completed, is used in simple or general conditions, usually fulfilled or certain of fulfillment. With לוּ or לוּלֵא the perf. usually indicates an unreal or contrary-to-fact condition.

§38.6332 The *imperfect*, action incomplete, is used with simple or general conditions, usually not yet fulfilled or being fulfilled, and with future conditions. When found in other types of cond. cls., either textual corruption is suggested, or there is some reason to be discovered.

§38.6333 The *conv. perf.* and *conv. impf.* are used in the apod. like the impf. and perf. respectively.

§38.6334 The *jussive, cohortative,* and *imperative* are approximately the same as the impf. in usage in the cond. cl.

§38.6335 The *participle* is used in the protasis, principally as a "dangling" substantive (*casus pendens*), often after כֹּל and without a cond. conj., in simple and general conditions. *Ges.* §166*w*.

§38.64 With these preliminary observations, the student should study a number of conditional clauses *in context*. Grammarians make *selections* of passages to illustrate the principles they have set forth, and there are many exceptions (just as in Eng. or Greek) to simple rules, when composing cond. cls.

§38.641 Examples of the *simple* condition: Gen. 18:3, 'If I have found favor in your sight (אִם־נָא מָצָאתִי, ʾ*im* + perf.), do not pass by (אַל־נָא תַעֲבֹר, neg. juss. Num. 12:14, 'If her father had only spit in her face (וְאָבִיהָ יָרֹק יָרַק, *wāw*, perf. + 60), would she not have been humiliated . . . ?' (הֲלֹא תִכָּלֵם, impf. interrog. Judg. 9:16-19 has 4 protases, all עֲשִׂיתֶם, perf., preceded by a single אִם, and 2 apodoses, שִׂמְחוּ, impv., and וְיִשְׂמַח, juss. Gen. 44:22, 'If he leaves his father (וְעָזַב, perf. with *wāw*, possibly conv.) he shall die' (וָמֵת, conv. perf. Judg. 6:13, 'If YHWH is with us (וְיֵשׁ יהוה עִמָּנוּ, verbless), why has all this happened to us?' (מְצָאַתְנוּ, perf., interrog. Gen. 27:46, 'If Jacob takes a wife of the Hittites (אִם־לֹקֵחַ, perf. = fut. perf., 'shall have taken'), what is life to me?' (nonverbal, interrog. Gen. 43:9, 'If I don't bring him back to you (אִם־לֹא הֲבִיאֹתִיו, ʾ*im* +

perf., future, 'if I shall not have . . . '), then let me bear the blame forever' (וְחָטָאתִי, conv. perf., 'I shall be guilty.'

§38.642 Examples of the *general* condition: Ps. 104:28, 'If you give to them (תִּתֵּן לָהֶם, impf. = 'whenever you give') they gather' (יִלְקֹטוּן, impf.). Neh. 1:8, 'If you revolt (אַתֶּם תִּמְעָלוּ, impf.), I will scatter you (אֲנִי אָפִיץ, impf.). Ps. 104:20, 'You appoint darkness (תָּשֶׁת־חֹשֶׁךְ, juss.), then let it be night' (וִיהִי, juss. with *wāw*, expressing a general condition; a result clause probably would have been in impf.). Gen. 42:18, 'Do this (עֲשׂוּ, impv. = 'if you do this') and live' (וִחְיוּ, impv., = 'you will live'). Num. 5:27, 'If she has defiled herself (אִם־נִטְמְאָה, N21) and has acted unfaithfully against her husband (וַתִּמְעֹל, Gc21), then the water shall enter into her . . . ' (וּבָאוּ, Gc15, a general law hence a general cond.). Gen. 9:6, 'If anyone sheds the blood of man (שֹׁפֵךְ דַּם, ptcp., cf. §38.6335, 'anyone shedding'), by man his blood shall be shed' (יִשָּׁפֵךְ, impf.).

§38.643 Examples of the *future* condition: Gen. 18:26, 'If I find in Sodom 50 righteous (אִם אֶמְצָא, impf.), I will spare the place for their sake' (וְנָשָׂאתִי, Gc14, possibly a simple cond.). Gen. 28:20, 'If the Lord God will be with me (verbless after *ʾim*), and (if) he will keep me ... (וּשְׁמָרַנִי, Gc10s4), and (if) he will give me . . . (וְנָתַן, Gc10), then YHWH shall be my God' (וְהָיָה, Gc10; again, is this a simple condition?). Isa. 1:18, 'If your sins are like scarlet (אִם־יִהְיוּ, impf.), they shall be white like snow' (יַלְבִּינוּ, impf., possibly concessive). Gen. 13:16, '. . .if anyone shall be able to count the dust of the earth (אִם־יוּכַל, impf.), so also shall your seed be counted' (יִמָּנֶה, impf. Without subjunctive or optative, it is almost impossible to distinguish the general and future conditions – probably the Hebrews didn't make a difference.

§38.644 Examples of the *contrary-to-fact* (*unreal*) condition. Judg. 8:19, 'If you had spared them (לוּ הַחֲיִתֶם, perf. after *lû*), I would not have killed you' (לֹא הָרַגְתִּי, perf., future certainty). Deut. 32:29, 'If they were wise (לוּ חָכְמוּ, perf., 'if they had achieved wisdom'), they would understand this' (יַשְׂכִּילוּ, impf.). Job 16:4, 'I, too, would speak as you do (אֲדַבֵּרָה, cohort., apodosis precedes), if you were in my place' (לוּ־יֵשׁ, verbless, 'were your soul in place of my soul'). Num. 22:29, 'Were there a sword in my hand (לוּ־יֶשׁ, verbless), for now I would kill you' (הֲרַגְתִּיךְ, perf. after *kî*; possibly *lû* 'would that' and *kî* causal). Judg. 14:18, 'If you had not plowed with my heifer (לוּלֵא חֲרַשְׁתֶּם, perf. after *lûlêʾ*), you would not have discovered my riddle' (לֹא מְצָאתֶם, perf.). Ps. 94:17, 'If the Lord had not been my help (לוּלֵי + verbless cl.), in a little while my soul would have dwelt in Dumah' (שָׁכְנָה, perf. = fut. perf.). Deut. 32:27, 'I would have said . . . (אָמַרְתִּי, perf., apodosis precedes), had I not been in constant conflict with the enemy' (לוּלֵי ... אָגוּר, impf., repeated state in the past?). Gen. 43:10, 'If we hadn't delayed (לוּלֵא הִתְמַהְמָהְנוּ, perf.), we would have been back twice by now' (שַׁבְנוּ, perf.).

§38.645 Doubtless other patterns can be found, and doubtless other grammarians will give a different analysis in many cases. In checking the more questionable statements with the Greek, I found that LXX agreed with me about 60% of the time. The student must learn to do his/her own observing and analyzing.

§38.646 Other particles are used to introduce the cond. cl. כִּי: Exod. 21:22, 'If men struggle and hurt a pregnant woman (וְכִי־יִנָּצוּ, *kî* + N25), . . . he shall be fined (עָנוֹשׁ יֵעָנֵשׁ, G60 + N20) . . . and he shall pay . . . ' (וְנָתַן, Gc10). הֵן: 'What shall we eat (מַה־נֹּאכַל, impf., 1st apod. precedes) . . . if we have not sowed (הֵן לֹא נִזְרָע, *hēn* + impf. [or is it N10/50?]) . . . and we are not gathering the crops?' (נֶאֱסֹף, impf., 2d apod. follows prot.). אֲשֶׁר: Deut. 11:27, '. . . the blessing (verbless apod.) if you obey (אֲשֶׁר תִּשְׁמְעוּ) . . . and the curse (verbless) if you do not obey . . .' (אִם־לֹא תִשְׁמְעוּ, note the parallel of *ʾim lôʾ* and *ʾăšer*, note also ellipsis in the two apodoses).

§38.647 לוּ in prot. without apod. serves to express a strong wish, "Would that!" Num. 14:2, 'Would that we had died in Egypt . . . !' (לוּ מַתְנוּ, *lû* + perf.). Gen. 17:18, 'Would that Ishmael might live in thy sight!' (לוּ יִשְׁמָעֵאל יִחְיֶה, *lû* + impf.).

§38.648 אִם and אִם־לֹא are used to express oaths or asseverations (*Ges.* §149). They are often found after חַי יהוה 'as YHWH lives!,' and generally are translated in just the opposite way (*ʾim* 'if not,' *ʾim lôʾ* 'if'), the theory being that a statement is left unexpressed such as "May YHWH do so to me *ʾim* if I do . . . = 'I will not do.' Ezek. 14:15, 'As I live, says the Lord YHWH, they shall not save sons or daughters!' (אִם־בָּנִים וְאִם־בָּנוֹת יַצִּילוּ). 1 Sam. 3:17, 'May God do thus to you, and then some, if you hide anything from me!' (אִם־תְּכַחֵד, = 'You shall not hide anything from me!'). 2 Sam. 11:11, 'As the Lord lives . . . I will not do this thing' (אִם־אֶעֱשֶׂה).

§38.649 *Ellipsis* (§30.14) is often found in conditional sentences. 1 Sam. 2:16, 'Now give, and if not (אִם־לֹא) I will take it by force.' Exod. 32:32, 'And now, if thou wilt forgive their sin (do so) . . . ' (אִם־תִּשָּׂא).

§38.65 The *concessive* clause admits or concedes some fact or condition *in spite of which* the predication of the main cl. is set forth. The protasis in Eng. is generally introduced by *although, even if, though*, or a similar concessive conjunction. Most of what has been said about conditional cls. applies also to concessive cls. *Ges.* §160.

§38.651 In Heb. the concess. cl. may be introduced by אִם 'if, though,' גַּם כִּי 'even if, though,' עַל 'notwithstanding,' and other particles.

§38.652 Examples of concess. cls.: Job 9:15, 'Though I am innocent (אִם־צָדַקְתִּי), I shall not answer.' Ps. 23:4, 'Even though I should walk in a valley of deep darkness (גַּם כִּי־אֵלֵךְ), I would not fear evil.' Isa. 53:9, 'And he appointed his grave with the wicked, and with the rich man in his death, even though he had done no violence (עַל לֹא־חָמָס עָשָׂה) . . . .' 2 Sam. 18:12, 'Even if I were weighing in my hand 1,000 shekels of silver (וְלֹא אָנֹכִי שֹׁקֵל), I would not lay a hand on the king's son.' Isa. 26:10, 'Even though the wicked is shown mercy (יֻחַן רָשָׁע, no conj.), still he does not learn righteousness.'

§38.66 A conditional clause may be placed within another conditional clause as a subcondition, cf. Num. 21:9; Lev. 15:24; 4:2-3, etc.

§38.7 A *clause of comparison* modifies a main cl. by comparing it with some other predication. Since this often involves manner or circumstance, there is much overlapping, cf. §38.56. A special kind of comparison is the cl. of *degree.*

§38.71 Comparison may be set forth in *juxtaposition* of dependent cls. *kî-ʾāḏām lᵉʿāmāl yûllāḏ ûḇᵉnê-réšep̄ yag̅bîhû ʿûp̄* 'Man is born unto trouble, and the sparks (sons of flame) fly upward' (Job 5:7).

§38.72 The compar. cl. may be introduced by כַּאֲשֶׁר. Est. 6:10, 'Take the clothing and the horse, *as you have spoken* (כַּאֲשֶׁר דִּבַּרְתָּ).'

§38.73 Because of the extensive use of noun (verbless) clauses in Heb., clauses of degree tend to become adverbial phrases. A statement such as Gen. 3:1, 'And the serpent was more subtle than any beast of the field,' is essentially two clauses, 'The serpent was subtle,' and 'more than any beast of the field was subtle.' In Heb. the main cl. has a pred. adj. (עָרוּם), and a phrase *mikkōl ḥayyaṯ haśśāḏêʰ*, which appears to be modifying *ʿārûm*. Even more obscure is the clause of comparison in Est. 6:6, 'To whom would the king delight to do honor more than me *(yôṯēr mimménnî)*?'

§38.74 Correlative conjunctions are sometimes used in clauses of comparison. Exod. 1:12 reads *wᵉḵaʾăšer yᵉʿannû ʾōṯô ḵēn yirbêʰ wᵉḵēn yip̄rōṣ*, lit., 'And just as they [the Egyptian taskmasters] afflicted him [the Israelites], so he multplied and so he overran [his allotted territory].' RSV translates, 'But the more they were oppressed, the more they multiplied and the more they spread abroad.' Main cls.: 'they multiplied,' 'they spread out'; compar. cl.: 'to the degree that the Egyptians oppressed them.'

§38.8 *Direct and Indirect Discourse.* After verbs of *saying, thinking, perceiving, commanding, denying,* and the like (*verba cordis*), a clause is required which sets forth the object of the mental action. This statement or question is a complement of the verb in the main cl. (§34.14), but it is usually considered separately as direct or indirect discourse or direct or indirect question.

§38.81 Direct discourse (*oratio recta*) is the presentation of the exact words, thoughts, commands, etc., of the subject of the main cl. (Whether or not they *are* the exact words, or indeed, whether the words were ever spoken, is beside the point. In fiction, an author can quote the exact words of an imaginary character.) 'And the king said, "Let him come in (יָבוֹא)" ' (Est. 6:5). Cf. Est. 4:13.

§38.811 Direct question is simply qirect quotation of an interrogative quotation. 'And the king said, "Who is in the court (מִי בֶחָצֵר)?" ' (Est. 6:4).

§38.812 The quotation *may* (but need not) be introduced by כִּי, like the *ὅτι recitativum* of Greek). If it is used, it must be *omitted* in translation.

§38.813 There is nothing special to learn about direct discourse. It can be short or long, simple or complex, and all features of syntax can be found in it.

§38.82 Indirect discourse (*oratio obliqua*) is the paraphrase of a quotation, author making no attempt to give the exact words. Direct, "He said, 'I will go.' " Indirect, "He said that he would go." It may be introduced by כִּי, אֲשֶׁר, or by no conjunction.

§38.821 With כִּי: Gen. 6:5, 'And YHWH saw *that the wickedness of man was great*' (כִּי רַבָּה רָעַת הָאָדָם).

§38.822 With אֲשֶׁר: Est. 3:4, 'For he told them *that he was a Jew*' (אֲשֶׁר־הוּא יְהוּדִי).

§38.823 With no conj.: Gen. 12:13, אִמְרִי־נָא אֲחֹתִי אָתְּ 'Say *that you are my sister*.'

§38.824 Indirect discourse may also be expressed as a noun clause, generally by means of an infinitive construct. 'Don't think *that you will be safe in the king's house*' (לְהִמָּלֵט, lit. 'don't think to escape') Est. 4:13.

§38.825 Indirect question is simply the presentation of an interrogative statement in the indirect discourse, cf. Gen. 8:8; 15:5; Jer. 5:1. It may be introduced by הֲ– or אִם. *Ges.* §150*i*.

§38.826 Since there is no apparent alteration of tense or mood, we may assume that the Heb.-speaking people made no grammatical distinction between direct and indirect discourse (such as, e.g., the alteration of *will* to *would* in Eng. indirect discourse).

Part 3
SYNOPTIC PARADIGMS

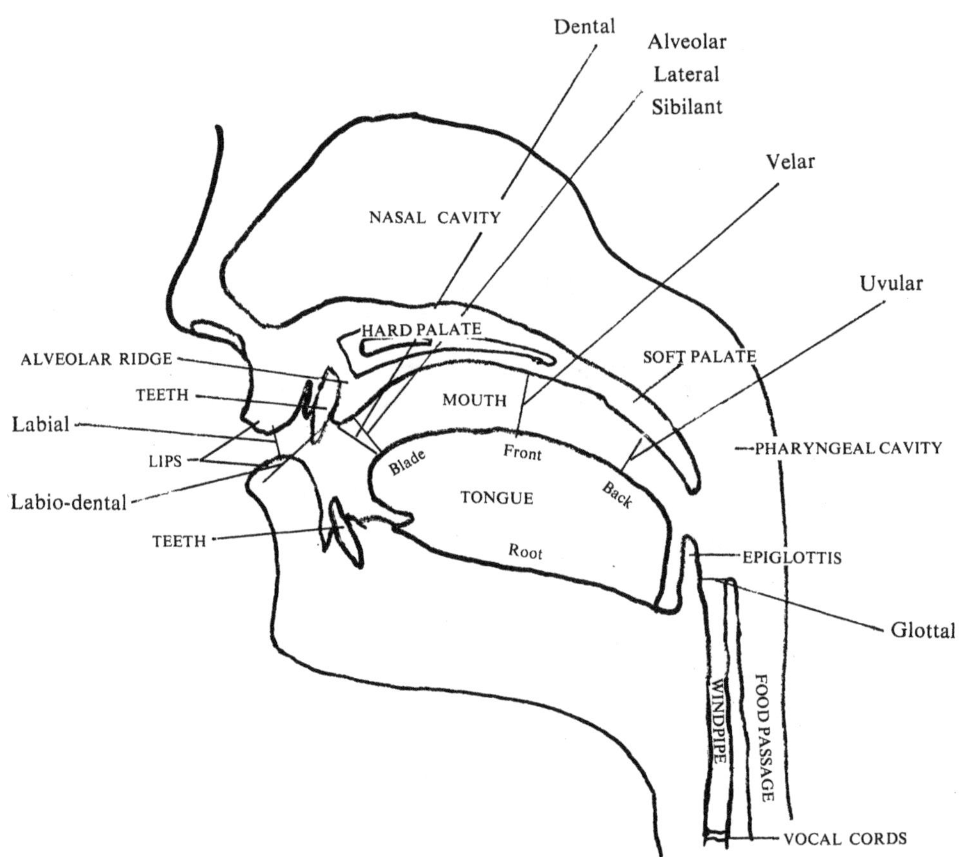

FIGURE 9. THE ORGANS OF SPEECH

Speech, except for implosives (clicks), is produced by the passage of air through the windpipe and mouth and/or nasal cavity, with or without the vibration of the vocal cords, and usually with some restriction caused by the tongue, uvula, palate, teeth, and lips, or combinations of these organs.

1a. A *dagesh* in a *begadkepat* at the beginning of a word or following a shewa is a light dagesh, indicating stopped pronunciation (§11.44). A dagesh in any other letter, or in a begadkepat in any other position, is a strong dagesh, indicating a geminate (doubled) consonant (§11.43). A strong dagesh in a begadkepat both doubles and hardens it (§11.442).

1b. Consonants with shewa, except begadkepat and מּ, frequently lose the strong dagesh (§13.41). This particularly applies to יּ.

2a. *Pure-long vowels* do not reduce except in originally-closed syllables (§15.22), where they become the corresponding short vowel, subject to the short-vowel rules (§15.222)

2b. Long *â* became long *ô* in the Canaanite dialects (§14.11).

3. Words joined by maqqeph and words in construct have only one major accent (§17.12).

4. Original short vowels in final open syllables have generally vanished (§§15.51, ,52).

5. A doubly-closed syllable never occurs within a word and rarely occurs at word-end (§16.34).

6. When a doubly-closed syllable would result from the loss of a short vowel (Rule 4), one of the following occurs:
  a. If a geminate consonant would result, it loses gemination (§13.42);
  b. If a consonantal cluster would result, an anaptycitic vowel is inserted (§15.61);
  c. In a few cases, the doubly-closed syllable remains (§16.3423).

7. Syllables do not begin with consonantal clusters, except in forms of the word for 'two' (§16.35).

8. The conjunction —וְ, when it occurs before labials (בּ, מּ, פּ, called *bûmep̄*), or before consonants with shewa, develops to vocalic וּ *û*; before yod with shewa, however, long *î* is formed (§15.652).

9. At word-end, original *-cw > *-cû* and *-cy > *-cî* (§15.67).

10a. *Gutturals* reject dagesh (§11.432); before א, ע, and ר there is compensatory lengthening (§15.141*.
  b. Gutturals do not take simple vocal shewa (§15.42).
  c. Gutturals often vocalize a silent shewa (§15.421).
  d. Gutturals prefer *a*-class vowels, especially before them (§15.43).
  e. At word-end, ע, ח, or הּ (*he*ʰ with mappiq) attract pattaḥ furtive after *i*- or *u*-class vowels (§15.4321).
  f. *i* > *e* (*ḥîrîq* > *sᵉgôl*) before nonfinal gutturals (§15.434).
  g. Initial א prefers *i*-class vowels when near the accent (§15.433).
  h. א at word-end and frequently at syllable-end is quiescent (§15.54).

11. Nun נ assimilates to a following consonant when no vowel separates (§13.111).

12. In HtD forms, when the first radical is a dental or a sibilant, metathesis, assimilation, or both occur (§13.112, §13.61)

13. Short vowels normally *lengthen* in accented or near-open syllables, and *reduce* in distant-open syllables (§15.11, §15.12, §15.23)
  b. Compensatory vowels do not reduce (§15.233).

c. The original vowel of a segolate does not reduce in sg. cstr. (§15.232). It does, however, reduce in pl. abs. forms.

d. In many forms, *ṣērê* does not reduce (§15.223).

14. Short *a* does not lengthen in *erstwhile doubly-closed syllables* except in pause (§15.111, cf. §15.132).

15. Short *a* does not lengthen in accented-closed syllables in finite verbal forms, except in pause (§15.113).

16. In *near-open* syllables, *i*- or *u*-class short vowels *reduce* to shewa when preceded by a long *syllable* or by no syllable at all (§15.241).

17. In finite verbal forms *without sufformatives,* the accent is on the *ultima* (§17.21). In such forms *with sufformatives,* the following rules prevail:

a. If the *ultima* is *closed,* the accent is on the ultima, and the form follows the short-vowel chart (§17.221).

b. If the *ultima* is *open* and the *penult* is *long,* the accent is on the *penult,* and the form follows the short-vowel chart (§17.222).

c. If the *ultima* is open and the *penult* is *short,* in *nonpausal* forms the accent is on the *ultima,* the vowel of the *penult* reduces to shewa, and the vowel of the antepenult ha its pausal form (lengthened) and is marked by metheg (§17.223).

d. Under the same conditions (17c) but in *pausal form,* the accent is on the *penult,* and the form follows the short-vowel chart (§17.2231).

18. Short *a* frequently attenuates to short *i* in unaccented closed syllables (§15.32).

19. When two successive simple (vocal) shewas would occur, the first becomes *ḥîrîq* and the second becomes zero-shewa (§15.651).

20. In originally closed accented syllables, in certain forms original short *i* becomes short *a* (§15.33).

21. When *simple (vocal) shewa* would occur before *compound shewa,* the simple shewa is changed to the normal short vowel of the same vowel-class as the compound shewa (§15.653).

22. When *compound shewa* would occur before simple (vocal) shewa, the compound shewa develops to its corresponding normal short vowel, and the simple shewa becomes zero shewa (§15.2532).

23. The connecting vowel of a pronominal suffix, if any, takes the accent (§17.32). If a shewa precedes the suffix, it is zero shewa and the ךְ/כ of the suffix is spirantized.

24. In verbal forms, thematic *a* in G-perf. generally yields thematic *u* in G-impf., and thematic *i* or *u* in G-perf. yields thematic *a* in G-impf. (§27.331).

25. In G-impf., the vowell of the preformative is determined usually by the thematic vowel, as follows: thematic *a* preformative *i,* thematic *i* or *u* preformative *a* (§27.332).

26. When adding a consonantal sufformative (i.e. one which begins with a consoant) to a CC[2] verb which ends in a geminated consonant, the consonantal cluster which would occur is avoided by the insertion of a long vowel before the sufformative, namely וֹ (*ô*) in the perf. and ֶי (*ê*[y]) in the impf. (§15.64).

27. Nonpausal converted impf. form· which have a closed ultima and an open penult are accented on the *penult* (§17.341)

28. Nonpausal converted perf. forms ending in תָּ (-*tā*) or תִּי (-*tî*) generally are accented on the *ultima* (§17.342).

TABLE A. THE ALPHABET

	Modern Printed Alphabet	Modern Greek Print
ʾā́lep̄	א	Α
bêṯ	בּ	Β
gîmel	גּ	Γ
dā́leṯ	דּ	Δ
hêʾ	ה	Ε
wāw	ו	F
záyin	ז	Ζ
ḥêṯ	ח	Η
têṭ	ט	Θ
yôḏ	י	Ι
kap̄	כּ	Κ
kap̄ sôp̄îṯ	ך	Κ
lā́meḏ	ל	Λ
mêm	מ	Μ
mêm sôp̄îṯ	ם	Μ
nûn	נ	Ν
nûn sôp̄îṯ	ן	Ν
sā́meḵ	ס	Ξ
ʿáyin	ע	Ο
pê	פּ	Π
pê sôp̄îṯ	ף	Π
ṣāḏê	צ	
ṣāḏê sôp̄îṯ	ץ	
qôp̄	ק	
rêš	ר	Ρ
šîn	שׁ	Σ
śîn	שׂ	Σ
tāw	תּ	Τ

TABLE B. THE CONSONANTS

Name and		Transliteration	Pronunciation	
א	ʾ	*ʾā́lep̄*	[ʔ]	slight glottal stop
בּ	*b*	*bêṯ*	[b]	*b* as in *bob*
ב	*ḇ*	”	[v]	*v* as in *valve*
גּ	*g*	*gîmel*	[g]	*g* as in *gag*
ג	*ḡ*	”	[γ]	*g* as in Ger. *Tage*, now [g]
דּ	*d*	*dā́leṯ*	[d]	*d* as in *dud*
ד	*ḏ*	”	[ð]	*th* as in *then*, now [d]
ה	*h*	*hêʾ*	[h]	*h* as in *hay*
ו	*w*	*wāw*	[w]	*w* as in *wow* or [v]
ז	*z*	*záyin*	[z]	*z* as in *zoo*
ח	*ḥ*	*ḥêṯ*	[x]	*ch* as in Ger. *ach!* or [ḥ] as in Arab. *ḥ*
ט	*ṭ*	*ṭêṯ*	[t]	*t* as in *tote*, emphatic
י	*y*	*yôḏ*	[i̯]	y as in *yes*
כּ	*k*	*kāp̄*	[k]	*k* as in *kick*
כ	*ḵ*	”	[ç]	*ch* as in Ger. *ich*, often [x]
ך	*ḵ*	*kāp̄ sôp̄îṯ*	[ç]	” ”
ל	*l*	*lā́meḏ*	[l]	*l* as in *loll*
מ	*m*	*mêm*	[m]	*m* as in *mum*
ם	*m*	*mêm sôp̄îṯ*	[m]	”
נ	*n*	*nûn*	[n]	*n* as in *noon*
ן	*n*	*nûn sôp̄îṯ*	[n]	”
ס	*s*	*sā́meḵ*	[s]	*s* as in *sister*
ע	ʿ	*ʿáyin*	[ʿ]	strong glottal stop
פּ	*p*	*pê*	[p]	*p* as in *pep*
פ	*p̄*	”	[f]	*f* as in *fife*
ף	*p̄*	*pê sôp̄îṯ*	[f]	”
צ	*ṣ*	*ṣāḏê*	[s]	*s* as in *saw*, emphatic, or [ts] as in *hats*
ץ	*ṣ*	*ṣāḏê sôp̄îṯ*	”	” ”
ק	*q*	*qôp̄*	[q]	*c* as in *coop*, further back in mouth
ר	*r*	*rêš*	[r]	*r* as in Span. *pero,* or [R] as in Fr. *rue*
שׁ	*š*	*šîn*	[ʃ]	*sh* as in *sheen*
שׂ	*ś*	*śîn*	[s]	*s* as in *seen*
תּ	*t*	*tāw*	[t]	*t* as in *teach*
ת	*ṯ*	”	[θ]	*th* as in *thin*, now [t]

For details, see §§11.–11.143, and §12.5

For the letters בּ גּ דּ כּ פּ תּ see §11.44.
For the letters ך ם ן ף ץ see §§11.13ff.

TABLE C. THE VOWELS

Name and Transliteration			Pronunciation
◌ַ	*a*	*paṯṯāḥ*	[ɑ] *à la mode*
◌ָ	*ā*	*qāmāṣ*	[ɑ:] *father*
◌ֶ	*e*	*s^{e}gôl*	[ɛ] *met*
◌ֵ	*ē*	*ṣêrê*	[e] *favorite, they*
◌ִ	*i*	*ḥîrîq*	[i] *iniquity, Paul'ine*
◌ֹ	*ō*	*ḥôlām*	[o] *obey*
◌ָ	*o*	*qāmāṣ ḥăṭûp̄*	[ɔ] *soft*
◌ֻ	*u*	*qubbuṣ*	[u] *moon*, Ger. *Fuß*
◌ֲ	*ă*	*ḥăṭap̄ paṯṯāḥ*	[ă] [ɒ] *alone, anniversary*
◌ֱ	*ĕ*	*ḥăṭap̄ s^{e}gôl*	[ĕ] [ə] *enemy*
◌ֳ	*ŏ*	*ḥăṭap̄ qāmāṣ*	[ŏ] *colloquial*
◌ְ	^{e}	*š^{e}wā*	[ə] *mathematics*
[הַ]	^{a}	*paṯṯāḥ g^{e}nûḇā^h*	[͵] *we're* (very slight vowel)
וֹ	*ô^w*	*ḥôlām mālē^{ʾ}*	[o:] *open*
◌ִי	*î^y*	*ḥîrîq gāḏôl*	[i:] *machine*
◌ֵי	*ê^y*	*ṣêrê yôḏ*	[e:] *they, navy*
וּ	*û*	*šûrûq*	[u:] *pool*, Ger. *Buch*

For discussion, see §§14.–14.232 and §§15.–15.67.

THE VOWEL TRIANGLE

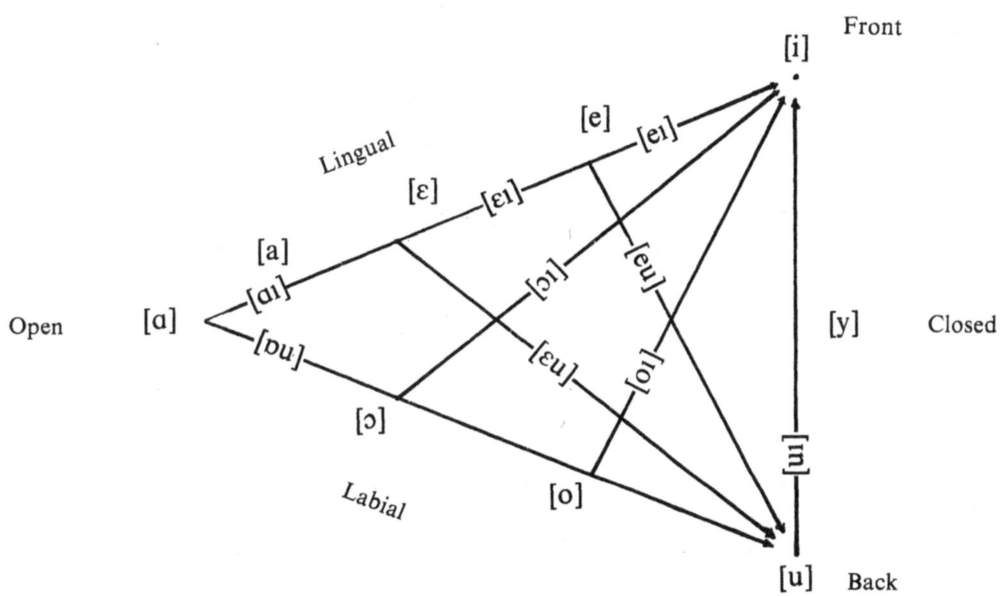

TABLE D. HAND-WRITTEN HEBREW

א	ב	ג	ד	ה	ו	ז	ח	ט	י	כ ך	ל
Aleph	Beth	Gimel	Daleth	Hè	Wāw	Záyin	Ḥeth	Ṭeth	Yŏdh	Kaph	Lāmedh (or)

מ ם	נ ן	ס	ע	פ ף	צ ץ	ק	ר
Mêm	Nûn	Sāmekh	‘Ayin	Pè	Tsadde	Qoph	Resh

שׁ	שׂ	ת
Shîn	Śîn	Taw

בּ גּ דּ כּ פּ תּ

יון יז וז גנ דר הח חת בכ טמ סם עצ

יון יז וז גנ דר הח חת בכ טמ סם עצ

אֱלֹהִים אַבְרָהָם יִצְחָק יַעֲקֹב מֹשֶׁה

אלהים אברהם יצחק יעקב משה

יִשְׂרָאֵל אֵלִיָּהוּ יְשַׁעְיָהוּ דָּוִד הַמֶּלֶךְ

ישראל אליהו ישעיהו דוד המלך

TABLE E. THE SHORT-VOWEL CHART

Character of Syllable	*a*-type vowel	*i*-type vowel	*u*-type vowel
unaccented-closed	–ַ	–ֶ | –ִ [1]	–ָ | –ֻ [1]
accented or near-open	–ָ	–ֵ	–ֹ
distant-open	–ְ	–ְ	–ְ
distant open עחהא	–ֲ | –ֱ	–ֱ | –ֲ	–ֳ

[1]These forms generally occur before the strong dagesh.

TABLE F. THE DIPHTHONG CHART

Character of syllable		*ay*-diphthong	*aw*-diphthong
accented-closed		–ַיִ	–ָוֶ
accented-closed	(less often)	–ֵ	–וֹ–
accented-open	(medial)	–ֶי	–וֹ–
accented-open	(final)	–ֶה	–וֹ
unaccented	(end of singular)	–ֵה	–וֹ
unaccented (all other)		–ֵי	–וֹ

TABLE G. THE DEFINITE ARTICLE CHART

Form of Article		Before
הֶ–	*he–*	חָ– *ḥa–* (not *ḥo–*)
הֶ–	*he–*	עָ– *ʿā́–* or הָ– *hā́–* (in near-open)
הָ–	*hā–*	א– *ʾ–*, ר– *r–*, ע– *ʿ–* usually (not near-open)
הַ–	*ha–*	ה– *h–*, ח– *ḥ–*, and sometimes ע– *ʿ–*
הַ–ּ	*ha- + dāgēš*	everything else

TABLE H. THE PRONOMINAL SUFFIXES

GENITIVE							
	Added to Prepositions				Added to Singular Nouns Ending in		Added to Dual/Plural Nouns
					Vowel	Consonant	
s0 (3ms)	בּוֹ	כָּמֹהוּ	מִמֶּנּוּ	אֵלָיו	הוּ– ו–	ֵ–הוּ ה–ֹו–	ָ–יו ָ–יהוּ
s1 (3fs)	בָּהּ	כָּמוֹהָ	מִמֶּנָּה	אֵלֶיהָ	הָ–	ָ–הּ ֶ–הָ	ֶ–יהָ
s2 (2ms)	בְּךָ בָּךְ	כָּמֹכָה	מִמְּךָ מִמֶּךָּ	אֵלֶיךָ	ךָ–	ְ–ךָ ֶ–ךָ	ֶ–יךָ
s3 (2fs)	בָּךְ		מִמֵּךְ	אֵלַיִךְ	ךְ–	ֵ–ךְ ָ–ךְ	ַ–יִךְ ַ–יִךְ
s4 (1cs)	בִּי	כָּמוֹנִי	מִמֶּנִּי	אֵלַי	י–	ִ–י	ַ–י ַ–י
s5 (3mp)	בָּהֶם בָּם	כּוֹהֶם כָּהֶם	מֵהֶם מֵהֵמָּה	אֲלֵיהֶם	הֶם– מוֹ–	ָ–ם ָ–מוֹ	ֵ–יהֶם ֵ–ימוֹ
s6 (3fp)	בָּהֶן	כָּהֵנָּה כָּהֵן	מֵהֵנָּה מֵהֶן	אֲלֵיהֶן	הֶן– הֶן–	ָ–ן	ֵ–יהֶן
s7 (2mp)	בָּכֶם	כָּכֶם כְּמוֹכֶם	מִכֶּם	אֲלֵיכֶם	כֶם–	ְ–כֶם	ֵ–יכֶם
s8 (2fp)					כֶן–	ְ–כֶן	ֵ–יכֶן
s9 (1cp)	בָּנוּ	כָּמוֹנוּ	מִמֶּנּוּ	אֵלֵינוּ	נוּ–	ֵ–נוּ ֵ–וּ	ֵ–ינוּ

TABLE H. THE PRONOMINAL SUFFIXES

ACCUSATIVE						
Added to אֵת	Added to Perf. Verbs Ending in Vowel	Added to Perf. Verbs Ending in Consonant	Added to Impf. Verbs Ending in Vowel	Added to Impf. Verbs Ending in Consonant	Added to Verbs with Nun Energicum	
אֹתוֹ	־הוּ ־ו	־ָהוּ ־וֹ/־ֹה	־הוּ ־ו	־ֵהוּ	־ֶנּוּ ־ֶנְהוּ/־נּוּ	s0 (3ms)
אֹתָהּ	־הָ	־ָהּ	־הָ	־ֶהָ ־ָהּ	־ֶנָּה	s1 (3fs)
אֹתְךָ אֹתָךְ	־ךָ	־ְךָ ־ָךְ/־ֶךָ	־ךָ	־ָךְ ־ֶךָ	־ְךָ ־ֶנְךָּ	s2 (2ms)
אֹתָךְ	־ךְ	־ָךְ ־ֶ־ָךְ/־ֵךְ	־ךְ	־ֵךְ		s3 (2fs)
אֹתִי	־נִי	־ַנִי ־ָנִי	־נִי	־ֵינִי	־ֶנִּי ־ֶנִּי	s4 (1cs)
אֹתָם	־הֶם ־ם	־ָם ־ֶ־ָם/־ָמוֹ	־ם	־ֵם ־ֶ־ָם/־ֵמוֹ		s5 (3mp)
אֹתְהֶן אֹתָן	־ן ־הֶן	־ָן ־ֶ־ָן		־ֵן		s6 (3fp)
אֶתְכֶם	־כֶם	־ְכֶם	־כֶם	־ְכֶם		s7 (2mp)
						s8 (2fp)
אֹתָנוּ	־נוּ	־ָנוּ	־נוּ	־ֵנוּ	־ֶנּוּ	s9 (1cp)

TABLE J. THE NUMERALS

The Cardinals

	WITH MASCULINE				WITH FEMININE			
	ABS.		CSTR.		ABS.		CSTR.	
'3'	שְׁלֹשָׁה	*š^{e}lôšā^{h}*	שְׁלֹשֶׁת	*š^{e}lôšeṯ*	שָׁלֹשׁ	*šālôš*	שְׁלֹשׁ	*s^{e}lôš*
'4'	אַרְבָּעָה	*'arbāʿā^{h}*	אַרְבַּעַת	*'arbáʿaṯ*	אַרְבַּע	*'arbaʿ*	אַרְבַּע	*'arbaʿ*
'5'	חֲמִשָּׁה	*ḥămiššā^{h}*	חֲמֵשֶׁת	*ḥămēšeṯ*	חָמֵשׁ	*ḥāmēš*	חֲמֵשׁ	*ḥămēš*
'6'	שִׁשָּׁה	*šiššā^{h}*	שֵׁשֶׁת	*šéšeṯ*	שֵׁשׁ	*šēš*	שֵׁשׁ	*šēš*
'7'	שִׁבְעָה	*šiḇʿā^{h}*	שִׁבְעַת	*šiḇʿaṯ*	שֶׁבַע	*šéḇaʿ*	שֶׁבַע	*šéḇaʿ*
'8'	שְׁמֹנָה	*š^{e}mônā^{h}*	שְׁמֹנַת	*š^{e}mônaṯ*	שְׁמֹנֶה	*š^{e}mônê^{h}*	שְׁמֹנֶה	*š^{e}mônê^{h}*
'9'	תִּשְׁעָה	*tišʿā^{h}*	תְּשַׁעַת	*tišʿaṯ*	תֵּשַׁע	*téšaʿ*	תֵּשַׁע	*téšaʿ*
'10'	עֲשָׂרָה	*ʿăśārā^{h}*	עֲשֶׂרֶת	*ʿăśéreṯ*	עֶשֶׂר	*ʿéśer*	עֶשֶׂר	*ʿéśer*

	WITH MASCULINE		WITH FEMININE	
'11'	אַחַד עָשָׂר	*'aḥaḏ ʿāśār*	אַחַת עֶשְׂרֵה	*'aḥaṯ ʿeśrē^{h}*
or	עַשְׁתֵּה עָשָׂר	*'aštê^{h} ʿāśār*	עַשְׁתֵּה עֶשְׂרֵה	*'aštê^{h} ʿeśrē^{h}*
'12'	שְׁנֵים עָשָׂר	*šnê^{y}m ʿāśār*	שְׁתֵּים עֶשְׂרֵה	*štê^{y}m ʿeśrē^{h}*
'13'	שְׁלֹשָׁה עָשָׂר	*š^{e}lôšā^{h} ʿāśār*	שְׁלֹשׁ עֶשְׂרֵה	*š^{e}lôš ʿeśrē^{h}*
'14'	אַרְבָּעָה עָשָׂר	*'arbāʿā^{h} ʿāśār*	אַרְבַּע עֶשְׂרֵה	*'arbaʿ ʿeśrē^{h}*
'15'	חֲמִשָּׁה עָשָׂר	*ḥămiššā^{h} ʿāśār*	חֲמֵשׁ עֶשְׂרֵה	*ḥămēš ʿeśrē^{h}*
'16'	שִׁשָּׁה עָשָׂר	*šiššā^{h} ʿāśār*	שֵׁשׁ עֶשְׂרֵה	*šēš ʿeśrē^{h}*
'17'	שִׁבְעָה עָשָׂר	*šiḇʿā^{h} ʿāśār*	שְׁבַע עֶשְׂרֵה	*š^{e}ḇaʿ ʿeśrē^{h}*
'18'	שְׁמֹנָה עָשָׂר	*š^{e}mônā^{h} ʿāśār*	שְׁמֹנֶה עֶשְׂרֵה	*š^{e}mônê^{h} ʿeśrē^{h}*
'19'	תִּשְׁעָה עָשָׂר	*tišʿā^{h} ʿāśār*	תְּשַׁע עֶשְׂרֵה	*t^{e}šaʿ ʿeśrē^{h}*

'20'	עֶשְׂרִים	*ʿeśrîm*
'30'	שְׁלוֹשִׁים	*š^{e}lôšîm*
'40'	אַרְבָּעִים	*'arbāʿîm*
'50'	חֲמִשִּׁים	*ḥămiššîm*
'60'	שִׁשִּׁים	*šiššîm*
'70'	שִׁבְעִים	*šiḇʿîm*
'80'	שְׁמֹנִים	*š^{e}mônîm*
'90'	תִּשְׁעִים	*tišʿîm*

'100' מֵאָה *mēʾā^{h}* cst. מְאַת *m^{e}ʾaṯ* pl. מֵאוֹת *mēʾôṯ*

'1,000' אֶלֶף *ʾélep̄*

The Ordinals

'2d'	שֵׁנִי		*šēnî*	שֵׁנִית	שְׁנִיָּה	*šēnîṯ*	*š^{e}nîyā^{h}*
'3d'	שְׁלִישִׁי		*š^{e}lîšî*	שְׁלִישִׁית	שְׁלִשִׁיָּה	*š^{e}lîšîṯ*	*š^{e}lîšîyā^{h}*
'4th'	רְבִיעִי		*r^{e}ḇîʿî*	רְבִיעִית		*r^{e}ḇîʿîṯ*	
'5th'	חֲמִישִׁי	חֲמִשִׁי	*ḥămîšî*	חֲמִישִׁית		*ḥămîšîṯ*	
'6th'	שִׁשִּׁי		*šiššî*	שִׁשִּׁית		*šiššîṯ*	
'7th'	שְׁבִיעִי		*š^{e}ḇîʿî*	שְׁבִיעִית		*š^{e}ḇîʿîṯ*	
'8th'	שְׁמִינִי		*š^{e}mînî*	שְׁמִינִית		*šînîṯ*	
'9th'	תְּשִׁיעִי		*t^{e}šîʿî*	תְּשִׁיעִית		*t^{e}šîʿîṯ*	
'10th'	עֲשִׂירִי		*ʿăśîrî*	עֲשִׂירִית	עֲשִׂירִיָּה	*ʿăśîrîṯ*	*ʿăśîrîyā^{h}*

PARADIGM V-1. SYNOPSIS OF THE HEBREW VERB

Hp Hophal	H Hiphil	HtD Hithpael	Dp Pual	D Piel	N Niphal	G Qal	
הָקְטַל	הִקְטִיל	הִתְקַטֵּל	קֻטַּל	קִטֵּל	נִקְטַל	קָטַל	Perf. (10)
יָקְטַל	יַקְטִיל	יִתְקַטֵּל	יְקֻטַּל	יְקַטֵּל	יִקָּטֵל	יִקְטֹל	Impf. (20)
	הַקְטֵל	הִתְקַטֵּל		קַטֵּל	הִקָּטֵל	קְטֹל	Impv. (32)
	הַקְטִיל	הִתְקַטֵּל		קַטֵּל	הִקָּטֵל	קְטֹל	Inf.Cstr. (65)
הָקְטֵל	הַקְטֵל	הִתְקַטֵּל	קֻטֹּל	קַטֹּל[4]	הִקָּטֹל[3]	קָטוֹל	Inf.Abs. (60)
	מַקְטִיל			מְקַטֵּל		קוֹטֵל	Ptcp.Act. (50)
		מִתְקַטֵּל			נִקְטָל		Ptcp.Refl.
מָקְטָל			מְקֻטָּל			קָטוּל	Ptcp.Pass.

[1] גִּדֵּל

[2] יְכַבֵּד

[3] נִקְטָל

[4] קַטֵּל

PARADIGM V-2. SYNOPSIS OF THE G-PERFECT

Type	G65	G60	Gp50	G50	G17/18	G12/14/19	G13	G11/15/16	G10
CCCa	קְטֹל	קָטוֹל	קָטוּל	קוֹטֵל	קְטַלְתֶּם	קָטַלְתָּ	קָטַלְתְּ	קָטְלָה	קָטַל
	קָטְלוֹ			קֹטֶלֶת	קְטַלְתֶּן	קָטַלְתִּי		קָטֲלָה	קָטָל
				קֹטְלִים		קָטַלְנוּ		קָטְלוּ	
CCCi	לִכְבַּד[1]	כָּבוֹד	כָּבוּד	כָּבֵד	כְּבַדְתֶּם	כָּבַדְתִּי	כָּבַדְתְּ	כָּבְדָה	כָּבֵד
CCCu		קָטוֹן		קָטֹן	קְטָנְתֶּם	קָטֹנְתִּי	קָטֹנְתְּ	קָטְנָה	קָטֹן
ʾCC	אֱכֹל[2]	אָכוֹל	אָכוּל	אוֹכֵל	אֲכַלְתֶּם	אָכַלְתִּי	אָכַלְתְּ	אָכְלָה	אָכַל
GCC	עֲמֹד	עָמוֹד	עָמוּד	עוֹמֵד	עֲמַדְתֶּם	עָמַדְתִּי	עָמַדְתְּ	עָמְדָה	עָמַד
NCC	גֶּשֶׁת[3]	נָגוֹשׁ	נָגוּשׁ	נוֹגֵשׁ	נְגַשְׁתֶּם	נָגַשְׁתִּי	נָגַשְׁתְּ	נָגְשָׁה	נָגַשׁ
WCC	שֶׁבֶת[4,5]	יָשׁוֹב	יָשׁוּב	יוֹשֵׁב	יְשַׁבְתֶּם	יָשַׁבְתִּי	יָשַׁבְתְּ	יָשְׁבָה	יָשַׁב
YCC	יְטֹב	יָטוֹב	יָטוּב	יֹטֵב	יְטַבְתֶּם	יָטַבְתִּי	יָטַבְתְּ	יָטְבָה	יָטַב
CGCi	שְׁחֹט	שָׁחוֹט	שָׁחוּט	שׁוֹחֵט	שְׁחַטְתֶּם	שָׁחַטְתִּי	שָׁחַטְתְּ	שָׁחֲטָה	שָׁחַט
CGCa	קוּם	קוֹם	קוּם	קָם	קַמְתֶּם	קַמְתִּי	קַמְתְּ	קָמָה	קָם
CWC	בּוֹא	מוֹת		מֵת	מַתֶּם	מַתִּי	מַתְּ	מֵתָה	מֵת
CYC	דִּין	בִּין		דָּן	דַּנְתֶּם	דַּנְתִּי	דַּנְתְּ	דָּנָה	דָּן
CC²	סֹב[6]	סָבוֹב	סָבוּב	סוֹבֵב	סַבּוֹתֶם	סַבּוֹתִי	סַבּוֹת	סַבָּה	סַב
CC²	לִסְבֹּב[1]							סָבֲבָה	סָבַב
CCʾa	מְצֹא[7]	מָצוֹא	מָצוּא	מוֹצֵא	מְצָאתֶם	מָצָאתִי	מָצָאת	מָצְאָה	מָצָא
CCʾi		מָלוֹא	מָלוּא	מָלֵא	מְלֵאתֶם	מָלֵאתִי	מָלֵאת	מָלְאָה	מָלֵא
CCG	שְׁלֹחַ	שָׁלוֹחַ	שָׁלוּחַ	שׁוֹלֵחַ	שְׁלַחְתֶּם	שָׁלַחְתִּי	שָׁלַחַתְּ	שָׁלְחָה	שָׁלַח
CCW				שָׁלֵו		שָׁלַוְתִּי		שָׁלוּ	שָׁלָה
CCY	גְּלוֹת	גָּלֹה	גָּלוּי	גֹּלֶה	גְּלִיתֶם	גָּלִיתִי	גָּלִית	גָּלְתָה	גָּלָה
היה	הֱיוֹת[8]	הָיֹה		הוֹיֶה	הֱיִיתֶם	הָיִיתִי	הָיִית	הָיְתָה	הָיָה

[1] with ־לְ
[2] לֵאמֹר
[3] לִנְפֹּל
[4] דַּעַת
[5] לִיסֹד
[6] בֹּר
[7] צֵאת
[8] לִהְיוֹת

PARADIGM V-3. SYNOPSIS OF THE G-IMPERFECT

G40	Gc20	G38	G33/37	G32	G26/28	G23/25/27	G24	G20/21/22/29	Type
יִקְטֹל	וַיִּקְטֹל	קְטֹלְנָה	קִטְלִי	קְטֹל	תִּקְטֹלְנָה	תִּקְטְלִי	אֶקְטֹל	יִקְטֹל	CCCu
			קִטְלוּ			יִקְטְלוּ		תִּקְטֹל	
						תִּקְטְלוּ		נִקְטֹל	
יִכְבַּד	וַיִּכְבַּד	כְּבַדְנָה	כִּבְדִי	כְּבַד	תִּכְבַּדְנָה	יִכְבְּדוּ	אֶכְבַּד	יִכְבַּד	ʾCC
	וַיֶּאֱחֹז		אֶחֱזוּ	אֱחֹז			אֶאֱסֹף	יֶאְסֹר[1]	ʾCC
	וַיֶּאֱהַב		אִמְצוּ	אֱמַץ	תֶּאֱרַכְנָה		אֵהַב	יֶאְשַׁב[2]	ʾCCa
	וַיֹּסֶף		אִכְלוּ	אֱכֹל	תֹּאבַדְנָה	יֹאבְדוּ	אֹחֵז	יֹאסֵף	ʾ CCi
	וַיַּעֲמֹד	עֲמֹדְנָה	עִמְדִי	עֲמֹד	תַּעֲמֹדְנָה	יַעַמְדוּ[4]	אֶעֱמֹד	תַּחְמֹל[3]	GCCu
	וַיֶּחֱזַק	חֲזַקְנָה	חִזְקִי	חֲזַק	תֶּחֱזַקְנָה	יֶחְמְרוּ[6]	אֶחְפַּץ	יֶחְמַץ[5]	GCCa
יִפֹּל	וַיִּפֹּל	נְפֹלְנָה	נִפְלִי	נְפֹל	תִּפֹּלְנָה	יִפְּלוּ	אֶפֹּל	יִפֹּל	NCCu
יִגַּשׁ	וַיִּגַּשׁ	גַּשְׁנָה	גְּשִׁי	גַּשׁ	תִּגַּשְׁנָה	יִגְּשׁוּ	אֶגַּשׁ	יִגַּשׁ	NCCa
	וַיִּתֵּן		תְּנִי	תֵּן		יִתְּנוּ	אֶתֵּן	יִתֵּן	NCCi
	וַיִּירַשׁ			יְרָא	תִּירַשְׁנָה	יִירְשׁוּ	אִירַשׁ	יִירַשׁ	WCCa
	וַיֵּשֶׁב	שֵׁבְנָה	שְׁבִי	שֵׁב[7]	תֵּשַׁבְנָה	יֵשְׁבוּ	אֵשֵׁב	יֵשֵׁב	WCCi
	וַיִּיטַב				תִּיטַבְנָה	יִיטְבוּ	אִיטַב	יִיטַב	YCCa
	וַיֶּאֱחֹז		אֶחֱזִי	נְעֹל				יִנְהֹם	CGCu
יִשְׁחַט	וַיִּשְׁחַט	שְׁחַטְנָה	שַׁחֲטִי	שְׁחַט	תִּשְׁחַטְנָה	יִשְׁחֲטוּ	אֶשְׁחַט	יִשְׁחַט	CGCa
יָקֹם	וַיָּקָם	קֹמְנָה	קוּמִי	קוּם	תְּקוּמֶינָה	יָקוּמוּ	אָקוּם	יָקוּם	CûC
	וַיֵּאֹר		אֹורִי	בּוֹא	תָּאֹרְנָה			יָבוֹא[8]	CâC ?
יָשֵׁת	וַיָּשֶׁת		בִּינִי	בִּין	תָּגֵלְנָה	יָגִילוּ	אָגִיל	יָדִין	CîC
	וַיָּסָב	סְבֶּינָה	סֹבִּי	סֹב	תְּסֻבֶּינָה	יָסֹבּוּ	אָסֹב	יָסֹב	CC²u
					תִּסֹּבְנָה	יִסְּבוּ	אֶסֹּב	יִסֹּב	CC²u
	וָאֵקַל					יֵחַמּוּ	אִיתַם	יֵקַל	CC²a
	וַיָּגֶל				תְּעַלֶּינָה	יֵקַלּוּ		יָגֵן	CC²i
		מְצֶאנָה	מִצְאִי	מְצָא	תִּמְצֶאנָה	יִמְצְאוּ	אֶמְצָא	יִמְצָא	CCʾa
				טְבֹחַ			אֶסְלַח		CCGu
יִשְׁלַח	וַיִּשְׁלַח	שְׁלַחְנָה	שִׁלְחִי	שְׁלַח	תִּשְׁלַחְנָה	יִשְׁלְחוּ	אֶשְׁלַח	יִשְׁלַח	CCGa
יִגֶל	וַיִּגֶל	גְּלֶינָה	גְּלִי	גְּלֵה	תִּגְלֶינָה	יִגְלוּ	אֶגְלֶה	יִגְלֶה	CCY
יְהִי	וַיְהִי		הֱיִי	הֱיֵה	תִּהְיֶינָה	יִהְיוּ	אֶהְיֶה	יִהְיֶה	היה

[1] יֶאֱסֹף
[2] יֶאֱנַף
[3] יַעֲמֹד
[4] תַּחְמְלוּ
[5] יֶעֱרַב
[6] יֶחֶזְקוּ
[7] דַּע
[8] יֵבוֹשׁ

PARADIGM V-4. SYNOPSIS OF THE D-STEM (Perfect)

Type	D65	D60	D50	D17/18	D12/14/19	D13	D11/15/16	D10[1]
CCCi	קַטֵּל	קַטֵּל	מְקַטֵּל	קִטַּלְתֶּם	קִטַּלְתָּ	קִטַּלְתְּ	קִטְּלָה	קִטֵּל
		קַטֵּל		קִטַּלְתֶּן	קִטַּלְתִּי		קִטְּלוּ	
					קִטַּלְנוּ			
CCCa		לַמֵּד	מְלַמֵּד		גִּדַּלְתִּי	לִמַּדְתְּ		גִּדֵּל
ʾCC	אַבֵּד	אַבֵּד	מְאַמֵּץ	אִבַּדְתֶּם	אִבַּדְתִּי	אִמַּצְתְּ		אִמֵּץ[2]
GCC	הַלֵּךְ		מְחַשֵּׁב		חִשַּׁבְתִּי	חִבַּרְתְּ	חִשְּׁבָה	חִבֵּר
NCC	נַשֵּׁק		מְנַצֵּחַ	נִצַּלְתֶּם	נִקַּמְתִּי			נִתֵּץ
WCC	יַסֵּד	יַסֹּת	מְיַהֵל		יִהַלְתִּי	יִדַּעַתְּ	יִסְּדוּ	יִסֵּד
YCC	יַשֵּׁר		מְיַשֵּׁר		יִשַּׁרְתִּי			
CGCi	בָּעֵר			בִּעַרְתֶּם	בִּעַרְתִּי	בִּעַרְתְּ	בִּעֲרוּ	בֵּאֵר[3]
CGCa		בָּרֵךְ	מְבָרֵךְ	בֵּרַכְתֶּם	בֵּרַכְתִּי	בֵּרַכְתְּ	בֵּרְכָה	בֵּרַךְ[4]
CWC	קוֹמֵם	קוֹמֵם	מְקוֹמֵם	קוֹמַמְתֶּם	קוֹמַמְתִּי		קוֹמֲמָה	קוֹמֵם[5]
CYC	בּוֹנֵן							
CC²	סוֹבֵב	סוֹבֵב	מְסוֹבֵב	סוֹבַבְתֶּם	סוֹבַבְתִּי	סוֹבַבְתְּ	סוֹבְבָה	סוֹבֵב
CCʾ	מַצֵּא	מַצֵּא[7]	מְמַצֵּא	מִצֵּאתֶם	מִצֵּאתִי	טִמֵּאת	טִמְּאוּ	מִצֵּא[6]
CCG	שַׁלֵּחַ	שַׁלֵּחַ	מְשַׁלֵּחַ	שִׁלַּחְתֶּם	שִׁלַּחְתִּי	שִׁלַּחַתְּ	שִׁלְּחָה	שִׁלַּח
CCY	צַוּוֹת	גַּלֵּה	מְגַלֶּה	גִּלִּיתֶם	גִּלִּיתִי	גִּלִּית	גִּלְּתָה	גִּלָּה

Type	Dp65	Dp60	Dp50	Dp17/18	Dp12/14/19	Dp13	Dp11/15/16	Dp10
CCC		קֻטַּל	מְקֻטָּל	קֻטַּלְתֶּם	קֻטַּלְתָּ	קֻטַּלְתְּ	קֻטְּלָה	קֻטַּל
				קֻטַּלְתֶּן				
GCC							אֻכְּלוּ	חֻבַּר
CGC			מְבֹרָךְ	בֹּרַכְתֶּם	בֹּרַכְתָּ		בֹּרְכוּ	בֹּרַךְ
CWC			מְקוֹמָם	קוֹמַמְתֶּם	קוֹמַמְתָּ		קוֹמֲמָה	קוֹמַם
CC²			מְחוֹלָל					
CC²			מְסֻבָּב					סוֹבַב
CCʾ			מְמֻלָּא	מֻצֵּאתֶם	מֻצֵּאתָ		מֻצְּאוּ	מֻצָּא
CCG			מְשֻׁלָּח	שֻׁלַּחְתֶּם	שֻׁלַּחְתָּ		שֻׁלְּחוּ	שֻׁלַּח
CCY			מְגֻלֶּה	גֻּלֵּיתֶם	גֻּלֵּיתִי		גֻּלּוּ	גֻּלָּה

[1]קַטֵּל [4]רִחַק [7]קַנֵּא

[2]אִבֵּד [5]קִיֵּם

[3]בִּעֵר [6]דִּכָּא

PARADIGM V-4. SYNOPSIS OF THE D-STEM (Imperfect)

D40	Dc20	D38	D33/37	D32	D26/28	D23/25/27	D24	D20/21/22/29	Type
יְקַטֵּל	וַיְקַטֵּל	קַטֵּלְנָה	קַטְּלִי קַטְּלוּ	קַטֵּל	תְּקַטֵּלְנָה	תְּקַטְּלִי יְקַטְּלוּ תְּקַטְּלוּ	אֲקַטֵּל	יְקַטֵּל תְּקַטֵּל נְקַטֵּל	CCC
	וַתְּאַבֵּד			אַבֵּד		תְּאַבְּדוּ		יְאַבֵּד	ʾCC
	וַיְחַבֵּר			הַלֵּךְ		יְחַשְּׁבוּ	אֲהַלֵּךְ	יְחַכֵּם	GCC
	וַיְנַסֵּךְ		נַשְּׁקוּ	נַשֵּׁק		יְנַכְּרוּ	אֲנַתֵּק	יְנַתֵּק	NCC
				יַסֵּד				תְּיַבֵּשׁ	WCC
			יַשְּׁרוּ				אֲיַשֵּׁר	יְיַשֵּׁר	YCC
	וַתְּמָאֵן		מַהֲרוּ	בָּעֵר		יְבַעֲרוּ		תְּבַהֵל	CGC
			קוֹמְמִי	קוֹמֵם	תְּקוֹמֵמְנָה	יְקוֹמְמוּ	אֲקוֹמֵם	יְקוֹמֵם	CWC
								יְבוֹנֵן	CYC
יְשׁוֹחֵחַ			סוֹבְבִי	סוֹבֵב	תְּסוֹבֵבְנָה	יְסוֹבְבוּ	אֲסוֹבֵב	יְסוֹבֵב	CC²
			מַצְּאוּ	מַצֵּא	תְּמַצֶּאנָה	יְמַצְּאוּ	אֲמַצֵּא	יְמַצֵּא	CCʾ
	וַיְשַׁלַּח		שַׁלְּחִי	שַׁלַּח	תְּשַׁלַּחְנָה	יְשַׁלְּחוּ	אֲשַׁלַּח	יְשַׁלַּח	CCG
תְּגַל	וַיְגַל		גַּלִּי	צַוֵּה[1]	תְּגַלֶּינָה	יְגַלּוּ	אֲגַלֶּה	יְגַלֶּה	CCY

Dp40	Dpc20	Dp26/28	Dp23/25/27	Dp24	Dp20/21/22/29	Type
יְקֻטַּל	וַיְקֻטַּל	תְּקֻטַּלְנָה	תְּקֻטְּלוּ	אֲקֻטַּל	יְקֻטַּל	CCC
			תְּאֻכְּלוּ		יְחֻפַּשׂ	GCC
				אֲבֹרַךְ	יְבֹרַךְ	CGC
		תְּקוֹמַמְנָה	יְחוֹלָלוּ		יְקוֹמַם	CC²
		תְּמֻצֶּאנָה	יְמֻצְּאוּ	יְמֻצָּא	יְמֻצָּא	CCʾ
		תְּשֻׁלַּחְנָה			יְשֻׁלַּח	CCG
			תְּגֻלִּי		יְגֻלֶּה	CCY

[1] גַּל

PARADIGM V-5. SYNOPSIS OF THE H-STEM (Perfect)

Type	H65	H60	H50	Hp17/18	H12/14/19	H13	H11/15/16	H10
CCC	הַקְטִיל	הַקְטֵל	מַקְטִיל	הִקְטַלְתֶּם הִקְטַלְתֶּן	הִקְטַלְתָּ הִקְטַלְתִּי הִקְטַלְנוּ	הִקְטַלְתְּ	הִקְטִילָה הִקְטִילוּ	הִקְטִיל
ʾCC	הַאֲכִיל		מַאֲכִיל	הֶאֱכַלְתֶּם	הֶאֱכַלְתִּי	הֶאֱכַלְתְּ	הֶאֱכִילָה	הֶאֱכִיל
GCC	הַעֲמִיד	הַעֲמֵד	מַעֲמִיד	הֶעֱמַדְתֶּם	הֶעֱמַדְתִּי	הֶעֱמַדְתְּ	הֶעֱמִידָה	הֶעֱמִיד
NCC	הַגִּישׁ	הַגֵּשׁ	מַגִּישׁ	הִגַּשְׁתֶּם	הִגַּשְׁתִּי	הִגַּשְׁתְּ	הִגִּישָׁה	הִגִּישׁ
WCC	הוֹשִׁיב	הוֹשֵׁב	מוֹשִׁיב	הוֹשַׁבְתֶּם	הוֹשַׁבְתִּי	הוֹשַׁבְתְּ	הוֹשִׁיבָה	הוֹשִׁיב
YCC	הֵיטִיב	הֵיטֵב	מֵיטִיב	הֵיטַבְתֶּם	הֵיטַבְתִּי	הֵיטַבְתְּ	הֵיטִיבָה	הֵיטִיב
CGC			מַבְעִיר		הִבְעַרְתִּי			הִבְהִיל
CWC	הָקִים	הָקֵם	מֵקִים	הֲקִימוֹתֶם	הֲקִימוֹתִי	הֲקִימוֹת	הֵקִימָה	הֵקִים
CYC								
CC^2	הָסֵב	הָסֵב	מֵסֵב	הֲסִבּוֹתֶם	הֲסִבּוֹתִי	הֲסִבּוֹת	הֵסֵבָּה	הֵסֵב[1]
CCʾ	הַמְצִיא	הַמְצֵא	מַמְצִיא	הִמְצֵאתֶם	הִמְצֵאתִי	הִמְצֵאת	הִמְצִיאָה	הִמְצִיא
CCG	הַשְׁלִיחַ	הַשְׁלֵחַ	מַשְׁלִיחַ	הִשְׁלַחְתֶּם	הִשְׁלַחְתִּי	הִשְׁלַחַתְּ	הִשְׁלִיחָה	הִשְׁלִיחַ
CCY		הַגְלֵה	מַגְלֶה	הִגְלֵיתֶם	הִגְלֵתִי	הִגְלִית[2]	הִגְלְתָה	הִגְלָה

Type	Hp65	Hp60	Hp50	Hp17/18	Hp12/14/19	Hp13	Hp11/15/16	Hp10
CCC	הָקְטַל	הָקְטֵל	מָקְטָל	הָקְטַלְתֶּם הָקְטַלְתֶּן	הָקְטַלְנוּ הָקְטַלְתָּ	הָקְטַלְתְּ	הָקְטְלוּ הָקְטְלָה	הָקְטַל
ʾCC	הָאֳכַל		מָאֳכָל	הָאֳכַלְתֶּם	הָאֳכַלְתִּי	הָאֳכַלְתְּ	הָאָכְלָה	הָאֳכַל
	הָעֳמַד	הָעֳמֵד	מָעֳמָד	הָעֳמַדְתֶּם	הָעֳמַדְתִּי	הָעֳמַדְתְּ	הָעָמְדָה	הָעֳמַד
NCC	הֻגַּשׁ	הֻגֵּשׁ	מֻגָּשׁ	הֻגַּשְׁתֶּם	הֻגַּשְׁתָּ	הֻגַּשְׁתְּ	הֻגְּשָׁה	הֻגַּשׁ
WCC	הוּשַׁב		מוּשָׁב	הוּשַׁבְתֶּם	הוּשַׁבְתִּי	הוּשַׁבְתְּ	הוּשְׁבָה	הוּשַׁב
CWC			מוּקָם	הוּקַמְתֶּם	הוּקַמְתָּ	הוּקַמְתְּ	הוּקְמָה	הוּקַם
CYC								
CC^2		הָשַׁמָּה	מוּסָב	הוּסַבּוֹתֶם	הוּסַבּוֹתָ	הוּסַבּוֹת	הוּסַבָּה	הוּסַב
CCʾ				הָמְצֵאתֶם	הָמְצֵאתִי	הָמְצֵאת	הָמְצְאָה	הָמְצָא
CCG	הָשְׁלַח	הָשְׁלֵחַ	מָשְׁלָח	הָשְׁלַחְתֶּם	הָשְׁלַחְתָּ	הָשְׁלַחַתְּ	הָשְׁלְחָה	הָשְׁלַח
CCY		הָגְלֵה	מָגְלֶה	הָגְלֵיתֶם	הָגְלֵיתִי	הָגְלֵית	הָגְלְתָה	הָגְלָה

[1] הֵסַב

הִגְלֵית

PARADIGM V-5. SYNOPSIS OF THE H-STEM (Imperfect)

[1]H40	Hc20	H38	H33/37	H32	H26/28	H23/25/27	H24	H20/21/22/29	Type
יַקְטֵל	וַיַּקְטֵל	הַקְטֵלְנָה	הַקְטִילִי	הַקְטֵל	תַּקְטֵלְנָה	תַּקְטִילִי	אַקְטִיל	יַקְטִיל	CCC
			הַקְטִילוּ			יַקְטִילוּ			
				הַאֲכֵל			אֹבִיד	יַאֲכִיל	ʾCC
יַעֲמֵד	וַיַּעֲבֵר	הַעֲמֵדְנָה	הַעֲמִידִי	הַעֲמֵד	תַּעֲמֵדְנָה	יַעֲמִידוּ	אַעֲמִיד	יַעֲמִיד	GCC
יַגֵּשׁ	וַיַּסֵּף	הַגֵּשְׁנָה	הַגִּישִׁי	הַגֵּשׁ	תַּגֵּשְׁנָה	יַגִּישׁוּ	אַגִּישׁ	יַגִּישׁ	NCC
יוֹשֵׁב	וַיּוֹשֶׁב	הוֹשֵׁבְנָה	הוֹשִׁיבִי	הוֹשֵׁב	תּוֹשֵׁבְנָה	יוֹשִׁיבוּ	אוֹשִׁיב	יוֹשִׁיב	WCC
יֵיטֵב	וַיֵּיטֶב	הֵיטֵבְנָה	הֵיטִיבִי	הֵיטֵב	תֵּיטֵבְנָה	תֵּיטִיבוּ	אֵיטִיב	יֵיטִיב	YCC
	וַיַּבְעֵר					יַבְהִילוּ		תַּבְעִיר	CGC
יָקֵם	וַיָּקֶם	הָקֵמְנָה	הָקִימִי	הָקֵם	תָּקֵמְנָה[4]	יָקִימוּ	אָקִים	יָקִים	CWC
	וַיָּבֵא								CYC
	וַיָּסֶב	הֲסִבֶּינָה	הָסֵבִּי	הָסֵב	תְּסִבֶּינָה	יָסֵבּוּ[3]	אָסֵב	יָסֵב[2]	CC²
יַנְצֵא		הַמְצֶאנָה	הַמְצִיאִי	הַמְצֵא	תַּמְצֶאנָה	יַמְצִיאוּ	אַמְצִיא	יַמְצִיא	CCʾ
יַשְׁלַח		הַשְׁלַחְנָה	הַשְׁלִיחִי	הַשְׁלַח	תַּשְׁלַחְנָה	יַשְׁלִיחוּ	אַשְׁלִיחַ	יַשְׁלִיחַ	CCG
יֶגֶל		הַגְלֶינָה	הַגְלִי	הַגְלֵה	תַּגְלֶינָה	יַגְלוּ	אַגְלֶה	יַגְלֶה	CCY

Hp26/28	Hp23/25/27	Hp24	Hp20/21/22/29	Type
תָּקְטַלְנָה	יָקְטְלוּ	אָקְטַל	נָקְטַל	CCC
			יָאֳכַל	ʾCC
תֻּגַּשְׁנָה	יֻגְּשׁוּ	אֻגַּשׁ	יֻגַּשׁ	NCC
תּוּשַׁבְנָה	יֻשְׁבוּ	אוּשַׁב	יוּשַׁב	WCC
				YCC
תּוּקַמְנָה	יוּקְמוּ	אוּקַם	יוּקַם	CWC
				CYC
תּוּסַבֶּינָה	יוּסַבּוּ	אוּסַב	יֻסַּב	CC²
תֻּמְצֶאנָה	יֻמְצְאוּ	אֻמְצָא	יֻמְצָא	CCʾ
תָּשְׁלַחְנָה	יָשְׁלְחוּ	אָשְׁלַח	יָשְׁלַח	CCG
תָּגְלֶינָה	יָגְלוּ	אָגְלֶה	יָגְלֶה	CCY

[1]תְּקִימֶינָה [2]יַסֵּב [3]יִסַּבּוּ

PARADIGM V-6. SYNOPSIS OF THE N-STEM (Perfect)

Type	N65	N60	N50	N17/18	N12/14/19	N13	N11/15/16	N10
CCC	הִקָּטֵל	הִקָּטֹל נִקְטֹל	נִקְטָל	נִקְטַלְתֶּם נִקְטַלְתֶּן	נִקְטַלְתָּ נִקְטַלְתִּי נִקְטַלְנוּ	נִקְטַלְתְּ	נִקְטְלָה נִקְטְלוּ	נִקְטַל
ʾCC	הֵאָכֵל	הֵאָסֵף	נֶאֱכָל				נֹאחֲזוּ	נֶאֱכַל
GCC	הֵעָמֵד	נַעֲמוֹד	נֶעֱמָד	נַעֲמַדְתֶּם	נַעֲמַדְתִּי	נֶעֱמַדְתְּ	נֶעֶמְדָה	נַעֲמַד[1]
NCC	הִנָּגֵשׁ	הִנָּגֵשׁ[2]	נִגָּשׁ	נִגַּשְׁתֶּם	נִגַּשְׁתִּי	נִגַּשְׁתְּ	נִגְּשָׁה	נִגַּשׁ
WCC			נוֹשָׁב	נוֹשַׁבְתֶּם	נוֹשַׁבְתִּי	נוֹשַׁבְתְּ	נוֹשְׁבָה	נוֹשַׁב
YCC								
CGC	הִשָּׁחֵט	נִשְׁחוֹט	נִשְׁחָט	נִשְׁחַטְתֶּם	נִשְׁחַטְתִּי	נִשְׁחַטְתְּ	נִשְׁחֲטָה	נִשְׁחַט
CWC	נָקוֹם	הִקּוֹם[3]	נָקוֹם	נְקוּמוֹתֶם	נְקוּמוֹתִי	נְקוּמוֹת	נָקוֹמָה	נָקוֹם
CYC			נָבוֹן	נְבוּנוֹתֶם	נְבוּנוֹתִי	נְבוּנוֹת	נָבוֹנָה	נָבוֹן
CC²	הִסֵּב	הִסּוֹב[6]	נָסָב[8,5]	נְסַבּוֹתֶם	נְסַבּוֹתִי	נְסַבּוֹת	נָסַבָּה	נָסַב[4]
CCʾ	הִמָּצֵא	נִמְצֹא	נִמְצָא	נִמְצֵאתֶם	נִמְצֵאתִי	נִמְצֵאת	נִמְצְאָה	נִמְצָא
CCG	הִשָּׁלַח	נִשְׁלוֹחַ	נִשְׁלָח	נִשְׁלַחְתֶּם	נִשְׁלַחְתִּי	נִשְׁלַחַתְּ	נִשְׁלְחָה	נִשְׁלַח
CCW								
CCY	הִגָּלוֹת	נִגְלֹה[7]	נִגְלֶה	נִגְלֵיתֶם	נִגְלֵיתִי	נִגְלֵית	נִגְלְתָה	נִגְלָה
היה			נִהְיָה[8]		נִהְיֵיתָ		נִהְיְתָה	נִהְיָה

[1] נֶהֱלַךְ [5] נְסַבָּה

[2] נָגוֹף [6] הִמֵּס

[3] נָסוֹג [7] הִנָּקֵה

[4] נָמֵס [8] fem.

PARADIGM V-6. SYNOPSIS OF THE N-STEM (Imperfect)

N40	Nc20	N38	N33/37	N32	N26/28	N23/25/27	N24	N20/21/22/29	Type
יִקָּטֵל	וַיִּקָּטֵל	הִקָּטַלְנָה	הִקָּטְלִי	הִקָּטֵל	תִּקָּטַלְנָה	הִקָּֽטְלִי	אֶקָּטֵל	יִקָּטֵל	CCC
			הִקָּֽטְלוּ			יִקָּֽטְלוּ		תִּקָּטֵל	
			הֵאָֽחֲזוּ	הֵאָכֵל		יֵאָֽחֲזוּ		יֵאָכֵל	ʾCC
תֵּעָשׂ		הֵעָמַדְנָה	הֵעָֽמְדִי	הֵעָמֵד	תֵּעָמַדְנָה	יֵעָֽמְדוּ	אֵעָמֵד	יֵעָמֵד	GCC
		הִנָּגַשְׁנָה	הִנָּֽגְשִׁי	הִנָּגֵשׁ	תִּנָּגַשְׁנָה	יִנָּֽגְשׁוּ	אֶנָּגֵשׁ	יִנָּגֵשׁ	NCC
	וַיִּוָּדַע								WCC
									YCC
	וַיִּבָּהֵל	הִשָּׁחַטְנָה	הִשָּֽׁחֲטִי	הִשָּׁחֵט	תִּשָּׁחַטְנָה	יִשָּֽׁחֲטוּ	אֶשָּׁחֵט	יִשָּׁחֵט	CGC
			הִקֹּֽומִי	הִקּוֹם		יִקֹּֽומוּ	אֶקּוֹם	יִקּוֹם	CWC
									CYC
		הִסַּבֶּינָה	הִסַּֽבִּי	הִסַּב	תִּסַּבֶּינָה	יִסַּֽבּוּ	אֶסַּב	יִסַּב	CC²
	וַיִּמָּלֵא	הִמָּצֶאנָה	הִמָּֽצְאִי	הִמָּצֵא	תִּמָּצֶאנָה	יִמָּֽצְאוּ	אֶמָּצֵא	יִמָּצֵא	CCʾ
	וַתִּלָּקַח	הִשָּׁלַחְנָה	הִשָּֽׁלְחִי	הִשָּׁלַח	תִּשָּׁלַחְנָה	יִשָּֽׁלְחוּ	אֶשָּׁלַח	יִשָּׁלַח	CCG
יִגָּל		הִגָּלֶינָה	הִגָּלִי	הִגָּלֵה	תִּגָּלֶינָה	יִגָּלוּ	אִגָּלֶה	יִגָּלֶה	CCY

PARADIGM V-7. SYNOPSIS OF THE HtD-STEM (Perfect)

Type	HtD65	HtD60	HtD50	HtD17/18	HtD12/14/19	HtD13	HtD11/15/16	HtD10
CCC	הִתְקַטֵּל	הִתְקַטֵּל	מִתְקַטֵּל	הִתְקַטַּלְתֶּם הִתְקַטַּלְתֶּן	הִתְקַטַּלְתָּ הִתְקַטַּלְתִּי הִתְקַטַּלְנוּ	הִתְקַטַּלְתְּ	הִתְקַטְּלָה הִתְקַטְּלוּ	הִתְקַטֵּל
CCCa			מִתְנַפֵּל					הִתְאַנַּף
ʾCC							הִתְאַפָּקוּ	הִתְאַנַּף
GCC			הִתְהַלֵּךְ	הִתְעַנַּגְתֶּם	הִתְהַלַּכְתִּי		הִתְהַלְּכוּ	תִּתְחַכַּם[1]
NCC	הִתְנַחֵל	הִתְנַחֵל	מִתְנַפֵּל[5]	הִתְנַחַלְתֶּם	הִתְנַפָּלְתִּי			
WCC		הִתְוַדַּע	מִתְוַדֶּה					הִתְוַדָּה
YCC			מִתְיַהֲדִים[15]					
CGC			מִתְבָּרֵךְ	הִתְבָּרַכְתֶּם	הִתְבָּרַכְתִּי	הִתְבָּרַכְתְּ	הִתְבָּרֲכָה	הִתְבָּרֵךְ
CWC			מִתְגֹּרֵר		הִתְעֹרַרְתִּי		הִתְמוֹטְטָה	
CYC								הִתְבּוֹנָן
CC²		הִשְׁתָּרֵר[2]	מִסְתּוֹלֵל[2]	הֲסִבּוֹתֶם	הִתְחַנַּנְתָּה		הִתְפּוֹרְרָה[3]	
CCʾ			מִתְמַצֵּא	הִתְמַצֵּאתֶם	הִתְמַצֵּאתִי	הִתְמַצֵּאת	הִתְמַצְּאָה	הִתְמַצֵּא
CCG		הִשְׁתַּלַּח[2]	מִשְׁתַּלֵּחַ[2]	הִשְׁתַּלַּחְתֶּם[2]	הִשְׁתַּלַּחְתִּי[2]	הִשְׁתַּלַּחַתְּ[2]	הִשְׁתַּלְּחָה[2]	הִשְׁתַּלַּח[2]
CCY			מִתְגַּלֶּה	הִתְגַּלִּיתֶם	הִתְגַּלֵּיתִי	הִתְגַּלִּית	הִתְגַּלְּתָה	הִתְגַּלָּה
SCC[16]			מִשְׁתַּכֵּר[2]					
DCC[17]			מִטַּהֵר[4]		הִטַּהַרְנוּ[4]			
ECC[18]								

[1] הִתְהַלֵּךְ
[2] metathesis
[3] הִתְגַּלְגְּלוּ
[4] assimilation
[5] מְנַאֵץ
[6] feminine
[7] מִתְגּוֹלֵל
[8] יִתְוַכָּח
[9] תִּכּוֹנָנִי
[10] יִתְבּוֹלָן
[11] יִתְחַטָּא
[12] יִשְׁתּוֹמֵם
[13] אֶתְרוֹעָע
[14] יִתְיָעֲצוּ
[15] plural
[16] sibilant
[17] dental
[18] emphatic

PARADIGM V-7. SYNOPSIS OF THE HtD-STEM (Imperfect)

HtD40	HtDc20	HtD38	HtD33/37	HtD32	HtD26/28	HtD23/25/27	HtD24	HtD20/21/22/29	Type
יִתְקַטֵּל	וַיִּתְקַטֵּל	הִתְקַטֵּלְנָה	הִתְקַטְּלִי	הִתְקַטֵּל	תִּתְקַטֵּלְנָה	תִּתְקַטְּלִי	אֶתְקַטֵּל	יִתְקַטֵּל	CCCi
			הִתְקַטְּלוּ			יִתְקַטְּלוּ		תִּתְקַטֵּל	
						תִּתְקַטְּלוּ		נִתְקַטֵּל	
	וַיִּתְאַנַּף			הִתְעַנַּג		תִּתְחַטָּאוּ	אֶתְאַפָּק	יִתְחַטָּא	CCCa
	וַיִּתְאַנַּף					יִתְאַמְּרוּ	אֶתְחַבַּת	תִּתְאַפַּק	ʾCC
			הִתְהַלְּכוּ	הִתְהַלֵּךְ	תִּתְהַלַּכְנָה	יִתְחַבְּרוּ	אֶתְנַפֵּל	יִתְחַשֵּׁב	GCC
	וַיִּתְנַכֵּר		הִתְנַגְּשׁוּ			יִתְנַגְּפוּ	אֶתְוַדֶּה	תִּתְנַקֵּם	NCC
	וַיִּתְיַלְדוּ			הִתְיַצֵּב		יִתְוַדּוּ[14]		תִּתְיַפֵּחַ[8]	WCC
		הִתְבָּרֵכְנָה	הִתְבָּרְכִי	הִתְבָּרֵךְ	תִּתְבָּרֵכְנָה	יִתְבָּרְכוּ	אֶתְבָּרֵךְ	יִתְבָּרֵךְ	CGC
	וַנִּתְעוֹדָד			יהִתְחוֹלֵל	תִּתְמוֹגַגְנָה	יִתְרוֹעֲעוּ[9]	אֵרוֹמֵם[1.4]	יִתְכּוֹנָן[9]	CWC
	וַתִּתְחַלְחַל					יִתְבּוֹנָנוּ	אֶתְבּוֹנֵן	יִתְלוֹנָן	CYC
	וַתִּתְחַנֵּן		הִתְהוֹלְלוּ			יִתְהוֹלָלוּ	אֶתְחַנָּן	תִּתְחַנֵּן[10]	CC²
		הִתְמַצֶּאנָה	הִתְמַצְּאִי	הִתְמַצֵּא	הִתְמַצֶּאנָה	יִתְחַטְּאוּ	אֶתְמַצֵּא	יִתְמַצֵּא[11]	CCʾ
		הִשְׁתַּלַּחְנָה[2]	הִשְׁתַּלְּחִי[2]	הִשְׁתַּלַּח[2]	תִּשְׁתַּלַּחְנָה[2]	יִשְׁתַּלְּחוּ[2]	אֶשְׁתַּלַּח[2]		CCG
יִתְגַּל	וַיִּתְגַּל	הִתְגַּלֶּינָה	הִתְגַּלִּי	הִתְגַּלֵּה	תִּתְגַּלֶּינָה	יִתְגַּלּוּ	אֶתְגַּלֶּה	יִתְגַּלֶּה	CCY
								יִסְתַּבֵּל[12.2]	SCC[16]
			הִטַּהֲרוּ[4]			יִטַּמְּאוּ[4]		יִטַּמָּא[4.2]	DCC[17]
								נִצְטַדָּק[4.2]	ECC[18]

PARADIGM N-1. NOUNS WITH TWO CONSONANTS (CvC, Cv̂C)

Type	PLURAL -cvc	-v/-cv	cstr.	abs.	SINGULAR -cvc	-cv	-v	cstr.	abs.
CaC	בְּנֵיכֶם	בָּנַי			יֶדְכֶם	יָדְךָ	יָדִי	יַד	יָד
CiC		עֵצֵינוּ	עֲצֵי	גֵּבִים	שִׁמְכֶם	בִּנְךָ	בְּנוֹ	בֶּן[1]	בֵּן
CuC						כֹּחֲךָ	כֹּחִי	כֹּחַ	כֹּחַ
CâC	שׁוֹטֵיכֶם	שׁוֹטַי	שׁוֹטֵי	שׁוֹטִים	שׁוֹטְכֶם	שׁוֹטְךָ	שׁוֹטִי	שׁוֹט	טוֹב
CâC		עָבָיו	עָבֵי	עָבִים			אֲלָתִי	עָב	עָב
CîC		שָׁרֶיךָ	רִיבֵי	שִׁירִים			שִׁירִי	שִׁיר	שִׁיר
CûC		שׁוּלַיִךְ	צוּרֵי			רוּחֲךָ	רוּחִי	רוּחַ	רוּחַ
CaCat		יְדֹתֶיהָ	יְדוֹת	יָדוֹת			דְּגָתוֹ	דְּגַת	דָּגָה
CiCat							עֲדָתִי		עֵדָה
CuCat									
CâCat		טוֹבֹתָיו		קָלוֹת		דֹּדָתְךָ	דֹּדָתוֹ	טוֹבַת	דּוֹדָה
CîCat	קִינוֹתֵיהֶם	קִירֹתָיו	קִירוֹת	קִירוֹת					קִינָה
CûCat		חוּצֹתָיו	לְחֹת	גּוּפוֹת		סוּפָתְךָ		גּוּפַת	
CaCt									
CiCt					בִּתֵּנוּ	בִּתְּךָ	בִּתִּי	בַּת	בַּת

DUAL

cstr.	abs.
יְדֵי	יָדַיִם
	לְחֹתַיִם

[1] בֶּן. בֵּן

PARADIGM N-2. TRICONSONANTAL NOUNS WITH ONE VOWEL (CvCC)

PLURAL				SINGULAR					
-cvc	-v/-cv	cstr.	abs.	-cvc	-cv	-v	cstr.	abs.	Type
מַלְכֵיכֶם	מַלְכַי	מַלְכֵי	מְלָכִים	מַלְכְּכֶם	מַלְכְּךָ	מַלְכּוֹ	מֶלֶךְ	מֶלֶךְ	CaCC
סִפְרֵיכֶם	סְפָרַי	סִפְרֵי	סְפָרִים	סִפְרְכֶם	סִפְרְךָ	סִפְרִי	סֵפֶר	סֵפֶר	CiCC
קָדְשֵׁיכֶם	קֳדָשַׁי	קָדְשֵׁי	חֳדָשִׁים	קָדְשְׁכֶם	קָדְשְׁךָ	קָדְשִׁי	קֹדֶשׁ	קֹדֶשׁ	CuCC
נַעֲרֵיכֶם	נְעָרַי	נַעֲרֵי	נְעָרִים	נַעַרְכֶם	נַעַרְךָ	נַעֲרוֹ	נַעַר	נַעַר	CaGC
פָּעֳלֵיכֶם	פְּעָלַי	פָּעֳלֵי	פְּעָלִים	פָּעָלְכֶם	פָּעָלְךָ	פָּעֳלוֹ	פֹּעַל	פֹּעַל	CuGC
					זַרְעֲךָ	זַרְעִי	זֶרַע	זֶרַע	CaCG
נִצְחֵיכֶם	נְצָחַי	נִצְחֵי	נְצָחִים	נִצְחֲכֶם	נִצְחֲךָ	נִצְחִי	נֵצַח	נֵצַח	CiCG
				מֽוֹתְכֶם	מֽוֹתְךָ	מוֹתִי	מוֹת	מָוֶת	CaWC
זֵיתֵיכֶם	זֵיתַי	זֵיתֵי	זֵיתִים	זֵיתְכֶם	זֵיתְךָ	זֵיתִי	זֵית	זַיִת	CaYC
יַמֵּיכֶם	יַמַּי	יַמֵּי	יַמִּים	יַמְּכֶם	יַמְּךָ	יַמִּי	יַם	יָם	CaC²
			עִזִּים	אִמְּכֶם	אִמְּךָ	אִמּוֹ	אֵם	אֵם	CiC²
חֻקֵּיכֶם	חֻקַּי	חֻקֵּי	חֻקִּים	חָקְכֶם	חָקְךָ	חֻקִּי	חָק־	חֹק	CuC²
		גְּדָיֵי	גְּדָיִים					גְּדִי	CaCY
לְחָיֵהֶם	לְחָיַי	לְחָיֵי	לְחָיַיִם	פֶּרְיְכֶם	פֶּרְיְךָ	פִּרְיִי	פְּרִי	פְּרִי	CiCY
						לֶחֱיוֹ		חֳלִי	CuCY
	DUAL								
	רַגְלַי	רַגְלֵי	רַגְלַיִם						CaCC
	מָתְנַי	מָתְנֵי	מָתְנַיִם						CuCC
	שִׁנַּי	שִׁנֵּי	שִׁנַּיִם						CiC²
	כַּפַּי	כַּפֵּי	כַּפַּיִם						CaC²

PARADIGM N-3. FEMININE NOUNS FROM CvCC

PLURAL				SINGULAR				
-cvc	-v/-cv	cstr.	abs.	-cvc	-v/-cv	cstr.	abs.	Type
מַלְכוֹתֵיהֶם	מַלְכוֹתַי	מַלְכוֹת	מְלָכוֹת	מַלְכַּתְכֶם	מַלְכָּתִי	מַלְכַּת	מַלְכָּה	CaCCat
		חֶרְפּוֹת	חֲרָפוֹת	חֶרְפַּתְכֶם	חֶרְפָּתִי	חֶרְפַּת	חֶרְפָּה	CiCCat
	חָרְבוֹתַי	חָרְבוֹת	חֳרָבוֹת	חָרְבַּתְכֶם	חָרְבָּתִי	חָרְבַּת	חָרְבָּה	CuCCat
	חֻקּוֹתַי	חֻקּוֹת	חֻקּוֹת	חֻקַּתְכֶם	חֻקָּתִי	חֻקַּת	חֻקָּה	CuC²at
	כִּלְיוֹתַי	כִּלְיוֹת	כְּלָיוֹת		אִמְרָתִי		כִּלְיָה	CiCYat
שִׁפְחוֹתֵיכֶם			שְׁפָחוֹת			שִׁפְחַת	שִׁפְחָה	CiCGat
מִנְחֹתֵיכֶם	מִנְחֹתֶיךָ				מִנְחָתִי	מִנְחַת	מִנְחָה	CiCCat
			חַיּוֹת		חַיָּתִי	חַיַּת	חַיָּה	CaC²at
			חָכְמוֹת (?)		חָכְמָתִי	חָכְמַת	חָכְמָה	CuCCat
	שַׁלְוֹתַיִךְ					שַׁלְוַת	שַׁלְוָה	CaCWat

PARADIGM N-4. NOUNS WITH TWO SHORT VOWELS (CvCvC)

Type	PLURAL -cvc	PLURAL -v/-cv	PLURAL cstr.	PLURAL abs.	SINGULAR -cvc	SINGULAR -v/-cv	SINGULAR cstr.	SINGULAR abs.
CaCaC	דִּבְרֵיכֶם	דְּבָרַי	דִּבְרֵי	דְּבָרִים	דְּבַרְכֶם	דְּבָרְךָ	דְּבַר	דָּבָר
CaCiC	זִקְנֵיכֶם	זְקֵנַי	זִקְנֵי	זְקֵנִים		זְקֵנִי	זְקַן	זָקֵן[1]
CaCuC								עָמֹק[1]
CiCaC				צְלָעִים		שִׁכְבָהּ	שְׁכַב[2]	לֵבָב
CiCiC						שִׁכְמוֹ		שְׁכֶם
CuCuC					אֲמָרְכֶם	שָׁכְבְךָ	קְטֹל[2]	
GaCaC	חַכְמֵיכֶם	חֲכָמַי	חַכְמֵי	חֲכָמִים	חֲכַמְכֶם	חֲכָמִי	חֲכַם	חָכָם
GaCiC	חַצְרֵיכֶם	חֲצָרַי	חַצְרֵי	חֲצֵרִים		חֲצֵרִי	חֲצַר	חָצֵר
CaCaY	פְּנֵיכֶם	פָּנַי	פְּנֵי	פָּנִים		שָׂדְךָ	שְׂדֵה	שָׂדֶה
CiCiC						שִׁכְמוֹ		שְׁכֶם
		DUAL						
CvCvC	כַּנְפֵיכֶם	כְּנָפַי	כַּנְפֵי	כְּנָפַיִם				

[1]G50 stative
[2]G65

PARADIGM N-5. FEMININE NOUNS FROM CvCvC

Type	PLURAL -cvc	PLURAL -v/-cv	PLURAL cstr.	PLURAL abs.	SINGULAR -cvc	SINGULAR -v/-cv	SINGULAR cstr.	SINGULAR abs.
CaCaCat		צִדְקוֹתַי	צִדְקוֹת	צְדָקוֹת	צִדְקַתְכֶם	צִדְקָתִי	צִדְקַת	צְדָקָה
CaCiCat			בַּהֲמוֹת	בְּהֵמוֹת			בֶּהֱמַת	בְּהֵמָה
CaGaCat			עַטְרוֹת	עֲטָרוֹת	זַעֲקַתְכֶם	זַעֲקָתִי	זַעֲקַת	זְעָקָה
GaCaCat			צַלְעוֹת	צְלָעוֹת			עֲטֶרֶת	עֲטָרָה
CaCiCt		יְרֵכַי		יְרֵכַיִם				חֲבֶרֶת
ʾaCiNt						אֲמִתּוֹ		אֱמֶת
CiCuCt								נְחֹשֶׁת
CiCaCat							שִׁכְבַת	שְׁכָבָה
		DUAL						
	שִׂפְתֵיכֶם	שְׂפָתַי	שִׂפְתֵי	שְׂפָתַיִם				

PARADIGM N-6. NOUNS WITH A LONG AND A SHORT VOWEL (CṽCvC)

PLURAL				SINGULAR				
-cvc	-v/-cv	cstr.	abs.	-cvc	-v/-cv	cstr.	abs.	Type
עוֹלְמֵיכֶם	עוֹלָמַי	עוֹלְמֵי	עוֹלָמִים	עוֹלַמְכֶם	עוֹלָמְךָ	עוֹלַם	עוֹלָם	CâCaC
אֹיְבֵיכֶם	אֹיְבַי	אֹיְבֵי	אֹיְבִים	אֹיִבְכֶם	אֹיְבִי	אֹיֵב	אוֹיֵב[1]	CâCiC
					מָגִנִּי	מָגֵן	מָגֵן	CâCiC
			שׁוּעָלִים		עוּגָבִי		עוּגָב	CûCaC
חֹזֵיכֶם	חֹזַי	חֹזֵי	חֹזִים	חֹזֶכֶם	חֹזְךָ	חֹזֵה	חוֹזֶה	CâCaY
					בֹּרַאֲךָ		בּוֹרֵא	CâCaʾ
	יוֹנְקוֹתֶיהָ	יוֹנְקוֹת		יוֹנַקְתְּכֶם	יוֹנַקְתִּי	יוֹנֶקֶת	יוֹנֶקֶת	CâCiCt
	אֹמְרוֹת	קֹטְלוֹת	קוֹטְלוֹת	קוֹטַלְתְּכֶם	קוֹטַלְתִּי	קוֹטְלַת	אֹמְרָה	CâCiCat
							יוֹדַעַת	CâCiGt

[1] G50 fientive verbs

PARADIGM N-7. NOUNS WITH A SHORT AND A LONG VOWEL (CvCv̂C)

Type	PLURAL -cvc	PLURAL -v/-cv	PLURAL cstr.	PLURAL abs.	SINGULAR -cvc	SINGULAR -v/-cv	SINGULAR cstr.	SINGULAR abs.
CaCâC		גְּדוֹלֶיהָ	גְּדֹלֵי	גְּדֹלִים		גָּדְלָם	גְּדֹל	גָּדוֹל[1]
CaCîC	פְּקִידֵיכֶם	פְּקִידַי	פְּקִידֵי	פְּקִידִים	פְּקִידְכֶם	פְּקִידְךָ	פְּקִיד	פָּקִיד
CaCûC			אֱמוּנֵי	אֱמוּנִים			אֱמוּן	אֵמֻן
CiCâC	חֲמוֹרֵיהֶם	חֲמֹרֵינוּ		חֲמֹרִים		חֲמֹרְךָ	חֲמוֹר	חֲמוֹר
CiCâC	כְּתָבֵיכֶם	כְּתָבַי	כְּתָבֵי	כְּתָבִים	כְּתָבְכֶם	כְּתָבִי	כְּתָב	כְּתָב
CiCâG	אֱלֹהֵיכֶם	זְרֹעָיו	אֱלֹהֵי	אֱלֹהִים		זְרֹעֲךָ	זְרֹעַ	אֱלוֹהַּ
CiCîC			כְּסִילֵי	כְּסִילִים			כְּסִיל	כְּסִיל
CiCûC		גְּבוּלֶיךָ		גְּבוּלִים		גְּבֻלְךָ	גְּבוּל	גְּבוּל
CaCîY	עֲנִיֵּיכֶם		עֲנִיֵּי	עֲנִיִּים			עֲנִי	עָנִי
CaCî'			בְּרִיאֵי	בְּרִאִים				בָּרִיא
CaCâCat		תְּעָלֹתֶיהָ	תְּעָלוֹת	תְּעָלוֹת			תְּעָלַת	תְּעָלָה
'iCûCat	תְּבוּאֹתֵיכֶם			אֱמוּנוֹת		אֱמוּנָתִי	אֱמוּנַת	אֱמוּנָה
CaCî'at								בְּרִיאָה
CaCûG				יְדֻעִים				יָדוּעַ[2]

FEMININE

Type	PLURAL -cvc	PLURAL -v/-cv	PLURAL cstr.	PLURAL abs.	SINGULAR -cvc	SINGULAR -v/-cv	SINGULAR cstr.	SINGULAR abs.
CaCàCat			גְּדֹלוֹת	גְּדוֹלוֹת			גְּדֹלַת	גְּדוֹלָה
CaCâCat		תְּעָלוֹת	תְּעָלוֹת				תְּעָלַת	תְּעָלָה
CaCîCt				גְּבָרוֹת	גְּבִרְתְּכֶם	גְּבִרְתִּי	גְּבֶרֶת	גְּבֶרֶת
CiCâCat		זְרוֹעֹתָי	זְרוֹעוֹת			בְּשׂוֹרָי		
CiCûCat		גְּבוּרֹתֶךָ	גְּבֻלוֹת	גְּבוּרוֹת		גְּבֻלָתוֹ	גְּבוּרַת	גְּבוּלָה
'iCûCat				אֱמוּנוֹת				אֱמוּנָה

[1]Cf. G60

[2]Cf. Gp50

PARADIGM N-8. NOUNS WITH TWO LONG VOWELS (Cv̂Cv̂C)

PLURAL -cvc	PLURAL -v/-cv	PLURAL cstr.	PLURAL abs.	SINGULAR -cvc	SINGULAR -v/-cv	SINGULAR cstr.	SINGULAR abs.	Type
כִּידוֹנֵיהֶם	כִּידוֹנֶיךָ	כִּידוֹנֵי	כִּידוֹנִים	כִּידוֹנְכֶם	כִּידֹנְךָ	כִּידוֹן	כִּידוֹן	CîCâC
	סָרִיסֶיהָ	סָרִיסֵי	סָרִיסִים			סְרִיס !	סָרִיס	CâCîC
					תִּירוֹשִׁי		תִּירוֹשׁ	CîCâC
מוֹכְחֵיכֶם	מוֹכִיחֶיהָ	מוֹכִיחֵי	מוֹכִיחִים[2]	מוֹכִיחֲכֶם	הֹורִישָׁם	הוֹרִישׁ[1]	מוֹכִיחַ	caWCîC
		מֵטִיבֵי	מֵיטִבִים		הֵיטִֽבְךָ	הֵינִיק[4]	מֵיטִיב[3]	caYCîC
	מֵינִיקֹתַיִךְ		מֵינִיקוֹת		מֵינִקְתּוֹ	מֵינֶקֶת	מֵינֶקֶת	caYCaCt

[1]H65 WCC

[2]H50 WCC

[3]H50 YCC

[4]H65 YCC

PARADIGM N-9. NOUNS WITH DOUBLED MIDDLE RADICAL (CvC^{2}vC)

Type	PLURAL -cvc	PLURAL -v/-cv	PLURAL cstr.	PLURAL abs.	SINGULAR -cvc	SINGULAR -v/-cv	SINGULAR cstr.	SINGULAR abs.
CaC^{2}aC	קַטְּלֵיהֶם	קַטָּלָיו	קַטְּלֵי	קַטָּלִים	קַטַּלְכֶם	קַטָּלִי	קַטַּל	קַטָּל
CaC^{2}aC						שַׁבָּתוֹ	שַׁבַּת	שַׁבָּת
CaC^{2}iC					מַקֶּלְכֶם	מַקְּלִי	מַקֵּל	קַדֵּשׁ
CiC^{2}aC			כִּכְּרֵי	כִּכָּרִים			כִּכַּר	כִּכָּר
CaG^{2}aC			חָרָשֵׁי	חָרָשִׁים			חָרַשׁ	חָרָשׁ
CiG^{2}iC				חֵרְשִׁים				חֵרֵשׁ
CiC^{2}âC	אִכָּרֵיכֶם			אִכָּרִים				אִכָּר
CiC^{2}âC		גִּבּוֹרֶיךָ	שִׁכּוֹרֵי	שִׁכּוֹרִים			צִפּוֹר	שִׁכּוֹר
CaC^{2}îC	אַדִּירֵיהֶם	אַדִּירֶיךָ	אַדִּירֵי	אַדִּירִים		אַדִּירוֹ	אַדִּיר	אַדִּיר
CiC^{2}ûC			לִמֻּדֵי	שִׁקּוּצִים			שִׁקּוּץ	שִׁקּוּץ
CaC^{2}ûC			עַמּוּדֵי	עַמּוּדִים			עַמּוּד	עַמּוּד
FEMININE								
CaC^{2}aCat	קַטְּלוֹתֵיהֶם	קַטְּלוֹתַי	קַטְּלוֹת	קַטָּלוֹת	קַטַּלְתְּכֶם	קַטְּלָתוֹ	קַטְּלַת	קַטָּלָה
CaC^{2}aCat				טַבָּחוֹת				חַטָּאָה
CaC^{2}aCt						אַדַּרְתּוֹ	אַדֶּרֶת	אַדֶּרֶת
CaC^{2}aGt			טַבְּעוֹת	טַבָּעֹת		טַבַּעְתּוֹ		טַבַּעַת
CaC^{2}a't		חַטֹּאתָיו	חַטֹּאות	חַטָּאוֹת	חַטַּאתְכֶם	חַטָּאתִי	חַטַּאת	חַטָּאת
CiC^{2}aCt		כִּסְאוֹתָם		כִּסְאוֹת[1]		עִוַּלְתִי		עִוֶּלֶת
CuC^{2}iCt								כֻּסֶּמֶת
CuC^{2}uCt		כָּתְנֹתָם		כֻּתֳּנוֹת		כֻּתָּנְתּוֹ		כֻּתֹּנֶת
CaC^{2}uCat		חַבֻּרוֹתָי		חַבֻּרוֹת		חַבֻּרָתִי		שַׁכּוּלָה

[1]Rule 1b

PARADIGM N-10. NOUNS WITH DOUBLED THIRD RADICAL (CvCvC^2)

PLURAL				SINGULAR				
-cvc	-v/-cv	cstr.	abs.	-cvc	-v/-cv	cstr.	abs.	Type
נְמַקֵּיכֶם	נְמַקֵּינוּ	קְטַנֵּי	קְטַנִּים	נְמַקְּכֶם	קְטַנָּם	קְטַן	קָטָן	CaCaC^2
חֲמִשֵּׁיהֶם	חֲמִשָּׁיו		חֲמִשִּׁים			חֲמֵשׁ	חָמֵשׁ	CaCiC^2
	עֲנִיֶּיךָ	עֲנִיֵּי	עֲנִיִּים		עֲנִיֶּךָ		עָנִי	CaCiY^2
עֵירֻמֵּיכֶם	עֵירֻמַּיִךְ	עֵירֻמֵּי	עֲמֻקִּים	עֵירֻמְּכֶם	עֵירֻמֵּךְ	עֵירֹם	עָמוֹק	CvCuC^2
מוּסַכֵּיהֶם	מוּסַכֵּינוּ	מוּסַכֵּי	מוּסַכִּים	מוּסַכְּכֶם	מוּסַכְּךָ	מוּסַךְ	מוּסָךְ	C$\hat{v}$CaC^2
			קְטַנּוֹת			קְטַנַּת	קְטַנָּה	CaCaC^{2}at
						חֲמֶשֶׁת	חֲמִשָּׁה	CaCiC^{2}at
אֲגֻדּוֹתֵיכֶם	אֲגֻדּוֹתַי	אֲגֻדּוֹת	עֲמֻקּוֹת	אֲגֻדַּתְכֶם	גְּדוּלָּרוֹ	גְּדֻלַּת	עֲמֻקָּה	CaCuC^{2}at
אֲמִתּוֹתֵיכֶם	אֲמִתּוֹתֶיהָ	אֲמִתּוֹת	אֲמִתּוֹת	אֲמִתְּכֶם	אֲמִתִּי	אֱמֶת	אֱמֶת	CaCiNt
							עֲנִיָּה	CaCiY^{2}at
		אֳנִיּוֹת	אֳנִיּוֹת				אֳנִיָּה	CuCiY^{2}at
	עֲלִיּוֹתָיו		עֲלִיּוֹת		עֲלִיָּתוֹ	עֲלִיַּת	עֲלִיָּה	CaCiY^{2}at
			שַׁאֲנַנִּים				שַׁאֲנָן	
			רַעֲנַנִּים				רַעֲנָן	
			נַאֲפוּפִים				שַׁפְרוּר	

PARADIGM N-11. NOUNS WITH REDUPLICATION (q^{e}*taltal, qalqal*)

Type	PLURAL				SINGULAR			
	-cvc	-v/-cv	cstr.	abs.	-cvc	-v/-cv	cstr.	abs.
CaCCaC	קַלְקְלֵיכֶם	קַלְוָלַי	קַלְקְלֵי	קַלְקָלִים	קַלְקַלְכֶם	קַלְקְלִי	קַלְקַל	קַלְקָל
CaCCaC²		גַּלְגַּלָּיו	זַלְזַלֵּי	זַלְזַלִּים		זַלְזַלִּי	גַּלְגַּל	גַּלְגַּל
CuCCuC	קָדְקֳדֵיכֶם		קָדְקֳדֵי	קָדְקֳדִים	קָדְקָדְכֶם	קָדְקֳדִי	קָדְקֹד	קָדְקֹד
CuCCuCt	גֻּלְגְּלוֹתֵיהֶם	גֻּלְגְּלוֹתֶיהָ	גֻּלְגְּלוֹת	גֻּלְגְּלוֹת	גֻּלְגָּלְתְּכֶם	גֻּלְגָּלְתִּי	גֻּלְגֹּלֶת	גֻּלְגֹּלֶת
CaCCâC			כַּדְכֹּדֵי	כַּדְכֹּדִים			כַּדְכֹּד	כַּדְכֹּד
CaCCûC			בַּקְבֻּקֵי	בַּקְבֻּקִים			בַּקְבֻּק	בַּקְבֻּק
CvCaCCûC			אֲסַפְסֻפֵי	אֲסַפְסוּפִים			אֲסַפְסוּף	אֲסַפְסוּף
CvCaCCaCt								אֲדַמְדֶּמֶת
CvCaCCaC²at								יְרַקְרַקָּה

PARADIGM N-12. NOUNS WITH PREFORMATIVE ELEMENTS

PLURAL				SINGULAR				
-cvc	-v/-cv	cstr.	abs.	-cvc	-v/-cv	cstr.	abs.	Type
מִפְעֲלֵיכֶם	מִקְדָּשַׁי	מִקְדְּשֵׁי	מִקְדָּשִׁים	מִפְעַלְכֶם	מִדְבָּרָהּ	מִדְבַּר	מִדְבָּר	maCCaC
				מַאֲכַלְכֶם	מַאֲכָלוֹ	מַאֲכַל	מַאֲכָל	maGCaC
		מַלְקוֹחֵי	מַלְקוֹחִים		מַלְקוֹחוֹ	מַלְקוֹחַ	מַלְקוֹחַ	maCCâC
					מַדְרִיכוֹ	מַבְדִּיל	מַבְדִּיל	maCCîC
						מַלְבּוּשׁ	מַלְבּוּשׁ	maCCûC
מִקְרֵיכֶם	מִקְרָיו	מִקְרֵי	מִקְרִים	מִקְרְכֶם	מִקְרָהּ	מִשְׁתֵּה	מִשְׁתֶּה	maCCaY
מוֹצָאֵיהֶם	מוֹצָאָיו	מוֹשְׁבֵי	מוֹשָׁבִים	מוֹצַאֲכֶם	מוֹצָאֲךָ	מוֹשַׁב	מוֹשָׁב	maWCaC
מִסְפְּדֵיכֶם	מִסְפְּדֵינוּ	מִסְפְּדֵי	מִסְפְּדִים	מִזְבַּחֲכֶם	מִזְבְּחִי	מִזְבַּח	מִזְבֵּחַ	miCCiC
					מַטּוֹ	מַטֵּה	מַטֶּה	maNCaY
		מָעֻזֵּי	מָעֻזִּים	מָעֻזְּכֶם	מָעֻזִּי	מָעוֹז	מָעוֹז	maCuC²
		מַמְלְכוֹת	מַמְלָכוֹת		מַמְלַכְתִּי	מַמְלֶכֶת	מַמְלָכָה	maCCaCat
		מִלְחֲמוֹת	מִלְחָמוֹת		מִלְחַמְתְּךָ	מִלְחֶמֶת	מִלְחָמָה	miCCaCat
מִשְׁמְרוֹתֵיהֶם	מִשְׁמְרוֹתָם	מִשְׁמְרוֹת	מִשְׁמָרוֹת		מִשְׁמַרְתִּי	מִשְׁמֶרֶת	מִשְׁמֶרֶת	miCCaCt
		תּוֹשָׁבֵי	תּוֹשָׁבִים		תּוֹשָׁבְךָ	תּוֹשַׁב	תּוֹשָׁב	taWCaC
							תֵּימָן	taYCaC
							תַּשְׁבֵּץ	taCCiC
תַּלְמִידֵיהֶם	תַּלְמִידָיו	תַּלְמִידֵי	תַּלְמִידִים		תַּלְמִידוֹ	תַּלְמִיד	תַּלְמִיד	taCCîC1
תַּמְרוּקֵיהֶן	תַּמְרוּקֶיהָ	תַּמְרוּקֵי	תַּמְרוּקִים				תַּמְרוּק	taCCûC
					תּוֹחַלְתִּי	תּוֹחֶלֶת	תּוֹחֶלֶת	taWCaCt
					תִּפְאַרְתִּי	תִּפְאֶרֶת	תִּפְאֶרֶת[1]	tiCCaCt
	תּוֹרֹתַי		תּוֹרוֹת		תֹּרָתוֹ	תּוֹרַת	תּוֹרָה	taWCaY
		תְּהִלּוֹת	תְּהִלֹּת		תְּהִלָּתְךָ	תְּהִלַּת	תְּהִלָּה	tvCiC²at
				הַלְבִּישְׁכֶם	הַלְבִּיוֹי	הַאֲכִיל	הַלְבִּישׁ[2]	haCCîC
				הוֹרִידְכֶם	הוֹרִידִי	הוֹרִיד	הוֹרִיד[2]	haWCîC
					הִוָּסֶרְכֶם	הִשָּׁלְחוֹ	הִשָּׁלֵחַ[3]	hinCaCiC
					הִסֹּגִי	הִכּוֹן[3]		hinCûC
				הִשְׁתַּכֶּרְכֶם	הִתְמַלַּאֲךָ	הִתְגַּלַּח[4]		hitCaC²iC
				הִתְגַּלּוֹתְךָ		הִתְגַּלּוֹת[4]		hitCaC²aY

[1]תִּפְאָרָה

[2]H65

[3]N65

[4]HtD65

PARADIGM N-13. NOUNS WITH SUFFORMATIVE ELEMENTS

Type	PLURAL -cvc	PLURAL -v/-cv	PLURAL cstr.	PLURAL abs.	SINGULAR -cvc	SINGULAR -v/-cv	SINGULAR cstr.	SINGULAR abs.
CvCCôn	פַּעֲמוֹנֵיכֶם	פַּעֲמוֹנָיו	פַּעֲמֹנֵי	פַּעֲמוֹנִים	חֶשְׁבּוֹנְכֶם	חֶשְׁבּוֹנָהּ	חֶשְׁבּוֹן	חֶשְׁבּוֹן
CvC²vCôn	זִכְרֹנֵיכֶם			גִּלְיֹנִים		חֶזְיֹנוֹ	חֶזְיוֹן	חִזָּיוֹן
CvCYôn					רְצֹנְכֶם	רְצוֹנוֹ	רְצוֹן	רָצוֹן
Ci'Côn				רִאשֹׁנִים				רִאשׁוֹן
CîCôn								חִיצוֹן
Ci'Cônat				רִאשֹׁנוֹת				רִאשֹׁנָה
taCCût	תַּרְבֻּיוֹתֵיכֶם	תַּרְבֻּיוֹתֶיךָ	תַּרְבֻּיוֹת	תַּרְבֻּיוֹת	תַּרְבּוּתְכֶם	תַּרְבּוּתָהּ	תַּרְבּוּת	תַּרְבּוּת
CaCCût						מַלְכוּתוֹ		מַלְכוּת
CâCût						גָּלוּתֵינוּ		גָּלוּת
CaCîCût							יְדִדוּת	
CvCît	בְּכִיּוֹתֵיהֶם	בְּכִיּוֹתַי	בְּכִיּוֹת	בְּכִיּוֹת	בְּכִיתְכֶם	בְּכִיתוֹ	בְּכִית	בְּכִית
maCCît					מַרְבִּיתָם	מַרְבִּית	מַרְבִּית	תאֹם
taCCît						תַּעֲנִיתִי	תַּבְנִית	תַּרְבִּית
CvCiCît						שְׁאֵרִיתֵךְ	שְׁאֵרִית	שְׁאֵרִית
CiC²ît				עִלִּיּוֹת				עִלִּית
CaCCî				רַגְלִים				רַגְלִי
CiCCî				עִבְרִים				עִבְרִי
CvCîCî				שְׁלִשִׁים				שְׁלִישִׁי
CvCîCît						שְׁלִשְׁתֵּךְ	רְבִעִית	שְׁבִיעִית
CaCCônî								אַדְמֹנִי
CiCCîyat				עִבְרִיּוֹת				עִבְרִיָּה
CaCCònî				קַדְמֹנִים				קַדְמֹנִי
CaCCônît				קַדְמֹנִיּוֹת				קַדְמֹנִית

PARADIGM N-14. IRREGULAR FORMATIONS

PLURAL					SINGULAR				
-cvc	-cv	-v	cstr.	abs.	-cvc	-cv	-v	cstr.	abs.
אֲבֹתֵיכֶם	אֲבֹתֵינוּ	אֲבֹתַי	אֲבוֹת	אָבוֹת	אֲבִיכֶם	אָבִיהָ	אָבִי	אֲבִי	אָב
אֲחֵיהֶם	אַחֵינוּ	אֶחָיו	אֲחֵי	אַחִים	אֲחִיהֶם	אָחִיהָ	אָחִיךָ	אֲחִי	אָח
אַחְיוֹתֵיהֶם		אַחְיוֹתַי	אַחְיוֹת	אֲחָיוֹת	אֲחֹתָם	אֲחוֹתְךָ	אֲחֹתִי	אֲחוֹת	אָחוֹת
אַנְשֵׁיהֶן	אֲנָשֵׁינוּ	אֲנָשָׁיו	אַנְשֵׁי	אֲנָשִׁים			אִישִׁי	אִישׁ	אִישׁ
נְשֵׁיהֶם	נָשֵׁינוּ	נָשָׁיו	נְשֵׁי	נָשִׁים		אִשְׁתְּךָ	אִשְׁתִּי	אֵשֶׁת	אִשָּׁה
אַמְהֹתֵיכֶם	אַמְהֹתֶיהָ	אַמְהֹתַי	אַמְהוֹת	אֲמָהוֹת		אֲמָתְךָ	אֲמָתִי	אֲמַת	אָמָה
בָּתֵּיהֶן	בָּתֶּיךָ		בָּתֵּי	בָּתִּים	בֵּיתְכֶם	בֵּיתְךָ	בֵּיתוֹ	בֵּית	בַּיִת
בְּנֵיכֶם	בָּנֶיךָ	בָּנַי	בְּנֵי	בָּנִים		בִּנְךָ	בְּנִי	בֶּן־	בֵּן
בְּנֹתֵיכֶם	בְּנֹתֶיהָ	בְּנֹתַי	בְּנוֹת	בָּנוֹת	בִּתְּכֶם	בִּתֵּךְ	בִּתִּי	בַּת	בַּת
יְמֵיהֶם	יָמֶיהָ	יָמַי	יְמֵי	יָמִים			יוֹמוֹ	יוֹם	יוֹם
מֵימֵיהֶם	מֵימֶיךָ	מֵימַי	מֵי	מַיִם					מַי
עָרֵיהֶם	עָרֶיךָ	עָרַי	עָרֵי	עָרִים		עִירְךָ	עִירִי	עִיר	עִיר
				פִּיּוֹת	פִּיכֶם	פִּיךָ	פִּי	פִּי	פֶּה
רָאשֵׁיהֶם	רָאשֵׁינוּ	רָאשָׁיו	רָאשֵׁי	רָאשִׁים	רֹאשְׁכֶם	רֹאשָׁהּ	רֹאשִׁי	רֹאשׁ	רֹאשׁ
שְׁמוֹתָם			שְׁמוֹת	שֵׁמוֹת	שִׁמְכֶם	שִׁמְךָ	שְׁמוֹ	שֵׁם	שֵׁם
שְׁמֵיכֶם	שָׁמֶיךָ	שָׁמָיו	שְׁמֵי	שָׁמַיִם					שָׁמַי

Part 4
BASIC VOCABULARY

A BASIC VOCABULARY

This list contains all the Hebrew words that occur 15 times or more in the Hebrew Bible, with the exception of personal and place names, arranged alphabetically. Meanings are generally taken from Brown-Driver-Briggs (BDB), but I have edited where I felt it to be more useful. I have translated all pointed forms literally (e.g. אָמַר *he said,* בּוֹא *to enter*, etc.). References to BDB are given except where they are the same as the previous entry. Numbering follows *Strong's Concordance* and the recent edition of *The Englishman's Hebrew Concordance.* Notes such as H_{229} indicate frequency *in that stem.* Other frequency symbols are explained in the table below.

A1	> 200x	C1	40-49x	E1	17-19x
A2	100-199x	C2	30-39x	E2	15-16x
B1	70- 99x	D1	25-29x	F1	13-14x
B2	50- 69x	D2	20-24x	F2	12x

א

1 A1 אָב *father, originator, ancestor* BDB 3
7 A1 אָבַד *he perished, was lost, vanished;* D *he killed,* H *he put to death* BDB 1
14 B2 אָבָה *he was willing, consented* BDB 2
34 B2 אֶבְיוֹן *needy, poor*
47 E1 אַבִּיר *strong, valiant; stallion*
56 C2 אָבַל *he mourned, lamented* (G_{18}, HtD_{19}) BDB 5
60 D2 אֵבֶל *mourning rites, funeral ceremony* BDB 5
69 A1 אֶבֶן *stone, precious stone, weight* BDB 6
113 A2 אָדוֹן *lord, master* BDB 10f.
117 D1 אַדִּיר *majestic* BDB 12
120 A1 אָדָם *man, mankind* BDB 9
127 A1 אֲדָמָה *ground, land, earth* BDB 9
134 B2 אֶדֶן *base, pedestal,* mostly pl. BDB 10
157 A1 אָהֵב *he loved*; often G50 *friend,* D50 *lover* BDB 12
160 C2 אַהֲבָה *love* BDB 13
162 E2 אֲהָהּ *alas! oh! ah!*
168 A1 אֹהֶל *tent, dwelling* BDB 13
176 A1 אוֹ *or, or rather, or if, if perchance* BDB 14f.
178 E1 אוֹב *familiar spirit, necromancer; skin-bottle* BDB 15
183 D1 אָוָה *he desired, longed after* (D, HtD) BDB 16
188 D2 אוֹי *woe!* BDB 17
191 D1 אֱוִיל *foolish, fool* BDB17
194 C1 אוּלַי *peradventure, if perhaps* BDB 19
197 E1 אוּלָם *porch* BDB 17
199 E1 אוּלָם *but indeed* BDB 19
200 D1 אִוֶּלֶת *folly* BDB 17
202 E1 אוֹן *wealth, strength, vigor* BDB 20
205 B1 אָוֶן *trouble, iniquity, vanity, sorrow* BDB 19f
215 C1 אוֹר *it became light;* H *it gave light, lighted up, he made to shine* BDB 21
216 A2 אוֹר *light, luminary* BDB 21
226 B1 אוֹת *sign, symbol, miracle* BDB 16f.
227 B1 אָז *at that time, then* BDB 23
238 C1 אָזַן *he gave ear, listened, heard* (H) BDB 24

241 A2 אֹזֶן *ear* BDB 23f.
247 E2 אָזַר *he put on, girded* BDB 25
249 E1 אֶזְרָח *native, indigenous* BDB 280
251 A1 אָח *brother*; אִישׁ אָחִיו *one ... another* BDB 26
259 A1 אֶחָד *one*; pl. *a few* BDB 25f.
268 C1 אָחוֹר *the back part, backwards* BDB 30
269 A2 אָחוֹת *sister* BDB 27f.
270 B2 אָחַז *he took hold, grasped, held, seized* BDB 28
272 B2 אֲחֻזָּה *possession* BDB 28
309 E1 אָחַר *he tarried*; D *he hindered, caused delay*
310 A1 אַחַר *behind, after, afterwards*; often pl. אַחֲרֵי BDB 29f.
312 A2 אַחֵר *another, different, strange* BDB 29
314 B2 אַחֲרוֹן *following, behind, hindermost, last* BDB 30
319 B2 אַחֲרִית *end, latter, posterity* BDB 31
335 C1 אֵי *where?*; often + pron. suff. BDB 32
339 C2 אִי *island, coastland, region* BDB 15
340 A1 אָיַב *he was hostile (to)*; G50 *enemy* BDB 33
343 D2 אֵיד *calamity, distress* BDB 15
346 C1 אַיֵּה *where?* BDB 32
349 B2 אֵיךְ *how? why? how!* BDB 32
351 D2 אֵיכָה *how? in what manner? where?*
352 A2 אַיִל *ram; leader, chief* BDB 17f.
352aD2 אַיִל *pillar* BDB 18
361 E2 אֵילָם only Ezek. *porch*; cf. #199 BDB 19
367 E1 אֵימָה *terror, dread, fright* BDB 33
369 A1 אַיִן, usually cstr. אֵין *nothing, is not, was not, etc*, often with pron. suff. BDB 34f.
370 E1 אַיִן only in מֵאַיִן *whence? from where?* BDB 32
374 C2 אֵיפָה *ephah*, a barley-measure BDB 35
376 A1 אִישׁ *man, male* (not woman, not animal, not God) BDB 35f.
389 A2 אַךְ *surely, only*; see BDB 36
398 A1 אָכַל *he ate, fed* BDB 37f.
400 C1 אֹכֶל *food* BDB 38
402 E1 אָכְלָה *'oklā^h^, food, eating* (mostly in Ezek.) BDB 38
403 E1 אָכֵן *surely, but indeed, nevertheless*
408 A1 אַל *not*, see BDB 39
410 A1 אֵל *God, god* BDB 42f.
413 A1 אֶל, אֶל־ *to, towards, into, see* BDB 39ff.
423 C2 אָלָה *oath, curse* BDB 46
428 A1 אֵלֶּה *these* BDB 41
430 A1 אֱלֹהִים *God; gods, judges, angels*, see BDB 43f.
433 B2 אֱלוֹהַּ *God, god* BDB 43
441 B2 אַלּוּף *chief, chiliarch* BDB 49
457 D2 אֱלִיל *worthless, worthless thing, idol* BDB 47
481 D2 אָלַם N *he was dumb, mute;* D *he bound* BDB 47f.
490 B2 אַלְמָנָה *widow* BDB 48
504 A1 אֶלֶף *thousand; clan* BDB 48f.
517 A1 אֵם *mother* BDB 51f.
518 A1 אִם *if;* also interrog. part. BDB 49f.

519 B2 אָמָה *handmaid* BDB 51
520 A1 אַמָּה *cubit*, length of forearm BDB 52
530 C1 אֱמוּנָה *faithfulness, fidelity, firmness* BDB 53
535 E2 אָמַל *it was weak*, Dp *he grew feeble, languished* BDB 51
539 A2 אָמַן G50 *one who or that which supports*, N *he confirmed, established, was reliable, faithful*, H *he stood firm, trusted, believed;* see BDB 52.
543 D1 אָמֵן *surely, verily, Amen* BDB 53
553 C1 אָמֵץ *he was strong*, D *he strengthened, hardened*, H *he exhibited strength*, HtD *he strengthened himself, determined* BDB 54f.
559 A1 אָמַר *he said*, N *he was called* BDB 55f.
561 B2 אֹמֶר *word, saying, utterance* BDB 56
571 A2 אֱמֶת *faithfulness, stability, truth* BDB 54
572 E2 אַמְתַּחַת *sack* BDB 607
575 D1 אָנָה, אָן *whither? to where? where?* BDB 33
582 C1 אֱנוֹשׁ, pl. אֲנָשִׁים *man, mankind, persons* BDB 60
587 A2 אֲנַחְנוּ *we* BDB 59
589 A1 אֲנִי *I* (1st com. sg. pron.) BDB 58f.
595 A1 אָנֹכִי *I*, see BDB 59
615 E2 אַסִּיר, אָסִיר *prisoner(s)* BDB 64 [BDB 62f.
622 A1 אָסַף *he gathered, removed*, N *they assembled, gathered, were gathered (died)* ↑
631 B1 אָסַר *he bound, imprisoned* BDB 63f.
637 A2 אַף *also* BDB 64f.
639 A1 אַף *nose, anger* (root *'np*) BDB 60
644 D1 אָפָה *he baked* BDB 66
646 B2 אֵפוֹד *ephod* BDB 65
650 E1 אָפִיק *channel* BDB 67
651 D2 אֲפֵלָה, אֹפֶל *darkness, gloom, calamity* BDB 66
657 C1 אֶפֶס *end, nought, none at all;* אֶפֶס כִּי *howbeit* BDB 67
665 D2 אֵפֶר *ashes* BDB 68
676 C2 אֶצְבַּע *finger* BDB 840
681 B2 אֵצֶל *beside, proximity* BDB 69
693 C1 אָרַב *he lay in wait for, ambushed* BDB 70
697 D2 אַרְבֶּה *locust* BDB 916
703 A1 אַרְבַּע *four* BDB 916f.
705 A2 אַרְבָּעִים *forty* BDB 917
713 C2 אַרְגָּמָן *purple* BDB 71
727 A1 אֲרוֹן *chest, ark (of covenant)* BDB 75
730 B1 אֶרֶז *cedar* BDB 72
734 B2 אֹרַח *way, path; traveller* BDB 73
738 B1 אַרְיֵה, אֲרִי *lion* BDB 71
748 C2 אָרַךְ *it was long*, H *he prolonged, it grew long* BDB 73
750 E2 אָרֵךְ *long* BDB 74
753 B1 אֹרֶךְ *length* BDB 73
776 A1 אֶרֶץ *earth, land, country* BDB 75f.
779 B2 אָרַר *he cursed, called a curse upon* BDB 76
784 A1 אֵשׁ *fire* BDB 77
801 B2 אִשֶּׁה *an offering made by fire* BDB 77f.
802 A1 אִשָּׁה *woman, female* BDB 61

817 C1 אָשָׁם *guilt, guilt-offering* BDB 79f.
819 E1 אַשְׁמָה *guiltiness, wrong-doing, guilt* BDB 80
833 E2 אָשַׁר *he went straight,* D *he went straight. set right, pronounced happy* BDB 80
834 A1 אֲשֶׁר *which, where,* see BDB 81-84
802 A1 אֵשֶׁת *woman,* see #802 BDB 61
853 A1 אֵת, אֶת־, –אֹת sign of def. dir. obj. BDB 84f.
854 A1 אֵת, –אִת *with,* see BDB 85ff.
857 D2 אָתָה *he came,* H *he brought* BDB 87
859 A1 אַתְּ *you, thou* (fem. sg.) BDB 61
859bA1 אַתָּה *you, thou* (masc. sg.) BDB 61
859cA1 אַתֶּם *you* (masc. pl.) BDB 61
860 C2 אָתוֹן *she-ass* BDB 87

ב

A1 –בְּ *in, with, by* bound prep., see BDB 88-91
875 C2 בְּאֵר *dug-well, pit* BDB 91
877 בֹּאר *cistern,* see #953
887 E1 בָּאַשׁ *it had a bad smell, stank* BDB 92f.
898 B2 בָּגַד *he dealt treacherously/deceitfully* BDB 93
899 A1 בֶּגֶד *garment, covering* (*biḡd-*)
905 A2 בַּד *alone, separation,* see לְבַד BDB 94
906 D2 בַּד *white linen* (mostly Lev. Ezk.) BDB 94
906bD2 בַּדִּים *parts, members, rods, poles*
914 C1 בָּדַל H *he divided, separated;* N *he separated, withdrew* BDB 95
926 C2 בָּהַל N *he was terrified, dismayed;* D H *he terrified, hastened* BDB 96
929 A1 בְּהֵמָה *animal, beast, cattle* BDB 96
935 A1 בּוֹא *to enter, come in, go in;* H *bring in,* see BDB 97ff.
953 B2 בּוֹר *pit, cistern, well,* cf. #877 BDB 92
954 A2 בּוֹשׁ *he was ashamed,* H *he made ashamed* BDB 101f.
957 D1 בַּז *spoil, plunder, robbery* (*bizzô*) BDB 103
959 C1 בָּזָה *he despised, regarded with contempt* BDB 102
962 C1 בָּזַז *he plundered, spoiled*
970 C1 בָּחוּר *young man* BDB 104
974 C2 בָּחַן *he examined, tried* BDB 103
977 A2 בָּחַר *he chose, tested* BDB 104f.
982 A2 בָּטַח *he trusted, was confident;* H *he made secure* BDB 105
983 C1 בֶּטַח *security, securely*
990 B1 בֶּטֶן *belly, womb, body* BDB 105f. (*biṭnēḵ*)
995 A2 בִּין *he discerned, perceived:* N *he was discerning, intelligent;* H *he understood, gave understanding;* HtL *he was attentive, considered diligently, showed himself discerning* BDB 106
996 A1 בֵּין *between,* see BDB 107
998 C2 בִּינָה *understanding,* see BDB 108
1002 E1 בִּירָה *castle, palace, citadel*
1004 A1 בַּיִת *house,* see BDB 108ff.
1058 A2 בָּכָה *he wept, bewailed* BDB 113
1060 A2 בְּכוֹר *first-born* BDB 114

1061 E1 בִּכּוּרִים *first-fruits* BDB 114
1065 C2 בְּכִי *weeping* BDB 113
1062 E2 בְּכֹרָה *right of first-born, birthright* BDB 114
1077 B2 בַּל *not* (31x in Ps.) BDB 115
1086 E2 בָּלָה *it wore out, became old,* D *he consumed, used, wore out* BDB 115
1097 B2 בְּלִי *not, without,* see BDB 115f.
1100 D1 בְּלִיַּעַל *worthless, good-for-nothing, worthlessness* BDB 116
1101 C1 בָּלַל *he mixed, confounded, mingled* BDB 117
1104 C1 בָּלַע *he swallowed, swallowed up* BDB 118
1107 E1 בִּלְעֲדֵי *except, apart from, besides* BDB 116
1115 A2 בִּלְתִּי *except, not*; see לְבִלְתִּי, BDB 116f.
1116 A2 בָּמָה *high place* (of worship) BDB 119
1121 A2 בֵּן *son*; see BDB 119-122
1129 A1 בָּנָה *he built* BDB 124f.
5668 C1 בַּעֲבוּר *for the sake of, in order that* BDB 721
1157 A2 בְּעַד, בַּעַד *away from, behind, about, on behalf of*; see BDB 126
1166 E2 בָּעַל *he married, was lord over* BDB 127
1167 B1 בַּעַל *owner, lord, husband, Baal* (*ba'lî*) BDB 127
1197 B1 בָּעַר *it burned* (tr. and intr.), D H *he burned, consumed* BDB 128f.
1204 E2 בָּעַת N *he was terrified*, D *he fell upon, overwhelmed* BDB 129f.
1214 E2 בָּצַע *he cut off, gained by violence*; D *he finished* BDB 130
1215 D2 בֶּצַע *unjust gain, profit from violence*
1219 D1 בָּצַר *he cut off, enclosed*; D *he fortified, made inaccessible* BDB 130f.
1234 B2 בָּקַע *he cleft, split, broke open* BDB 131f.
1237 D2 בִּקְעָה *valley, plain* BDB 132
1241 A2 בָּקָר *herd, large cattle* BDB 133
1242 A2 בֹּקֶר *morning,* see BDB 133f.
1245 A1 בִּקֵּשׁ D *he sought* BDB 134
1254 B2 בָּרָא *he created, fashioned* BDB 135
1259 D1 בָּרָד *hail, hailstone* BDB 135f.
1265 D2 בְּרוֹשׁ *cypress, fir, Phoenician juniper* BDB 141
1270 B1 בַּרְזֶל *iron* BDB 137
1272 B2 בָּרַח *he passed through, fled*; H *he chased* BDB 137f.
1281 C1 בְּרִיחַ *bar, bolt* BDB 138
1285 A1 בְּרִית *covenant, contract,* see BDB 136f.
1288 A1 בָּרַךְ *he knelt, blessed* (mostly D) BDB 138f.
1290 D1 בֶּרֶךְ *knee* BDB 139
1293 B2 בְּרָכָה *blessing* BDB 139
1295 E1 בְּרֵכָה *pool, pond* BDB 140
1300 D2 בָּרָק *lightning*
1305 E1 בָּרַר *he was pure, purified, cleansed* BDB 140f.
1310 D1 בָּשַׁל *it grew ripe, he boiled* (mostly D) BDB 143
1314 B2 בֹּשֶׂם, בֶּשֶׂם *spice, balsam* BDB 141f.
1322 C2 בֹּשֶׁת *shame, shameful thing* BDB 102
1319 D2 בִּשֵּׂר D *he announced/bore good news* BDB 142
1320 A1 בָּשָׂר *flesh*
1323 A1 בַּת (< *bint*) *daughter* BDB 123
1330 B1 בְּתוּלָה *unmarried woman, virgin* BDB 143f.

ג

1346 E1 גַּאֲוָה *majesty, pride* BDB 144
1347 C1 גָּאוֹן *exaltation, majesty, pride*
1350 A2 גָּאַל *he redeemed, acted as kinsman (gô'ēl)* BDB 145
1353 E2 גְּאֻלָּה *redemption,* see BDB 145
1361 C2 גָּבַהּ *it was high, he was exalted* BDB 146f.
1363 E1 גֹּבַהּ *height, haughtiness* BDB 147
1364 C2 גָּבֹהַּ *high, exalted, haughty*
1366 A1 גְּבוּל *border, boundary, territory* BDB 147f.
1368 A2 גִּבּוֹר *strong, mighty, hero, mighty man* BDB 150
1369 B2 גְּבוּרָה *strength, might, valor*
1389 B2 גִּבְעָה *hill* BDB 149
1396 D1 גָּבַר *he was strong*; D, H *he made strong, confirmed*
1397 B2 גֶּבֶר *man* (not woman), *male* BDB 149f.
1406 C2 גַּג *roof, top* BDB 150f.
1416 C2 גְּדוּד *band, troop, foray* BDB 151
1419 A1 גָּדוֹל *great, greatness* BDB 152f.
1423 E1 גְּדִי *kid, young goat* BDB 152
1431 A2 גָּדַל *he grew up, became great*; D *he made great*; H *he magnified, did great things*
1438 D2 גָּדַע *he hewed down, cut off* BDB 154
1471 A1 גּוֹי *nation, people, gentile* BDB 156
1473 C1 גּוֹלָה *exile, captivity, exiles* BDB 163
1478 D2 גָּוַע *he expired, perished, died* BDB 157
1481 A2 גּוּר *to sojourn, dwell* BDB 157
1486 B1 גּוֹרָל *lot, portion* BDB 174
1494 E2 גָּזַז *he sheared, cut off* BDB 159
1497 C2 גָּזַל *he tore away, seized, robbed* BDB 159f.
1513 E1 גַּחֶלֶת, גֶּחָלִים *coal, glowing coals/stones* BDB 160f.
1516 D2 גַּיְא, גַּי *valley* BDB 161
1523 C1 גִּיל, גּוּל *he exulted, rejoiced* BDB 162
1530 C2 גַּל *heap of stones, wave of sea* BDB 164
1540 A2 גָּלָה *he uncovered, revealed, removed, went into exile* BDB 162f.
1544 C1 גִּלּוּל pl. *idols, amulets* (39x in Ezk.) BDB 165
1547 E2 גָּלוּת *exile, captivity; exiles* BDB 163
1548 D2 גָּלַח D *he shaved (off)* BDB 164
1556 E1 גָּלַל *he rolled, rolled away*
1571 A1 גַּם *also, moreover, even, yea* BDB 168f.
1576 E1 גְּמוּל *dealing, recompence, benefit* BDB 168
1580 D2 גָּמַל *he dealt fully, bountifully, recompensed, she weaned*
1581 B2 גָּמָל *camel*
1588 B2 גַּן (*gann-*) *garden* BDB 171
1589 C2 גָּנַב *he stole, stole away* BDB 170
1590 E1 גַּנָּב *thief* (13x in Ex. 22)
1606 E2 גְּעָרָה *rebuke* BDB 172
1612 B2 גֶּפֶן *vine*
1616 B1 גֵּר *stranger, sojourner,* see BDB 158
1624 E2 גָּרָה D HtD *he stirred up strife, engaged in strife* BDB 173
1637 C2 גֹּרֶן *threshing-floor* BDB 175

1639 D2 גָּרַע *he diminished, restrained, withdrew*

1644 C1 גָּרַשׁ *he drove out/away, cast out* BDB 176f.

1653 C2 גֶּשֶׁם *rain* BDB 177

ד

1687 E2 דְּבִיר *innermost room of temple* BDB 184

1692 B2 דָּבַק *he clung to, kept close to* BDB 179f.

1696 A1 דָּבַר *he spoke* (mostly D) see BDB 180ff.

1697 A1 דָּבָר *speech, word, thing, matter;* see BDB 182ff.

1698 C1 דֶּבֶר *pestilence, plague* BDB 184

1706 B2 דְּבַשׁ *honey* BDB 185

1709 E1 דָּג *fish*

1710 E2 דָּגָה *fish*

1715 C1 דָּגָן *grain, corn* BDB 186

1730 B2 דּוֹד *loved one, beloved; uncle, friend,* see BDB 187

1777 D1 דִּין *to judge, execute judgment* BDB 192

1755 A2 דּוֹר *age, generation, lifetime, dwelling-place* BDB 189f.

1758 E2 דּוּשׁ, דִּישׁ *to tread, thresh, trample* BDB 190

1767 C2 דַּי *enough,* see BDB 191

1779 E1 דִּין *legal case, judgment* (17x Dt.) BDB 192

1792 E1 דָּכָא D *he crushed* BDB 193f.

1800 C1 דַּל *weak, poor, oppressed* BDB 195

1817 B1 דֶּלֶת *door, gate*

1818 A1 דָּם *blood,* pl. *blood shed in violence,* see BDB 196f.

1819 C2 דָּמָה *he resembled, was like*; D *he likened, imagined* BDB 197f.

1823 D2 דְּמוּת *likeness, pattern* (14x Ezk.) BDB 198

1826 C2 דָּמַם *he was still, silent, motionless, dumb* BDB 198f.

1832 D2 דִּמְעָה *tears, weeping* (mostly Jer., Pss.)

1847 B1 דַּעַת *knowledge, discernment,* see BDB 395f. (40x Prov.)

1864 E1 דָּרוֹם *south* (12x Ezk.) BDB 204f.

1869 B2 דָּרַךְ *he tread, marched* BDB 201f.

1870 A1 דֶּרֶךְ *way, road, manner* BDB 202ff.

1875 A2 דָּרַשׁ *he sought, inquired, consulted* BDB 205

1880 E2 דֶּשֶׁן *fat, fatness, ashes mixed with fat* BDB 206

1881 D2 דָּת *decree, law, usage* (Persian loan-word)

ה

A1 הַ· *the* (def. art.), see BDB206-09

A1 הֲ— interrog. part., see BDB 209f.

A1 —ָהּ *her* (pron. suf. s1)

A1 —ָה *to, at,* loc. part.

1892 B1 הֶבֶל *breath, vapor, vanity* (37x Eccl.) BDB 210f.

1897 D1 הָגָה *he growled, groaned, uttered, mused* BDB 211

1926 C2 הָדָר *ornament, splendor, glory* BDB 214

1931 A1 הוּא *he, that,* see BDB 214ff.

1931bA1 הִיא (Pent. הִוא) *she, that,* see BDB 214ff.

1935 D2 הוֹד *splendor, majesty, vigor* BDB 217

1942 E1 הַוָּה *ruin, destruction, desire*

1945 C1 הוֹי *woe! alas!* (21x Is.) BDB 222f.

1961 A1 הָיָה *he was, became, it happened,* see BDB 224-28

1964 B1 הֵיכָל *temple, palace* BDB 228
1969 D2 הִין *hin* (liquid measure; 12x Num.)
1973 E2 הָלְאָה *onwards, further, out there* BDB 229
1980 A1 הָלַךְ *he walked, went, came,* see BDB 229-37
1984 A2 הָלַל *he was boastful,* D *he praised* BDB 237ff.
1992 A1 הֵם, הֵמָּה *they, those* (m.) BDB 241f.
A1 ־הֶם *their, them* (pron. suf. s5)
1993 C2 הָמָה *he murmured, growled, roared* BDB 242
1995 B1 הָמוֹן *murmur, roar, tumult, crowd* BDB 242
2004 הֵן, הֵנָּה *they, those* (f.) BDB 241f.
־הֶן *their, them* (f. pron. suf. s6)
2009 A1 הֵן, הִנֵּה *lo! behold!* BDB 243
2015 B1 הָפַךְ *he overturned, turned (back)* BDB 245f.
2022 A1 הַר *mountain, hill, hill-country* BDB 249ff.
2026 A2 הָרַג *he slew, killed,* see BDB 246f.
2029 C1 הָרָה fem. *she conceived, became pregnant* BDB 247f.
2030 E2 הָרָה *pregnant* BDB 248
2040 C1 הָרַס *he threw down, broke down* BDB 248f.

ו

A1 ־וְ *and, but,* study BDB 251-55
A1 ־וַ conv. *wāw* BDB 253f.
A1 ־וֹ *his, him* (pron. suf. s0)

ז

2063 A1 זֹאת *this* (f.) BDB 260ff.
2076 A2 זָבַח *he slaughtered for sacrifice* BDB 256f.
2077 A2 זֶבַח *sacrifice* (*zibḇ-*) BDB 257f.
2088 A1 זֶה *this* (m.) BDB 260ff.
2091 A1 זָהָב *gold* BDB 262f.
2094 D2 זָהַר H, N *he instructed, warned* (Ezk. 16x) BDB 264
2100 C1 זוּב *to flow, gush* BDB 264
2108 E2 זוּלָה (cstr. only) *except, only* BDB 265f.
2181 C2 זוֹנָה *harlot* (Dt. 25x) BDB 275
2114 B1 זוּר *to be a stranger* (mostly G50), *stranger* BDB 266
2132 C2 זַיִת *olive, olive tree* BDB 268
2142 A1 זָכַר *he remembered* BDB 269ff.
2143 D2 זֵכֶר *remembrance, memory, memorial* BDB 271
2145 B1 זָכָר *male* BDB 271
2146 D2 זִכָּרוֹן *memorial, remembrance* BDB 272
2154 D1 זִמָּה *plan, evil device, licentiousness* BDB 273
2167 C1 זָמַר D *he praised, sang praises* BDB 274
2181 B1 זָנָה *he committed fornication* BDB 275f.
2186 D2 זָנַח G H *he rejected, spurned* BDB 276
2195 D2 זַעַם *anger, indignation* BDB 276f.
2199 B1 זָעַק *he cried (out), called* BDB 277
2201 E1 זְעָקָה *outcry, cry, clamor*
2204 D1 זָקֵן *he was/became old* BDB 278
2205 A2 זָקֵן *old person, elder* BDB 278f.
2206 E1 זָקָן *beard,* (f.) *chin* BDB 278

2114 B2 זָר *strange, stranger* BDB 266
2219 C1 זָרָה *he fanned, winnowed, scattered* BDB 279f.
2220 B1 זְרֹעַ (of man) *strength* BDB 283f.
2224 E1 זָרַח *he rose, it shone, came forth* BDB 280
2232 B2 זָרַע *he scattered seed, sowed* BDB 281ff.
2233 A1 זֶרַע *seed, sowing, offspring* BDB 282f.
2236 C2 זָרַק *he tossed, threw, sprinkled* BDB 284

ח

2244 C2 חָבָא *he hid himself* BDB 285
2254 E1 חָבַל *he bound, took as pledge* BDB 286
2256 B2 חֶבֶל *cord, band, measured part*
2266 D1 חָבַר *he was joined, united,* D *he joined* BDB 287f.
2280 C2 חָבַשׁ *he bound on/up, twisted* BDB 289f.
2282 B2 חַג *feast, festival* (*ḥagg-*) BDB 290f.
2287 E2 חָגַג *he made a pilgrimage, kept a feast*
2296 C1 חָגַר *he girded himself* BDB 291f.
2308 B2 חָדַל *he ceased, it came to an end* BDB 292f.
2315 C2 חֶדֶר *chamber, room*
2319 B2 חָדָשׁ *new, recent, fresh* BDB 294
2320 A1 חֹדֶשׁ *new moon, month* BDB 294f.
7817 E1 חָוָה HtŠ *to bow down, worship* BDB 1005f.
2342 C1 חוּל, חִיל *to whirl, dance, writhe* BDB 296f.
2344 D2 חוֹל *sand* BDB 297
2346 A2 חוֹמָה *wall* (usually of city) BDB 327
2347 D2 חוּס *he pitied, looked with compassion* BDB 299
2351 A2 חוּץ *outside (city, camp, etc.), abroad* BDB 299f.
2363 D2 חוּשׁ *to make haste* BDB 301
2372 B2 חָזָה *he saw, beheld,* followed by בְּ *looked intensely* BDB 302
2374 E1 חֹזֶה *seer* BDB 302f.
2377 C2 חָזוֹן *vision, sight, divine communication* BDB 302f.
2388 A1 חָזַק *he grew strong, was firm, it was urgent;* D *he strengthened* BDB 304f.
2389 B2 חָזָק *hard, strong, firm, severe* BDB 305
2398 A1 חָטָא *he missed, went wrong, sinned*; D *he made a sin-offering* BDB 306f.
2399 C2 חֵטְא *guilt, punishment* (of sin), *offence* BDB 307f.
2400 E1 חַטָּא *sinful, sinners* BDB 308
2403 A1 חַטָּאת *sin, sin-offering,* see BDB 308ff.
2406 C2 חִטָּה *wheat, wheat-harvest* BDB 334f.
2416 A1 חַי *alive, living* (*ḥayy-*) BDB 311f.
2420 E1 חִידָה *riddle, enigma* BDB 295
2416 A2 חַיָּה *animal, wild animal, living being, life* BDB 312
2421 A1 חָיָה *he lived*; D *he quickened, made alive*; H *he preserved alive* BDB 310f.
2416 A2 חַיִּים *life, sustenance* BDB 313
2428 A1 חַיִל *power, wealth, valor; force, army* BDB 298f.
2435 D2 חִיצוֹן *outer, external* (Ezk. 17x) BDB 300
2436 C2 חֵיק, חֵק *bosom* BDB 300f.
2441 E1 חֵךְ *roof of mouth, gums, palate* BDB 335
2449 D1 חָכַם *he was wise*; D *he made wise* BDB 314
2450 A2 חָכָם *skillful, wise, clever* BDB 314f.
2451 A2 חָכְמָה *wisdom, experience, skill* BDB 315

2459 B1 חֵלֶב *fat, choice* (Lev. 47x) BDB 316f.
2461 C1 חָלָב *milk*
2470 B1 חָלָה *he became weak, was sick* BDB 317f.
2472 B2 חֲלוֹם *dream* BDB 321
2483 D2 חֳלִי *sickness* BDB 318
2474 D חַלּוֹן *window* BDB 319
2486 D2 חָלִילָה *ad profanum! far be it!* BDB 321
2490 A2 חָלַל N *he was defiled*; D *he defiled, profaned*; H *he began* BDB 320
2491 B1 חָלָל *pierced, slain* BDB 319
2498 D1 חָלַף *he passed on, away, through*; H *he changed* BDB 322
2502 C1 חָלַץ *he drew off*; D *he delivered, rescued* BDB 322
2505 B2 חָלַק *he divided, apportioned, distributed* BDB 323f.
2507 B2 חֵלֶק *portion, share, territory* BDB 324
2513 D2 חֶלְקָה *portion* (of ground)
2530 D2 חָמַד *he desired, took pleasure in* BDB 326
2532 E2 חֶמְדָּה *desire, delight, desirable*
2534 A2 חֵמָה *heat, rage, fury; poison* BDB 404f.
2543 B1 חֲמוֹר *he-ass* BDB 331
2549 C1 חֲמִישִׁי *fifth* BDB 332
2550 C1 חָמַל *he spared, had compassion* BDB 328
2552 D1 חָמַם *he was/became warm* BDB 328
2555 B2 חָמָס *violence, wrong* BDB 329
2556 E1 חָמֵץ *leaven, leavened* (mostly Exod.)
2563 E1 חֹמֶר *mortar, cement, clay* BDB 330
2568 A1 חָמֵשׁ *five* BDB 331f.
2568 A1 חֲמִשָּׁה *five*
2572 A1 חֲמִשִּׁים *fifty* BDB 332
2580 B2 חֵן *favor, grace, charm, acceptance* BDB 336
2583 A2 חָנָה *it declined, he encamped* BDB 333
2595 C1 חֲנִית *spear* BDB 333f.
2600 C2 חִנָּם *for nothing, in vain* BDB 336
2603 B1 חָנַן *he was gracious, he extended favor*
2618 A1 חֶסֶד *kindness covenant love*, see BDB 338f.
2620 C2 חָסָה *he sought refuge* BDB 340
2623 C2 חָסִיד *pious, godly, kind* BDB 339 (26x Ps.)
2637 D2 חָסֵר *he lacked, it diminished* BDB 341
2638 E1 חָסֵר *needy, lacking, in want of* (13x Prov.)
2654 B1 חָפֵץ *he delighted in, had pleasure in* BDB 342f.
2656 C2 חֵפֶץ *delight, desire, pleasure* BDB 343
2658 D2 חָפַר *he dug, searched, explored* BDB 343
2659 E1 חָפֵר *he was abashed, ashamed* BDB 344
2670 E1 חָפְשִׁי (*ḥopšî*) *free, manumitted*
2664 D2 חָפַשׂ *he searched for, thought out, tested*
2671 B2 חֵץ *arrow* BDB 346
2672 D1 חָצַב *he hewed out, divided* BDB 345
2673 E2 חָצָה *he divided, halved*
2677 A2 חֲצִי *half, middle*
2682 D2 חָצִיר *grass, green herbage* BDB 348
2689 D1 חֲצֹצְרָה *clarion, trumpet* (16x Chr.)

2691 A2 חָצֵר *enclosure, court* BDB 346f.
2706 A2 חֹק *statute, prescribed portion, decree* BDB 349
2708 A2 חֻקָּה *statute* BDB 349f.
2710 E1 חָקַק *he inscribed, cut in, decreed* BDB 349
2713 D1 חָקַר *he searched (for), explored* BDB 350
2717 C2 חָרֵב *it was dry, dried up*; H *he dried up* BDB 351
2713 D1 חָקַר *he searched (for), explored* BDB 350
2717 C2 חָרֵב *it was dry, dried up;* H he dried up BDB 351
2719 A1 חֶרֶב *sword* BDB 352f.
2721 E1 חֹרֶב *drought, parching heat* BDB 351
2723 C1 חָרְבָּה *waste, ruin, desolation* BDB 352
2729 C2 חָרַד *he was terrified, trembled, it quaked* BDB 353
2734 B1 חָרָה *it was kindled, burned* (of anger) BDB 354
2740 C1 חָרוֹן *(burning) anger* [BDB 355f.
2763 B2 חָרַם H *he banned, devoted (to a deity), exterminated, completely destroyed* ↑
2764 D1 חֵרֶם *devotion, person/place devoted* BDB 356
2778 C1 חָרַף *he reproached, taunted* (mostly D) BDB 357
2781 B1 חֶרְפָּה *reproach, taunt, contumely* BDB 357f.
2790 D1 חָרַשׁ *he engraved, plowed, devised* BDB 360
2790aC1 חָרַשׁ H *he was silent, dumb* BDB 361
2796 C2 חָרָשׁ *artisan, graver, artificer* BDB 360
2789 E1 חֶרֶשׂ *earthen vessel, potsherd*
2803 A2 חָשַׁב *he thought, devised, reckoned, regarded* BDB 362f.
2814 E2 חָשָׁה *he was silent, still* BDB 364
2821 E1 חָשַׁךְ *it grew dark* BDB 364f.
2822 B1 חֹשֶׁךְ *darkness* (lit. and fig.), see BDB 365
2833 D2 חֹשֶׁן *breast-plate, sacred pouch* (of high priest) (23x Ex.)
2820 D1 חָשַׂךְ *he withheld, kept back, restrained* BDB 362
2856 D1 חָתַם *he sealed (with a seal), sealed up* BDB 367f.
2860 D2 חָתָן *son-in-law, bridegroom* BDB 368
2865 B2 חָתַת *it was shattered, he was dismayed* BDB 369

ט

2874 E2 טֶבַח *slaughter, slaughtering* BDB 370
2876 E1 טַבָּח *cook, bodyguard* BDB 371
2881 E2 טָבַל *he dipped* (tr. and intr.)
2885 C1 טַבַּעַת *signet-ring, seal*
2889 B1 טָהוֹר *clean, pure* (Ex.-Lev. 49x) BDB 373
2891 B1 טָהֵר *he was clean, pure*; D *he cleansed* (Lev. 44x) BDB 372
2895 B1 טוֹב *he was good, pleasing* BDB 373
2896 A1 טוֹב *good, pleasant*, see BDB 373-75
2896aA2 טוֹבָה *welfare, benefit, good things* BDB 375
2905 D1 טוּר *row, course, series* BDB 377
2919 C2 טַל *dew, night-mist* BDB 378
2930 A2 טָמֵא *he was/became unclean*; D *he defiled* BDB 379
2931 B1 טָמֵא *unclean* (Lev. 46x) BDB 379f.
2932 C2 טֻמְאָה *uncleanness* (Lev. 18x) BDB 380
2934 C2 טָמַן *he hid, concealed, buried*
2945 C1 טַף *little children* BDB 381f.
2962 B2 טֶרֶם *not yet*; בְּטֶרֶם *before*, see BDB 382

2963 D1 טָרַף *he tore, rent* BDB 382f.
2964 D2 טֶרֶף *prey, food* BDB 383

2974 E1 יָאַל H *he was pleased, willing, he undertook* BDB 383f.
2986 E1 יָבַל H *he carried, carried along* BDB 384f.
3001 B2 יָבֵשׁ *it was dried up, withered* BDB 386
3018 E2 יְגִיעַ *toil, product* (of toil) BDB 388
3021 D1 יָגַע *he toiled, grew weary*
3027 A1 יָד *hand*; for many meanings see BDB 388-91
3034 A2 יָדָה H *he gave thanks, praised, confessed,* see BDB 392
3045 A1 יָדַע *he knew*; for many meanings see BDB 393ff.
3051 C2 יָהַב, only G impv. הַב *give* BDB 396
3104 D1 יוֹבֵל *ram's horn, 50th year* (Jubilee) BDB 385
3117 A1 יוֹם *day*; note usage in BDB 398-401
3119 B2 יוֹמָם *daytime, by day, daily* BDB 401
3123 C2 יוֹנָה *dove* BDB 401f.
3162 C1 יַחַד *unitedness, in union, together* BDB 403
3162bC1 יַחְדָּו *together*
3176 C1 יָחַל N *he tarried,* H *he awaited* BDB 403f.
3187 D2 יָחַשׂ HtD *he enrolled, was enrolled* (by genealogy; (15x Chr.) BDB 405
3190 A2 יָטַב *it went well,* H *he did good* BDB 405f.
3196 A2 יַיִן *wine* BDB 406
3198 B2 יָכַח H *he judged, convicted, reproved, rebuked* BDB 406f.
3201 A2 יָכֹל *he was able,* see BDB 407f.
3205 A1 יָלַד, 208x יָלְדָה *she bore, gave birth*; H *he begat* BDB 408f.
3206 B1 יֶלֶד *child, boy,* f. *girl* BDB 409
3213 C2 יָלַל H *he howled* BDB 410
3220 A1 יָם *sea; west, westward* BDB 410f.
3225 A2 יָמִין *right (hand); south* (for *orientation* you face east) BDB 411f.
3238 D2 יָנָה *he suppressed, oppressed* BDB 413
3243 D2 יָנַק *he sucked, nursed*; H *to suckle, nurse* BDB 413
3245 C1 יָסַד *he established, founded* BDB 413f.
3247 D2 יְסוֹד *foundation, base* BDB 414
3254 A1 יָסַף *he added*: H172 *to add* + inf. *to do again/more*; see BDB 414f.
3256 C1 יָסַר *he admonished, disciplined*; D *to establish, found* BDB 415f.
3259 D1 יָעַד *he appointed*; N *to meet/assemble by appointment* BDB 416f.
3276 D2 יָעַל H *he profited, benefited* BDB 418
3289 B1 יָעַץ *he advised, counseled*; N *consult together* BDB 419f.
3293 B2 יַעַר *wood, forest, thicket* BDB 420
3303 C1 יָפֶה *fair, beautiful* BDB 421
3308 E1 יֳפִי (*yōpy-*) *beauty* BDB 421
3318 A1 יָצָא *he came/went forth*; H *to bring out, produce* BDB 422-25
3320 C1 יָצַב HtD *to set/station self, take one's stand* BDB 426
3322 E2 יָצַג H *he set, placed* BDB 426
3323 D2 יִצְהָר *fresh oil* BDB 844
3332 B2 יָצַק *he poured (out), cast* BDB 427
3335 B2 יָצַר *he formed, fashioned* (21x Is. 40-55) BDB 427f.
3341 C2 יָצַת *it burned,* H *he kindled* BDB 428

3342 E2 יֶקֶב *wine-vat, wine-press* BDB 428
3366 E1 יְקָר *precious(ness), price, honor* BDB 430
3368 C2 יָקָר *precious, rare, splendid, costly* BDB 429f.
3372 A1 יָרֵא *he was afraid, feared, stood in awe* BDB 431
3374 C1 יִרְאָה *fear, reverence, awe* BDB 432
3381 A1 יָרַד *he went down, descended* BDB 432ff.
3384 B1 יָרָה *he threw, cast, shot, taught* (mostly H); [there seems to be no sound basis for distinguishing 2 roots, see BDB 434f.]
3394 D1 יָרֵחַ *moon* BDB 437
3407 B2 יְרִיעָה *curtain, tent-cloth* (43x Ex.) BDB 438
3409 B2 יָרֵךְ *thigh, loins, side* BDB 437f.
3411 D1 יַרְכָה *back, side*; du. *remote parts* BDB 438
3423 A1 יָרַשׁ *he took possession, inherited,* see BDB 439f.
3426 A2 יֵשׁ *existence of, there is/are*; often + pron. suf., see BDB 441f.
3427 A1 יָשַׁב *he sat, stayed, dwelt* BDB 442f.
3444 B1 יְשׁוּעָה *salvation, deliverance, victory* BDB 447
3462 D1 יָשֵׁן *he slept* BDB 445
3467 A1 יָשַׁע H *to deliver, save, give victory,* see BDB 446f.
3468 C2 יֶשַׁע *deliverance, salvation, safety* (20x Ps.) BDB 447
3474 D1 יָשַׁר *he was pleasing;* D *to make straight, approve,* see BDB 448
3477 A2 יָשָׁר *straight, right, upright, just,* see BDB 449
3489 D2 יָתֵד *peg, tent-pin* BDB 450
3490 C1 יָתוֹם *orphan, fatherless* BDB 450
3498 A2 יָתַר N *it was left over*; H *to leave (over), excel, have more than enough* BDB 451
3499 B1 יֶתֶר *remainder, rest, excess, pre-eminence* BDB 451f.

כ

A1 כְּ– *like, as;* note carefully usage in BDB 453ff.
A1 ךָ– *your, you* (m.sg. pron.suf. s2)
A1 ךְ– *your, you* (f.sg. pron. suf. s3)
כַּאֲשֶׁר *according as, in so far as, when,* see BDB 455 [BDB 457f.
3513 A2 כָּבֵד *he was heavy,* N *to be honored,* D *to honor, glorify,* H *to make heavy* ↑
3515 C1 כָּבֵד *heavy, burdensome, grievous* BDB 458
3518 D2 כָּבָה *it was quenched, extinguished,* D to quench BDB 459
3519 A1 כָּבוֹד *glory, honor,* see BDB 458
3526 B2 כָּבַס D *he washed* (31x Lev.) BDB 460
3533 E2 כָּבַשׁ *he subdued, dominated, brought into bondage* BDB 461
3532 A2 כֶּבֶשׂ *lamb* BDB 455
3537 E1 כַּד *water-jar* (9x Gen. 24)
3541 A1 כֹּה *thus, here, till now,* see BDB 462
3547 D2 כָּהַן D *to act as priest* (12x Ex.) BDB 464
3548 A1 כֹּהֵן *priest* BDB 463f.
3556 C2 כּוֹכָב *star* BDB 456f.
3557 C2 כּוּל *to comprehend*; mostly R *to sustain, support* BDB 465
3559 A1 כּוּן N *to be established, fixed, firm, proper*; H *to establish, make firm/ready; to set up, establish, make, direct,* study BDB 465ff.
3563 C2 כּוֹס *cup* BDB 468
3576 E2 כָּזַב D *to tell a lie* BDB 469
3581 A2 כֹּחַ *strength, power* BDB 470f.

3582 C2 כָּחַד D H *to hide, efface, annihilate* BDB 470
3584 D2 כָּחַשׁ *D to deceive* BDB 471
3588 A1 כִּי *that, for, when, because*; study BDB 471-74
A2 כִּי אִם *except, unless*, see BDB 474f.
3595 D2 כִּיּוֹר *pot, basin* BDB 468
3602 C2 כָּכָה *thus* (more emphatic than כֹּה) BDB 462
3603 B2 כִּכָּר *round, round weight (talent)* BDB 503
3606 A1 כָּל־, כֹּל *all, every* BDB 481ff.
3607 E1 כָּלָא *he shut up, restrained, withheld* BDB 476
3611 C2 כֶּלֶב *dog* BDB 476f.
3615 A1 כָּלָה *it was complete, finished*; D*to complete* BDB 477f.
3617 D2 כָּלָה *complete destruction, consumption, annihilation* BDB 478
3618 C2 כַּלָּה *daughter-in-law, bride* BDB 483
3627 A1 כְּלִי *utensil, vessel, instrument* BDB 479f.
3629 C2 כְּלָיוֹת pl. *kidneys* BDB 480
3632 E2 כָּלִיל *entire, whole, holocaust (whole burnt-offering)* BDB 483
3637 C2 כָּלַם N *he was humiliated*; D *to humiliate* BDB 483f.
3639 C2 כְּלִמָּה *insult, reproach, ignominy* BDB 484
A1 ־כֶם *your, you* (pl. pron. suf. s7)
3644 A2 כְּמוֹ־ *like, as, when*, see BDB 455f.
3651 A1 כֵּן *so, thus*, see BDB 485ff.
־כֶן *your, you* (f.pl. pron.suf. s8)
3658 C1 כִּנּוֹר *lyre* BDB 490
3665 C2 כָּנַע N *to humble self, be humbled*; H *to humble, subdue* BDB 488
3671 A2 כָּנָף *wing, extremity* BDB 489
3678 A2 כִּסֵּא *throne, royal dignity* BDB 490f.
3680 A2 כָּסָה D *to cover, conceal, clothe* BDB 491f.
3684 B1 כְּסִיל *fool, stupid fellow* (70x, 49x Prov., 18x Eccl.) BDB 493
3701 A1 כֶּסֶף *silver, money* BDB 494
3707 B2 כָּעַס *he was angry*; H *to provoke to anger* BDB 494f.
3708 D2 כַּעַס *vexation, anger* BDB 495
3709 A2 כַּף *palm of hand, sole of foot, hollow item* BDB 496f.
3715 C2 כְּפִיר *young lion*, see BDB 498
3722 A2 כִּפֶּר D *to cover over, make propitiation, atone*, see BDB 497f.
3727 D1 כַּפֹּרֶת *propitiatory, atonement* (19x Exod.) BDB 498
3742 B1 כְּרוּב *cherub* (32x Ezek.) BDB 500f.
3754 B1 כֶּרֶם *vineyard* BDB 501
3759 E2 כַּרְמֶל *garden, orchard* BDB 502 (the same word also means *Carmel*)
3766 C2 כָּרַע *he bowed down* BDB 502
3772 A1 כָּרַת *he cut, cut down*, esp. *cut a covenant*, see BDB 503f.
3782 B2 כָּשַׁל *he stumbled, staggered, tottered* BDB 505f.
3789 A1 כָּתַב *he wrote*, see BDB 507f.
3792 E1 כְּתָב *writing, document, register* (9x Est.) BDB 508
3801 D1 כְּתֹנֶת, כֻּתֹּנֶת *tunic, inner garment* BDB 509
3802 B2 כָּתֵף *shoulder-blade, shoulder* (of man, beast, mountain) BDB 509
3805 D2 כּוֹתֶרֶת *capital of pillar* (18x 1-2 Kg.) BDB 509
3807 E1 כָּתַת *he beat, crushed, hammered* BDB 510

ל

A1 ל– *to, for, inregard to*, etc.; see BDB 510-18
3939 A1 לֹא, לוֹא *no, not;* see BDB 518ff.
3811 E1 לָאָה *he was weary, impatient* BDB 521
3816 C1 לְאֹם *people, folk* BDB 522
3820 A1 לֵב *heart, mind, will*; cf. #3824, BDB 524f.
3824 A1 לֵבָב *heart, mind, will*; cf. #3820. BDB 523f.
905 A1 לְבַד, לְבַד– usually with pron. suf. *by ...self/selves* BDB 94
3830 C2 לְבֻשׁ, לְבוּשׁ *garment, clothing, raiment* BDB 528
1115 B1 לְבִלְתִּי *so as not ..., in order not ...,* see BDB 116
3836 D1 לָבָן *white* (18x in Lev. 13) BDB 526
3828 D2 לְבֹנָה *frankincense* BDB 526
3847 A2 לָבַשׁ, לָבֵשׁ *he put on, wore, was clothed*; H trans. BDB 527f.
3863 D2 לוּא, לוּ *if, if only ...! would that ...!* BDB 530
3871 C1 לוּחַ *tablet, board* BDB 531f
3885 B1 לִין, לוּן *to lodge, pass the night* BDB 533
3885bE1 לוּן (לנן ?) N, H *to murmur*, see BDB 534
3895 D2 לְחִי *jaw, cheek*
3898 A2 לָחַם N *to fight, do battle* BDB 535
3899 A1 לֶחֶם *bread, food* BDB 536
3905 E1 לָחַץ *he squeezed, pressed, oppressed* BDB 537
3915 A1 לַיְלָה, לַיִל *night, at night* BDB 538f
3887 D1 לִיץ *to scorn*; for H, L, HtL see BDB 539 (18x Prov.)
3920 A2 לָכַד *he captured, seized, caught* BDB 539f.
3651 A2 לָכֵן *therefore* BDB 486, 3,d
3925 B1 לָמַד *he learned, trained;* D *he taught* BDB 540
4100 A1 לָמָּה *why? for what reason?* BDB 554, 4,d
4616 A2 לְמַעַן *for the sake of, on account of, in order that,* see BDB 775
5704 D2 לָעַד *forever* BDB 723, 2,d
3932 E1 לָעַג *he mocked, derided;* N *to stammer* BDB 541
3947 A1 לָקַח *he took* BDB 542ff.
3950 C2 לָקַט *he gathered, gleaned* BDB 544f.
3887 E2 לֵץ *scorner*, G50 of לִיץ BDB 539
3956 A2 לָשׁוֹן *tongue; language* BDB 546
3957 C1 לִשְׁכָּה *room, chamber, hall, cell* (23x Ezek.) BDB 545

מ

A1 ם– (pron. suf. s.5) *them, their*
3966 A1 מְאֹד *very, exceedingly, greatly* BDB 547
3967 A1 מֵאָה *hundred* BDB 547f.
3971 D2 מְאוּם, מוּם, מאוּם *blemish, defect* BDB 548
3972 C2 מְאוּמָה *anything,* + neg. *nothing* BDB 548f.
3974 E1 מָאוֹר *luminary, light-source* BDB 22
3976 E2 מֹאזְנַיִם *scales, balances* BDB 24f.
310 B2 מֵאַחֲרֵי *from behind* BDB 30, 4a
370 E1 מֵאַיִן *whence? from where?* BDB 32
3978 C2 מַאֲכָל *food* BDB 38

3985 C1 מָאֵן D *he refused* BDB 549
3988 B1 מָאַס *he rejected, despised* BDB 549
3967bE1 מָאתַיִם *two hundred* BDB 548.1b
3996 D1 מָבוֹא *entrance, entering, sunset* BDB 99f.
4013 C2 מִבְצָר *fortification* BDB 131
4026 B2 מִגְדָּל *tower* BDB 153f.
4039 D2 מְגִלָּה *roll, scroll* (of writing) BDB 166
4043 B2 מָגֵן *shield, buckler* BDB 171
4046 D1 מַגֵּפָה *fatal blow, slaughter, plague, pestilence* BDB 620
4054 A2 מִגְרָשׁ *common/open land, pasture* BDB 177
4057 A2 מִדְבָּר *steppe, wilderness* BDB 184f.
4058 B2 מָדַד *he measured* BDB 551
4060 B2 מִדָּה *measure, measurement, extent, portion* BDB 551
4066 D2 מָדוֹן *strife, contention* (19x Prov.) BDB 193
4069 B1 מַדּוּעַ *wherefore? why?* BDB 396
4082 B2 מְדִינָה *province* BDB 193
4100 A1 מָה (for other forms, BDB 552) *what? whatever* BDB 552ff.
4116 B2 מָהַר D *he hastened, hurried* (also trans.) BDB 554f.
4118 E1 מַהֵר *quickly, speedily* BDB 555
4120 D2 מְהֵרָה *haste, quickly, hastily* BDB 555
4127 E1 מוּג *to melt,* N *to melt away,* L *to soften, dissolve,* HtL *to melt* BDB 556
4131 C1 מוֹט *to totter, slip, shake* BDB 556f.
4136 C2 מוֹל, מוּל *in front of* BDB 557
4135 C2 מוּל *to circumcise* BDB 557
4137 C2 מוֹלֶדֶת *kindred, birth, offspring* BDB 409
4148 B2 מוּסָר *discipline, chastening, correction* BDB 416
4150 A1 מוֹעֵד *appointed time, place, meeting* BDB 417f.
4159 C2 מוֹפֵת *wonder, sign, portent* BDB 68f.
4161 D1 מוֹצָא *place/act of going forth, issue, export, source* BDB 425
4170 D1 מוֹקֵשׁ *bait, lure, snare* BDB 430
4171 E2 מוּר H *to change, alter, exchange* BDB 558
4185 D2 מוּשׁ *to depart,* H *to take away* BDB 559
4186 C1 מוֹשָׁב *seat, dwelling-place, assembly* BDB 444
4191 A1 מוּת *to die* BDB 559f.
4194 A2 מָוֶת *death* BDB 560
4196 A1 מִזְבֵּחַ *altar* BDB 258f.
4201 E1 מְזוּזָה *door-post, gate-post* BDB 265
4209 E1 מְזִמָּה *purpose, discretion (wicked) device* BDB 273
4210 B2 מִזְמוֹר *psalm, melody* BDB 274
4217 B1 מִזְרָח *(place of) sunrise, east* BDB 280f.
4219 C2 מִזְרָק *bowl, basin* (14x in Num. 7) BDB 284
4229 C2 מָחָה *he wiped, wiped out, blotted out* BDB 562
4242 E2 מְחִיר *price, hire* BDB 564
4256 C1 מַחֲלֹקֶת *share, division, course* (mostly in Chr.) BDB 324f.
4261 E2 מַחְמָד (*maḥmadd-*) *desire, desirable thing* BDB 326f.
4264 A1 מַחֲנֶה *camp, encampment* BDB 334
4268 D2 מַחְסֶה, מַחֲסֶה *refuge, shelter* BDB 340
4276 E2 מַחֲצִית *half, middle* BDB 345f.

4279 B2 מָחָר *tomorrow, in future time* BDB 563f.
4283 C2 מָחֳרָת *on the morrow, on the following day* BDB 564
4284 B2 מַחֲשָׁבָה *thought, device* BDB 364
4289 D2 מַחְתָּה *fire-holder, censer, snuff-dish* (11x Num. 16-17) BDB 367
4294 A2 מַטֶּה *staff, rod, scepter, branch, tribe* BDB 641
4295 E1 מַטָּה *downwards, below, beneath* (note accent) BDB 641
4296 D1 מִטָּה *couch, bed* BDB 641f
4305 E1 מָטַר H *to rain* BDB 565
4306 C2 מָטָר *rain* BDB 564
4307 E2 מַטָּרָה *guard, ward, prison; target, mark* (11x Jer.) BDB 643
4310 A1 מִי *who? whoever* see BDB 566f.
4325 A1 מַיִם *water* BDB 565f.
4327 D1 מִין *kind, species* (17x in Gen. 1, 6, 7) BDB 568
4334 D2 מִישׁוֹר *level place, table-land, uprightness,* see BDB 449
4339 E1 מֵישָׁרִים *evenness, level, uprightness, equity*
4341 E2 מַכְאוֹב *pain* BDB 456
4347 C1 מַכָּה *blow, wound, beating; slaughter, defeat* BDB 646f.
4349 E1 מָכוֹן *fixed/established place, foundation* BDB 467
4350 D2 מְכוֹנָה *base, stand, fixed resting-place* (15x 1 Kg. 7) BDB 467
4372 E2 מִכְסֶה *covering* (of ark, of tent of meeting) BDB 492
4376 B1 מָכַר *he sold;* G50 *seller* BDB 569
4390 A1 מָלֵא *it was full;* D *to fill* BDB 569f.
4392 B2 מָלֵא *full* BDB 570f.
4393 C2 מְלֹא *fulness, mass, multitude,* see BDB 571
4394 E2 מִלֻּאִים *setting* (of stones), *installation* (of priests) BDB 571 [521
4397 A1 מַלְאָךְ *messenger, angel,* (esp. *angel of* י׳ in Num. 22, Judg. 6, 13) BDB ↑
4399 A2 מְלָאכָה *occupation, work, business, workmanship* BDB 521f.
905 C2 מִלְּבַד *besides* BDB 94 II.1e
4405 C2 מִלָּה *word, speech, utterance* BDB 576
4410 D2 מְלוּכָה *kingship, royalty, kingly office* BDB 574
4421 A1 מִלְחָמָה *battle, war* BDB 536
4422 B1 מָלַט N *to slip away, escape*; D *to let escape, deliver* BDB 572
4427 A1 מָלַךְ *he was/became king*; H *to crown, cause to reign* BDB 573f.
4428 A1 מֶלֶךְ *king* BDB 572f.
4436 C2 מַלְכָּה *queen* (25x Est.) BDB 573
4438 B1 מַלְכוּת *royalty, kingship, reign, kingdom* BDB 574f.
4467 A2 מַמְלָכָה *kingdom, dominion, sovereignty, reign* BDB 575
4475 E2 מֶמְשָׁלָה *rule, dominion, realm* BDB 606
4478 E2 מָן *manna* BDB 577
4480 A1 מִן *from;* study usage in BDB 577-583
4487 D1 מָנָה *he counted, numbered, reckoned, assigned* BDB 584
4496 D2 מְנוּחָה *resting-place, rest* BDB 629f.
4501 C2 מְנוֹרָה *lampstand* BDB 633
4504 A1 מִנְחָה *gift, tribute, offering, cereal offering* BDB 585
4513 D1 מָנַע *he withheld, held back* BDB 586
4522 D2 מַס *(mass-) corvée, labor-gang, forced service, serfdom* BDB 586f.
4526 E1 מִסְגֶּרֶת *border, rim, fastness* BDB 689
4539 D1 מָסָךְ *covering, screen* (16x Exod.) BDB 697

4541 D1 מַסֵּכָה *molten metal, image; libation* BDB 651
4546 D1 מְסִלָּה *highway, raised road* (in open country) BDB 700
4549 D2 מָסַס N *to melt* (intrans.), *dissolve*; H trans. BDB 587f.
4553 E2 מִסְפֵּד *wailing* BDB 704
4557 A2 מִסְפָּר *number, tally, tale* BDB 708f.
4581 C2 מָעוֹז *place/means of safety, protection, stronghold* BDB 731f.
4591 D2 מָעַט *he was/became small, few*; H *to make small* BDB 589
4592 A2 מְעַט *a little, a few, fewness* BDB 589f.
4598 D1 מְעִיל *robe* BDB 591
4578 C2 מֵעִים only pl.cstr. and suf. *bowels, inward parts,* see BDB 588f.
4599 D2 מַעְיָן *spring, source* (of water) BDB 745f.
4603 C2 מָעַל *he acted unfaithfully/treacherously* BDB 591
4600 D1 מַעַל *unfaithful, treacherous* BDB 591
4605 A2 מַעַל, מִמַּעַל *on top, above,* מַעְלָה, לְמַעְלָה *upwards* BDB 751f.
4608 E1 מַעֲלֶה *ascent, stairs* BDB 751
4609 C1 מַעֲלָה *step, stairs, stories, ascent* BDB 752
4631 C1 מְעָרָה *cave* BDB 792
4634 E1 מַעֲרָכָה *row, rank, battle-line* BDB 790
4639 A1 מַעֲשֶׂה *deed, work* BDB 795f.
4643 C2 מַעֲשֵׂר *one-tenth, tithe* BDB 798
4672 A1 מָצָא *he found, encountered,* see BDB 592ff.
4676 C2 מַצֵּבָה, מַצֶּבֶת *pillar, stump, sacred pillar* BDB 663
4682 C1 מַצָּה *unleavened bread, matzah* BDB 595
4687 A2 מִצְוָה *commandment, mitzvah* BDB 846
4692 C2 מָצוֹר *siege entrenchment/enclosure* BDB 848f.
4720 B1 מִקְדָּשׁ *sanctuary, holy place* BDB 874
4725 A1 מָקוֹם *place, standing-place, station, locality* BDB 879f.
4726 E1 מָקוֹר *source, spring, fountain,* see BDB 881
4731 E1 מַקֵּל *rod, staff, tree branch, wand* BDB 596
4733 D2 מִקְלָט *refuge, asylum* (mostly Num. Josh.) BDB 886
4735 B1 מִקְנֶה *cattle* (usually only small cattle), *possession* BDB 889
4736 E2 מִקְנָה *purchase, purchase-price, possession* BDB 889
4744 D1 מִקְרָא *convocation, sacred assembly, reading* (12x Lev.) BDB 896
4751 C2 מַר (*marr-*) *bitter, bitterness* BDB 600
4758 A2 מַרְאֶה *sight, appearance, vision* BDB 909
4775 D1 מָרַד *he rebelled, revolted* BDB 597
4784 C1 מָרָה *he was disobedient, rebellious, stubborn*; H *to display* this quality BDB 598
4791 B2 מָרוֹם *height, elevation, high place* BDB 928f.
4801 E1 מֶרְחָק *distant place, distance* BDB 935
4805 D2 מְרִי *rebellion, rebellious* (16x Ezek.) BDB 598
4818 C1 מֶרְכָּבָה *chariot* BDB 939
4820 C2 מִרְמָה *deceit, treachery, treacherous* BDB 941
4843 E2 מָרַר *he was bitter*; D H *to make bitter, show bitterness* BDB 600
4886 B1 מָשַׁח *he smeared, anointed, consecrated* BDB 602f.
4888 D2 מִשְׁחָה *ointment, anointed portion* (22x Exod. Lev., 1x Num.) BDB 603
4899 C2 מָשִׁיחַ *anointed, anointed one, messiah* BDB 603
4900 C2 מָשַׁךְ *he drew, led, dragged, drew out, prolonged* BDB 604
4904 C1 מִשְׁכָּב *couch, place of lying, act of lying* BDB 1012

4908 A2 מִשְׁכָּן *dwelling-place, tabernacle, abode* of YHWH BDB 1015f.
4911 E1 מָשַׁל *he spoke in proverbs* BDB 605
4912 C2 מָשָׁל *proverb, parable, similitude* BDB 605
4929 D2 מִשְׁמָר *jail, prison, guard, act of guarding* BDB 1038
4931 B1 מִשְׁמֶרֶת *guard, watch, charge, function* BDB 1038
4932 C2 מִשְׁנֶה *double, copy, second* BDB 1041
4940 A1 מִשְׁפָּחָה *clan, division of a tribe* BDB 1046f.
4941 A1 מִשְׁפָּט *judgment* (act, place, case, sentence, execution of) see BDB 1048f.
4948 C1 מִשְׁקָל *weight* BDB 1054
4961 C1 מִשְׁתֶּה *feast, banquet, drink* (23x Est.) BDB 1059
4853 B2 מַשָּׂא *load, burden, lifting, bearing, tribute* BDB 672
4864 E2 מַשְׂאֵת *uprising, uplifting, burden, utterance, portion, gift* BDB 673
4869 E1 מִשְׂגָּב *secure height, stronghold, refuge* BDB 960
4885 E1 מָשׂוֹשׂ *exultation* BDB 965
4970 C1 מָתַי *when?*; for idioms see BDB 607
4962 D2 מְתִים pl. *men, males* (also generic disregarding sex) BDB 607
4976 D2 מַתָּן coll. *gifts, gift, offering* BDB 682 incl. מַתָּנָה
4975 C1 מָתְנַיִם (*moṯnáyim*) *loins*, see BDB 608

נ

ן– (pron. suf. s6) *her*
4994 A1 נָא *I pray, prithee*, see BDB 609
5002 A1 נְאֻם *utterance/revelation of* BDB 610
5003 C2 נָאַף *he committed adultery* (man with another's wife) BDB 610
5006 D2 נָאַץ *he contemned, held contemptible, spurned* BDB 610f.
5012 A2 נָבָא N *to prophesy*; HtD *to act as a prophet* BDB 612
5027 B1 נָבַט H *to look, look at, regard, show regard for* BDB 613
5030 A1 נָבִיא *one called as spokesman, prophet* BDB 611f.
5034 D1 נָבֵל *he sank, dropped down, it withered, faded*, see BDB 615
5035 C2 נֵבֶל, נֶבֶל *harp, lute, guitar*; also *skin-bottle, jar* BDB 614
5036 E1 נָבָל *foolish, stupid, impious, churlish* BDB 614
5038 C1 נְבֵלָה *carcass, corpse* BDB 615
5045 A2 נֶגֶב *south-country, Negev* BDB 616
5046 A1 נָגַד H *to declare, tell, publish, proclaim, set out in front* BDB 616f.
5048 A2 נֶגֶד *in front of, in sight of, opposite to*, see BDB 617
5051 D2 נֹגַהּ *brightness* BDB 618
5057 C1 נָגִיד *leader, one placed in front, ruler, prince* BDB 617f.
5059 E2 נָגַן D *to play* (an instrument) BDB 618 [BDB 619
5060 A2 נָגַע *he touched, reached, struck*; H *to cause to touch, apply, arrive, reach* ↑
5061 B1 נֶגַע *stroke, wound, mark, plague* (60x in Lev.) BDB 619
5062 C1 נָגַף *he struck, smote* BDB 619
5066 A2 נָגַשׁ *he drew near, approached* BDB 620f.
5065 D2 נָגַשׂ *he drove, exacted*; G50 *taskmaster, driver* BDB 620
5068 E1 נָדַב *he incited, impelled*; HtD *to volunteer, offer freewill-offerings* BDB 621
5071 D1 נְדָבָה *voluntariness; freewill-offering* BDB 621
5074 D1 נָדַד *he fled, retreated, wandered, strayed*; H *to chase away* BDB 622
5079 C2 נִדָּה *impurity, impure thing* BDB 622
5080 B2 נָדַח H *to thrust out, impel, banish*; N pass. BDB 623
5081 D1 נָדִיב *willing, generous, noble* BDB 622
5087 C2 נָדַר *he vowed* BDB 623

5088 B2 נֶדֶר *vow* BDB 623f.
5090 C2 נָהַג G and D *he drove, drove away, led* BDB 624
5104 A2 נָהָר *stream, river* BDB 625f.
5110 D1 נוּד *to move to and fro, wander, waver, shake with grief* BDB 626f.
5116 C2 נָוֶה *abode of shepherd/flock, habitation* BDB 627
5117 A2 נוּחַ *to rest, settle down and remain, have rest* BDB 628f.
5127 A2 נוּס *to flee, escape, depart* BDB 630f.
5128 C1 נוּעַ *to wave, tremble, vibrate, totter* BDB 631
5130 C2 נוּף H *to wield, shake, wave, swing, brandish* BDB 631f.
5137 D2 נָזָה H *to sprinkle, cause to spurt* (15x Lev.) BDB 633
5139 E2 נָזִיר *consecrated one, Nazirite* BDB 634
5140 E1 נָזַל *it trickled, flowed* BDB 633
5141 E1 נֶזֶם *nose-ring, earring* BDB 633f.
5145 D2 נֵזֶר *crown* (sign of consecration), *Naziriteship* (12x in Num. 6) BDB 634
5148 C2 נָחָה G and H *he led, brought, guided* BDB 634f.
5157 B2 נָחַל *he took possession, inherited*; H *to cause to inherit, give as a possession* ↑ [BDB 635f.
5158 A2 נַחַל *torrent-valley, wadi, torrent* BDB 636
5159 A1 נַחֲלָה *inheritance, possession, property* BDB 635
5162 A2 נָחַם N *to be sorry, have compassion, repent*; D *to comfort* BDB 636f.
5175 C2 נָחָשׁ *serpent* BDB 638
5178 A2 נְחֹשֶׁת *copper, bronze; fetters* BDB 638f.
5186 A1 נָטָה *he stretched out, extended, spread out, turned, bent, inclined;* H often the same BDB 639f.
5193 B2 נָטַע *he planted* BDB 642
5197 E1 נָטַף G and H *it dripped, dropped, he dripped* (utterance as prophecy) BDB 642f.
A1 –נִי (pron. suf. s4) *me*
5203 C1 נָטַשׁ *he left, forsook, abandoned,* see BDB 643f.
5221 A1 נָכָה H *to strike, smite* BDB 645f.
5227 C2 נֹכַח *in front of*; for usage see BDB 647
5234 B2 נָכַר H *to regard, observe, recognize, acknowledge* BDB 647f.
5237 C1 נָכְרִי (*nokrî*) *foreign, alien* BDB 648f.
5251 D2 נֵס (*niss-*) *ensign, signal, sign, flag* BDB 651f.
5254 C2 נָסָה D *he tested, tried, attempted, proved* BDB 650
5258 D1 נָסַךְ G, H *he poured out, offered* (a libation) BDB 650
5262 B2 נֶסֶךְ *drink-offering* (33x Num.) BDB 651.
5265 A2 נָסַע *he pulled up* (tent-pegs), *set out, journeyed* BDB 652
5271 C1 נְעוּרִים f.pl. *youth, early life* BDB 655
5275 D2 נַעַל *sandal, shoe* BDB 653
5288 A1 נַעַר *boy, youth, servant* BDB 654f.
5291 B1 נַעֲרָה *girl, damsel, maids* (only pl.) BDB 655
5307 A1 נָפַל *he fell, lay* BDB 656ff.
5310 D2 נָפַץ *it shattered*; D *to dash in pieces* (12x Jer.) BDB 658
5315 A1 נֶפֶשׁ *soul, living being, self, person*; see BDB 659ff.
5324 B1 נָצַב N *to take one's stand, be stationed*; H *to station, set up, fix* BDB 662
5329 B2 נָצַח D *to act as director, overseer, choirmaster,* see BDB 663f.
5331 C1 נֵצַח, נֶצַח *eminence, enduring, everlastingness* BDB 664
5337 A1 נָצַל H *to snatch away, rescue, deliver* BDB 664f.
5341 B2 נָצַר *he watched, guarded, kept, observed, kept secret* BDB 665f.

5344 D2 נָקַב *he bored, pierced, pricked off, designated* BDB 666
5347 D2 נְקֵבָה *female* (all Pent. exc. Jer. 31:22; 12x Lev.) BDB 666
5352 C1 נָקָה N *to be cleaned out, purged, empty, free from obligation*; D *to acquit* BDB 667
5355 C1 נָקִי *clean, innocent, free from, exempt*
5358 C2 נָקַם *he avenged, took vengeance* BDB 667f.
5359 E1 נָקָם *vengeance* BDB 668
5360 D1 נְקָמָה *vengeance*
5362 E1 נָקַף H *to go around, surround, emcompass, enclose* BDB 668f.
5369 C1 נֵר *lamp* BDB 632
5377 E2 נָשָׁא H *to beguile, deceive*; N pass. BDB 674
5378 E1 נָשָׁא (6x), נָשָׁה (11x) *to give on loan, be a creditor*; see BDB 673, 674
802 A1 נָשִׁים *women*
5391 E2 נָשַׁךְ *he bit* BDB 675
5397 D2 נְשָׁמָה *breath, breathing thing* BDB 675
5401 C2 נָשַׁק *he kissed* BDB 676
5404 D1 נֶשֶׁר *griffon-vulture, eagle* BDB 676f.
5375 A1 נָשָׂא *he lifted, carried, took* BDB 669-72
5381 B2 נָשַׂג H *to reach, overtake, attain, cause to reach* BDB 673
5387 A2 נָשִׂיא *one lifted up, prince, chief* BDB 672
5411 E1 נְתִינִים *temple servants, Nethinim* (Ezr.-Neh. exc. 1x) BDB 682
5413 D2 נָתַךְ *it poured forth*; H *to pour out* BDB 677f.
5414 A1 נָתַן *he gave*; for many meanings, see BDB 678-681
5422 C1 נָתַץ *he pulled down, broke down* BDB 683
5423 D1 נָתַק *he pulled apart, tore apart/away*
5428 D2 נָתַשׁ *he pulled/plucked up, rooted out* BDB 684

ס

5437 A2 סָבַב *he turned, turned around, surrounded,* see BDB 685f.
5349 A1 סָבִיב *round about, the surrounding region*; מִסָּבִיב *from every side* BDB 686f.
5461 E1 סֶגֶן, only pl. סְגָנִים *prefects, rulers, nobles* BDB 688
5462 B1 סָגַר *he shut, closed* BDB 688f.
5472 D2 סוּג, erroneously שׂוּג N *to turn away, backslide* BDB 690f.
5475 D2 סוֹד *secret counsel/council* BDB 691
5483 A2 סוּס *horse* BDB 692
5492 E2 סוּפָה *storm-wind* BDB 693 [BDB 693f.
5493 A1 סוּר G_{161} *to turn aside, depart*; H_{133} *to cause to turn aside, remove, take away* ↑
5496 E1 סוּת H *to incite, allure, instigate* BDB 694
5503 E1 סָחַר *he went about, traveled around in*; G50 *trader* BDB 695
5518 C2 סִיר *pot* BDB 696
5521 C2 סֻכָּה *thicket, booth* (made of interwoven boughs) BDB 697
5536 E2 סַל (*sallî*) *basket* BDB 700
5542 B1 סֶלָה *lift up! Selah!* (71x, all Ps.) BDB 699f.
5545 C1 סָלַח *he forgave, pardoned* BDB 699
5553 B2 סֶלַע *cliff, crag, rock* BDB 700f.
5560 B2 סֹלֶת *fine flour* (34x Lev. Num.) BDB 701
5561 E2 סַמִּים pl. only *spice, perfume* (used in incense) (11x Exod.) BDB 702
5564 C1 סָמַךְ *he leaned, lay* (hand), supported, upheld, see BDB 701f.

5591 D2 סַעַר *tempest* BDB 704
5592 D2 סַף (*sipp-*) *threshold, sill* BDB 706
5594 C2 סָפַד *he wailed, lamented* BDB 704
5595 D2 סָפָה *he swept/snatched away, caught up* BDB 705
5608 A2 סָפַר *he counted, numbered*; D *to recount, tell, relate* BDB 707f.
5612 A2 סֵפֶר *writing, document, book* BDB 706f.
5619 D2 סָקַל *he stoned to death* BDB 709
5631 C1 סָרִיס *eunuch, officer* BDB 710
5633 D2 סֶרֶן, only pl. סְרָנִים *tyrants, lords* (Philistine title) BDB 710
5637 E1 סָרַר *he was stubborn, rebellious* BDB 710f.
5641 B1 סָתַר N *to hide self, be concealed* BDB 711
5643 C2 סֵתֶר *hiding-place, covering, secrecy* BDB 712

ע

5645 C2 עָב *dark cloud, cloud-mass, thicket* BDB 728
5647 A1 עָבַד *he worked, served* BDB 712f.
5650 A1 עֶבֶד *slave, servant, man-servant, subject,* see BDB 713f.
5656 A2 עֲבֹדָה *labor, work, service* BDB 715
5668 C1 עֲבוּר, see בַּעֲבוּר, *for, because of* BDB 721
5674 A1 עָבַר *he passed over/through/by, he passed away,* see BDB 716-19
5676 B1 עֵבֶר *region across/beyond, opposite side* BDB 719
5678 C2 עֶבְרָה *overflow, arrogance, fury* BDB 720
5688 D2 עֲבֹת *twisted cord, rope, cordage-work* BDB 721
5695 C2 עֵגֶל *calf* BDB 722
5699 D1 עֲגָלָה *cart; war-chariot* (Ps. 46:10) BDB 722
5704 A1 עַד *up to, until*; see discussion BDB 723ff.
5704aC1 עַד, וָעֶד *for ever* BDB 723.I
5707 B2 עֵד *witness, evidence* BDB 729
5712 A2 עֵדָה *congregation* BDB 417
5713 D2 עֵדוֹת pl. *testimonies* (13x in Ps. 119) BDB 730
5715 C1 עֵדוּת (19x), עֵדֻת (27x) *testimony,* see BDB 730
5739 C2 עֵדֶר *flock, herd* BDB 727
5749 C1 עוּד H *to admonish, bear witness, cause to testify* BDB 729f.
5750 A1 עוֹד *still, yet, again*; see discussion BDB 728f.
5766 D2 עָוֶל *injustice, unrighteousness* BDB 732
5766 C2 עַוְלָה (*'awlā*) *injustice, deeds of injustice* BDB 732
5768 D2 עוֹלֵל, עוֹלָל *child* BDB 760
5769 A1 עוֹלָם *long duration* (past or future), *'eternity'* BDB 761ff.
5771 A1 עָוֹן (*'āwôn*) *iniquity, guilt, punishment,* see BDB 730f.
5774 D1 עוּף *to fly* BDB 733
5776 B1 עוֹף *flying things, fowl, insects*
5782 B1 עוּר *to awake, rouse oneself* BDB 734f.
5785 B1 עוֹר *skin* (of men 55x, of animals 44x) (53x Lev.) BDB 736
5787 D1 עִוֵּר (*'iwwēr*) *blind, blind man* BDB 734
5794 D2 עַז (*'azzā*^{h}) *strong, mighty, fierce* BDB 738
5795 B1 עֵז (*'izzîm*) f. *she-goat* BDB 777
5797 E2 עֹז (*'ozz-* or *'uzz-*) *strength, might, stronghold* BDB 738f.
5800 A1 עָזַב *he left, forsook, abandoned, set loose* BDB 736f.
5826 B1 עָזַר *he helped, succored* BDB 740

5828 D2 עֵזֶר *help, succor* BDB 740
5833 D1 עֶזְרָה, עֶזְרַת, עֶזְרָתָה *help, succor, assistance* BDB 740f.
5844 E1 עָטָה *he wrapped himself with, enveloped himself* BDB 741f.
5850 D2 עֲטָרָה *crown, wreath* BDB 742
5869 A1 עַיִן *eye* BDB 744f.
5869bD1 עַיִן *spring of water* BDB 745 (connection with previous word dubious)
5889 E1 עָיֵף *faint, weary* BDB 746
5892 A1 עִיר *town, city*
5921 A1 עַל *upon*, study usage in BDB 752-759
5923 C1 עֹל (*'ull-*) *yoke* BDB 760
5927 A1 עָלָה *he went up, ascended*, see BDB 748ff.
5929 E1 עָלֶה *leaf, leafage* BDB 750
5930 A1 עֹלָה *holocaust, whole burnt-offering*, see BDB 750
5937 E1 עָלַז *he exulted, triumphed* BDB 759
5944 D2 עֲלִיָּה *upper room, roof-chamber* BDB 751
5945 B2 עֶלְיוֹן *high, highest, upper(most); Most High* (God) 19x BDB 751 I, II
5949 D2 עֲלִילָה *wantonness, deed, practices* BDB 760
5953 D2 עָלַל L *he acted arbitrarily toward*, see BDB 759f.
5971 A1 עַם, עָם (*'amm-*) *people* BDB 766f.
5973 A1 עִם (*'imm-*) *with*; study usage in BDB 767f. [BDB 763ff.
5975 A1 עָמַד *he stood, took his stand*; H *he stood* (tr.), *caused to stand, stationed* ↑
5980 C2 עֻמָּה *close by, parallel to, agreeing with*, see BDB 769
5982 A2 עַמּוּד *pillar, column* BDB 765
5998 D2 עָמַל *he labored, toiled* BDB 765
5999 B2 עָמָל *labor, toil* (19x Eccl.) BDB 765
6010 B2 עֵמֶק *valley, deep place* BDB 770f.
6013 E1 עָמֹק *deep* BDB 771
6025 E1 עֵנָב coll. *grapes* BDB 772
6030 A1 עָנָה *he answered, replied, responded* BDB 772f.
6031 B1 עָנָה *he was bowed down, afflicted* BDB 776
6040 C2 עֳנִי *affliction, poverty* BDB 777
6041 B1 עָנִי *poor, needy, weak, afflicted* BDB 776f.
6051 B1 עָנָן *cloud-mass* BDB 777f.
6035 D2 עָנָו *poor, afflicted, humble, meek* BDB 776
6083 A2 עָפָר *dust, dry earth* BDB 779f.
6086 A1 עֵץ *tree, trees*; pl. *articles of wood, pieces of wood* BDB 781f.
6087 E2 עָצַב *he grieved, it pained, hurt*, see BDB 780
6091 E1 עֲצַבִּים pl. *idols* BDB 781
6098 B1 עֵצָה *counsel, advice* BDB 420
6099 C2 עָצוּם *mighty, numerous* BDB 783
6105 E1 עָצַם *he was mighty, vast, numerous* BDB 782
6106 A2 עֶצֶם *bone, substance, self*, see BDB 782f.
6113 C1 עָצַר *he restrained*; (late) *he retained* BDB 783
6118 E2 עֵקֶב *consequence, because, as a consequence of, reward* BDB 784
6148 D2 עָרַב *he took/gave on pledge* BDB 786
6153 A2 עֶרֶב *evening, sunset* BDB 787f.
6160 B2 עֲרָבָה *desert-plain, steppe, Arabah* BDB 787
6172 B2 עֶרְוָה *nakedness, pudenda* (31x Lev.) BDB 788f.

6174 E2 עָרוֹם (*ʿărummā*[h]) *naked* BDB 736
6184 D2 עָרִיץ *awe-inspiring, terror-striking, ruthless* BDB 792
6186 B1 עָרַךְ *he arranged, set in order* BDB 789
6187 C2 עֵרֶךְ *order, row, estimate* (27x Lev.), see BDB 789f.
6189 C2 עָרֵל *having foreskin, uncircumcised* (15x Ezek.) BDB 790
6190 E2 עָרְלָה (*ʿorlā*[h]) *foreskin* BDB 790
6203 C2 עֹרֶף *(back of) neck, stiffnecked* BDB 791
6205 E2 עֲרָפֶל *choud, heavy cloud* BDB 791
6206 E2 עָרַץ *he trembled, caused to tremble*
6223 D2 עָשִׁיר *rich, wealthy* BDB 799
6227 D1 עָשָׁן *smoke* BDB 798
6231 C2 עָשַׁק *he oppressed, wronged, extorted* BDB 798f.
6238 E1 עָשַׁר *he was/became rich* BDB 799
6239 C2 עֹשֶׁר *riches*
6212 C2 עֵשֶׂב *herb, herbage* BDB 793
6213 A1 עָשָׂה *he did, made;* for usage see BDB 793ff.
6218 E2 עָשׂוֹר *a ten, decade, ten* (or *the 10th) of*, see BDB 797
6224 D1 עֲשִׂירִי *tenth* (ordinal) BDB 798
6235 A1 עֶשֶׂר, עֲשָׂרָה *ten* BDB 797f.
6235bA1 עָשָׂר, עֶשְׂרֵה *teen* (used after units to make 11-19) BDB 797
6241 C2 עִשָּׂרוֹן *tenth part* (of ephah; 27x Num.) BDB 798
6242 A1 עֶשְׂרִים *twenty* BDB 797f.
6249 E1 עַשְׁתֵּי, used with #6235b to form *eleven* BDB 799
6256 A1 עֵת (*ʿint-*) *time* BDB 773
6260 D1 עַתּוּד only pl. *he-goat* (12x Num. 7) BDB 800
6279 D2 עָתַר G H *he prayed, made supplication*; N (God) *was entreated)* BDB 801

פ

6285 B1 פֵּאָה *corner, side* (47x Ezek. 41-48) BDB 802
6293 C1 פָּגַע *he reached, met, encountered*, see BDB 803
6297 D2 פֶּגֶר *corpse, carcass*
6299 B2 פָּדָה *he ransomed* BDB 804
6310 A1 פֶּה *mouth* BDB 804f
6311 B2 פֹּה, פוֹ, פֹּא *here, hither* (פוֹ 23x Ezek 40-41) BDB 805f.
6315 E2 פּוּחַ H *to puff, snort, breath out*, see BDB 806
6327 B2 פּוּץ *it was dispersed, scattered*; N *to be scattered* BDB 806f.
6341 D1 פַּח (*pḥḥ*) *bird-trap, snare* BDB 809
6342 D1 פָּחַד *he dreaded, was in fear/awe, trembled* BDB 808
6343 C1 פַּחַד *dread*
6346 D1 פֶּחָה *governor* (*pḥḥ* or possibly *pḥḥ*?)
6370 C2 פִּילֶגֶשׁ, פִּלֶגֶשׁ *concubine* BDB 811
6381 B1 פָּלָא N *to be extraordinary, difficult to understand*; H *to do wonderfully, to do marvelous things*; נִפְלָאוֹת *wonderful acts* (of YHWH) BDB 810
6403 D1 פָּלַט D *to cause to escape, bring to security*; H *to deliver* BDB 812
6412 E1 פָּלִיט *escaped one, fugitive*
6413 D1 פְּלֵיטָה *escape, deliverance*
6419 B1 פָּלַל D *to mediate, judge*; HtD80 *to intercede, pray* BDB 813
6435 A2 פֶּן־ *lest* BDB 814f.
6437 A2 פָּנָה *he turned, faced* BDB 815

6438 D1 פִּנָּה *corner* BDB 819
6440 A1 פָּנִים always pl. *face*, also *faces*, see BDB 815-819
6440bA1 פְּנֵי with preps. to form improper preps., esp. לִפְנֵי, בִּפְנֵי, see BDB 816-19
6442 C2 פְּנִימִי *inner* (24x Ezek.) BDB 819
6453 C1 פֶּסַח *Passover* (sacrifice, festival) BDB 820
6456 D2 פְּסִלִים, פְּסִילִים pl. *idols* BDB 820f.
6459 C2 פֶּסֶל *idol, image*; cf. pl. above BDB 820
6466 B2 פָּעַל *he did, made* BDB 821
6467 C2 פֹּעַל *doing, deed, work*
6471 A2 פַּעַם *time, occurrence* BDB 821f.
6475 E2 פָּצָה *he opened* (mouth), *uttered* BDB 822
6485 A1 פָּקַד G234 *he attended to, visited, visited upon, mustered, appointed*; H29 *to make overseer, commit, entrust;* see BDB 823f.
6486 C2 פְּקֻדָּה *oversight, mustering, visitation, charge* BDB 824
6490 D2 פִּקּוּדִים only pl. cstr. *precepts* (21x Ps. 119)
6491 D2 פָּקַח *he opened* (eyes, once ears)
6499 A2 פַּר (*prr*) *young bull, steer* BDB 830f.
6504 D1 פָּרַד N to divide, be divided, separate; H *to make a division, separation* BDB 825
6505 E2 פֶּרֶד *mule*
6509 D1 פָּרָה *he was fruitful, bore fruit* (15x Gen.) BDB 826
6524 C2 פָּרַח *it budded, put forth shoots, sprouted* BDB 827
6525 E2 פֶּרַח *bud, sprout*
6529 A2 פְּרִי *fruit* BDB 826
6532 D1 פָּרֹכֶת *curtain* before Holy of Holies in tabernacle BDB 827
6541 D2 פַּרְסָה *hoof* BDB 828
6544 E2 פָּרַע *he let go, loosed, let alone* BDB 828f.
6555 B2 פָּרַץ *he broke through/down/into/out, broke in pieces* BDB 829
6556 E1 פֶּרֶץ *bursting forth, breach*
6565 B2 פָּרַר H *to break, frustrate* BDB 830
6571 B2 פָּרָשׁ (prob. *parraš*) *horseman* BDB 832
6566 B2 פָּרַשׂ *he spread out, spread* BDB 831
6584 C1 פָּשַׁט *he stripped off, made a dash*; D, H *to strip* BDB 832f.
6586 C1 פָּשַׁע *he rebelled, transgressed* BDB 833
6587 B1 פֶּשַׁע *transgression, rebellion* BDB 833
6593 E2 פֵּשֶׁת *flax, linen*
6581 D2 פָּשָׂה *it spread, was divulged* (only in Lev. 13-14) BDB 832
6597 D1 פִּתְאֹם *suddenness, suddenly* BDB 837
6605 A1 פָּתַח *he opened* BDB 834f.
6607 A2 פֶּתַח *opening, doorway, entrance* BDB 835f.
6612 E1 פֶּתִי *simple, simple-minded* (15x Prov.) BDB 834

צ

6629 A1 צֹאן *flock, small cattle, sheep and goats* BDB 838
6635 A1 צָבָא *army, host*; י׳ צְבָאוֹת *Y. of hosts, Y. Sabaoth* BDB 838f.
6654 C2 צַד (*ṣadd-*) *side* BDB 841
6662 A1 צַדִּיק *just, righteous* BDB 843
6663 C1 צָדַק, צָדֵק *he was just, righteous*; H *to declare righteous, justify* BDB 842f.
6664 A2 צֶדֶק *rightness, righteousness* BDB 841f.
6666 A2 צְדָקָה *righteousness, truthfulness, justification*, see BDB 842

6672 D2 צָהֳרַיִם (*ṣohŏráyim*) *noon, midday* BDB 843
6677 C1 צַוָּאר *neck, back of neck* BDB 848
6679 E2 צוּד *he hunted* BDB 844
6680 A1 צִוָּה D *he charged, gave command, ordered* BDB 845f.
6684 D2 צוּם *to abstain from food, fast* BDB 847
6685 D1 צוֹם *fast, fasting*
6696 C2 צוּר *to confine, bind, besiege, shut in*
6697 B1 צוּר *rock, cliff* BDB 849
6718 E1 צַיִד *hunting, game* BDB 844
6723 E2 צִיָּה *dryness, drought, desert* BDB 851
6731 E2 צִיץ *blossom, flower, shining thing* BDB 847
6738 C1 צֵל (*ṣill-*) *shadow, shade* BDB 853
6743 B2 צָלַח, צָלֵחַ *he advanced, prospered*; H *to make prosperous, bring to successful conclusion* BDB 852
6755 E1 צֶלֶם *image* BDB 853f.
6757 E1 צַלְמָוֶת *deep shadow, death-shadow, darkness* (10x Job) BDB 853
6763 C2 צֵלָע *rib, side, ridge/terrace* (of hill) BDB 854
6772 E1 צָמָא *thirst*
6776 E2 צֶמֶד *couple, pair; area that can be plowed by a span of oxen in a day* BDB 855
6779 C2 צָמַח *it sprouted, sprang up*
6785 E2 צֶמֶר *wool* BDB 856
6789 E2 צָמַת *he put an end to*; N *to be ended*; H *to exterminate, annihilate*
6793 D2 צִנָּה *large shield* BDB 857
6810 D2 צָעִיר *little, small, young, insignificant* BDB 859
6817 B2 צָעַק *he cried out, called, summoned* BDB 858
6818 D2 צְעָקָה *outcry, cry of distress*
6823 C1 צָפָה D *he overlay, plated* BDB 860
6828 A2 צָפוֹן *north* BDB 860f.
6833 C1 צִפּוֹר *bird* BDB 861f.
6845 C2 צָפַן *he hid, treasured up* BDB 860
6862 B2 צַר (*ṣrr*) *adversary, foe* BDB 865
6862bD1 צַר *straits, distress*
6869 B1 צָרָה *distress, straits*
6879 D2 צָרַע Gp50 *leper*; Dp *to be leprous* BDB 863f.
6883 C2 צָרַעַת *leprosy*, some kind of fungus or mold, apparently not Hansen's dis-[ease, BDB 863
6884 C2 צָרַף *he smelted, refined, tested* BDB 864
6887 C2 צָרַר (**ṣrr*) *he bound up, restricted; it was narrow* BDB 864
6887bD1 צָרַר (**ḍrr*) *he showed hostility toward, vexed, harassed* BDB 865

ק

6908 A2 קָבַץ *he gathered, collected, assembled* BDB 867f.
6912 A2 קָבַר *he buried*, G_{86} N_{39} BDB 868
6913 B2 קֶבֶר *grave, sepulchre, burial-place*
6915 E2 קָדַד *he bowed/knelt down* BDB 869
6918 A2 קָדוֹשׁ *sacred, holy* BDB 872
6921 B2 קָדִים *east, east wind, east side* (52x Ezek.) BDB 870
6923 D1 קִדֵּם D *he met, confronted, went before, anticipated* BDB 869f.
6924 B2 קֶדֶם *front, east, aforetime, beginning* BDB 869
6924bD1 קֵדְמָה (loc. ה) *eastward, toward the east* BDB 870

6937 E1 קָדַר *it was dark, he was in mourning* BDB 871 [see BDB 872f.
6942 A2 קָדַשׁ N *to be consecrated*; D *to dedicate, set apart, observe as holy, hallow*; ↑
6944 A1 קֹדֶשׁ *holiness, sacredness, apartness* BDB 871f.
6950 C2 קָהַל N *to assemble* (intr.); H *to assemble* (trans.) BDB 874f.
6951 A2 קָהָל *assembly, convocation* BDB 874
6957 E1 קַו *line, measuring-line* BDB 876
6960 C1 קָוָה G50 *one waiting for*; D *to wait, look for, lie in wait for* BDB 875
6963 A1 קוֹל *voice, sound* BDB 876f.
6965 A1 קוּם *to arise, stand* (intr.); H146 *to raise, stand* (tr.), set up, build BDB 877ff.
6967 C1 קוֹמָה *height* BDB 879
6996 C1 קָטָן *small, young, little, unimportant* BDB 881f.
6994 B2 קָטֹן *small, young, insignificant* BDB 882
6999 A2 קָטַר D, H *to burn sacrifices, make smoke* BDB 882f.
7004 B1 קְטֹרֶת *(sweet) smoke* (of sacrifice), *incense* (41x Ex., Lv., Nu.) BDB 882
7015 E1 קִינָה *elegy, dirge* BDB 884
6974 D2 קִיץ H *to awake, show signs of waking*
7019 E1 קַיִץ *summer, summer-fruit*
7023 B1 קִיר *wall* BDB 885
7036 E1 קָלוֹן *ignominy, dishonor, disgrace* BDB 885f.
7043 B1 קָלַל *it was slight, swift, trifling* BDB 886
7045 C2 קְלָלָה *curse* BDB 887
7050 E2 קֶלַע *curtain, hanging* (13x Exod.)
7065 C2 קָנָא D *he was jealous, zealous, envious, excited to anger* BDB 888
7068 C1 קִנְאָה *jealousy, zeal*
7069 B1 קָנָה *he got, acquired, bought* (G 81x out of 84) BDB 888f.
7070 B2 קָנֶה *stalk, reed, measuring-rod* (11x Ezek. 40, 42) BDB 889
7080 D2 קָסַם *he practised divination* BDB 890
7086 E1 קְעָרָה *dish, platter* (15x in Num.) BDB 891
7093 B2 קֵץ *end, extremity* BDB 893f.
7097 B1 קָצֶה *end, extremity* BDB 892
7105 B2 קָצִיר *harvesting, harvest, crop, time of harvest* BDB 894
7107 C2 קָצַף *he was wroth, angry* BDB 893
7110 D1 קֶצֶף *wrath*
7114 E2 קָצַר, קָצֵר *it was short, he was impatient*, see BDB 894
7114bC2 קָצַר *he reaped, harvested*
7121 A1 קָרָא *he called, proclaimed, read aloud* BDB 894ff. [BDB 897f.
7126 A1 קָרַב, קָרֵב *he drew near, approached*; H177 *to bring near, offer, present* ↑
7130 A1 קֶרֶב *inward part, midst* BDB 899
7133 B1 קָרְבָּן (*qorbān*) *offering, oblation* BDB 898
7136 D1 קָרָה *he encountered, met, it befell* BDB 899
7138 B1 קָרוֹב *near* BDB 898
7151 D1 קִרְיָה *town, city* BDB 900
7161 B1 קֶרֶן *horn* BDB 901f.
7167 B2 קָרַע *he tore, rent* BDB 902
7179 E2 קַשׁ (*qš̌š*) *stubble, chaff* BDB 905
7181 C1 קָשַׁב H *to give attention, attend* BDB 904
7185 D1 קָשָׁה *it was hard, difficult, severe*
7186 C2 קָשֶׁה *hard, difficult, severe*

קָשַׁר – רְכוּשׁ   Basic Hebrew

7194 C1 קָשַׁר *he bound, conspired* BDB 905
7198 B1 קֶשֶׁת *bow* (weapon, rainbow) BDB 905f.

ר

7200 A1 רָאָה *he saw;* N *to appear;* H *to show* BDB 906-09
7218 A1 רֹאשׁ *head* BDB 910f.
7223 A2 רִאשׁוֹן *foremost, former, first, chief* BDB 911f.
7225 B2 רֵאשִׁית *beginning, first, chief* BDB 912
7227 A1 רַב (rabb-) *much, many, great* BDB 912f.
7227bC1 רַב (rabb-) *chief* BDB 913
7230 A2 רֹב (rubb-) *multitude, abundance, greatness* BDB 913f.
7231 D2 רָבַב *he was/became many/great* BDB 912
7233 E2 רְבָבָה *multitude, myriad, ten thousand* BDB 914
7235 A1 רָבָה *he was/became great, many, much;* H_{162} *to make many, multiply, increase* BDB 915f.
7244 B2 רְבִיעִי *fourth* BDB 917f.
7257 C2 רָבַץ *he stretched out, lay down* BDB 918
7264 C1 רָגַז *he was agitated, excited, he quivered, quaked* BDB 919
7270 D1 רָגַל D *to explore, spy out, slander;* T *to teach to walk* BDB 920
7272 A1 רֶגֶל *foot; see* BDB 919f.
7275 E2 רָגַם *he stoned, killed by stoning* BDB 920
7281 D2 רֶגַע *moment, twinkling* BDB 921
7287 D2 רָדָה *he ruled, had dominion* BDB 921f.
7291 A2 רָדַף *he pursued, chased, persecuted* BDB 922f.
7301 E2 רָוָה *he drank his fill, was saturated, sated* BDB 924
7307 A1 רוּחַ *breath, wind, spirit; see* BDB 924ff.
7311 A2 רוּם *he was exalted, lifted, high;* L H *to raise, erect, exalt* BDB 926f.
7321 C1 רוּעַ H *to raise a shout, give a blast* BDB 929
7323 A2 רוּץ *to run* BDB 930
7337 D1 רָחַב *he was/grew large, wide;* H *to enlarge* BDB 931
7341 A2 רֹחַב *breadth, width* (54x Ezek. 40-48) BDB 931f.
7342 D2 רָחָב *wide, broad, spacious* BDB 932
7339 C1 רְחוֹב *plaza, broad open place*
7350 B1 רָחוֹק *distant, far; distance* BDB 935
7355 C1 רָחַם D *to have compassion, be compassionate* BDB 933
7358 D1 רֶחֶם, רַחַם *womb* BDB 933
7356 C2 רַחֲמִים *compassion*
7364 B1 רָחַץ *he bathed, washed* (tr. and intr.) BDB 934
7368 B2 רָחַק *he was/became distant, it was far* BDB 934f.
7378 B2 רִיב *to strive, contend, conduct a [legal] case, suit* BDB 936
7379 B2 רִיב *strife, dispute, case at law* BDB 936f.
7381 B2 רֵיחַ *scent, odor; esp. odor of sacrifice* (35x Lev.-Num.) BDB 926
7324 E1 רִיק H *to empty out, pour out/down* BDB 937f.
7387 E2 רֵיקָם *emptily, vainly, without effect* BDB 938
7326 D2 רִישׁ, רוּשׁ *he was in want, poor;* HtL *to impoverish self* BDB 930
7390 E2 רַךְ *tender, delicate, soft* BDB 940
7392 B1 רָכַב *he mounted (and rode), rode* BDB 938f.
7393 A2 רֶכֶב *chariotry, chariot; rider, millstone* BDB 939
7399 D1 רְכוּשׁ, רְכָשׁ *property, goods, movable possessions* BDB 940

7402 E1 רֹכֵל G50 of רכל *trader* (11x Ezek. 27)
7416 C2 רִמּוֹן *pomegranate* (tree, fruit, decoration) BDB 941f.
7420 E2 רֹמַח *lance, spear* BDB 942
7423 E2 רְמִיָּה *slackness, looseness, laxness; deceit, treachery* BDB 941
7429 E1 רָמַס *he trampled, trod* BDB 942
7430 E1 רָמַשׂ *he crept, moved lightly/about*; see BDB 942f.
7431 E1 רֶמֶשׂ *creeping/gliding things* (10x Gen.) BDB 943
7440 C2 רִנָּה *ringing cry, exultation*
7442 B2 רָנַן *he cried* (in joy, exultation, distress)
7451bA2 רַע *evil, distress, calamity, injury, bad(ness)* BDB 948f.
7453aA1 רַע *bad, evil*; BDB 948.I; the distinction between adj. and n., as indicated in BDB, can hardly be defended
7453 A2 רֵעַ *friend, companion, fellow* BDB 945f.
7455 E1 רֹעַ *badness, evil* BDB 947f.
7457 D2 רָעֵב *hungry* BDB 944
7458 A2 רָעָב *famine, hunger*
7451 A1 רָעָה (r'') *evil, misery, distress, injury* (cf. #7451) BDB 949
7462 A2 רָעָה (r'y) *he tended, pastured, grazed* BDB 944f.
7488 E1 רַעֲנָן *luxuriant, fresh, flourishing* BDB 947
7489 B1 רָעַע *he was evil/bad*; H70 *to hurt, do evil* BDB 949
7493 C2 רָעַשׁ *it quaked, shook*; H *to cause to quake* BDB 950
7494 E1 רַעַשׁ *quaking, shaking, earthquake*
7495 B2 רָפָא *he healed* BDB 950f.
7503 C1 רָפָה *it sank down, dropped, he relaxed*; H *to abandon* BDB 951f.
7521 B2 רָצָה *he was pleased with, accepted* BDB 953
7522 B2 רָצוֹן *goodwill, favor, acceptance, will*
7523 C1 רָצַח *he murdered, slew* BDB 953f.
7533 E1 רָצַץ *he crushed, oppressed*; Gp50 *the oppressed* BDB 954
7535 A2 רַק *only, surely, altogether*, see BDB 956
7549 E1 רָקִיעַ *extended surface, expanse, firmament* (9x Gen. 1)
7561 C2 רָשַׁע *he acted wickedly*; H *to condemn as guilty* BDB 957f.
7562 C1 רֶשַׁע *wickedness* BDB 957
7563 A1 רָשָׁע *wicked, criminal*
7568 D2 רֶשֶׁת *net* BDB 440

שׁ

–שֶׁ *who, which, that*; see BDB 979f. (but *not* abbrev. from אשר)
7580 D2 שָׁאַג *he roared* BDB 980
7585 B2 שְׁאוֹל *underworld, Sheol* BDB 982f.
7588 E1 שָׁאוֹן *roar, din, uproar, crash* BDB 981
7592 A2 שָׁאַל *he asked, inquired, asked for, borrowed* BDB 981f.
7604 A2 שָׁאַר N93 *to remain, be left over*; H *to leave over, spare* BDB 983f.
7605 D1 שְׁאָר *rest, residue, remnant* BDB 984
7607 E2 שְׁאֵר *flesh, blood-relation* BDB 984f.
7611 B2 שְׁאֵרִית *rest, residue, remnant, remainder* BDB 984
7617 C1 שָׁבָה *he took captive* BDB 985
7620 D2 שָׁבוּעַ *heptad, period of seven, week* BDB 988f.
7621 C2 שְׁבוּעָה *oath, curse* BDB 989f.
7626 A2 שֵׁבֶט *rod, staff, scepter; tribe* (145x) BDB 986f.

7628 B2 שְׁבִי *captivity, captives* (coll.) BDB 985
7622 C2 שְׁבִית, שְׁבוּת *captivity* BDB 986
7637 B1 שְׁבִיעִי *seventh* BDB 988
7641 E2 שִׁבֹּלֶת *ear* (of grain) (10x Gen. 41) BDB 987
7650 A2 שָׁבַע N *to swear, 'seven' oneself* BDB 989
7651 A1 שֶׁבַע, שִׁבְעָה *seven* BDB 987f.
7657 B1 שִׁבְעִים *seventy* BDB 988
7665 A2 שָׁבַר *he broke* (G_{53}, N_{57}, D_{36}) BDB 990f.
7666 D2 שָׁבַר *he bought grain*; H *to sell (cause to buy) grain* (14x Gen.) BDB 991
7667 C1 שֶׁבֶר, שֵׁבֶר *breaking, fracture, crushing, breach*; see BDB 991 [BDB 991f.
7673 B1 שָׁבַת G_{27} *he ceased, desisted, rested*; H_{40} *to cause to cease, end, destroy* ↑
7676 A2 שַׁבָּת *Sabbath*; see BDB 992
7684 E1 שְׁגָגָה *sin of error, inadvertence* (mostly Lev. Num.) BDB 993
7686 D2 שָׁגָה *he erred, sinned ignorantly or inadvertently, went astray*
7699 D2 שַׁד (root *šd*, not *šdd*) *breast* (usually du.) BDB 994
7701 D1 שֹׁד *violence, havoc, devastation, ruin*
7703 B2 שָׁדַד *he dealt violently with, despoiled, ruined*
7725 A1 שׁוּב G_{685} *to turn back, return, repent*; H_{353} *to bring back, turn back, cause to return*; see discussion in BDB 996-1000
7737 D2 שָׁוָה *he was like, resembled;* D *to smoothe, level* BDB 1000f.
7768 D2 שָׁוַע D *to cry for help* BDB 1002
7778 C2 שׁוֹעֵר *porter, door/gate-keeper* (20x Chr.) BDB 1045
8199 B2 שׁוֹפֵט *judge* BDB 1047f.
7782 B1 שׁוֹפָר *ram's horn, trumpet, Shofar* BDB 1051
7785 E1 שׁוֹק *leg, thigh* BDB 1003
7789 E2 שׁוּר *to behold, regard*
7794 B1 שׁוֹר *single head of cattle*; see BDB 1004
7799 E1 שׁוּשַׁן, שׁוֹשָׁן, שׁוֹשַׁנָּה *lily*
7806 D2 שָׁזַר Hp50 only *twisted* (only in Exod.) BDB 1004f.
7810 D2 שֹׁחַד *bribe* BDB 1005
7812 A2 שָׁחָה (should be listed as HtŠ of חָוָה) *to bow down* BDB 1005
7817 E1 שָׁחַח *he bowed, was prostrated/humbled* BDB 1005f.
7819 B1 שָׁחַט *he slaughtered*; Gp50 *hammered, beaten* BDB 1006
7834 D2 שַׁחַק *fine dust, cloud* BDB 1007
7837 D2 שַׁחַר *dawn, at dawn* [1007f.
7843 A2 שָׁחַת N *to be marred, spoiled, corrupt*; D H_{103} *to spoil, ruin, corrupt* BDB ↑
7845 D2 שַׁחַת *pit, grave* BDB 1001
7848 D1 שִׁטָּה *acacia tree/wood* (25x Exod. 25–38) BDB 1008
7857 C2 שָׁטַף *it flowed, overflowed, he rinsed* BDB 1009
7860 D1 שֹׁטֵר *officer, official* (originally, *scribe*)
7891 B1 שִׁיר *to sing*, L_{26} BDB 1010
7892 B1 שִׁיר *song*
7896 B1 שִׁית *to put, set, appoint, fix* BDB 1011
7901 A1 שָׁכַב *he lay down*; see BDB 1011f.
7911 A2 שָׁכַח *he forgot* BDB 1013
7921 D2 שָׁכֹל, שָׁכַל *he was bereaved*; D *to make childless, cause barrenness*
7925 B2 שָׁכַם H *to rise early, make an early start* BDB 1014
7926 D2 שְׁכֶם *shoulder*

7931 A2 שָׁכַן, שָׁכֵן *he settled down, abode, dwelt* BDB 1014f.
7934 D2 שָׁכֵן *inhabitant, neighbor* BDB 1015
7937 E1 שָׁכַר *he was/became drunk*; D H *to make drunken* BDB 1016
7941 D2 שֵׁכָר *strong/intoxicating drink*
7950 D2 שֶׁלֶג *snow* BDB 1017
7965 A1 שָׁלוֹם *completeness, soundness, welfare, peace* BDB 1022f.
7971 A1 שָׁלַח *he sent, stretched out* (hand) BDB 1018f.
7979 B1 שֻׁלְחָן *table* BDB 1020
7991 E1 שָׁלִישׁ *adjutant, officer* (perhaps *third man* on chariot) BDB 1026
7992 A2 שְׁלִישִׁי *third* (ordinal, sometimes fraction) BDB 1026
7993 A2 שָׁלַךְ H$_{112}$ *to throw fling, cast* BDB 1020f.
7997 E2 שָׁלַל *he spoiled, plundered* BDB 1021
7998 B1 שָׁלָל *spoil, booty, plunder, prey* BDB 1021f.
7999 A2 שָׁלֵם *he was complete, sound*; D$_{89}$ *to complete, finish, restore, recompense, reward* BDB 1022
8002 B1 שֶׁלֶם, all but once pl. שְׁלָמִים *peace-offering* (49x Lev.-Num.) see BDB 1023
8025 D1 שָׁלַף *he drew out/off* BDB 1025
7969 A1 שָׁלֹשׁ, שְׁלֹשָׁה *three* BDB 1025f.
7970 B2 שְׁלֹשִׁים *thirty* BDB 1026
8032 D1 שִׁלְשֹׁם *3 days ago, day before yesterday*
8033 A1 שָׁם *there, thither*; שָׁמָּה *thither* BDB 1027
8034 A1 שֵׁם *name*, see BDB 1027f. [BDB 1029
8045 B1 שָׁמַד N *to be annihilated, exterminated*; H$_{69}$ *to annihilate, exterminate* ↑
8052 D1 שְׁמוּעָה *report, tidings, mention* BDB 1035
8064 A1 שָׁמַיִם *heaven(s), sky* BDB 1029f
8066 C2 שְׁמִינִי *eighth* BDB 1033
8074 B1 שָׁמֵם *he was appalled, desolated* BDB 1030f.
8077 B2 שְׁמָמָה *devastation, waste* BDB 1031
8081 A2 שֶׁמֶן *fat, oil, olive-oil* BDB 1032
8083 A2 שְׁמֹנֶה *eight* BDB 1032f.
8084 C2 שְׁמֹנִים *eighty* BDB 1033
8085 A1 שָׁמַע G$_{1052}$ *he heard*, H$_{63}$ *to cause to hear* BDB 1033f.
8088 E1 שֵׁמַע *hearing, report* BDB 1034
8104 A1 שָׁמַר *he kept, watched, preserved* BDB 1036f.
8121 A2 שֶׁמֶשׁ *sun* BDB 1039
8127 B2 שֵׁן *(šinn-) tooth, ivory* BDB 1042
8138 B1 שָׁנָה *he changed* (intr.); D *to remove, change* (trans.) BDB 1039
8141 A1 שָׁנָה, pl. שָׁנִים *year* BDB 1040
8142 D2 שֵׁנָה *sleep* BDB 446
8144 C1 שָׁנִי *scarlet* (26x Exod.) BDB 1040
8145 A2 שֵׁנִי, שֵׁנִית *second, 2nd* BDB 1041
8147 A1 שְׁנַיִם, שְׁתַּיִם, שְׁנֵי, שְׁתֵּי *two* BDB 1040f.
8172 D2 שָׁעַן N *to lean on, support oneself* BDB 1043
8179 A1 שַׁעַר *gate* BDB 1044f.
8198 B2 שִׁפְחָה *maid, maid-servant* (28x Gen.) BDB 1046
8199 A1 שָׁפַט *he judged, governed* BDB 1047f.
8196 E2 שְׁפָטִים *acts of judgment* (10x Ezek.) BDB 1048 under שֶׁפֶט
8210 A2 שָׁפַךְ *he poured (out)* BDB 1049f.

8213 D1 שָׁפֵל *he was/became abased/low* BDB 1050
8217 E1 שָׁפָל *low* (in height or station)
8219 D2 שְׁפֵלָה *lowland, Shephelah*
8245 E1 שָׁקַד *he kept watch, was wakeful* BDB 1052
8248 B1 שָׁקָה H *to irrigate, water, give to drink*
8251 D1 שִׁקּוּץ *detested thing, abominable thing* BDB 1055
8252 C2 שָׁקַט *he was quiet, undisturbed* BDB 1052f.
8254 D2 שָׁקַל *he weighed, weighed out* BDB 1053
8255 B1 שֶׁקֶל *shekel* (a weight, later a coin) BDB 1053f.
8259 D2 שָׁקַף N, H *to overhang, look out and down* BDB 1054
8267 A2 שֶׁקֶר *lie, deceit, deception, falsehood* BDB 1055
8318 E2 שֶׁרֶץ (coll.) *swarming creatures* BDB 1056
8330 C2 שֹׁרֶשׁ *root* BDB 1057
8334 B1 שָׁרַת D *to minister, serve* BDB 1058
8336 C2 שֵׁשׁ *byssus, fine linen* (32x Exod.) BDB 1058
8337 A1 שֵׁשׁ, שִׁשָּׁה *six* BDB 995
8345 D1 שִׁשִּׁי, שִׁשִּׁית *sixth* BDB 995
8346 B2 שִׁשִּׁים *sixty*
8354 A1 שָׁתָה *he drank* BDB 1059
8147 A1 שְׁתַּיִם, שְׁתֵּי *two* BDB 1040f.

שׂ

7639 E2 שְׂבָכָה *lattice-work, network* BDB 959
7646 B1 שָׂבַע *he was sated, satisfied*
7682 D2 שָׂגַב *it was (inaccessibly) high* BDB 960
7704 A1 שָׂדֶה *open field/land, field* BDB 961
7716 C1 שֶׂה *one of a flock, sheep, goat* BDB 961f.
7760 A1 שׂוּם, שִׂים *to put, place, set* BDB 962ff.
7797 D1 שׂוּשׂ, שִׂישׂ *to exult, rejoice* BDB 965
7832 C2 שָׂחַק *he laughed*; D *to play, jest, make sport* BDB 965f.
7854 D1 שָׂטָן *adversary, Satan* (20x, 14x Job 1-2) BDB 966
7872 E1 שֵׂיבָה *grey hair, hoary head, old age*
7878 D2 שִׂיחַ *he complained, mused, talked of* (14x Prov.) BDB 967
7916 E1 שָׂכִיר *hired, hireling* BDB 969
7919 B1 שָׂכַל *he was prudent*; H *to prosper, ponder, give attention to*; see BDB 968
7922 E2 שֶׂכֶל, שֵׂכֶל *prudence, insight*
7936 D2 שָׂכַר *he hired* BDB 968f.
8008 E2 שַׂלְמָה (cf. #8071) *mantle, wrapper* BDB 971
8040 B2 שְׂמֹאל *left (hand), north* BDB 969
8055 A2 שָׂמַח, שָׂמֵחַ *he was glad*; D *to gladden* BDB 970
8056 D2 שָׂמֵחַ *glad, joyful, merry*
8057 B1 שִׂמְחָה *gladness, mirth, joy* (46x of religious joy in Pss., Chr.)
8071 C2 שִׂמְלָה *mantle, wrapper* BDB 971
8130 A2 שָׂנֵא *he hated*
8135 E1 שִׂנְאָה *hating, hatred* BDB 971f.
8163 B2 שָׂעִיר *he-goat, buck* BDB 972
8181 C2 שֵׂעָר *hair* (animal, human)
8184 C2 שְׂעֹרָה *barley*, pl. the grains, measured, cooked, etc., see BDB 972
8193 A2 שָׂפָה *lip* (of mouth, lake), *speech, shore* BDB 973f.

8242 C1 שַׂק *sack, sackcloth* BDB 974
8269 A1 שַׂר (*śarr-*) *prince, ruler, chieftain* BDB 978f.
8300 D1 שָׂרִיד *survivor, one who or that which escaped* BDB 975
8313 A2 שָׂרַף *he burned* (70x + בָּאֵשׁ) BDB 976f.
8342 D2 שָׂשׂוֹן *exultation, rejoicing* BDB 965

ת

8379 D2 תַּאֲוָה *longing, desire* BDB 16 (*sic*)
8384 C2 תְּאֵנָה *fig, fig-tree* BDB 1061
8389 E2 תֹּאַר *outline, form*
8392 D1 תֵּבָה *(Noah's) ark, (Moses') vessel* (26x Gen.) BDB 1061
8393 C1 תְּבוּאָה *product, revenue, yield, income* BDB 100
8394 C1 תְּבוּנָה *understanding* BDB 108
8398 C2 תֵּבֵל *world* (the planet) BDB 385
8401 E1 תֶּבֶן *straw, fodder, chaff* BDB 1061f.
8403 D2 תַּבְנִית *construction, pattern, figure* BDB 125
8414 D2 תֹּהוּ *formlessness, confusion, unreality, emptiness* (11x Isa.) BDB 1062
8415 C2 תְּהוֹם *deep (subterranean waters), sea, abyss* BDB 1062f.
8416 B2 תְּהִלָּה *(song of) praise* (29x Pss.) BDB 239f.
8426 C2 תּוֹדָה *thanksgiving, thank-offering,* see BDB 392f.
8432 A1 תָּוֶךְ, oft. cstr. תּוֹךְ (+ בְּ) *midst* BDB 1063
8433 D2 תּוֹכַחַת *argument, reproof* (16x Prov.) BDB 407
8435 C2 תּוֹלְדוֹת pl. *generations* (a man and his descendants) BDB 410
8438 C2 תּוֹלֵעָה, תּוֹלַעַת *worm, grub*; also *crimson* from such, *crimson cloth* (26x Exod.) BDB 1069
8441 A2 תּוֹעֵבָה *abomination,* see BDB 1072f.
8444 D2 תּוֹצָאוֹת pl. *extremities, sources* (14x Josh.) BDB 426
8446 D1 תּוּר *to seek out, spy out, explore* BDB 1064
8451 A1 תּוֹרָה *instruction, law, direction, Torah* BDB 435f.
8457 D2 תַּזְנוּת *fornication* (only in Ezek. 16, 23) BDB 276
8462 D2 תְּחִלָּה *beginning* BDB 321
8467 D1 תְּחִנָּה *favor, supplication for favor* BDB 337
8469 E1 תַּחֲנוּנִים *supplication for favor* BDB 337
8478 A1 תַּחַת *under, beneath, below, instead of*; see BDB 1065f.
8486 D2 תֵּימָן *south, south wind* BDB 412
8492 C2 תִּירוֹשׁ *must, new wine* BDB 440
8504 C1 תְּכֵלֶת *violet, violet thread/stuff* (34x Exod.) BDB 1067
8505 E1 תָּכַן *he estimated*; N *to be estimated, adjusted*; D *to mete out, regulate* BDB 1067
8518 C2 תָּלָה *he hanged, put to death by hanging* BDB 1067f.
8535 E2 תָּם *complete, perfect, wound, whole* BDB 1070f.
8537 D1 תֹּם *completeness, integrity* BDB 1070
8543 D2 תְּמוֹל (also אֶתְמוֹל) *yesterday, recently*; see BDB 1069f. [1026
8543bE2 תְּמוֹל שִׁלְשֹׁם *day before yesterday, yesterday and the day before, recently* BDB ↑
8548 A2 תָּמִיד *continuity, continually, continuously* BDB 556
8549 B1 תָּמִים *complete, sound, whole, innocent* BDB 1071
8551 D2 תָּמַךְ *he grasped, lay hold of, supported, attained* BDB 1069
8552 B2 תַּם, תָּמַם *it was complete, finished*; see BDB 1070
8561 E1 תִּמֹרָה, prob. תִּמֹּרָה *palm(-tree) figure used as ornament* BDB 1071

8573 C2 תְּנוּפָה *swinging, brandishing, wave-offering* BDB 632
8574 E2 תַּנּוּר *(portable) stove, fire-pot* BDB 1072
8581 D2 תָּעַב N *to be abhorred*; D *to regard as* or *to cause to be an abomination*; H *to do abominably* BDB 1073
8582 B2 תָּעָה *he erred*
8596 E1 תֹּף *(tupp-) timbrel, tamborine* BDB 1074
8597 C1 תִּפְאֶרֶת *beauty, glory, honor* BDB 802
8605 B1 תְּפִלָּה *prayer* BDB 813
8610 B2 תָּפַשׂ *he grasped, lay hold of, wielded* BDB 1074f.
8615 C2 תִּקְוָה *hope* BDB 876
8628 B2 תָּקַע *he thrust, drove, gave a blast/blow, struck, clapped* BDB 1075
8641 B1 תְּרוּמָה *contribution, offering* BDB 929
8643 C2 תְּרוּעָה *shout/blast of war/alarm/joy* BDB 929f.
8655 E2 תְּרָפִים pl. *idols, household gods, Teraphim* BDB 1076
8672 B2 תְּשַׁע, תִּשְׁעָה *nine* BDB 1077
8668 C2 תְּשׁוּעָה *deliverance, salvation* BDB 448
8671 E1 תְּשִׁיעִי *ninth* BDB 1077
8673 E1 תִּשְׁעִים *ninety*

According to my count, this list contains 1,539 words, including bound morphemes that serve as words (e.g. –וְ *and*, –וֹ *his*, etc.). The distribution is as follows:

A1	> 200x	242	=	242
A2	100-199x	164	=	406
B1	70- 99x	120	=	526
B2	50- 69x	146	=	672
C1	40- 49x	130	=	802
C2	30- 39x	184	=	986
D1	25- 29x	115	=	1,101
D2	20- 24x	184	=	1,285
E1	17- 19x	148	=	1,433
E2	15- 16x	106	=	1,539

The Book of Esther

Specially Edited for Inclusion in

HANDBOOK OF BIBLICAL HEBREW
by
WILLIAM SANFORD LA SOR

www.ingramcontent.com/pod-product-compliance
Lightning Source LLC
Chambersburg PA
CBHW081143290426
44108CB00018B/2422

* 9 7 8 0 8 0 2 8 0 4 4 4 0 *

מגלת אסתר
THE BOOK OF ESTHER

פרק א CHAPTER 1

א וַיְהִ֖י בִּימֵ֣י אֲחַשְׁוֵר֑וֹשׁ ה֣וּא אֲחַשְׁוֵר֗וֹשׁ הַמֹּלֵךְ֙ מֵהֹ֣דּוּ וְעַד־
2 כּ֔וּשׁ שֶׁ֛בַע וְעֶשְׂרִ֥ים וּמֵאָ֖ה מְדִינָֽה: בַּיָּמִ֣ים הָהֵ֔ם כְּשֶׁ֣בֶת ׀
הַמֶּ֣לֶךְ אֲחַשְׁוֵר֗וֹשׁ עַ֚ל כִּסֵּ֣א מַלְכוּת֔וֹ אֲשֶׁ֖ר בְּשׁוּשַׁ֥ן הַבִּירָֽה:
3 בִּשְׁנַ֤ת שָׁלוֹשׁ֙ לְמָלְכ֔וֹ עָשָׂ֣ה מִשְׁתֶּ֔ה לְכָל־שָׂרָ֖יו וַעֲבָדָ֑יו
חֵ֣יל ׀ פָּרַ֣ס וּמָדַ֗י הַֽפַּרְתְּמִים֙ וְשָׂרֵ֣י הַמְּדִינ֔וֹת לְפָנָֽיו:
4 בְּהַרְאֹת֗וֹ אֶת־עֹ֙שֶׁר֙ כְּב֣וֹד מַלְכוּת֔וֹ וְאֶ֨ת־יְקָ֔ר תִּפְאֶ֖רֶת
ה גְּדוּלָּת֑וֹ יָמִ֣ים רַבִּ֔ים שְׁמוֹנִ֥ים וּמְאַ֖ת יֽוֹם: וּבִמְל֣וֹאת ׀ הַיָּמִ֣ים
הָאֵ֗לֶּה עָשָׂ֣ה הַמֶּ֡לֶךְ לְכָל־הָעָ֣ם הַנִּמְצְאִים֩ בְּשׁוּשַׁ֨ן הַבִּירָ֜ה
לְמִגָּד֣וֹל וְעַד־קָטָ֗ן מִשְׁתֶּ֛ה שִׁבְעַ֥ת יָמִ֖ים בַּחֲצַ֕ר גִּנַּ֥ת בִּיתַ֖ן
הַמֶּֽלֶךְ: ח֣וּר ׀ כַּרְפַּ֣ס וּתְכֵ֗לֶת אָחוּז֙ בְּחַבְלֵי־ב֣וּץ וְאַרְגָּמָ֔ן
6 עַל־גְּלִ֥ילֵי כֶ֖סֶף וְעַמּ֣וּדֵי שֵׁ֑שׁ מִטּ֣וֹת ׀ זָהָ֣ב וָכֶ֗סֶף עַ֛ל רִֽצְפַ֥ת
7 בַּהַט־וָשֵׁ֖שׁ וְדַ֥ר וְסֹחָֽרֶת: וְהַשְׁקוֹת֙ בִּכְלֵ֣י זָהָ֔ב וְכֵלִ֖ים
8 מִכֵּלִ֣ים שׁוֹנִ֑ים וְיֵ֥ין מַלְכ֛וּת רָ֖ב כְּיַ֥ד הַמֶּֽלֶךְ: וְהַשְּׁתִיָּ֥ה
כַדָּ֖ת אֵ֣ין אֹנֵ֑ס כִּי־כֵ֣ן ׀ יִסַּ֣ד הַמֶּ֗לֶךְ עַ֚ל כָּל־רַ֣ב בֵּית֔וֹ
9 לַעֲשׂ֖וֹת כִּרְצ֥וֹן אִישׁ־וָאִֽישׁ: גַּ֚ם וַשְׁתִּ֣י הַמַּלְכָּ֔ה עָשְׂתָ֖ה
מִשְׁתֵּ֣ה נָשִׁ֑ים בֵּ֚ית הַמַּלְכ֔וּת אֲשֶׁ֖ר לַמֶּ֥לֶךְ אֲחַשְׁוֵרֽוֹשׁ: בַּיּוֹם֙
י הַשְּׁבִיעִ֔י כְּט֥וֹב לֵב־הַמֶּ֖לֶךְ בַּיָּ֑יִן אָמַ֡ר לִ֠מְהוּמָן בִּזְּתָ֨א
חַרְבוֹנָ֜א בִּגְתָ֤א וַאֲבַגְתָא֙ זֵתַ֣ר וְכַרְכַּ֔ס שִׁבְעַת֙ הַסָּרִיסִ֔ים

v. 5. ובמלאת קרי   v. 6. ח' רבתי   v. 8. א' מ"א ר' בקמץ   v. 13. ס' רבתי י"ב

11 הַמְשָׁרְתִ֕ים אֶת־פְּנֵ֖י הַמֶּ֥לֶךְ אֲחַשְׁוֵרֽוֹשׁ׃ לְ֠הָבִיא אֶת־
וַשְׁתִּ֧י הַמַּלְכָּ֛ה לִפְנֵ֥י הַמֶּ֖לֶךְ בְּכֶ֣תֶר מַלְכ֑וּת לְהַרְא֨וֹת הָֽעַמִּ֤ים
12 וְהַשָּׂרִים֙ אֶת־יָפְיָ֔הּ כִּֽי־טוֹבַ֥ת מַרְאֶ֖ה הִֽיא׃ וַתְּמָאֵ֞ן הַמַּלְכָּ֣ה
וַשְׁתִּ֗י לָבוֹא֙ בִּדְבַ֣ר הַמֶּ֔לֶךְ אֲשֶׁ֖ר בְּיַ֣ד הַסָּרִיסִ֑ים וַיִּקְצֹ֤ף
13 הַמֶּ֙לֶךְ֙ מְאֹ֔ד וַחֲמָת֖וֹ בָּעֲרָ֥ה בֽוֹ׃ וַיֹּ֣אמֶר הַמֶּ֔לֶךְ
לַחֲכָמִ֖ים יֹדְעֵ֣י הָֽעִתִּ֑ים כִּי־כֵן֙ דְּבַ֣ר הַמֶּ֔לֶךְ לִפְנֵ֕י כָּל־יֹדְעֵ֖י
14 דָּ֥ת וָדִֽין׃ וְהַקָּרֹ֣ב אֵלָ֗יו כַּרְשְׁנָ֤א שֵׁתָר֙ אַדְמָ֣תָא תַרְשִׁ֔ישׁ
מֶ֥רֶס מַרְסְנָ֖א מְמוּכָ֑ן שִׁבְעַ֞ת שָׂרֵ֣י ׀ פָּרַ֣ס וּמָדַ֗י רֹאֵי֙ פְּנֵ֣י
טו הַמֶּ֔לֶךְ הַיֹּשְׁבִ֥ים רִאשֹׁנָ֖ה בַּמַּלְכֽוּת׃ כְּדָת֙ מַה־לַּעֲשׂ֔וֹת
בַּמַּלְכָּ֖ה וַשְׁתִּ֑י עַ֣ל ׀ אֲשֶׁ֣ר לֹא־עָשְׂתָ֗ה אֶֽת־מַאֲמַר֙ הַמֶּ֣לֶךְ
16 אֲחַשְׁוֵר֔וֹשׁ בְּיַ֖ד הַסָּרִיסִֽים׃ וַיֹּ֣אמֶר מוּמְכָ֗ן* לִפְנֵ֤י הַמֶּ֙לֶךְ֙
וְהַשָּׂרִ֔ים לֹ֤א עַל־הַמֶּ֙לֶךְ֙ לְבַדּ֔וֹ עָוְתָ֖ה וַשְׁתִּ֣י הַמַּלְכָּ֑ה כִּ֚י
עַל־כָּל־הַשָּׂרִים֙ וְעַל־כָּל־הָ֣עַמִּ֔ים אֲשֶׁ֕ר בְּכָל־מְדִינ֖וֹת
17 הַמֶּ֥לֶךְ אֲחַשְׁוֵרֽוֹשׁ׃ כִּֽי־יֵצֵ֤א דְבַר־הַמַּלְכָּה֙ עַל־כָּל־הַנָּשִׁ֔ים
לְהַבְז֥וֹת בַּעְלֵיהֶ֖ן בְּעֵינֵיהֶ֑ן בְּאָמְרָ֗ם הַמֶּ֣לֶךְ אֲחַשְׁוֵר֡וֹשׁ אָמַ֞ר
18 לְהָבִ֨יא אֶת־וַשְׁתִּ֧י הַמַּלְכָּ֛ה לְפָנָ֖יו וְלֹא־בָֽאָה׃ וְֽהַיּ֨וֹם הַזֶּ֜ה
תֹּאמַ֣רְנָה ׀ שָׂר֣וֹת פָּֽרַס־וּמָדַ֗י אֲשֶׁ֤ר שָֽׁמְעוּ֙ אֶת־דְּבַ֣ר הַמַּלְכָּ֔ה
19 לְכֹ֖ל שָׂרֵ֣י הַמֶּ֑לֶךְ וּכְדַ֖י בִּזָּ֥יוֹן וָקָֽצֶף׃ אִם־עַל־הַמֶּ֣לֶךְ ט֗וֹב
יֵצֵ֣א דְבַר־מַלְכוּת֮ מִלְּפָנָיו֒ וְיִכָּתֵ֛ב בְּדָתֵ֥י פָֽרַס־וּמָדַ֖י וְלֹ֣א
יַעֲב֑וֹר אֲשֶׁ֨ר לֹא־תָב֜וֹא וַשְׁתִּ֗י לִפְנֵי֙ הַמֶּ֣לֶךְ אֲחַשְׁוֵר֔וֹשׁ
כ וּמַלְכוּתָהּ֙ יִתֵּ֣ן הַמֶּ֔לֶךְ לִרְעוּתָ֖הּ הַטּוֹבָ֥ה מִמֶּֽנָּה׃ וְנִשְׁמַע֩
פִּתְגָ֨ם הַמֶּ֤לֶךְ אֲשֶׁר־יַעֲשֶׂה֙ בְּכָל־מַלְכוּת֔וֹ כִּ֥י רַבָּ֖ה הִ֑יא
21 וְכָל־הַנָּשִׁ֗ים יִתְּנ֤וּ יְקָר֙ לְבַעְלֵיהֶ֔ן לְמִגָּד֖וֹל וְעַד־קָטָֽן׃ וַיִּיטַב֙

v. 14. בנ״א דרי בקמץ   v. 16. ממוכן קרי

הַדָּבָר בְּעֵינֵי הַמֶּלֶךְ וְהַשָּׂרִים וַיַּעַשׂ הַמֶּלֶךְ כִּדְבַר מְמוּכָן׃
22 וַיִּשְׁלַח סְפָרִים אֶל־כָּל־מְדִינוֹת הַמֶּלֶךְ אֶל־מְדִינָה וּמְדִינָה
כִּכְתָבָהּ וְאֶל־עַם וָעָם כִּלְשׁוֹנוֹ לִהְיוֹת כָּל־אִישׁ שֹׂרֵר
בְּבֵיתוֹ וּמְדַבֵּר כִּלְשׁוֹן עַמּוֹ׃

ב CHAPTER 2 פרק ב

א אַחַר הַדְּבָרִים הָאֵלֶּה כְּשֹׁךְ חֲמַת הַמֶּלֶךְ אֲחַשְׁוֵרוֹשׁ זָכַר
אֶת־וַשְׁתִּי וְאֵת אֲשֶׁר־עָשָׂתָה וְאֵת אֲשֶׁר־נִגְזַר עָלֶיהָ׃
2 וַיֹּאמְרוּ נַעֲרֵי־הַמֶּלֶךְ מְשָׁרְתָיו יְבַקְשׁוּ לַמֶּלֶךְ נְעָרוֹת בְּתוּלוֹת
3 טוֹבוֹת מַרְאֶה׃ וְיַפְקֵד הַמֶּלֶךְ פְּקִידִים בְּכָל־מְדִינוֹת
מַלְכוּתוֹ וְיִקְבְּצוּ אֶת־כָּל־נַעֲרָה־בְתוּלָה טוֹבַת מַרְאֶה אֶל־
שׁוּשַׁן הַבִּירָה אֶל־בֵּית הַנָּשִׁים אֶל־יַד הֵגֶא סְרִיס הַמֶּלֶךְ
4 שֹׁמֵר הַנָּשִׁים וְנָתוֹן תַּמְרוּקֵיהֶן׃ וְהַנַּעֲרָה אֲשֶׁר תִּיטַב
בְּעֵינֵי הַמֶּלֶךְ תִּמְלֹךְ תַּחַת וַשְׁתִּי וַיִּיטַב הַדָּבָר בְּעֵינֵי
ה הַמֶּלֶךְ וַיַּעַשׂ כֵּן׃ אִישׁ יְהוּדִי הָיָה בְּשׁוּשַׁן הַבִּירָה
6 וּשְׁמוֹ מָרְדֳּכַי בֶּן* יָאִיר בֶּן־שִׁמְעִי בֶּן־קִישׁ אִישׁ יְמִינִי׃ אֲשֶׁר
הָגְלָה מִירוּשָׁלַיִם עִם־הַגֹּלָה אֲשֶׁר הָגְלְתָה עִם יְכָנְיָה
7 מֶלֶךְ־יְהוּדָה אֲשֶׁר הֶגְלָה נְבוּכַדְנֶצַּר מֶלֶךְ בָּבֶל׃ וַיְהִי אֹמֵן
אֶת־הֲדַסָּה הִיא אֶסְתֵּר בַּת־דֹּדוֹ כִּי אֵין לָהּ אָב וָאֵם
וְהַנַּעֲרָה יְפַת־תֹּאַר וְטוֹבַת מַרְאֶה וּבְמוֹת אָבִיהָ וְאִמָּהּ
8 לְקָחָהּ מָרְדֳּכַי לוֹ לְבַת׃ וַיְהִי בְּהִשָּׁמַע דְּבַר־הַמֶּלֶךְ וְדָתוֹ
וּבְהִקָּבֵץ נְעָרוֹת רַבּוֹת אֶל־שׁוּשַׁן הַבִּירָה אֶל־יַד הֵגָי
וַתִּלָּקַח אֶסְתֵּר אֶל־בֵּית הַמֶּלֶךְ אֶל־יַד הֵגַי שֹׁמֵר הַנָּשִׁים׃
9 וַתִּיטַב הַנַּעֲרָה בְעֵינָיו וַתִּשָּׂא חֶסֶד לְפָנָיו וַיְבַהֵל אֶת־

בּ׳ v. 5. סגול בלא מקף

תַּמְרוּקֶיהָ וְאֶת־מָנוֹתֶהָ לָתֵת לָהּ וְאֵת שֶׁבַע הַנְּעָרוֹת
הָרְאֻיוֹת לָתֶת־לָהּ מִבֵּית הַמֶּלֶךְ וַיְשַׁנֶּהָ וְאֶת־נַעֲרוֹתֶיהָ
י לְטוֹב בֵּית הַנָּשִׁים׃ לֹא־הִגִּידָה אֶסְתֵּר אֶת־עַמָּהּ וְאֶת־
11 מוֹלַדְתָּהּ כִּי מָרְדֳּכַי צִוָּה עָלֶיהָ אֲשֶׁר לֹא־תַגִּיד׃ וּבְכָל־
יוֹם וָיוֹם מָרְדֳּכַי מִתְהַלֵּךְ לִפְנֵי חֲצַר בֵּית־הַנָּשִׁים לָדַעַת
12 אֶת־שְׁלוֹם אֶסְתֵּר וּמַה־יֵּעָשֶׂה בָּהּ׃ וּבְהַגִּיעַ תֹּר נַעֲרָה
וְנַעֲרָה לָבוֹא ׀ אֶל־הַמֶּלֶךְ אֲחַשְׁוֵרוֹשׁ מִקֵּץ הֱיוֹת לָהּ כְּדָת
הַנָּשִׁים שְׁנֵים עָשָׂר חֹדֶשׁ כִּי כֵּן יִמְלְאוּ יְמֵי מְרוּקֵיהֶן שִׁשָּׁה
חֳדָשִׁים בְּשֶׁמֶן הַמֹּר וְשִׁשָּׁה חֳדָשִׁים בַּבְּשָׂמִים וּבְתַמְרוּקֵי
13 הַנָּשִׁים׃ וּבָזֶה הַנַּעֲרָה בָּאָה אֶל־הַמֶּלֶךְ אֵת כָּל־אֲשֶׁר
תֹּאמַר יִנָּתֵן לָהּ לָבוֹא עִמָּהּ מִבֵּית הַנָּשִׁים עַד־בֵּית הַמֶּלֶךְ׃
14 בָּעֶרֶב ׀ הִיא בָאָה וּבַבֹּקֶר הִיא שָׁבָה אֶל־בֵּית הַנָּשִׁים
שֵׁנִי אֶל־יַד שַׁעַשְׁגַז סְרִיס הַמֶּלֶךְ שֹׁמֵר הַפִּילַגְשִׁים לֹא־
תָבוֹא עוֹד אֶל־הַמֶּלֶךְ כִּי אִם־חָפֵץ בָּהּ הַמֶּלֶךְ וְנִקְרְאָה*
טו בְשֵׁם׃ וּבְהַגִּיעַ תֹּר־אֶסְתֵּר בַּת־אֲבִיחַיִל ׀ דֹּד מָרְדֳּכַי אֲשֶׁר
לָקַח־לוֹ לְבַת לָבוֹא אֶל־הַמֶּלֶךְ לֹא בִקְשָׁה דָּבָר כִּי אִם
אֶת־אֲשֶׁר יֹאמַר הֵגַי סְרִיס־הַמֶּלֶךְ שֹׁמֵר הַנָּשִׁים וַתְּהִי
16 אֶסְתֵּר נֹשֵׂאת חֵן בְּעֵינֵי כָּל־רֹאֶיהָ׃ וַתִּלָּקַח אֶסְתֵּר אֶל־
הַמֶּלֶךְ אֲחַשְׁוֵרוֹשׁ אֶל־בֵּית מַלְכוּתוֹ בַּחֹדֶשׁ הָעֲשִׂירִי הוּא־
17 חֹדֶשׁ טֵבֵת בִּשְׁנַת־שֶׁבַע לְמַלְכוּתוֹ׃ וַיֶּאֱהַב הַמֶּלֶךְ אֶת־
אֶסְתֵּר מִכָּל־הַנָּשִׁים וַתִּשָּׂא־חֵן וָחֶסֶד לְפָנָיו מִכָּל־הַבְּתוּלוֹת
18 וַיָּשֶׂם כֶּתֶר־מַלְכוּת בְּרֹאשָׁהּ וַיַּמְלִיכֶהָ תַּחַת וַשְׁתִּי׃ וַיַּעַשׂ
הַמֶּלֶךְ מִשְׁתֶּה גָדוֹל לְכָל־שָׂרָיו וַעֲבָדָיו אֵת מִשְׁתֵּה

v. 14. הרי בח״ק

אֶסְתֵּ֔ר וַהֲנָחָ֥ה לַמְּדִינ֖וֹת עָשָׂ֑ה וַיִּתֵּ֥ן מַשְׂאֵ֖ת כְּיַ֥ד הַמֶּֽלֶךְ׃
19 וּבְהִקָּבֵ֥ץ בְּתוּל֖וֹת שֵׁנִ֑ית וּמָרְדֳּכַ֖י יֹשֵׁ֥ב בְּשַֽׁעַר־הַמֶּֽלֶךְ׃
כ אֵ֣ין אֶסְתֵּ֗ר מַגֶּ֤דֶת מֽוֹלַדְתָּהּ֙ וְאֶת־עַמָּ֔הּ כַּאֲשֶׁ֛ר צִוָּ֥ה עָלֶ֖יהָ מָרְדֳּכָ֑י וְאֶת־מַאֲמַ֤ר מָרְדֳּכַי֙ אֶסְתֵּ֣ר עֹשָׂ֔ה כַּאֲשֶׁ֛ר הָיְתָ֥ה בְאָמְנָ֖ה אִתּֽוֹ׃
21 בַּיָּמִ֣ים הָהֵ֔ם וּמָרְדֳּכַ֖י יֹשֵׁ֣ב בְּשַֽׁעַר־הַמֶּ֑לֶךְ קָצַף֩ בִּגְתָ֨ן וָתֶ֜רֶשׁ שְׁנֵֽי־סָרִיסֵ֤י הַמֶּ֙לֶךְ֙ מִשֹּׁמְרֵ֣י הַסַּ֔ף
22 וַיְבַקְשׁוּ֙ לִשְׁלֹ֣חַ יָ֔ד בַּמֶּ֖לֶךְ אֲחַשְׁוֵרֹֽשׁ׃ וַיִּוָּדַ֤ע הַדָּבָר֙ לְמָרְדֳּכַ֔י וַיַּגֵּ֖ד לְאֶסְתֵּ֣ר הַמַּלְכָּ֑ה וַתֹּ֧אמֶר אֶסְתֵּ֛ר לַמֶּ֖לֶךְ בְּשֵׁ֥ם מָרְדֳּכָֽי׃
23 וַיְבֻקַּ֤שׁ הַדָּבָר֙ וַיִּמָּצֵ֔א וַיִּתָּל֥וּ שְׁנֵיהֶ֖ם עַל־עֵ֑ץ וַיִּכָּתֵ֗ב בְּסֵ֛פֶר דִּבְרֵ֥י הַיָּמִ֖ים לִפְנֵ֥י הַמֶּֽלֶךְ׃

פרק ג CHAPTER 3

א אַחַ֣ר ׀ הַדְּבָרִ֣ים הָאֵ֗לֶּה גִּדַּל֩ הַמֶּ֨לֶךְ אֲחַשְׁוֵר֜וֹשׁ אֶת־הָמָ֧ן בֶּֽן־הַמְּדָ֛תָא הָאֲגָגִ֖י וַֽיְנַשְּׂאֵ֑הוּ וַיָּ֙שֶׂם֙ אֶת־כִּסְא֔וֹ מֵעַ֕ל כָּל־הַשָּׂרִ֖ים אֲשֶׁ֥ר אִתּֽוֹ׃
2 וְכָל־עַבְדֵ֨י הַמֶּ֜לֶךְ אֲשֶׁר־בְּשַׁ֣עַר הַמֶּ֗לֶךְ כֹּרְעִ֤ים וּמִֽשְׁתַּחֲוִים֙ לְהָמָ֔ן כִּי־כֵ֖ן צִוָּה־ל֣וֹ הַמֶּ֑לֶךְ וּמָ֨רְדֳּכַ֔י לֹ֥א יִכְרַ֖ע וְלֹ֥א יִֽשְׁתַּחֲוֶֽה׃
3 וַיֹּ֨אמְר֜וּ עַבְדֵ֥י הַמֶּ֛לֶךְ אֲשֶׁר־בְּשַׁ֥עַר הַמֶּ֖לֶךְ לְמָרְדֳּכָ֑י מַדּ֙וּעַ֙ אַתָּ֣ה עוֹבֵ֔ר אֵ֖ת מִצְוַ֥ת הַמֶּֽלֶךְ׃
4 וַיְהִ֗י *בְּאָמְרָם אֵלָיו֙ י֣וֹם וָי֔וֹם וְלֹ֥א שָׁמַ֖ע אֲלֵיהֶ֑ם וַיַּגִּ֣ידוּ לְהָמָ֗ן לִרְאוֹת֙ הֲיַֽעַמְדוּ֙ דִּבְרֵ֣י מָרְדֳּכַ֔י כִּֽי־הִגִּ֥יד לָהֶ֖ם אֲשֶׁר־ה֥וּא יְהוּדִֽי׃
5 וַיַּ֣רְא הָמָ֔ן כִּי־אֵ֣ין מָרְדֳּכַ֔י כֹּרֵ֥עַ וּמִֽשְׁתַּחֲוֶ֖ה ל֑וֹ וַיִּמָּלֵ֥א הָמָ֖ן חֵמָֽה׃
6 וַיִּ֣בֶז בְּעֵינָ֗יו לִשְׁלֹ֤חַ יָד֙ בְּמָרְדֳּכַ֣י לְבַדּ֔וֹ כִּֽי־הִגִּ֥ידוּ ל֖וֹ אֶת־עַ֣ם מָרְדֳּכָ֑י וַיְבַקֵּ֣שׁ הָמָ֗ן לְהַשְׁמִ֧יד אֶת־כָּל־הַיְּהוּדִ֛ים אֲשֶׁ֛ר בְּכָל־מַלְכ֥וּת אֲחַשְׁוֵר֖וֹשׁ

ג׳ v. 4. כאמרם קרי

עִם מָרְדֳּכָֽי׃ ⁷ בַּחֹ֤דֶשׁ הָרִאשׁוֹן֙ הוּא־חֹ֣דֶשׁ נִיסָ֔ן בִּשְׁנַת֙ שְׁתֵּ֣ים עֶשְׂרֵ֔ה לַמֶּ֖לֶךְ אֲחַשְׁוֵר֑וֹשׁ הִפִּ֣יל פּוּר֩ ה֨וּא הַגּוֹרָ֜ל לִפְנֵ֣י הָמָ֗ן מִיּ֧וֹם ׀ לְי֛וֹם וּמֵחֹ֥דֶשׁ לְחֹ֛דֶשׁ שְׁנֵים־עָשָׂ֖ר הוּא־חֹ֥דֶשׁ אֲדָֽר׃ ⁸ וַיֹּ֤אמֶר הָמָן֙ לַמֶּ֣לֶךְ אֲחַשְׁוֵר֔וֹשׁ יֶשְׁנ֣וֹ עַם־אֶחָ֗ד מְפֻזָּ֤ר וּמְפֹרָד֙ בֵּ֣ין הָֽעַמִּ֔ים בְּכֹ֖ל מְדִינ֣וֹת מַלְכוּתֶ֑ךָ וְדָתֵיהֶ֞ם שֹׁנ֣וֹת מִכָּל־עָ֗ם וְאֶת־דָּתֵ֤י הַמֶּ֙לֶךְ֙ אֵינָ֣ם עֹשִׂ֔ים וְלַמֶּ֥לֶךְ אֵין־שֹׁוֶ֖ה לְהַנִּיחָֽם׃ ⁹ אִם־עַל־הַמֶּ֣לֶךְ ט֔וֹב יִכָּתֵ֖ב לְאַבְּדָ֑ם וַעֲשֶׂ֨רֶת אֲלָפִ֜ים כִּכַּר־כֶּ֗סֶף אֶשְׁקוֹל֙ עַל־יְדֵי֙ עֹשֵׂ֣י הַמְּלָאכָ֔ה לְהָבִ֖יא אֶל־גִּנְזֵ֥י הַמֶּֽלֶךְ׃ ¹⁰ וַיָּ֧סַר הַמֶּ֛לֶךְ אֶת־טַבַּעְתּ֖וֹ מֵעַ֣ל יָד֑וֹ וַֽיִּתְּנָ֗הּ לְהָמָ֧ן בֶּֽן־הַמְּדָ֛תָא הָאֲגָגִ֖י צֹרֵ֥ר הַיְּהוּדִֽים׃ ¹¹ וַיֹּ֤אמֶר הַמֶּ֙לֶךְ֙ לְהָמָ֔ן הַכֶּ֖סֶף נָת֣וּן לָ֑ךְ וְהָעָ֕ם לַעֲשׂ֥וֹת בּ֖וֹ כַּטּ֥וֹב בְּעֵינֶֽיךָ׃ ¹² וַיִּקָּרְאוּ֩ סֹפְרֵ֨י הַמֶּ֜לֶךְ בַּחֹ֣דֶשׁ הָרִאשׁ֗וֹן בִּשְׁלוֹשָׁ֨ה עָשָׂ֣ר יוֹם֮ בּוֹ֒ וַיִּכָּתֵ֣ב כְּֽכָל־אֲשֶׁר־צִוָּ֣ה הָמָ֡ן אֶ֣ל אֲחַשְׁדַּרְפְּנֵֽי־הַ֠מֶּלֶךְ וְֽאֶל־הַפַּח֞וֹת אֲשֶׁ֣ר ׀ עַל־מְדִינָ֣ה וּמְדִינָ֗ה וְאֶל־שָׂ֤רֵי עַם֙ וָעָ֔ם מְדִינָ֤ה וּמְדִינָה֙ כִּכְתָבָ֔הּ וְעַ֥ם וָעָ֖ם כִּלְשׁוֹנ֑וֹ בְּשֵׁ֨ם הַמֶּ֤לֶךְ אֲחַשְׁוֵרֹשׁ֙ נִכְתָּ֔ב וְנֶחְתָּ֖ם בְּטַבַּ֥עַת הַמֶּֽלֶךְ׃ ¹³ וְנִשְׁל֨וֹחַ סְפָרִ֜ים בְּיַ֣ד הָרָצִים֮ אֶל־כָּל־מְדִינ֣וֹת הַמֶּלֶךְ֒ לְהַשְׁמִ֡יד לַהֲרֹ֣ג וּלְאַבֵּ֣ד אֶת־כָּל־הַ֠יְּהוּדִים מִנַּ֨עַר וְעַד־זָקֵ֜ן טַ֤ף וְנָשִׁים֙ בְּי֣וֹם אֶחָ֔ד בִּשְׁלוֹשָׁ֥ה עָשָׂ֛ר לְחֹ֥דֶשׁ שְׁנֵים־עָשָׂ֖ר הוּא־חֹ֣דֶשׁ אֲדָ֑ר וּשְׁלָלָ֖ם לָבֽוֹז׃ ¹⁴ פַּתְשֶׁ֣גֶן הַכְּתָ֗ב לְהִנָּ֤תֵֽן דָּת֙ בְּכָל־מְדִינָ֣ה וּמְדִינָ֔ה גָּל֖וּי לְכָל־הָֽעַמִּ֑ים לִהְי֥וֹת עֲתִדִ֖ים לַיּ֥וֹם הַזֶּֽה׃ ¹⁵ הָרָצִ֞ים יָצְא֤וּ דְחוּפִים֙ בִּדְבַ֣ר הַמֶּ֔לֶךְ

ג׳ v. 12. קמץ בז״ק

וְהַדָּת נִתְּנָה בְּשׁוּשַׁן הַבִּירָה וְהַמֶּלֶךְ וְהָמָן יָשְׁבוּ לִשְׁתּוֹת
וְהָעִיר שׁוּשָׁן נָבוֹכָה׃

CHAPTER 4 פרק ד

ד

א וּמָרְדֳּכַי יָדַע אֶת־כָּל־אֲשֶׁר נַעֲשָׂה וַיִּקְרַע מָרְדֳּכַי אֶת־
בְּגָדָיו וַיִּלְבַּשׁ שַׂק וָאֵפֶר וַיֵּצֵא בְּתוֹךְ הָעִיר וַיִּזְעַק זְעָקָה
2 גְדוֹלָה וּמָרָה׃ וַיָּבוֹא עַד לִפְנֵי שַׁעַר־הַמֶּלֶךְ כִּי אֵין לָבוֹא
3 אֶל־שַׁעַר הַמֶּלֶךְ בִּלְבוּשׁ שָׂק׃ וּבְכָל־מְדִינָה וּמְדִינָה מְקוֹם
אֲשֶׁר דְּבַר־הַמֶּלֶךְ וְדָתוֹ מַגִּיעַ אֵבֶל גָּדוֹל לַיְּהוּדִים וְצוֹם
4 וּבְכִי וּמִסְפֵּד שַׂק וָאֵפֶר יֻצַּע לָרַבִּים׃ וַתָּבוֹאינָה נַעֲרוֹת
אֶסְתֵּר וְסָרִיסֶיהָ וַיַּגִּידוּ לָהּ וַתִּתְחַלְחַל הַמַּלְכָּה מְאֹד
וַתִּשְׁלַח בְּגָדִים לְהַלְבִּישׁ אֶת־מָרְדֳּכַי וּלְהָסִיר שַׂקּוֹ מֵעָלָיו
ה וְלֹא קִבֵּל׃ וַתִּקְרָא אֶסְתֵּר לַהֲתָךְ מִסָּרִיסֵי הַמֶּלֶךְ אֲשֶׁר
הֶעֱמִיד לְפָנֶיהָ וַתְּצַוֵּהוּ עַל־מָרְדֳּכָי לָדַעַת מַה־זֶּה וְעַל־
6 מַה־זֶּה׃ וַיֵּצֵא הֲתָךְ אֶל־מָרְדֳּכָי אֶל־רְחוֹב הָעִיר אֲשֶׁר
7 לִפְנֵי שַׁעַר־הַמֶּלֶךְ׃ וַיַּגֶּד־לוֹ מָרְדֳּכַי אֵת כָּל־אֲשֶׁר קָרָהוּ
וְאֵת ׀ פָּרָשַׁת הַכֶּסֶף אֲשֶׁר אָמַר הָמָן לִשְׁקוֹל עַל־גִּנְזֵי
8 הַמֶּלֶךְ בַּיְּהוּדִיִּים לְאַבְּדָם׃ וְאֶת־פַּתְשֶׁגֶן כְּתָב־הַדָּת אֲשֶׁר־
נִתַּן בְּשׁוּשָׁן לְהַשְׁמִידָם נָתַן לוֹ לְהַרְאוֹת אֶת־אֶסְתֵּר וּלְהַגִּיד
לָהּ וּלְצַוּוֹת עָלֶיהָ לָבוֹא אֶל־הַמֶּלֶךְ לְהִתְחַנֶּן־לוֹ וּלְבַקֵּשׁ
9 מִלְּפָנָיו עַל־עַמָּהּ׃ וַיָּבוֹא הֲתָךְ וַיַּגֵּד לְאֶסְתֵּר אֵת דִּבְרֵי
י 11 מָרְדֳּכָי׃ וַתֹּאמֶר אֶסְתֵּר לַהֲתָךְ וַתְּצַוֵּהוּ אֶל־מָרְדֳּכָי׃ כָּל־
עַבְדֵי הַמֶּלֶךְ וְעַם מְדִינוֹת הַמֶּלֶךְ יוֹדְעִים אֲשֶׁר כָּל־אִישׁ
וְאִשָּׁה אֲשֶׁר־יָבוֹא אֶל־הַמֶּלֶךְ אֶל־הֶחָצֵר הַפְּנִימִית אֲשֶׁר

v. 4. יתיר י׳ v. 7. יתיר י׳

לֹא־יִקָּרֵא אַחַת דָּתוֹ לְהָמִית לְבַד מֵאֲשֶׁר יוֹשִׁיט־לוֹ הַמֶּלֶךְ
אֶת־שַׁרְבִיט הַזָּהָב וְחָיָה וַאֲנִי לֹא נִקְרֵאתִי לָבוֹא אֶל־
12 הַמֶּלֶךְ זֶה שְׁלוֹשִׁים יוֹם׃ וַיַּגִּידוּ לְמָרְדֳּכָי אֵת דִּבְרֵי אֶסְתֵּר׃
13 וַיֹּאמֶר מָרְדֳּכַי לְהָשִׁיב אֶל־אֶסְתֵּר אַל־תְּדַמִּי בְנַפְשֵׁךְ
14 לְהִמָּלֵט בֵּית־הַמֶּלֶךְ מִכָּל־הַיְּהוּדִים׃ כִּי אִם־הַחֲרֵשׁ
תַּחֲרִישִׁי בָּעֵת הַזֹּאת רֶוַח וְהַצָּלָה יַעֲמוֹד לַיְּהוּדִים מִמָּקוֹם
אַחֵר וְאַתְּ וּבֵית־אָבִיךְ תֹּאבֵדוּ וּמִי יוֹדֵעַ אִם־לְעֵת כָּזֹאת
טו הִגַּעַתְּ לַמַּלְכוּת׃ וַתֹּאמֶר אֶסְתֵּר לְהָשִׁיב אֶל־מָרְדֳּכָי׃
16 לֵךְ כְּנוֹס אֶת־כָּל־הַיְּהוּדִים הַנִּמְצְאִים בְּשׁוּשָׁן וְצוּמוּ עָלַי
וְאַל־תֹּאכְלוּ וְאַל־תִּשְׁתּוּ שְׁלֹשֶׁת יָמִים לַיְלָה וָיוֹם גַּם־אֲנִי
וְנַעֲרֹתַי אָצוּם כֵּן וּבְכֵן אָבוֹא אֶל־הַמֶּלֶךְ אֲשֶׁר לֹא־כַדָּת
17 וְכַאֲשֶׁר אָבַדְתִּי אָבָדְתִּי׃ וַיַּעֲבֹר מָרְדֳּכָי וַיַּעַשׂ כְּכֹל אֲשֶׁר־
צִוְּתָה עָלָיו אֶסְתֵּר׃

CHAPTER 5 פרק ה

ה
א וַיְהִי ׀ בַּיּוֹם הַשְּׁלִישִׁי וַתִּלְבַּשׁ אֶסְתֵּר מַלְכוּת וַתַּעֲמֹד בַּחֲצַר
בֵּית־הַמֶּלֶךְ הַפְּנִימִית נֹכַח בֵּית הַמֶּלֶךְ וְהַמֶּלֶךְ יוֹשֵׁב עַל־
2 כִּסֵּא מַלְכוּתוֹ בְּבֵית הַמַּלְכוּת נֹכַח פֶּתַח הַבָּיִת׃ וַיְהִי
כִרְאוֹת הַמֶּלֶךְ אֶת־אֶסְתֵּר הַמַּלְכָּה עֹמֶדֶת בֶּחָצֵר נָשְׂאָה
חֵן בְּעֵינָיו וַיּוֹשֶׁט הַמֶּלֶךְ לְאֶסְתֵּר אֶת־שַׁרְבִיט הַזָּהָב אֲשֶׁר
3 בְּיָדוֹ וַתִּקְרַב אֶסְתֵּר וַתִּגַּע בְּרֹאשׁ הַשַּׁרְבִיט׃ וַיֹּאמֶר לָהּ
הַמֶּלֶךְ מַה־לָּךְ אֶסְתֵּר הַמַּלְכָּה וּמַה־בַּקָּשָׁתֵךְ עַד־חֲצִי
4 הַמַּלְכוּת וְיִנָּתֶן לָךְ׃ וַתֹּאמֶר אֶסְתֵּר אִם־עַל־הַמֶּלֶךְ טוֹב
יָבוֹא הַמֶּלֶךְ וְהָמָן הַיּוֹם אֶל־הַמִּשְׁתֶּה אֲשֶׁר־עָשִׂיתִי לוֹ׃

v. 12. קמץ בז״ק

ה וַיֹּאמֶר הַמֶּלֶךְ מַהֲרוּ אֶת־הָמָן לַעֲשׂוֹת אֶת־דְּבַר אֶסְתֵּר
וַיָּבֹא הַמֶּלֶךְ וְהָמָן אֶל־הַמִּשְׁתֶּה אֲשֶׁר־עָשְׂתָה אֶסְתֵּר׃
6 וַיֹּאמֶר הַמֶּלֶךְ לְאֶסְתֵּר בְּמִשְׁתֵּה הַיַּיִן מַה־שְּׁאֵלָתֵךְ וְיִנָּתֵן
7 לָךְ וּמַה־בַּקָּשָׁתֵךְ עַד־חֲצִי הַמַּלְכוּת וְתֵעָשׂ׃ * וַתַּעַן
8 אֶסְתֵּר וַתֹּאמַר שְׁאֵלָתִי וּבַקָּשָׁתִי׃ אִם־מָצָאתִי חֵן בְּעֵינֵי
הַמֶּלֶךְ וְאִם־עַל־הַמֶּלֶךְ טוֹב לָתֵת אֶת־שְׁאֵלָתִי וְלַעֲשׂוֹת
אֶת־בַּקָּשָׁתִי יָבוֹא הַמֶּלֶךְ וְהָמָן אֶל־הַמִּשְׁתֶּה אֲשֶׁר אֶעֱשֶׂה
9 לָהֶם וּמָחָר אֶעֱשֶׂה כִּדְבַר הַמֶּלֶךְ׃ וַיֵּצֵא הָמָן בַּיּוֹם הַהוּא
שָׂמֵחַ וְטוֹב לֵב וְכִרְאוֹת הָמָן אֶת־מָרְדֳּכַי בְּשַׁעַר הַמֶּלֶךְ
וְלֹא־קָם וְלֹא־זָע מִמֶּנּוּ וַיִּמָּלֵא הָמָן עַל־מָרְדֳּכַי חֵמָה׃
י וַיִּתְאַפַּק הָמָן וַיָּבוֹא אֶל־בֵּיתוֹ וַיִּשְׁלַח וַיָּבֵא אֶת־אֹהֲבָיו
11 וְאֶת־זֶרֶשׁ אִשְׁתּוֹ׃ וַיְסַפֵּר לָהֶם הָמָן אֶת־כְּבוֹד עָשְׁרוֹ
וְרֹב בָּנָיו וְאֵת כָּל־אֲשֶׁר גִּדְּלוֹ הַמֶּלֶךְ וְאֵת אֲשֶׁר נִשְּׂאוֹ
12 עַל־הַשָּׂרִים וְעַבְדֵי הַמֶּלֶךְ׃ וַיֹּאמֶר הָמָן אַף לֹא־הֵבִיאָה
אֶסְתֵּר הַמַּלְכָּה עִם־הַמֶּלֶךְ אֶל־הַמִּשְׁתֶּה אֲשֶׁר־עָשָׂתָה
13 כִּי אִם־אוֹתִי וְגַם־לְמָחָר אֲנִי קָרוּא־לָהּ עִם־הַמֶּלֶךְ׃ וְכָל־
זֶה אֵינֶנּוּ שֹׁוֶה לִי בְּכָל־עֵת אֲשֶׁר אֲנִי רֹאֶה אֶת־מָרְדֳּכַי
14 הַיְּהוּדִי יוֹשֵׁב בְּשַׁעַר הַמֶּלֶךְ׃ וַתֹּאמֶר לוֹ זֶרֶשׁ אִשְׁתּוֹ וְכָל־
אֹהֲבָיו יַעֲשׂוּ־עֵץ גָּבֹהַּ חֲמִשִּׁים אַמָּה וּבַבֹּקֶר ׀ אֱמֹר לַמֶּלֶךְ
וְיִתְלוּ אֶת־מָרְדֳּכַי עָלָיו וּבֹא עִם־הַמֶּלֶךְ אֶל־הַמִּשְׁתֶּה שָׂמֵחַ
וַיִּיטַב הַדָּבָר לִפְנֵי הָמָן וַיַּעַשׂ הָעֵץ׃

ו CHAPTER 6 פרק ו

א בַּלַּיְלָה הַהוּא נָדְדָה שְׁנַת הַמֶּלֶךְ וַיֹּאמֶר לְהָבִיא אֶת־

ה׳ v. 7. חצי הספר בפסוקים

סֵ֣פֶר הַזִּכְרֹנוֹת֙ דִּבְרֵ֣י הַיָּמִ֔ים וַיִּהְי֥וּ נִקְרָאִ֖ים לִפְנֵ֥י הַמֶּֽלֶךְ׃

2 וַיִּמָּצֵ֣א כָת֗וּב אֲשֶׁר֩ הִגִּ֨יד מָרְדֳּכַ֜י עַל־בִּגְתָ֣נָא וָתֶ֗רֶשׁ שְׁנֵי֙ סָרִיסֵ֣י הַמֶּ֔לֶךְ מִשֹּׁמְרֵ֖י הַסַּ֑ף אֲשֶׁ֤ר בִּקְשׁוּ֙ לִשְׁלֹ֣חַ יָ֔ד בַּמֶּ֖לֶךְ אֲחַשְׁוֵרֽוֹשׁ׃

3 וַיֹּ֣אמֶר הַמֶּ֔לֶךְ מַֽה־נַּעֲשָׂ֞ה יְקָ֧ר וּגְדוּלָּ֛ה לְמָרְדֳּכַ֖י עַל־זֶ֑ה וַיֹּ֨אמְר֜וּ נַעֲרֵ֤י הַמֶּ֙לֶךְ֙ מְשָׁ֣רְתָ֔יו לֹא־נַעֲשָׂ֥ה עִמּ֖וֹ דָּבָֽר׃

4 וַיֹּ֥אמֶר הַמֶּ֖לֶךְ מִ֣י בֶחָצֵ֑ר וְהָמָ֣ן בָּ֗א לַחֲצַ֤ר בֵּית־הַמֶּ֙לֶךְ֙ הַחִ֣יצוֹנָ֔ה לֵאמֹ֣ר לַמֶּ֔לֶךְ לִתְלוֹת֙ אֶֽת־מָרְדֳּכַ֔י עַל־הָעֵ֖ץ אֲשֶׁר־הֵכִ֥ין לֽוֹ׃

5 וַיֹּ֨אמְר֜וּ נַעֲרֵ֤י הַמֶּ֙לֶךְ֙ אֵלָ֔יו הִנֵּ֥ה הָמָ֖ן עֹמֵ֣ד בֶּחָצֵ֑ר וַיֹּ֥אמֶר הַמֶּ֖לֶךְ יָבֽוֹא׃

6 וַיָּבוֹא֮ הָמָן֒ וַיֹּ֤אמֶר לוֹ֙ הַמֶּ֔לֶךְ מַה־לַעֲשׂ֕וֹת בָּאִ֕ישׁ אֲשֶׁ֥ר הַמֶּ֖לֶךְ חָפֵ֣ץ בִּיקָר֑וֹ וַיֹּ֤אמֶר הָמָן֙ בְּלִבּ֔וֹ לְמִ֞י יַחְפֹּ֥ץ הַמֶּ֛לֶךְ לַעֲשׂ֥וֹת יְקָ֖ר יוֹתֵ֥ר מִמֶּֽנִּי׃

7 וַיֹּ֥אמֶר הָמָ֖ן אֶל־הַמֶּ֑לֶךְ אִ֕ישׁ אֲשֶׁ֥ר הַמֶּ֖לֶךְ חָפֵ֥ץ בִּיקָרֽוֹ׃

8 יָבִ֙יאוּ֙ לְב֣וּשׁ מַלְכ֔וּת אֲשֶׁ֥ר לָֽבַשׁ־בּ֖וֹ הַמֶּ֑לֶךְ וְס֗וּס אֲשֶׁ֨ר רָכַ֤ב עָלָיו֙ הַמֶּ֔לֶךְ וַאֲשֶׁ֥ר נִתַּ֛ן כֶּ֥תֶר מַלְכ֖וּת בְּרֹאשֽׁוֹ׃

9 וְנָת֨וֹן הַלְּב֜וּשׁ וְהַסּ֗וּס עַל־יַד־אִ֞ישׁ מִשָּׂרֵ֤י הַמֶּ֙לֶךְ֙ הַֽפַּרְתְּמִ֔ים וְהִלְבִּ֙ישׁוּ֙ אֶת־הָאִ֔ישׁ אֲשֶׁ֥ר הַמֶּ֖לֶךְ חָפֵ֣ץ בִּיקָר֑וֹ וְהִרְכִּיבֻ֤הוּ עַל־הַסּוּס֙ בִּרְח֣וֹב הָעִ֔יר וְקָרְא֣וּ לְפָנָ֔יו כָּ֚כָה יֵעָשֶׂ֣ה לָאִ֔ישׁ אֲשֶׁ֥ר הַמֶּ֖לֶךְ חָפֵ֥ץ בִּיקָרֽוֹ׃

10 וַיֹּאמֶר֩ הַמֶּ֨לֶךְ לְהָמָ֜ן מַהֵ֗ר קַ֤ח אֶת־הַלְּבוּשׁ֙ וְאֶת־הַסּ֔וּס כַּאֲשֶׁ֖ר דִּבַּ֑רְתָּ וַֽעֲשֵׂה־כֵן֙ לְמָרְדֳּכַ֣י הַיְּהוּדִ֔י הַיּוֹשֵׁ֖ב בְּשַׁ֣עַר הַמֶּ֑לֶךְ אַל־תַּפֵּ֣ל דָּבָ֔ר מִכֹּ֖ל אֲשֶׁ֥ר דִּבַּֽרְתָּ׃

11 וַיִּקַּ֤ח הָמָן֙ אֶת־הַלְּב֣וּשׁ וְאֶת־הַסּ֔וּס וַיַּלְבֵּ֖שׁ אֶֽת־מָרְדֳּכָ֑י וַיַּרְכִּיבֵ֙הוּ֙ בִּרְח֣וֹב הָעִ֔יר וַיִּקְרָ֣א לְפָנָ֔יו כָּ֚כָה יֵעָשֶׂ֣ה לָאִ֔ישׁ אֲשֶׁ֥ר הַמֶּ֖לֶךְ חָפֵ֥ץ בִּיקָרֽוֹ׃

v. 2. פתח באתנח   v. 9. כ״א והלבישו

12 וַיָּ֥שָׁב מָרְדֳּכַ֖י אֶל־שַׁ֣עַר הַמֶּ֑לֶךְ וְהָמָן֙ נִדְחַ֣ף אֶל־בֵּית֔וֹ אָבֵ֖ל
13 וַחֲפ֥וּי רֹֽאשׁ׃ וַיְסַפֵּ֨ר הָמָ֜ן לְזֶ֤רֶשׁ אִשְׁתּוֹ֙ וּלְכָל־אֹ֣הֲבָ֔יו
אֵ֖ת כָּל־אֲשֶׁ֣ר קָרָ֑הוּ וַיֹּ֣אמְרוּ ל֩וֹ* חֲכָמָ֨יו וְזֶ֜רֶשׁ אִשְׁתּ֗וֹ אִ֣ם
מִזֶּ֣רַע הַיְּהוּדִ֡ים מָרְדֳּכַ֞י אֲשֶׁר֩ הַחִלּ֨וֹתָ לִנְפֹּ֤ל לְפָנָיו֙ לֹא־
14 תוּכַ֣ל ל֔וֹ כִּֽי־נָפ֥וֹל תִּפּ֖וֹל לְפָנָֽיו׃ עוֹדָם֙ מְדַבְּרִ֣ים עִמּ֔וֹ
וְסָרִיסֵ֥י הַמֶּ֖לֶךְ הִגִּ֑יעוּ וַיַּבְהִ֙לוּ֙ לְהָבִ֣יא אֶת־הָמָ֔ן אֶל־הַמִּשְׁתֶּ֖ה
אֲשֶׁר־עָשְׂתָ֥ה אֶסְתֵּֽר׃

ז CHAPTER 7 פרק ז

א 2 וַיָּבֹ֤א הַמֶּ֙לֶךְ֙ וְהָמָ֔ן לִשְׁתּ֖וֹת עִם־אֶסְתֵּ֥ר הַמַּלְכָּֽה׃ וַיֹּאמֶר֩
הַמֶּ֨לֶךְ לְאֶסְתֵּ֜ר גַּ֣ם בַּיּ֤וֹם הַשֵּׁנִי֙ בְּמִשְׁתֵּ֣ה הַיַּ֔יִן מַה־שְּׁאֵלָתֵ֛ךְ
אֶסְתֵּ֥ר הַמַּלְכָּ֖ה וְתִנָּ֣תֵֽן לָ֑ךְ וּמַה־בַּקָּשָׁתֵ֛ךְ עַד־חֲצִ֥י הַמַּלְכ֖וּת
3 וְתֵעָֽשׂ׃ וַתַּ֨עַן אֶסְתֵּ֤ר הַמַּלְכָּה֙ וַתֹּאמַ֔ר אִם־מָצָ֨אתִי חֵ֤ן
בְּעֵינֶ֙יךָ֙ הַמֶּ֔לֶךְ וְאִם־עַל־הַמֶּ֖לֶךְ ט֑וֹב תִּנָּֽתֶן־לִ֤י נַפְשִׁי֙
4 בִּשְׁאֵ֣לָתִ֔י וְעַמִּ֖י בְּבַקָּשָׁתִֽי׃ כִּ֤י נִמְכַּ֙רְנוּ֙ אֲנִ֣י וְעַמִּ֔י לְהַשְׁמִ֖יד
לַהֲר֣וֹג וּלְאַבֵּ֑ד וְאִלּוּ֩ לַעֲבָדִ֨ים וְלִשְׁפָח֤וֹת נִמְכַּ֙רְנוּ֙ הֶחֱרַ֔שְׁתִּי
ה כִּ֣י אֵ֥ין הַצָּ֛ר שֹׁוֶ֖ה בְּנֵ֥זֶק הַמֶּֽלֶךְ׃ וַיֹּ֙אמֶר֙ הַמֶּ֣לֶךְ
אֲחַשְׁוֵר֔וֹשׁ וַיֹּ֖אמֶר לְאֶסְתֵּ֣ר הַמַּלְכָּ֑ה מִ֣י ה֥וּא זֶה֙ וְאֵי־זֶ֣ה
6 ה֔וּא אֲשֶׁר־מְלָא֥וֹ לִבּ֖וֹ לַעֲשׂ֥וֹת כֵּֽן׃ וַתֹּ֣אמֶר אֶסְתֵּ֔ר אִ֚ישׁ
צַ֣ר וְאוֹיֵ֔ב הָמָ֥ן הָרָ֖ע הַזֶּ֑ה וְהָמָ֣ן נִבְעָ֔ת מִלִּפְנֵ֥י הַמֶּ֖לֶךְ
7 וְהַמַּלְכָּֽה׃ וְהַמֶּ֜לֶךְ קָ֤ם בַּחֲמָתוֹ֙ מִמִּשְׁתֵּ֣ה הַיַּ֔יִן אֶל־גִּנַּ֖ת
הַבִּיתָ֑ן וְהָמָ֣ן עָמַ֗ד לְבַקֵּ֤שׁ עַל־נַפְשׁוֹ֙ מֵאֶסְתֵּ֣ר הַמַּלְכָּ֔ה כִּ֣י
8 רָאָ֔ה כִּֽי־כָלְתָ֥ה אֵלָ֛יו הָרָעָ֖ה מֵאֵ֥ת הַמֶּֽלֶךְ׃ וְהַמֶּ֡לֶךְ שָׁב֩
מִגִּנַּ֨ת הַבִּיתָ֜ן אֶל־בֵּ֣ית ׀ מִשְׁתֵּ֣ה הַיַּ֗יִן וְהָמָן֙ נֹפֵ֔ל עַל־הַמִּטָּה֙

* v. 13. ל׳ דגושה

אֲשֶׁר אֶסְתֵּר עָלֶיהָ וַיֹּאמֶר הַמֶּלֶךְ הֲגַם לִכְבּוֹשׁ אֶת־
הַמַּלְכָּה עִמִּי בַּבָּיִת הַדָּבָר יָצָא מִפִּי הַמֶּלֶךְ וּפְנֵי הָמָן חָפוּ׃
9 וַיֹּאמֶר חַרְבוֹנָה אֶחָד מִן־הַסָּרִיסִים לִפְנֵי הַמֶּלֶךְ גַּם הִנֵּה־
הָעֵץ אֲשֶׁר־עָשָׂה הָמָן לְמָרְדֳּכַי אֲשֶׁר דִּבֶּר־טוֹב עַל־הַמֶּלֶךְ
עֹמֵד בְּבֵית הָמָן גָּבֹהַּ חֲמִשִּׁים אַמָּה וַיֹּאמֶר הַמֶּלֶךְ תְּלֻהוּ
י עָלָיו׃ וַיִּתְלוּ אֶת־הָמָן עַל־הָעֵץ אֲשֶׁר־הֵכִין לְמָרְדֳּכָי וַחֲמַת
הַמֶּלֶךְ שָׁכָכָה׃

ח CHAPTER 8 פרק ח

א בַּיּוֹם הַהוּא נָתַן הַמֶּלֶךְ אֲחַשְׁוֵרוֹשׁ לְאֶסְתֵּר הַמַּלְכָּה אֶת־
בֵּית הָמָן צֹרֵר הַיְּהוּדִיִּים וּמָרְדֳּכַי בָּא לִפְנֵי הַמֶּלֶךְ כִּי־
2 הִגִּידָה אֶסְתֵּר מַה הוּא־לָהּ׃ וַיָּסַר הַמֶּלֶךְ אֶת־טַבַּעְתּוֹ
אֲשֶׁר הֶעֱבִיר מֵהָמָן וַיִּתְּנָהּ לְמָרְדֳּכָי וַתָּשֶׂם אֶסְתֵּר אֶת־
3 מָרְדֳּכַי עַל־בֵּית הָמָן׃ וַתּוֹסֶף אֶסְתֵּר וַתְּדַבֵּר לִפְנֵי
הַמֶּלֶךְ וַתִּפֹּל לִפְנֵי רַגְלָיו וַתֵּבְךְּ וַתִּתְחַנֶּן־לוֹ לְהַעֲבִיר אֶת־
רָעַת הָמָן הָאֲגָגִי וְאֵת מַחֲשַׁבְתּוֹ אֲשֶׁר חָשַׁב עַל־הַיְּהוּדִים׃
4 וַיּוֹשֶׁט הַמֶּלֶךְ לְאֶסְתֵּר אֵת שַׁרְבִט הַזָּהָב וַתָּקָם אֶסְתֵּר
ה וַתַּעֲמֹד לִפְנֵי הַמֶּלֶךְ׃ וַתֹּאמֶר אִם־עַל־הַמֶּלֶךְ טוֹב וְאִם־
מָצָאתִי חֵן לְפָנָיו וְכָשֵׁר הַדָּבָר לִפְנֵי הַמֶּלֶךְ וְטוֹבָה אֲנִי
בְּעֵינָיו יִכָּתֵב לְהָשִׁיב אֶת־הַסְּפָרִים מַחֲשֶׁבֶת הָמָן בֶּן־
הַמְּדָתָא הָאֲגָגִי אֲשֶׁר כָּתַב לְאַבֵּד אֶת־הַיְּהוּדִים אֲשֶׁר
6 בְּכָל־מְדִינוֹת הַמֶּלֶךְ׃ כִּי אֵיכָכָה אוּכַל וְרָאִיתִי בָּרָעָה
אֲשֶׁר־יִמְצָא אֶת־עַמִּי וְאֵיכָכָה אוּכַל וְרָאִיתִי בְּאָבְדַן
7 מוֹלַדְתִּי׃ וַיֹּאמֶר הַמֶּלֶךְ אֲחַשְׁוֵרֹשׁ לְאֶסְתֵּר הַמַּלְכָּה

ח׳ v. 1. יתיר י׳ v. 6. מלרע ibid. מלרע

וּלְמָרְדֳּכַי הַיְּהוּדִי הִנֵּה בֵית־הָמָן נָתַתִּי לְאֶסְתֵּר וְאֹתוֹ
8 תָּלוּ עַל־הָעֵץ עַל אֲשֶׁר־שָׁלַח יָדוֹ בַּיְּהוּדִיים׃ וְאַתֶּם
כִּתְבוּ עַל־הַיְּהוּדִים כַּטּוֹב בְּעֵינֵיכֶם בְּשֵׁם הַמֶּלֶךְ וְחִתְמוּ
בְּטַבַּעַת הַמֶּלֶךְ כִּי־כְתָב אֲשֶׁר־נִכְתָּב בְּשֵׁם־הַמֶּלֶךְ וְנַחְתּוֹם
9 בְּטַבַּעַת הַמֶּלֶךְ אֵין לְהָשִׁיב׃ וַיִּקָּרְאוּ סֹפְרֵי־הַמֶּלֶךְ בָּעֵת־
הַהִיא בַּחֹדֶשׁ הַשְּׁלִישִׁי הוּא־חֹדֶשׁ סִיוָן בִּשְׁלוֹשָׁה
וְעֶשְׂרִים בּוֹ וַיִּכָּתֵב כְּכָל־אֲשֶׁר־צִוָּה מָרְדֳּכַי אֶל־
הַיְּהוּדִים וְאֶל הָאֲחַשְׁדַּרְפְּנִים וְהַפַּחוֹת וְשָׂרֵי הַמְּדִינוֹת
אֲשֶׁר ׀ מֵהֹדּוּ וְעַד־כּוּשׁ שֶׁבַע וְעֶשְׂרִים וּמֵאָה מְדִינָה
מְדִינָה וּמְדִינָה כִּכְתָבָהּ וְעַם וָעָם כִּלְשֹׁנוֹ וְאֶל־הַיְּהוּדִים
י כִּכְתָבָם וְכִלְשׁוֹנָם׃ וַיִּכְתֹּב בְּשֵׁם הַמֶּלֶךְ אֲחַשְׁוֵרֹשׁ וַיַּחְתֹּם
בְּטַבַּעַת הַמֶּלֶךְ וַיִּשְׁלַח סְפָרִים בְּיַד הָרָצִים בַּסּוּסִים
11 רֹכְבֵי הָרֶכֶשׁ הָאֲחַשְׁתְּרָנִים בְּנֵי הָרַמָּכִים׃ אֲשֶׁר נָתַן
הַמֶּלֶךְ לַיְּהוּדִים ׀ אֲשֶׁר בְּכָל־עִיר־וָעִיר לְהִקָּהֵל וְלַעֲמֹד
עַל־נַפְשָׁם לְהַשְׁמִיד לַהֲרֹג וּלְאַבֵּד אֶת־כָּל־חֵיל עַם
12 וּמְדִינָה הַצָּרִים אֹתָם טַף וְנָשִׁים וּשְׁלָלָם לָבוֹז׃ בְּיוֹם
אֶחָד בְּכָל־מְדִינוֹת הַמֶּלֶךְ אֲחַשְׁוֵרוֹשׁ בִּשְׁלוֹשָׁה עָשָׂר
13 לְחֹדֶשׁ שְׁנֵים־עָשָׂר הוּא־חֹדֶשׁ אֲדָר׃ פַּתְשֶׁגֶן הַכְּתָב
לְהִנָּתֵן דָּת בְּכָל־מְדִינָה וּמְדִינָה גָּלוּי לְכָל־הָעַמִּים וְלִהְיוֹת
14 הַיְּהוּדִיים עֲתוּדִים לַיּוֹם הַזֶּה לְהִנָּקֵם מֵאֹיְבֵיהֶם׃ הָרָצִים
רֹכְבֵי הָרֶכֶשׁ הָאֲחַשְׁתְּרָנִים יָצְאוּ מְבֹהָלִים וּדְחוּפִים בִּדְבַר
טו הַמֶּלֶךְ וְהַדָּת נִתְּנָה בְּשׁוּשַׁן הַבִּירָה׃ וּמָרְדֳּכַי יָצָא ׀
מִלִּפְנֵי הַמֶּלֶךְ בִּלְבוּשׁ מַלְכוּת תְּכֵלֶת וָחוּר וַעֲטֶרֶת זָהָב

v. 7. יתיר י׳ v. 13. יתיר י׳ ibid. עתידים קרי

גְּדוֹלָה וְתַכְרִיךְ בּוּץ וְאַרְגָּמָן וְהָעִיר שׁוּשָׁן צָהֲלָה וְשָׂמֵחָה׃
16 17 לַיְּהוּדִים הָיְתָה אוֹרָה וְשִׂמְחָה וְשָׂשֹׂן וִיקָר׃ וּבְכָל־
מְדִינָה וּמְדִינָה וּבְכָל־עִיר וָעִיר מְקוֹם אֲשֶׁר דְּבַר־הַמֶּלֶךְ
וְדָתוֹ מַגִּיעַ שִׂמְחָה וְשָׂשׂוֹן לַיְּהוּדִים מִשְׁתֶּה וְיוֹם טוֹב
וְרַבִּים מֵעַמֵּי הָאָרֶץ מִתְיַהֲדִים כִּי־נָפַל פַּחַד־הַיְּהוּדִים
עֲלֵיהֶם׃

ט CHAPTER 9 פרק ט

א וּבִשְׁנֵים עָשָׂר חֹדֶשׁ הוּא־חֹדֶשׁ אֲדָר בִּשְׁלוֹשָׁה עָשָׂר יוֹם
בּוֹ אֲשֶׁר הִגִּיעַ דְּבַר־הַמֶּלֶךְ וְדָתוֹ לְהֵעָשׂוֹת בַּיּוֹם אֲשֶׁר
שִׂבְּרוּ אֹיְבֵי הַיְּהוּדִים לִשְׁלוֹט בָּהֶם וְנַהֲפוֹךְ הוּא אֲשֶׁר
2 יִשְׁלְטוּ הַיְּהוּדִים הֵמָּה בְּשֹׂנְאֵיהֶם׃ נִקְהֲלוּ הַיְּהוּדִים
בְּעָרֵיהֶם בְּכָל־מְדִינוֹת הַמֶּלֶךְ אֲחַשְׁוֵרוֹשׁ לִשְׁלֹחַ יָד
בִּמְבַקְשֵׁי רָעָתָם וְאִישׁ לֹא־עָמַד בִּפְנֵיהֶם כִּי־נָפַל פַּחְדָּם
3 עַל־כָּל־הָעַמִּים׃ וְכָל־שָׂרֵי הַמְּדִינוֹת וְהָאֲחַשְׁדַּרְפְּנִים
וְהַפַּחוֹת וְעֹשֵׂי הַמְּלָאכָה אֲשֶׁר לַמֶּלֶךְ מְנַשְּׂאִים אֶת־
4 הַיְּהוּדִים כִּי־נָפַל פַּחַד־מָרְדֳּכַי עֲלֵיהֶם׃ כִּי־גָדוֹל מָרְדֳּכַי
בְּבֵית הַמֶּלֶךְ וְשָׁמְעוֹ הוֹלֵךְ בְּכָל־הַמְּדִינוֹת כִּי־הָאִישׁ
ה מָרְדֳּכַי הוֹלֵךְ וְגָדוֹל׃ וַיַּכּוּ הַיְּהוּדִים בְּכָל־אֹיְבֵיהֶם מַכַּת־
6 חֶרֶב וְהֶרֶג וְאַבְדָן וַיַּעֲשׂוּ בְשֹׂנְאֵיהֶם כִּרְצוֹנָם׃ וּבְשׁוּשַׁן
הַבִּירָה הָרְגוּ הַיְּהוּדִים וְאַבֵּד חֲמֵשׁ מֵאוֹת אִישׁ׃

7 וְאֵת ׀
פַּרְשַׁנְדָּתָא וְאֵת ׀
דַּלְפוֹן וְאֵת ׀

v. 15 קמץ בלא אסיף   v. 7 ס״א ש׳ זעירא. ת׳ זעירא

8 אַסְפָּתָא׃ וְאֵת ׀
פּוֹרָתָא וְאֵת ׀
אֲדַלְיָא וְאֵת ׀
9 אֲרִידָתָא׃ וְאֵת ׀
פַּרְמַשְׁתָּא וְאֵת ׀
אֲרִיסַי וְאֵת ׀
אֲרִדַי וְאֵת ׀
י וַיְזָתָא׃ עֲשֶׂרֶת
בְּנֵי הָמָן בֶּן־הַמְּדָתָא צֹרֵר הַיְּהוּדִים הָרָגוּ וּבַבִּזָּה לֹא
11 שָׁלְחוּ אֶת־יָדָם׃ בַּיּוֹם הַהוּא בָּא מִסְפַּר הַהֲרוּגִים בְּשׁוּשַׁן
12 הַבִּירָה לִפְנֵי הַמֶּלֶךְ׃ וַיֹּאמֶר הַמֶּלֶךְ לְאֶסְתֵּר הַמַּלְכָּה
בְּשׁוּשַׁן הַבִּירָה הָרְגוּ הַיְּהוּדִים וְאַבֵּד חֲמֵשׁ מֵאוֹת אִישׁ
וְאֵת עֲשֶׂרֶת בְּנֵי־הָמָן בִּשְׁאָר מְדִינוֹת הַמֶּלֶךְ מֶה עָשׂוּ
13 וּמַה־שְּׁאֵלָתֵךְ וְיִנָּתֵן לָךְ וּמַה־בַּקָּשָׁתֵךְ עוֹד וְתֵעָשׂ׃ וַתֹּאמֶר
אֶסְתֵּר אִם־עַל־הַמֶּלֶךְ טוֹב יִנָּתֵן גַּם־מָחָר לַיְּהוּדִים אֲשֶׁר
בְּשׁוּשָׁן לַעֲשׂוֹת כְּדָת הַיּוֹם וְאֵת עֲשֶׂרֶת בְּנֵי־הָמָן יִתְלוּ
14 עַל־הָעֵץ׃ וַיֹּאמֶר הַמֶּלֶךְ לְהֵעָשׂוֹת כֵּן וַתִּנָּתֵן דָּת בְּשׁוּשָׁן
טו וְאֵת עֲשֶׂרֶת בְּנֵי־הָמָן תָּלוּ׃ וַיִּקָּהֲלוּ הַיְּהוּדִיִּים אֲשֶׁר־
בְּשׁוּשָׁן גַּם בְּיוֹם אַרְבָּעָה עָשָׂר לְחֹדֶשׁ אֲדָר וַיַּהַרְגוּ
בְשׁוּשָׁן שְׁלֹשׁ מֵאוֹת אִישׁ וּבַבִּזָּה לֹא שָׁלְחוּ אֶת־יָדָם׃
16 וּשְׁאָר הַיְּהוּדִים אֲשֶׁר בִּמְדִינוֹת הַמֶּלֶךְ נִקְהֲלוּ ׀ וְעָמֹד
עַל־נַפְשָׁם וְנוֹחַ מֵאֹיְבֵיהֶם וְהָרוֹג בְּשֹׂנְאֵיהֶם חֲמִשָּׁה
17 וְשִׁבְעִים אָלֶף וּבַבִּזָּה לֹא שָׁלְחוּ אֶת־יָדָם׃ בְּיוֹם־שְׁלוֹשָׁה

v. 9. ס"א ר' זעירא ibid. ש' ות' זעירא ibid. ר' רבתי ibid. ד' זעירא

עָשָׂר לְחֹדֶשׁ אֲדָר וְנוֹחַ בְּאַרְבָּעָה עָשָׂר בּוֹ וְעָשֹׂה אֹתוֹ
18 יוֹם מִשְׁתֶּה וְשִׂמְחָה׃ וְהַיְּהוּדִיים אֲשֶׁר־בְּשׁוּשָׁן נִקְהֲלוּ
בִּשְׁלוֹשָׁה עָשָׂר בּוֹ וּבְאַרְבָּעָה עָשָׂר בּוֹ וְנוֹחַ בַּחֲמִשָּׁה
19 עָשָׂר בּוֹ וְעָשֹׂה אֹתוֹ יוֹם מִשְׁתֶּה וְשִׂמְחָה׃ עַל־כֵּן הַיְּהוּדִים
הַפְּרָוזִים הַיֹּשְׁבִים בְּעָרֵי הַפְּרָזוֹת עֹשִׂים אֵת יוֹם אַרְבָּעָה
עָשָׂר לְחֹדֶשׁ אֲדָר שִׂמְחָה וּמִשְׁתֶּה וְיוֹם טוֹב וּמִשְׁלֹחַ
כ מָנוֹת אִישׁ לְרֵעֵהוּ׃ וַיִּכְתֹּב מָרְדֳּכַי אֶת־הַדְּבָרִים הָאֵלֶּה
וַיִּשְׁלַח סְפָרִים אֶל־כָּל־הַיְּהוּדִים אֲשֶׁר בְּכָל־מְדִינוֹת
21 הַמֶּלֶךְ אֲחַשְׁוֵרוֹשׁ הַקְּרוֹבִים וְהָרְחוֹקִים׃ לְקַיֵּם עֲלֵיהֶם
לִהְיוֹת עֹשִׂים אֵת יוֹם אַרְבָּעָה עָשָׂר לְחֹדֶשׁ אֲדָר וְאֵת
22 יוֹם־חֲמִשָּׁה עָשָׂר בּוֹ בְּכָל־שָׁנָה וְשָׁנָה׃ כַּיָּמִים אֲשֶׁר־נָחוּ
בָהֶם הַיְּהוּדִים מֵאֹיְבֵיהֶם וְהַחֹדֶשׁ אֲשֶׁר נֶהְפַּךְ לָהֶם מִיָּגוֹן
לְשִׂמְחָה וּמֵאֵבֶל לְיוֹם טוֹב לַעֲשׂוֹת אוֹתָם יְמֵי מִשְׁתֶּה
וְשִׂמְחָה וּמִשְׁלֹחַ מָנוֹת אִישׁ לְרֵעֵהוּ וּמַתָּנוֹת לָאֶבְיֹנִים׃
23 וְקִבֵּל הַיְּהוּדִים אֵת אֲשֶׁר־הֵחֵלּוּ לַעֲשׂוֹת וְאֵת אֲשֶׁר־כָּתַב
24 מָרְדֳּכַי אֲלֵיהֶם׃ כִּי הָמָן בֶּן־הַמְּדָתָא הָאֲגָגִי צֹרֵר כָּל־
הַיְּהוּדִים חָשַׁב עַל־הַיְּהוּדִים לְאַבְּדָם וְהִפִּל פּוּר הוּא
כה הַגּוֹרָל לְהֻמָּם וּלְאַבְּדָם׃ וּבְבֹאָהּ לִפְנֵי הַמֶּלֶךְ אָמַר עִם־
הַסֵּפֶר יָשׁוּב מַחֲשַׁבְתּוֹ הָרָעָה אֲשֶׁר־חָשַׁב עַל־הַיְּהוּדִים
26 עַל־רֹאשׁוֹ וְתָלוּ אֹתוֹ וְאֶת־בָּנָיו עַל־הָעֵץ׃ עַל־כֵּן קָרְאוּ
לַיָּמִים הָאֵלֶּה פוּרִים עַל־שֵׁם הַפּוּר עַל־כֵּן עַל־כָּל־דִּבְרֵי
הָאִגֶּרֶת הַזֹּאת וּמָה־רָאוּ עַל־כָּכָה וּמָה הִגִּיעַ אֲלֵיהֶם׃
27 קִיְּמוּ וְקִבְּלֻ הַיְּהוּדִים ׀ עֲלֵיהֶם ׀ וְעַל־זַרְעָם וְעַל כָּל־

v. 15. 18. יתיר י׳ v. 19. יתיר ו׳ v. 24. ט׳ כ״א והפיל v. 27. וקבלו קרי

הנלוים עליהם ולא יעבור להיות עשים את־שני הימים
28 האלה ככתבם וכזמנם בכל־שנה ושנה׃ והימים האלה
נזכרים ונעשים בכל־דור ודור משפחה ומשפחה מדינה
ומדינה ועיר ועיר וימי הפורים האלה לא יעברו מתוך
29 היהודים וזכרם לא־יסוף מזרעם׃ ותכתב
אסתר המלכה בת־אביחיל ומרדכי היהודי את־כל־
ל תקף לקים את־אגרת הפרים הזאת השנית׃ וישלח
ספרים אל־כל־היהודים אל־שבע ועשרים ומאה מדינה
31 מלכות אחשורוש דברי שלום ואמת׃ לקים את־ימי
הפרים האלה בזמניהם כאשר קים עליהם מרדכי היהודי
ואסתר המלכה וכאשר קימו על־נפשם ועל־זרעם דברי
32 הצומות וזעקתם׃ ומאמר אסתר קים דברי הפרים
האלה ונכתב בספר׃

CHAPTER 10 פרק י

י

א 2 וישם המלך אחשרש ׀ מס על־הארץ ואיי הים׃ וכל־
מעשה תקפו וגבורתו ופרשת גדלת מרדכי אשר גדלו
המלך הלוא־הם כתובים על־ספר דברי הימים למלכי
3 מדי ופרס׃ כי ׀ מרדכי היהודי משנה למלך אחשורוש
וגדול ליהודים ורצוי לרב אחיו דרש טוב לעמו ודבר
שלום לכל־זרעו׃

סכום פסוקי דמגלת אסתר מאה וששים ושבעה. וסימנו כבדני נא נגד זקני עמי. וחציו ותען אסתר ותאמר. וסדריו חמשה. וסימנו וזה גב המזבח׃

v. 29. ת׳ רבתי v. 1. י׳ אחשורוש קרי ibid. כ״א פסיק